The Mindful Legal Writer

Aspen Coursebook Series

The Mindful Legal Writer

Mastering Predictive and Persuasive Writing

Heidi K. Brown

Director, Legal Writing Program
Associate Professor of Law
Brooklyn Law School

Wolters Kluwer

Published by Wolters Kluwer in New York.

Wolters Kluwer Legal & Regulatory US serves customers worldwide with CCH, Aspen Publishers, and Kluwer Law International products. (www.WKLegaledu.com)

To contact Customer Service, e-mail customer.service@wolterskluwer.com, call 1-800-234-1660, fax 1-800-901-9075, or mail correspondence to:

Wolters Kluwer
Attn: Order Department
PO Box 990
Frederick, MD 21705

Printed in the United States of America.

1 2 3 4 5 6 7 8 9 0

ISBN 978-1-4548-3617-9

Library of Congress Cataloging-in-Publication Data

Names: Brown, Heidi K. (Heidi Kristin), 1970- author.
Title: The mindful legal writer : mastering predictive and persuasive writing/
    Heidi K. Brown, Director, Legal Writing Program, Associate Professor of
    Law, Brooklyn Law School.
Description: First edition. | New York : Wolters Kluwer, [2016] | Series:
    Aspen coursebook series
Identifiers: LCCN 2016012483 | ISBN 9781454836179
Subjects: LCSH: Legal composition. | Law—United States—Language.
Classification: LCC KF250 .B766 2016 | DDC 808.06/634—dc23
LC record available at http://lccn.loc.gov/201601248

About Wolters Kluwer Legal & Regulatory US

Wolters Kluwer Legal & Regulatory US delivers expert content and solutions in the areas of law, corporate compliance, health compliance, reimbursement, and legal education. Its practical solutions help customers successfully navigate the demands of a changing environment to drive their daily activities, enhance decision quality, and inspire confident outcomes.

Serving customers worldwide, its legal and regulatory portfolio includes products under the Aspen Publishers, CCH Incorporated, Kluwer Law International, ftwilliam.com, and MediRegs names. They are regarded as exceptional and trusted resources for general legal and practice-specific knowledge, compliance and risk management, dynamic workflow solutions, and expert commentary.

To my students.

Scribo ergo sum.

Summary of Contents

Part 1   Predictive Writing **1**

Section 1   Becoming a Mindful Legal Writer: An Opportunity
for Personal and Professional Reinvention **3**

Section 2   The Mindful Legal Writer's Raw Materials **43**

Section 3   The Mindful Legal Writer's Framework **89**

Section 4   The Mindful Legal Writer's Work **103**

Contents

Chapter 2: Pondering Professional Judgment 25

Chapter 3: Strategies for Starting a New Legal Writing Assignment 35

Section 2: The Mindful Legal Writer's Raw Materials

Chapter 4: Understanding the Sources of Legal Rules 45

Chapter 5: Learning How to Read Statutes 59

Chapter 6: Learning How to Read and Brief
Cases 69

Chapter 7: Learning How to Read Regulations 83

Section 3: **The Mindful Legal Writer's Framework**

Section 4: **The Mindful Legal Writer's Work**

Chapter 11: Basic Legal Citation for Legal Memoranda **129**

Chapter 12: Rule Application: Applying the Rule to the Client's Facts **143**

Chapter 13: Putting the Memorandum Together: Introductions, Transitions, Headings, and Conclusions **153**

Chapter 14: Locking in Logic and Abolishing Assumptions in Legal Analysis **169**

Chapter 15: Writing the Memorandum Header, the Question Presented, and the Short Answer 175

Chapter 16: Writing a Statement of Facts in a Legal Office Memorandum 187

Section 5: Adjustment, Refinement, and Perfection

Chapter 17: Preparing for Legal Writing Feedback . . . 193

Chapter 18: Becoming an Expert Self-Editor 199

Chapter 19: Adding Levels of Sophistication to a Legal Analysis 215

Section 6: Expanding and Contracting IREAC/CREAC to Fit an Audience's Needs

Chapter 20: Tackling a Multi-Issue Legal Office Memorandum Assignment **221**

Chapter 21: Drafting Shorter Memoranda and E-mail Communications **225**

Part 2: Persuasive Writing

Section 7: Context

Introduction to Part 2: Transitioning from Predictive to Persuasive Legal Writing **239**

Section 8: Writing Persuasive Letters in the Litigation Context

Section 9:   Writing Persuasive Pleadings in the Litigation Context

Chapter 24: Drafting a Persuasive Complaint **289**

Chapter 25: Drafting a Persuasive Answer **305**

Chapter 26: Drafting a Persuasive Counterclaim, Third-Party Claim, or Cross-Claim **315**

Section 10: Persuasion in the Scheduling Phase of Litigation

Section 11: Writing Persuasive Motions and Briefs in the Litigation Context

Chapter 30: Drafting Persuasive Opposition and Reply Briefs **423**

Chapter 31: Drafting an Appellate Brief **445**

Section 12: Persuasion Through Oral Argument

Section 13: Drafting Persuasive Mediation/Arbitration Papers

Section 14: **Persuasive Writing in the Transactional Context**

Appendices **487**

Preface

Practicing Mindfulness in Legal Writing

I am not an expert on mindfulness by any means. But I am a rabid aspirational fan. And an activist. And living proof that the concept makes the practice, teaching, and learning of law a more healthy experience for those who open themselves to its ripple effects. This world unequivocally needs more mindful lawyers, law professors, and law students.

Throughout law school and fifteen years of law practice, I was not mindful. At all. In fact, I was mind*less*. I was an introvert playing in the extrovert world, trying to fake it until I made it, forcing myself to be something I so profoundly was not. I suffered from extreme public speaking anxiety—and yet I chose a career in litigation because I was rudderless. I succumbed to the Nike "Just Do It" pressure to bungee-jump off the courtroom cliff in a swell of fabricated confidence, when really all I wanted to do was burrow deep in the most remote carrel of the law firm's library where I could research, write, and think—in enveloping quiet. I was happiest when those still moments were carved out for me, by perceptive mentors (such as Julian Hoffar, my first writing champion) who realized and then overtly declared that not every law firm associate needed to be a fist-pounding orator. They let me write. And think. And research. And write again. And made me feel appreciated and intelligent for it. Through writing, I found my "lawyer voice."

So what exactly does mindfulness mean? Jon Kabat-Zinn, Professor of Medicine Emeritus and creator of the Stress Reduction Clinic and the Center for Mindfulness in Medicine, Health Care, and Society at the University of Massachusetts Medical School, describes mindfulness as "paying attention in a particular way: on purpose, in the present moment, and nonjudgmentally."[1] I have studied mindfulness in the context of helping law students conquer extreme public speaking anxiety, and in overcoming my own struggle with that specific challenge. A helpful psychology-based research source I consulted, Steve Flowers's book, *The Mindful Path Through Shyness*, defines mindfulness as "the awareness that grows from being present in the unfolding moments of our lives without judging or trying to change anything that we experience."[2]

A dedicated cadre of law professors who have called for an integration of mindfulness into legal pedagogy offer the following definitions:

---

[1] Jon Kabat-Zinn, *Wherever You Go There You Are* 4 (1994).
[2] Steve Flowers, MFT, *The Mindful Path Through Shyness*, 3 (New Harbinger Publications, Inc. 2009).

- Professor Leonard Riskin, C.A. Leedy Professor of Law and director of the Center for the Study of Dispute Resolution and the Initiative on "Mindfulness in Law and Dispute Resolution" at the University of Missouri-Columbia School of Law, defines mindfulness as "paying attention deliberately, moment to moment, and without judgment, to whatever is going on in the mind and body."[3]
- Professor Nathalie Martin, Frederick M. Hart Chair in Consumer and Clinical Law at the University of New Mexico School of Law, summarizes mindfulness as "present awareness of one's thoughts as they arise and minute-to-minute awareness of one's existence. . . . [M]indfulness allows you to pay clear and particular attention to the things around you, so you can do what is best for yourself, those you care about, and the world at large, if you take it that far."[4]
- Professor Larry Krieger, Clinical Professor of Law and Director of Clinical Externship Programs at Florida State University College of Law, and Past Chair of the American Association of Law Schools' Section on Balance in Legal Education, summarizes mindfulness as "the state of being consciously open and attentive to one's experience."[5]

What is my understanding of mindfulness as it applies to legal writing? Slowing down the pace of law school, law teaching, and law practice, and allowing an aspiring lawyer time to think, to be . . . to touch, feel, and taste the law without striving to be something he or she is not quite yet prepared to be. The cadence of law school and law practice is extraordinarily fast. My hope for law students and their teachers and eventual law office mentors is that we can decelerate our tempo without losing rigor. Bequeath ourselves and our students time to think. Sit with the shades of the rules, the nuances of the facts, the notion of what law is and why it matters. Give ourselves permission to cleave a space of quietude to become better writers by pausing and pondering what we individually and collectively want to say. Reduce the Pavlov pressure to respond instantaneously to a text, a tweet, an instant message, an e-mail, a Socratic question we need a moment to process, an eleventh hour motion filed by opposing counsel. Slow down, or even better, stop. Read. Reflect. Be confounded. Scrunch up our faces in confusion at the complexity of a legal concept. Acknowledge what we don't know or understand without being embarrassed or ashamed. Steep with our thoughts, ideas, and words. And then, when ready, mindfully respond. And figure it out.

---

[3] Leonard L. Riskin, *The Place of Mindfulness in Healing and the Law*, in *Shifting the Field of Law & Justice* 99-120 (2007).
[4] Nathalie Martin, *Think Like A (Mindful) Lawyer: Incorporating Mindfulness, Professional Identity, And Emotional Intelligence Into The First Year Law Curriculum*, 36 U. Ark. Little Rock L. Rev. 413, 416 (2014).
[5] Lawrence S. Krieger, *Human Nature As A New Guiding Philosophy For Legal Education And The Profession*, 47 Washburn L.J. 247, 285-286 (Winter 2008), citing Kirk W. Brown & Richard M. Ryan, *The Benefits of Being Present: Mindfulness and Its Role in Psychological Well-Being*, 84 J. Personality & Soc. Psychol. 822, 822 (2003).

I strongly believe that learning, teaching, and practicing the art and science of legal writing is the ideal opportunity for students, law professors, and lawyers to apply the concept of mindfulness. My aspiration is that, in reading this book, students will understand the value of approaching legal writing in a deliberate, slow-paced manner— starting with visualizing the structural framework of a legal analysis, imagining the play-by-play of a client's factual scenario like a movie, honing the legal issue extracting the applicable legal rule from an array of research sources, carefully considering how best to illustrate the rule of law through vivid examples, methodically and thoughtfully applying the rule to the client's circumstances, and then either predicting a concrete logical outcome derived through this contemplative process (predictive legal writing) or selecting the right words to persuade a reader that the proposed outcome is the correct one (persuasive legal writing). We do not need to start out as experts on mindfulness practice to aspire to experiment with its techniques in our everyday commitment to legal writing excellence. We can begin by paying attention—to words, ideas, rules, facts—and lingering with them longer than we normally might, increasing our awareness of how they might inspire us as counselors-at-law representing human beings, refraining from too-soon reflex judgments about their effects. The more contemplative or meditative we are about client factual scenarios and their interaction with rules of law, the more creative we will be in conceiving effective solutions to legal problems.

I hope that this book inspires law professors and students to step away from the often frantic fray of law school, and commit to a thoughtful approach to writing about the law. I also hope that you will share your observations and reflections as you traverse this circuitous and adventurous lifelong writing trail. Please write me at heidi@theintrovertedlawyer.com. I would love to hear from you.

Heidi K. Brown
April 2016

Acknowledgments

For eight years and counting, it has been an honor to be a member of the legal writing academy. I am grateful to have witnessed and absorbed the creativity, dedication, and inspiration of my legal writing colleagues.

As every legal writing professor knows, we learn and absorb so much from: (a) our colleagues at our own institutions and throughout the academy, (b) contributors to the LWI Listserv and other online communities, (c) the creative and collaborative legal writing conferences across the nation, and (d) the various textbooks and articles written by our cadre of talented legal writing experts. All of my teaching ideas sprouted and then were further influenced, developed, honed, and tweaked over the last eight years through my interaction with all the foregoing resources.

My teaching career started eight years ago through collaboration with my colleagues at Chapman University School of Law (now the Dale E. Fowler School of Law): specifically, Professor Stephanie Lascelles, Professor Jenny Carey, Professor Moujan Walkow, Professor Rita Barnett, Professor Carolyn Larmore, Professor Robin Wellford Slocum, and the Chapman library staff. Due to a larger-than-usual new 1L class, I was hired at the last minute in August 2008 for the Fall semester (I got the call on a Friday and had to teach my first law school class EVER the following week). My Chapman colleagues brought me up-to-speed quickly by sharing their class plans, teaching ideas, and assignments. Their generosity provided a strong foundation for me (as a new teacher) to experiment with creative ideas—some which flopped miserably (!) and others which remain in my classroom wheelhouse today.

After three years at Chapman, my teaching philosophy, ideas, and assignments were further influenced, nurtured, and developed through daily teamwork and collaboration with my Legal Practice colleagues at New York Law School under the leadership of Professor Anne Goldstein. I cannot give enough credit to Professor Goldstein, Professor Kim Hawkins, Professor Erika Wood, Professor Jodi Balsam, Professor Lynnise Pantin, Professor Lynn Su, Professor David Epstein, Professor Cynara McQuillan, Professor Melynda Barnhart, Professor Kirk Burkhalter, Professor Daniel Warshawsky, Professor Parisa Tafti, Professor Chaumtoli Huq, Professor Marcia Levy, Professor Monte Givhan, and Professor Sandra Janin for their influence on my legal writing teaching, and to the New York Law School library staff for their thoughtful research curriculum. I also credit the mentorship of Professor Frank Bress, Professor Doni

Gewirtzman, Professor Kris Franklin, Dean Carol Buckler, and Dean Mariana Hogan.

I have attended numerous legal writing conferences throughout the country over the past eight years, and have been inspired by many creative ideas from the speakers and workshops. I further have learned a great deal from the books and articles written by our talented colleagues throughout the academy, including the following textbooks that have informed and influenced my teaching:

- Robin Wellford Slocum, *Legal Reasoning, Writing, and Persuasive Argument* (LexisNexis 2d. ed).
- Linda H. Edwards, *Legal Writing and Analysis* (Wolters Kluwer 3d 3d.).
- Helene S. Schapo, Marilyn R. Walter, Elizabeth Fajans, *Writing and Analysis in the Law* (Foundation Press, 5th ed.).
- Christine Coughlin, Joan Malmud, Sandy Patrick, *A Lawyer Writes: A Practical Guide to Legal Analysis* (Carolina Academic Press 2d ed).
- Linda J. Barris, *Understanding and Mastering The Bluebook, A Guide for Students and Practitioners* (2d ed. Carolina Academic Press 2010).

I wish to thank the marvelous editing team at Wolters Kluwer, especially Dana Wilson.

Further, I am most appreciative of the education I received from The University of Virginia—in both the College of Arts and Sciences, and the Law School—where I learned to love writing in general, and legal writing specifically (thanks to Professor Jan Levine). I also want to thank the law firm of Watt, Tieder, Hoffar & Fitzgerald, LLP for instilling in me the importance of legal writing excellence from the time I was a rookie associate.

As always, thank you to my family, friends, and students who continue to embolden my twisty voyage on the meandering road less traveled.

Happy writing!

Heidi K. Brown
heidi@theintrovertedlawyer.com
Heidi.Brown@brooklaw.edu
April 2016

Part 1

Predictive Writing

Section 1

Becoming a Mindful Legal Writer: An Opportunity for Personal and Professional Reinvention

Introduction to Part 1

Congratulations and welcome. Just by investing the time in reading this Introduction, you are taking a huge step toward your goal of obtaining a law degree, joining many interesting, intelligent, creative, ambitious folks who have journeyed this same path. In doing so, you also are embarking on a career as a *writer*, like many journalists, novelists, memoirists, poets, screenwriters, playwrights, songwriters, and others. You may find this thought exciting if you enjoy putting words on paper or crafting that perfect phrase to capture a thought. However, you might find this "writing career" idea surprising, and a bit daunting if, in the past, you have felt that writing is one big chore. Or perhaps your college major or pre-law-school profession focused more heavily on science, math, or economics—where writing may not have been emphasized as strongly as other areas of study or competence. Do not fear. This book "evens the playing field" for novice legal writers like you and gives you a solid foundation to find your "lawyer voice" through the written word.

Even if you have substantial writing experience in other fields, learning how to write like a lawyer requires an open-mindedness—to embrace a completely new writing structure and style. Like any other writing genre, legal writing has its own "formula" that legal audiences expect to see so they can process a written intellectual analysis of a complex legal issue.

Imagine this: If you were to sit down at your laptop and write a haiku, a sonnet, or a screenplay, you would follow the expected structures of those media. A haiku—a form of Japanese poetry—consists of 17 "*on*" (similar to syllables), in 3 lines comprised of 5, 7, and 5 syllables. A Shakespearean sonnet entails 14 lines, 10 syllables each, written in iambic pentameter, a rhythm of unstressed and stressed syllables. Screenplays, too, are written in a traditional format—in Courier 12-point font, with a page of text usually translating to one minute of screen time. The screenplay genre reflects strict industry guidelines for the page layout of scene headings, dialogue, and transitions, and a writing style that conveys what the reader would see and hear on a screen. If you sat down to write in one of these genres, you would not simply click away on your laptop in your own style and structure, and expect the intended audience to rave. If you submitted a screenplay to a Hollywood agent in your own unique format and style, your creative endeavor likely would end up in the recycling bin, even if the story idea presented the newest spin on the vampire-superhero-wizard craze and offered blockbuster potential. Any time writers experiment with a new category of written communication, they adapt to the audience's expected structural parameters. Even with text messaging, Facebook, and Twitter, new writers learn how to be witty in short sound-bites or 140 characters.

Legal writing requires the same open-minded attitude and commitment. Our eventual audiences—supervising attorneys, opposing counsel, and judges—expect legal documents to follow a certain logic flow, leading the reader down a clear path to a well-reasoned conclusion. This logic thread usually follows some derivation of a writing structure called IRAC (Issue, Rule, Application/Analysis, and Conclusion), or IREAC (Issue, Rule, Explanation, Application/Analysis, and Conclusion), or CREAC (Conclusion, Rule, Explanation, Application/Analysis, and Conclusion). As a novice legal writer, if you embrace this simple formula, you are guaranteed to include all the necessary logic components so your reader can follow your thought process and understand why your ultimate conclusion makes sense. In contrast, if you ignore this formula and construct your own logic configuration—thinking you are novel, clever, and singlehandedly about to change written advocacy for all time—you run the risk of omitting necessary logic "building blocks" and leaving the reader confused, guessing, and frustrated—not a good scenario for your eventual *clients*.

In fact, you must always consider the *client factor* as you learn and then practice legal writing. In college, your written work likely was assignment-based: A professor assigned a writing project that you performed for a grade. No third party relied on your written work for a desired result affecting a person's property, economic well-being, liberty interests, health, or welfare. Law school and law practice are quite different in this respect. They require you to evolve from an assignment-based mindset to an advocacy-based one. Start thinking of every piece of legal writing, no matter how small, as a "voice" for a client. This client needs your expertise, your logical reasoning, your commitment, and your careful analysis on behalf of his or her cause. He or she may have a lot riding on how well you advocate.

The more you regard yourself as a legal apprentice rather than simply a continuing student, the more thoughtful and emotionally engaged your legal writing will be, and the more it will resonate with your reader. Thoughtful and emotionally engaged writing is not soft or sentimental. Yes, "thoughtful" can mean "heedful anticipation of the needs and wants of others," but in the context of legal writing, the more apt definition is "characterized by careful reasoned thinking."[1] As a thoughtful legal writer, you will put more intention and

---

[1] Merriam-Webster Dictionary, http://www.merriam-webster.com/dictionary/thoughtful (last visited Oct. 11, 2014).

consideration into researching your client's issue. You will go deeper than surface level in your research by: (1) organizing the sources of law you find; (2) thinking hard about how these legal principles affect your client's situation; (3) brainstorming about the best way to communicate the application of legal rules to a client's scenario; (4) taking the utmost care to write with clarity, precision, and passion; (5) and then perfecting that piece of writing in its logic flow, phrasing, and presentation.

Also consider what being a mindful legal writer and law student means. "Mindfulness" is defined as "being fully conscious and aware of one's actions and surroundings"[2] or "an awareness that arises through paying attention, on purpose, in the present moment."[3] Law school can be overwhelming: the amount of nightly reading, the pressure to zealously embrace the Socratic method, the competitive dialogue in the hallways about who has outlined the fastest. The pace can feel frantic. Students often cope by racing through piles of reading assignments, sprinting through writing projects, and plowing through study outlines. Slow down the pace if you can, be more deliberate and intentional as you read and write, and pay attention to the twists and turns along the learning path. It doesn't matter whether you process the material as quickly as others; it matters whether the content makes sense to you. Be mindful of what you understand, and acknowledge and note what you don't.

Legal writing is both a science and an art. *Merriam-Webster* defines "science" as "knowledge or a system of knowledge covering general truths or the operation of general laws especially as obtained and tested through scientific method."[4] If this definition sounds confusing, extract the instructive words: "knowledge," "system," "truths," "laws," "tested," and "method." Science gives us systems to use to find answers—through experiments, tests, dissection, and procedure. Science helps us figure out how things work, by analyzing their internal anatomy, structure, and mechanisms.

As a novice legal writer, you need to begin at an elemental level—with the science, the mechanics, the blueprints. You can become a clear, convincing, and interesting legal writer by starting slowly and methodically with basic fundamentals and by embracing formulas. As you practice those structural set-ups, you will begin to recognize and identify gaps in logic, clarity, and presentation. Then, after mastering those simple, straightforward formulas and learning how to identify and correct deficiencies, you will build from that foundation by adding more complex legal sources as examples for the reader and more sophisticated analysis

---

[2] *Observation Skills May be Key Ingredient to Creativity*, Ass'n for Psychol. Sci. (June 26, 2014), http://www.psychologicalscience.org/index.php/news/minds-business/observation-skills-may-be-key-ingredient-to-creativity.html.

[3] Carolyn Gregoire, *13 Things Mindful People Do Differently Every Day*, Huffington Post (May 1, 2014), *quoting* Jon Kabat-Zinn, http://www.huffingtonpost.com/2014/04/30/habits-mindful-people_n_5186510.html.

[4] Merriam-Webster Dictionary, http://www.merriam-webster.com/dictionary/science (last visited Oct. 11, 2014).

and application of rules to client facts. Finally, and the most fun part of all, you will experiment with your lawyer voice and stylistic flair. That is the moment when legal writing becomes art.

Merriam-Webster defines "art" in part as "the conscious use of skill and creative imagination especially in the production of aesthetic objects."[5] The dictionary distinguishes between "skill" and "art." Skill "stresses technical knowledge and proficiency," while art "implies a personal, unanalyzable creative power: the art of choosing the right word."[6] To gain the skill of legal writing, first you will become technically proficient at finding the right legal rules and applying them logically and clearly to your client's situation—as a scientist. Then, you will develop and nurture your personal, creative power to communicate the "right" result to your audience—as an artist. Your creative power will shine through choices of words, themes, imagery, and emotional triggers, but also through contemplative selection of illustrative case law, citation methods, organization of key points, descriptive headings, and so on.

This book breaks down legal writing into step-by-step manageable formulas that may seem overly simplistic and rigid at first glance. However, if you adopt these formulas as a new legal writer, and become comfortable with them as they build on one another to create a powerful whole, you will never inadvertently omit critical logic components from your analysis. Then, once you master these formulas, you can experiment with more sophisticated and advanced structural and stylistic techniques, while at the same time adding your own lawyer voice.

Consider this: Resist the urge to do too much too soon. If you wanted to try snowboarding for the first time, you probably would not buy the fastest, most high-tech equipment and a plane ticket to the wildest mountain with the "shreddiest" slopes on the globe. Instead, you might sign up for a lesson or two, in which an instructor would start by explaining, in basic vocabulary, the physics of the sport and familiarize you with alien equipment, snow conditions, and pitfalls for novices. Then, you would try out the equipment, getting comfortable with the boots, the board, and your balance, noticing how even the most minimal foot adjustments have significant directional effects on which way the fancy piece of plywood takes you. You might learn how to fall, so it seems less intimidating or hurts less. And then you would practice, and fall, a lot.

Approach legal writing the same way. Start slowly. Learn—and really understand—the most basic writing mechanics and why they are important and function well. Listen to your professor—he or she likely really loves this science and art, and is quite good at it, and excited for you to love it too. Practice the fundamentals repeatedly. Then observe, and appreciate, how minor tunings can have dramatic effects. Slowly, experiment with more advanced techniques and thoughtfully inject your personal lawyering style.

---

[5] *Id.*, http://www.merriam-webster.com/dictionary/art.
[6] *Id.*

Taken seriously, legal research and writing can be the most exhilarating part of being an attorney. At moments in your career, you will find that needle-in-a-haystack magical case that miraculously produces a viable argument for your client, when you thought one did not exist. You will spend hours writing a brief, painstakingly trying to explain to a judge why your proposed result makes the most logical sense—and is the truly fair thing to do—and months later, you will receive an order from the court awarding summary judgment, saving your client thousands, perhaps even hundreds of thousands, of dollars and countless hours of stress navigating a trial. These are moments that YOU will create through professional creative power.

As you begin this quest, remain open-minded. If legal writing feels unnatural at first or if your professor writes voluminous constructive criticism on your papers—yet you are accustomed to receiving high marks of praise—do not resist. Embrace and practice the formulas, even if they seem overly simplistic or rigid. Transition quickly out of the college-level, assignment-based mindset and into an apprentice attitude. Soon you will have a unique opportunity to speak on behalf of a client—a person who trusts you—and right a wrong, change something for the better, or create a positive outcome where none existed. Use the law to be a creative solution maker. Don't stop at the easy "yes" or easy "no" answer in your research or your analysis. Think about what the right, fair, best outcome could be—even if it is a result that has never been achieved previously.

You might feel buried under piles of writing rules, first from your professor, eventually from your supervising attorneys, and certainly from the judges before whom you will practice. Welcome these standards and make it your personal mission to satisfy, and hopefully exceed, the expectations of your audience by following these mandates in your written work product. Too many practicing attorneys think court rules are just "recommendations" and then aggravate the judge (and opposing counsel) by submitting briefs and other court submissions that flout these requirements, creating more work for the court staff and slowing down the system for everyone else. Taking writing rules seriously, and using them to make your legal writing the best it can be, enhances your credibility with your audience and paves the way for your substance to resonate with your reader.

Finally, enjoy this learning process. Of course, law school will challenge you and sometimes feel all-consuming. Use your Legal Research and Writing, Lawyering, and Legal Practice classes as a haven for finding the intellectual thrill in law school. In the legal writing classroom, you can experiment with finding your lawyer voice and take on a lawyer persona from day one.

You are the future of legal practice in the United States and beyond. Let legal research and writing be your powerful advocacy tools to effect positive change.

Chapter 1
Putting Legal Writing in Context

The first few weeks of law school might feel a bit daunting: You're already struggling under stacks of reading, trying to make sense of the Socratic method, learning new vocabulary and a fresh way of analyzing complex subjects, and figuring out where you fit in. You're not even sure where the library is. But you can do this. The Roman poet Ovid offers an inspiring quote that readily applies to law school: "Perfer et obdura; dolor hic tibi proderit olim," or "Be patient and tough; someday this pain will be useful to you."

So, let's get your legal research and writing[1] class off to a great start.

Flash forward three years. You have graduated from law school, have passed the bar exam, and are starting your new job as a practicing lawyer. Your sleek office phone rings. The caller is your supervising attorney assigning your first research and writing project: drafting a set of interrogatories for a case pending in federal court. The deadline is Friday. You hang up the phone. You gaze at your quickly scribbled notes and realize that you do not know what an interrogatory is, what it looks like, what purpose it serves, or how it helps your client. Instead of panicking, your first step is to "get context."

One of the aspects of law practice that new lawyers struggle with the most is how a particular written work product fits into a client's or case's big picture. This is "context." If you approach a legal writing project as a stand-alone, one-off

---

[1] The class for which you're using this book may be called Legal Research and Writing, Legal Methods, Lawyering, Legal Practice, or some other iteration of those titles. Law school educators and lawyers nationwide have realized the critical importance of providing students a strong foundation in legal research and writing early in their legal careers, and so this class will be a key part of your law school curriculum. This class may require more written work on a weekly basis than some of your other courses (which culminate in a single final exam, with perhaps a midterm test as well), but you will learn key competencies in this course that will help you write better law school exam essays, perform well in your summer jobs, excel on the bar exam, and serve your clients productively in a hopefully long and fruitful legal career.

"assignment"—like a college term paper—the end result might not truly serve its intended, and most effective, purpose. So, from the very beginning of your journey as a legal writer, it is important to understand and ponder how different types of legal writing are used in a relationship with a client. Envisioning how a piece of written work fits into the big picture of a legal case enables you to craft more effective documents. This is true whether your client seeks general legal assistance, such as setting up a business or entering into a contract (examples of "transactional" legal work), or is hiring a law office to resolve a dispute with another individual or entity (often referred to as "litigation" work).[2]

Regardless of the client's ultimate need or goal, legal writing typically involves these activities:

(1) identifying the legal issue(s) impacting the client;
(2) pinpointing the applicable legal rules;
(3) possibly explaining those legal rules, either briefly or in detail, depending on the audience;
(4) applying those rules to the client scenario; and/or
(5) stating a conclusion (either objectively or persuasively, depending on the audience).

The level of specificity the legal writer provides for each category always depends on the audience and the purpose of the written document. If the document is an internal client document (meaning, it will not be circulated to the opposing party or to the court), the writer might make recommendations, weighing the pros and cons of different legal options and the strengths and weaknesses of the client's position. If the document is an external communication to a third party in a pending contract negotiation, or opposing counsel or the judge in a lawsuit, the conclusions will be points of persuasion, to convince the audience to agree with the author's contentions.[3]

In legal writing, your audience might include one or more of the following people:

- A supervising attorney, who asked you to identify the client's issue, research the applicable law, apply the law to the client scenario, and predict the likely outcome
- Your client (sometimes clients are in-house lawyers at companies, but often they are nonlawyers)[4]

---

[2] Law practice generally falls into two categories (though with lots of subcategories): transactional work and dispute resolution. No matter which type of practice in which you decide you are interested, the fundamental analytical and writing skills you learn in your writing class will improve your lawyering competencies.

[3] "Contentions" are your assertions, arguments, claims, or positions.

[4] If you are drafting a document to communicate information directly to the client, you will assess the level of legal knowledge of your reader by considering whether your reader is an in-house corporate attorney or a layperson who does not have a law degree, and adjust your explanation of the legal rules and terminology accordingly.

- A third party in a transactional setting (in a non–dispute resolution scenario)
- Opposing counsel
- A judge, a mediator, or an arbitrator

The first half of this book focuses on written communications between you and your supervising attorney who will then convey recommendations to the client—emphasizing predictive or objective legal analysis. Typically, these communications are protected from disclosure to opposing parties by the attorney-client privilege and/or the attorney work product doctrine (which protects the mental impressions and legal theories of an attorney). The second half of this book will focus on written communications between you and (1) the court and (2) opposing counsel—emphasizing persuasive legal analysis.[5]

However, first, as an overview, the next section of this chapter will provide examples of different types of legal documents lawyers create in (1) dispute resolution and (2) transactional legal work.

I. Legal Writing in Dispute Resolution

Legal writing is an essential part of any dispute resolution scenario. Written legal analysis helps clients, lawyers (on both sides of a case), and judges make smart decisions about how to resolve a case.

Most legal cases follow a typical progression and involve similar types of legal documents. To understand how the pieces fit together, envision the following chronology of events.

A. Preliminary Client Advisory Phase

A client—an individual or an entity (via a representative)—contacts a law office seeking legal advice on a potential dispute with another party.

Step 1: Checking for Ethical Conflicts: The first step a lawyer takes before agreeing to represent a client is to conduct a "conflicts check." This process ensures that a potential attorney-client relationship does not create any ethical "conflicts of interest." Many law offices have computer systems that perform these conflicts checks. Also, attorneys often circulate conflicts check e-mails to other lawyers within the firm. Once the lawyer confirms that no ethical conflicts exist, the fact-gathering phase begins.

---

[5] In your legal career, you also might write transmittal letters, e-mails, contracts, client interview outlines, deposition outlines, witness examination outlines, jury instructions, articles, and a whole slew of other types of documents. Depending on your interests (transactional, litigation, law office management), you might consider choosing elective courses in law school that will give you experience in these other types of legal writing as well.

Step 2: Fact Gathering: The lawyer's goal in the initial client contact—whether on the phone or in person—is to (1) gather the relevant facts triggering to the dispute and (2) begin to identify the legal issue(s) to research. During this phase, it is important for the attorney to establish a rapport with the client so he or she feels comfortable and trusting enough to reveal both favorable and unfavorable facts. Lawyers need to know the client's backstory to effectively apply the governing law to the client's situation and predict a realistic outcome. During this phase, attorneys take thorough notes to keep track of what they learn, but also follow up with questions[6] if they sense gaps in the client's narrative.

After a client meeting, some lawyers begin drafting a "master chronology" of the facts gleaned from the initial client interview. Attorneys add to the chronology as they further flesh out the facts. Any notes taken or chronologies drafted constitute "attorney work product" and should be protected from disclosure to the potential parties on the other side of the case.

During this initial phase, attorneys also send the client an **engagement letter**, describing the terms of the representation and providing information about billing rates and fees. State bar association websites provide ethical guidelines of items to include in a client engagement letter.

Step 3: Identifying the Legal Question: Once the attorney reflects on the client's facts, the next step is to identify the precise legal question posed. Is the client asking whether he has the right to demand that his neighbor cut down a decaying tree that poses a safety hazard on the client's property? Is the client inquiring whether her daughter's school principal overstepped the bounds of privacy by searching the daughter's locker without permission? Is the client requesting advice on whether he has a claim against a company for using his picture in an advertisement without his permission? Once the lawyer knows the basic legal question, legal research commences.

Step 4: Researching the Governing Law and Narrowing the Legal Question: Next, the lawyer searches for governing statutes, regulations, and case law that interpret and apply legal rules to different factual scenarios. (Chapter 4 explains these various sources of law and how to read them and break them down into understandable frameworks.) Depending on the topic, legal research can take several hours or even days, or it might demand just a few minutes if the researcher knows exactly what to look for and the answer is readily available. Lawyers conduct legal research in a law library, using books that codify the governing laws and rules,[7] or by accessing online databases such Westlaw, Lexis,

---

[6] For guidance on client interviewing, see Stefan H. Krieger & Richard K. Neumann, Jr., *Essential Lawyering Skills* (4th ed. 2011).

[7] When you first learn about various sources of law such as statutes and cases, it often helps to look at hardcopy books containing these resources. While this might seem like an "old school" tactic in our high-tech digital age, legal research is complicated and requires open-mindedness and slow, deliberate learning of new skills—at first. Seeing how the sources of law physically cross-reference one another (e.g., statutes contain "Notes of Decisions" that help you find cases; cases describe statutes; "digests" include summaries of cases;

Bloomberg Law, and others. The goal of the legal research phase is to narrow the legal question further—and identify the governing "rule."

Step 5: Preparing a Legal Research Memorandum: Once the lawyer gathers the client facts and performs careful legal research, it is time to synthesize the legal research results. Research might reveal a single source describing one clear or obvious "rule" or a pile of sources that require sifting. (Chapter 9 explains how to synthesize legal research results.) The first type of legal writing most new law students learn is how to draft a **legal research memorandum**. The memorandum is the vehicle lawyers use to identify the client's pertinent legal issue, describe the applicable rule(s), apply the rule(s) to the client's factual scenario, and objectively predict a realistic outcome. This book explains the step-by-step process for preparing a legal research memorandum in Chapters 8 to 20.

Usually, a legal research memorandum is an internal law office document, meaning that a junior attorney drafts it for a supervising attorney. It should be protected from disclosure to the potential opposing party by the attorney work product doctrine. The supervising attorney uses the written analysis to advise the client on how to handle a legal issue.[8] The legal query could relate to a general question about a particular law or to a specific dispute with a third party. The memo's analysis helps the attorney recommend what action or next steps, if any, the client should take.

Step 6: Advising the Client on the Next Course of Action: Once the legal analysis is complete, lawyers advise the client on the recommended course of action, either in person, on the phone, or via an **opinion letter** or **opinion e-mail**. To create these two types of documents, a lawyer converts the internal legal research memorandum into an appropriate external communication to the client. As long as the client does not distribute the letter or e-mail to anyone else, the attorney-client privilege should protect the document's contents from disclosure to the potential opposing party. During this advisory phase, the lawyer counsels[9] the client on next steps, such as dispute resolution options (including settlement) or procedures for filing a lawsuit.[10]

---

legal encyclopedias refer to statutes and cases) can help you visualize this interconnectedness on paper before you make the leap to online research where the visual connections and links might be more hidden. (You eventually will learn how to follow online research "bread crumbs" and access hyperlinks.) When you start researching online, if you find it difficult to understand how sources of law fit together, consider this strategy. Look first at the same sources in hard-copy books— to understand the big picture.

[8] Sometimes the supervising attorney decides the junior lawyer's memo is so well written that he or she transmits the document directly to the client.

[9] For valuable guidance on client counseling, see Krieger & Neumann, *supra* note 6.

[10] Sometimes parties choose arbitration over litigation. Litigation is explained in detail in Section I.C. Arbitration is a form of alternative dispute resolution in which parties can choose a neutral third person (or a panel of three impartial individuals) to resolve their dispute. The arbitrators typically are people with expertise in the particular industry or subject matter that is the subject of the dispute (e.g., construction, insurance, sports). Arbitration is often faster and less expensive than litigation if the parties agree to limited "discovery" (investigation of the facts of the case through document exchange, witness interviews, and so forth), but drawbacks include the fact that the arbitration panel is the sole decision maker (there is no jury), and typically the parties waive the right to an appeal. Arbitration is described further in Chapter 34.

B. Prelitigation Settlement

Clients often choose to settle a case short of filing a lawsuit, a decision that saves money, time, and energy fighting in court. In these situations, an attorney may use a favorable analysis extracted from the internal legal research memorandum to convince the opposing party (or his or her attorney if the party is represented by counsel) that the client has a valid argument and would likely prevail at trial. The lawyer can use the research and analysis from the internal legal research memorandum to draft a persuasive **settlement demand letter** to the other side. The demand letter sets forth the legal arguments demonstrating how and why the client would prevail at trial, but might offer to compromise for a particular amount of money or a specific action. Usually, such a letter includes a deadline for compromise and warns the recipient that, if settlement is not reached by that date, the client is prepared to file a legal complaint in the appropriate court.

If settlement is reached, the attorneys draft a **settlement agreement**, summarizing the terms of the compromise and any deadlines for compliance—which the parties sign. Settlement letters and agreements are discussed in Chapters 22 and 23.

C. Phases of Litigation

1. Pleadings

A lawsuit commences when a party, the "plaintiff," files a **complaint** in the appropriate court. When drafting a complaint, a lawyer researches which court has appropriate jurisdiction over the parties and the subject matter of the client's case. (Chapter 4 explains jurisdiction, a concept that is also taught in Civil Procedure class.) The document that an attorney files with the court to launch a case is called a **pleading** because the party is making a "plea" to the court.

A complaint starts off with a "caption" of the case, which includes the parties' full individual or corporate names and designations (plaintiff(s) and defendant(s)), the court's name, and the title of the pleading (i.e., complaint) so the court clerk can keep track of each document filed in the case. Then, in numbered paragraphs, the attorney describes

- the court's jurisdiction over the case,
- the basic facts giving rise to the dispute, and
- the legal "causes of action" asserted by the plaintiff.

Causes of action are the legal claims that the plaintiff must prove; examples include breach of contract, negligence, fraud, defamation, and slander. Each cause of action has certain required "elements," or component parts, that must be alleged in the complaint. Lawyers research what elements are essential to plead for each cause of action (see, e.g., the boxed example below). The drafter of the complaint needs to make sure the pleading does not omit mandatory elements of a cause of action, which would cause the complaint to fail.

Six Elements of a Cause of Action for Fraudulent Misrepresentation in Nebraska

A plaintiff must allege

(1) a person made a representation;
(2) the representation was false;
(3) the person knew the representation was false, or made it recklessly without knowledge of whether it was true or false;
(4) the person intended that the plaintiff rely on the representation;
(5) the plaintiff did rely on it; and
(6) the plaintiff suffered damage as a result.

Finally, the complaint states the "remedy," or the result that the plaintiff seeks. The remedy can include monetary damages or performance by the defendant—such as return of a tangible item, or the act of chopping down a rotting tree on adjoining land, or refraining from publishing a compromising photo in a tabloid.

The attorney signs the complaint and then files it with the appropriate court, usually paying a filing fee. Courts may allow and/or require electronic filing, which means the document is uploaded onto the court's electronic database and is assigned a case number (also called a docket number) from the clerk of the court. The complaint is then "served"[11] on the defendant, and the case begins.

After receiving the complaint, the defendant has a certain number of days (defined in the particular court's rules) to file a **motion to dismiss the complaint** or to file an **answer**. A "motion" is a form of legal writing in which an attorney "moves" or requests the court to take a certain action. If the defendant can demonstrate (based on legal research) that the complaint fails to state a viable cause of action or contains various other flaws (which you will learn in Civil Procedure class), a court might grant the motion to dismiss the complaint. The complaint is dismissed, and the lawsuit stops.

Alternatively, the defendant files an answer—which includes the same case caption at the top of the document (adding the case or docket number assigned by the court clerk and the title of "Answer")—and then responds, in numbered paragraphs corresponding to those in the complaint, to each allegation, either admitting or denying each statement. The defendant also uses the answer to assert

---

[11] "Service" is delivery of legal documents to another party, providing notice of the legal matter.

"defenses" to the causes of action in the complaint. Like the complaint, the answer is called a pleading.

Sometimes, parties also will add new litigants to the case, filing "third-party complaints," or may serve a "cross-complaint" on a co-party. Once all the pleadings have been filed, the case quickly moves into the scheduling phase.

2. Scheduling

Courthouses are very busy places. Courts all over the country manage hundreds of thousands of cases involving numerous parties and attorneys. Scheduling is critical. Many courts promulgate rules that require the attorneys on both sides of a case to work out a litigation management schedule between themselves, as soon as the pleadings phase ends. Often, counsel for one party coordinates a conference call or a face-to-face meeting with the lawyers representing the other party or parties. Together, the attorneys peruse their calendars and hammer out dates and deadlines for exchanging documents, taking depositions (interviews of witnesses under oath), responding and objecting to written discovery requests, engaging experts, exchanging expert reports, filing written motions to narrow issues for trial, submitting pretrial documents, and filing pretrial evidentiary motions. The parties also try to agree on how many days or weeks of trial are necessary. Hopefully, the attorneys can agree on all these items, but that is not always possible.

At the end of this conference call or meeting, the lawyers draft a **proposed joint case management plan** or **scheduling order** and present it to the court, identifying all items agreed on and those that remain sticking points. The court might accept the plan or adjust it, and then the judge signs the official "case management order" or "scheduling order" for the case. Once the judge issues the order, the case schedule is set, and time extensions are difficult to obtain. Thus, in the scheduling phase, attorneys must take the time to think through realistic durations for completing the numerous activities involved in preparing a case for trial.

3. Fact Discovery

In the fact discovery phase, lawyers become investigators and sleuths. They brainstorm about the many possible witnesses, documents, physical items, or tidbits of information that might be helpful in building and defending the client's case, and then ask for them—nicely—in written documents called **discovery requests**. In litigation, there are four main categories of discovery:

(1) Requests for production of documents or things: Categories of documents or physical objects that the attorneys believe will help them learn the facts of the case and prove or defend the causes of action in the complaint or the defenses in the answer

(2) Interrogatories: Written questions that parties must answer in writing, under oath

(3) Requests for admissions: Written statements that parties must admit or deny

(4) Depositions: Attorneys' interviews of witnesses who testify under oath; court reporters transcribe the questions and answers[12]

Clearly, the discovery phase of a case requires an assortment of legal writing.[13] Lawyers draft voluminous discovery requests to serve on opposing parties. The attorneys receiving the discovery requests draft written **objections** to any requests that the responding party considers to be beyond the scope of the court's discovery rules, and written **responses** to appropriate requests. Depositions also require legal writing: **notices of deposition** or **subpoenas**, and **deposition outlines** of questions to ask the witness and key topics to exhaust during the limited time available.

The discovery phase of litigation can take months, depending on the complexity of the case. Unfortunately, during this phase, lawyers have a habit of getting embroiled in their own quarrels and sometimes accuse one another of withholding key case information. This unpleasant scenario might require a party to file a **motion to compel discovery**, which requires court intervention to resolve the disagreement. However, many judges are disinclined to spend time refereeing discovery disputes and strongly encourage attorneys to work out these issues among themselves instead of consuming valuable judicial resources.

4. Expert Discovery

Some cases necessitate the assistance of expert witnesses to explain important aspects of the case to the jury or judge. For example, different cases might require experts on handwriting, fingerprints, car mechanics, heart surgery, art restoration, weapons, violin construction, or other specialized topics. An expert does not necessarily need advanced degrees or a history of employment at prestigious corporations; in a case involving a vending machine accident, for example, a lawyer could call an experienced local vending machine repair person to testify as an expert on an issue of the particular machine's operation that is beyond the experience of the average layperson. However, there are certain legal standards that a party proposing a certain expert at trial must meet. Legal research is important here as well to ensure that a client does not spend money engaging an expert that the judge later will not allow to testify at trial.

Lawyers work closely with experts in reviewing the case facts and provide the experts with whatever pertinent case documents and deposition transcripts they need to render opinions on the particular subject matter.

---

[12] Some cases might necessitate a fifth type of discovery—a request for a physical or mental examination of a party—but these requests require a motion by a party and a court order.
[13] Courts might require that parties exchange "initial disclosures" of categories of documents, potential witnesses, damages summaries, and insurance coverage—which help launch the discovery phase of the case.

The types of legal writing that lawyers perform during the expert phase of litigation include **engagement letters** (identifying the scope and boundaries of an expert's role in the case), **expert deposition outlines**, and **motions** to exclude another party's expert from trial if the expert's opinions do not meet the legal standards of the particular jurisdiction. During this phase, experts draft "expert reports" summarizing their opinions, which are provided to the other party in advance of depositions and trial. Sometimes lawyers are involved in recommending stylistic edits to these reports so they read clearly, but lawyers should not be the substantive authors of the reports.

5. Pretrial

The court's case management order, or scheduling order, typically sets a hard deadline for the cutoff date of all discovery, both fact- and expert-related. After that date, the parties shift gears and begin preparing pretrial submissions, to streamline the case as much as possible before trial. The types of legal writing that lawyers perform during the pretrial phase include the following.

- **Motions to narrow the substantive legal issues** (e.g., motions for summary judgment in which parties request the court to render judgment on a part or all of a cause of action in the complaint)
- **Motions regarding evidentiary issues** ("motions in limine") (e.g., motions requesting the court to decide whether a certain piece of evidence is "admissible" under the court's rules of evidence)
- **Jury instructions**[14] (if the case involves a jury), which explain the law governing the various causes of action in the complaint and the defenses in the answer, in language the jury can understand
- **Exhibit lists**, identifying all the exhibits the parties plan to present as evidence at trial
- **Witness lists**, identifying all the witnesses the parties plan to call to testify at trial

During this phase, litigants often revisit the possibility of settling the case. If a compromise is reached, the attorneys draft the settlement agreement.

6. Trial

The trial is the "big show"—a presentation of the facts and law to the decision maker. Even during trial, attorneys spend hours writing. The types of legal writing lawyers perform during trial include the following:

---

[14] In jury trials, lawyers also might be required to draft voir dire questions. *Voir dire* is old French for "to speak the truth." Lawyers and/or judges ask potential jurors voir dire questions during the jury selection phase of a trial to uncover whether jurors are biased, have relationships with any of the parties, or should be removed from the jury pool for any other legitimate reasons.

- **Opening statements**
- **Witness outlines**, including direct and cross-examination
- Additional **motions** regarding issues that arise during trial
- **Closing arguments**

7. Posttrial

Even after the judge or jury delivers a decision, lawyers still write. A prevailing (winning) party may be entitled to recover interest, attorneys' fees, or other costs; the attorney must file a motion requesting and proving the amounts of these items. The nonprevailing party has a certain number of days to file an appeal, which involves writing **briefs** to the appellate court.

II. Legal Writing in Transactional Lawyering

Many clients seek legal counsel for reasons that have nothing to do with a dispute. For example, individuals and companies seek legal advice regarding property ownership, taxes, real estate purchases, business start-ups and transactions, mergers, estate planning, and contract negotiation. These can all be positive "win-win" experiences for everyone involved, but still require legal research, analysis, and well-thought-out recommendations. The types of legal writing that lawyers do in these scenarios might involve the following:

- Corporate filings
- Legal research memoranda
- Deal "term sheets" (summaries of terms agreed on in a contract negotiation that have not yet been formalized in a contract)
- Negotiation Letters
- Contracts
- Wills
- Leases
- Loan documents

Whatever the type of legal writing, an attorney's goal is to make sure she

- knows all the legally significant facts that affect the client's legal question;
- thoroughly researches and understands the applicable law;
- properly applies the legal rules to the client scenario; and
- communicates clearly in the written document so the drafter and the reader are both fully aware of its intent, purpose, and legal effect.

PRACTICE TIPS

You now have a basic familiarity of the types of legal writing that lawyers do in various phases of a client's representation. When you receive a new assignment from a supervising attorney, take a moment to think about what phase the case or client relationship is in, and how the writing project will be used, perhaps in one of the following stages.

- In the initial stage of a client relationship, to provide advice on what course of action the client should take in a transaction or in a dispute with another individual or company
- In the middle of a case, to gather factual information from an opposing party or demand that the other side provide information to which the client is entitled under the governing rules
- At any phase of a client relationship, to convince a third party or the court to give the client the result or remedy he seeks

Knowing the ultimate purpose of your written work product makes all the difference in how you approach the task of preparing to write it.

PRACTICE CHECKLIST: TYPES OF LEGAL WRITING ATTORNEYS DO

Legal Writing in Dispute Resolution

Prelitigation

- ☑ Client Engagement Letter
- ☑ Master Fact Chronology
- ☑ Legal Research Memorandum
- ☑ Client Opinion Letter (or E-mail)
- ☑ Settlement Demand Letter
- ☑ Settlement Agreement

Pleadings Phase

- ☑ Complaint
- ☑ Motion to Dismiss
- ☑ Opposition to Motion to Dismiss
- ☑ Answer
- ☑ Third-Party Pleadings

Scheduling Phase

☑ Joint Proposed Scheduling Plan (or Case Management Plan)

Fact Discovery

☑ Any Court-Required Initial Disclosures
☑ Requests for Production of Documents or Things
☑ Interrogatories
☑ Requests for Admissions
☑ Motions for Physical or Mental Examination
☑ Written Objections and Responses to Discovery
☑ Notices of Deposition and/or Subpoenas
☑ Deposition Outlines
☑ Motions to Compel Discovery
☑ Oppositions to Motions to Compel

Expert Discovery

☑ Engagement Letters
☑ Reviewing (but not Drafting) Expert Reports
☑ Expert Deposition Outlines
☑ Motions in Limine to Exclude an Expert
☑ Oppositions to Motions in Limine

Pretrial Phase

☑ Motions for Summary Judgment
☑ Motions in Limine on Evidentiary Issues
☑ Oppositions to Motions
☑ Jury Instructions
☑ Voir Dire Questions
☑ Exhibit Lists
☑ Witness Lists
☑ Settlement Agreement

Trial Phase

☑ Opening Statements
☑ Witness Direct-Examination and Cross-Examination Outlines
☑ Trial Motions (and Oppositions)
☑ Closing Arguments

Posttrial Phase

- ☑ Motions for Interest, Attorneys' Fees, and/or Costs
- ☑ Appeal Brief

Legal Writing in Transactional Lawyering

- ☑ Client Engagement Letter
- ☑ Corporate Filings
- ☑ Legal Research Memorandum
- ☑ Deal Term Sheet
- ☑ Negotiation Letters
- ☑ Contract
- ☑ Wills
- ☑ Lease
- ☑ Loan Document

Chapter 2
Pondering
Professional Judgment

Now that you are on your way to becoming a lawyer, you will be using the word "judgment" (spelled "judgment," rather than "judgement") on a regular basis. In the litigation context, the term means "[a] court's final determination of the rights and obligations of the parties in a case"[1]—in other words, the court's decision in a litigation. However, consider engaging with a different kind of judgment in your first few weeks of law school, and every week of your career thereafter: professional judgment.

You probably are going to hear a lot about "professionalism" throughout your law school experience. *Black's Law Dictionary* offers an elegant definition of this term: "The practice of a learned art in a characteristically methodical, courteous, and ethical manner."[2] Likewise, various glossaries define "judgment" as

- "the ability to . . . make a decision, or form an opinion objectively, authoritatively, and wisely, especially in matters affecting action."[3]
- "good sense, or discretion."[4]
- "the ability to make considered decisions or come to sensible conclusions."[5]

So, what does it mean to exercise professional judgment and be "methodical, courteous, and ethical" as a law student? Can judgment, good sense, discretion, or sensibility be learned or taught, or is it innate?

---

[1] *Black's Law Dictionary* (9th ed. 2009).
[2] *Id.*
[3] Dictionary.com, http://dictionary.reference.com/browse/judgment (last visited Oct. 13, 2014).
[4] *Id.*
[5] Oxford Dictionaries, http://oxforddictionaries.com/us/definition/american_english/judgment (last visited Oct. 13, 2014).

Carve out some time to think about these words and what professional judgment means to you. Make a commitment to contemplate how you can enhance your professional judgment, starting now as a 1L student. Even if you have been in professional workplace environments before, you are entering a new vocation in which clients will rely on you for advice often in complex, emotionally charged, stressful circumstances. The colleagues, adversaries, parties, authority figures, and decision makers we encounter as lawyers are part of a system greater than ourselves. Acquiring, and then enriching, professional judgment requires new lawyers to reflect on how they fit into the legal system as a whole. What role do you want to play? What role should you play? How will exercising good judgment get you where you want to be?

In law school, you will engage in relationships with classmates, section-mates, professors, administrative staff, alumni, potential employers, family, significant others, friends, and acquaintances. Perhaps you presented yourself a certain way in college (the ambitious achiever? the fun-loving athlete? the happy-go-lucky jokester? the master-of-all-nighters?). Maybe you projected a particular persona in graduate school or in the workforce prior to law school. As you commence this new life phase, grant yourself flexibility to shift the way you portray yourself as a law student and an attorney. Now is your chance to reinvent yourself—into the newer, more professional "you."

> "It is not by muscle, speed, or physical dexterity that great things are achieved, but by reflection, force of character, and judgment."
> ● *Marcus Tullius Cicero*

I. Respect Rules

Law is a profession swaddled in rules. Yet, people break the rules all the time: criminals, contracting parties, vehicle drivers, taxpayers, and yes, unfortunately even lawyers. In law school, you will learn many types of rules, including substantive legal rules and procedural rules. Developing professional judgment includes embracing legal rules, deconstructing confusing mandates into understandable components, being interested in the context (the "why") behind these requirements, and respecting the law enough to follow substantive and procedural rules for a greater purpose.

A. Substantive Rules

In law school, rules are a law student's friend; rules are the vehicle for answering legal questions. When in doubt, ask yourself, "Well, what is the legal rule?" Classes such as Contracts, Torts, Criminal Law, Property, Civil Procedure,

Constitutional Law, and Evidence abound with "substantive" rules. "Substantive" means that they "create and define rights and duties."[6] Your job as a law student is to read statutes, regulations, and case law with an eye toward extracting substantive legal rules about parties' entitlements and obligations, and then experiment with applying them to factual scenarios. Often, you will have to "synthesize," or pare down, a single unified rule from a combination of more than one legal source; for example, you might read a collection of cases and notice common themes or patterns, and then consolidate these ideas into a well-constructed, cohesive rule. In analyzing and understanding rules, lawyers are investigators, problem solvers, surgeons—of words. Rules are simply words, with legal significance.

B. Procedural Rules

In contrast to substantive rules, legal "procedural" rules focus on logistical steps, instructions, processes, or ways of facilitating legal results.[7] Procedural rules in law school are just as important as substantive ones. Understanding and following the procedural rules that your law professors use to govern your classes will give you practice in exercising professional judgment regarding the observance of rules issued by courts, arbitrators, regulatory agencies, corporate governance boards, and similar entities later in your career.

Professors invest significant time and energy in structuring law school courses, whether they involve large lecture classes, small legal research/writing classes or seminars. To ensure a rewarding educational experience for each student, professors aspire to create a comprehensive yet reasonably paced "substantive arc" of the course (i.e., the breadth of the subject matter covered), in addition to clear procedures that govern

- daily class preparation,
- class participation,
- submission of written assignments or other "assessments" (such as midterms or exams),
- deadlines,
- interaction with the professors and/or teaching fellows/assistants,
- office hours,
- lateness or absence, and
- grading.

---

[6] Merriam-Webster Dictionary, http://www.merriam-webster.com/dictionary/substantive (last visited Oct. 13, 2014).
[7] *Id.*, http://www.merriam-webster.com/dictionary/procedure.

These procedural rules are designed to help students excel, not falter. Yet, too often, students do not recognize the importance of these rules, and—burdened by an overwhelming workload or the inherent stress of law school—forget about them, ignore them, or resist them. The discussion throughout this chapter may seem obvious; "Yes, we get it, follow the rules." But as you embark on a career based on the "rule of law," it is important to contemplate how respect for rules becomes a crucial component of professional judgment in law school and beyond.

II. Beware the Dreaded "Benchslap"

In an alarming multitude of written judicial opinions, judges reprimand lawyers for violating nonnegotiable substantive and procedural rules. Legal "blawgers" affectionately dub these public reprimands "benchslaps."[8] Judges meting out these admonishments take time out of adjudicating a case to describe how the lawyers did not follow the rules and, more importantly, how those rule violations detrimentally affected the court's ability to do its job. Certainly, these written opinions are often entertaining to read, and at first glance, you might think to yourself, "Well, I would never break the rules like that, so a benchslap would never happen to me!" But the truth is, this happens more often than you might think and yet is so easily avoidable. Benchslaps tend to focus on eight categories of legal writing shortcomings:

(1) Written work product that the court cannot understand because it lacks structural logic and clear phrasing

(2) Written work product that is missing substantive components required in the rules (e.g., statements of facts, procedural case history, legal questions presented)

(3) Written work product that poorly handles the case facts (e.g., misstates facts or improperly cites to the factual record)

(4) Written work product that inadequately explains the governing law (e.g., ignores law that is adverse to the lawyer's client or improperly cites legal sources)

(5) Written work product that violates clear procedural and formatting rules (e.g., page/word limits, line spacing, margins)

(6) Written work product riddled with rampant typographical, grammatical, or general proofreading errors

(7) Written work product infused with a disrespectful tone toward the court, opposing counsel, or other parties

(8) Late submissions, in violation of clear court-imposed deadlines

---

[8] According to the *Urban Dictionary*, the term "benchslap" was popularized by David Lat of Above-TheLaw.com (when he was blogging for UnderneathTheirRobes.com). See also Josh Blackman, *The 8 Best Benchslaps of 2012*, Josh Blackman's Blog (Dec. 18, 2012), http://joshblackman.com/blog/2012/12/18/the-8-best-benchslaps-of-2012/.

In many of these benchslap cases,[9] judges emphasize why these rule viola-tions, or displays of less-than-professional judgment, impede the court's ability to do its work in processing a legal case. First, on a positive note, many judges accentuate that lawyers who exercise *good* professional judgment, and submit written work product that thoughtfully presents substantive rules and applies them clearly to client facts, enable courts to process complex intellectual material efficiently, so judges can "forge enlightened decisions."[10] Remember, as lawyers, you are representing third parties—the clients—and want judges to render deci-sions that help clients achieve a fair result or right a wrong. Your professional judgment, displayed often through the vehicle of legal writing, can help courts resolve cases in ways that facilitate equitable outcomes.

Second, on another encouraging note, judges often point out in these written opinions that lawyers who exercise *good* professional judgment and submit written work product that complies with the court's procedural rules help ensure "fairness and orderliness" in the judicial process.[11] Courts' procedural rules are designed to "ensure fairness by providing litigants with an even playing field."[12] This means that lawyers and parties on either side of a case must follow the same set of rules so neither side reaps an unfair advantage. This notion might seem odd in a compet-itive environment like law school or the legal arena, but just like on the sports field, a clear and consistently applied set of rules enhances the experience for everyone.

Further, procedural rules facilitate "orderliness by providing courts with a means for the efficient administration of crowded dockets."[13] Courts handle countless legal matters in a single day, processing numerous legal documents whether in hard copy or electronically. When lawyers exercise professional judg-ment and respect court procedures, court clerks can process all the necessary paperwork more efficiently so judges have ready access to the documents they need to get up-to-speed on each case and so justice can be served for every client.

Overall, a lawyer's professional judgment is one of the most important factors affecting a client's representation. An attorney's poor judgment in submitting substantively weak legal writing hampers a judge's ability to understand the parties' claims and render fair decisions, jeopardizing the client's interests. Like-wise, a lawyer's imprudence in submitting written work product that defies procedural rules unfairly increases the workload of others, including courthouse staff and opposing counsel.

---

[9] See Appendix A for a survey of these benchslap cases.

[10] As the United States Court of Appeals for the First Circuit (a federal court) explained so succinctly in a case called *Reyes-Garcia v. Rodriguez & Del Valle, Inc.*, 82 F.3d 11, 14 (1st Cir. 1996), "rules establish a framework that helps courts to assemble the raw material that is essential for forging enlightened decisions." Deficiencies in legal writing "frustrate any reasonable attempt to understand [a party's] legal theories." *Id.* Further, "Since appellate judges are not haruspices, they are unable to decide cases by reading goats' entrails. They must rely on lawyers and litigants to submit briefs that present suitably developed argumentation. . . ." *Id.* (Chapter 11 explains the use of "*id.*" in legal citations.)

[11] *Id.*

[12] *Id.*

[13] *Id.*

III. Respect Procedural Rules in the Law School Classroom

Most law professors provide a detailed, sometimes lengthy syllabus and course policies governing their law school courses. Answers to students' questions about how to excel in the class are almost always found in these two documents. These documents are wide-open windows into the mind of the professor and what he or she is looking for in an excellent student who exhibits the utmost professional judgment.

Substantively, whether the syllabus is cursory or voluminous, it provides an overview of the big picture (or substantive arc) of the course, start to finish. Before you begin the assigned reading in the first week of a law school class, get to know the syllabus as a whole. Notice any particular headings the professor uses to separate subject matter or assign readings. The headings typically offer guidance to the main coverage topics in the course and their sub-components. Consider trying to diagram the headings of a syllabus on your own, to see whether you can understand how the course is designed overall.

Procedurally, the syllabus and course policies furnish guidelines for exhibiting professional judgment in several different categories listed below. The right-hand column identifies some potential questions that mindful law students often ask themselves as they undertake each classroom task.

Professional Judgment Opportunity	Information Likely Provided in the Syllabus	Self-Prompts if the Answer is Not Readily Apparent in the Syllabus/Policies
Class preparation	Advance reading assignments; substantive topics covered	• In a voluminous reading assignment, what details does my professor care about the most for class discussion? • How does this professor typically ask questions in class? Does he or she have a pattern of questioning? • How can I best prepare my reading notes to be able to answer those types of questions?
Class participation	Whether students will be "on-call," "cold-called," or are encouraged to volunteer	• How can I answer questions in class in a professional way that shows I am interested and engaged in deep thinking about the material? • Even if I am nervous about talking in class, how can I prepare myself to at least try to demonstrate my interest and preparation (even if my answers do not sound perfect)?
Laptop/technology usage	Whether laptops are permitted in class; any restrictions	• Am I tempted to check e-mail, Facebook, or instant messages during class? • Is my laptop behavior distracting to classmates around me? • Would I be better off simply resisting temptation, closing my laptop and shutting off my phone, and taking notes the "old-fashioned" way?

Professional Judgment Opportunity	Information Likely Provided in the Syllabus	Self-Prompts if the Answer is Not Readily Apparent in the Syllabus/Policies
Submission of written assignments	E-mail submission requirements (information required in e-mail headers to professors); word count/page limits; font; margins; line spacing; use of footnotes; hard-copy submissions; single-sided or double-sided paper; use of anonymous grading numbers	*Note:* While some of these formatting rules might seem picky, your professor (like a court) has important logistical reasons for requiring written documents to be submitted a certain way: • *Font size:* easy to read and process large quantities of information • *Word count/page limits:* teaching you to be concise; also processing large numbers of student papers efficiently to provide reasonable turnaround of feedback; creating an "even playing field" for all students • *E-mail headers:* keeping track of timeliness of multiple submissions of different types of documents across several sections of students or different courses altogether • If I ask for "special treatment" or skirt or ignore the rules, am I adding to the professor's workload or being unfair to colleagues who complied with the rules? Am I being perceived as disrespectful?
Deadlines	When all graded and nongraded assignments are due throughout the semester	• If I know I am going to be late in submitting an assignment and I have a legitimate reason (i.e., serious illness, family emergency), should I let my professor know in advance? • How much personal information is "too much information" regarding a lateness excuse? • If I ask for special treatment for a particular excuse, am I being fair to my classmates who submitted their work on time? • By submitting assignments late, without advance notice, am I showing disrespect to my professor (who is grading me)?
Interaction with my professor/attending office hours	Whether your professor prefers e-mail questions, telephone conferences, scheduled office hours appointments, drop-ins	• If I drop by my professor's office without an appointment, am I being disrespectful to his or her time? • Even if I have a friendly relationship with a professor, how should I craft professional e-mails to him or her? • If I have a question about a class-related issue, have I first tried to find the answer myself (e.g., in the syllabus, policies, or readings)? • If I have an appointment with a professor, what preparation should I do in advance? • Should I print out a copy of whatever document I want to discuss with the professor so he or she does not have to strain to look at my computer?

Professional Judgment Opportunity	Information Likely Provided in the Syllabus	Self-Prompts if the Answer is Not Readily Apparent in the Syllabus/Policies
Lateness or absence	Whether your professor wants to know in advance if you will be late to, or absent from, class; excused v. unexcused absences; follow-up for missed classes	• If I know I am going to be late to, or absent from, a class and I have a legitimate reason (i.e., serious illness, family emergency), should I let my professor know in advance? • How much personal information is "too much information" regarding a lateness/absence excuse? • What follow-up can I do on my own if I miss a class (rather than asking my professor to repeat what he or she covered in class)?
Grading and feedback	Rules governing graded assignments; how assignments will be graded; application of a curve	• If a professor asks students to wait a certain time period after receiving a grade before seeking an appointment to discuss it, am I being disrespectful by asking for an exception to this policy? • Before I meet with a professor about a grade, have I taken the time to review and process his or her comments on my work?

As you read various course syllabi and policies and apply those rules in your everyday use, try to practice professional judgment in understanding the reasoning behind them. Like courts, professors create these rules not to be onerous or punitive, but to process substance more effectively, maintain fairness among all participants, and facilitate orderliness in evaluating large quantities of individual work product.

In a competitive environment like law school, it might seem counterintuitive to think about fairness to your classmates. It also might feel awkward to respect a system you do not yet fully understand. However, think of law school as practice for the real world of law. Respect for the system is important and requires professional courtesy toward for your colleagues and adversaries alike.

IV. Consider Professional Judgment When Communicating as a Law Student

Use the following real-life examples of students' writing to law professors to spark your own thoughts about exhibiting professional judgment, being mindful in your written communications in law school, and thoughtfully addressing individuals who eventually may serve as references or mentors.

Example 1: (E-mail from a student to an academic support professor referred by another professor who was worried about the student's nervousness when speaking in class)

prof. i need to meet. i am free after 4 M/T/Th

Example 2: (E-mail from a student who missed a legal writing draft deadline and did not respond to his professor's four reminder e-mails—over a four-day period including a weekend—to set up a one-on-one writing conference)

I just got to school this morning from being away all break[14] and saw your messages. I had not signed up for the meeting yet because I couldn't remember if there was a time we had already set. Can you check and get back to me?

Example 3: (E-mail from a student who was displeased with a grade on a written assignment that he turned in late and that exceeded the professor's word count by 276 words)

I'm pretty shocked about this grade, regardless of the 8 point deduction for word count and the 5 points off for being late which wasn't my fault—I had computer problems. When can we meet so we can try and figure this out? It doesn't look like the curve will help me much on this one.

Example 4: (E-mail from a student who missed a 9 a.m. class)

Sorry I missed today's class. I felt really tired and wound up over sleeping until 11. Outside of going over the logistics of the brief is there anything important I missed?

Example 5: (E-mail from a student who scheduled a 2 p.m. appointment with a professor over a holiday break to obtain advice about a cover letter; the e-mail was sent an hour after the scheduled appointment time)

Hii,
I could not make it to your office today!! I overslept. I was working on that letter until 4 am! Will you be there after 4pm? I am so sorry!!

Examples of Good Professional Judgment from Law Students

Example 1: Dear Professor: I am writing to let you know in advance that, regrettably, I need to miss Legal Practice class this Thursday to attend a funeral of a family friend. I plan to do the reading and obtain the class notes from a colleague. Please let me know if you would like me to provide any additional information about my absence or perform any extra work outside of class. Thank you very much for your understanding.

Example 2: Dear Professor: I have received my grade on my Memo 1 assignment, and I have taken the time to review your comments in detail. I still have a few questions on certain areas that I would like to improve in my next assignment. May I make an appointment during your next Office Hours to discuss three specific points in my Memo 1 assignment? Thank you very much for your time.

Example 3: Dear Professor: I am looking forward to meeting with you for our Memo 1 conference scheduled next week. Unfortunately, I just realized that my scheduled conference time conflicts with a mandatory professional development seminar. I fully understand that your conference schedule likely is fully booked; however, I spoke with a classmate who offered to switch time slots with me, upon your approval. Would that be possible? Thank you very much for your consideration.

---

[14] By "break" this student was referring to a normal law school weekend, not a holiday.

EXERCISE: DEVELOPING YOUR OWN PROFESSIONAL JUDGMENT CHECKLIST

Set aside 30 minutes to develop a set of professional judgment "aspirations"[15] for your law school experience. Or do so with a small group of classmates, as if you are creating your own law firm and agreeing on a set of professional judgment objectives for the office. Think about how you want to exercise professional judgment in the following areas.

- Preparing in a thoughtful manner for all your classes
- Participating in class in a respectful and engaged way (tone, volunteering, respectfully disagreeing with a professor or classmate)
- Respecting your professors' course policies, expectations, and experience
- Using (or not using) your own technology in the classroom (laptops, iPads, smartphones, Facebook)
- Representing yourself in law school–related social media postings
- Communicating with classmates and professors (via e-mail and in person)
- Showing up on time to classes, meetings, and appointments (and how/when to communicate regarding unavoidable lateness or absence)
- Capturing learning in class (laptops, note taking)
- Presenting yourself in a professional manner while still maintaining your own personality
- Following up with the professor in a courteous manner if you miss a class
- Handling lateness in submitting assignments (legitimate excuses, respectful requests for time extensions/accommodations)
- Interacting with professors outside of class
- Studying with others
- Helping others struggling in law school
- Representing your school off campus
- Conducting yourself in a job search
- Asking for help or seeking mentors to address law school anxiety or substantive questions
- Holding yourself accountable for all of the above

---

[15] An "aspiration" is "a strong desire to achieve something high or great." Merriam-Webster Dictionary, http://www.merriam-webster.com/dictionary/aspiration (last visited Oct. 13, 2014).

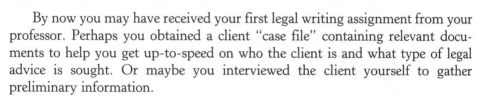

Chapter 3

Strategies for Starting a New Legal Writing Assignment

By now you may have received your first legal writing assignment from your professor. Perhaps you obtained a client "case file" containing relevant documents to help you get up-to-speed on who the client is and what type of legal advice is sought. Or maybe you interviewed the client yourself to gather preliminary information.

To approach this assignment as a real lawyer would, gather your case file documents and a fresh legal pad (or your laptop), and then answer the following questions.

☑ Who is the client?

☑ What is the client's role in society?

☑ What is the general situation that caused the client to seek legal advice?

☑ What type of document am I being asked to write? What is the expected format of my written work product? Letter? Memorandum? E-mail? Bullet-point outline?

☑ Who is my intended audience?

☑ What is my deadline? Do I have an internal deadline? An external deadline? Interim deadlines for drafts? (Tip: Check the syllabus.)

☑ Are there rules I need to follow for producing and submitting my work product? Law office rules? Supervising attorney rules? Court rules? (Tip: Check the course policies.)

☑ How long should the final document be? Is there a word count or page limit?

☑ Are there budget limits on the amount of time I can spend on this project? (Tip: In a law office environment, lawyers need to consider the client's budget.)

☑ Are there limits on the sources I can consult when researching the legal issue? (Tip: Has the supervising attorney already given you the sources of law? Are you instructed to conduct additional research? Is online research permitted?)

☑ What is the purpose of the assignment for the client? Why am I being asked to prepare this document? In what phase or stage of the client representation am I joining the client team (see Chapter 1)?

☑ What documents can I consult to get me up-to-speed quickly on the facts of the client's legal matter?

I. Creating a Client Case File

The next task you should undertake when given a new client matter is to create your own physical, hard-copy client case file. This can be a three-ring binder or some sort of folder to which you add documents as they are created (i.e., in chronological order). It is fine to maintain a case file on your computer. However, if you also print a hard copy, the documents will be more readily accessible for you to jot notes, circle or highlight key items, organize facts in chronological order, and visualize how the facts and legal issues relate. Also, when your professor (or a law firm supervisor) asks you to refer to a document quickly in class (or in a meeting), you have the case file handy instead of having to scramble to find an item on the computer.

In a law school assignment, the initial case file may include an instructional memo from the supervising attorney, factual documents (contracts, letters, e-mails, photographs, etc.), and perhaps statutes, regulations, or cases.[1] Print out these documents, put them in a binder or folder, and bring them to class, or in the law firm environment, to every meeting with the client or supervising attorney. You can experiment with different ways of organizing your case file, but anticipate that it will expand as you perform additional fact-gathering, research, and writing activities. You may need more than one file folder or binder.

Some lawyers organize case files chronologically, with individual sections for different categories of documents:

- Internal law office memoranda (to/from members of the client team within the law office)
- Correspondence
  o To/from the client (including initial client engagement letter, printed e-mails, letters, legal fee bills)

---

[1] Often your first legal research assignment in a law school writing class is a "closed universe" assignment—meaning that your professor provides the applicable law; you will not conduct any research on your own. In an "open universe" assignment, you conduct the research yourself. And, of course, in real law practice, your supervising attorney may or may not give you a statute, a regulation, or a case citation to get you started; you likely will conduct the remaining research yourself.

- o To/from opposing parties/counsel
- o To/from third parties (e.g., copy vendors, deposition court reporters, couriers)
- Client factual documents (e.g., contracts, e-mails, letters, photographs)
- Legal research (e.g., copies of statutes, regulations, cases)
- Pleadings (e.g., complaint, answer) and motions
- Court orders

II. Who Is the Client?

After you create your case file, think carefully about who your client is. Is she an individual? A company? Another type of organization? What does the client do for a living? Where does she live or work? How old is she? What is her role in society? Is her life experience similar to or different from yours?

Now review the case file and identify the general situation that has prompted the client to call the law office and seek legal advice. Is the client contemplating entering into a contract or a business transaction? Is the client in a dispute with someone else? Is the client concerned about possibly being sued?

Do not worry if the precise legal issue is not yet clear from the preliminary information provided. This is normal. Your legal research and synthesis/analysis of the law will help illuminate the precise legal issue and governing rule(s). Your initial job is to identify the general reason the client is seeking legal advice. It might help to start off just by brainstorming about what body of law might govern the question: Contract law? Criminal law? Property law? Tort law? Constitutional law? Marital law? Juvenile law? Immigration law? Maritime law? Animal law?

III. What Exactly Am I Expected to Write?

The next questions you will ask yourself are "what, who, when, why, and how?" First, identify exactly *what* type of document the supervising attorney is asking you to prepare: A legal research memorandum? A letter? An e-mail? An outline? If this is your first assignment in law school, the desired product is likely a **legal research memorandum**. Since presumably you have never written one of these before, first obtain a visual image of what one looks like. In the reading assignments on your syllabus, your professor probably has identified samples of documents that he considers to be examples of solid legal writing in the format he expects to see.[2] Skim these examples (for formatting only) to identify the

---

[2] There is a sample single-issue legal office memorandum in Appendix B. However, note that there is not a one-size-fits-all perfect model of a legal office memorandum; different audiences (such as professors and

various components included in a legal research memorandum; scan and note headings and sections throughout the document.[3]

Next, find out how long or short the end product of your writing assignment should be, and whether there is any word count or page limit.

You also should determine whether your intended audience has imposed any particular rules for submission of the document; professors and some attorneys and law offices have particular formatting requirements, and courts usually have strict rules about written submissions. Obtain copies of these rules before you even begin working on the project. Your legal writing class rules might appear in the course policies or in a separate document in the case file.

IV. Who Is My Audience?

Next, identify your hypothetical audience: The supervising attorney? The client? Opposing counsel? A judge? For your first legal research memorandum, your audience probably is your professor playing the role of a supervising attorney. Think about *who* will be reading the document and how your written work will affect that person's ability to do her job. Strive to make each piece of legal writing as useful as possible to the reader. Picture the person physically reading your document and then using its contents to make some type of challenging decision. Imagine a supervising attorney as a flesh-and-blood human being, either sitting at a desk or racing off to court or a meeting: What is his daily schedule? What is his role in the law office? Where physically will he be reading your document: At a desk? On a plane? In a taxi? In a conference room? On a train? Why has he assigned this particular task to you? How much time will he take to read your document?

V. When Is My Work Product Due?

Next, identify when the document is due. In law school, check the syllabus and identify any interim deadlines for drafts, dates of writing conferences with the professor to discuss the preliminary version, and the final deadline. In a law office setting, ask the supervising attorney when she would like the final product and whether she would like to see a draft earlier than the final deadline.

---

supervising attorneys) have varying preferences of writing style. It is wise to review sample legal documents for overall structure and formatting, but still approach each of your own writing assignments by tailoring the structure specifically to the substantive legal matters at hand and to your particular audience.

[3] In the law firm setting, you should obtain examples of similar documents written or used by your supervising attorney so you can grasp visually how each document is constructed (i.e., what the various components are and how they are organized).

Lawyers are reigned by calendars: their own, the clients', the courts', the opposing counsels', and others'. Now is a good time for you to experiment with and choose a calendaring system that will help you plan how to complete and submit drafts and final work product on time, while balancing an abundance of other commitments. As you learn the step-by-step process of drafting the incremental parts of a legal office memorandum in the upcoming chapters, you will write each component part individually and they will build on each other. Legal writing is not a "night-before-the-due-date" all-nighter type of experience. It requires layers of careful thought and adjustments—which take contemplation, concentration, patience, reflection, and revision.

VI. Why Am I Being Asked to Write This Document?

Chapter 1 explains how various types of legal writing fit into different phases of a client representation. Think about what stage the client representation is in and how this particular type of legal writing will assist you or the supervising attorney in helping the client make a decision or move the case forward. If you are not sure about the phase or stage of the case, that is a good question to ask the person assigning the legal writing project. You want to make your work product as useful as possible to your supervising attorney, the client, and, of course, yourself.

VII. What Time or Budget Limits Should I Consider?

In real law practice, time is money. Many lawyers bill clients based on hourly rates, often in increments of tenths of the hour (i.e., "2.3 hours reviewing client documents; 7.2 hours researching, outlining, and drafting a legal research memorandum"). New lawyers sometimes are surprised at how quickly time spent on a particular project adds up. Before you start each research and writing project, especially in a law office environment, ascertain any governing time and budget restrictions. Also, you might face constraints on using certain legal research resources, like online databases, as they can be expensive. It always helps to obtain this information prior to starting a project, so you know how much latitude you have to get your work done thoroughly yet efficiently. Since you are new at this and still on the learning curve, practice legal research and writing as much as you can in law school so that when you graduate, you already have a solid foundation to perform these tasks efficiently.

VIII. How Should I Get Started?

Now that you have a basic idea of your project parameters, it is time to begin the actual "heavy lifting." Appendix D at the end of this book provides an office memorandum drafting checklist, with step-by-step instructions for how to get started writing a legal research memorandum; each step is described in detail in the subsequent chapters of this book.

The initial phase of any legal assignment is to become familiar with the *facts* of the client's case and use them to identify the precise legal *issue* to research. So, dig in and get acquainted with the case file. Sources of client facts might include a summary memo from the supervising attorney, notes from a client interview, and evidentiary documents provided by the client, such as e-mails, letters, photographs, contracts, blueprints, diaries, telephone logs, and/or transcripts. Begin building a chronology of events. Familiarize yourself with the key documents and identify factual gaps so you can seek out additional information from the client or the supervising attorney. Once you have a framework of the facts, it is time to put that attorney mind to work and start researching the law.

New Assignment Worksheet

Who is the client?_____

Client billing/matter number (for law office timesheets):_____

Who are the opposing parties? Any other key characters/players?_____

_____

What is the general situation that has caused the client to seek legal advice?____

_____

What type of document am I being asked to write?_____

Who will be reading this document?_____

What is my deadline? Is there an internal deadline and an external deadline? Are there interim deadlines?_____

What is the expected format of my end product? Letter? Memorandum? E-mail? Bullet-point outline? _____

Are there rules I need to follow for the expected format? Supervising attorney rules? Court rules?_____

Do I have a complete, up-to-date copy of these rules?_____

_____

How long should my document be? Is there any word count or page limit?_____

_____

Are there budget limits on the amount of time I can spend on the project?_____

_____

Are there limits on the sources I can consult when researching the legal issue?_____

_____

What is the purpose of the assignment in the law office's legal representation of the client? In what stage of the client representation is the case in, and how will this document be used to advance the client's case?_____

_____

What documents can I consult to get up-to-speed quickly on the facts of the client's legal matter?_____

_____

Any additional questions for the supervising attorney?_____

_____

Facts Known So Far[4]

1. Key players/characters in the client "story"?

2. Key events or dates?

3. Key documents?

4. Key physical objects?

5. Any themes appearing so far in the facts?

---

[4] Some or all of these facts eventually appear in your memorandum. (See Chapter 16, "Writing a Statement of Facts in a Legal Office Memorandum.")

Section 2

The Mindful Legal Writer's Raw Materials

Chapter 4
Understanding the Sources of Legal Rules

Once a lawyer has a basic idea of what factual circumstance is prompting the client to seek legal advice, the next step is finding the appropriate sources of law to answer the legal question. To do this, you need to understand how the American legal system works. So let's start with a few refresher civics lessons.

The U.S. legal system is comprised of a federal system and a state system. According to the Tenth Amendment to the U.S. Constitution,[1] "The powers not delegated to the United States by the Constitution, nor prohibited by it to the States, are reserved to the States respectively, or to the people."

I. Branches of Federal Government

The U.S. Constitution establishes **three** branches of our government: legislative, executive, and judicial.

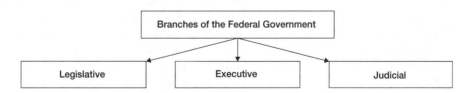

---

[1] *Merriam-Webster* defines "constitution" as "the basic principles and laws of a nation, state, or social group that determine the powers and duties of the government and guarantee certain rights to the people in it." Merriam-Webster Dictionary, http://www.merriam-webster.com/dictionary/constitution (last visited Nov. 11, 2014). But the dictionary also defines the word as "the structure, composition, physical makeup, or nature of something." Our federal Constitution gives structure to our legal system.

A. Legislative Branch

Article I, Section 1, of the Constitution states, "All legislative Powers herein granted shall be vested in a Congress of the United States, which shall consist of a Senate and House of Representatives." Congress makes laws, in the form of legislation (which we call **statutes**). These statutes are published in the *United States Code*. (Chapter 5 explains statutes in detail.)

B. Executive Branch

Article II, Section 1, of the Constitution vests executive power in the president of the United States. The president implements and enforces the laws written by Congress by appointing a cabinet, which includes heads of federal agencies "responsible for the day-to-day enforcement and administration of federal laws."[2] Well-known examples of federal agencies include the Bureau of Alcohol, Tobacco, and Firearms (ATF); the Drug Enforcement Administration (DEA); and the Federal Aviation Administration (FAA).

Federal agencies are given certain authority—under the Administrative Procedure Act (APA), which is a statute—to issue **regulations** that explain *how* federal laws (statutes) should be enforced. Agency regulations are published in the *Code of Federal Regulations*. Examples of regulations include Securities and Exchange Commission (SEC) regulations, Food and Drug Administration (FDA) regulations, and Federal Communications Commission (FCC) regulations.

C. Judicial Branch

Federal Court System

U.S. Supreme Court
(highest court)
U.S. Courts of Appeals
(appellate court)
U.S. District Courts
(trial court)

Article II, Section 1, of the Constitution establishes the judiciary, including the U.S. Supreme Court and lower-level trial courts and courts of appeals. The trial-level courts in the federal system are called U.S. District Courts. The intermediate appeals courts are called the U.S. Courts of Appeals. The U.S. Supreme Court is the highest court in our nation. Federal courts "interpret the law, determine the constitutionality of the law, and apply it to individual

---

[2] *The Executive Branch*, The White House, http://www.whitehouse.gov/our-government/executive-branch (last visited Oct. 16, 2014).

Sources of Federal Law

- Constitution
- Statutes (enacted by the legislative branch)
- Regulations (issued by agencies appointed by the executive branch)
- Common law (in opinions written by the judicial branch)

cases."[3] When a federal court renders a decision, the written **opinion** becomes **precedent**. We call this **common law** (see Section III below).

Many federal cases are published in "reporters," such as the *United States Reports* (U.S. Supreme Court decisions), the *Federal Reporter* (U.S. Courts of Appeals decisions), and the *Federal Supplement* (U.S. District Court decisions). Unpublished decisions from the U.S. Courts of Appeals are found in the *Federal Appendix*.

II. Branches of State Government

According to the Tenth Amendment to the U.S. Constitution, mentioned above, "The powers not delegated to the United States by the Constitution, nor prohibited by it to the States, are reserved to the States respectively, or to the people." Article IV, Section 4, of the Constitution states, "The United States shall guarantee to every State in this Union a Republican Form of Government." State governments consist of the same three branches as the federal government: executive (led by a governor), legislative (comprised of elected representatives), and judicial (usually a court hierarchy similar to the federal system involving lower-tiered trial-level courts and higher appellate courts).

III. How a Common Law System Works

The U.S. judiciary system is based on "common law." This system differs from a civil law system (common in continental Europe, Latin America, Scotland, and Louisiana[4]), in which statutes are the dominant source of law. In a common law system, judges decide cases under two primary principles: precedent and stare decisis. Two other principles—jurisdiction and type of authority—further impact the effect of common law decisions.

Stand by things decided

---

[3] *The Judiciary Branch*, The White House, http://www.whitehouse.gov/our-government/judicial-branch (last visited Oct. 16, 2014).
[4] *Black's Law Dictionary* (9th ed. 2009).

A. Precedent and Stare Decisis

Before entering law school, many of us defined the term "precedent" as something like "an earlier occurrence of something similar" or "a person or thing that serves as a model."[5] In law school, this term takes on weighty legal significance. *Black's Law Dictionary* defines "precedent" as a "decided case that furnishes a basis for determining later cases involving similar facts or issues." "Stare decisis" (pronounced "star-ay dee-sigh-sis") is Latin for "to stand by things decided." *Black's Law Dictionary* defines this term as the "doctrine of precedent, under which a court must follow earlier judicial decisions when the same points arise again in litigation."[6] The purpose of this doctrine—under which courts *must* follow prior decisions when adjudicating new cases—is to promote certainty, predictability, and stability in the law. In a community governed by the rule of law, individuals need to know what those laws are and how they will be applied consistently.

B. Jurisdiction and Type of Authority

There are limits to what categories of precedent courts are required to follow, based on two other concepts: (1) jurisdiction and (2) mandatory (as opposed to persuasive) authority. The doctrine of "vertical stare decisis" requires courts to follow only decisions rendered by **higher courts** within the same **jurisdiction**. (See Figure 4-1.)

Figure 4-1. Federal Court System Vertical Hierarchy

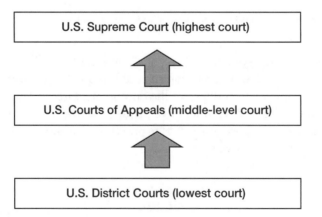

[5] Merriam-Webster Dictionary, http://www.merriam-webster.com/dictionary/precedent (last visited Oct. 16, 2014).
[6] *Black's Law Dictionary, supra* note 4.

Decisions by higher courts within the same jurisdiction are referred to as "mandatory authority," meaning that the lower court *must* follow such precedent. If the prior case was decided by a court at the *same* hierarchical level, at a *lower* hierarchical level, or in a *different* jurisdiction, the court *may* rely on such precedent, but is *not required* to follow it; this is "persuasive authority" as opposed to "mandatory authority."

So, you might be asking, what is "jurisdiction," and how do I know the hierarchy of the courts within a particular jurisdiction? Let's look at some examples.

1. Federal Court Hierarchy

Before you begin reading this section, consider logging onto a website that visually depicts how the federal court system is organized. One excellent online resource is http://www.uscourts.gov, especially the site's court map at http://www.uscourts.gov/about-federal-courts/federal-courts-public/court-website-links. In the chart below the map find either the state in which you were born or in which you are attending law school so you can absorb how the federal court system governing your chosen location is structured i.e., how many federal district courts exist in that state.

As mentioned in Chapter 1, lawsuits typically start off in a trial-level court. Once a decision is rendered in that court, a party may be able to appeal to an appellate court. In our federal system, the trial-level courts are called federal district courts. Each state has its own federal district court (or courts, depending on the size of the state).[7] Overall, there are "94 federal judicial districts; each state has at least one district, as do the District of Columbia, Puerto Rico, the Virgin Islands, Guam, and the Northern Mariana Islands."[8] The U.S. Courts of Appeals are the first level of appeal for parties who wish to have a higher court review a judgment rendered in a trial-level district court. The courts of appeals are divided into "circuits," or federal appellate jurisdictions. Eleven circuits cover the 50 states; two additional circuits are the District of Columbia Circuit and the Federal Circuit.[9]

Let's look at an example. If you are attending law school in, for instance, New York, and you find the New York State in the chart below the court map on the federal court website map (http://www.uscourts.gov/about-federal-courts/federal-courts-public/court-website-links), you would learn that New York

---

[7] To find the names of the federal district courts in your state, locate your state in the chart below the map found at http://www.uscourts.gov/about-federal-courts/federal-courts-public/court-website-links. You can see how many different district courts are in your jurisdiction. The different districts will have distinct geographical titles and may include (depending on the state): Eastern, Western, Central, Northern, and/or Southern.

[8] *District Courts*, United States Courts, http://www.uscourts.gov/about-federal-courts/court-role-and-structure (last visited January 27, 2016).

[9] The Court of Appeals for the Federal Circuit has jurisdiction over "specialized cases, such as those involving patent laws and cases decided by the Court of International Trade and the Court of Federal Claims." *Courts of Appeals*, United States Courts, http://www.uscourts.gov/about-federal-courts/court-role-and-structure (last visited January 27, 2016). The Court of Federal Claims is a special trial court with jurisdiction over "most claims for money damages against the United States, disputes over federal contracts, unlawful 'takings' of private property by the federal government, and a variety of other claims against the United States." *District Courts*, *supra* note 8.

Figure 4-2. Federal Court System Governing the State of New York

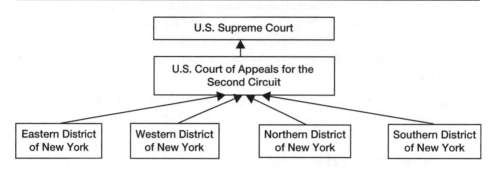

State has four district courts: the Eastern District, the Western District, the Northern District, and the Southern District.[10] From the map on the federal courts website, you also would glean that cases appealed from New York federal district courts (trial-level courts) are heard at the Court of Appeals for the Second Circuit (denoted by the number 2 on the color-coded map)—which also covers federal appeals in Connecticut and Vermont. After that, the case would be appealed to the U.S. Supreme Court. (See Figure 4-2.)

Let's try this again with the Commonwealth of Virginia. If you find Virginia in the chart below the federal court map (http://www.uscourts.gov/about-federal-courts/federal-courts-public/court-website-links), you learn that Virginia has only two districts: the Eastern District and the Western District. Further, appeals from the federal district courts in Virginia are heard by the U.S. Court of Appeals for the Fourth Circuit (denoted by the number 4 on the color-coded map) —which also

Figure 4-3. Federal Court System Governing the Commonwealth of Virginia

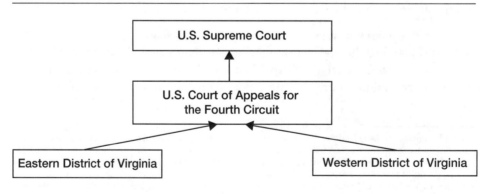

---

[10] Find a map on the Internet that shows the geographical coverage of the federal districts in your state (but be sure not to confuse the federal and state courts). As the next section explains, state courts often are organized in a different geographical manner from the federal courts in the same state.

covers federal appeals in Maryland, West Virginia, North Carolina, and South Carolina. Cases appealed from the Fourth Circuit are sent to the U.S. Supreme Court. (See Figure 4-3.)

 EXERCISE   Locate your state on the federal court map. From the chart below the map, determine how many federal district courts are in your state. Returning to the map, identify the Federal circuit in which your court of appeals sits.

2. State Court Hierarchies

States have their own court hierarchies, with names for particular courts that may vary from state to state. For instance, California trial courts are called superior courts. There are 58 superior courts in California, one for each county. To appeal a superior court decision, a litigant takes the case to the California Court of Appeal. There are six appellate districts in California, and one appeal court for each district.[11] The highest court in California is the Supreme Court of California. (See Figure 4-4.)

Figure 4-4. California State Court System

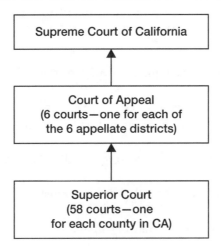

In contrast, in New York, the court system can appear much more complicated, with varying terminology. For example, the lowest court (the trial level) is

---

[11] *California Courts of Appeal*, California Courts, http://www.courts.ca.gov/courtsofappeal.htm (last visited January 27, 2016).

called the Supreme Court.[12] In the New York City area, the first level of appellate courts are referred to as the Appellate Terms (divided into "departments," which cover various "districts"). The intermediate appeals court for New York City is called the Appellate Division (also divided into judicial "departments"). The highest appellate court is the Court of Appeals for the State of New York.

EXERCISE	Search online for your state's court structure. Find color-coded maps and charts that help define and describe the trial-level courts and the various levels of appeals, and the proper terminology for each.

3. Determining Which Court Has Jurisdiction over a Case

We've all heard the term "jurisdiction" when watching a crime show on TV. Picture the scene: Local police are in the midst of handling a criminal investigation when suddenly the FBI swoops in; the characters turn to one another and ask, "Who has jurisdiction here? The state or the feds?" In our legal system, federal courts have jurisdiction over certain cases, and state courts over others. The word "jurisdiction" means a "court's power to decide a case or issue a decree."[13] Jurisdiction is important for determining whether the prior case law that attorneys find in their research is mandatory authority (that the court must follow) or persuasive authority (that can inform the court but that it is not required to follow).

Federal district courts have jurisdiction over the following types of cases:

(1) Cases involving a federal question (i.e., an action arising under the Constitution, a constitutional amendment, a federal statute, an act, or a treaty)

(2) Admiralty or maritime cases ("arising out of commerce on or over navigable water")[14]

(3) Cases affecting ambassadors, other public ministers (such as diplomats), and consuls

(4) Cases in which the United States is a party

(5) Cases between states

---

[12] Other trial-level courts in New York include the Court of Claims, the Family Courts, the Surrogate's Courts, and, outside New York City, the County Courts. New York State Unified Court System, http://www.courts.state.ny.us/courts/structure.shtml (last visited January 27, 2016).

[13] *Black's Law Dictionary, supra* note 4.

[14] *Id.* ("*Id.*" is Latin for "the same"; in legal citation, it means that the item cited comes from the same source as the prior citation. See Chapter 11 for more about legal citation.)

(6) Cases involving a state and citizens of another state
(7) Cases involving "diversity of citizenship"—meaning that no plaintiffs and defendants are citizens[15] of the same state—if the amount in controversy exceeds $75,000, not including interest and costs

Separate units of the federal district courts handle bankruptcy matters.

State courts have jurisdiction over the following types of cases:

(1) Most cases involving state laws and constitutions (unless the parties can satisfy the requirements for federal court jurisdiction under the "diversity of citizenship" rule, the $75,000 threshold, and certain other requirements)
(2) Most criminal cases (although violations of federal criminal laws are handled by federal courts)
(3) Cases involving wills and estates
(4) Most contract cases
(5) State tort cases (personal injuries)
(6) Cases involving family law (i.e., marriages, divorces, adoptions)[16]

In some cases, both federal and state courts could have jurisdiction, so the parties might have a choice.

4. Determining Mandatory v. Persuasive Authority

So, you already learned earlier in this chapter that courts adjudicating new cases follow the doctrine of stare decisis, which means judges rely on precedent when deciding new legal matters. However, two criteria come into play to determine whether a prior case is mandatory authority (the court *must* follow the prior decision in ruling on a new case with similar facts) or persuasive authority (the court may be guided by the prior decision but is not required to follow it): (1) whether the pending case is in the *same* jurisdiction as the earlier case; and (2) whether the decision was rendered by a court of *higher* authority within the same jurisdiction.

Thus, when you begin researching a legal issue, it will be important for you to understand what *jurisdiction* your client's case is in (or likely to be in, if the case is not yet filed) and whether prior decisions were rendered in that jurisdiction by courts of higher authority. Take a look at the following example of mandatory authority in a federal jurisdiction.

Imagine you represent a client in a lawsuit pending in the Southern District of New York—at the trial level. Figure 4-2 shows you that the **mandatory authority** will

---

[15] Citizenship is based on state of domicile, which is the state in which an individual, intentionally resides (for a person) or the state of incorporation or principal place of business (for a corporate entity).
[16] *Comparing Federal and State Courts*, United States Courts http://www.uscourts.gov/about-federal-courts/court-role-and-structure/comparing-federal-state-courts (last visited January 27, 2016).

come from the higher courts: the U.S. Court of Appeals for the Second Circuit and the U.S. Supreme Court. **Persuasive authority** might come from courts on the same hierarchical level within the New York federal jurisdiction—the Eastern, Western, and Northern Districts. Persuasive authority also might come from courts outside the New York court's jurisdiction (e.g., the District of New Jersey or the Middle District of Pennsylvania).

Now consider an example of mandatory authority in a state jurisdiction (you might consider searching for an online map of California's appellate court system as you review the following scenario).

Imagine you represent a California client in an appeal to the Second District Court of Appeal, which covers appeals from the Los Angeles, Ventura, Santa Barbara, and San Luis Obispo Superior Courts. **Mandatory authority** for this state court of appeals will come from the only higher court in California (the Supreme Court of California) (see Figure 4-4) and the highest court in the United States (the U.S. Supreme Court). Cases from the other five California appellate district courts—which are on the same level as the Second District Court of Appeal—will be only **persuasive authority**. Cases from other states (different jurisdictions) will also serve solely as **persuasive authority**.

Now, it can get a bit confusing when trying to discern what, if any, state cases might be mandatory authority in federal courts and vice versa—since federal and state courts are different jurisdictions. Let's break this down as well.

a. Whether Federal Courts Must Follow State Court Decisions

By federal statute, "[t]he laws of the several states, except where the Constitution or treaties of the United States or Acts of Congress otherwise require or provide, shall be regarded as rules of decision in civil actions in the courts of the United States, in cases where they apply."[17] Now, if this statutory language sounds a bit like gobbledygook, let's translate the language into plain English. The question is: when must federal courts follow state court decisions? Remember, in general, federal courts use federal law in deciding cases, so state law often would not be pertinent. However, in situations in which the federal court has jurisdiction based on "diversity of citizenship" (remember that, for a federal court to have diversity jurisdiction, no plaintiffs can be citizens of the same state as any defendants, and the amount in controversy must exceed $75,000), the federal court could be adjudicating an issue of state law.

For consistency and fairness, the federal court must follow the substantive state law that governs the parties' dispute. So, federal courts (with diversity jurisdiction) must apply state statutes and also are bound by the decisions of the state's

---

[17] 28 U.S.C. § 1652 (1948). (This format for a federal statute is explained in detail in Chapters 5 and 11.)

highest court—as *mandatory authority*. These federal courts do not need to follow decisions on the issue rendered by lower state courts if such decisions conflict with the highest state court.

It is possible that a federal court might be presented with a state law issue that the highest state court has never analyzed and decided. In that scenario, the federal court must "give great weight" to the intermediate (middle-level) appellate decisions and try to predict how the state's highest court would rule on the issue.[18] In other words, these federal courts are not bound by these intermediate decisions as mandatory authority, but such cases are regarded as strong persuasive authority.

b. Whether State Courts Must Follow Federal Court Decisions

Here is a chart to help sort out when and whether state courts must follow decisions rendered by federal courts.

	Decision by the U.S. Supreme Court	Decision by a federal district court or circuit court of appeals interpreting a matter of state law	Decision by a federal district court or circuit court of appeals interpreting a federal procedural rule
State court's obligation to follow the federal precedent	Mandatory authority	Not mandatory authority, but may be persuasive authority	Not mandatory, but may be persuasive if the state rules are patterned after the federal rules

5. Cases of First Impression

Because U.S. law is constantly evolving to adjust to societal changes, a court may encounter a case involving legal matters that have never been decided in that jurisdiction or a case applying an established law to a completely new factual scenario. We call this a "case of first impression." In that circumstance, mandatory authority directly on point might not exist, but the court may gather analogous cases from different jurisdictions as persuasive authority to guide its decision.

---

[18] 32 Am. Jur. 2d *Federal Courts* § 367, n.1 (2014), *citing Lucini Italia Co. v. Grappolini*, 231 F. Supp. 2d 764 (N.D. Ill. 2002). "Am. Jur." is an abbreviation for *"American Jurisprudence,"* which is a legal encyclopedia that lawyers refer to as "secondary authority." (See the discussion in Section IV for the distinction between primary authority (statutes, regulations, cases) and secondary authority ("[a]uthority that explains the law but does not itself establish it, such as a treatise, annotation, or law-review article." *Black's Law Dictionary, supra* note 4).)

IV. Primary v. Secondary Authority

So far in this chapter, you have learned about various sources of law, including statutes enacted by a legislative body, regulations issued by a federal agency established by the executive branch, and case law generated by the judiciary. We call these sources of law "primary authority," which means "authority that issues directly from a law-making body."[19] As you learned above, citizens must follow these laws, and courts adjudicating subsequent cases rely on these sources of law when making decisions in pending cases.

There is another source of legal information that lawyers consult when researching laws and rules, to get a "bigger picture" or clearer understanding of how the law works: "secondary authority." Judges, lawyers, professors, and law students have written thousands of helpful compilations, like legal encyclopedias, treatises, hornbooks, law review articles, and journal publications that help explain the law more clearly. You should not confuse these with sources of law—like statutes, regulations, or case law—but you can use them to grasp the fundamentals of a particular area of law and begin to explore how to apply the rules to a specific client factual situation.

Commonly used secondary sources include the following:

- *American Jurisprudence*
- *Corpus Juris Secundum*
- *Wright & Miller's Federal Practice & Procedure*
- Restatements of the Law
- American Law Institute-American Bar Association Continuing Legal Education materials
- Treatises, hornbooks, and nutshells
- Law review articles and law journals

Various states have their own well-known secondary sources, such as *New York Jurisprudence, Arkansas Civil Practice and Procedure,* and Strong's North Carolina Index.

LEGAL SOURCES CHECKLIST

- ☑ The U.S. legal system is divided into a federal system and a state system.
- ☑ Each system has three branches of government: executive, legislative, and judicial.

---

[19] *Black's Law Dictionary, supra* note 4.

☑ Legal research breaks down into primary authority and secondary authority.

☑ Four sources of primary authority are constitutions, statutes, regulations, case law (common law).

☑ Secondary authority includes encyclopedias, treatises, Restatements, and law review articles.

☑ Common law breaks down into mandatory authority and persuasive authority.

☑ Stare decisis means "to stand by things decided."

☑ Mandatory authority depends on jurisdiction and hierarchy of court.

☑ Federal court hierarchy: U.S. District Courts → U.S. Court of Appeals (for the various circuits) → U.S. Supreme Court.
  o 94 federal district courts
  o 11 circuits, plus the District of Columbia Circuit and Federal Circuit
  o 1 Supreme Court (9 Justices)

☑ State court hierarchy: trial courts → intermediate appellate courts → courts of last resort.

☑ A case of first impression is a "case that presents the court with an issue of law that has not previously been decided by any controlling legal authority in that jurisdiction."[20]

CHECKLIST FOR BEGINNING TO REVIEW SOURCES OF LAW IN A LEGAL WRITING ASSIGNMENT

☑ In what state is my client's case taking place?

☑ Does federal or state law govern the legal issues affecting my client?

☑ Has a case been filed in a particular court?

☑ Is the court a state court or a federal court?

☑ Locate an online map or chart of the applicable state or federal court system.

☑ From the court system map/chart, learn the hierarchy of the courts in the applicable jurisdiction.

☑ Identify the names of the courts within the jurisdiction that occupy a higher level of authority than the court where the case is pending. (Prior cases from these courts will be mandatory authority.)

---

[20] *Id.*

Chapter 5

Learning How to Read Statutes

If you are starting to tackle your first legal writing assignment in law school, your professor may have given you a case file and a "closed universe" of legal sources—perhaps a **statute**, **regulation**, and/or a handful of **cases**. Alternatively, you may be experimenting with finding the research on your own. This chapter focuses on one of the "raw materials" attorneys use in conducting a legal analysis: **statutes**.

I. Deciphering Statutes

Remember from Chapter 4 that the legislative branch of government enacts laws, which are called statutes. Before learning how to decode statutes, it will help to recall how statutes are drafted and become law in the first place. After all, we are dealing with interpreting written words, so let's see how a writer's words transform into an enforceable law.

A. How Federal Statutes Are Enacted

In the U.S. federal legislative system, law making begins with a document called a **bill** that is introduced to Congress. A bill can range from one or two pages to more than a thousand, depending on the complexity of the proposed law (and the verbosity of its drafters). An original bill might be drafted by members of

Congress or their staff, citizens, lobbyists, and/or advocacy groups.[1] A member of Congress becomes the sponsor of the bill and then submits it for consideration by the House of Representatives or the Senate. Committees and subcommittees review the bill and conduct hearings to analyze its language and legal effect. The relevant policy committee votes to approve the bill. If it is not approved, the bill does not progress. If it is approved, the House of Representatives or the Senate places the bill on its calendar for consideration. Debate over the bill ensues, and eventually either the House or the Senate votes to approve the bill. A bill must pass both the House and the Senate before it is sent to the president for consideration. Interestingly, the wording of versions of the same bill coming from the House and from the Senate might vary:

> Though the Constitution requires that the two bills have the exact same wording, this rarely happens in practice. To bring the bills into alignment, a Conference Committee is convened, consisting of members from both chambers. The members of the committee produce a conference report, intended as the final version of the bill. Each chamber then votes again to approve the conference report. Depending on where the bill originated, the final text is then enrolled by either the Clerk of the House or the Secretary of the Senate, and presented to the Speaker of the House and the President of the Senate for their signatures. The bill is then sent to the President.[2]

When presented with a bill, the president may either sign it into law or veto it. You might have seen the president signing bills on television, using special pens often given as commemorative souvenirs to key players in the law's creation. If the president vetoes a bill, Congress has the power to override a presidential veto with a two-thirds vote of the House and the Senate.

If the president signs the bill into law or Congress overrides a presidential veto, the bill is printed in the Statutes at Large. The Government Printing Office (GPO) has authority to publish and print statutes under the direction of the Office of the Federal Register. When first printed, new statutes are called public laws and given a number.

Public laws frequently are written as amendments to the *United States Code*, which is a compilation of federal statutes organized by subject matter to enable lawyers to research and find law on particular legal issues. The *United States Code* has 51 subject matter titles, such as Agriculture, Bankruptcy, Copyrights, Education, Intoxicating Liquors, Labor, Patents, and Transportation. The Office of the Law Revision Counsel of the U.S. House of Representatives prepares and publishes the *United States Code*.[3]

---

[1] *Legislative Process: How a Senate Bill Becomes a Law*, United States Senate, http://www.senate.gov/reference/resources/pdf/legprocessflowchart.pdf (last visited January 27, 2016).
[2] *The Legislative Branch*, The White House, http://www.whitehouse.gov/our-government/legislative-branch (last visited January 27, 2016).
[3] *About the Office and the United States Code*, Office of the Law Revision Counsel, United States Code, http://uscode.house.gov/about/info.shtml (last visited January 27, 2016).

B. How State Statutes Are Enacted

State statutes follow similar procedures. Once state statutes are passed by the state legislature and approved by the governor, they become a public law, or a public act, and are assigned a number. Each state has procedures under which these consecutively numbered public laws are organized into subject matter areas and incorporated into the state statutory codes. Statutes might be organized by chapters or titles, and have a table of contents, a list of definitions, and/or an index.

C. Techniques for Parsing and Deciphering Statutes

Merriam-Webster defines the word "parse" as "to resolve (as a sentence) into component parts of speech and describe them grammatically." The dictionary defines the word "decipher" as "to make out the meaning of, despite indistinctness or obscurity." When analyzing statutes, lawyers do both: (1) "parse" or break down statutory sentences into understandable parts, and (2) use analytical techniques to decipher convoluted legal concepts into clear workable terms. Lawyers approach statutes grammatically—looking for key "indicator" words, phrasing, transitions, and punctuation—to extract clarity from sometimes murky or complex writing. At a basic level, statutes fall into four different categories:

(1) Statutes authorizing or permitting an action
(2) Statutes mandating or requiring an action
(3) Statutes barring or prohibiting an action
(4) Statutes affording a decision maker discretion in handling an action

An example of a law *authorizing or permitting* an action is a section of Maine's Medical Use of Marijuana Act.

Me. Rev. Stat. Ann. tit. 22, § 2423-C (2011)

A person *may* provide a qualifying patient or a primary caregiver with marijuana paraphernalia for purposes of the qualifying patient's medical use of marijuana in accordance with this chapter and be in the presence or vicinity of the medical use of marijuana as allowed under this chapter. [Emphasis added.]

An example of a law *mandating* or *requiring* an action is New Jersey's law requiring physicians to report gunshot wounds to the police, under its statutory framework entitled "Licensing and Other Provisions Relating to Firearms."

N.J. Stat. Ann. § 2C:58-8 (West 2011)

Every case of a wound, burn or any other injury arising from or caused by a firearm, destructive device, explosive or weapon *shall* be reported at once to the law enforcement agency of the municipality where the person reporting is located and to the Division of State Police by the physician consulted, attending or treating the case or the administrator or administrator's designee, whenever such case is presented for treatment or treated in a general hospital. . . . [Emphasis added.]

An example of a statute *prohibiting* or *barring* an action is Iowa's Alcoholic Beverage Control statute forbidding the sale of alcohol to minors.

Iowa Code Ann. § 123.47 (West 2014)

A person *shall not* sell, give, or otherwise supply alcoholic liquor, wine, or beer to any person knowing or having reasonable cause to believe that person to be under legal age. [Emphasis added.]

An example of a statute giving a decision maker discretion is Alabama's rule governing penalties and remedies against a property owner who allows a drug-related nuisance to affect a neighbor. In Ala. Code § 6-5-156.3 (1996), if a court determines that a property owner has created a drug-related nuisance, the court has discretion to (1) assess damages against the property owner; (2) require the property owner to cover the attorneys' fees accrued in the nuisance lawsuit or prosecution; (3) impose a fine; (4) order the owner to clean up the property and make repairs; (5) suspend or revoke any business, housing, operational, or liquor license; and (6) mandate the owner to install secure locks on doors, hire private security personnel, increase lighting in common areas, and use videotaped surveillance of the property and adjacent alleyways, sidewalks, and parking lots, and so on.

When reading statutes to determine whether they authorize, mandate, or prohibit behavior, lawyers look for "indicator verbs" like "may," "must," "shall," "must not," or "shall not." To identify discretionary statutes, attorneys hunt for phrases like "shall have power to," "shall exercise discretion," and "shall consider."

II. Understanding the Difference Between Statutory Elements and Factors

After determining the basic function of a statute—to authorize, mandate, prohibit, or allow discretion—lawyers assess whether the rule includes an inventory of required "elements" that must be satisfied or itemizes a list of "factors" that the evaluator must weigh and measure to determine whether the law has been satisfied or violated. Nonlawyers often use the terms "element" and "factor" interchangeably. However, in the context of statutory rules, these words mean different things. An analogy to help understand how elements work is the operation of a vehicle. To start a Volkswagen beetle and drive it off a parking lot, the driver must have (a) a key, (b) fuel, (c) a working battery, and (d) four inflated tires. Without one of these elements, the driver cannot drive the car off the lot. All the elements are required.

In contrast, factors are typically a list of items considered, balanced, and/or weighed, but not all are necessary for a law to apply. The end result can still be achieved even when one or more factors is lacking. A helpful analogy for comprehending how factors work is a house or apartment hunt. When deciding where to live, a renter might consider (a) neighborhood; (b) price; (c) size of the dwelling; and (d) amenities such as new appliances, closet space, gym access, storage space, and so on. The renter weighs the presence or absence of certain factors in each option and ultimately may compromise on some; not all the factors are required for the renter to make a decision so long as most of them are satisfied.

A. Examples of Statutes with Required Elements

An example of a statute with required elements is New York's "right of privacy" statute; this law states that it is a misdemeanor for an individual or a company to use another living person's name, portrait, or picture for advertising purposes without written consent.

N.Y. Civ. Rights Law § 50 (McKinney 2014)

A person, firm or corporation that uses for advertising purposes, or for the purposes of trade, the name, portrait or picture of any living person without having first obtained the written consent of such person, or if a minor of his or her parent or guardian, is guilty of a misdemeanor.

The required elements of this statute are

- the use of a *living person's name, portrait* or *picture*
- for purposes of *advertising* or *trade*
- without that person's *written consent*

If any one of these elements is missing, there is no violation. For example, if the person is no longer living, there is no violation of this statute. If the person's initials are used instead of his or her name, there is likely no violation. If the person's portrait was used for artistic purposes, instead of advertising or trade, there is no violation. If the person gave written consent, there is no violation.

Another example of a statute with elements is the California rule governing vehicle theft.

Cal. Veh. Code § 10851 (West 2011)

Any person who drives or takes a vehicle not his or her own, without the consent of the owner thereof, and with intent either to permanently or temporarily deprive the owner thereof of his or her title to or possession of the vehicle, whether with or without intent to steal the vehicle . . . is guilty of a public offense. . . .

To identify the elements of this statute, lawyers look for connector punctuation (like commas) and words like "and," "either," and "or."

So the elements of the crime of vehicle theft are (1) driving or taking, (2) a vehicle, (3) that is not one's own, (4) without consent of the owner, (5) with the intent to permanently or temporarily deprive the owner of title to or possession of the vehicle. All of these items are required.

Diagramming the Vehicle Code Statute

Any person who:

- drives OR
- takes
  - o a vehicle
  - o not his or her own,
  - o without the consent of the owner thereof, AND
  - o with intent EITHER to
    - o permanently OR
    - o temporarily deprive the owner thereof of his or her title to or possession of the vehicle,
- whether with or without intent to steal the vehicle . . .

B. Examples of Statutes with Factors

An example of a statute that includes factors (instead of elements) is Arizona's law governing the criteria under which an individual may obtain a license to sell lottery tickets.

Ariz. Rev. Stat. Ann. § 5-562 (West 2012)

Before issuing a license as a lottery sales agent to any person, the director shall consider factors such as the financial responsibility and security of the person and the nature of the person's business activity, the person's background and reputation in the community, the accessibility of the person's place of business or activity to the public, the accessibility of existing licensees to serve the public convenience and the volume of expected sales.

So, the director of the state lottery shall consider the following factors.

- The applicant's financial responsibility and security
- The nature of the person's business activity
- The person's background and reputation in the community
- The accessibility of the place of business to the public
- Whether existing licensees serve the public's convenience
- Volume of expected sales

Each of these factors are weighed and balanced.

Similarly, in Hawaii's Crime Victim Compensation statute, the court considers several factors when deciding what type of fee to impose on a convicted defendant to compensate a crime victim, including (1) the seriousness of the offense; (2) the circumstances surrounding the commission of the offense; (3) the economic gain, if any, realized by the defendant; (4) the number of victims; and (5) the defendant's earning capacity, including future earning capacity.[4]

III. Looking for Indicator or Connector Words and Punctuation

Rules of law are not always models of clarity; lawyers refer to some statutes as "inartfully drafted." To make sense of complex or intricate statutes, attorneys hunt for "indicator" or "connector" words, phrases, and punctuation to help outline or diagram the rule and identify lists of elements or factors.

- Assess whether the law is authorizing, mandating, or prohibiting action, or affording discretion.
  - o Authorizing indicator words: "may," "can"
  - o Mandating indicator words: "must," "shall," "will"
  - o Prohibiting indicator words: "must not," "shall not," "will not," "violation," "guilty of"
  - o Discretionary indicator words: "shall have power to," "shall exercise discretion," "may consider" "shall consider"
- Look for key connector words like "and," "or," "either," "both," and commas and semicolons to identify required elements or lists of factors to weigh.

---

[4] Haw. Rev. Stat. § 351-62.6 (West 2005).

EXERCISE: IDENTIFYING REQUIRED ELEMENTS IN A STATUTE

Read the following statutes. Look for—and underline, circle, or highlight—indicator words to determine whether this statute is authorizing, mandating, or prohibiting action. Then outline the required *elements* of the statute (look for connector words and punctuation).

1. Haw. Rev. Stat. § 142-63 (1975)

If any cattle, horse, mule, ass, swine, sheep, or goat, trespasses on any properly fenced cultivated ground, the owner thereof shall pay upon proof, the full amount of the damage or loss to the landowners, or to any person in possession of the land, whoever suffers the damage or loss. *Mandating*

Outline:

2. Mich. Penal Code § 750.529a (West 2004)

A person who in the course of committing a larceny of a motor vehicle uses force or violence or the threat of force or violence, or who puts in fear any operator, passenger, or person in lawful possession of the motor vehicle, or any person lawfully attempting to recover the motor vehicle, is guilty of carjacking, a felony punishable by imprisonment for life or for any term of years.

Outline:

3. Fla. Stat. Ann. § 837.055 (West 2012)

Whoever knowingly and willfully gives false information to a law enforcement officer who is conducting a missing person investigation or a felony criminal investigation with the intent to mislead the officer or impede the investigation commits a misdemeanor of the first degree.

Outline:

4. Cal. Health & Safety Code § 11362.795 (West 2004)

Any person who is to be released on parole from a jail, state prison, school, road camp, or other state or local institution of confinement and who is eligible to use medical marijuana . . . may request that he or she be allowed to use medical marijuana during the period he or she is released on parole. A parolee's written conditions of parole shall reflect whether or not a request for a modification of the conditions of his or her parole to use medical marijuana was made, and whether the request was granted or denied.

Outline:

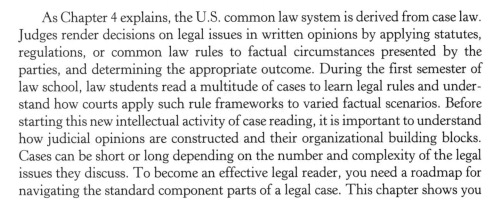

Chapter 6
Learning How to Read and Brief Cases

As Chapter 4 explains, the U.S. common law system is derived from case law. Judges render decisions on legal issues in written opinions by applying statutes, regulations, or common law rules to factual circumstances presented by the parties, and determining the appropriate outcome. During the first semester of law school, law students read a multitude of cases to learn legal rules and understand how courts apply such rule frameworks to varied factual scenarios. Before starting this new intellectual activity of case reading, it is important to understand how judicial opinions are constructed and their organizational building blocks. Cases can be short or long depending on the number and complexity of the legal issues they discuss. To become an effective legal reader, you need a roadmap for navigating the standard component parts of a legal case. This chapter shows you

- how cases are organized and what constituent parts to look for when reading judicial opinions,
- how to actively "mark up" an opinion while reading it, and
- how to "brief" a case in a way that is useful for law school class discussion and analysis of a client's legal problem.

I. Typical Components of a Case Opinion

A judicial opinion summarizes the factual background of the parties' dispute, the applicable rules of law, the legal analysis, the court's holding, and the reasoning behind the court's decision. When reading a case for the first time, consider first scanning the opinion to highlight the following component parts, so you can see how the case is organized.

Caption: Case captions help court clerks keep track of numerous documents (i.e., pleadings, briefs, and pre-trial submissions) filed by parties in a case. A caption in a judicial opinion includes (a) the name of the court (indicating the governing jurisdiction), (b) the names of the parties (and their designation as "plaintiff" or "defendant"), (c) the case file number assigned by the clerk, and (d) the date of the court's decision. Near the caption, you can also find the case citation—the name of the reporter in which the decision is published (or the online legal research database in which you can find an unpublished case), the volume of the reporter, and the page number on which the case begins. The citation helps you find the case in the hard-copy books in your law library or in an online legal database such as Westlaw, Lexis, or Bloomberg Law.

Synopsis: Beneath the case caption, legal publishers often include a brief background, summary, or synopsis of the case's substance and procedural history. This abstract is not part of the judge's opinion, but is written by lawyers or other legal analysts hired by the publishers. In your legal writing, you should not cite to this material because it does not reflect the "voice" of the court; nonetheless, these summaries are very useful in legal research because they provide a snapshot of the case.

Headnotes: Legal publishers like West Publishing, LexisNexis, and Bloomberg Law also hire attorneys or legal analysts to write numbered "headnotes," which summarize—for lawyers conducting legal research—the legal rules discussed in the opinion. Headnote numbers indicate where the same concepts are discussed in the body of the court's opinion. Headnotes in cases published by West implement a research tool called the Key Number System, which organizes legal doctrines into more than 400 Topics and 80,000 Key Numbers. LexisNexis also links case headnotes into a Topic index. Lawyers can use these Topics and Key Numbers to locate additional cases discussing the same legal issues.

Attorneys and Judges: Between the headnotes and the beginning of the court's substantive analysis, the judicial opinion might identify the names of the attorneys representing the parties and the name of the presiding judge.

Procedural History: Often at the beginning of the opinion, the court recaps the procedural history of the case, which might summarize the complaint and its causes of action, any relevant defenses asserted by the responding party, any motions filed by the parties, any hearings conducted, and prior decisions rendered or orders issued by the court on those motions. The presiding judge uses the procedural history to lay the groundwork for why the court is deciding the particular issue at that point in time.

Facts: Next, the court usually describes the legally significant facts triggering the legal issue. The court conveys the parties' respective stories, relying on the evidence and documentation provided by the litigants. If the parties disagree about certain facts, the court may summarize each side's point of view.

Look for IRAC

One traditional and easy-to-follow structure of a legal analysis (discussed in detail in subsequent chapters) is known as IRAC: Issue, Rule, Analysis, Conclusion. When reading a case for the first time, see whether you can locate the issue, the rule of law, the analysis (or application of the rule to the facts of the case), and the conclusion.

Issues: Next, the court sets forth the precise legal issue (or issues) it is tasked with deciding. When reading a case, determine how many legal issues the court is analyzing. Follow the analysis of one distinct issue at a time.

Rule: Within the opinion, the court describes the applicable rule(s) of law. The rule could be derived from an excerpt from the Constitution, a statute, a regulation, or a common law rule based on elements, factors, or a definition of a legal term synthesized from prior cases.

Analysis/Discussion:

- **Arguments raised by various parties:** Before conducting its own analysis, the court may describe each party's argument(s) on the legal issue at hand and the reasons each party believes the court should rule in its favor.
- **Holding on each issue:** The court conducts its analysis and then issues the holding: the court's answer to each legal question posed. Search for the court's holding by looking for phrases such as "the court holds," "the court finds," "we hold," or "we find."[1]
- **Rationale behind each holding:** The reasoning, or rationale, underlying the court's holding might be a few sentences or paragraphs, explaining the court's analysis. If the court is applying the elements or factors of a rule to render its overall decision, the court will analyze each element or factor— one at a time—as justification for its holding. The court also might explain "public policy" reasons supporting its holding—such as objectives that benefit society as a whole. Examples of public policy considerations include fairness, equality, efficiency, safety, health and welfare of citizens.
- **Dicta:** One sometimes overlooked component of a court's analysis is called dicta. The origin of the word dicta is the Latin phrase *obiter dictum* ("something said in passing"). Judges sometimes include sentences in case opinions that mention how they would rule under different facts or

---

[1] Even though the court may use the term "we," law students and lawyers should refrain from using pronouns such as "I/we/our/my/you" in legal writing. Chapter 17 explains how these words detract from the formality of a lawyer's legal writing.

circumstances. These sentences are not mandatory authority that would govern the outcome of future cases, but they may be used as persuasive argument. Dicta can sometimes be difficult to distinguish from the rationale of a court's holding; this demarcation takes practice.

Judgment: The judgment in a case is different from the court's holding. The judgment reflects the procedural and substantive *action* to be taken in the case and directly affects the parties. For example, a trial-level court might

- grant a motion to dismiss a case (and "order" such dismissal);
- deny a motion to dismiss a case (and thus, the case would proceed);
- grant a motion for "summary judgment" on a legal issue or "cause of action" (and "order" that the clerk enter judgment in favor of one party);
- deny a motion for summary judgment on a cause of action, and therefore allow the "cause of action" to proceed;
- issue a "declaratory judgment," declaring that a party is entitled to a certain action by the other party;
- issue some form of "equitable" relief, such as a temporary restraining order or preliminary/permanent injunction—to force another party to either do or stop doing something;
- award monetary damages in a certain amount;
- impose a sentence, sanction, penalty or fine in a certain amount;
- award attorneys' fees, interest, and/or court costs.

A court of appeals might

- reverse the trial court's judgment;
- affirm the trial court's judgment;
- remand (send back) the case to the lower court for further action; or
- vacate (cancel, invalidate, nullify) the decision of the trial court.

The court's decision is put into effect via the court's written "order," which is the court's directive that the mandated action occur.

Concurring or Dissenting Opinions: At the appeals court level, if one or more of the judges[2] agrees with the judgment rendered by the majority of the court, but believes in a different reasoning or rationale to support the decision, such judge(s) may author a concurring opinion, explaining the alternate analysis. If one or more of the judges disagrees with the judgment rendered by the majority, such judge(s) may write a dissenting opinion. The judges' names will appear before such concurring or dissenting opinion, along with a note as to whether the additional opinion is a concurrence or a dissent. These parts of the case opinion are not mandatory authority but may have persuasive value.

---

[2] A trial court has only one judge. An appellate court usually is comprised of a panel of judges.

II. Marking Up the Structural Components in a Case Opinion

Let's look for the various components discussed above in the following case example.

Synopsis: At trial, the jury found Appellant, Dylan Fontaine ("Fontaine"), guilty of the crime of felonious assault with a deadly weapon. The facts are: Fontaine removed a Jimmy Choo high-heel stiletto shoe from her foot and threw it at a local bartender, Jamie Dunham ("Dunham"). She yelled curse words at Dunham while throwing the shoe, and the pointed heel of the stiletto shoe hit Dunham in the forehead, causing a deep gash requiring emergency medical attention. Fontaine appealed the jury verdict, arguing that a stiletto shoe does not constitute a deadly weapon. The Court of Appeals affirmed the conviction.

Headnotes:

[1] Felonious Assault:

Under Ohio Rev. Code § 2903.11(A) (2008), the felonious assault statute states that "[n]o person shall knowingly . . . [c]ause or attempt to cause physical harm to another . . . by means of a deadly weapon or dangerous ordnance."

[2] Deadly Weapon:

Ohio Rev. Code § 2923.11(A) (2013) defines a "deadly weapon" as "any instrument, device, or thing capable of inflicting death, and designed or specially adapted for use as a weapon, or possessed, carried, or used as a weapon."

[3] Deadly Weapon:

When evaluating whether an otherwise innocuous item qualifies as a deadly weapon under the felonious assault statute, Ohio courts consider (1) the size and weight of the item, (2) the shape and design of the item, (3) the ability of the item to be grasped in the hands of the user in such a way that it may be used on or directed against the body of another, and (4) the ability of the item to be used in a manner and with sufficient force to kill the other person.

Headnotes

Attorneys: Christopher Brown, Esq., for the Appellant, Prosecuting Attorney, Peter Gartner, Esq.

Attorneys

Judges: Aquino, J., Schonfeld, J., and Prager, J.

Judges

OPINION, per curiam.

Start of opinion

The issue before the court is whether a stiletto high-heel shoe can constitute a deadly weapon under Ohio law.

Legal issue

The facts of this case are as follows. Appellant, Dylan Fontaine ("Fontaine"), is a twenty-seven-year-old resident of Cleveland, Ohio, where she works for an advertising and marketing agency. She is a frequent patron of an upscale wine bar called Enoteca located in Shaker Heights, Ohio. On New Year's Eve, Fontaine attended a party at the wine bar. Prior to midnight, she ordered a bottle of Spanish wine from the bartender, Jamie Dunham ("Dunham"). At midnight, Fontaine still had not received the bottle of wine she ordered and began to get agitated; she felt the bartender was ignoring her requests. She requested the bottle again. Finally, Dunham responded to Fontaine, "Dylan, I can't serve you any more. I'm cutting you off." Fontaine reacted angrily. A few moments later, witnesses saw her remove from her foot a size 7 champagne-colored suede Jimmy Choo high-heel stiletto shoe. The shoe was a platform "peep-toe" stiletto constructed of suede, leather, and steel. The heel measured 3.9 inches in height and was plated in a gold-colored metal; the point of the heel was affixed to a small rubber sole. The platform part of the shoe was less than half an inch wide.

Facts

Witnesses observed Fontaine throw the shoe with force at Dunham while yelling curse words. The pointed heel of the stiletto shoe hit Dunham directly in the forehead. He immediately fell backwards and into the bar, and then collapsed onto the floor. The point of the stiletto heel caused a deep gash in his forehead. Bystanders called paramedics to the scene. Police arrived as well, and they arrested

Fontaine for felonious assault. Dunham's forehead required emergency medical attention, including stitches and treatment for a concussion. Paramedics transported him to the hospital where he spent one night; he was released the next afternoon.

> Facts

Fontaine was charged with the crime of felonious assault with a deadly weapon. Ohio Rev. Code § 2903.11(A) (2008)—the felonious assault statute—states that "[n]o person shall knowingly . . . [c]ause or attempt to cause physical harm to another . . . by means of a deadly weapon or dangerous ordnance." Ohio Rev. Code § 2923.11(A)(2013) defines a "deadly weapon" as "any instrument, device, or thing capable of inflicting death, and designed or specially adapted for use as a weapon, or possessed, carried, or used as a weapon."

> Rules

It is undisputed that Fontaine knowingly caused physical harm to Dunham by throwing her Jimmy Choo high-heel stiletto shoe directly at him. Therefore, the sole question is whether the shoe qualifies as a "deadly weapon" under Ohio law.

> Court's narrowing of legal issue

When evaluating whether an otherwise innocuous item qualifies as a deadly weapon under the felonious assault statute, Ohio courts consider (1) the size and weight of the item, (2) the shape and design of the item, (3) the ability of the item to be grasped in the hands of the user in such a way that it may be used on or directed against the body of another, and (4) the ability of the item to be used in a manner and with sufficient force to kill the other person.

> Beginning of analysis/ discussion and identification of rule factors

Ohio courts have applied the foregoing factors to numerous household items that normally would not be considered weapons in their everyday uses. For example, in *State v. Redmon*, No. CA-7938, 1990 WL 94745 (Ohio Ct. App. June 25, 1990), a home intruder, who had smoked cocaine earlier in the evening, broke into a house, picked up a wicker rocking chair, approached the homeowner who was sitting on her couch, and told her that he was going to kill her. *Id.* at *1. The intruder swung the rocker at the woman's face. While she was able to duck and run into the kitchen, the intruder continued swinging the chair as he made his way to the kitchen. He swung the rocker at the homeowner again, missed, and finally threw the object away. *Id.* After an ongoing struggle and a 911 call, eventually the police arrived and arrested the intruder for the crime of felonious assault. *Id.*

> Precedent case explaining the rule

The intruder argued that the wicker rocking chair was not a deadly weapon. *Id.* However, the court held that the chair was indeed a deadly weapon as defined by Ohio law. *Id.* at *2. The court explained, "[a]n instrument, no matter how innocuous when not in use, is a deadly weapon if it is of sufficient size and weight to inflict death upon a person, when the instrument is wielded against the body of the victim or threatened to be so wielded." *Id.* The court considered the following factors: (1) the size and weight of the chair, (2) the shape and design of the chair, (3) the ability of the chair to be grasped in the hands of the intruder and swung at the victim, (4) the ability of the chair to be used in a manner and with sufficient force to kill the victim. *Id.* Applying these factors, the court emphasized that the intruder swung the wicker rocking chair at the victim's head, while telling her that he was going to kill her. She ducked and the chair missed her face by one-and-a-half feet. These factors supported the court's finding that the chair constituted a deadly weapon. *Id.*

Similarly, in *State v. Ware*, No. 57546, 1990 WL 151499 (Ohio Ct. App. Oct. 11, 1990), an ex-boyfriend entered his ex-girlfriend's home and, as she was putting a broom behind a door, struck her on the head with an iron and said, "I am going to kill you." *Id.* at *1. The man continued to strike the woman with the iron while she screamed for help. She struggled toward her bed and grabbed a pillow to protect herself from the blows of the iron. The man continued to swing the iron, hitting her and the wall, until the iron fell apart. Eventually, she got away. *Id.* The ex-boyfriend was charged with felonious assault with a deadly weapon. He argued that the iron did not qualify as a "deadly weapon." *Id.*

| Precedent case explaining the rule |

The court held that the iron was a deadly weapon. *Id.* at *6. Applying the above-mentioned factors to determine whether the iron was capable of inflicting death, the court emphasized that the ex-boyfriend used the iron in such a manner by striking the victim several times and caused her to sustain multiple abrasions and lacerations, requiring several stitches. The court found this sufficient to qualify the iron as capable of inflicting death. *Id.*

Further, in *State v. Maydillard*, No. CA99-06-060, 1999 WL 988822 (Ohio Ct. App. Nov. 1, 1999), an inmate at a correctional institution in Ohio entered the cell of another inmate carrying a plastic shaving razor from which he had removed the plastic guards to expose the blades. The first inmate brandished the razor at the second inmate in an attempt to collect a debt owed. *Id.* at *1. A struggle ensued. Guards arrived at the cell, pulled the inmates apart, and handcuffed them. During a pat-down search, a guard found the razor. The inmate was charged with possession of a deadly weapon while under detention. *Id.*

| Precedent case explaining the rule |

In applying the statutory definition of a "deadly weapon" to the razor, the *Maydillard* court held that the razor possessed by the inmate was a "deadly weapon" by the manner of its use or adaptation. *Id.* at *4. The court explained that cases that have found a razor not to be a deadly weapon involved circumstances where the razor was used or possessed in a manner consistent with its legitimate purpose, such as a barber's razor or a pocket knife used for cutting packing tape and rope. *Id.* at *3. However, this inmate had adapted the razor, by removing the plastic guards, to function as a deadly weapon. *Id.* at *4. Further, he brandished it as a weapon. Finally, the court emphasized that the inmate presented no testimony that he was using the razor in a manner consistent with its legitimate purpose. *Id.*; *see also State v. Salinas*, No. F-84-8, 1985 WL 7568 (Ohio Ct. App. July 26, 1985) (holding that a jury reasonably could find that a baseball bat constituted a deadly weapon when the perpetrator swung the bat at a victim, causing injury to his jaw, ribs, and arms); *State v. Deboe*, 406 N.E.2d 536 (Ohio Ct. App. 1977) (holding that a club-like instrument three inches in diameter wrapped in spongy material, which the perpetrator swung rapidly at the victim, hitting him 15 or 20 times on the head, arms, back, shoulders, and kidneys, causing black and blue welts and bruises, constituted a deadly weapon).

> Signal citations of precedent cases explaining the rule

In contrast, in *State v. Kaeff*, No. 20519, 2004 WL 2245095 (Ohio Ct. App. Sept. 24, 2004), a husband was indicted for one count of domestic violence and one count of felonious assault with a deadly weapon after using only his hands to attempt to strangle the victim, his wife. *Id.* at *1. The husband filed a motion to dismiss the count of felonious assault on the ground that a person's hands cannot, as a matter of law, be considered a deadly weapon. The trial court granted the motion and dismissed the count. The prosecution appealed the court's ruling. *Id.*

> Precedent case explaining the rule

The prosecution argued that hands (1) fit within the definition of an "instrument," (2) are capable of inflicting death, and (3) can be used as a weapon. However, the court held that hands do not meet the definition of a deadly weapon. *Id.* at *4. The *Kaeff* court reasoned that the factors defining a deadly weapon suggest the use of an object apart from one's own body. Thus, one's hands are not within the scope of the statutory definition. *Id.*

In evaluating whether Fontaine's Jimmy Choo stiletto qualifies as a deadly weapon, this court must consider (1) the size and weight of the shoe, (2) the shape and design of the shoe, (3) the ability of the shoe to be grasped in the hands of the user in such a way that it may be used on or directed against the body of another, and (4) the ability of the shoe to be used in a manner and with sufficient force

> Transition to Court's analysis of facts

to kill the other person. Applying these factors, we hold that the stiletto shoe was a deadly weapon."

> Holding

The facts indicate that Fontaine's "instrument" was a size 7 champagne-colored Jimmy Choo high-heel stiletto shoe. The shoe was constructed of suede and leather and was a platform peep-toe stiletto. The heel height measured 3.9 inches and was constructed of steel with a gold-colored point attached to a small rubber sole. The platform part of the shoe was less than half an inch. The shoe was neither lightweight nor small. Further, the pointy shape of the nearly four-inch metal heel, and the weight of the platform peep toe structure, rendered the shoe capable of causing harm when thrown with force. Fontaine was able to grasp the heavy unwieldy shoe in her hand and hurl it toward the body of Dunham, specifically his head. The weight and shape of the shoe, when thrown in the manner Fontaine propelled it, likely had sufficient force to kill another person.

> Rationale

Unlike the perpetrator in *Maydillard* who modified an everyday razor by removing plastic safety guards, Fontaine did not modify or adapt the shoe from its original purpose. Further, unlike the assailants in *Redmon*, *Ware*, and *Deboe*, who swung their respective weapons—a rocking chair, an iron, and a sponge-covered bat—numerous times against the body of their victims, Fontaine heaved the shoe only one time at Dunham. However, given the shoe's size, weight, shape, design, and ability to be grasped by Fontaine in such a way to be hurled at Dunham with sufficient force to gravely injure him and possibly kill him, this court finds that the shoe meets the definition of a "deadly weapon."

Because Fontaine knowingly caused physical harm to Dunham by means of a deadly weapon, the jury properly found her guilty of felonious assault under Ohio Rev. Code § 2903.11(A).

> Judgment

We affirm the verdict.

SO ORDERED.

III. Drafting Useful Case Briefs

One key to success in your first semester of law school will be for you to learn how to read numerous and voluminous legal cases in an efficient manner and pare them down into key discussion components, identifying the major characters and events in the parties' factual story, the legal issue, the rule of law, the holding on the particular legal issue, the rationale/reasoning behind the holding, and the judgment (or procedural result) in the case. When you extract this information from a complex case opinion and condense it into "talking points," you are creating a "case brief." Each student, professor, and lawyer has a different way of processing, managing, and presenting this information. Develop a case brief template that works for you and fits the way your individual brain handles complex and dense information. The goal is to condense the critical components of a lengthy case into a one- or two-page document so you can refer to a streamlined summary of the case in class discussion instead of searching through numerous pages to track down the important information.

The following describes one possible strategy for creating a case brief template.

Step One: Print out a hard copy of the case; you want to be able to write on the document and circle, highlight, and mark up text on the paper. Skim the structure of the case as a whole before reading it closely to see whether you can identify some of the component parts mentioned in this chapter. Use a highlighter to identify these items, underline them, circle them, or make notes in the margins. It is okay, and recommended, to "get your hands dirty" and "get messy" when dissecting a case. No one will see your markup but you. Remember, statutes and cases are some of the raw materials of a lawyer's creative process. It's okay to be a bit of a mad scientist or untamed artist when working with these tools.

Step Two: Create a case briefing template on your computer or on a sheet of paper with the following categories.

- Case name: Who are the parties? What do they do for a living? What is their role in society? What is their relationship to one another? Instead of referring to the parties as "plaintiff" or "defendant,"[3] can you give each party a more useful descriptive term such as "employer," "perpetrator," "celebrity," "contractor," "property owner," or "victim"? Do not refer to the parties by their actual names; eventually it will be easier to apply the principles of the case to your client's factual circumstances if you assign role labels to the key players in the precedent cases rather than using their real names.
- Jurisdiction: In what court is the case pending? State or federal? What level does the court occupy in the judicial hierarchy—trial level, appeal, or court of last resort? (Consider searching for an online color-coded map of the particular state or federal court's hierarchy so you understand how the specific case fits within the vertical framework.)
- Date: When was this case decided? Was there anything notable or important about the political culture in our country at the time? Was anything major happening in the particular state or the United States then?

---

[3] An exception to this suggestion is in the context of criminal case law; when briefing criminal cases, it is okay to designate the "accused" as the "defendant" since that is a clear indication of the individual's role in the legal matter.

- Facts: What happened between the parties? Who is unhappy with whom? What led to the lawsuit? Can you capture the "story" of the case in a few sentences? Can you create a brief chronology of events?
- Procedure: What court documents have been filed so far in the case? What is the procedural "status" of the case? What procedural event in the litigation prompted the court to write an opinion at this time?
- Legal issue: What specific legal question are the parties asking the court to answer or resolve? Do the litigants want the court to resolve more than one legal issue?
- Rule of law: What rule of law governs the particular legal question? Is there an applicable statute or regulation? Have other cases provided a common law rule? Does the court break down the rule into a list of elements? Factors? Does the court define legal terms?
- Arguments made by the parties: What arguments does the plaintiff (or appellant or petitioner) make to persuade the court to rule in its favor? What arguments does the defendant (or appellee or respondent) assert to persuade the court to rule in its favor? Try to pare down the arguments for both sides into three or four bullet points.
- Holding: How does the court answer the legal question? Look for words like "the court holds," "the court finds," "we hold," or "we find." This is the substantive answer to the legal question (usually not a procedural step).
- Rationale or reasoning: What are the three or four reasons the court provides to support its holding? Does the court itemize a list of elements or factors and make a decision on each one? Does the court emphasize any public policy reasons for its decision (e.g., fairness, equality, efficiency, judicial economy, safety, health, welfare of citizens)?
- Judgment: What is the court's judgment? More specifically, what procedural step does the court order? Does the court grant or deny a motion? Does the court order the entry of judgment in one party's favor? Does the court award damages to one party or impose a penalty against another party? Does the court order "equitable relief" such as a temporary restraining order or an injunction? Does the court direct the clerk to take any procedural action?

Step 3: Go through the case again and begin to fill in your case brief template. If you encounter words in the opinion that you do not recognize or understand, look them up in a legal dictionary and keep a running definition list that accompanies your case briefs.

Step 4: Proofread and edit your case brief so it reads clearly. Use bolded or underlined headings so you can locate the different case components easily if questioned about them in class.

Step 5: Print out your completed case brief. Keep a folder of printed hard copies of your case briefs and take them to class so you do not have to search for answers to your professor's questions on your computer, but instead have all the answers neatly typed up on your printouts.

Sample "Best Practices" Case Brief

Case Name (Parties): State of Ohio v. Marci Hersh (she is a woman who worked at Case Western Reserve University, who was accused of stalking a coworker)

Jurisdiction: Court of Appeals of the State of Ohio, Eighth District, Cuyahoga County (Ohio is divided into 12 appellate districts, each of which is served by a court of appeals)

Date: August 23, 2012

Legally Significant Facts: The accused stalker was convicted of the crime of "menacing by stalking" in a bench trial and appealed. In 2006, she allegedly stalked a worker by harassing her on a daily basis. They lived in the same apartment building and worked at the same university. The defendant was found guilty of menacing by stalking in 2008. In 2009, the defendant had encounters with the stalking victim's parents, and then on a single occasion in 2009, the defendant followed the victim in a supermarket from aisle to aisle, but left the premises before the victim departed the store.

Procedure: The defendant was convicted of "menacing by stalking" (for the supermarket incident) in a bench trial and appealed.

Legal Issue: Whether the evidence was sufficient to establish a "pattern of conduct" as required to convict a defendant of "menacing by stalking" under the applicable Ohio statute, Rev. Code § 2903.211(A)(1) (2014), which states: "No person by engaging in a pattern of conduct shall knowingly cause another person to believe that the offender will cause physical harm to the other person or cause mental distress to the other person."

Rule of Law: "Pattern of conduct" is defined as "two or more actions or incidents closely related in time, whether or not there has been a prior conviction based on any of those actions or incidents."

Arguments Made by the Parties: The defendant argued that the supermarket encounter was the only encounter, and that the other encounters in 2006 were not "closely related in time." The prosecutor argued that the defendant's 2009 encounters with the victim's parents served as the basis for a "pattern of conduct."

Holding: The prosecution failed to present sufficient evidence of a "pattern of conduct."

Rationale or Reasoning: The cases cited by the prosecution did not support the argument that a "pattern of conduct" can be established by a defendant's alleged menacing interactions with *third parties* associated with a victim. Even if the court considered the encounters with the parents, the prosecution failed to present sufficient evidence that the encounters knowingly caused the victim to believe that the defendant would cause her physical harm or mental distress. The parents encountered her in public places; she said "hello" to them but did not otherwise talk to them. The victim did not testify that her parents' encounter made her believe that the defendant would cause her physical harm or mental distress.

> For tips on how to conquer anxiety about the Socratic method and answering a professor's questions in class about a case, see Appendix E.

Judgment: Court ordered that the conviction be vacated.

Chapter 7
Learning How to Read Regulations

In addition to statutes and cases, lawyers often review regulations promulgated by government agencies when researching a client's legal issue. Regulations explain how to apply and administer statutes. As explained in Chapter 4, the Constitution vests executive power in the president of the United States to appoint a cabinet to implement and enforce the statutes written by Congress. The cabinet consists of the vice president of the United States and heads of federal agencies "responsible for the day-to-day enforcement and administration of federal laws."[1] The heads of the 15 executive departments represented in the cabinet are the secretaries of agriculture, commerce, defense, education, energy, health and human services, homeland security, housing and urban development, interior, labor, state, transportation, treasury, veterans affairs, and the attorney general.

A statute known as the Administrative Procedure Act (APA)[2] grants federal agencies authority to issue the regulations that explain how federal statutes should be enforced. In the 1930s, Congress enacted the Federal Register Act[3] to establish two publications that document these federal regulations: (1) the daily *Federal Register*, and (2) the *Code of Federal Regulations* (CFR), the official codification of final agency regulations. The *Federal Register* (the "daily journal of the United States Government"[4]) contains four types of documents:

(1) "notices of public meetings, hearings, investigations, grants and funding, environmental impact statements, information collections, statements of

---

[1] *The Executive Branch*, The White House, http://www.whitehouse.gov/our-government/executive-branch (last visited January 27, 2016).
[2] 5 U.S.C.A. § 500 *et seq.* (West 2014).
[3] 44 U.S.C.A. § 1501 *et seq.* (West 2014).
[4] *The Federal Register: The Daily Journal of the United States Government*, Federal Register, https://www.federalregister.gov (last visited January 27, 2016).

organization and functions, delegations, and other announcements of public interest";[5]

(2) proposed new regulations;

(3) final regulations (before they are officially published in the CFR); and

(4) presidential documents such as executive orders, proclamations, administrative orders, and presidential memoranda.

I. Understanding the Rulemaking Process

When a statute is enacted, if regulations are necessary to implement the statute, Congress designates the appropriate government agency to develop the text of the regulations (called a rule) within an established timeline. The "rulemaking process" commences, and the agency begins shaping the rule. Under the APA, the agency publishes a Notice of Proposed Rulemaking in the daily *Federal Register*, presenting the proposed rule, summarizing the issues, stating why the rule is necessary, and inviting public comments.[6] Through such comments, the public can provide information, facts and figures, viewpoints, or positions. At the conclusion of the notice-and-comment process, the agency finalizes the rule by publishing it in the *Federal Register* as an amendment to the CFR. This *Federal Register* version includes the purpose of the new rule, a detailed summary of the background of the rule, a discussion of the rule, regulatory analyses, helpful tables, the effective date, contact information for the rulemakers, and any supplementary information (such as acronyms). Then, Government Printing Office personnel begin "processing the material for codification into the CFR."[7]

II. Understanding the Structure of Government Agency Regulations

To read regulations, it is important to know how they are structured. The CFR consists of 50 topical titles (such as "Energy," "Food and Drugs," and "Telecommunication"). Each title breaks down into chapters designated to the agencies assigned to issue regulations pertaining to the title's subject matter. More than one agency may share responsibility for each title. Each chapter splits into parts (each covering a particular agency program), which further are divided into sections—the basic unit of the CFR—and shorter paragraphs therein.

---

[5] *What's in the Federal Register: Notices*, Federal Register, https://www.federalregister.gov (last visited January 27, 2016).

[6] *A Guide to the Rulemaking Process Prepared by the Office of the Federal Register*, Federal Register, https://www.federalregister.gov/uploads/2011/01/the_rulemaking_process.pdf (last visited January 27, 2016).

[7] *Id.*

Title	Broad subject matter area of the regulation
Chapter	Individual agency coverage of the relevant subject area
Part	Agency coverage of a single program/function
Section	One category of program/function rules
Paragraph	A detailed, specific rule

Each title of the CFR is revised and reissued once each year on the following staggered schedule:

Titles 1-16 updated as of January 1
Titles 17-27 updated as of April 1
Titles 28-41 updated as of July 1
Titles 42-50 updated as of October 1

Consider this example. Suppose meteorologists are predicting that a dangerous hurricane will make landfall in a certain region in the United States. As a law student or lawyer, imagine you want to research the circumstances under which the president might declare a state of emergency or a major disaster in your region. To find a pertinent agency regulation governing presidential declarations related to natural disasters, peruse the list of titles in the CFR. Title 44 refers to "Emergency Management and Assistance."

Next, the chapters in title 44 show which agencies have promulgated rules on this topic.[8] Two chapters indicate agencies with overlapping responsibilities: (1) Federal Emergency Management Agency (FEMA), which is part of the Department of Homeland Security (DHS); and (2) Department of Commerce and Department of Transportation. FEMA certainly sounds familiar when we consider government agencies that respond to natural disasters, so a law student or lawyer might focus on that chapter first. The table of contents in the FEMA chapter of title 44 lists several subchapters:

Subchapter A—General
Subchapter B—Insurance and Hazard Mitigation
Subchapter C—Fire Prevention and Control
Subchapter D—Disaster Assistance
Subchapter E—Cerro Grande Fire Assistance
Subchapter F—Preparedness

---

[8] The CFR includes tables of contents providing lists of all CFR titles, subtitles, chapters, and parts, as well as the names of agencies assigned to the CFR chapters.

"Disaster Assistance" in subchapter D sounds like it is on point. It is divided into parts:

Part 201—Mitigation Planning
Part 204—Fire Management Assistance Grant Program
Part 206—Federal Disaster Assistance
Part 207—Management Costs
Part 208—National Urban Search and Rescue Response System
Part 209—Supplemental Property Acquisition and Elevation Assistance

Scanning the parts, the one entitled "Federal Disaster Assistance" seems the most promising. This part has the following subparts:

Subpart A—General
Subpart B—The Declaration Process
Subpart C—Emergency Assistance
Subpart D—Federal Assistance to Individuals and Households
Subpart E—Individual and Family Grant Programs
Subpart F—Other Individual Assistance
Subpart G—Public Assistance Project Administration
Subpart H—Public Assistance Eligibility
Subpart I—Public Assistance Insurance Requirements
Subpart J—Coastal Barrier Resources Act
Subpart K—Community Disaster Loans
Subpart L—Fire Suppression Assistance
Subpart M—Minimum Standards
Subpart N—Hazard Mitigation Grant Program

Subpart B, the "Declaration Process," is relevant since your legal question relates to how the government declares a state of emergency or disaster. Next, each subpart contains sections:

§ 206.31 Purpose
§ 206.32 Definitions
§ 206.33 Preliminary Damage Assessment
§ 206.34 Request for Utilization of Department of Defense (DoD) Resources
§ 206.35 Requests for Emergency Declarations
§ 206.36 Requests for Major Disaster Declarations
§ 206.37 Processing Requests for Declarations of a Major Disaster or Emergency
§ 206.38 Presidential Determination
§ 206.39 Notification
§ 206.40 Designation of Affected Areas and Eligible Assistance
§ 206.41 Appointment of Disaster Officials
§ 206.42 Responsibilities of Coordinating Officers
§ 206.43 Emergency Support Teams
§ 206.44 FEMA–State Agreements

§ 206.45 Loans of Non-Federal Share

§ 206.46 Appeals

§ 206.47 Cost-Share Adjustments

Sections 206.35 and 206.36 sound pertinent, but take a look at § 206.38.

44 C.F.R. § 206.38

§ 206.38 Presidential determination.

(a) The Governor's request for a major disaster declaration may result in either a Presidential declaration of a major disaster or an emergency, or denial of the Governor's request.

(b) The Governor's request for an emergency declaration may result only in a Presidential declaration of an emergency, or denial of the Governor's request.

Credits

[55 FR 5458, Feb. 15, 1990]

SOURCE: 54 FR 11615, March 21, 1989; 55 FR 2288, Jan. 23, 1990; 55 FR 2292, Jan. 23, 1990; 55 FR 35529, Aug. 30, 1990; 58 FR 47996, Sept. 14, 1993; 61 FR 7224, Feb. 27, 1996; 61 FR 19201, May 1, 1996; 62 FR 45330, Aug. 27, 1997; 67 FR 8852, Feb. 26, 2002; 68 FR 15668, April 1, 2003; 71 FR 40027, July 14, 2006; 72 FR 57875, Oct. 11, 2007; 72 FR 61565, Oct. 31, 2007; 74 FR 15345, April 3, 2009; 77 FR 67290, Nov. 9, 2012; 78 FR 49961, Aug. 16, 2013, unless otherwise noted.

AUTHORITY: Robert T. Stafford Disaster Relief and Emergency Assistance Act, 42 U.S.C. 5121 through 5207; Homeland Security Act of 2002, 6 U.S.C. 101 et seq.; Department of Homeland Security Delegation 9001.1; sec. 1105, Pub.L. 113–2, 127 Stat. 43 (42 U.S.C. 5189a note).

Current through June 26, 2014; 79 FR 36240.

Before analyzing the text of the regulation, take note of its other component parts. First, the information "44 C.F.R. § 206.38" is the citation; the number 44 reflects the title, the designation "C.F.R." refers to the *Code of Federal Regulations*, the symbol "§." means "section," and the number "206.38" is the precise section of the regulation where a law student or lawyer can find the particular text.

There are a few other pieces of useful information: (1) source and (2) authority. The source lists the citations to the *Federal Register* entries containing the notices and preliminary versions of the regulation that eventually became codified into the final rule. The authority provides the particular reference to the statutes granting the agencies the authority to issue the regulation in the first place. The CFR also provides the date when the particular text was last published.

In analyzing the language of the regulation, lawyers employ the same techniques they use in parsing statutes, looking for indicator words like "must," "shall," "may," and "must not," as well as key connector words, phrases, and punctuation. At first glance, the two sentences in paragraphs (a) and (b) above sound quite similar. But note a few key language differences:

> (a) The Governor's request for a *major disaster* declaration *may* result *in either* a Presidential declaration of *a major disaster* **or** *an emergency*, *or* denial of the Governor's request.
> (b) The Governor/s request for an *emergency* declaration *may* result *only* in a Presidential declaration of *an emergency*, *or* denial of the Governor's request. [Emphasis added.]

In paragraph (a), if the governor of a certain state requests the president to declare a "major disaster" resulting from the hurricane, for example, there are *three* possible results: (1) a declaration of a major disaster, (2) a declaration of an emergency, or (3) a denial of the request. In contrast, in paragraph (b), if the governor of a certain state requests the president to declare an "emergency" resulting from the hurricane, for example, there are only *two* possible results: (1) a declaration of an emergency, or (2) a denial of the request. Why does this difference matter? According to FEMA, major disasters and emergencies trigger different federal funding responses. For a major disaster to elicit supplemental federal aid, the event must require federal assistance beyond what state or local governments can address independently. If the required threshold is met, long-term recovery funding may be activated.[9] An emergency declaration is more limited in scope and will not stimulate the same level of long-term recovery funding that a major disaster can. This regulation indicates that if a governor requests a declaration of a major disaster, the president can decide to "downgrade" the event to an emergency, but not vice versa.

III. Tackling Regulations in a Legal Writing Assignment

If your legal writing assignment involves a regulation, identify (1) the general topic and subject matter of the regulation; (2) the agency (or agencies) involved in creating the regulation; and (3) the names of the pertinent title, chapter, part, and section. Then, use the same skills you apply in reading statutes (see Chapter 5) to understand the text of the rule.

---

[9] *The Disaster Process and Disaster Aid Programs: Response and Recovery*, FEMA, https://www.fema.gov/disaster-process-disaster-aid-programs (last updated January 27, 2016).

Section 3

The Mindful Legal Writer's Framework

Chapter 8

Introduction to the Format of a Single-Issue Legal Office Memorandum

Often, the first assignment legal writing students embark on in law school is a legal research memorandum (also called a law office memorandum) focused on a single legal issue. This type of document is a perfect introduction to the art and science of legal writing because it allows new legal writers to experiment with building a logical legal analysis using a basic foundational structure. The process is simple and yet provides all the fundamental tools you need to start an objective/predictive legal writing project. Through this assignment, you will

- first assess the facts of the hypothetical client's situation and then identify the narrow legal issue affecting the client's rights or interests;
- review statutes, regulations, and/or cases to pinpoint the rule of law governing the issue;
- possibly further narrow the rule of law to a particular element or set of factors to analyze;
- learn how to clearly explain the rule of law to your reader (who might have years of legal experience but still might be unfamiliar with the law you are analyzing);
- apply each part of the rule to the client's facts and perform a legal analysis;
- conclude by predicting how a court would rule on the legal issue.

Real-Life Scenarios of Supervising Attorneys Using Legal Memoranda

- A law firm partner schedules a conference call with in-house counsel to a corporate client and uses the law office memorandum to explain a complex statute to the client.
- A law firm partner boards a flight across the country to attend a settlement meeting with opposing counsel and reads the memorandum on the plane to understand the law and how a court likely will rule on the key legal issue.
- A law firm partner reviews the legal memorandum to evaluate what the client must prove in order to prevail in the case and then makes a list of necessary witnesses to contact and documents to gather.

I. Functional Context: How Do Supervising Attorneys Use Legal Research Memoranda?

Before beginning the task of writing a law office memorandum, it is important to understand how practicing lawyers use these types of documents in real life. As explained in Chapter 1, lawyers write legal research memoranda in many stages of a case. Often, supervising attorneys identify legal issues affecting a client or a case and then assign junior associates to write memoranda on these topics. Junior associates conduct the research and write (hopefully) clear predictive analyses so the supervising attorney can quickly grasp the law on the issue without having to research it independently. The supervising attorney then uses the memo to advise the client on the likely outcomes, empowering the client to make the best possible strategic decision. Legal memoranda are excellent tools to enable supervising attorneys and clients to make wise tactical choices in a case. Lawyers refer to legal research memoranda as "objective" or "predictive" because they are internal documents—not revealed to opposing parties—in which lawyers realistically evaluate both the strengths and weaknesses of the client's case and impartially apply the law to predict the most likely outcome. This process is different from persuasive legal writing (which you likely will learn about in your second semester of law school, and which is explained in the second half of this book) in which the lawyer takes a stand on the client's side of the issue and focuses on the strengths of that position.

II. Visual Context: What Does a Legal Research Memorandum Look Like?

Most single-issue legal research memoranda contain the following: (1) a header (To, From, Date, Re:); (2) a Question Presented; (3) a Brief Answer;

Single-Issue Legal Memorandum Template

MEMORANDUM

TO:
FROM:
DATE:
RE:

Question Presented

Brief Answer

Statement of Facts

Discussion

(I) ISSUE (Umbrella/Overview/Roadmap Paragraph)

(R) RULE (Relevant Statute, Regulation, or Common Law Rule)

(E) Rule Explanation (using case law to explain the Rule)

(A) Rule Application

(C) Conclusion

(4) a Statement of Facts; (5) a Discussion section organized around a legal formula called IRAC or IREAC (or alternatively CREAC)[1]; and (6) a final Conclusion, summarizing the attorney's prediction of the likely outcome on the legal issue presented.

III. Drafting Context: How the Legal Memo-Writing Process Differs from College-Style Drafting

When writing a term paper in college or graduate school, you may have started the project by drafting the first word of the paper's introduction and continued typing away until you reached the final words of your conclusion. In legal writing, however, lawyers do not necessarily *draft* a legal document in the chronological order that its final component parts appear on the page. For an analytical piece of legal writing to be cogent and well reasoned, a lawyer's drafting process often starts from the "inside out." When first learning how to write a legal

---

[1] IRAC stands for Issue-Rule-Application/Analysis-Conclusion. IREAC stands for Issue-Rule-Explanation-Application/Analysis-Conclusion. Some law professors use CREAC: Conclusion-Rule-Explanation-Application/Analysis-Conclusion.

research memorandum, law students typically benefit from drafting the discussion section first. Later, once you have pinpointed the precise legal question (which might not be apparent at first glance) and established the correct answer to that question, you can go back and draft the formal question presented and brief answer. You also might write the formal statement of facts after you determine which legally significant facts are essential to the analysis.

Similarly, new legal writers benefit from constructing the discussion section from the "inside out," starting with the "meat" of IREAC—extracting the issue and the rule in conjunction with one another, explaining or illustrating the rule through case examples, applying the rule to the client facts, and then going back and writing the introduction (in an "umbrella," "overview," or "roadmap" paragraph) that summarizes what the reader will learn in the discussion section. To teach you how to draft a memorandum like a lawyer, this book follows the progression of steps shown in the following table.[2]

	Task	Completed?
Step 1	Assessing the Big Picture (Envisioning the Six Major Parts of a Legal Memorandum)	
Step 2	Understanding the Component Parts of IREAC	
Step 3	Gathering the Client Facts	
Step 4	Researching and Extracting the Overall Governing Rule from a Statute/Regulation/Case Law	
Step 5	Clarifying the Precise Issue (or Component of the Rule) the Client Needs Addressed (the I in IREAC)	
Step 6	Synthesizing a More Precise Governing Rule for the Pertinent Legal Issue (the R in IREAC)	
Step 7	Drafting one (or more) Rule Explanation Paragraph(s) (the E in IREAC)	
Step 8	Drafting one (or more) Rule Application Paragraph(s) (the A in IREAC)	
Step 9	Drafting the Umbrella/Overview/Roadmap Paragraph (the I in IREAC)	
Step 10	Drafting the Conclusion (the C in IREAC)	
Step 11	Constructing the Question Presented (QP)	
Step 12	Crafting the Brief Answer (BA)	
Step 13	Writing the Statement of Facts (SOF)	
Step 14	Commencing the (Nonnegotiable) Foolproof, Ten-Step Editing Process (see Chapter 18)	

---

[2] Your professor might prefer a different chronological progression. In the end, as long as all the component parts are present, the memorandum should provide your reader with a logical analysis.

IRAC = ISSUE → RULE → APPLICATION → CONCLUSION
IREAC = ISSUE → RULE → EXPLANATION → APPLICATION → CONCLUSION

So, now that you can envision the process, let's talk about IRAC or IREAC.

Why do lawyers use IRAC or IREAC? Well, quite simply, this formula creates a logical flow to any legal analysis that most readers can easily understand. The goal in every piece of legal writing is to simplify complex concepts and guide the audience down the path of understanding, to a particular prediction (in objective legal writing) or a specific favorable result for your client (in persuasive legal writing).

To start, it is essential to clearly identify the legal *issue* for the reader (the I in IRAC or IREAC). When you are just beginning to learn the art and science of legal writing, you likely will be addressing a *single* issue in your first law school writing assignment. The issue part of IREAC will sweep away any distractions in the predicament posed by the client and focus the reader exclusively on the precise legal issue the memorandum will address. Your job in crafting the issue part of IREAC is to pare down the client's question into the exact legal question you will answer through your research and analysis, and steer the reader away from tangential topics that may seem interesting but are not at issue. (Chapter 9 teaches how to describe the issue clearly and concisely.)

In the second component of IREAC, the legal writer explains to the reader— ideally in plain English rather than legalese—the applicable *rule* derived from a statute, regulation, and/or common law. Warning: This next tip may spark flashbacks to grammar school, but lawyers often use sentence diagramming techniques to break down a rule into understandable and workable parts, such as definitions, elements, or factors.

Sample Statute Diagram (see Chapter 5)

Impersonating a Law Enforcement Officer
Any person →
    who shall falsely →
        assume the functions, powers, duties and privileges of a OR
        pretend to be a →
            sheriff,
            police officer,
            marshal, OR
            other peace officer →
                shall be deemed guilty of a misdemeanor.

Modified from Va. Code Ann. § 18.2-174 (West 2013).

"Elements" and "factors" might sound like interchangeable terms to a layperson, but remember the legal distinction drawn in Chapter 5. Elements are required items that *must* be satisfied for the rule to apply. For example, if you trot out to the driveway to start your car, you must have the keys, gas in the car, a functioning battery, and four inflated tires; otherwise, you will not be able to drive the vehicle to your destination. Any missing items will prevent you from moving forward.

Applying Required Elements

Keys?	☑
Gas?	☑
Functioning battery?	☑
Four inflated tires?	☑

In contrast, factors are options that a decision maker weighs and balances; not all are required. For example, if you are considering a new place to live, you might deliberate over location, price, square footage, and amenities. You will weigh the various characteristics, but in making your final decision you might compromise on one or two of them if the majority of your primary preferences are present.

The same concept applies to legal rules: some rules have a checklist of required elements, while others balance a range of factors. In your legal writing, you will describe the applicable rule to the reader by creating descriptive and organized lists of the elements or factors governing the client's issue. Readers often can understand and process well-structured lists more readily than a lengthy statutory quote or case excerpt.

Third, after you communicate the rule to the reader (hopefully in a clear definition or a workable list of elements or factors), you employ another formula called a Rule Explanation (abbreviated as RE)[1] to illustrate how prior courts have

Weighing Factors

	Convenience to law school	Price	Square footage	Amenities
High-rise condo near Wall Street	Ten-block walk	$350/month more than your original budget	Size of a postage stamp	Modern kitchen, walk-in closet, Wi-Fi, elevator
Renovated warehouse loft in Brooklyn	Thirty-minute subway ride	$100/month less than your original budget	Size of a larger postage stamp	Appliances from the early 1990s; fifth-floor walkup (no elevator)

---

[1] Professors might use different terminology for this memorandum component as well, such as Case Illustration or Case Explanation.

applied the same rule in either similar or different factual situations. One RE formula that is easy for a reader to understand is the following:

Rule Statement → Case Citation → Facts → Holding → Rationale

In a RE, legal writers introduce the rule (or a subrule) in an introductory sentence and use legal citation rules (explained in detail in Chapter 11) to cite the case that supports the statement of the rule or subrule. Then, to commence the RE, the writer describes the "legally significant facts" of the precedent case applying that rule—in a few sentences. The writer might not include all the case facts; some cases are many pages long and include tomes of background information and interesting but legally irrelevant details. Instead, the legal writer chooses the legally significant facts that tell the story and that also tie directly to the elements or factors of the legal rule.

RE Formula Example

Rule statement

   Under Florida law, an "assault" is (1) an intentional, unlawful threat, (2) by word or act to do violence, (3) to the person of another, (4) coupled with an apparent ability to do so, and (5) doing some act that creates a well-founded fear in such other person that violence is imminent. Fla. Stat. Ann.

Citation
Facts

§ 784.011 (West 1975). In *Rogan v. State*, 203 So. 2d 24 (Fla. Dist. Ct. App. 1967), a man standing outside a residence picked up a heavy flower pot full of dirt and threw the pot into a window of the residence. The man could see the victim inside the residence, seated in a chair five feet from the window, and yelled at her. *Id.* at 25. The flower pot broke the glass but did not penetrate the screen. The screen also held out the broken glass, but dirt from the flower pot spilled through onto the floor of the room. *Id.*

Holding
Rationale

   The court held that the perpetrator was guilty of the crime of assault. *Id.* at 26. The court reasoned that, while the flower pot was not a deadly weapon, the elements of the crime of assault were established: (1) the man intentionally hurled the flower pot in the direction of the victim; (2) at the same time, he yelled a threat of bodily harm to her; (3) he had the ability to harm her; and (4) his proximity prompted her well-founded fear. *Id.*

Next, the memo drafter states the court's holding (or decision) on the legal issue presented in the precedent case, using the phrase, "The court held . . ." Finally, the writer describes the court's reasoning in several sentences, starting with phrases like these: "The court reasoned . . . ," "The court explained . . . ," "The court relied on . . . ," or "The court emphasized . . ."

Your goal in writing the RE is to paint a vivid picture of how a court applied the legal rule to the facts in the precedent case. If the legal writer follows the "facts, holding, rationale" formula in crafting the RE, the reader should be able to grasp (1) the factual circumstances of the case, to eventually compare and contrast to the client's facts; (2) the court's decision on the precise legal issue—the same issue on which the client seeks an answer; and (3) the reasoning behind the court's decision in the precedent case.

Whether you include a single RE paragraph or multiple RE paragraphs in a legal memorandum depends on factors such as the number of relevant cases bearing on the client's legal issue and the appropriate length of the document.

After the RE, the legal writer moves onward to the Rule Application (abbreviated as RA)—the A in IREAC. In the RA, the memo drafter applies each part of the applicable legal rule to the client's fact pattern, compares or contrasts the client's facts to the precedent cases explained in the RE section, and analyzes the impact. RAs also can follow a formula. First, a strong RA starts off with a transition sentence, foreshadowing the ultimate conclusion on the legal issue. Then the RA addresses each component of the applicable legal rule, element by element or factor by factor. This can be accomplished in one paragraph, if the analysis is not too long, or the analysis can be broken into individual well-structured paragraphs (with a beginning, middle, and end). While applying each part of the rule to the client's facts, a thoughtful memo drafter weaves in the case(s) explained in the RE(s), comparing precedent cases to the client's case or distinguishing them, using comparison phrases such as, "Like the passenger in *Ramos* . . . ," "Just as the company in *Dehranian* . . . ," or "Similar to the aggrieved homeowner in *Mandell*. . . ." Legal writers also use phrases that connote contrast: "In contrast to the bystander in *Ng* . . . " or "Unlike the perpetrator in *Del Giacco* . . ."

After applying all parts of the rule to the client's circumstances, the memo drafter ends the memorandum by concluding and predicting the ultimate outcome. This is the C in IREAC.

Based on the foregoing case law, our client, Cruz, will likely prevail in its cause of action against Howell for fraud.

Example of IREAC

The following is an annotated example of an IREAC analysis.

Issue

Our client, Dylan Fontaine ("Fontaine"), seeks legal advice regarding whether she likely will be found guilty of the crime of felonious assault with a deadly weapon, as defined under Ohio law. Ohio Rev. Code § 2903.11(A) (2011)—the felonious assault statute—states that "[n]o person shall knowingly . . . [c]ause or attempt to cause physical harm to

Rule

another . . . by means of a deadly weapon or dangerous ordnance." Ohio Rev. Code § 2923.11(A) (2013) defines a "deadly weapon" as "any instrument, device, or thing capable of inflicting death, and designed or specially adapted for use as a weapon, or possessed, carried, or used as a weapon." The parties do not dispute that Fontaine knowingly caused physical harm to Jamie Dunham ("Dunham") by throwing her Jimmy Choo high-heel stiletto shoe directly at him. Thus, the sole question is whether the shoe qualifies as a "deadly weapon" under Ohio law.

Factors helping to explain the rule

When evaluating whether an otherwise innocuous item qualifies as a deadly weapon under the felonious assault statute, Ohio courts consider (1) the size and weight of the item, (2) the shape and design of the item, (3) the ability of the item to be grasped in the hands of the user in such a way that it may be used upon or directed against the body of another, and (4) the ability of the item to be used in a manner and with sufficient force to kill the other person. Applying these factors to Fontaine's shoe, a court likely will construe the stiletto to be a deadly weapon. Thus, Fontaine likely will be found guilty of the crime of felonious assault with a deadly weapon.

RE

Courts have applied the foregoing factors to numerous household items that would not normally be considered a weapon in their everyday use. For example, in *State v. Redmon*, No. CA-7938, 1990 WL 94745 (Ohio Ct. App. June 25, 1990), a home intruder, who had smoked cocaine earlier in the evening, broke into a house, picked up a wicker rocking chair, approached the homeowner who was sitting on her couch, and told her that he was going to kill her. *Id.* at *1. The intruder swung the rocker at the woman's face. While she was able to duck and run into the kitchen, the intruder continued swinging the chair as he made his way to the kitchen. He swung the rocker at the homeowner again, missed, and finally threw it away. *Id.* After an ongoing struggle and a 911 call, eventually the police arrived and arrested the intruder for the crime of felonious assault. *Id.*

The intruder argued that the wicker rocking chair was not a deadly weapon. *Id.* However, the court held that the chair was indeed a deadly weapon as defined by Ohio law. *Id.* at *2. The court explained, "[a]n instrument, no matter how innocuous when not in use, is a deadly weapon if it is of sufficient size and weight to inflict death upon a person, when the instrument is wielded against the body of the victim or threatened to be so wielded." *Id.* The court considered the following factors: (1) the size and weight of the chair, (2) the shape and design of the chair, (3) the ability of the chair to be grasped in the hands of the intruder and swung at the victim, (4) the ability of the chair to be used in a manner and with sufficient force to kill the victim. *Id.* Applying these factors, the court emphasized that the intruder swung the wicker rocking chair at the victim's head, while telling her that he was going to kill her. She ducked and the chair missed her face by one-and-a-half feet. These factors supported the court's finding that the chair constituted a deadly weapon. *Id.*

Second RE Similarly, in *State v. Ware*, No. 57546, 1990 WL 151499 (Ohio Ct. App. Oct. 11, 1990), an ex-boyfriend entered his ex-girlfriend's home and, as she was putting a broom behind a door, struck her on the head with an iron and said, "I am going to kill you." *Id.* at *1. The man continued to strike the woman with the iron while she screamed for help. She struggled toward her bed and grabbed a pillow to protect herself from the blows of the iron. The man continued to swing the iron, hitting her and the wall, until the iron fell apart. Eventually, she got away. *Id.* The ex-boyfriend was charged with felonious assault with a deadly weapon. He argued that the iron did not qualify as a "deadly weapon." *Id.*

The court held that the iron was a deadly weapon. *Id.* at *6. Applying the above-mentioned factors to determine whether the iron was capable of inflicting death, the court emphasized that the ex-boyfriend used the iron in such a manner by striking the victim several times, and caused her to sustain multiple abrasions and lacerations, requiring several stitches. The court found this sufficient to qualify the iron as capable of inflicting death. *Id.*

Third RE Further, in *State v. Maydillard*, No. CA99-06-060, 1999 WL 988822 (Ohio Ct. App. Nov. 1, 1999), an inmate at a correctional institution in Ohio entered the cell of another inmate, carrying a plastic shaving razor from which he had removed the plastic guards to expose the blades. The first inmate brandished the razor at the second inmate in an attempt to collect a debt owed. *Id.* at *1. A struggle ensued. Guards arrived at the cell, pulled the inmates apart, and handcuffed them. During a pat-down search, a guard found the razor. The inmate was charged with possession of a deadly weapon while under detention. *Id.*

In applying the statutory definition of a "deadly weapon" to the razor, the *Maydillard* court held that the razor possessed by the inmate was a "deadly weapon" by the manner of its use or adaptation. *Id.* at *4. The court explained that cases which have found a razor not to be a deadly weapon involve circumstances where the razor was used or possessed consistent with its legitimate purpose, such as a barber's razor or a pocket knife used for cutting packing tape and rope. *Id.* at *3. However, this inmate had adapted the razor, by removing the plastic guards, to function as a deadly weapon. *Id.* at *4. Further, he brandished it as a weapon. Finally, the court emphasized that the inmate presented no testimony that he was using the razor in a manner consistent with its legitimate purpose. *Id.; see also State v. Salinas*, No. F-84-8, 1985 WL 7568 (Ohio Ct. App. July 26, **Signal cites** 1985) (holding that a jury reasonably could find that a baseball bat consti**adding** tuted a deadly weapon when the perpetrator swung the bat at a victim, **additional** causing injury to his jaw, ribs and arms); *State v. Deboe*, 406 N.E.2d 536 **case law** (Ohio Ct. App. 1977) (holding that a club-like instrument three inches in diameter wrapped in spongy material, which the perpetrator swung rapidly at the victim, hitting him 15 or 20 times on the head, arms, back, shoulders, and kidneys, causing black and blue welts and bruises, constituted a deadly weapon).

Fourth RE

In contrast, in *State v. Kaeff*, No. 20519, 2004 WL 2245095 (Ohio Ct. App. Sept. 24, 2004), a husband was indicted for one count of domestic violence and one count of felonious assault with a deadly weapon, after using only his hands to attempt to strangle the victim, his wife. *Id.* at *1. The husband filed a motion to dismiss the count of felonious assault on the ground that a person's hands cannot, as a matter of law, be considered a deadly weapon. The trial court granted the motion and dismissed the count. The prosecution appealed the court's ruling. *Id.*

The prosecution argued that hands (1) fit within the definition of an "instrument," (2) are capable of inflicting death, and (3) can be used as a weapon. However, the court held that hands do not meet the definition of a deadly weapon. *Id.* at *4. The *Kaeff* court reasoned that the factors defining a deadly weapon suggest the use of an object apart from one's own body. Thus, one's hands are not within the scope of the statutory definition. *Id.*

RA

In evaluating whether Fontaine's Jimmy Choo stiletto qualifies as a deadly weapon, a court will consider (1) the size and weight of the shoe, (2) the shape and design of the shoe, (3) the ability of the shoe to be grasped in the hands of the user in such a way that it may be used upon or directed against the body of another, and (4) the ability of the shoe to be used in a manner and with sufficient force to kill the other person. Applying the foregoing factors, the court likely will find the stiletto constitutes a deadly weapon. Regarding the size and weight of the shoe, the facts indicate that Fontaine's "instrument" was a size 7 champagne-colored Jimmy Choo high-heel stiletto shoe. The shoe was constructed of suede and leather and was a platform peep-toe stiletto. The heel height measured 3.9 inches and was constructed of steel with a gold-colored point attached to a small rubber sole. The platform part of the shoe was less than half an inch. The shoe was neither lightweight nor small. Further, the pointy shape of the nearly four-inch metal heel, and the weight of the platform peep toe structure, rendered the shoe capable of causing harm when thrown with force. Fontaine was able to grasp the heavy unwieldy shoe in her hand, and hurl it toward the body of Dunham, specifically his head. The weight and shape of the shoe, when thrown in the manner Fontaine propelled it, likely had sufficient force to kill another person.

Conclusion

Unlike the perpetrator in *Maydillard* who modified an everyday razor by removing plastic safety guards, Fontaine did not modify or adapt the shoe from its original purpose. Further, unlike the assailants in *Redmon*, *Ware*, and *Deboe*, who swung their respective weapons—a rocking chair, an iron, and a sponge-covered bat—numerous times against the body of their victims, Fontaine only heaved the shoe one time at Dunham. Nonetheless, given the shoe's size, weight, shape, design, and ability to be grasped by Fontaine in such a way to be hurled at Dunham with sufficient force to gravely injure him and possibly kill him, a court will likely find that the shoe meets the definition of a "deadly weapon."

Section 4

The Mindful Legal Writer's Work

Chapter 9

Identifying the Legal Issue, and Extracting and Synthesizing the Rule

IREAC Map

Issue
Rule
(Rule) Explanation
(Rule) Application
Conclusion

Chapter 3 discussed general strategies for starting a new legal writing assignment. Part of that process includes initially identifying the *reason* the client contacted the law office to seek legal advice. A client may come to an attorney's office and ask questions like: "Do I have a case?" "Can I sue my neighbor ... a company ... the driver of a car that hit me ... ?" "Should I accept the terms of this contract?" "Am I entitled to a refund?" "Can I stop paying rent until my landlord fixes my plumbing?" These are "client-mindset" questions, but they might not represent the precise *legal* issue the lawyer needs to research. The attorney's job is to listen to the questions the client is asking, identify the governing area of law, and then pinpoint the specific legal issue and rule that will determine the answer to the client's question.

For example, imagine a client arrives at your law office and asks whether he is entitled to reimbursement from his neighbor for the loss of a prized vintage car that was ruined when the neighbor's landscape irrigation system malfunctioned and flooded the client's garage. Since no *contract* or obvious *crime* is involved, you might identify *torts* as the relevant legal subject area. Then, you could start by researching the legal issue of negligence, identifying the four elements of negligence (duty, breach, causation, and damages), and determining whether the neighbor owed a duty to his neighbor, the client. Through this process, the legal question might become: Does a landowner owe a duty to a neighbor to protect the latter's property from damage caused by water originating on the landowner's property? For now, you might set aside the other elements of breach, causation, and damages until you assess and predict the answer to the threshold "duty" question.

Similarly, visualize a client visiting your law office and asking whether she can be found guilty of the crime of check fraud when she wrote a personal check to the Apple store for $250, knowing that she had only $200 in her account; she was hoping her paycheck of $800 would clear before the Apple store cashed her check. First, you would research the elements of the felony of check fraud: (1) the issuance of a check in the amount of $200 or more, (2) for payment for property or another thing of value, (3) with knowledge that there were insufficient funds in the check writer's bank account, and (4) with specific intent to defraud the recipient of the check. The first three elements likely are satisfied by our client's facts: (1) she wrote a check for $250, (2) the check was for an Apple product, and (3) she knew she had only $200 in her account. So you would focus the precise legal issue on the last element: What constitutes a specific intent to defraud the recipient of the check?

I. Narrowing Down the Legal Issue from a Statute

To narrow down a legal issue for a memorandum assignment, first determine whether a statute governs your client scenario. If so, use the tips in Chapter 5 to diagram the parts of the statute and determine whether it includes required elements or a list of factors that comprise the applicable rule. Consider creating a chart of the elements and/or factors. Then review your client's fact documents and begin inserting the key facts in columns next to the appropriate element or factor.

Consider the California Vehicle Code statute from Chapter 5 as an example:

Any person who
- drives OR takes
  - a vehicle
  - not his or her own,
  - without the consent of the owner thereof, AND
  - with intent EITHER to
    - permanently OR
    - temporarily deprive the owner thereof of his or her title to or possession of the vehicle,
- whether with or without intent to steal the vehicle.

Imagine you have a client who works as a car valet at a fancy hotel. A hotel guest arrives in an expensive BMW Z8 roadster, worth more than $100,000. The hotel guest asks the car valet to park the vehicle in front of the hotel rather than putting it in the garage where it might get scratched. The valet takes the keys to the Z8, drives it around the traffic circle in front of the hotel, and parks it near a row of limousines. An hour later, an ambulance arrives at the hotel, and the EMT explains to the car valets that they need to move the limousines (and the Z8) so the ambulance has room to park and load an ill guest. The car valet hops in the Z8 and, deciding to go on an early lunch break, takes the car for a drive on the coastal highway, where a police officer pulls him over for speeding and issues a ticket. When the owner of the Z8 finds out about the valet's "joy ride," he wants to press charges for vehicle theft under the California Vehicle Code. An element chart to help nail down the precise legal issue might look like this:

Element	Client Facts
Driving or taking a vehicle	The car valet drove the BMW.
Not his or her own	The BMW did not belong to the car valet.
Without the consent of the owner	Did the car valet have consent from the owner to drive the vehicle at all? Within certain limits?
With intent to permanently OR temporarily deprive the owner of his or her title to or possession of the vehicle	Did the car valet intend to permanently or temporarily deprive the Z8 owner of title to or possession of the vehicle?

From this chart, you might realize you need to conduct additional research about the definition and scope of "consent" and "intent to permanently or temporarily deprive the owner of title or possession" of his car. In your research, you would search for cases specifically interpreting these two elements of the statutory rule.

If your legal rule is derived from regulations (Chapter 7), you can look for elements and factors within the text of the regulation, and create charts to apply these components to the client's facts.

II. Using Case Law to Further Define a Legal Issue and Governing Rule

Chapter 6 provides guidance on how to read and brief a case. In researching and writing your first legal memorandum, you will apply those reading skills to several cases, learn how to isolate the precise legal issue affecting the client, and synthesize the rule governing the outcome. When lawyers conduct legal research, they might find 5, 10, or 20 or more cases addressing the client's legal issue. However, a legal research memorandum does not have room to describe all 5, 10, or 20 cases—and a legal reader certainly will not have the patience to read a serial summary of every judicial opinion on point. Thus, it is important to learn the skill of (1) reviewing a group of cases; (2) recognizing patterns in how the rules, themes, and analyses overlap and build on each other; and (3) condensing that information into a concise "synthesized rule" that governs the client's case.

Discerning a single clear legal rule from more than one case might seem difficult at first, until you realize that you do this type of synthesizing all the time in your daily life. Here is an example of synthesis in a nonlegal context.

Nonlegal Example of Case Synthesis: Predicting Movie Reviews

Imagine that a movie called *Savages* directed by Oliver Stone just came out, and you're deciding whether it is worth spending $13 on a box office ticket. You first might try to predict whether the film will be any good, so you look at how critics have reviewed other films involving similar actors, genres, themes, settings, and so on.

Your "question presented" might be: Will the film critic (i.e., the "court") issue a "thumbs up" or a "thumbs down" ruling for the Oliver Stone crime thriller film *Savages*?

Known Facts About *Savages*

(1) The film stars Blake Lively as the mutual girlfriend of two Laguna Beach marijuana growers, Salma Hayak as the reigning queen of a Mexican drug cartel, Benicio del Toro as the drug cartel's ruthless chainsaw-wielding enforcer, and John Travolta as a fast food–loving DEA agent.

(2) The film is based on the novel by Don Winslow.

(3) Genre: Crime/Thriller

(4) Plot: A pair of likeable marijuana entrepreneurs and best friends (Chon and Ben) hailing from the West Coast town of Laguna Beach are the target of an extortion scheme by a vicious Mexican Baja drug cartel. Ben is a dedicated Buddhist and global philanthropist, and his buddy Chon is a former mercenary who trained as a Navy SEAL. They have a stunning mutual girlfriend named Ophelia (Blake Lively). Just as Chon and Ben are hitting record profits in their marijuana business, the cartel decides it wants a precentage of their market. Their merciless leader La Reina Elena (Salma Hayak) orders her enforcer, Lado (Benicio del Toro), to kidnap the golden Ophelia and threatens to kill her unless the Laguna boys kowtow to her demands.

(5) Theme: The film involves drugs, violence, and mayhem (including chainsaw massacres and roadside shootouts), contrasted with beautiful scenery—beaches of Southern California and hills of Mexico.

(6) Setting: Laguna Beach and Mexico

Now, consider the facts, holdings, and rationales of the following "precedent cases."

Precedent Case	Girl with the Dragon Tattoo	Sahara	Eat Pray Love	Under the Tuscan Sun	Da Vinci Code
Facts	• Action/Thriller • Based on the best-selling book by Stieg Larsson • Involves cyber-spying, journalistic intrigue, international travel, murder • Setting: Sweden	• Starring Matthew McConaughey as the master explorer Dirk Pitt (hero of best-selling author Clive Cussler's action-adventure novels) • Based on the novel Sahara by Clive Cussler • Action-packed adventure through Africa	• Starring Julia Roberts • Based on best-selling divorce recovery memoir by Elizabeth Gilbert • Travel/Romance set in Italy, Bali, and India	• Starring Diane Lane • Based on the best-selling travel memoir (true story about an American who moves to Tuscany) by Frances Mayes • Travel/Romance set in Italy	• Starring Tom Hanks and Audrey Tautou • Based on the best-selling novel by Dan Brown • Mystery/Thriller • Action-packed adventure through Europe
Holding	THUMBS WAY UP Rationale: "The Swedish winter scenery was stunning. The plot stays true to the novel and expertly juxtaposes action-packed raw violence (i.e., there is a tattoo gun involved) and the pain of loss against the beauty of love. Daniel Craig's star power did not overshadow newcomer Rooney Mara—the two exuded chemistry."	THUMBS DOWN Rationale: "While the travel intrigue was a plus, Matthew McConaughey seems to play a similar role in every action/adventure movie and fell short in portraying Clive Cussler's brilliant-yet-buff hero, Dirk Pitt—an adventurer bent on saving the world. Further, fans of Cussler's novels were disappointed at the film's departure from the book's story line."	THUMBS DOWN Rationale: "The film did not live up to the book except for the travel imagery. The book was a pure treasure. Julia Roberts was too huge a star for average fans of Elizabeth Gilbert's book to relate to. . . . Her 'pain' was not palpably felt. Plus, she had minimal chemistry with Javier Bardem . . . ."	THUMBS WAY UP Rationale: "The book was slow in parts. But Diane Lane brought the story to life. She was the perfect acting choice and did not overshadow the author's story of falling in love with Italy. Men and women alike could relate to her vulnerability on the big screen."	THUMBS UP Rationale: "Notwithstanding Tom Hanks' major star status, he didn't overshadow Audrey Tautou and enabled the audience to connect with the characters. He allowed other stars to shine, like Jean Reno and Paul Bettany. The film did the book justice, and left fans of Dan Brown satisfied. The European travel was a plus too."

Now, commence the synthesizing process by asking the following questions.

Synthesizing Process

1. What common themes/factors can be derived from the precedent cases? What factors about these movies does the court tend to favor or disfavor?
   a. The court rules "thumbs up" in favor of "movie cases" that have the following:
      i.
      ii.
      iii.
      iv.
   b. The court rules "thumbs down" in "movie cases" that have the following:
      i.
      ii.
      iii.
2. Does the client case (*Savages*) have more "thumbs up" factors than "thumbs down" factors?
3. So, what is the predicted result?
4. Finally, which "precedent" cases are best used to explain which themes/factors?

III. Case Synthesis

In the foregoing movie example, hopefully you were able to determine pretty readily that the factors the "court" considered included (a) the connection of the film's plot to the storyline of the original book, (b) the presence of intriguing international settings and scenery, and (c) the existence of chemistry between the actors without one dominating the rest of the cast. As you begin to read real court cases addressing the legal issues governing your memorandum assignment, consider creating a similar case chart (inserting the facts, holdings, and, rationales) to visualize and draw links among common themes, elements, or factors across a range of court opinions. This process will help you synthesize a more precise legal rule.

Legal Example of Case Synthesis

Now try a legal example. Imagine a client visits your law office after being ticketed by the New York Police Department for selling colorful, artistic, painted roller-derby skates on a city sidewalk without a vendor's license, in violation of New York City Administrative Code § 20-453. The client wants to know whether the ticket is legally justified or whether her sale of the skates—which she considers "expressive art"—is constitutionally protected under her First Amendment right of freedom of expression, in which case she would not need a vendor's license.

Case Name	People v. Saul	People v. Chen Lee	Mastrovincenzo v. City of New York	People v. Franqui	People v. Ndiaye
Facts	• Defendant was charged with selling playing cards on the street without a general vendor's license. • The playing cards showed photographic images and names/ranks of military and political figures associated with the war in Iraq.	• Defendant was charged with selling decorative coasters/tiles on the street without a vendor's license. • The coasters were small tiles with photographs glued onto them.	• Freelance artists were charged with selling clothing painted with hip-hop-style graffiti without a vendor's license. • The artists individually decorated t-shirts and hats "with text and images in what they label a graffiti style."	• Defendant was charged with selling costume jewelry without a street vendor's license. • Defendant had been an artist for 25 years and made jewelry "using wires, shells, and other objects."	• Defendant was charged with selling costume jewelry without a vendor's license. • She claimed the jewelry was "wearable sculpture."
Legal issue	• Whether the playing cards were a form of written or visual expression and therefore protected by the First Amendment and, thus, did not require a vendor's license	• Whether the coasters were predominantly expressive (which would be protected by the First Amendment) or more like regular commercial goods (requiring a vendor's license)	• Whether the t-shirts were predominantly expressive or commercial goods	• Whether the jewelry served a predominately expressive purpose	• Whether the sale of the jewelry was sufficiently expressive to warrant First Amendment protection
Holding	• The cards were not expressive art.	• The coasters were exclusively expressive.	• The t-shirts were predominantly expressive.	• Jewelry was not automatically artistic work entitled to protection.	• First Amendment protects speech, not objects; costume jewelry was not art.
Court's rationale	• The cards are merely photographic images of Iraqi military or political figures. • There is nothing artistically noteworthy about the photographic images on the cards. • They do not constitute the seller's own artistic endeavor. • They do not communicate ideas, opinions, emotions, or a point of view. • They contain no written expression. • They are more like collectibles.	• The defendant decorated ceramic tiles with photographs of Marilyn Monroe, local sports arenas, and the storefront of Vesuvio Bakery. • The tiles are not usable as functional coasters or for any other practical commonplace purpose.	• The clothing had expressive or communicative elements (including words). • However, the clothing also had nonexpressive purposes ("shielding the eyes and head from the sun, calming and controlling unruly hair"). • The price varied based on the complexity of the design. • The artists created the designs themselves to communicate artistic ideas.	• List of materials used and the fact that the seller was the artist were not enough to prove the items were predominantly for an "expressive purpose."	• Costume jewelry was not art; it was not sculpture. • The jewelry had a utilitarian purpose as well.

To address the client's question, imagine that you diligently conducted legal research and found the foregoing five cases. From these five cases, synthesize a list of the factors courts might consider when determining whether an item being sold on the streets of New York City qualifies either as (1) expressive art not requiring a vendor's license or (2) a commercial item requiring a vendor's license.

Factors the various courts considered:

1.
2.
3.
4.
5.

To introduce a synthesized rule, you might start by saying, "When evaluating whether an item being sold by a street vendor is predominantly expressive art or instead a commercial item, courts consider the following factors: (1) . . . , (2) . . . , (3) . . . ."

Chapter 10

Rule Explanation: Explaining and Illustrating a Legal Rule Through Case Law

IREAC Map

Issue

Rule

(Rule) Explanation

(Rule) Application

Conclusion

The first moment you put pen to paper (or fingertips to keyboard) in beginning to craft a law office memorandum, consider writing a Rule Explanation (abbreviated as RE)[1] paragraph (or paragraphs) first. As mentioned in previous chapters, legal writers do not necessarily sit down to write a legal memo and start with typing the words "Question Presented" and continue clacking away busily until they, in a satisfied flourish, reach the last word of the conclusion. Instead, one option for developing a logical IREAC or CREAC analysis, especially while you are learning the building blocks of legal writing, is to draft a legal memorandum "from the inside out," starting with the more manageable internal components of the discussion section. This process should help you better understand the rule you are applying (the R in IREAC or CREAC), clearly explain and illustrate such rule to your reader (through carefully selected case examples—the E in IREAC or CREAC), and then apply the parts of the rule to the client's facts in a rule application (the A in IREAC or CREAC). After you perform this carefully constructed analysis,

---

[1] Remember that your professor may use different terminology for this component of a legal memorandum's Discussion section, such as Case Illustration or Case Explanation.

you add on the "extras": the overview/umbrella/roadmap paragraph (the I in IREAC or the first C in CREAC), the conclusion, the question presented, the brief answer, the statement of facts, and possibly some internal headings as signposts to the reader. This step-by-step, inside-out process ensures that you do not make any logic leaps or any faulty assumptions that will leave the reader confused.

This chapter focuses on how to write a rule explanation (RE) for a single judicial opinion—taking one precedent case and writing about it in a concise, organized, logical way. Instead of having to read the case independently, the memo reader can use the RE to grasp what happened to the parties in the case and how the court applied the particular rule to the underlying facts.

An RE actually can be one of the most fun tasks in the process of learning how to write like a lawyer because it follows a very simple formula; if you start by following this formula, your REs will be coherent, crisp, and informative. Later, you can adjust the formula as needed for more sophisticated analyses; for now, embrace this straightforward formula as a foundational tool.

So far, you might have read three or four cases for your first memorandum assignment. You have briefed the cases, discussed them in class, and used them to extract or synthesize the rule that governs your client's factual scenario. Through the REs, you will illustrate the rule to your reader in the memorandum. Take a look at the length of your case briefs, and then consider the word count or page limit that your professor has designated for the memorandum assignment. In a legal memorandum, lawyers do not have the luxury of stringing along an endless series of case briefs; plus, such a repetitive structural arrangement would not be very pleasant to read. So instead, attorneys carefully choose cases[1] and construct RE paragraphs to illustrate precedent cases in a more succinct, instructive, and elegant fashion. Through REs, the legal writer does the intellectual legwork for the memorandum audience and brings cases to life through a nicely packaged sketch of the rule statement, the citation, the legally significant facts in the case, the holding on the relevant legal issue, and the court's rationale (or reasoning) underlying its decision. This is the formula for a strong, clear RE:

> *Rule statement* (often followed by the *citation* of the case: the source of the rule)
> *Facts* of the precedent case (a few concise sentences to paint a vivid picture for the reader of what happened between the parties, focusing on context but also "legally significant" facts relevant to the court's decision)
> Court's *holding* on the relevant legal issue (one sentence: "The court held . . .")

---

[1] Most legal memoranda involve more than one illustrative case. Chapter 13 provides guidance on how to decide which cases to use and how to organize them.

> Court's *rationale* (reasoning) for its decision (a few sentences explaining *why* the court decided the case the way it did, using the elements/ factors of the rule)

Consider each component part of this RE formula.

I. RE Component 1: Rule Statement

To introduce the first RE in a memorandum, you start by stating the legal rule that you plan to illustrate via the case. If this is the first time in the body of the memorandum that you are identifying the governing rule, this could comprise the main R in your overall IREAC or CREAC. Alternatively, as Chapter 13 discusses, you may decide to describe the overall rule first in your overview/ umbrella/roadmap paragraph and then transition to your RE with a subrule, or narrower version of the main rule, that will be further illustrated via that case. This distinction will make more sense once you learn about the overview/umbrella/roadmap paragraph, but for now, take a look at some examples of rule statements for REs. Your rule might be extracted from a statute or a single case, or it might be synthesized from a group of cases.

A. Using Statutory Language to Write a Rule Statement

If the law governing the client's case comes from a statute, your main rule will be the elements or requirements of that statute. For example, if a rule involves several elements of the crime of assault, you might state the rule as follows:

> Under Florida law, an "assault" is (1) an intentional, unlawful threat; (2) by word or act to do violence; (3) to the person of another; (4) coupled with an apparent ability to do so; and (4) doing some act (5) which creates a well-founded fear in such other person (6) that such violence is imminent.

Here is another example of a statutory rule relating to the crime of impersonating a police officer:

> Under North Carolina law, a person makes a false representation that he is a sworn law enforcement officer if he (1) verbally informs another that he is a sworn law enforcement officer; (2) displays any badge or identification signifying to a reasonable individual that the person is a sworn law enforcement officer; (3) unlawfully operates a vehicle on a public street, highway, or public vehicular area with an operating red light; or (4) unlawfully operates a vehicle on a public street, highway, or public vehicular area with an operating blue light.

B. Crafting a Synthesized Rule Statement from Case Law

Alternatively, perhaps your main rule comes from a statute, but then the case law you researched provides more helpful or descriptive information about that rule by providing a list of factors that further define a particular word, phrase, or element of the statute. Here is an example of a list of factors defining whether a photograph constitutes "obscene printed material":

> When determining whether a photograph qualifies as "obscene," courts use modern societal standards to evaluate whether (1) the photograph "appeals to a shameful or morbid interest in nudity or sex"; (2) the photograph is "patently offensive"; and (3) the photograph has any "literary, scientific, political, or artistic value."[2]

C. Not Too Narrow, Not Too Broad

A Rule Statement in a RE should not be so detailed or focused exclusively on the precedent case that it becomes irrelevant to your client's case. It also should not be so overbroad that it becomes useless to the reader. Your goal in a well-crafted Rule Statement is to summarize the rule from a precedent case in a way that your memorandum audience can apply it readily to the client's case. Take a look at a few nonlegal examples so you can see how this works.

1. Nonlegal Example 1: Go Bears!

Let's say you are trying to predict whether the Chicago Bears football team is likely to win a particular football game being played in the rain in November at its home stadium, with a backup quarterback. You have a "precedent case" in which the Bears won a home game in the snow in November using a backup wide receiver—obviously a different yet still informative scenario.

> **Too Narrow Rule Statement:** "The Bears win football games played in the snow with backup wide receivers." This is too narrow because the facts of your client scenario involve rain and a quarterback, not snow and a wide receiver.

> **Too Broad Rule Statement:** "The Bears win football games." This is too broad because it does not tell the reader the circumstances under which the team has won in the past.

> **Useful Rule Statement:** "The Bears have won football games in inclement weather using backup players in key positions." This rule statement covers rain **or** snow and backup players in **either** the quarterback or wide receiver position.

---

[2] *State of La. v. Walden Book Co.*, 386 So. 2d 342 (La. 1980).

2. Nonlegal Example 2: Let's Dine Out!

Now imagine you are trying to predict whether your hard-to-please future mother-in-law will enjoy a hip new local restaurant when she comes to visit your city next month. You know she prefers to eat in a restaurant that has a pleasant view, serves healthy food, and is not overly noisy. You have a "precedent case" in which a similarly cantankerous mother-in-law approved of a Thai restaurant that served vegetarian entrees, had a view of a park in which cherry blossoms were blooming, and played soothing harp music in the background.

> **Too Narrow Rule Statement:** "Difficult mothers-in-law approve of Thai restaurants with harp music and views of cherry blossoms."

> **Too Broad Rule Statement:** "Difficult mothers-in-law approve of multi-cultural restaurants with music and a view."

> **Helpful Rule Statement:** "Difficult mothers-in-law approve of restaurants offering vegetarian options, views of nature, and accompanying soothing music."

3. Legal Example of Too Broad and Too Narrow Rule Statements

Remember the client from Chapter 9 who sold colorful, artistic, painted roller derby skates? Suppose your legal question involves whether an item being sold by a street vendor is predominantly expressive art (which does not require a vendor's license) or a commercial item (which does require a vendor's license). Further, as support for your analysis, you have selected the precedent case of *Mastrovincenzo v. City of New York*, which involved freelance artists who were charged with selling clothing painted with hip-hop-style graffiti without a vendor's license. The artists had decorated t-shirts and hats "with text and images in what they label[ed] a graffiti style."[3] The court held the t-shirts were predominantly "expressive" rather than "commercial," and focusing on the following factors: (1) the clothing had artistically expressive or communicative elements, including words; (2) the clothing also had nonexpressive functional purposes ("shielding the eyes and head from the sun, calming and controlling unruly hair");[4] (3) the price of the items varied based on the complexity of the design; and (4) the artists created the designs themselves to communicate artistic ideas.

> **Too Broad Rule Statement:** "All wearable items sold on the street constitute predominantly expressive art, not requiring a vendor's license."

This statement is overbroad because it assumes that all "wearable items" have the same characteristics as the clothing in the *Mastrovincenzo* case.

---

[3] 435 F.3d 78, 86 (2d Cir. 2005).
[4] *Id.* at 96.

Too Narrow Rule Statement: "All individually decorated hip-hop t-shirts and hats with artistic graffiti-style text and images constitute predominantly expressive art, not requiring a vendor's license."

This is too narrow because the current client's "art" is painted roller derby skates—not "individually decorated hip-hop t-shirts and hats"—so the rule would sound irrelevant to the reader.

Helpful Rule Statement: This rule statement extracts the specific factors about the "art" that apply generally to other kinds of clothing, shoes, or skates:

When evaluating whether items sold on the street without a vendor's license constitute predominantly expressive art or commercial items, courts evaluate whether: (1) the items have artistically expressive or communicative elements, including words; (2) the items also have nonexpressive functional purposes; (3) the prices of the items vary based on design complexity; and (4) the artists created the designs themselves to communicate artistic ideas or purchased them from someone else.[5]

See how this rule statement can be applied to hip-hop clothing *or* roller derby skates? The process of writing a well-balanced, helpful rule statement takes time and practice. One helpful technique is to write the rule statement *last*, after you have written the other components of the RE (explained below) and you fully understand the important aspects of the precedent case that apply to the client's scenario.

II. RE Component 2: Case Citation

The next component of the RE is the case citation. (Chapter 11 discusses the basics of legal citation.[6]) Citing the case achieves two foundational purposes: (1) to tell the reader the source of the rule statement, and (2) to enable the reader to find the case if he or she wants to read it (hopefully, your reader will find your RE so helpful that he or she will not need to read the case). The citation itself also provides other helpful information:

---

[5] Also, notice how this rule statement is structured; it introduces a numbered list whose components are written in parallel grammatical structure. See how each of the parts of the list, if read separately, match the grammar of the list's introduction? When constructing these types of helpful lists, it is important to check that the introductory language feeding into the list makes sense when read aloud with each individual component part of the list. Also, each component of the list should be in the same grammatical form: all nouns or all standalone sentences like the example above.

[6] Legal citation rules appear in two primary guidebooks: (1) *The Bluebook: A Uniform System of Citation*, compiled by the editors of the Columbia Law Review, the Harvard Law Review, the University of Pennsylvania Law Review, and the Yale Law Journal; and (2) the *ALWD Citation Manual: A Professional System of Citation*, written and edited by legal writing professors and experts affiliated with the Association of Legal Writing Directors. There are some very helpful workbooks in the market that provide step-by-step instructions on how to understand and become proficient at these sometimes confusing citation rules. (Chapter 11 provides a few basic introductory steps to citation that you can use as you write your first legal memorandum.)

Case Citation Components

Full name of case (underlined or italicized)
Comma
Case reporter volume #
Name of reporter (the book where the case can be found)
First page #
In parentheses: court and year
Period

Examples

Christian Louboutin S.A. v. Yves Saint Laurent Am. Holding, Inc., 709 F.3d 140 (2d Cir. 2013).

Basic Citation Template: [Plaintiff v. Defendant] [comma] [Volume 709] [Third Series of the *Federal Reporter* books] [case starts on page 140] [case was decided in the U.S. Court of Appeals for the Second Circuit] [case was decided in 2013].

Only the case name gets italicized or underlined. The rest of the cite is in regular typeface. Because the citation is its own standalone sentence, it ends with a period. (Chapter 11 explains slight variations in citation form for cases decided in different courts, but for the most part, the foregoing formula is standard for citing cases.)

III. RE Component 3: Case Facts

In the facts section of the RE, you paint a vivid picture for the reader of what legally significant events happened to, or between, the parties in the case. This is a balancing act: you want to provide sufficient details about the legally relevant facts so the reader understands what occurred, but not be so verbose in your storytelling that you take up too much space in your memorandum. A good starting place is to describe the first key player in the case and why he, she, or it is disgruntled.

> **Example 1:** In *Christian Louboutin*, a French footwear designer sued an American competitor brand, alleging that the brand infringed on the designer's trademark by copying its signature shiny red-soled shoes.

> **Example 2:** In *Rogan*, a man standing outside a residence picked up a heavy flower pot full of dirt and threw the pot into a window of the residence. The man could see the homeowner inside the residence, seated in a chair five feet from the window, and yelled at her. *Id.* at 25. The flower pot broke the glass but did not penetrate the screen. The screen held out the broken glass, but dirt from the flower pot spilled through onto the floor of the room. *Id.*

In the facts section of the RE, as Detective Joe Friday advised in a vintage TV series called *Dragnet*, stick to "just the facts, ma'am"; focus solely on necessary background facts and the legally relevant facts that tell the story of the precedent case in a concise manner. "Legally relevant" or "legally significant" facts are those that ultimately influence the court's decision. Trim away details that might be interesting but are not necessarily legally significant.

Items to Note in Example 1 Above

- In the recitation of the facts, use descriptive terms that can transfer or relate to your own client's role rather than using the actual names of the parties in the case. For example, the author above uses terms like "footwear designer" and "brand" instead of the parties' names. Good legal writers try not to burden their readers with extraneous hard-to-remember details; ideally, your reader should need to keep track of only the names of the characters involved in the client's case. Some legal writing professors also advise students against using terms like "plaintiff" and "defendant" to describe the players in a precedent case; using descriptive nouns is more informative to a reader.
- Because the rule statement, if included, would cite the case in full, the facts section uses a short cite (*Christian Louboutin*). (Full and short case cites are explained in further detail in Chapter 11.)

Items to Note in Example 2 Above

- Again, the writer uses terms like "man" and "homeowner" rather than the parties' names. When writing your REs, ask yourself: What nouns can I use to describe my client? "Business"? "Advertiser"? "Athlete"? How about the other parties? "Street entertainer"? "Police officer"? "Airline passenger"?
- All the facts in the RE are framed in the past tense.
- The Latin term "*Id.*" is used as a short case citation. *Id.* (which means "the same") is used in a legal citation to refer to the authority cited immediately before. "*Id.* at 25" means that the particular fact referenced in the previous sentence is found on page 25 of the case. The repetition of "*Id.*" after the last sentence (without a new page number) means that fact is also found on the same exact page as the prior cite. (Chapter 11 explains the use of *id.* and other short cites in more detail.)

IV. RE Component 4: Court's Holding on the Relevant Legal Issue

The holding arguably is the easiest component of an RE to write because it should always start with the same three words: "The court held . . ." There is no need to strive for professional creativity with the holding. Simply write the words "The court held . . ." and then state the court's decision on the precise legal question at issue in the precedent case. This is not the time to describe the court's "judgment"—remember, the court's holding and procedural judgment are two different items (see Chapter 6). If you are not sure how to find the holding, go back and ask yourself again: What is the precise legal issue pending in my client's case? That is the same legal issue you should be referring to in the sentence describing the holding in the RE.

For example, if the issue in your client's case is whether a party committed an assault, the holding in your RE should be whether the key player in that case committed an assault.

> **Example 1:** The court held that the perpetrator was guilty of the crime of assault. *Id.* at 26.

Alternatively, if the issue in your client's case is whether a person expressing his political views via Facebook is protected under the First Amendment right to freedom of speech, the holding in your RE should be whether the speech by the key player in that case was protected under the First Amendment.

> **Example 2:** The *Citizen Publishing* court held that the letter to the editor of the newspaper was free speech protected under the First Amendment. *Id.* at 519.

In Example 2, notice how the writer inserted the name of the case in the sentence describing the holding, using the short cite of the case (*Citizen Publishing*). Typically, in the holding section of an RE, you do not mention rules of procedure, or procedural results, such as dismissals, summary judgments, reversals, affirmances, or remands—unless the procedural steps are relevant to your own client's case. A good rule of thumb when first experimenting with drafting REs is to keep the holdings short: Simply write "The court held . . ." plus a concise statement of what exactly the court decided on the legal issue. Stop, and then start a new sentence to explain *why* the court held the way it did in the rationale component of the RE.

V. RE Component 5: Court's Rationale for Its Decision

This final component of the RE[7] is the legal writer's opportunity to explain—succinctly—*why* the court held the way it did. The easiest and most logical way to write the rationale section is to use phrases like, "The court evaluated . . . ," "The court determined . . . ," "The court reasoned . . . ," "The court emphasized . . . , "The court explained . . . ," "The court considered . . ."

The rationale can be several sentences and should tie closely to the rule that the court applied to the facts of the case. A well-organized rationale paragraph will

---

[7] Some legal writing professors and lawyers prefer to flip the order of the holding and rationale—placing the rationale before the holding. You should discuss these options with your professor. Regardless, the goal is to make sure your REs include all of the logic-driven components: rule statement, citation, facts, holding, rationale.

Holding	The court held that the perpetrator was guilty of the crime of assault. *Id.* at 26.
Rationale (tracking the ele- ments of the crime of assault)	The court reasoned that, while the flower pot was not a deadly weapon, the elements of the crime of assault were nonetheless established. First, the man intentionally hurled the flower pot in the direction of the victim. *Id.* Second, at the same time, he yelled a threat of bodily harm to her. *Id.*

track each rule element or factor the court considered. It is acceptable, and encouraged, to incorporate the key legally significant facts that the court relied on in its decision. You might feel like you are repeating the facts. However, in the rationale you are using the facts for a different purpose; you are tying the facts to the rule. The goal in the rationale is to explain the logic behind the court's decision, to help the memo reader understand how a court likely will handle the client's factual scenario.

VI. RE Recap

Your overall objective in drafting an effective RE is to capture the facts, holding, and rationale of the precedent case, and to present them in a concise yet engaging way so your memorandum reader does not need to read the case him- or herself to understand what happened. If you follow the described formula—rule statement, citation, facts, holding, rationale—you cannot possibly leave out any key logic components.

Further, if you avoid using the names of the actual parties in the precedent cases, but instead use descriptive nouns or labels that parallel the roles of the key players in your own client's case, you will help the reader grasp the storyline without burdening him or her with extraneous details to remember. Use the fact section to paint the scene; use vivid visual descriptors so the reader can imagine the play-by-play of what happened.

Do *not* be creative with the holding: stick to "The court held . . ." plus the legal decision. Stop, and then start again to explain the rationale, tying your sentences as closely as possible to the key parts of the rule the court applied to the precedent case and that you will apply to your client's case.

This chapter also provides (1) a rule explanation checklist, (2) an RE template, (3) a sample annotated RE so you can visualize how the five component parts fit together, and (4) an RE annotation exercise.

RULE EXPLANATION CHECKLIST

Rule Statement

☑ Accurately captures the applicable rule or a useful sub-rule.

☑ Not too general, but also not too narrow—the reader needs to be able to readily apply the rule to the client's scenario.

Citation

☑ Case name gets italicized or underlined (choose one style and use it consistently).

☑ The numbering part (volume, reporter, page, court, date) is not italicized or underlined.

☑ Include the court and date in the "full cite" (use the full cite the first time you cite the case).

☑ Italicize or underline *Id.*

☑ Place a period after *Id.*

☑ Place a period before *Id.* to end the prior sentence.

☑ Use lowercase "a" for "at" after *Id.* (your word processing system might automatically capitalize the word so you will need to double-check and fix the "a").

☑ Do not place brackets around cites (you may see brackets or parentheses in case cite hyperlinks on Westlaw, Lexis, or Bloomberg Law, but that format is not proper "Bluebooking").

☑ Use the page numbers from the case reporter volumes, not the Westlaw/Lexis/Bloomberg printouts. No asterisks are needed unless the case is unpublished. (See Chapter 11 for an explanation of page numbering in citing cases.)

Verb Tense

☑ Use the present verb tense when writing the rule statement. "Courts consider the following factors . . ."

☑ Use the past verb tense for precedent case facts, the court's holding, and the rationale. "In *Christian Louboutin*, the court held . . . ," "In *Rogan*, the court reasoned . . ."

Facts

☑ If possible, use generic, readily identifiable terms like "celebrity," "company," "business," "claimant" when describing the parties in the precedent cases; avoid using personal (e.g., Chris Maloney) or company (e.g., Citibank) names.

☑ Do not make legal conclusions in your fact section (e.g., "The woman clearly assaulted the distracted man."). Stick to the basic facts and refrain from making judgments or assumptions. Instead of using legal terms, refer to the factual terms. Save the "legal conclusions" for the rationale section.

Holdings and Rationales

☑ When referring to the court, avoid using "humanistic" verbs like "felt," "said," "believed." Instead, use verbs like "held," "stated," "determined," "confirmed," "concluded."

☑ The court is an "it," not a "they."

☑ To state the holding correctly, start with "The court held . . ." and answer the legal question posed; avoid mentioning procedural consequences (unless the procedure is relevant to your client's scenario as well).

☑ Remember that your memo reader probably is not as familiar with the elements/factors of the legal rule as you are, so, in the rationale, avoid using one- or two-word abbreviations or shortcut descriptions of the legal terms that you may have used in class discussion. Instead, write out each element or factor so that its meaning is 100 percent clear to a reader who is unfamiliar with the case.

☑ It is okay to repeat some case facts in the rationale; the facts transform into factors there, so the writing might be slightly repetitive. That is normal.

General Writing

☑ Use active voice instead of passive voice whenever you can [Active voice = an actor + an action verb. For example: The baseball player swung the bat. Passive voice = an object being manipulated by an actor. For example: The bat was swung by the baseball player.].

☑ Avoid the temptation to speak in "legalese." Your normal "voice" is better, though your phrasing will be more formal than regular conversation.

☑ Avoid contractions in legal writing: "can't," "didn't."

☑ Use pronouns correctly. The pronouns "they" and "their" are plural and therefore cannot refer to singular nouns or indefinite pronouns such as "everyone," or "no one." So, for example, refer to the court as "it" and to "everyone" as "he," "she," or "he or she."

EXHIBIT 10A

Rule Explanation Template

[*The first sentence of your rule explanation is a one- or two-sentence summary of the rule of law from the case, also known as the rule statement.*][1] [*Insert full case citation here (if this is the first time you are citing the case in the memorandum).*][2] In [*insert short case name*],[3] _____ [*describe the legally significant facts from the precedent case*][4]_____

_____.

The _____[5] court held _____

_____[6].

The court reasoned _____

_____[7].

---

[1] The rule statement is the hardest part of drafting the RE because the legal writer needs to pare down the rule (which might include elements, factors, or both) into one or two clear and concise sentences. Experiment—this takes practice.

[2] Legal writers always cite the source of the rule statement. Chapter 11 provides all the information you need to experiment with citing cases in the REs. Attorneys either underline or italicize case names. Whichever style you choose, be consistent within the body of the same memorandum.

[3] You will learn more about short cites in Chapter 11, but for now, insert the name of the first party of the case. (use the last name only if the first party is a person instead of a corporate entity). If, however, the first party's name could confuse the reader if the same party is involved in several precedent cases within the memorandum (i.e., in criminal matters, the State might be the first party in more than one precedent case), use the second party's name instead. *State v. Horowitz*, for example, would be shortened to *Horowitz*.

[4] Your case facts might take up a few sentences.

[5] Insert the shortened name of the case, as in note 3.

[6] This is the holding.

[7] The rationale might take up a few sentences.

EXHIBIT 10B

Sample Annotated Rule Explanation

When evaluating whether an otherwise innocuous item qualifies as a deadly weapon under the felonious assault statute, Ohio courts consider (1) the size and weight of the item, (2) the shape and design of the item, (3) the ability of the item to be grasped in the hands of the user in such a way that it may be used on or directed against the body of another, and (4) the ability of the item to be used in a manner and with sufficient force to kill the other person. *State v. Deboe*, 406 N.E.2d 536 (Ohio Ct. App. 1977). For example, in *Deboe*, a carpet salesman visited a customer's home to estimate the cost of carpet installation. While the salesman took measurements in a front room in the house, a man came out of a room and struck the salesman with a club-like instrument. *Id.* at 537. The club possessed features similar to a softball or baseball bat, and was three or four inches in diameter. The perpetrator held the club like a baseball bat, swung it fast at the victim, and struck him rapidly 15 or 20 times on the head, arms, back, shoulders, and kidneys. *Id.* The perpetrator then stole the victim's money, watch, cigarette lighter, and a roll of carpet. *Id.*

The *Deboe* court held that the club was a deadly weapon. *Id.* The court explained "an instrument, no matter how innocuous when not in use, is a deadly weapon if it is of sufficient size and weight to inflict death upon a person, when the instrument is wielded against the body of the victim or threatened to be so wielded." *Id.* The manner of use of the instrument, its threatened use, and its nature determine its capability to inflict death. Based on these factors, the court emphasized the facts that (1) the club-like instrument was three to four inches in diameter wrapped in spongy material; (2) the perpetrator swung it rapidly at the victim, hitting him 15 or 20 times on the head, arms, back, shoulders, and kidneys; and (3) the blows caused black and blue welts and bruises. *Id.* The court concluded that, based on the size and weight of the item, and the manner in which it was used, the perpetrator wielded a deadly weapon on the body of the victim. *Id.*

Rule
statement

Citation

Facts

Holding

Rational

EXHIBIT 10C

Rule Explanation Annotation Exercise

Assignment: Label the following parts of the two rule explanations below: (1) rule statement, (2) citation, (3) facts, (4) holding, (5) rationale.

Example 1: Courts closely examine the facts known to an airline when examining whether a decision to remove a passenger was arbitrary and capricious. *Schaeffer v. Cavallero*, 54 F. Supp. 2d 350 (S.D.N.Y. 1999). In *Schaeffer*, an attorney bought an airline ticket and boarded his flight. A flight attendant informed the passenger that he was not allowed to bring two pieces of luggage on board. *Id.* at 351. He protested, reluctantly gave up one of his bags, and demanded a receipt. *Id.* The attorney became increasingly cantankerous. After the flight attendant asked him to deplane, the passenger refused. Police arrived and escorted him off the plane. *Id.* He sued the airline.

The *Schaeffer* court held that the airline did not have the right to remove the passenger from his flight as he was not in fact "inimical to safety." *Id.* The court stated that "to say that, any time an impolite or unpleasant passenger debates a non-safety issue with an airline employee in a boisterous or abusive manner, he automatically poses a potential threat to safety" would set no limit to an airline's discretion. *Id.* at 352. The court determined that the pilot's decision to remove the passenger from the flight because he argued with the flight attendant merely about a receipt and luggage was arbitrary and capricious. *Id.*

Example 2: Courts allow a pilot to rely on the facts relayed to him from an airline employee when deciding whether to remove a passenger from a flight, unless no responsible decision maker would credit the information provided. *Christel v. AMR Corp.*, 222 F. Supp. 2d 335 (E.D.N.Y. 2002). In *Christel*, the pilot relied solely on a flight attendant's report that a passenger was being disruptive (without performing his own investigation), and subsequently removed the traveler from the flight. *Id.* at 338. The flight attendant had told the passenger, who was listening to music, to stow his bag under the seat in front of him and turn off all electronic devices. Annoyed by this admonition, the passenger yelled, kicked his bag, and threw it into the aisle. *Id.*

The court held that the pilot's decision to remove the passenger was not arbitrary and capricious based on the flight attendant's representations that the passenger yelled and threw his bag in the aisle. *Id.* at 340. The court stated that even if the "battle of the egos" escalated, and the flight attendant made exaggerated or false representations to the pilot, the latter was not required to leave the cockpit to investigate the truthfulness of her statements. *Id.*

Chapter 11
Basic Legal Citation for Legal Memoranda

What is legal citation? You already know that lawyers conduct substantial legal research to find statutes, regulations, case law, and other sources to determine the legal rules that govern clients' factual scenarios. When lawyers write about these rules and legal authorities, they need a standardized way of conveying to all readers the source of those rules. Legal writers accomplish that task through legal citation.

Black's Law Dictionary defines citation as "[a] reference to a legal precedent or authority, such as a case, statute, or treatise, that either substantiates or contradicts a given position," or "[a] reference to another document in support of an argument." There are very precise rules governing the format of legal citation, which are different from the citation rules you may have used in college or business-style writing. These rules may seem confusing (or even exasperating) at first, but the more you practice them, the more they will become second nature.

Two primary guidebooks summarize legal citation rules: (1) *The Bluebook: A Uniform System of Citation*, currently in its 19th edition, compiled by the editors of the *Columbia Law Review*, the *Harvard Law Review*, the *University of Pennsylvania Law Review*, and the *Yale Law Journal*; and (2) the *ALWD Citation Manual: A Professional System of Citation*, currently in its 5th edition, written and edited by legal writing professors and experts affiliated with the Association of Legal Writing Directors. There also are some very helpful workbooks in the publishing marketplace that provide step-by-step instructions on how to understand and become proficient at these sometimes befuddling rules. This chapter teaches a few introductory steps to citation that you can apply right away as you write your first legal memorandum. This chapter implements the *Bluebook* citation form, rather than *ALWD*.

I. Why Is Citation Important?

Law students sometimes resist learning citation rules. This is normal. The rules and citation formats look strange—like a foreign language. However, embracing the art and science of legal citation is important for four reasons. First, you will use legal citation to educate and inform your readers about the legal sources you diligently found and analyzed, why these sources are pertinent to your legal analysis, and how the reader can find those sources. Just by following structural citation rules, you convey multiple pieces of information to your reader. For example, by using proper citation form in citing a case, you efficiently transmit details about the parties' names, whether they are individuals or companies, who is suing whom, the jurisdiction and court, the decision date, and the volume and page number of the case reporter in which the decision is published. Further, you will use even more precise page citations called pinpoint cites (also called pin or jump cites) to show the reader the exact page within a multipage case where a particular quotation or concept is found.

The second beneficial aspect of citation is that it demonstrates the effort you put into your legal research. Citations communicate to the reader, "Hey! Look how many cases I found!" or "Check out this recent case that is directly on point and shows a result favoring our client!" or "Marvel at how many cases weigh in favor of the result our client seeks!"

Along those same lines, the third benefit to good citation is that it enhances a legal writer's credibility with the reader, not only because it conveys substantive information but, when used properly, shows mastery of a legal skill.

Finally, perfect citation—like proofreading—boosts the professionalism of the overall presentation of a legal document. Conversely, messy or sloppy citation—like typographical errors and grammar problems—chips away at the professionalism of a lawyer's work product.

This chapter explains basic citation rules for the following types of legal references law students often use in a basic office memorandum:

- Statutes
- Cases
- Full cites
- Short cites
- *Id.* cites
- Pinpoint cites
- String cites and explanatory parentheticals

As you read this chapter, have your *Bluebook* handy so you can look up the various citation forms in the table of contents or index. The *Bluebook* is divided into three major sections: (1) Bluepages, (2) Rules, and (3) Tables. It also offers an index in the back of the book. Consider tabbing the relevant pages you use

> **Practical Note**
>
> One lawyer compares legal citation to writing in a foreign language. When she studied French and Italian in high school and college, and had to write term papers entirely in those languages, she would reserve extra time at the end of her editing process to look up each foreign word to see whether it required an accent. She had difficulty remembering whether the accents veered to the left ("è") or the right ("é"). It didn't take too long to look up the words, yet making sure all the accents were correct gave her paper that extra veneer of professionalism. As an attorney, she applied the same techniques to perfecting her citation, reserving at least an hour of editing time solely to check the *Bluebook* for proper citation form. Eventually the citation rules became second nature.

regularly, so you can find them more quickly. The more comfortable you become with the citation guidebooks, the less frustrating this aspect of legal writing will be, and the more fun you will have conquering each citation challenge.

II. Citing Statutes

A. Federal Statutes

Federal statutes are published in the *United States Code*. During your research, you might encounter cites from the "official" code and the "annotated" code. The official code provides the exact text of the statute as written by the legislators. Annotated statutes include an added research bonus: The publisher took the time to gather and publish historical notes, commentaries, and synopses of federal and state cases interpreting and applying the statutory text. This is a wealth of helpful information during a lawyer's legal research process. The distinction between the official code and the annotated code is important for this particular chapter because they each have their own citation form.[1]

Federal Statute Citation Formula

Official code: [Title no.] [Code name] [§] [Section no.] [(Year)].

Annotated code: [Title no.] [Code name] [§] [Section no.] [(Publisher Year)].[2]

---

[1] For how to cite to the U.S.C. (the official code), see *The Bluebook: A Uniform System of Citation* 120 (Columbia Law Review Ass'n et al. eds., 20th ed. 2015). For how to cite to the U.S.C.A. (the annotated code), see *id.* at 123.

[2] The brackets in these examples are simply to show you the various component parts of the citation. You do not put brackets around each component.

Example

18 U.S.C.A. § 2331 (West 2013).

The terms "international terrorism" and "domestic terrorism" are defined in the annotated federal statute with the citation: 18 U.S.C.A. § 2331 (West 2013). The "18" is the title number of the statute (which, in this terrorism statute, refers to the title of "Crimes and Criminal Procedure"). The code name is the *United States Code Annotated*. The squiggly symbol ("§") means "section."[3] The number 2331 is the section containing the text of this statute. "West" is the publisher of the annotated code, and 2013 is the year the code was published.

Want to try?

What is the correct citation for the federal statute relating to using weapons of mass destruction, found in the 2013 version of Section 2332a of Title 18 of the *United States Code Annotated* published by West? _____

B. State Statutes

Each state has its own format for citing its statutes. The *Bluebook*'s tables describe how to cite statutes in every state. For example, the New York statute citation formula is:

New York Statute Citation Formula

N.Y. [Subject] Law § [Section Number] [(McKinney [Year])].[4]

Example

New York's Right to Privacy statute is cited as N.Y. Civ. Rights Law § 50 (McKinney 2011).

Want to try?

(1) What is the proper citation for Section 2 of the 2012 McKinney's New York Volunteer Firefighters' Benefit Law?

_____

(2) What *Bluebook* table shows how to cite statutes in your home state? On what page of the Bluebook can you find your home state's citation rules?

_____

---

[3] This is an important word processing symbol for you to familiarize yourself with—immediately. Find "symbols" in your computer's word processing program and locate the section symbol.
[4] *Bluebook, supra* note 1, at 280 tbl. T1; *id.* at B12.1.

III. Citing Cases

A. Federal Cases

1. Federal Trial and Appellate Courts

Every federal case citation for trial and appellate court decisions has the following component parts.

Federal Case Citation Formula

[Name of the case (underlined or *italicized*)], [Volume no.] [Reporter name] [First page no. of case] [(Court and Year)].[5]

Remember from Chapter 4 that trial courts in the federal judicial system are called U.S. District Courts, and appellate courts are known as U.S. Courts of Appeals for the various numbered circuits. Knowing where the court deciding a cited case fits in the judicial hierarchy is important when assessing how much, if at all, the case may affect your client's situation (recall the difference between mandatory and persuasive authority discussed in Chapter 4). Fortunately for legal researchers, federal case citations automatically reveal the particular court in two places: (1) in the parentheses, just before the year; and (2) through the name of the reporter.

The first location is self-evident. Simply look within the parentheses for the abbreviated court name, such as "D.N.J"—for District of New Jersey—or "E.D. Va."—for Eastern District of Virginia.[6] Or at the appellate level, you might see the abbreviation "9th Cir."—for the U.S. Court of Appeals for the Ninth Circuit—or "1st Cir."—for the U.S. Court of Appeals for the First Circuit. The second location for ascertaining the applicable court in a federal citation (i.e., the case reporter) requires a little extra knowledge. Each category of federal reporter specializes in publishing cases from only certain levels of courts. Since 1932, for example, the *Federal Reporter* has published U.S. Court of Appeals and Court of Federal Claims decisions. A cite, then, that contains one of the *Federal Reporter*'s three abbreviations—"F.," "F.2d," or "F.3d"—is either a U.S. Court of Appeals or (less commonly) a Court of Federal Claims decision. In contrast, the *Federal Supplement* ("F. Supp.," "F. Supp. 2d," or "F. Supp. 3d") only publishes cases decided by the U.S. District Courts. So, just as you would not look for a word definition in a thesaurus or a chili recipe in a phonebook, you would not look for a U.S. Court of Appeals case in the *Federal Supplement*.

---

[5] Again, do not include brackets around the component parts in the actual citation. The brackets here are simply to show you the components of a full statute cite.

[6] 28 U.S.C.A. §§ 81-131 (West 2014) list the various districts (and divisions thereof) within each state jurisdiction. Consider looking up the statute that lists the federal district courts in your home state. The *Bluebook* explains how to abbreviate each district court for purposes of citation.

Tips for Citing Cases

(1) Omit the first names of people in case names; only use last names of people.
(2) Cite only one party from either side of the case.
(3) In "non-people" (corporate or governmental) party names, find *Bluebook* abbreviations for common words like "Incorporated" or "Corporation" (see *Bluebook* tbl. T6).
(4) Use proper *Bluebook* abbreviations for case reporters (*Bluebook* tbl. T1) and the courts (tbls. T7, BT2).
(5) Follow the *Bluebook* rules for spacing after periods (*Bluebook* R6).
(6) Use a lowercase "v." (not "vs." or "V.") between adversarial parties' names.

Example

Burck v. Mars, Inc., 571 F. Supp. 2d 446 (S.D.N.Y. 2008).[7]

Consider the aforementioned case involving a street entertainer named Robert Burck—better known on the streets of New York City as The Naked Cowboy—who performs in Times Square. He sued the candy company, Mars, Incorporated, and its advertising agency, Chute Gerdeman, Incorporated. The case was decided in the U.S. District Court for the Southern District of New York in 2008. The case was published in Volume 571 of the second series of the *Federal Supplement* reporter. The case started on page 446.

Want to try?

Write accurate case names for the following:

- Chris Robinson, Jr. against American Marketing Company and the Tuono Media Company:

  _____

- High Maintenance Productions Limited versus Kimberly Randall South:

  _____

- Bridgton University and Victor Ramirez versus All-Pro Marketing Group:

  _____

---

[7] For examples of how to cite federal reporters, see *Bluebook, supra* note 1, at 235 tbl. T1. For a list of federal court abbreviations, see *id.* at 498 tbl. T7.

2. U.S. Supreme Court Cases

The *Bluebook* rule for citing U.S. Supreme Court cases is slightly different from other federal cases decided in the lower federal courts.[8] Supreme Court decisions are published in three different printed collections, but the official cite is to the *United States Reports*, abbreviated as "U.S." The other two (unofficial) reporters are called *Supreme Court Reporter* ("S. Ct.") and *Supreme Court Reports, Lawyers' Edition* ("L. Ed."). In the citation formula for Supreme Court cases, because it is obvious from the name of the reporter (U.S.) that the case was decided by the Supreme Court, lawyers do not need to put the court name inside the parentheses. Remember: This is different from how lawyers cite other cases—where the legal writer typically includes the jurisdiction in the parentheses.

Supreme Court Case Citation Formula

[Name of the case (*underlined or italicized*)], [Volume] [Reporter] [First Page of Case] [(Year)].

Example

Tinker v. Des Moines Indep. Cmty. Sch. Dist., 393 U.S. 503 (1969).

Want to try?

Convert the following two U.S. Supreme Court cases to proper *Bluebook* form:

● Walter Chaplinsky versus State of New Hampshire. Volume 315 of the United States Reporter. Page 568. Date: 1942.

_____

_____

● Millard Gooding, Appellant versus Johnny C. Wilson. Volume 405 of the United States Reporter. Page 518. Date: 1972.

_____

_____

3. *Federal Appendix* Cases

Some federal appellate court decisions not selected for official publication are still reported in a hard-copy reporter called the *Federal Appendix*.

Federal Appendix Citation Formula

[Name of case (<u>underlined</u> or *italicized*)], [Volume no.] F. App'x [Page no.] ([Court and Year]).

---

[8] The rule is found at *Bluebook, supra* note 1, at 233 tbl T1.1.

Example

U.S. v. Payan-Paz, 31 F. App'x 836 (5th Cir. 2002).

Want to try?

Use proper *Bluebook* form to cite the following case using its *Federal Appendix* cite: United States Court of Appeals, Ninth Circuit. Elina Shaffy, Plaintiff-Appellant, v. United Airlines, Inc., Defendant-Appellee. December 10, 2009. Volume 360 of the *Federal Appendix*, starting on page 729.

_____

_____

_____

B. State Cases

The *Bluebook* also contains tables that list the names of the state courts in every jurisdiction. Typically, state case citations follow the same general format as federal cases:

Sample State Case Citation Formula

[Name of the case (underlined or *italicized*)], [Volume no.] [Reporter name] [First page of case] [(Court and Year)].

However, some states use variations of that formula, so you'll need to check the Bluebook tables for your state's rules.

Want to try?

Find the table in the *Bluebook* that shows how to cite cases in your home state: _____

C. Unpublished Cases

Not every state and federal case is published in the case reporters. However, lawyers can find unpublished cases through Lexis, Westlaw, and Bloomberg Law. Various courts have rules regarding whether lawyers are permitted to cite to, or rely on, unpublished cases in briefs submitted to the court. Thus, when you learn how to write persuasive briefs (in the second half of this book and often in the second semester of law school), it will be important to research the local court rules of the governing jurisdiction in your client's matter and ascertain whether such court permits citation of unpublished cases. Of course, there are *Bluebook* rules for citing unpublished cases as well.

Unpublished Case Citation Formula

[Case name (underlined or *italicized*)], [Docket no.], [Database ID and document no.], at * [Pinpoint page no.] ([Court and Full date]).

Example

State v. Connely, No. 1CA–CR10–0786, 2012 WL 988586, at *3 (Ariz. Ct. App. Mar. 22, 2012).

Note the differences between the citation form of an unpublished case and a published case: The unpublished case includes the court docket number, an asterisk before the page number (because the number refers to an electronic page rather than an actual printed page), and the full date instead of just the year.

Want to try?

Use proper *Bluebook* format to cite to page 4 of the following unpublished case: United States Court of Appeals, Ninth Circuit. Elina Shaffy, Plaintiff-Appellant, v. United Airlines, Inc., Defendant-Appellee. Docket No. 08-56307. 2009 WL 4882662. December 10, 2009.

_____

_____

_____

D. Short Cites

Once you have cited a case "in full" in a legal memorandum, thereafter you use "short cites," with "pinpoint" (or "pin" or "jump") cites to the exact pages from which you are quoting or paraphrasing. Let's say, for example, you have just full-cited case A. The way you cite case A the next time it is mentioned in the memorandum will depend on whether (1) you are continuing to discuss case A without interruption by mention of case B (or perhaps a statute), or (2) you already switched to discussion of case B (or a statute) and are now returning to case A.

1. Citing the Same Case Without an Intervening Cite

If you are citing case A again in the same or subsequent paragraph (without any other intervening cite—i.e., case B or a statute—between your two case A cites), you will use an "*Id.*" cite. (Recall from Chapter 10 that "*Id.*" is Latin for "the same.") If the particular page you are citing differs from the previous page reference, however, you must use a pinpoint cite to refer to the new page reference: "*Id.* at 245." If the page reference remains the same as the prior case A cite, you simply use "*Id.*" with no additional page number. "*Id.*" is italicized or underlined, just like the original case name. Do not switch back and forth between italics and underlining of case names and "Id." Choose one style for your entire memorandum.

2. Citing a Case After an Intervening Citation

If you cite case A in full, and then move on to mention or discuss case B (or a statute), and subsequently return to case A, you would use a "short cite" with the following format:

> [First party name (underlined or *italicized*)], [Volume no.] [Reporter name] at [Pinpoint page cite].

Example:

Burck, 571 F. Supp. 2d at 449.

Then, if you continue along in the same paragraph citing only to that case, you may use *"Id."* until you switch again to a new case or other source of law.

Want to try?

(1) Rewrite the following case in proper *Bluebook* form: Muhammad Ali, Plaintiff versus Playgirl, Incorporated, Tony Yamada and Independent News Company, Defendants. United States District Court for the Southern District of New York. Volume 447. Federal Supplement. Page 723. Date: 1978.

_____

_____

(2) What would the short cite of the Mohammed Ali case be if you switched to discussing another case and now are returning to the Ali case later in the memorandum and citing to page 725?

_____

(3) What would the short cite be if you cite to page 728 in the next sentence? _____

IV. Using Signal Citations

So far in your legal writing class, you may have started to experiment with writing your first Rule Explanation about a single case. Perhaps you have read three or four other cases analyzing the legal issue affecting your client, and you are thinking about which judicial opinions you want to write about, or should write about, in your legal memorandum. Meanwhile, your professor—like most courts—probably has established either a word-count limit or a page limit for the assignment. Remember from Chapter 2, this limit is not designed to be unfair or onerous; it simply is a good early lesson to learn about following rules, but also about writing as concisely as possible. While supervising attorneys may not impose a strict page limit on the memoranda you submit internally within the law office, they will want you to be succinct; indeed, most courts impose fixed limits on the length of attorney submissions, to (1) encourage lawyers to be crisp in their analyses and arguments, and (2) ensure an even playing field among all litigants in the same case (allowing both sides the same volume of text to convey their arguments—no more and no less).

You may have already started thinking about which cases might be most useful or interesting to include as full Rule Explanations in your memo. However, in the event you do not have room for all the cases you have spent time reviewing and analyzing, the *Bluebook* offers a fabulous citation trick that enables lawyers to concisely weave extra cases into an analytical document: the "signal cite + explanatory parenthetical." Lawyers use this citation technique to include cases in a document without writing a full Rule Explanation. The technique has three component parts: (1) the proper "signal" to introduce the cite, (2) the cite itself, and (3) a helpful "explanatory parenthetical" that pithily captures the facts, holding, and rationale of the cited case in three to four lines of text or less.

A. Introductory Signals

Signals allow lawyers to introduce an extra case (or cases) into a written discussion, "signaling" the reader to consider the case as additional support or comparison for the analysis. Take a look at the different types of signals summarized in the *Bluebook* at B1.2 and R1.2.

Signals Indicating Support	Signals Indicating Comparison	Signals Indicating Contradiction	Signals Indicating Background
[No signal] *See* *See also* *See, e.g.,* *Accord*	*Compare . . . with . . .*	*But see*	*See generally*

It is important to choose the correct signal so the reader does not get confused about whether the case supports or contradicts a statement in the discussion.

Type of Signal	When the Signal Is Used
No signal	The cite following the signal stands exactly for the proposition you just stated, perhaps even in a direct quote.
See	The cite following the signal stands exactly for the proposition you just stated.
See also	The cite following the signal provides additional support for the proposition you just described in another case.
See, e.g.,	The cite following the signal provides an illustrative example of the proposition you just stated.
But see	The cite following the signal contrasts with the statement or the cases you just explained.

Signal Citation Formula

[Proper signal] [case citation] [helpful explanatory parenthetical].

B. Explanatory Parentheticals

The use of signals to introduce a citation, accompanied by an explanatory parenthetical, is a great way to include a relevant court decision in a memo if there is not enough room to write an entire Rule Explanation on the case. However, you need to take some time in crafting the explanatory parenthetical so it is as helpful to the reader as a full Rule Explanation, but much more abridged. Typically, parentheticals should be no more than three to four lines of text; otherwise, you might as well write an entire Rule Explanation.

Signal Cite + Explanatory Parenthetical Formula

[Proper signal] [case citation] [explanatory parenthetical].

Example

See, e.g., Citizen Publ'g Co. v. Miller, 115 P.3d 107 (Ariz. 2005) (holding that a rude and arguably racist letter-to-the-editor of a newspaper did not constitute "fighting words" because it was not made in a face-to-face confrontation with the target of the remarks and contained no personally abusive words or epithets).

Formula of a Good Explanatory Parenthetical

(holding that [*concisely state holding on the key legal issue*] when [*concisely state facts in ten words or less*] because [*concisely state court's reasoning in a way that emphasizes the key elements/factors/facts on which the court relied in making its decision*])

Hints for Drafting a Useful Explanatory Parenthetical

(1) Typically, start with an *-ing* word, like "holding that . . . ," "emphasizing that . . . ," "demonstrating that . . . ."
(2) Do not exceed three to four lines of text.
(3) Provide enough information about the case to make it useful (capturing the facts, holding, and rationale of the case in an abridged but informative manner).
(4) Punctuate using only commas and semicolons—no periods or full sentences.

Example

State v. Deboe, 406 N.E.2d 536 (Ohio Ct. App. 1977) (holding that a club-like instrument three inches in diameter wrapped in spongy material, which a perpetrator swung rapidly at his victim, hitting him 15 or 20 times on the head, arms, back, shoulders, and kidneys, causing black and blue welts and bruises, constituted a deadly weapon).

C. String Cites Plus Explanatory Parentheticals

Another citation technique takes signal cites to the next (even more sophisticated) level. Imagine you have a series of cases that stand for the same proposition or support the same legal concept. You do not want to waste space in the memo writing a series of lengthy Rule Explanations about a single idea, but you might want to inform the reader that this string or line of cases exists. The *Bluebook* furnishes lawyers with another trick for incorporating a series of cases into a memorandum: the "string cite." String cites-plus-explanatory parentheticals are useful to link a series of cases supporting the same concept. Legal writers use these sparingly (they can be tedious for a reader if inserted too often), but the occasional string cite can be a powerful yet concise way to demonstrate considerable support for a statement made in a memorandum.

Example

Other jurisdictions follow the same doctrine. *See, e.g., New Port Richey Med. Investors, LLC v. Stern*, 14 So. 3d 1084 (Fla. Dist. Ct. App. 2009) (applying a Florida statute, and finding that a nursing home resident agreement requiring American Arbitration Association (AAA) arbitration was still enforceable even after the AAA no longer accepted such cases because there was no evidence the chosen forum was integral to the agreement to

Hints for String Cites + Explanatory Parentheticals

(1) Use the proper signal to introduce the string cite.
(2) Separate cases with semicolons.
(3) Place cases in the following order:
  • Federal cases go before state cases.
  • Federal cases go in order of highest court to lowest.
  • State cases go in alphabetical order (and in reverse chronological order within each state).

**A signal or string cite goes at the very end of an RE of another case, never in the middle. You will confuse the reader if you toss a signal or string cite in the middle of an RE (stopping the flow of the RE) and then switch back to the RE case. Always place the signal or string cite after the last period at the end of the RE of the other case.

arbitrate); *Royce Homes, L.P. v. Bates*, 315 S.W.3d 77, 89 (Tex. App.–Hous. 2010) (finding that, when homeowners argued against the enforcement of an arbitration provision in a development contract based on a "mechanical breakdown in the process of appointing an arbitrator," the appointment of a substitute arbitrator was proper under Section 5 of the Federal Arbitration Act); *In re Brock Specialty Servs. Ltd.*, 286 S.W.3d 649 (Tex. App.–Corpus Christi 2009) (holding the nonexistence or unavailability of the arbitrator chosen in an arbitration clause does not render the clause unenforceable; the choice of forum was not integral to the agreement, and thus, the court can appoint a different arbitrator).

EXERCISE   As you start to think about how you plan to outline and draft your first legal memorandum, consider which cases you have read that might be most appropriate for a full Rule Explanation. Practice writing out the full citation, short citation, and *Id.* citation for each. With any remaining cases, evaluate whether they are similar to, or contrast with, the cases in your Rule Explanations. If a case is similar to a case you want to use in a Rule Explanation (or relates to the same rule element or factor), think about crafting a *"See also"* signal-cite-plus-explanatory-parenthetical for that additional case. Or, if an extra case provides a holding that contrasts with the Rule Explanation case, consider constructing a *"But see"* signal-cite-plus-explanatory-parenthetical for that additional case.

Chapter 12

Rule Application: Applying the Rule to the Client's Facts

In a legal memorandum, after explaining the rule clearly (the R in IREAC or CREAC) and illustrating it via Rule Explanations (the E or RE), next the legal writer transitions to the Rule Application section (the A or RA). This is the analytical component of the legal memorandum that provides the most insight to the reader (the supervising attorney). This section applies the narrowly focused legal rule to the client's scenario, analyzes the client facts in the framework of such rule, and predicts as best as possible how a court likely would decide the legal question if presented with the client's particular circumstances.

I. Crafting an Effective Rule Application

The most important qualities of the RA component of a legal memorandum are (1) logic, (2) clarity, and (3) completeness. A good RA contains the following:

- A smooth transition from the RE so the reader knows the writer is shifting from illustrations of the rule through *other* cases (REs) to the actual facts of *the client's* case (RA)
- A strong organizational structure built around the elements or factors of the rule, perhaps allocating one paragraph per rule element or factor

- Clear topic/thesis sentences introducing each paragraph
- Transitions between paragraphs (through mini-conclusions and new topic/thesis sentences)
- Within each paragraph, comparisons and contrasts between the illustrated RE cases and the client facts
- Momentum leading the reader along a path toward the most logical conclusion
- Ultimately, a clear prediction/conclusion (the C in IREAC/CREAC)

If, as a new legal writer, you struggle with creating a logical legal analysis, break the RA-drafting process down into two steps. First, spend some time thinking about the rule itself and consider whether its component parts (elements or factors) can provide a "logic framework" for the RA. This is called rule-based reasoning—a straightforward way to approach a legal analysis. By now, you already recognize that legal rules can be pretty complicated, but legal writers make them less convoluted by identifying elements or factors to create a structural scaffold or checklist. (Chapter 5 explains the difference between elements and factors.)

For example, if your rule has three required elements that must be satisfied, you know you need to apply each individual element to the facts of your client's case to determine the likely outcome. Regard the rule elements as a mental checklist, and construct your RA in an organized, logical fashion so you are tackling one element at a time.

Alternatively, your rule might involve a set of factors extracted from a statute or synthesized from a collection of cases. If your legal rule is based on factors, you might consider organizing your RA by factor, analyzing one at a time. Allow yourself some space to "work the rule."

Second, take a step back from the morass of law and ask yourself, "Does my reasoning make sense? Do my analysis and ultimate predicted result reflect good common sense? Does the projected outcome seem fair or practical?" In this process, think about your client as a human being or a real company, even if you are dealing with a law school hypothetical. If this were a real-world scenario, would your analysis seem rational?

II. Remembering the Purpose of the Legal Memorandum

As you write the RA section, remember the underlying purpose of the legal memorandum and your role in its creation. A supervising attorney has asked you to research a client's legal issue, locate and analyze the governing rule, break it down into workable parts, explain the rule in a clear and understandable fashion, apply the rule to the client's facts, and predict an outcome. The supervising attorney assigned you this legal issue because she does not know the answer. This is not a test to see whether you know what she knows. Instead, there is an information gap, and you are the one filling it. The supervising attorney is relying on you to do the best job you can in analyzing the law and facts and forecasting an outcome, so the attorney can advise the client on the most appropriate course of action.

Remember also that this is an internal attorney-client privileged document, so it is appropriate, and encouraged, for you to explore the strengths and weaknesses of your client's case. The opposing party will never see this memorandum. By ruminating over and describing the advantages and disadvantages of your client's position, you are helping the supervising attorney and the client make the best strategic decision possible in circumstances that may involve money, property, freedom, relationships, or other important concerns.

Understandably, you may be a bit nervous in making your first definitive and concrete prediction of a legal outcome. That is why logic is such an important "ally." If you let the rule of law be your guide and use the RA section of the memorandum to "work the rule," the organizational structure will steer you to the most logical conclusion. As long as you process the information in a methodical, systematic way and give the supervising attorney your most well-reasoned prediction, you will have done your job. The answer might not always be the one the supervising attorney or the client wants to hear, and that is okay as long as you have diligently processed the rule.

Be prepared for the possibility that there may be more than one outcome or prediction. Your conclusion might be a close call. You might even have creative ideas for alternate arguments that would change the end result: a way to demonstrate professional creativity. Supervising attorneys will appreciate a junior attorney who conscientiously applies the rule, spends time mindfully thinking about the analysis (lingering in the intellectual moment instead of rushing through the analytical exercise and jumping to the easiest, most obvious resolution), and then predicts a logical outcome. They will also value a junior attorney who takes the analysis a step further and brainstorms other options the client can pursue if the first prediction is unfavorable.

Practical Uses of a Legal Memorandum

- Supervising attorney reads the memo and jumps on a conference call with the client to discuss the case.
- Supervising attorney uses your memo to craft an opinion letter to the client.
- Supervising attorney uses your memo to draft a pleading or a motion in a litigation.
- Your memo is retained in the file in the event someone later files a lawsuit against the client.

III. Using Element or Factor Charts to Organize the Rule Application

Writing an RA is not as simple as sitting down at the laptop and picking up from where you left off with your last RE. You first need to organize your thoughts. Some lawyers use charts to integrate three essential sources of information: (1) the parts of the rule, (2) the cases that best illustrate those rule components, and (3) the client facts tied to each part of the rule.

Apply Each Element or Factor of the Rule to the Client's Facts

Element/Factor	Precedent Case that Best Illustrates the Particular Rule Element/Factor	Client Facts

To draw comparisons or contrasts between your client's case and the precedent cases, ask yourself:

Are the facts of my client's case similar or comparable to the facts of a particular precedent case (or cases)? Which one(s)? _____ Why? _____

Are the facts of my client's case distinguishable or different from the facts of a particular precedent case (or cases)? Which one(s)?_____ Why? _____

IV. Transitioning from the Rule Explanation to the Rule Application

One vastly underestimated technique for converting a decent legal memorandum into a great one is the use of smooth transitions between the various memorandum components, gently nudging the reader onward while softening abrupt intellectual lurches. Have you ever ridden in a train, bus, or taxicab in which the conductor or driver clumsily applies pressure to the accelerator and the brakes, causing the vehicle to pitch forward with every jerky stop and start? Reading a legal memorandum without gentle transitions gives the reader the same headache-inducing experience.

Therefore, as you segue from the RE section to the RA segment, start with a transition sentence that summarizes the overall conclusion or prediction.

Example 1: Applying the foregoing elements of California's Vehicle Code Section 10851 to the client's circumstances, a court likely will find that the valet driver did not commit vehicle theft.

Example 2: Applying the foregoing factors to the merchandise our client sold at the street festival without a vendor's license, a court likely will find that the products did not qualify as "art," but rather constituted commercial items requiring a sales license.

V. Applying the Rule to the Client's Circumstances

If you are experiencing difficulty knowing where to begin constructing the RA, start with the ingredients of the rule. Think about all the different components of the rule you need to evaluate and consider dedicating an RA paragraph to each part. You can always edit later and combine short paragraphs if necessary, but for now, tackle each part of the rule one at a time.

Start each paragraph with a clear topic and/or thesis sentence[1]. A topic sentence announces to the reader what concept or idea the paragraph discusses, either through key words or phrases. A thesis sentence goes a step further and takes a *position* or declares *a conclusion* on the topic about to be discussed. In legal writing, a topic sentence in an RA paragraph triggers in the reader's mind which part of the rule the writer is poised to apply next. A thesis sentence goes ahead and summarizes the legal writer's conclusion on the particular portion of the rule. Different legal writing professors might have different preferences on whether you use topic sentences or thesis sentences; the important point is that each paragraph needs a "billboard" or a "'headline."

Example of a Topic Sentence

The first way a defendant may commit the crime of impersonating a law enforcement officer is by verbally informing another person that he is a duly authorized peace officer.

Example of a Thesis Sentence

Analyzing the first method in which a defendant may commit the crime of impersonating a law enforcement officer, which requires the defendant to verbally inform another person that he is a duly authorized peace officer, our client clearly informed the bartender that he is a member of the NYPD.

In legal writing, thesis sentences can be more helpful to the reader than topic sentences because they state a concrete position. As you begin writing RA paragraphs, however, you may not know yet what your position is on each part of the rule. That is okay. Your thoughtful analysis within each paragraph will help you discover your thesis. For each part of the rule, ponder how the client's facts satisfy, or do not satisfy, that element or factor. Consider all of the client's legally significant facts; do not omit substantive details simply because they are unfavorable. Again, this process is called rule-based reasoning. Then, you can always go back and convert topic sentences to thesis sentences once your position on each rule component is more firm.

---

[1] In legal writing, a thesis sentence is a "persuasive topic sentence." Kirsten K. Davis, *Persuasion Through Organization*, 42-SEP Ariz. Att'y 50 (2005) ("A thesis sentence not only gives the topic of the paragraph it introduces, it also furthers the writer's argument on a particular point.").

VI. Comparing and Contrasting Case Law to the Client's Facts

Another type of legal analysis is "analogical reasoning." The word "analogy" comes from the Greek word "analogia," and is a form of reasoning in which speakers or writers educate an audience by comparing or linking less familiar items or ideas to well-known objects or concepts. You already use analogies in everyday conversation all the time, comparing and contrasting things or experiences to illustrate a point.

Examples of Nonlegal Analogies

- "This political race is like the story of David and Goliath."
- "Getting my legal memorandum submitted on time feels like an uphill battle."
- "The study of law sometimes feels like learning a foreign language."
- "My teacher's comments on my paper resemble a Jackson Pollock painting."

In analogies, authors or orators use descriptions of events, things, or experiences that already resonate with the audience to help better explain and give context to unexplored concepts or ideas. In legal writing, you can accomplish the same goal by analogizing a precedent case (a past event/experience with a concrete result) to the client's facts (a new uncharted event/experience with, as yet, an uncertain outcome). In the RA, legal writers often compare and contrast the cases presented in REs to the client's facts.

Example 1: Like the street artists in *Mastrovincenzo*, who sold clothing they had hand-painted with hip-hop-style "expressive" graffiti, which was priced according to each piece's design complexity, our client hand-painted roller-derby skates to communicate artistic ideas about female athleticism and priced each pair according to color pattern.

Example 2: Unlike the assailants in *Redmon*, *Ware*, and *Deboe*, who swung their respective weapons—a rocking chair, an iron, and a sponge-covered bat—numerous times against the bodies of their victims, Fontaine heaved her Jimmy Choo stiletto shoe only one time at Dunham.

When comparing and contrasting precedent cases with the client's case, you can use terms such as

"similar to . . ." or "similarly, in_____"
"as . . ." or "like . . ."
"exactly like . . ."
"identical to . . ."

"comparable to . . ."

"just as in ____, . . ."

"in contrast to the ____ in ____, . . ."

"unlike . . ."

"distinguishable from . . ."

"far from . . ."

"distinct from . . ."

Avoid simply "ping-ponging" back and forth between precedent cases and your client's case; instead, make these factual links, comparisons, and contrasts, but take your writing a step further. Explain the consequence of each nexus or divergence: i.e., because the court ruled a certain way in the precedent case, which reflected similar facts, the court likely will rule the same way in the client's case. Or, in contrast, because the court ruled a certain way in the precedent case, which reflected facts *different* from the client's case, the court likely will rule an alternate way in the client's case because the factual distinctions are legally significant.

VII. Adding Mini-Conclusions to Each Section of the Rule Application

Just as topic/thesis sentences are important to give the reader signposts or headlines for what topics will be discussed in each paragraph of an RA, a good RA paragraph gives the reader closure at the end of each rule component. Consider ending each part of the RA analysis with a mini-conclusion on that particular part of the rule. If you are addressing an element, you can state whether that element likely is satisfied. If you are addressing a factor, you can assess whether that factor weighs in favor of or against a particular result.

When you are ready to move on to the next part of the rule, simply insert a paragraph break and craft your next topic/thesis sentence. By the end of the RA, you can consider whether all the elements of the rule are satisfied (or whether a majority of the factors of the rule are present), and then predict how a court likely would decide the legal issue affecting the client. This prediction will become your overall conclusion—the C in your IREAC or CREAC analysis.

VIII. Stepping Back and Reviewing the Rule Application for Logic

The first draft of an RA is complete when you have exhausted all the pertinent parts of the rule and have led the reader along a path toward a logical conclusion. Once you have a first draft finished, take a break from the analysis and return to it later with fresh eyes. At your next review, step back and read the RA to make sure it makes logical sense. Ask yourself: Have I applied all the legally significant facts of my client's case? Does the result seem fair under the circumstances? Have I skipped any critical steps? Can an unfamiliar reader understand how I arrived at the ultimate prediction?

IX. Adding Policy-Based Reasoning to a Rule Application

Throughout law school, you will hear professors and students using the term "public policy," but unless you have studied political science or a similar field in college, you may not be 100 percent familiar with that phrase. Public policy refers to "principles and standards regarded by the legislature or by the courts as being of fundamental concern to the state and the whole of society."[2] In other words, in law, courts and lawmakers often make decisions based on the "good of society," considering such issues as equality, economy, freedom, safety, health, and order.

In the RA, after you have performed rule-based reasoning, and perhaps some analogical reasoning drawing similarities or distinctions between the precedent cases and the client facts, you also might consider whether there are any public policy reasons supporting your predicted outcome. Does the forecasted result foster equality among citizens? Is it the best economical consequence? Will it preserve the health and safety of citizens? Will it promote order in society? Sometimes public policy reasoning can be communicated concisely in two or three sentences and yet really add a deeper dimension to a legal analysis.

 RULE APPLICATION CHECKLIST

☑ Craft a transition sentence between the RE and RA sections of the memorandum, foreshadowing the overall prediction of the client's legal outcome.

☑ Organize the RA around the components of the rule. (Elements? Factors? One element or factor per paragraph?) This is rule-based reasoning.

☑ Start each paragraph with a topic/thesis sentence.

☑ Apply one part of the rule at a time to the client's facts.

---

[2] *Black's Law Dictionary* (9th ed. 2009).

☑ Consider all the client's legally significant facts—do not omit unfavorable facts.

☑ Within a paragraph applying a particular part of the rule, consider comparing the client's facts to a precedent case or contrasting the client's facts with a precedent case (analogical reasoning).

☑ At the end of the analysis of each part of the rule, give the reader closure with a mini-conclusion solely on that aspect of the rule.

☑ Once you have applied each component of the rule, check to see whether the analysis of each component leads to a clear probable outcome. This will become the conclusion (final C of the IREAC/CREAC).

☑ Once you have completed a first draft of the RA, review it for logic. Does it make logical sense? Does the result seem fair? Will it make sense to an unfamiliar reader?

☑ Are there any public policy reasons that support the predicted outcome?

Also Remember

☑ Avoid using "I/my/we/our/us" or "you." Instead, state "the client."

☑ Avoid contractions ("can't," "didn't") in legal writing.

☑ Use active voice instead of passive voice whenever you can.

☑ Avoid the temptation to speak in "legalese." Your normal "voice" is better, though your writing should sound a bit more formal than regular conversation.

☑ Use pronouns correctly. The pronouns "they" and "their" are plural and therefore cannot refer to singular nouns or indefinite pronouns such as "everyone," or "no one." So, for example, refer to the court as "it" and to "everyone" as "he," "she," or "he or she."

☑ Use concrete, affirmative language whenever you can. Avoid the temptation to soften your analysis through statements like "it seems that," or "it might be the case that." It's okay to practice taking a stand or a position.

SAMPLE RULE APPLICATION

In evaluating whether Fontaine's Jimmy Choo stiletto qualifies as a deadly weapon, a court will consider (1) the size and weight of the shoe, (2) the shape and design of the shoe, (3) the ability of the shoe to be grasped in the hands of the user in such a way that it may be used on or directed against the body of another, and (4) the ability of the shoe to be used in a manner and with sufficient force to kill the other person.[3] Applying the foregoing factors, the court likely will find the stiletto constitutes a deadly weapon. Regarding the size and weight of the shoe, the facts indicate that Fontaine's "instrument" was a size 7 champagne-colored Jimmy Choo high-heel stiletto shoe. The shoe was constructed of suede and leather, and was a platform peep-toe stiletto. The heel height measured 3.9 inches and was constructed of steel with a gold-colored point attached to a small rubber sole. The platform part of the shoe was less than half an inch. The shoe was neither lightweight nor small. Further, the pointy shape of the nearly four-inch metal heel, and the weight of the platform peep toe structure, rendered the shoe capable of causing harm when thrown with force. Fontaine was able to grasp the heavy unwieldy shoe in her hand and hurl it toward the body of Dunham, specifically his head. The weight and shape of the shoe, when thrown in the manner Fontaine propelled it, likely had sufficient force to kill another person.

Unlike the perpetrator in *Maydillard*, who modified an everyday razor by removing plastic safety guards, Fontaine did not modify or adapt the shoe from its original purpose. Further, unlike the assailants in *Redmon*, *Ware*, and *Deboe*, who swung their respective weapons—a rocking chair, an iron, and a sponge-covered bat—numerous times against the bodies of their victims, Fontaine heaved the shoe only one time at Dunham.

Nonetheless, given the shoe's size, weight, shape, design, and ability to be grasped by Fontaine in such a way to be hurled at Dunham with sufficient force to gravely injure him and possibly kill him, a court likely will find that the shoe meets the definition of a "deadly weapon."

---

[3] This is an example of a short RA, so the factors are not broken down and analyzed in separate paragraphs. But notice how the legal writer performs rule-based reasoning in the first paragraph (applying each of the four factors from the rule) and then analogical reasoning in the second paragraph (comparing and contrasting the precedent cases and the client facts), before reiterating the ultimate conclusion.

Chapter 13

Putting the Memorandum Together: Introductions, Transitions, Headings, and Conclusions

IREAC Map

Issue
Rule
(Rule) Explanation
(Rule) Application
Conclusion

So far, if you have been following the memorandum drafting progression of the chapters of this book, you have constructed the discussion section from the inside out, starting with extracting the rule, perhaps synthesizing a more descriptive version of the rule through elements or factors, illustrating the rule through one or more Rule Explanations (REs), and, finally, "working the rule" by applying its components to the client's facts in a Rule Application (RA). As you continue to work on your memorandum draft, now it is time to flesh out the legal analysis into a full IREAC or CREAC.

Some law professors introduce new legal writers to legal analysis through the IREAC formula: starting with identifying the legal issue affecting the client (I); then leading the reader down the path of rule (R), explanation (E), application/ analysis (A); toward the likely outcome or conclusion (C). Other law professors prefer CREAC: starting with a conclusory statement about the predicted outcome (C), followed by the same progression: rule (R), explanation (E), application/analysis (A), conclusion (C). Either formula works; follow the preferences of your reader—your professor. In law practice, you may need to adjust the formula further to satisfy the preferences of your new reader—the supervising attorney.

I. Finishing the Discussion Section Draft: A Worksheet for Putting the Pieces Together

The completed discussion section of your legal memorandum will have the following parts:

- Heading (simply "Discussion" or perhaps a more informative or descriptive heading suggesting the ultimate conclusion)
- An umbrella[1] paragraph, introducing the discussion section, identifying the issue (I) and the rule (R) in IREAC (or the first C and R in CREAC)
- The REs, including a careful selection of the best cases to illustrate the rule, plus a smooth transition from the umbrella to the first RE, and transitions between each RE
- The RA, including a graceful transition from RE to RA, paragraphs organized around the rule, strong topic/thesis sentences, carefully selected and interwoven case analogies, mini-conclusions to each paragraph, and a clear logic flow toward the conclusion
- A well-reasoned conclusion, stating the predicted outcome of the client's legal question

The following worksheet will help you finalize the discussion section by putting the pieces together.

---

1. The general legal *question* the client has posed is _____

_____

[*This is the question the* client *asked, which may not be the precise legal* **issue** your memorandum analyzes in detail.]

2. The precise legal *issue* (the I) this memo will analyze is _____

---

[1] Professors use varying terminology for this paragraph: umbrella, overview, roadmap. This book uses the term umbrella. Regardless of the terminology, this is the first paragraph of the discussion section and can include the I in IREAC or the first C in CREAC, and the rule (R).

3. The applicable overall *legal rule* (the R) is _____
_____

[If the rule is confusing or complex, can it be broken into elements—required subparts? If not, simply state the rule the best you can.]

4. Are there any *elements* or parts of the rule that are already obviously established (and therefore, do not need to be analyzed in detail) in your client's case?_____
_____

5. Which *element* or part of the rule is not already obviously established by the client's facts? *[This aspect of the rule will be the primary focus of your analysis in the memorandum.]* _____
_____

6. Do the cases, synthesized together, provide a useful set of *factors* to explain how courts evaluate or define the element or part of the rule at issue? *[Note: Your rule may not have or need factors; if it does not, you may skip this question.]*
   a. _____
   b. _____
   c. _____
   d. _____

7. What are the best cases to help *explain* the rule (the E in IREAC or CREAC)?
   [For each rule element, part, or factor, choose the precedent case(s) that best explain(s) or defines that element, part, or factor. Carefully select the most helpful cases for each aspect of the rule and those that will provide the clearest support for your legal analysis. For example, you might choose cases that apply the rule in the most straightforward way; that give especially interesting or vivid illustrative facts to bring the rule to life; or that you personally understand the best and, therefore, can describe the most effectively. In writing your first few memoranda, experiment with these choices. Experimentation is the beauty of editing; you can always move your writing around, reprioritize cases, or swap out a case for a better one once you complete the first draft.]
   _____
   _____

Rule Element? Factor?	Best Illustrative Case(s) (briefly note to yourself why these cases are the best ones to demonstrate the parts of the rule in action)

8. After selecting the best cases to illustrate the rule in REs, consider whether any leftover cases could be tucked into the memo using the "signal citation + explanatory parenthetical" technique described in Chapter 11.

9. Now, to begin organizing the RA (the A in IREAC), go back to the work you did in Chapter 12 and apply each element or factor to your client's facts:

Element/Factor	Precedent Case that Best Illustrated the Particular Element/Factor	Client Facts

10. In the middle column in the chart above, think about which precedent cases might be useful to weave into the RA in a case analogy.

11. Ask yourself: Which precedent case(s) is/are most similar or comparable to the facts of the client's case? _____ Why? _____

12. **Ask yourself: Which precedent case(s) is/are most distinguishable or different from the facts of the client's case? _____ Why? _____**

13. **What is the overall conclusion on the issue presented (the C in IREAC)? What is the prediction of how a court would rule on the issue?**

_____

_____

II. Drafting the Umbrella Paragraph

A. Purpose of an Umbrella Paragraph

Beneath the heading of the discussion section (see the sample memorandum in Appendix B for standard headings), you will place your umbrella paragraph (or more than one introductory paragraph if necessary), which gives the reader the "big picture" of the memorandum. This requires a balancing act of providing key information in a concise manner. The goal of the umbrella paragraph(s) is three-fold: (1) identify the precise legal issue facing the client, (2) provide the formula of the rule for the reader that is easy to understand, and (3) briefly predict the likely outcome. Whether your professor prefers IREAC (the I referring to the issue), or CREAC (the C referencing the memorandum's conclusion), the umbrella paragraph encompasses both the issue and the rule, giving enough background context for the reader to be familiar with the client's problem.

Umbrella Paragraph for an IREAC Memorandum

- Issue: "Our client, _____, seeks legal advice regarding . . . ."
- Rule: "The rule regarding _____ is . . . ."
- Break down the rule into understandable parts. (Elements? Factors?)
- Identify any parts of the rule that are not at issue (and briefly identify why not).
- Briefly predict the outcome.

The umbrella in the sample memorandum in Appendix B reflects the foregoing structure.

B. Presenting the Client Issue

The first sentence of the umbrella paragraph reminds the reader why the client is seeking legal advice. Some students wonder why a junior attorney in a law office would need to remind the senior attorney about the subject matter of the assignment. Supervising attorneys routinely have multiple cases going on at the same time; thus, a clear opening sentence in an umbrella paragraph can jog the supervising attorney's memory about that particular client's issue. Further, lawyers often work in teams; lawyers other than your supervising attorney may pick up your memorandum to get up-to-speed on the case for the first time.

Examples

Our client, Food Truck Empire, Inc. ("FTE"), seeks legal advice regarding whether it violated New York law by parking near a city park and selling gourmet grilled cheese sandwiches without a permit.

Our client, high school student Violet Martin ("Martin"), seeks legal advice regarding whether her school improperly suspended her for posting inappropriate material on Facebook about a fellow classmate.

Our client, Randolph Jenkins ("Jenkins"), seeks legal advice regarding whether he has a cause of action against his neighbor, Melinda Carlisle ("Carlisle"), for intentional infliction of emotional distress arising out of the destruction of his prized Ferrari when Carlisle chopped down a rotting tree that fell onto Jenkins' driveway.

Our client, Louche Banking, Inc. ("Louche"), seeks legal advice regarding whether it is legally entitled to charge an 18 percent interest rate on a new credit card.

Remember that the client's request for legal advice might not reveal the exact legal issue that you will be analyzing in detail. Therefore, the rest of the umbrella paragraph needs to narrow this down for the reader.

C. Communicating, and Then Narrowing, the Applicable Rule and Issue of Focus for the Reader

While the client's query may be a general question about what action to take or avoid, the lawyer's job is to identify the governing rule and then pinpoint the part(s) of the rule that require analysis. This is the R part of IREAC or CREAC and is a critical part of the umbrella paragraph.

The second sentence in the umbrella paragraph recites the governing rule. However, as you already know from the few weeks you have spent in law school by now, these rules can be complex and can contain multiple parts, some of which might not even be in question in your client's case. If your rule can be broken down into elements, you can itemize those elements for the reader (perhaps in a numbered list), demonstrating that the client's legal matter involves, for example, a three-part test or a four-pronged analysis.

Next, take the opportunity to explain briefly to the reader which parts of the rule, if any, are *not* at issue and why. Some parts of the rule might already be obviously satisfied by the client's facts, leaving only one or more components that require analysis. Identify the part(s) of the rule—perhaps an element or a particular word or phrase that needs to be defined and analyzed in more detail—that will be the focus on the analysis in the memorandum.

Example 1

Our client, car valet Stefano Duran ("Duran"), seeks legal advice regarding whether he will be found guilty of the crime of stealing a hotel patron's BMW when he took the car for a brief "joy ride." The elements of the crime of vehicle theft under California Vehicle Code § 10851 (West 2011) are (1) a person drives or takes a vehicle not his or her own, (2) without the consent of the vehicle owner, and (3) with intent either to permanently or temporarily deprive the owner of his or her title to or possession of the vehicle. Duran clearly drove the hotel patron's BMW off the lot of the hotel, so the first prong of the statute is not at issue. However, further analysis is required to determine whether Duran had consent to drive the car in the way that he did, and whether he intended to permanently or temporarily deprive the owner of title to or possession of the vehicle.

Then, if a specific part of the rule can be broken down into a list of factors, the next part of the umbrella can itemize those factors.

Example 2

When evaluating whether items sold on the street without a vendor's license constitute predominantly "expressive art" or rather "commercial" items, courts consider whether (1) the items have artistically expressive or communicative elements, including words; (2) the items also have nonexpressive functional purposes; (3) the prices of the items vary based on design complexity or are consistent for all the merchandise; and (4) the seller created the designs himself to communicate artistic ideas or purchased them from someone else.

D. Briefly Predicting the Outcome

The end of the umbrella paragraph presents a one-sentence prediction of the outcome of the client's legal dilemma.

Example 1

Applying the foregoing rule, our client, Food Truck Empire, Inc.,[2] likely violated the city ordinance by parking near Madison Square Park without a license and selling gourmet grilled cheese sandwiches.

Example 2

Applying the foregoing factors, our client likely did not violate the New York ordinance requiring a street vendor's license for commercial goods because (1) the items she sold—painted roller-derby skates—had artistically expressive and communicative elements, including colors, designs, and words; (2) the prices of the pairs of skates varied based on design complexity; and (3) she created the designs herself to communicate artistic and political ideas about female empowerment.

Example of Well-Constructed Umbrella Paragraphs

Our client, Dylan Fontaine ("Fontaine"), seeks legal advice regarding whether she likely will be found guilty of the crime of felonious assault with a deadly weapon, as defined under Ohio law. Ohio Rev. Code § 2903.11(A) (2011)—the felonious assault statute—states that "[n]o person shall knowingly . . . [c]ause or attempt to cause physical harm to another . . . by means of a deadly weapon or dangerous ordnance." Ohio Rev. Code § 2923.11(A) (2013) defines a "deadly weapon" as "any instrument, device, or thing capable of inflicting death, and designed or specially adapted for use as a weapon, or possessed, carried, or used as a weapon." The parties do not dispute that Fontaine knowingly caused physical harm to Jamie Dunham ("Dunham") by throwing her Jimmy Choo high-heel stiletto shoe directly at him. Thus, the sole question is whether the shoe qualifies as a "deadly weapon" under Ohio law.

When evaluating whether an otherwise innocuous item qualifies as a deadly weapon under the felonious assault statute, Ohio courts consider (1) the size and weight of the item, (2) the shape and design of the item, (3) the ability of the item to be grasped in the hands of the user in such a way that it may be used on or directed against the body of another, and (4) the ability of the item to be used in a manner and with sufficient force to kill the other person. Applying these factors to Fontaine's shoe, a court likely will construe the stiletto to be a deadly weapon. Thus, Fontaine likely will be found guilty of the crime of felonious assault with a deadly weapon.

---

[2] In this example, you probably would have already abbreviated the client's name to FTE as shown in the example in Section II.B, above.

Importantly, the umbrella should not include any elaborate factual analyses or detailed application of the rule to the facts. The rest of your memorandum will take care of those tasks.

III. Crafting Thoughtful Transitions Between Components of a Discussion Section

As mentioned in Chapter 12, one technique for transforming a decent legal memorandum into a great one is the use of smooth transitions between the various component parts. Think about other genres of "performance" in which transitions help the audience understand what is going on or, conversely, in which missing or abrupt transitions leave the audience confused and bewildered. For example, imagine a stage play in which, between scenes, instead of the lights fading smoothly or the curtains closing gently while the stage is reset, new characters clomp onto the stage before a scene appropriately ends and stagehands begin assembling new scenery before the prior tableau is moved out of the way. Or, think of a poorly edited film in which there is no smooth transition between (1) a quiet romantic beach scene involving two characters deep in conversation and (2) a bar fight involving two unfamiliar characters. Consider a Battle of the Bands performance in which there is no transition between a soft acoustic guitar set and a loud heavy metal set. In each of these examples, the audience is unprepared. Transitions help the audience ease from one area of focus to the next, allowing for even a few moments of closure on one intellectual topic before having to shift attention to a different one.

Luckily, there are very obvious spots in a legal memorandum where purposeful and thoughtful transitions are useful and effective:

- Between the umbrella/overview/roadmap and the first RE
- Between REs
- Between the last RE and the RA section
- Between RA paragraphs

A. Transitioning from the Umbrella Paragraph to the First Rule Explanation

Chapter 10, which discusses how to craft REs, explains that the first sentence of an RE is usually a rule statement. The rule statement is a perfect transition from the umbrella to the first RE; instead of leaping into the facts, holding, and rationale of a case that is unfamiliar to the reader, you transition the reader by providing one sentence that further summarizes the rule in a concise manner. Be careful, however. If your umbrella paragraph already does a wonderful job of explaining the rule, the first sentence of your RE should not, under any circumstances, repeat that same rule statement. Many novice legal writers who are trying hard to follow the structure provided by their professor make the mistake of simply restating the same rule in their RE rule statements. This is not beneficial to the reader and simply wastes space.

Use the rule statement component of your first RE to (1) state the rule a different way from the umbrella paragraph (perhaps in a subrule—one that focuses on just one aspect of the overall rule), (2) provide more information on the types of factors courts consider when applying the rule, or (3) suggest a trend in how courts render decisions in a certain type of cases. Alternatively, if the RE case is simply an illustration of the clearly stated rule you just described in the umbrella paragraph(s), then you can delete the rule statement from the first sentence of your RE and use a much simpler type of transition: a phrase like, "For example, in *Sangati v. Spears* . . . ." In other words, you skip the duplicative rule statement, add transitional words, like "For example, in _____,"or "For instance, in _____," state the name of the case, and segue right into the factual component of the RE.

B. Transitioning Between Rule Explanations

Transitions between REs also enhance the readability of a memo. For example, if you are using two or three cases to illustrate the rule, start each subsequent RE with either (1) a more detailed or nuanced rule statement that provides more helpful information about the rule than already provided or (2) a transition word or phrase, like:

"Similarly, in *Brady v. Snyder*, . . ."
"Likewise, in *Aydin v. Miller Contracting Co.*, . . ."
"Further, in *Palmas v. Chen*, . . ."
"In contrast, in *Jacques v. Balsam Media, Inc.*, . . ."
"Conversely, in *Nardi Marketing, LLC v. Kutepova Engineering, Inc.*, . . ."

If you choose to draft a new rule statement rather than simply inserting one of the foregoing transition words or phrases, remember that you do not want to repeat the exact phrasing of the rule as set forth in the umbrella or the rule statement in the prior RE. Choose a new subrule or a more explanatory way of phrasing the rule to introduce the next RE.

C. Transitioning Between the Last Rule Explanation and the Rule Application

Mindful legal writers also cushion the transition from RE to RA sections. As explained in Chapter 12, as you shift from the RE section of the legal memorandum to the RA, use a transition sentence that summarizes or foreshadows the overall conclusion or prediction of how a court likely would decide the legal issue affecting the client.

Example 1

Applying the foregoing elements of California's Vehicle Code Section 10851 to our client's circumstances, a court likely will find that the valet driver did not commit vehicle theft.

Example 2

Applying the foregoing factors to the merchandise our client sold at the street festival without a vendor's license, a court likely will find that the objects for sale did not qualify as "art," but rather constituted commercial items requiring a license.

After the transition sentence, you then shift to the "meat" of the RA, as described in Chapter 12. If the RA is addressing several components of a multipart rule—such as elements and/or factors—consider devoting one paragraph to each component. Transitions between those paragraphs—in the form of mini-conclusions and topic/thesis sentences—are important to give the reader closure on each ingredient of the analysis before moving on to the next one.

IV. Drafting Descriptive Headings Within the Discussion Section

As shown in the sample single-issue memorandum in Appendix B, a legal memorandum should have basic headings (perhaps in bold typeface and/or underlined) for the question presented, the brief answer, the statement of facts, the discussion, and the conclusion. Depending on the length and complexity of the legal analysis in the discussion section, you also might consider crafting descriptive headings within the body of the discussion section that track the structure of the various parts of the rule you are analyzing. (See examples in the more complex sample multi-issue legal memorandum in Appendix C.)

A. Purpose of Descriptive Headings Within the Discussion Section

Descriptive headings within a discussion section of a memorandum break up long passages of text and give the reader signposts or headlines of what material will be covered next. These types of headings are typically used in longer memoranda addressing multiple issues or multipronged legal rules. However, even in a short memorandum, headings can be useful to organize a discussion section around a multipart rule.

A complex multipronged legal analysis (i.e., one involving three to five elements or factors of a complex rule) may lead naturally to breaking up sections of analysis with headings. You could experiment with the following structure of the discussion section:

- Provide the reader with an umbrella paragraph in which you present the multiple parts of the complex rule.
- Before transitioning to the first RE, insert a heading that introduces the first rule element or factor to be addressed.
- Underneath the heading, state a fully formed rule statement soley on that element or factor.
- Conduct an RE/RA analysis and include a mini-conclusion on that element or factor.
- Provide a second heading on the next element or factor, and proceed accordingly until all the elements or factors are completely analyzed.

Headings might sound like an easy writing task to complete, but headings in legal writing require thoughtful construction in substance and form. One- or two-word headings or sentence fragments are rather useless to a legal reader. Instead, the best types of headings are those that inform the reader about what part of the rule you will discuss next and, even more beneficial, concisely suggest how the part of the rule affects the client's case. Effective headings usually occupy no more than three single-spaced lines of text and form a complete sentence. The reader should be able to grasp all the key points of the memorandum's legal analysis simply by reading your headings.

B. Examples of Headings Based on Rule Factors

I. When Evaluating Whether an Object Qualifies as a Deadly Weapon, Courts Consider the Physical Proximity Between the Victim and the Object.

II. When Evaluating Whether an Object Qualifies as a Deadly Weapon, Courts Consider any Threats or Words Used by the Assailant.

III. When Evaluating Whether an Object Qualifies as a Deadly Weapon, Courts Consider the Size and Shape of the Object.

IV. When Evaluating Whether an Object Qualifies as a Deadly Weapon, Courts Consider the Object's Ability to Inflict Death or Serious Injury.

V. When Evaluating Whether an Object Qualifies as a Deadly Weapon, Courts Consider the Manner in Which the Defendant Used the Object.

C. Examples of Headings Directly Tying the Factors of a Rule to the Client's Facts

I. The Close Physical Proximity Between the Victim and Fontaine's Jimmy Choo Stiletto Weighs in Favor of a Finding That the High-Heeled Shoe Qualifies as a Deadly Weapon.

II. The Threatening Language Used by Fontaine When She Threw the Shoe at the Victim Weighs in Favor of a Finding That the High-Heeled Shoe Qualifies as a Deadly Weapon.

III. The Size and Shape of the Four-Inch Pointed Heel of the Shoe Weighs in Favor of a Finding That the Object Qualifies as a Deadly Weapon.

IV. The Ability of the Four-Inch Pointed Heel of the Shoe to Inflict Serious Injury Weighs in Favor of a Finding That the High-Heeled Shoe Qualifies as a Deadly Weapon.

V. The Manner in Which Fontaine Used the Object Weighs in Favor of a Finding That the High-Heeled Shoe Qualifies as a Deadly Weapon.

When crafting descriptive headings, make sure to use consistent grammatical structure throughout the flow of the headings and a uniform style of numbering, indentation, line spacing, typeface, and capitalization. You may bold and underline headings; further, many lawyers capitalize the initial letter of key words throughout the headings (rather than capitalizing the entire heading text, which can be hard to read).

V. Thoughtfully Selecting Cases for Rule Explanations or Signal Cites with Accompanying Explanatory Parentheticals

Hopefully, Chapter 10 and the worksheet at the beginning of this chapter gave you a jumpstart on how to choose the best cases to illustrate in full REs in your legal memorandum. However, if you are still unsure which cases to select, or the order in which to discuss them, let's think about why this decision matters.

First, consider whether your professor has set specific page or word-count limits for your memorandum assignment. Again, these types of boundaries are designed to mimic real-life court restrictions on the length of attorney submissions, to encourage concise analysis and facilitate efficient review of substance. It is important to learn the art and skill of concision early in your legal writing career. One way to save yourself the headache of having to trim a lot of substance after "overwriting" during the memorandum-drafting process is to take the time, in the organizing phase, to strategically think about how many, and which, cases will be most useful to your legal analysis. You certainly want to demonstrate the breadth of your research, but also need to strike a balance of illustrating the applicable rule thoroughly yet succinctly so the audience readily understands the law without being overwhelmed or inadvertently confused.

Second, when choosing cases for your initial draft, think about whether a case has the following qualities:

- This case is in the appropriate jurisdiction relevant to the client's legal dilemma.
- This case clearly explains the rule that affects the client's case and is not overly complicated or confusing.
- I understand this case perhaps better than some of the others, so I will be able to explain it clearly to my audience.
- This case has interesting facts that are similar or analogous to the client's case, so it will be engaging for the reader but also useful in the analysis.

Further, consider choosing cases that show *opposite* sides of the spectrum of a rule so the reader can compare (1) the type of factual scenario in which the court rules a certain way on the client's issue with (2) the type of factual scenario in which the court rules the opposite way.

Alternatively, you might select cases that favor your client's position on the issue and contrast those judicial decisions with others in which the court's rulings disfavor your client's position on the issue. In objective/predictive legal analysis, do not ignore a case simply because it has a negative implication for your client. When you are evaluating the strengths and weaknesses of your client's case—and discussing them freely with your supervising attorney and the client, subject to the confidentiality of the attorney-client privilege—you want to know "the good, the bad, and the ugly."

Remember, once you have picked the handful of cases to use in full REs, you can always use the handy citation technique of "signal cite + explanatory parenthetical" to tuck an additional case into the memorandum. If you experiment with that technique, follow these rules in addition to those discussed in Chapter 11:

- A signal cite goes at the very end of an RE of another case, never in the middle. You will confuse the reader if you toss a signal cite in the middle of an RE (stopping the flow of the RE) and then switch back to the RE case. Always place the signal cite after the last period at the end of the RE of the other case.

- Choose the appropriate signal. If, for example, the signal case has a similar holding to the RE case, use *"See also."* If the signal case has a contrasting holding to the RE case, use *"But see."*
- Make sure the parenthetical is informative enough to the reader. Follow the structural guidelines in Chapter 11 and try to capture the facts, holding, and rationale in three to four lines of text or less.

VI. Handling Counterarguments in the Rule Application

New legal writers often ask, "Where am I supposed to address counterarguments or weaknesses in the client's case?" The answer is: in the RA. Within each RA paragraph, you will apply the various parts of the rule to the client's facts. In almost every legal case, the client has helpful facts and some not-so-helpful facts. In objective/predictive legal analysis, legal writers address the unhelpful facts as well.

As you apply the law to the facts in the RA, you may feel that there is more than one possible outcome on a particular component of the rule. Go ahead and state both alternative arguments or results. One of these might be helpful for the client, and one of these might not be, but it is okay to describe both. You are simply presenting arguments and counterarguments and then, at the end of your analysis, making your best well-reasoned prediction of the likely overall result.[3] The more you experiment with this process, the more comfortable it will feel.

Practical Anecdote

A junior associate at a law firm confided that she used to somehow feel responsible for the client's "bad facts." If a horrible e-mail appeared in a document production or an incriminating answer emerged in a deposition, she felt that somehow she had not done her job. It took her a few years to realize that the facts are the facts. In litigation, clients usually contact lawyers *after* bad things have already happened. These facts are beyond the attorney's control. You cannot make them go away. And you do not need to feel responsible for them. You simply do your job: ethically analyze the facts and handle them appropriately.

---

[3] When you shift to persuasive writing (for example, in briefs to the court described in the second half of this book), you will emphasize and focus on the arguments that are helpful to your side.

VII. Writing a Helpful Informative Conclusion to a Legal Memorandum

The overall conclusion to a legal memorandum can be short, perhaps only a sentence or two. In the conclusion, you state, as clearly and concretely as possible, the answer to the client's legal question. You might use phrases like these:

"A court likely/unlikely will find . . ."
"A court probably will find. . . ."
"The client will be able to . . ."
"The client should be able to . . ."
"The client has a viable cause of action for . . ."

Avoid being wishy-washy; do not say, "It is possible . . . ." Try to provide a definite answer to the question: the bottom line.

Examples

Based on the foregoing analysis, our client likely is guilty of the crime of assault with a deadly weapon.

Therefore, applying the required statutory elements, our client has a viable cause of action for violation of his right to privacy.

Overall, our client has a valid defense against a claim of intentional infliction of emotional harm because his behavior was not "extreme and outrageous" as defined under Maryland law.

If you have suggestions or recommendations for alternative legal strategies the client might pursue, you might offer them in the conclusion. If you need more information to conduct further analysis, you can state that as well.

Chapter 14

Locking in Logic and Abolishing Assumptions in Legal Analysis

This chapter focuses on two substantive aspects of objective legal writing that many new legal writers struggle with: (1) structuring a legal analysis so it makes *logical* sense to the reader; and (2) avoiding *assumptions* about the reader's background knowledge that create unfortunate gaps between the author's communication and the reader's comprehension.

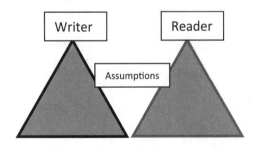

I. Examining Logic in Legal Writing

If you look up the word "logic" in a dictionary, you find all kinds of sophisticated intellectual definitions tied to mathematics, philosophy, or computer science. Scholars of logic use highbrow terminology like "inductive reasoning" (general propositions derived from specific examples), "abductive reasoning" (observations leading to a hypothesis), and "deductive reasoning" (specific examples derived from general propositions). Others discuss the concept of "syllogism": "a deductive scheme of a formal argument consisting of a major and a minor premise and a conclusion."[1] An example of a commonly used syllogism is:

> Major premise: All humans are mortal.
> Minor premise: All Greeks are humans.
> Conclusion: All Greeks are mortal.

Or . . .

> Major premise: All law school courses are challenging.
> Minor premise: Legal Writing is a law school course.
> Conclusion: Legal Writing is challenging.

Or . . .

> Major premise: All dogs are canines.
> Minor premise: Australian shepherds are a dog breed.
> Conclusion: Australian shepherds are canines.

If you find some of the above-referenced high-level definitions of logic confusing, this chapter proposes starting on a more fundamental level, approaching legal writing logic the same way you tackle practical real-life tasks.

In objective/predictive legal writing, you start at point A at which the client comes to the law office with a problem. You solve the problem by locating a rule and applying that rule to determine the predicted outcome and make a recommendation: point B.

| Point A: Client arrives at law office with a problem | Point B: Predicted outcome and recommendation |

Point A is the condition under which you have a dilemma but no solution, and point B is the predicted result and recommended course of action. Your goal in writing about the client's predicament is to guide the reader from point A to point B such that the reader understands clearly how you arrived at point B and could recreate the analytical stages herself by following your step-by-step analysis.

---

[1] Merriam-Webster Dictionary, http://www.merriam-webster.com/dictionary/syllogism (last visited Nov. 25, 2014).

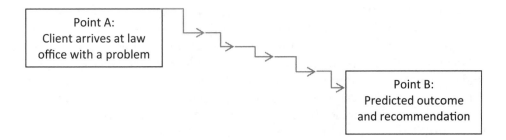

Think about how often people perform logical, step-by-step applications and analyses in daily life. Consider the following tasks involving logical procedures:

- A bartender mixing a rosewater rickey cocktail, which involves cherries brandied overnight, Angostura bitters, and a brulee flame torch
- A party host preparing boneless Buffalo chicken wings, which entails deboning a chicken and then battering and deep-frying the pieces
- A traveler figuring out how to journey from bustling Rome to a small coastal town called Ostuni 336 miles away via a high-speed train, a small regional connecting train, and a local bus
- A roommate assembling an IKEA bureau that arrives in 14 pieces accompanied by a plastic bag of knobs, screws, nails, and other fasteners

Each of these examples requires following incremental instructions in a certain order; otherwise, the end product likely will not end up tasting or looking like the desired product or functioning properly. For instance, a mixologist cannot concoct a rosewater rickey by dumping a jumble of ingredients into a Tom Collins glass and then firing up the flame torch to flambee the cherries now submerged at the bottom of the tumbler. Likewise, it would be impossible to get from Rome to Ostuni by taking the local Ostuni bus first, then a coastal regional train, before the high-speed train that departs from Rome.

Even though these are trivial examples, they illustrate the theme that logic does not have to be a complex concept fraught with intellectual terminology like syllogisms or inductive/deductive reasoning. It can simply mean organizing the paces of a task in a logical order that makes sense to you and your audience, and that can be repeated to achieve similar successful results. In legal writing, lawyers use the legal rule to guide their written logic. If the rule has three required elements, the analysis in the rule application must address each of the three parts. If the client's facts demonstrate that one of the elements is not satisfied, then the particular cause of action (e.g., negligence, breach of contract, car theft, or impersonating an officer) fails entirely. A good legal writer addresses each of the required elements one at a time and then generates a logical conclusion based on the checklist of elements being satisfied or not satisfied.

When a rule involves factors instead of elements, this analysis may seem more complicated at first glance, but the examination follows a similar logic flow.

A good legal writer takes each one of the factors—one at a time—and evaluates the particular factor in light of the facts of the client's case. At the end of the analysis, the legal writer considers how many factors are satisfied and how many are not satisfied. If more factors are fulfilled than not, the legal writer logically can conclude that a court would probably find that the requirements of the rule are met. A factor analysis requires balancing and weighing of factors against one another, but the mechanical approach is still the same. Think of elements as an "all-must-be-satisfied" approach and factors as a "most-must-be-satisfied" approach.

New legal writers lose logic flow, and confuse their readers, when they proceed too quickly or not precisely enough through the rule analysis, skip over steps, jumble steps together, or put the steps outside of a rational order. Sometimes these behaviors stem from a basic confusion about or misunderstanding of the rule in the first place; this can be fixed by slowing down, mindfully approaching the rule, acknowledging and lingering with any challenging concepts, and taking extra time to diagram and outline the rule to clearly and fully grasp the component parts and how they fit together. Other times, the foregoing writing mishaps occur when a legal writer takes shortcuts to save time, word space, hassle, and so on; resist that shortcut temptation—be thoughtful, methodical, organized, and thorough, and the logic will flow nicely.

> **Practice Tip**
>
> If you are having trouble organizing the logic of your analysis, try to imagine how you would explain the legal problem as a recipe, driving instructions, or directions for building a piece of furniture.

II. Avoiding Erroneous Assumptions

Some new legal writers leave gaps in their work product because they assume that their reader shares equal knowledge about (1) the facts of the client's case, (2) the key players involved, (3) the legal terminology necessary for an evaluation of the legal issue, and (4) the governing law. Especially in the law school environment, where professors and students spend weeks in class mulling over the subject matter of a single memorandum, novice legal writers understandably assume the professor is familiar with shorthand terminology for referring to client names, key events, and rule components, and therefore presume that shortcuts and abbreviations in references and explanations are acceptable. However, from the beginning of your legal writing career, resist making these types of faulty assumptions. Instead, always imagine your reader (a busy supervising attorney) and focus on his mindset. Remember that your supervising attorney will be handling many client matters, not just the one you are working on; so as you prepare your work product, avoid making erroneous assumptions about the depth of the supervising attorney's knowledge or recollection of the client's case and applicable law. Err on the side of being overly informative in referencing and giving background context to names, persons, nouns, events, and legal terminology. To envision how these types of assumptions impact a reader's understanding, consider the following exercises.

EXERCISE: ASSUMPTIONS

Pretend you are the supervising attorney reading the following umbrella paragraphs in two different memoranda. As you read these introductory paragraphs, highlight or circle places in the text where the writer has *assumed* erroneously that you already know certain facts of the case, aspects of the legal issue, or elements of the governing rule. Circle names, persons, nouns, events, and undefined legal terminology you do not recognize. Do the writer's assumptions inhibit your understanding of the client's case? How? What details would you like the writer to fill in to enhance your understanding?

Example 1: Our client, Dara Torres ("Torres"), seeks legal advice regarding whether she has a viable basis to seek asylum in the United States, on the grounds that she has been persecuted in Mexico on the basis of her sexual orientation. To be eligible for asylum, an alien must demonstrate that she is unable or unwilling to return to her home country because of "past persecution" on a statutorily protected ground. To establish eligibility for asylum based on "past persecution," an applicant must show (1) an incident that rises to the level of persecution and (2) such incident is committed by the government or forces the government is either unable or unwilling to control.

The court likely will grant asylum in this case because (1) Torres and Ramos both identify as homosexuals, satisfying the social group requirement; (2) the death threats and police targeting outside Secreto in Hermosillo constitute persecution on account of her homosexuality; (3) the tire-slashing incident outside her home rises to the level of persecution as defined in the case law; and (4) Miguel Longo and his drug cartel enforcers meet the private and government actor prong.

Example 2: Our clients, Matteo and Alexis Malta (the "Maltas"), seek legal advice regarding whether FlyGreen's decision to remove them was discriminatory. Under 49 U.S.C.A. § 44902(b) (2012), an airline can refuse an individual's transportation when (1) the "inimical to safety" standard is met, and (2) the pilot's decision is not arbitrary and capricious. In this case, in determining if the pilot justifiably deemed Matteo "inimical to safety" on the grounds of his behavior stemming from the disability, courts consider the decision in light of (1) the facts known to the airline at the time of the decision, (2) the pilot's reasonable reliance, (3) the time constraints faced by the pilot, and (4) the general security climate at the time.

The court likely will find that Matteo was "inimical to safety" and, therefore, his removal from the flight was proper because of (1) the flight attendant's statement; (2) Matteo's erratic actions, including his toy, language, and interaction with the passenger; (3) the weather; and (4) the recent security events in the other Louisiana airport. Therefore, the pilot's decision was not arbitrary and capricious.

Chapter 15

Writing the Memorandum Header, the Question Presented, and the Short Answer

---

<table>
<tr><td>

Memo Map

Header
Question Presented
Short Answer
Statement of Facts
Discussion (IREAC/CREAC
  Parts)
Conclusion

</td></tr>
</table>

Now that you have a working draft of the discussion section of the legal memorandum well underway, or perhaps near completion, it is time to go back to the overall memo structure and write (a) the memorandum header, (b) the question presented, and (c) the short answer (alternatively called the brief answer). Given that these items will appear on the *first* page of the legal memorandum, it might seem strange that you are writing these components almost *last* in the sequence of internal memorandum parts. However, once you learn how the question presented and short answer are structured, it will make more sense why it is important to start the memo-drafting process by first tackling the hard work of paring down the rule and performing the legal analysis, and then shaping that information into a concise question and answer.

As you learn how to write these two sections of the memo, keep in mind how the reader will *read* the document, rather than recalling the sequence in which you are writing the document. Considering the reader's thought process will help you avoid making erroneous assumptions about the extent of the reader's knowledge or recollection of the client's case. Because the question presented and short answer are likely the *first* items the supervising attorney will read (since they

> **Practical Note**
>
> Sometimes, your supervising attorney might read only the question presented and the short answer, and set aside the discussion section to read in more detail later. Therefore, it is important to be thorough yet concise in these two sections, generally limiting them to the first page (or less) of the memorandum.

appear on the first page of the memorandum), your goal is to capture the following information in an efficient but instructive manner:

- Client's full name (and possibly the opposing party's full name) plus any helpful abbreviations for these key players that you will use throughout the memorandum
- The governing body of law (jurisdiction? key statute? topical area of legal doctrine?)
- The legal question/issue affecting the client
- A snapshot of the legally significant facts
- The applicable rule (if possible, broken down into a more useful framework for the reader—i.e., elements or factors)
- A concise application of the rule to the client scenario (no more than a few sentences)
- A concrete prediction/conclusion of the likely outcome

Some lawyers describe the question presented and the short answer as the "30-second elevator pitch" to the supervising attorney. Imagine you step onto the elevator at your law office, ready to go home after a long but rewarding day of researching and writing. Your supervising attorney hops into the same elevator right before the door closes, and asks, "So what's the bottom line on the Penske file?" For the 30 to 60 seconds it takes for the elevator to reach the first floor, as you recap your question presented and short answer, your supervising attorney should have the primary information needed to advise the client.

I. Crafting an Informative Memorandum Header

The header portion of the legal memorandum will be the easiest thing you write as a lawyer (besides your own name), but that does not let you off the hook for making it perfect and useful to the reader. A memorandum header contains five parts: (1) the title of the document, (2) the recipient's name, (3) the author's name, (4) the date, and (5) a useful and informative reference line (for filing purposes and so the reader can discern the substance of the memorandum, especially in a case involving multiple legal research memoranda on various substantive issues). The header should look like this:

MEMORANDUM

TO: Lucy Van Pelt, Esq.
FROM: Charlie Brown, Summer Associate
DATE: March 26, 2017
RE: Woodstock, Inc.; Client File No. 3-26; Possible Cause of Action
            for Breach of an Employee's Noncompetition Agreement

---

Some law offices might prefer junior attorneys to use memorandum header templates reflecting the name of the law firm or company. If not, a standard memorandum includes the title "MEMORANDUM" in all capital letters. Then, it relays the full names of the recipient and author of the memorandum.

The date is also very important; it sets a time boundary for the universe of facts and governing law to which you had access when you conducted the analysis and rendered the conclusion. The law office team might unearth new facts after that date, or the law may change, so it is important to memorialize the date you completed your analysis so you are held accountable only for the facts and law available at that time.

The reference line might seem inconsequential, but you would be surprised how often law students and junior attorneys do not take the time to draft an informative reference line—which can confuse the reader. While this legal research and writing assignment might be your primary work activity during a given week, the supervising attorney might be handling 5, 10, or 20 other client matters. Also, given the size and complexity of the client's case, different junior attorneys might be working on a variety of legal memoranda for the same client matter at the same time. You do not want busy supervising attorneys to have to scan the substance of your particular document to remember what issue they assigned you to research and analyze. In the reference line, give the client's full name and the client's billing or file number, so the memorandum can be filed with the correct case; further, that information reminds the supervising attorney to which client and matter your work product is being billed or allocated, in the likely event the law office represents the client in more than one legal matter. Also, make sure you describe the subject matter of the memo in sufficient detail to trigger the supervising attorney's memory about the topic she assigned you to research. This reference line is useful especially in cases entailing multiple legal research memoranda by different attorneys.

II. Crafting a Helpful Question Presented

Beneath the "Memorandum" header, the "Question Presented" heading appears next. Other than the header reference line, the question presented is likely to be the first substantive component of the memorandum that your supervising attorney will read.

When writing questions presented, many law students and junior attorneys mistakenly assume that the supervising attorney possesses as much knowledge as they do about the case facts, applicable law, or even the original research/writing assignment. When you craft a question presented, assume that the supervising attorney has been so occupied handling other matters that he has forgotten exactly what he assigned you to research. Use the question presented to jog his memory and enable him to talk intelligently about the issue—for example, during a conference call with the client.

Example of Language That Improperly Assumes the Reader's Knowledge of the Law

The following examples of introductory language in questions presented erroneously assume the reader knows as much about the law as the author does:

"Under the *Rowan* doctrine . . ."
    What does "*Rowan*" refer to?
"Under the Nebraska laws of IIED . . ."
    What does "IIED" stand for?
"Under the carjacking statute . . ."
    Which carjacking statute? What state's law applies?
"Under Section 44.1970 of the statute . . ."
    Which statute?

A. Components of an Effective Question Presented

An effective question presented includes the following components:

- The client's full name (and the respectful abbreviation you plan to use throughout the memorandum), and if appropriate, the opposing parties or other key players in the client scenario
- Which body of law governs the client's circumstances
- The precise legal question/issue(s) the memorandum will address
- A concise description of the legally significant facts related to the issue

Like other parts of the memorandum discussed in prior chapters, there is a simple yet thorough formula for drafting an informative question presented: the "under/does/when" formula.

Formula

Under [*insert governing body of law*] does/can/is/has [*identify the client and abbreviate the name appropriately*] [*state the legal question/issue*] when [*describe the critical, relevant, legally significant facts that caused the issue to arise*]?

Example

Under Ohio law, is our client, Dylan Fontaine ("Fontaine"), guilty of the crime of assault with a deadly weapon when (1) she removed a Jimmy Choo high-heel stiletto shoe from her foot and threw it at the victim, local bartender Jamie Dunham ("Dunham"); (2) she yelled curse words at the victim while throwing the shoe; and (3) the pointed heel of the stiletto shoe hit the victim in the forehead, causing a deep gash requiring emergency medical attention?

The next sections explain each part of the formula in more detail.

B. "Under": The "Governing Law" Part of the Question Presented

The governing body of law can be, for example:

A particular state's laws	"Under Arizona law, . . ."
A certain federal or state statute	"Under New York's right of privacy statute, N.Y. Civ. Rights Law § 50 (McKinney 2011), . . ."
	"Under the federal statute regarding an airline's right to remove a passenger from a plane, 49 U.S.C. § 44902(b) (2013), . . ."
A certain area of law	"Under constitutional law, . . ." "Under federal immigration law, . . ." "Under federal tax law, . . ."

Remember, even though you probably have drafted your discussion section already and cited the applicable law many times therein, the question presented is the *first* time the reader is ascertaining the governing law in your memorandum. Resist taking shortcuts or using abbreviations for the legal rule. If you are using a statute, use proper citation form and cite it "in full" since it is the first time it is being referenced in the memorandum. (See Chapter 11 for guidance on basic legal citation rules for writing legal memoranda.)

C. "Does/Can/Is/Has": The "Legal Question" Part of the Question Presented

The next component of the question presented accomplishes two things: (1) introduces the client's full name for the first time in the body of the memorandum; and (2) concisely states the legal question/issue posed by or affecting the client. This is an opportunity to identify (in parentheses and quotation marks) an appropriate and respectful abbreviation for the client's name if using the full name throughout the document would be repetitive, cumbersome, or confusing.

Examples

". . . does our client, Woodstock, Inc. ("Woodstock"), . . ."

". . . has our client, Derek Jeter ("Jeter"), . . ."

". . . is our client, the National Football League ("NFL"), . . ."

". . . will our client, the Human Rights Coalition ("HRC"), . . ."

". . . can our client, Mark Ballas ("Ballas"), . . ."

Once you establish the client's name abbreviation in the question presented, do not use the full name again in the memorandum. (Good news: An appropriate abbreviation can help with word count and page limits.) You may use suitable acronyms to abbreviate company names, but do not shorten people's names to initials.

The trickiest part of the "does/can/is/has" component of the question presented is crafting the correct legal question or issue that the memorandum will address. In drafting the discussion section, you probably narrowed the broader, client-posed legal question (e.g., Does our client have a cause of action for negligence? Is our client liable for defamation? Can our client sue for intentional infliction of emotional harm?) to a specific fragment of the overall rule, such as defining the term "duty," or "breach," or "reasonable," by listing elements and then focusing on the particular prong of the rule at issue or by synthesizing and applying factors that interpret an element. However, since we are now back at the beginning of the memorandum, the question likely will be broadened again, making it more similar to the general query that prompted the client to contact the law office.

Examples

Under Michigan law, does our client, Kirby Slade ("Slade") who purchased a new iPhone, have a viable cause of action for fraudulent misrepresentation against the retail store when . . .

Under California law, does our client, Rowan Brown ("Brown"), have a valid claim for breach of her lease contract for a house when . . .

In the "legal question" part of the question presented, refrain from using shorthand or abbreviations for the legal terminology. From weeks of class discussion in law school (or a week or two of continuous legal research and writing on this subject in law practice), you will feel intimately familiar with the legal question and phrasing from drafting the rule, the rule explanations, and the rule applications in the discussion section. However, it is essential to remember that your reader has not performed all the foregoing work and is encountering your memorandum with fresh eyes. Thus, be thorough and complete in the language you choose to recite the client's legal issue in the question presented.

D. "When": The "Legally Significant Facts" Part of the Question Presented

The "when" part of the question presented is an opportunity to concisely but visually "sketch the scene" of your client's circumstances. You will use only legally significant facts rather than every interesting fact (which you do not have room to do). You might consider putting the "when" facts in a succinct, well-structured list format.

As it comes time for you to draft the "when" part of the question presented, you already know for certain which facts are legally significant because they are the client details you relied on most heavily in the rule application part of your legal analysis in the discussion section of the memo. To identify the legally significant facts for the question presented, review the worksheet in Chapter 13 and scan the facts inserted. Scrutinize the rule application paragraphs in the discussion section, and highlight the key client details you relied on in the analysis. Make a separate list of the extracted key facts. See whether you can pare these down into a list of three to five legally significant facts. Ideally, these storytelling details should track the important parts of the governing rule—perhaps certain required elements or factors considered by the court.

Example 1

Under Michigan law, does our client, Kirby Slade ("Slade"), who purchased a new iPhone, have a viable cause of action for fraudulent misrepresentation when (1) the seller made a statement about the phone's ability to download a Justin Timberlake ringtone that the seller knew was false, and (2) the purchaser (who possessed limited knowledge about cellphones and ringtones) relied on the statement in deciding to purchase the phone?

Example 2

Under California law, does our client, Rowan Brown ("Brown"), have a valid claim for breach of her lease contract for a house when (1) the plumbing in the bathroom emits a rancid odor; (2) the house is inhabited by two-inch-long bugs that extermination fails to eradicate; and (3) there is evidence of rodent activity in the kitchen, such that the tenant felt she had no choice but to stay in a hotel and begin searching for alternate housing?

Notice how the "when" facts in the examples reflect the storyline from the specific client scenarios. They sound more like client-specific narratives than legal terminology. This is good. You want the "when" facts to give the reader a snapshot of the client's story in as crisp a manner as possible.

One mistake that new legal writers make in drafting the "when" part of the question presented is to recite the legal terms from the elements or factors of the rule instead of the legally significant facts. One strategy for distinguishing between a legally significant fact and an element or a factor of a legal rule is to ask: Is this a colorful storytelling detail or a mundane, unexciting part of the legal rule? The "when" facts should use visual storytelling events—not legal jargon.

Two additional and very common challenges that new legal writers face when crafting helpful "when" facts are (1) constructing a grammatically proper list using parallel structure and (2) describing the facts in such a way that does not erroneously assume the reader knows certain details.

1. Using Parallel Structure in a List

Take a look at the following example of a list that lacks parallel grammatical structure.

Example of a List Lacking Parallel Grammatical Structure

Under Texas law, is our client, Dylan Fontaine ("Fontaine"), guilty of the crime of assault with a deadly weapon when (1) she removed a Jimmy Choo stiletto high-heel shoe from her foot and threw it at the victim, Jamie Dunham ("Dunham"); (2) threats and curse words; and (3) depending on whether the victim sustained an injury to his forehead?

This is a particularly egregious example and is rather nonsensical, but notice how the first fact is structured as a standalone sentence: "she removed a Jimmy Choo stiletto high-heel shoe from her foot and threw it at the victim, Jamie Dunham ("Dunham")." The second fact is comprised of two nouns: "threats and curse words." The third fact is a conditional phrase: "depending on whether the victim sustained an injury to his forehead." One way to catch a lack of parallel grammatical structure is to read the introduction to the list separately out loud with each component, pretending the other components are not present, and see whether they flow nicely. If they do not, the list lacks parallel structure. In the above example, the introduction to the list ("with a deadly weapon when . . .") matches the first component but does not match the other two. A better version of the question presented above is:

Example of a List with Parallel Structure

Under Texas law, is our client, Dylan Fontaine ("Fontaine"), guilty of the crime of assault with a deadly weapon when (1) she removed a Jimmy Choo stiletto high-heel shoe from her foot and threw it at the victim, Jamie Dunham ("Dunham"); (2) she yelled curse words at the victim while throwing the shoe; and (3) the pointed heel of the stiletto shoe hit the victim in the forehead, causing a deep gash requiring emergency medical attention?

These three list components have parallel grammatical structure because they are all standalone sentences that flow well when read in conjunction with the introduction to the list: (1) "when . . . she"; (2) "when . . . she"; and (3) "when . . . the pointed heel . . ."

2. Avoiding Factual Assumptions in a List

Once again, good legal writers describe the legally significant facts in the question presented such that they do not assume the reader knows about certain people, events, and facts that she actually does not recognize. Consider the following "assumed facts" version of a question presented related to the stiletto client scenario above.

Example of Improper Assumptions About a Reader's Familiarity with the Facts

Under Texas law, is our client, Dylan Fontaine ("Fontaine"), guilty of the crime of assault with a deadly weapon when (1) she removed the shoe from her foot and threw it at Dunham; (2) she yelled the phrase in question at the victim while throwing the shoe; and (3) the bartender sustained the alleged injuries?

This writer has assumed that the reader already knows the following facts:

- "[T]he shoe." What shoe?? Was it a Birkenstock? A clog? A flip-flop? No, it was a pointy-heeled Jimmy Choo stiletto.
- "Dunham." Who is Dunham? Jamie Dunham. The victim.
- "[T]he phrase in question." What phrase? Curse words? Were they threatening?
- "[T]he bartender." What bartender? Is the bartender the same person as Dunham?
- "[T]he alleged injuries." What injuries?

Always review the facts of the question presented with the reader in mind. If any names, key players, or contextual facts are not explained clearly enough, rephrase the language so that a reader unfamiliar with the details of the client's case can picture the basics of the scene. This process helps establish rapport between the writer and reader instead of distance.

III. Constructing a Concise, Informative Short Answer

A. Components of the Short Answer

The goal of the short answer is to respond to the question presented as it is phrased, providing logical reasons for the particular response. The short answer should accomplish the following:

- Answer the question presented in one or two words, and add a conclusory statement (either in the same or the next sentence).

- State the governing rule of law (the applicable statute or the primary rule synthesized from common law).
  - o Identify any required elements of the rule.
  - o State why any particular elements are not at issue or are already determined from the client's facts.
  - o List any applicable factors, if any, that help explain the element at issue.
- Briefly apply the rule to the client's circumstances in a few sentences.
- Predict the outcome.

If this sounds familiar, it should. The short answer is very similar to the umbrella paragraph in the body of the discussion section, even though they serve two very different purposes. The short answer is part of the "30-second elevator pitch" to the reader. The umbrella paragraph is the introduction to the discussion section.

B. Presenting a One-Word Answer + Conclusory Statement

First, answer the question presented either "yes" or "no." There is no "maybe" option. Your supervising attorney is looking for as close to a definitive answer as possible. If you need a little wiggle room, you can say "It is likely" or "It is unlikely," or "It is probable." Do not say, "It is possible." Anything is possible. Trust yourself that the detailed legal analysis you perform in the discussion section backs up your concrete answer: Yes. No. It is likely. Probably.

Examples

"No. Our client did not violate . . ."

"Yes. A court likely would find that our client violated . . ."

C. Providing the Rule Formula for the Reader

The rule formula for the short answer is the same one you included in the umbrella paragraph, though with slightly varied phrasing so the language does not sound overly repetitive and robotic in the two sections. Remember: The short answer (which appears on the first page of the memorandum) is the *first place* the supervising attorney sees the rule, so the recitation must be 100 percent clear and informative. Even though you already wrote about the rule when drafting the discussion section, resist the urge to use shorthand or abbreviations in phrasing when you describe the rule (now earlier chronologically in the memo) in the short answer. Clearly recite the governing rule, and decide whether you need to cite the source (e.g., a statute, synthesized case law). If the rule breaks down into required elements, list them and identify which elements, if any, are not at issue because they are already determined by the client's facts. If you can narrow down the focal point of the memo to a single legal issue, do so here.

If the particular element is better explained through a series of factors, go ahead and concisely list those in the short answer as well: for example, "When evaluating X, courts considering the following factors . . . ."

D. Briefly Applying the Rule to the Client Facts

After you have accurately summarized the applicable rule, very briefly apply the rule to the client's scenario in a few sentences, using the elements or factors. Once again, be careful not to assume the supervising attorney knows the facts as well as you do. If you refer to names, events, or terminology in this condensed application (which is fleshed out more thoroughly in the discussion section), ask yourself whether the supervising attorney will know what those words mean. If not, spend a few extra words defining them.

E. Concisely Predicting the Outcome

The last sentence of the short answer reiterates the predicted outcome. This sentence can be exactly the same as the final conclusion of the discussion section.

Examples

Based on the foregoing analysis, our client likely is guilty of the crime of assault with a deadly weapon.

Therefore, applying the required statutory elements, our client has a viable cause of action for violation of his right to privacy.

Overall, our client has a valid defense against a claim of intentional infliction of emotional harm because his behavior was not "extreme and outrageous" as defined under Maryland law.

Examples of short answers are provided in the sample memoranda in Appendices B and C.

Chapter 16

Writing a Statement of Facts in a Legal Office Memorandum

Memo Map

Header
Question Presented
Short Answer
Statement of Facts
Discussion (IREAC/CREAC Parts)
Conclusion

As you can see from the legal memoranda examples provided in Appendices B and C, a legal office memorandum typically includes a statement of facts summarizing the universe of client facts on which the legal writer based the legal analysis—as of the date the memorandum is completed and submitted to the supervising attorney. The statement of facts relays the client's story in an efficient, yet engaging, thorough, and well-organized fashion. This section of the memorandum contains *no* legal analysis, argument, statutes, case citations, or legal conclusions: "Just the facts, ma'am."

Because the typical legal memorandum is an objective, predictive, internal office document—not distributed to the opposing party—good legal writers include both favorable and unfavorable facts in the statement of facts. The reader (the supervising attorney) needs to know the compilation of facts (bad and good) affecting the legal analysis to properly advise the client of the range of realistic legal options.

The statement of facts should include the following:

- Parties' names, names of all key players in the client's factual scenario, and their relationships to one another

- Chronology of legally significant events that led to the client's request for legal advice
- Brief description of any key documents or tangible things that are legally relevant to the analysis
- Any background facts that help the reader understand the context of the client's situation
- Procedural history of the client's legal case, if pertinent to the legal analysis (e.g., pleadings served, substantive or discovery motions filed, court decisions rendered; see Chapter 1)

I. Purpose of the Statement of Facts

Some new legal writers ask why they need to spend time writing an entire section of a legal memorandum synopsizing the client's facts when the supervising attorney likely already knows some, if not all, of those very same details. However, remember that legal writers never want to make erroneous assumptions about the reader's knowledge or memory of the client's case. The supervising attorney may not have had the chance to read as much of the case file as you have, or he might be so busy handling matters for other clients that he does not remember the legally significant facts that bear on the legal analysis in the memorandum. Further, the law office might staff the particular legal case with more than one attorney, so individuals who have not been part of the case team from the beginning might read and rely on the memorandum.

Also, because the conclusion of a good legal memorandum predicts how a court would rule on the client's legal issue, the legal writer must memorialize the collection of facts that form the basis of the legal analysis at that snapshot in time. After a legal writer submits a memo to a supervising attorney, new facts may come to light or the law might change. Thus, the statement of facts helps document the boundaries of factual knowledge on the date the legal writer (or the supervising attorney or the law firm) made legal recommendations to the client. The supervising attorney also can use the statement of facts to verify or clarify factual issues with the client.

II. How to Write a Statement of Facts

Prior to reviewing the sources of law and writing the discussion portion of the legal memorandum, you reviewed the client case file and perhaps interviewed the client to gather background information and legally significant facts. You may have created your own written chronology of events. As you prepared to craft the Rule Application in the discussion section of the memorandum, you may have used the chart in Chapter 12 to evaluate the elements or factors of the rule against the client's circumstances. Then, in drafting the Rule Application, you presented and analyzed the client facts for their legal significance. You may have cross-checked the facts against each component part of the rule, and even compared and contrasted such facts from precedent cases. Also, in constructing the "when" part of the question presented, you synthesized the client facts into a short list of legally significant facts to frame the question (see Chapter 15).

Now, as you sit down to draft a concise, well-organized statement of facts, go through the foregoing work product and highlight the key background details and legally significant facts that relay the client's story. Then, as you start to write the statement of facts, consider whether it makes the most sense to communicate the client's narrative either (1) chronologically, introducing the reader to the key people, places, things, documents, and events in the order in which they occurred; or (2) topically, categorizing facts by issue, element, factor, or case theme. Either way is acceptable. The only restriction—and the golden rule of writing thorough statements of facts in legal memoranda—is that every single fact that you rely on in your discussion section (in the Rule Application(s)) *must also appear* in the statement of facts. It is very confusing for a supervising attorney to read a memorandum, think she grasps the factual scenario from a statement of facts appearing around page 2 of the memorandum, and yet suddenly be confronted with a new fact, without warning, in a Rule Application found on page 7 or 8 of the same document. For example, if a legal writer names and describes two key parties in the statement of facts but then introduces an unfamiliar third party several pages later in a Rule Application, the reader will be perplexed. If a legal writer references a particular piece of artwork in the statement of facts because it is the subject of the client's dispute with an opposing party, but then describes a new piece of client-related artwork in a Rule Application, the reader will be puzzled. If a legal writer encapsulates a key conversation between the parties in the statement of facts, but then quotes a completely new statement from one of those parties in a Rule Application, the reader might feel blindsided. It may feel redundant to mention the facts in both places—the statement of facts and the Rule Application—but the two memorandum components serve distinct roles. The statement of facts gives the supervising attorney a chronicle of the client's circumstances while the Rule Application applies the rule components to those facts to predict a logical outcome.

To ensure that you do not inadvertently omit an essential fact used in a Rule Application from the statement of facts, print out both parts of your memorandum, grab a highlighter, and cross-check all your Rule Application facts against the statement of facts, highlighting items as they appear in both places. Any detail in the Rule Application that is missing from the statement of facts needs to be added there. If there are pieces of information described in the statement of facts that are not used in the Rule Application, you can decide whether the detail provides helpful background information and should stay in the memorandum or whether it is tangential or extraneous information that can be safely deleted if you need to trim words to meet a word count or page limit.

III. Style Tips for Writing Statements of Facts

Keep the following style tips in mind when writing statements of facts:

- Be uniform in referring to client names. If you have abbreviated the party names in the question presented or short answer, use the same abbreviations in the statement of facts.
- Check spelling of client names.
- Avoid making assumptions about the reader's knowledge. When in doubt, provide context and more explanation.
- If quoting from case file documents or citing other factual documents, see *Bluebook* Rule B7.
- Tell the facts in an interesting way, but do not dramatize them or present them persuasively. Eventually, when transitioning from objective/predictive legal writing to persuasive writing (advocacy letters, briefs, and motions described in the second half of this book), you will learn when it is appropriate to couch client facts in a more dramatic or persuasive light.

Section 5

Adjustment, Refinement, and Perfection

Chapter 17

Preparing for Legal Writing Feedback

Sometime in the first month or two of law school, after you have written a first (or second, or third, etc.) draft of your legal memorandum, you likely will be meeting with your professor one-on-one or possibly in small groups to discuss your work. Your professor will review your latest version, either in advance of or "live" during the conference, and provide valuable feedback that you will incorporate during the editing process prior to submitting the final graded version. For new law students, this conference/feedback experience sometimes feels uncomfortable or initially can engender resistance or resentment. Thus, this chapter discusses (1) what to expect in a writing conference; (2) how best to prepare yourself intellectually, logistically, and emotionally for the experience; and (3) how to absorb the information you receive, process it constructively, and apply it to enhance your work product—in the legal writing classroom and beyond.

I. What to Expect in a Writing Conference: A Dialogue Rather Than an "Answer Key"

Preparing for a legal writing conference with a professor is another opportunity for you to envision the big picture of your development as a lawyer, and a chance to exercise professional judgment (discussed in Chapter 2). In college and pre-law-school professional experiences, you may have participated in meetings with professors or job supervisors in which the dialogue was one-directional: They talked, you listened, and you then returned to your cubicle and followed their instructions. A conference with a legal writing professor will be wildly different. Now, you are training to be a counselor-at-law, so the professor's goal is to develop *your* ability to evaluate your own work and identify areas of improvement so that you can eventually serve your client's needs on your own. Instead of handing you an "answer key," legal writing professors strive to equip you with competencies to self-appraise and evolve; after all, eventually, you will be the person sitting at your law office desk alone, writing memoranda and briefs on behalf of a client, under greater time pressure, and often for high stakes. Legal writing professors aspire to cultivate your ability and confidence to do this work. Of course, teachers understand that you need to *learn* these skills before employing them. However, if professors just furnish you "the answers" from the beginning, they are not developing your aptitude to generate excellent legal writing on your own. Thus, a conference with your legal writing professor will be a two-way street, with you doing much of the talking and the professor prompting you in ways that encourage you to identify the gaps in your writing so you can fill them yourself.

Some law students expect to arrive at the professor's office and watch him or her mark up the draft, so the student can simply grab the line-edited document, input a few changes, and then submit the final version. However, that is not how you will learn to be an excellent legal writer. Many times, legal writing professors hear the following types of requests from students:

"Can you just look at this and tell me what I need to fix?"
"What else do I need to do to get an A?"
"Is this right?"

Sometimes students think the professor is "hiding the ball" when he or she resists whipping out a red pen and "fixing" the document. Nonetheless, the following is the more likely way the feedback process will proceed: Your professor will read your draft and then identify, either in the margins or verbally, the areas that could use more "nurture." The professor will not line-edit your draft or mend its flaws. Instead, the professor will pinpoint areas that need attention and enrichment, such as

- missing components of IREAC/CREAC,
- overlooked pieces of a rule explanation (facts, holding, rationale),
- erroneous assumptions about a reader's knowledge of the client facts or law,
- logic gaps in the overall analysis,
- confusing phrasing,
- too much legalese instead of clear sentences, and/or
- omitted citation or support for the analysis.

The professor also might note issues with grammar, punctuation, and spelling, but this will not be the primary focus of the draft review. Instead, the emphasis will be on the logic and clarity of the legal analysis. The professor probably will ask you questions like the following—in the margins or verbally—that prompt you to perceive the gaps in the writing for yourself:

"Was this fact (relied on in the reasoning here) mentioned anywhere earlier in the discussion of the facts above, or does it appear out of the blue here? Will this be confusing to the reader?"

"This precedent case appears for the first time in this Rule Application analogy, but it is not discussed anywhere earlier in the memo. Will this be perplexing to the reader?"

"This paragraph uses abbreviations to refer to the parties in the case. Have these abbreviations been defined yet anywhere for the reader? Will this be puzzling to the reader who is not yet familiar with the key players?"

These types of questions will facilitate a dialogue between you and the professor about your writing, so that you can see where gaps in the analysis might confound your audience.

II. What to Expect in a Writing Conference: Time Boundaries

How many other students are in your legal writing class section? As one-on-one legal writing conferences approach, bear in mind that your professor will be reviewing drafts and meeting with all your classmates (not just you) and, depending on your professor's course load, perhaps an additional full section of students. Therefore, there are realistic constraints on the professor's time. The best way to maximize a legal writing conference experience is to be mindful of these scheduling limits and respect them. These boundaries inherently limit the logistical length of each conference to accommodate all students, the number of hours the professor can devote to the physical review of drafts, and the ability for additional follow-up after conferences. That is why it is so important to be prepared for the conference, be open-minded during your interaction with the professor, and take notes to capture the dialogue exchanged.

One misstep that new law students sometimes make when they arrive at the conference is to ask the professor to read a new draft from scratch and "tell me what I need to do to fix it." In a 20-, 30-, or even 40-minute block of time, this is neither realistic nor the best use of this valuable one-on-one opportunity. It is mentally challenging for a professor to read a paper for the first time with the author sitting across a desk or table and provide meaningful feedback on the entire document under such time pressure. The better option is for you to think through, in advance, specific areas of the document that you would like to discuss with the professor. Like you would in a law office, create a realistic agenda for the meeting.

Further, because of time restrictions, any run-through of an early version of your written work by the professor in advance of your final grade on that assignment may not be all inclusive—even if he or she is trying very hard to be. For instance, your professor may evaluate an interim draft for overall IREAC/ CREAC logic flow and not specifics like sentence structure, citation form, or grammar. If the professor gives written feedback on portions of an assignment, you should apply those same general suggestions throughout your work product. Do not assume that a scarcity of comments on a particular section of your memorandum means that text requires no additional refinement. You constantly should strive to edit and revise the entire work product to implement recommendations made in earlier sections of the document and on prior assignments, and produce the best quality of written work that you can.

You also should read your professor's course policies regarding review of drafts and any rules governing the conferences and postconference follow-up. Once your writing conference has occurred on each assignment, the professor likely will no longer review drafts of your paper. Respect this policy and refrain from requesting additional review of subsequent drafts after the conference and prior to the due date. As a final follow-up, your professor may have a specific policy about answering specific questions via e-mail or during office hours.

III. How to Prepare (Like a Lawyer) for the Writing Conference

Consider your writing conference to be a prime opportunity to demonstrate professional judgment. In your conference preparation, practice your new lawyer persona. Instead of assuming the professor will be enthusiastic about reading your document from a laptop screen or flipping through a crumpled paper yanked from your backpack, consider creating a lawyer-type "case file" for the writing project. Organize a folder or a three-ring binder containing the memorandum assignment, factual documents, pleadings or transcripts, sources of law (statutes, cases, regulations), the professor's rules or policies governing the assignment, and the memorandum draft. Have an extra hard copy of the latest version for your professor, unless he or she prefers to read from a computer screen.

Be on time. Legal writing conferences are important academic appointments. To accommodate all students within a quick turnaround time, these conferences are tightly scheduled. It is essential to be prompt and prepared, with the draft document in hand. It is often difficult for your professor to switch student time slots at the last minute or schedule new appointments; conference weeks are time-sensitive and can be intellectually exhausting for even the most energetic or experienced professor. Exercise professional judgment and help the professor perform his or her job efficiently.

Most important, approach the conference with a positive and open-minded attitude. Professors spend months creating and crafting interesting, challenging, yet balanced legal writing assignments, and appreciate when students show enthusiasm about learning how to be a skilled legal writer. This conference is a premier opportunity for you to forge a lasting bond with a legal professional, one who may eventually serve as a job reference or help you foster networking opportunities within the legal community. Respect the professor's course policies, time, and experience. Remain intellectually open to the feedback. Consider the writing conference as an opportunity to recruit an influential champion for your future as a successful attorney.

IV. Processing Legal Writing Feedback

After the conference, set aside time to craft a new and improved draft (which you will revise several more times using the techniques in Chapter 18 before submitting the final graded version). Consult your calendar and count how many days you have until the final due date. Instead of finalizing the document in one long sitting the day before the deadline, map out a foolproof editing program by carving out smaller increments of time over a period of days or a week, so that you can fulfill your other law school obligations and yet come back to the legal writing project with fresh eyes in each editing session.

First, make all the changes your professor recommended during the conference, and then take time to reflect on the specific questions he or she asked. Instead of just making small editorial modifications, consider how to transform your work product into a truly client-worthy document. Next, go back to your class notes and highlight helpful guidelines from your professor; he or she has been telling you all semester exactly how to be an excellent legal writer. Use the Legal Office Memorandum-Drafting Checklist in Appendix D and evaluate your work. If your professor provided other checklists or grading rubrics, definitely use them to assess your own writing. Follow all the steps in Chapter 18 to edit the memorandum. Read the entire document aloud a few times, in different sittings.

Overall, if you approach the legal writing feedback process as one that is designed to make you a stronger, smarter, more efficient lawyer, the benefits will be exponentially more useful.

LEGAL WRITING CONFERENCE CHECKLIST

☑ Follow the professor's instructions for signing up for a conference.

☑ Input the correct conference time into your calendar (with a reminder alert).

☑ Follow the professor's instructions and deadlines for submitting a memorandum draft in advance of the conference.

☑ Prepare a "case file" folder and print out two copies of the draft.

☑ Identify specific areas of the memorandum to focus on with the professor.

☑ Show up to the conference on time, with an open mind and a positive attitude.

☑ Listen to the professor's questions about the draft.

☑ Take notes, as appropriate.

☑ Say thank you!

☑ Respect the professor's postconference rules.

☑ After the conference, review the professor's recommendations and edit accordingly.

☑ Reflect on the professor's questions asked during the conference or in the margin comments within the draft.

☑ During the editing process, incorporate guidance from the professor's questions, class notes, checklists, and grading rubrics.

Chapter 18

Becoming an Expert Self-Editor

"If it sounds like writing, I rewrite it."

● Elmore Leonard (1925–2013)

I. Ten-Step Editing Process: Introduction

Law students and lawyers are busy people, and time constraints sometimes can impact their ability to polish the final draft of a document to its full potential. However, the appearance of written work product reflects the professionalism of the author, so it is essential to take the time to perfect the style and presentation of every legal document so the substance can shine. This chapter offers a ten-step editing and proofreading process to enable you to make your first legal memorandum as strong as possible. Each of these steps takes time, however, and many should be performed in separate sittings, so it is important to plan your editing timeline accordingly.

Recall Chapter 2's discussion of, and Appendix A's summary of, "benchslaps": courts' admonitions of lawyers for submitting shoddy work product and/or failing to follow court rules. Judges criticize lawyers for submitting written work product that

- lacks structural logic and clear phrasing, making the writing difficult to understand;
- omits substantive components required by the rules;
- misrepresents, fails to cite, or poorly handles the case facts;
- inadequately explains the governing law;
- violates clear procedural and formatting rules (e.g., electronic or paper filing conventions, page or word-count limits, line spacing, margins, font size);
- includes frequent typographical, grammatical, or proofreading errors;
- uses a disrespectful tone toward the court, opposing counsel, or other parties; and/or
- violates court-imposed filing deadlines.

The steps in this chapter will ensure that your work product can withstand scrutiny on all these levels—even for documents you are not yet submitting to a court but for which you aspire to exceed the expectations of your intended audience: a law professor, a supervising attorney, or potentially a client.

II. Editing Starting Point

> The most important lesson in the writing trade is that any manuscript is improved if you cut away the fat.
> ● *Robert Heinlein (1907-1988)*

Before you begin editing a legal memorandum, double-check three details: (1) the word-count or page limit for the assignment, (2) the due date, and (3) the formatting and submission rules governing the document (e.g., font, line spacing, margins, page numbering, electronic v. hard-copy submission, e-mail reference header requirements).

Check and recheck each of these details so you know exactly what the end product should look like and how and when you must transmit it to the professor. Once you have confirmed the due date, take out your calendar and start to map out a master editing plan. Because improving a single piece of legal writing involves so many nuances, angles, and layers, you cannot sit down at your computer the day before the due date and make all the editorial changes and conduct the levels of review necessary to generate top-notch legal work. The legal editing process differs from methods writers use in revising other written pieces. Because legal editing requires review for different substantive, logical, analytical, and technical purposes—each of which requires a different mental focus—it is wise to perform these steps in different sittings so you can bring a fresh perspective to the document each time.

This chapter recommends allocating ten separate editing sessions to review, revise, and polish each iteration of the draft for the following distinct purposes:

(1) Cross-checking each substantive component of the memorandum against a memorandum-drafting checklist.

(2) Reading the document as a whole in one sitting, focusing on the logic of the overall IREAC/CREAC analysis: Do the discussion and predicted outcome make logical sense?

(3) Reviewing the document at the section and/or paragraph level, focusing on the substantive logic of each standalone section and/or paragraph: Is each section and/or paragraph dedicated to a standalone topic that is addressed through an introduction (topic or thesis sentence), a discussion, and a mini-conclusion?

(4) Inspecting the document sentence-by-sentence: Will each sentence make grammatical and substantive sense to a reader who likely is unfamiliar with the subject matter? Is each sentence well structured, succinct, and understandable

(5) Reading the document on a word-by-word level to catch typographical and punctuation errors that are often missed during substantive reviews.

(6) Evaluating the document for professional and respectful tone and formality.

(7) Considering the document for audience interest: Is the client's story told in an engaging way? Will the reader care about the client's circumstances or the legal issue?

(8) Scanning the document at the full-page level (in hard copy) to catch formatting errors.

(9) Checking the accuracy of the legal citation throughout the document.

(10) Performing a final "out loud" read and conducting one last check to make sure the document conforms to the intended reader's formatting and submission rules.

These steps are most effective when they are performed separately, one at a time, in different editing sessions. Some levels of review will take longer than others. Before you begin editing, consult your calendar and map out a plan for tackling each step at a different time. Giving yourself even a short mental break between each task will make each round of review exponentially more effective. Of course, you already know how to proofread, but it is remarkable how many times an author can read a legal document and still miss picky details that a supervising attorney, client, judge, or opposing counsel will pick up right away at first glance. These steps will help you avoid that embarrassment and frustration.

III. Step 1: Cross-Checking the Document Against a Legal Memorandum-Drafting Checklists

Before you begin the substantive editing process, go through the following memorandum-drafting checklists to ensure that you followed the writing guidelines discussed in prior chapters and others provided by your professor.

The Question Presented Checklist

☑ Did I indicate what governing law applies? ("Under . . .")

☑ Did I identify the client by full name and give enough background context for a reader unfamiliar with the case to grasp the main legal issue to be discussed in the memo? ("Does . . .")

☑ Did I abbreviate the client's name in a respectful, clear manner and then use the same abbreviation throughout my memo? ("Does . . .")

☑ Did I ask the correct legal question posed by the client? ("Does . . .")

☑ Did I include the legally significant facts in a concise, organized, grammatically correct list, without assuming any prior knowledge by the reader? ("When . . .")

The Short Answer Checklist

- ☑ Did I answer the legal question "yes" or "no"?
- ☑ Did I cite the applicable rule?
  - ○ Can the rule be broken down into required *elements*, and if so, did I explain them clearly? Did I identify the element at issue (and, if applicable, carve out elements not at issue)?
  - ○ Can an element be further explained through a list of *factors* that a reader unfamiliar with the case could understand (e.g., avoiding abbreviations or shorthand not yet introduced)?
- ☑ Did I briefly and concisely apply the rule and predict a concrete outcome for the client?

The Statement of Facts (SOF) Checklist

- ☑ Did I describe *all* the legally significant facts that mirror the key parts of the rule (i.e., elements/factors)?
- ☑ Did I cross-check the discussion section against the SOF to make sure all the facts I relied on in my Rule Applications are also in the SOF?
- ☑ Did I properly cite to the factual record, if required?

The Discussion Section Checklist

Umbrella Paragraph

- ☑ Did I reiterate the issue, rule (and elements/factors, if applicable), and provide a concise prediction/conclusion?
- ☑ Did I vary the language from my short answer?

Rule Explanations (RE)

- ☑ Did I appropriately transition from the umbrella to the RE through a rule statement or a transition word/phrase?
- ☑ Did I follow the required RE format?
  - ○ Rule statement or transition, plus citation to the case
  - ○ Facts of the precedent case first
  - ○ A clear holding on the precise legal issue in question
  - ○ Rationale (describing each of the factors the court relied on in rendering its holding)
- ☑ Did I provide all the key case facts so an unfamiliar reader could understand the precedent case?
- ☑ Did I tie the holding to the legal issue being discussed and affecting my client as well?
- ☑ Did I use the past tense in describing the precedent case?

☑ Did I refrain from using the names of the parties in the precedent case (unless they are recognizable to the reader) and instead use readily applicable generic terms like "employee," "victim," or "officer"?

☑ Did I use transitions between multiple Rule Explanations?

Signal Cites and Explanatory Parentheticals (if applicable)

☑ Did I choose an appropriate signal to indicate that the case either supports or contrasts with the information just stated?

☑ Did I use proper citation form to cite the case?

☑ Did I start the explanatory parenthetical with an *-ing* word such as "holding that . . ."?

☑ Did I concisely weave in the facts, holding, and rationale of the case in three to four lines of text in the explanatory parenthetical?

☑ For punctuation within the explanatory parenthetical, did I stick to commas and semicolons (instead of using periods)?

Rule Applications (RA)

☑ Did I use a conclusory sentence to transition between my RE and RA?

☑ Did I organize the RA paragraphs around the components of the rule?

☑ Did I give each paragraph a topic/thesis sentence and a mini-conclusion?

☑ Did I address all the components of the rule and apply them to my client?

☑ If analogizing precedent cases to the client's case, did I italicize or underline the precedent case name (and not my client's name)?

☑ Did I consider adding a public policy argument?

Conclusion

☑ Did I state the prediction of the client's outcome in a clear manner so the reader can understand it and relay it to the client?

☑ Did I give a concrete answer to the client's question?

Once you have run through the entire set of memorandum-drafting checklists and made any necessary changes, print your memorandum in hard copy for the next phase of the master editing plan.

IV. Step 2: Reading for Overall Structure and Logic

The next step in the editing process is to take a *hard-copy* draft (you are much more likely to see errors on paper than on a computer screen) and read it straight through—cover to cover—solely for the purpose of evaluating its **structural logic and clarity**. The purpose of Step 2 is to check whether you lead the reader down a logical path. Is the rule framework clear? Does the analysis of the client's predicament—in light of that framework—make logical sense? Have you made any erroneous assumptions about your reader's knowledge of the case? At any point in the memo, have you accidentally assumed the reader knows as much about the facts and the law as you do? Does your analysis lead logically to the conclusion you provided?

As you read through this iteration of the document, seek out logic gaps and faulty assumptions, make notes in the margins, and circle areas that need to be clarified. When you are finished, fix those issues; then print the document again before moving on to the next editing phase.

V. Step 3: Reviewing Each Standalone Section and Paragraph for Structure and Clarity

Once you are satisfied that the structural logic of the overall memorandum will make sense to the reader, you are ready to move on to Step 3 in which you will review each standalone section and paragraph for organization and clarity. Now, rather than evaluating the document as a whole, you focus on the arc of each smaller component part.

For Step 3, in hard copy, read one section or paragraph of the memorandum at a time. Does each section or paragraph focus on a single key topic? Does it start with a clear topic/thesis sentence announcing that topic/thesis, address the subject concisely but thoroughly within the section or paragraph, and then conclude? During this examination, you may notice repetitive concepts or language that can be removed or rephrased. Watch, for instance, whether you state the rule in the umbrella paragraph and then repeat the same exact phrasing in the rule statement at the beginning of the first RE. Eliminate or replace words used too frequently. Your sections and paragraphs will tighten up and become more concise.

Good News if you are Having Word-Count or Page-Limit Problems

Step 3 will help you trim each section and paragraph. You will notice repetitiveness and see more clearly what text may be deleted.

"Be grateful for every word you can cut."
          • *William Zinsser* (author of *On Writing Well*)

During this editing phase, also notice whether you have smooth transitions between sections and paragraphs. Mini-conclusions at the end of one section/ paragraph and new topic/thesis sentences at the beginning of the next section/ paragraph facilitate effective transitions. Sometimes, simply adding a transition word or phrase might be all you need. Common transition words include "for example," "for instance," "further," "similarly," "likewise," "moreover," "in contrast," or "conversely."

Check the length of your paragraphs. Readers lose focus when a document requires them to absorb too much information without a natural mental break. Are any of your paragraphs getting close to a full page? Could you subdivide a long paragraph into two? Each paragraph should address a single, discrete topic. If you have a long paragraph covering nearly a page of precious memorandum real estate, assess whether you have combined two topics into the same paragraph and consider inserting a break. Your reader will appreciate it.

Once you finish Step 3, check your word-count or page limit, and then print the document in hard copy again.

VI. Step 4: Inspecting Each Sentence for Grammar, Clarity, and Concision

> "Every word that is unnecessary only pours over the side of a brimming mind."
> ● *Cicero (106-43 BC)*

The next phase of the editing process—sentence-level review—focuses on concision and precision. You cannot help but catch grammatical errors during this editing segment. Read each sentence as a standalone entity, and ask

- Are the terms used in this sentence readily identifiable to readers unfamiliar with the case? Or are names, events, or legal terms abbreviated without being explained previously?
- Are there any sentence fragments (incomplete thoughts) that should be converted into complete sentences?
- Are the subjects and verbs of each sentence clear?
- Are pronoun references (e.g., "it," "they," "he," "she") obvious?
- Is there any legalese that can be converted to your own "lawyer voice" in plain English?

A. Tips for Writing Concisely

Here are a few simple grammatical techniques for enhancing concision:

- Convert instances of passive voice to active voice, to tighten up sentences.

- Identify whether run-on sentences can be modified into a well-structured itemized list (using parallel grammatical structure).
- Eliminate legalese.
- Prune superfluous words and phrases to tighten each sentence.

1. Converting Passive Voice to Active Voice

You might remember from an English class in your distant past that there is a grammatical distinction between "active voice" and "passive voice." Here is a refresher.

A sentence uses active voice when it has the following sequence:

[A subject (the "actor")] + [an action verb] + [an object].

Example: The dog ate my legal memorandum.

A sentence uses passive voice when it has the following sequence:

[The object] + [verb] + [the actor].

Example: My legal memorandum was eaten by the dog.

Notice how the first sentence (using active voice) is six words while the second sentence (using passive voice) is eight words.

Consider another example:

Active: The police officer gave the driver a ticket. (8 words)

Passive: A ticket was given to the driver by the police officer. (11 words)

Active voice not only helps shorten sentences, even by trimming just a couple of words, but also creates a more engaging reading experience. The action moves faster and more vividly. Active voice also binds the actor to the act instead of creating distance between them. Consider one more example:

Passive: The motion that was filed by the plaintiff was decided by the judge in the plaintiff's favor. (17 words) *[Yuck.]*

Active: The judge granted the plaintiff's motion. (6 words)

The active voice example is punchier. You can almost hear the judge banging the gavel and saying "Motion granted."

Use active voice wherever possible; if you are not sure how to find instances of passive voice in the memo, do an electronic word search within the document for every instance of the word "was" or "were" and see whether you can make the sentence more action oriented. One tiny exception to this active voice preference is if you strategically need to create distance between a bad actor and a bad act. Some lawyers occasionally use passive voice to distance a perpetrator from a crime: "The retirement funds were depleted by the investment banker."

2. Creating Concise and Useful Lists, Using Parallel Grammatical Structure

Lists are a great way to combine a series of linked information in a succinct manner. Consider the following contrasting examples:

Examples

Version 1 (using passive voice and a series of nouns): She started her job at the law firm and was given a softball t-shirt. She also received a game schedule. Additionally, she was e-mailed a team sign-up sheet. (28 words)

Version 2 (using active voice and a list): The law firm gave the new associate a softball t-shirt, a game schedule, and a team sign-up sheet. (18 words)

Version 1 (using passive voice and a series of details): The robbery victim sustained an injury to the back of his head by a karate chop. His wallet and Rolex watch were stolen by the perpetrator. The victim's ATM card was used by the perpetrator to steal $200. (38 words)

Version 2 (using active voice and a list): The perpetrator karate-chopped the back of the victim's neck, stole his wallet and Rolex watch, and used his ATM card to pilfer $200. (23 words)

One crucial requirement in constructing concise and useful lists is the use of parallel grammatical structure when crafting the itemized components. Consider the following example:

Version 1 (list lacking parallel grammatical structure):

In evaluating whether to classify a beer bottle opener as a deadly weapon, Texas courts consider the following five factors: (1) physical proximity between the victim and the offending object; (2) the assailant communicated threats or words while using the object; (3) assessing the size and shape of the object; (4) whether the object has the ability to inflict death or serious injury; and (5) the manner in which the perpetrator used the object.

The five parts of this list constitute four different grammatical structures—presenting a challenging mental task for a reader. Items (1) and (5) are nouns. Item (2) is a complete sentence. Item (3) is a sentence fragment starting with a gerund (a verb ending with -*ing*). Item (4) is a conditional phrase. To make this list much stronger, the writer can re-write the five list components so they have parallel grammatical structure:

Version 2 (list using parallel grammatical structure):

In evaluating whether to classify a beer bottle opener as a deadly weapon, Texas courts consider the following five factors: (1) the physical proximity between the victim and the object; (2) any threats or words used by the assailant; (3) the size and shape of the object; (4) the object's ability to inflict death or serious injury; and (5) the manner in which the assailant used the object.

Now all five list components are nouns.

3. Eliminating Legalese and Instead Using Your Authentic Voice

Many new legal writers feel obligated to begin sentences with words or phrases that sound like something a lawyer would say but that really just take up valuable space on the page and communicate nothing of substance.

Examples

It is the party's position that . . .

It is the defendant's argument that . . .

It is the plaintiff's contention that . . .

One might make the assertion that . . .

One could argue that . . .

It appears that . . .

The client might have a good argument that . . .

The defendant could take the position that . . .

It seems that . . .

There is a possible argument that . . .

Look for sentences containing language such as "contention," "argument," "position," "assertion," "argue," etc., and see whether you need that phrasing at all to make the point.

4. Deleting Superflous Words

Most sentences can be shortened very easily by deleting superflous words.

Examples

Version 1: It makes sense that McKinney refused to comply with the subpoena because _____.

Version 2: McKinney challenged the subpoena because _____.

Version 1: Even though Meyer disputed any liability, she eventually made the resolution to settle the case.

Version 2: Although disputing liability, Meyer settled the case.

B. Tips for Using Direct Quotations from Legal Sources

If you are incorporating direct quotations from case file documents, statutes, or precedent cases, follow these tips:

- If you are including a direct quote in a memorandum, use the exact language from the source, put quotations around the text, and then provide the correct citation.

- If you delete words to shorten the quote (without changing the content or nature of the quote), use an ellipsis (three periods in a row) to indicate the deletion.
- If you need to add or modify words for a quotation to make grammatical sense or provide clarifying information, use [brackets] to indicate the addition or change.
- If you add bold typeface, italics, or underlining to a quote, put "emphasis added" in parentheses after the quote.
- If the quote runs longer than three lines of text, convert it to a block quote: insert a line space before the quote, indent the quote on both sides, single-space it, and do not put quotation marks around it. Then insert a line space after the quote and include the cite for the quote on the next line without indenting it.

VII. Step 5: Reading the Document Word by Word to Catch Typographical and Punctuation Errors

When editing an intellectually complex legal document for substance, logic, and clarity, it is difficult to catch proofreading errors because your mind is concentrating diligently on so many other things. It is essential to set aside a round of editing solely to check the spelling of each word and the punctuation in every sentence. One trick to this editing phase is to print the document and read it backwards. When your brain is not focused on processing substance, it is more likely to notice words that seem out of place, odd punctuation, or missing quotation marks.

Spellcheck will not catch every typographical error in a legal document; certain words that are very similar to legal terminology simply are not misspelled:

statute v. statue
contract v. contact
marital v. martial
trial v. trail

Read the document backwards and look for words that have no logical place in your memo.

Watch for the following common proofreading and editing errors:

- Misplaced or missing apostrophes: If you have two nouns next to each other, the first one likely needs an apostrophe, to demonstrate "possession." If you have a plural noun that is also possessing an item, the apostrophe goes after the "s" in the plural noun.
- The difference between semicolons and commas: Semicolons join two complete sentences (or can be used in lists). If the language on either side

of a semicolon cannot stand alone as a separate sentence or is not part of a list, use another form of punctuation (e.g., a comma, a colon). Hint: The word "however" appearing in the middle of a sentence often introduces a standalone concept. If so, it needs a semicolon before it.

- Incorrect use of pronouns: Many new legal writers mistakenly use the pronoun "they" to refer to a singular but gender-neutral entity—such as a court or a company. However, the pronouns "they" and "their" are plural and therefore cannot refer to singular noun. You should refer to the court or a company as "it."
- The word "it's" means "it is." "Its" is the possessive form.
- Take out all contractions in legal writing, such as "can't," "didn't," "isn't," and "they're."
- Do *not* omit articles ("a," "an," or "the") to save space.

VIII. Step 6: Evaluating the Document for a Professional, Respectful Tone and Formal Language

In today's world of text and e-mail messages, Facebook posts, and Twitter tweets, writers have become accustomed to informal, abbreviated language and emoticons. However, in legal writing—whether in the form of an e-mail to a boss, a legal memorandum, a letter to a client or opposing counsel, or a brief to the court—writers need to reengage with formal language, tone, and style. During Step 6 of the editing process, evaluate your document with the following advice in mind:

- Take out references to "I," "me," "we," and "you." Sometimes a new legal writer will communicate to the supervising attorney as though the written document is a face-to-face casual conversation, using language like "I believe we have a good case because . . ." Or "We should prevail because . . ." Focus not on yourself but on the client, the facts, the law, and what a court would do. Use nouns like "the court," "the client," or "the parties," or descriptive role labels like "the company," "the police officer," or "the customer."
- Remove all contractions, such as "can't," "didn't," "won't," or "she's."
- Avoid sarcasm or attempts at humor.
- Avoid slang, clichés, shortcuts, or euphemisms.
- Be respectful to the client's circumstances; no matter how outlandish you may personally believe the client's facts are, you must approach the legal analysis with at least some level of empathy and dedication to providing well-reasoned legal advice.
- Always assume your document will be circulated to individuals other than its originally intended recipient (including the client).

IX. Step 7: Reviewing the Document for Its Audience Interest and Engagement

Even though you are writing about important, serious, sometimes complex, or perhaps business-oriented legal topics, you can still make your writing interesting to read. Tell your client's story using visually descriptive language, active verbs, illustrative terminology to define the parties in the precedent cases (rather than simply "plaintiff" or "defendant"), and specific factual details to support the analysis (rather than simply stating "the elements are satisfied"). Even if your client is a corporate entity, you can still invoke a storytelling narrative to engage the reader.

X. Step 8: Scanning Each Page for Formatting Glitches

The next step of the editing process is the quickest and requires the least amount of brain power. Print out the document and literally flip through each page, solely scanning the page for visual formatting issues. Check and fix any glitches with the following:

- Dangling headings or one-liner "widow-orphan" sentences lingering at the bottom of the page (insert a page break to place the dangler at the top of the next page)
- Visual consistency in
    - heading format (spacing, bold typeface or underlining, capitalization)
    - font type and size
    - heading and paragraph indentation
    - spacing between paragraphs and beneath headings
    - margins
- Paragraph and sentence length
- Formatting of block quotations
- Page numbering

XI. Step 9: Checking Each Legal Citation

The next phase of the editing process is also rather simple and should not take as much time as some of the other steps. During Step 9, take a hard-copy printout of your document and highlight all the legal citations. Then solely focus on those citations, checking for proper *Bluebook* or *ALWD* form in full cites, short cites, and *"Id."* cites. This process will help you catch citation errors that your eyes might gloss over when reading for substance, logic, and standard proofreading. Note and fix inconsistencies in italicizing or underlining of case names, confusion between short cites and *"Id."* cites, and mistakes in pinpoint page references (i.e., the pinpoint page cites are referring to pages from a different reporter than the original full cite).

XII. Step 10: Final Review and Double-Checking the Formatting and Submission Guidelines

As you approach the memorandum deadline, print out the document one more time and read it aloud. One final read-aloud should help you catch any lingering longwinded sentences or awkward phrasing. If your professor provided a grading rubric, cross-check the final memorandum against the rubric to strive to meet and exceed expectations as much as possible. Review the formatting and submission guidelines in the course policies. Have you followed the rules for "anonymizing" your paper if your professor requires anonymous grading? Have you saved the document in a non-redline format so your "tracked changes" are not showing in the final version? Have you familiarized yourself with electronic submission requirements? If you are submitting the paper in hard copy, have you printed it out and again checked every page to make sure it printed correctly?

If you have followed all these steps, congratulations. As you submit your assignment, make sure you retain a time-stamp or copy of the submission e-mail (cc yourself to make sure the e-mail went through).

EDITING EXERCISES

Word Economy Exercises

1. Rewrite the following 102-word sentence into fewer than 25 words:

Our client, a winemaker and owner of a Long Island vineyard, Derek Zachary, has contacted this law firm in an effort to seek counsel with regards to a letter he received from lawyers of the New York law firm Tigre & Hammerhead, LLP, who are representing a professional basketball player named Jack Sampson, threatening legal action under the New York Civil Rights Act, N.Y. Civ. Rights Law §§50 & 51, as a result of a Photoshop label that our client decided to have transferred onto the side of a recent vintage of wine bottles that contain a particular type of Zinfandel.

_____

_____

_____

_____

2. Rewrite the following 105-word sentence into fewer than 25 words:

Unlike the claimant professional boxing champion who sued for violation of his right to privacy in *Ali*, the court likely will make a finding that the depiction on the side of Zachary's wine bottle does not reflect a recognizable likeness of at least the face of Sampson because the facial characteristics discussed by the court in *Ali*, which include but are not limited to the person's hair, eyes, cheekbones and mouth, are not recognizable as Sampson on the wine bottle because the face is completely blurry and therefore does not perpetuate the suggestion of the presumably famous NBA basketball player as a matter of law.

_____

_____

_____

_____

3. Rewrite the following 32-word sentence into fewer than 20 words:

Precedent cases under New York law provide us information about several factors that courts will consider in making a determination to hold whether or not an image constitutes a portrait or picture.

_____

_____

_____

_____

_____

Parallel Structure Exercises

1. Rewrite this sentence so that the list uses parallel structure (and make any other editing changes you think will help make it more concise):

> The courts of the State of New York have determined there are three essential and important factors used to make a decision with regard to whether an image might be considered to constitute a "portrait or picture": (1) is the image a "recognizable likeness" of the claimant, and not just a character, costume, or personality; (2) captures the "essence" of the claimant; and (3) recognizable to someone familiar with the person.

_____

_____

_____

2. Rewrite this sentence so that the list uses parallel structure:

> The staging of the video store print ad called to mind the characteristics of the famous actor, Woody Allen, in several ways: VCR cassettes of films directed by or acted in by the celebrity strategically were positioned on the store counter; the signature hairstyle and expression worn by the look-alike; the image included a lady smiling at the customer agape in enthusiasm at the presence of a celebrity; and the text next to the ad which stated, "Become a V.I.P. at National Video. We'll Make You Feel Like a Star," and "you don't need a famous face to be treated to some pretty famous service."

_____

_____

_____

3. Rewrite this sentence so that the list uses parallel structure:

> The court considered the factors that gave rise to the airline's decision to remove the passenger from the flight including but not limited to the existing flight delays due to a pending storm, whether the passenger refused to comply with the flight attendant's safety instructions, the passenger tried to enter the first class cabin without permission, refusal to stow luggage, and whether he was disruptive to fellow travelers.

_____

_____

_____

Chapter 19

Adding Levels of Sophistication to a Legal Analysis

Now that you have been through all the basic steps of drafting a well-structured first legal memorandum (based on the guidance in Chapters 1 to 18), you are ready to refine your technique with each subsequent writing project. The analytical processes and strategic decisions discussed in this chapter will help you add levels of sophistication to a new writing assignment. Once you have mastered the basic IREAC or CREAC formula, consider these steps to deepen your legal analysis and make it even more helpful to the reader.

I. Brainstorm Different Ways of Organizing a Legal Analysis Around the Components of the Rule

Sophisticated legal writers take time to organize and outline their analysis before writing. While the fundamental writing formulas (IREAC, CREAC) will remain largely the same from memorandum to memorandum, good legal writers make tweaks and adjustments as their writing skills evolve, to construct a written analysis in a way that best explains the rule to an unfamiliar reader and applies its component parts to the client facts. If you are writing about a complicated legal rule, take time to really ponder the best way to organize the memorandum to cover each component part of that particular rule. If the rule has three parts, consider whether the parts can be addressed collectively in one IREAC or whether they might be more helpful in three separate IREAC analyses (separated by descriptive headings). Try outlining the analysis a few different ways. You can always change your mind about the best organizational strategy, so allow yourself to get creative. What works best for a three-element rule in one memorandum might not work as effectively for a five-factor rule in another memorandum.

Experiment with different organizational frameworks to find the one that helps you write most clearly about the given legal issue.

II. Be Strategic in Choosing Case Law for the Memorandum

After writing your first legal research memorandum—which may have required analysis of only three or four cases selected by your professor—eventually you will be conducting your own research, which will yield a larger number of cases to synthesize and discuss. Mindful legal writers do not simply choose the first three or four cases that pop into their minds and then churn out Rule Explanations thereon. Instead, thoughtful writers take the time to carefully select the most informative cases that will illustrate the rule in the clearest and most accurate way possible, and then compare and contrast those cases with the client's facts. Consider creating a memorandum worksheet like the one described in Chapter 13 to prioritize the case law, create smaller subgroups of cases that most effectively illustrate subcomponents of the rule, and choose cases that would best serve as full Rule Explanations or as signal cites with explanatory parentheticals. Also evaluate the most useful chronological order in which to place the cases. You might consider organizing the cases by element or factor, by holdings that favor and then disfavor your client, or in a continuum of results (demonstrating to the reader where along the spectrum your client's case falls). Mindful legal writers include a substantial amount of precedent in a memorandum, but without overwhelming the reader. Choose the cases that best explain the rule, write succinct yet informative Rule Explanations, and consider using advanced citation (signal cites plus explanatory parentheticals) to incorporate additional case law into the memorandum without distracting from or cluttering the analysis.

III. Construct Helpful Headings and Smooth Transitions Between Parts of the Memorandum

Thoughtful legal writers craft informative and descriptive headings (see Chapter 13) between component parts of the memo, and insert elegant transitions between paragraphs and sections, to move the reader along seamlessly without jolting directional changes. Take some time to review your draft and discern where transitions (like road signs) are missing, too abrupt, or confusing. If you encounter several pages of text with no visual breaks, compose helpful headings to serve as billboards for the reader about what the next section covers. Make sure your headings are structured in a parallel grammatical format; develop a phrasing pattern or rhythm that the reader can easily follow.

IV. When Applying the Rule to Your Client's Facts, Think About the Underlying Societal Purpose of the Law

When applying a rule to a client's factual scenario, refined legal writers do not simply ping-pong back and forth between the rule elements or factors and the client facts and then robotically deliver a predicted result, like an automated receipt at an ATM. Indeed, thoughtful writers methodically apply each component of the rule to the client's facts and then predict a logical outcome, remaining mindful of the underlying societal purpose and function of the law. This is where a written reflection on public policy concepts can transform a basic legal analysis into a more sophisticated one. Think about what intention and objective the lawmakers had when originally creating the rule: Was it to promote fairness? Equity? Order? Economic benefit? Safety? Health? Consider writing a paragraph in the Rule Application section of the memorandum that weaves in a discussion of the public policy behind the rule and how the predicted result generated through your methodical analysis furthers that public policy goal.

V. Honing Your Prose

Mindful legal writers take time to sit with their writing, listen to the text speaking back from the page, and think carefully about whether changes to language choice and phrasing would enhance the readability of, and reader engagement with, the legal analysis, making it clear yet interesting for the reader. Instead of racing toward the editing finish line, let the document steep a bit. Read it aloud. Regard each word, sentence, paragraph, page, or section as an opportunity to tell the client's story and relay the narratives of the precedent cases to your supervising attorney. Have you incorporated enough description so that the reader can picture each scene? Have you varied the phrasing in your sentences and paragraphs so you are not repeating the same banal words or legal terminology over and over? Experiment with descriptive nouns and strong concrete verbs. Use active voice. Be visual and tangible.

VI. Check for Logic Gaps and Faulty Assumptions

Mindful legal writers care about and have empathy for their readers. They routinely ask themselves: Will this make sense to an audience unfamiliar with the facts or law? Consult Chapter 14 to learn how to spot and remedy logic leaps and faulty assumptions that will confuse and frustrate the reader. The more you envision your reader as a real human being sitting down at a desk with your memorandum in hand, and imagine how he or she will intellectually process the words on your pages, the more likely you are to identify clarity gaps, fill logic holes, and present a tightened-up final work product that makes analytical sense to your audience.

VII. Edit, Edit, Edit

Good legal writers constantly edit their work—in thoughtfully paced phases to approach each editing task with fresh eyes—until it absolutely must leave their hands. Use the ten-level editing process explained in Chapter 18 to continuously fine-tune your work. The more time spent performing each of the ten editing phases, the more second-nature your self-editing abilities will become. Your writing will continue to improve with every draft and new assignment.

Section 6

Expanding and Contracting IREAC/CREAC to Fit an Audience's Needs

Chapter 20

Tackling a Multi-Issue Legal Office Memorandum Assignment

Once you have successfully navigated the process of drafting a single-issue legal memorandum using the IREAC or CREAC formula, you may be tasked with writing a new memorandum addressing more than one legal issue or perhaps several elements of a rule in separate IREAC or CREAC analyses. Because longer, more complex memoranda are more challenging to write and read, adopting a clear organizational structure becomes even more critically important during the drafting process. Once you establish that your memorandum entails more than one issue or requires substantive examination of numerous prongs of a rule, take some time to thoughtfully outline an IREAC/CREAC framework for each issue or topic. Use interim headings as signposts or billboards to indicate to the audience when you are transitioning from one discussion point to the next.

For example, imagine your supervising attorney has asked you to write a legal memorandum predicting whether a criminal defendant likely will be found guilty of violating a particular subsection of New Jersey's multipart aggravated assault statute, specifically the subsection governing reckless assault with a deadly weapon. This particular subsection of the crime of aggravated assault has five elements. The perpetrator must

(1) recklessly
(2) cause
(3) bodily injury
(4) to another
(5) with a deadly weapon.

In this hypothetical example, after reviewing the facts of your newly assigned client matter, you are able to determine from the documentary record that the particular assailant's physical act indisputably caused bodily injury to another person; thus, elements 2 through 4 are not in question. However, the notions of whether the perpetrator acted "recklessly" (element 1) and whether she used a "deadly weapon" (element 5) require further scrutiny.

In this legal writing scenario, your memorandum should address these two discrete legal issues independently; each concept might require study and consideration of completely different case law (Rule Explanations) and an application of the synthesized rules from those cases to distinct sets of facts (Rule Applications). In a law office environment, a supervisory attorney could designate two different junior attorneys to write two completely separate memoranda, each tackling one prong of the statutory rule. Alternatively, one writer could address the dual legal issues in a single memoranda, so long as the document (1) incorporates clear headings subdividing the two analyses, and (2) presents two separate IREAC/CREAC structures, the first predicting an outcome on the "recklessness" issue and the second forecasting the likely result on the "deadly weapon" issue. Here is one possible organizational outline for the foregoing writing task.

MEMORANDUM

TO:
FROM:
DATE:
RE:

QUESTIONS PRESENTED

Overall Question Presented on whether the defendant likely will be found guilty of the crime of aggravated assault under the particular subsection of the New Jersey statute—which requires the defendant to have "recklessly caused bodily injury to another with a deadly weapon"

1. Sub-Question Presented #1 (whether the defendant acted "recklessly")
2. Sub-Question Presented #2 (whether the defendant used a "deadly weapon")

BRIEF ANSWERS

Overall Brief Answer
Global rule (the pertinent section of the aggravated assault statute: 5 elements)
Identification of the 3 statutory elements *not* at issue (causation, bodily injury, to another)
Narrowing of the 2 elements *at* issue (recklessness and deadly weapon)

1. Sub-Brief Answer #1 (answering the Question Presented of whether the defendant acted "recklessly")
2. Sub-Brief Answer #2 (answering the Question Presented of whether the defendant used a "deadly weapon")

Overall Outcome Prediction (based on the answers to the two sub-brief answers)

STATEMENT OF FACTS

DISCUSSION

Umbrella Paragraph

Issue: Overall issue of whether the defendant likely will be found guilty of the crime of aggravated assault under the particular subsection of the New Jersey statute ("recklessly causing bodily injury to another with a deadly weapon")

Rule: The particular subsection of the New Jersey statute setting forth the 5 elements of the crime of aggravated assault:

(1) Recklessly
(2) Caused
(3) Bodily injury
(4) To another
(5) Using a deadly weapon

Identification of elements *not* at issue (causation, bodily injury, to another)
Identification of the two elements *at* issue: (1) recklessness, (2) deadly weapon
Brief conclusory sentence foreshadowing of the overall prediction

I. Heading #1 (Well-Constructed Heading Summarizing the "Recklessness" Issue)

Umbrella Paragraph
 Issue: Sub-issue of whether the defendant acted "recklessly"
 Rule: Definition of "recklessness" (Statute? Synthesized case rule?)
 Brief conclusory sentence foreshadowing of prediction on "reckless-
 ness" issue
Rule Explanation(s) (REs): Choose the most appropriate cases to illustrate the rule through Rule Explanations and signal cites + explanatory parentheticals (with helpful transitions between REs)
Rule Application: Apply the rule defining "recklessness" to the facts
Mini-conclusion: Predict how a court would rule on the "recklessness" issue

II. Heading #2 (Well-Constructed Heading Summarizing the "Deadly Weapon" Issue)

Umbrella Paragraph
 Issue: Sub-issue of whether the defendant used a "deadly weapon"
 Rule: Definition of "deadly weapon" (Statute? Synthesized case rule?)
 Brief conclusory sentence foreshadowing of prediction on "deadly
 weapon" issue
Rule Explanation(s): Choose the most appropriate cases to illustrate the rule through Rule Explanations and signal cites + explanatory parentheticals (with helpful transitions between REs)
Rule Application: Apply the rule defining "deadly weapon" to the facts
Mini-conclusion: Predict how a court would rule on the "deadly weapon" issue

III. <u>Overall Conclusion</u>

Summarize how the court likely would rule on all 5 elements of the pertinent subsection of the New Jersey aggravated assault statute

The foregoing is just one example of how to construct a two-issue legal memorandum. Your memorandum might involve three or four issues or subsections of a rule, each of which deserves its own IREAC or CREAC treatment. So long as you (1) identify the discrete legal issues requiring individual attention, (2) use numbered or lettered headings and subheadings to separate each IREAC/CREAC discussion, and (3) methodically evaluate each legal issue through a thorough IREAC/CREAC examination, your reader should be able to follow even the most multifaceted memorandum.

Chapter 21

Drafting Shorter Memoranda and E-mail Communications

The law office memorandum format discussed throughout this book remains alive and well at law offices across the country. The memorandum remains a useful analytical tool for supervising attorneys advising clients. However, you also might work with lawyers who prefer shorter memoranda or even abbreviated e-mail communications transmitting research results and client recommendations. Some research assignments may be as simple as: "What is the statute of limitations in Georgia for a breach of contract action?" Or, "In a case pending in a federal court in Virginia, how many days does a party have to serve objections to a set of requests for production of documents?" Or, "In a medical malpractice case pending in Michigan, must a plaintiff offer expert testimony to the jury about the appropriate standard of care for doctors?" For these types of legal questions, a lengthy memorandum with the traditional format of question presented, brief answer, statement of facts, discussion (using IREAC or CREAC), and conclusion indeed may be excessive. Instead, it might suffice for you to provide (1) a short, succinct reminder to the supervising attorney of the issue you were asked to research, and (2) a clear and concrete answer to the question. This form of communication may require no more than a single paragraph. As always, the key is clarity and precision.

I. Short Memoranda Answering a Discrete Legal Question

Even if you are answering a simple, straightforward legal question (which some attorneys refer to as a "quick-hitter" research assignment), a supervising attorney still might prefer the research results to be delivered in writing instead of orally. Even in such an abbreviated mode of delivery, you still want your written work product to appear professional and readable.

If you are conveying your research results in a hard-copy written communication (rather than an e-mail), start by using the same memorandum header you would for a longer memorandum:

MEMORANDUM

TO: Lucy Van Dorn, Esq.
FROM: Chuck Brown, Summer Associate
DATE: March 26, 2017
RE: Michael McInerney; Client File No. 3-26; Requirement
             of Expert Testimony on the Applicable Standard of Care
             in a Medical Malpractice Action in Michigan

The header provides the supervising attorney with the same information a longer memorandum would: the date of the work product, the client name, the case file number, and a helpful description of the subject matter of the communication.

The body of an effective, short "quick-hitter" memorandum restates the legal question you were asked to answer and then provides a brief synopsis of your findings.

Example 1 (Short Memorandum Conveying an Answer to an Evidence Question)

You have asked me to research whether a plaintiff in a medical malpractice action in the State of Michigan is required to present an expert witness at trial to testify regarding the applicable standard of care of a doctor. The answer is yes. For example, in *Harrington v. Casale*, No. 291211, 2010 WL 4106688 (Mich. Ct. App. Oct. 19, 2010), a patient sued a doctor for negligence. The patient argued that her tort action against the doctor sounded in ordinary negligence because it did not raise questions of medical judgment beyond the realm of common knowledge and experience, and therefore, expert testimony was unnecessary to resolve the matter. *Id.* at *1. The trial court disagreed and granted summary disposition in favor of the doctor when the patient failed to present expert testimony regarding the applicable standard of care. *Id.* The court explained that, in order for the jury to determine whether the doctor's care and exercise of medical judgment was reasonable under the circumstances, the testimony of an expert—a member of the same profession and who practices in the same field as the doctor—would be necessary. *Id.*

Example 2 (Short Memorandum Transmitting a Discovery Rule)

Here is another example of a short "quick-hitter" memorandum assignment, answering a narrowly focused question about a discovery rule.

MEMORANDUM

TO: Lucy Van Dorn, Esq.
FROM: Chuck Brown, Summer Associate
DATE: March 26, 2017
RE: Atlantic Tinting Consultants; Case File 11-8; Deadline
            for Serving Discovery Objections

You have asked me to research the number of days within which a party must serve objections to discovery requests, including requests for production of documents, under the rules of the United States District Court for the Eastern District of Virginia. According to Local Rule 26(C) of the Rules of the United States District Court for the Eastern District of Virginia, a party has **fifteen (15) days** to serve discovery objections after receipt of the discovery requests, even though the actual responses are not due until thirty (30) days after receipt of the requests. The rule states as follows:

<u>Objections to Discovery Process</u>: Unless otherwise ordered by the Court, an objection to any interrogatory, request, or application under Fed. R. Civ. P. 26 through 37, shall be served within fifteen (15) days after the service of the interrogatories, request, or application; or, in a case removed or transferred to this Court after discovery was served, within fifteen (15) days after the date of removal or transfer.

Example 3 (Short Memorandum Communicating a Procedural Rule)

Here is another example of a short "quick-hitter" memorandum assignment, answering a straightforward question about a procedural rule.

MEMORANDUM

TO: Lucy Van Dorn, Esq.
FROM: Chuck Brown, Summer Associate
DATE: March 26, 2017
RE: Penske Appeal; Case File 1-14; Required Components
            of the Appellate Brief

You have asked me to research the required components for the appellate brief due on April 15, 2017, in the Penske Appeal. Rule 28 of the Alabama Rules of Appellate Procedure requires appellants to include eleven items in the appeal brief: (1) a statement requesting oral argument, (2) a table of contents, (3) a statement of jurisdiction, (4) a table of authorities, (5) a statement of the case, (6) a statement of the issues, (7) a statement of the facts, (8) a statement of the standard of review, (9) a summary of the argument, (10) the argument, and (11) a conclusion.

Example 4 (Short Memorandum Providing a Statute Cite)

Sometimes, a supervising attorney might ask you to find a citation for a statute that answers a very clear-cut legal question. You might convey your research results in a short memorandum as follows.

MEMORANDUM

TO: Lucy Van Dorn, Esq.
FROM: Chuck Brown, Summer Associate
DATE: March 26, 2017
RE: Statute of Limitations for a Breach of Contract Action Under
          Georgia Law

You asked me to find the statute of limitations for a breach of contract action under Georgia law. According to Ga. Code Ann. § 9-3-24 (West 2014), "All actions upon simple contracts in writing shall be brought within six years after the same become due and payable."

Example 5 (Short Memorandum Transmitting a Statute and a Case Cite)

Another time, a supervising attorney might ask you to find a single statute or a case that defines a particular legal term—without yet applying that definition to the client's facts. You might convey your research results in a short memorandum as follows.

MEMORANDUM

TO: Olivia Fields, Esq.
FROM: Sloan McDonald, Associate
DATE: July 1, 2017
RE: Dylan Fontaine; File No. 2-10; Case Defining
          "Deadly Weapon" Under Ohio Law

You have asked me to find an Ohio statute or case defining the legal term "deadly weapon." Ohio Rev. Code § 2923.11(A) (Baldwin 1972) defines a "deadly weapon" as "any instrument, device, or thing capable of inflicting death, and designed or specially adapted for use as a weapon, or possessed, carried, or used as a weapon." When evaluating whether an otherwise innocuous item qualifies as a deadly weapon under Ohio's felonious assault statute, courts consider (1) the size and weight of the item, (2) the shape and design of the item, (3) the ability of the item to be grasped in the hands of the user in such a way that it may be used on or directed against the body of another, and (4) the ability of the item to be used in a manner and with sufficient force to kill the other person. *See, e.g., State v. Redmon*, No. CA-7938, 1990 WL 94745 (Ohio Ct. App. June 25, 1990) (holding that a wooden rocking chair was a deadly weapon when swung by a perpetrator at a woman's head); *State v. Salinas*, No. F-84-8, 1985 WL 7568 (Ohio Ct. App. July 26, 1985) (holding that a jury reasonably could find that a baseball bat constituted a deadly weapon when the perpetrator swung the bat at a victim, causing injury to his jaw, ribs, and arms); *State v. Deboe*, 62 Ohio App. 2d 192, 406 N.E.2d 536 (1977) (holding that a club-like instrument three inches in diameter wrapped in spongy material, which the perpetrator swung rapidly at the victim, hitting him 15 or 20 times on the head, arms, back, shoulders, and kidneys, causing black and blue welts and bruises, constituted a deadly weapon).

Example 6 (Short Memorandum Summarizing a Contract Review)

Sometimes, a supervising attorney might ask you to review a particular legal document, like a contract, and highlight any key points or potential pitfalls. A short memo summarizing your findings might look like this.

MEMORANDUM

TO: Lucy Van Dorn, Esq.
FROM: Chuck Brown, Summer Associate
DATE: March 26, 2017
RE: The Anna Miller Gallery; Case File 6-3; Contract Review

Pursuant to your request, I performed a detailed review of the proposed Construction Contract between the Anna Miller Gallery ("Owner") and the Michelangelo Group ("Contractor"). In this memorandum, I have summarized key provisions to which Owner should pay close attention during contract negotiations, and have recommended changes to better protect Owner's interests. I also have marked some unusual provisions that Owner should review, be thoroughly familiar with, and further discuss with Contractor prior to executing the Agreement.

Contract Provisions

Article 1.6: "Third Party Consultant Services": In this provision, Contractor states that it will be reviewing and approving invoices of third parties. Owner might wish to consider inserting language stating "upon request by Owner" (if Owner wants to monitor whose invoices Contractor is reviewing and approving).

Article 1.7: "Payment to Third Parties": The last sentence should clarify who is making such payments and whether such entity is cross-checking such payment requests against the project budget.

[*This memo could be as short or as long as necessary to address all the key contract terms.*]

II. Short but Professional E-mails Communicating Research Results

If the supervising attorney is on the go, she may prefer to receive your research results in a professionally crafted, concise e-mail rather than in a printed document. The content of the e-mail should be the same as the "quick-hitter" memoranda discussed earlier in this chapter: no more than one or two paragraphs reminding the supervising attorney what she asked you to research and then precisely answering the question posed.

Example 1 (E-mail Summarizing the Definition of a Legal Term)

TO: rkbrowning@browningclayllp.com
FROM: clagrande@browningclayllp.com
DATE: September 11, 2017
RE: **Precipice Foundation LLC; Definition of "Common Interest" Privilege**

At your request, I researched the definition of the "common interest" privilege and its applicability to Precipice Foundation LLC's business activities with its affiliate, Edge & Associates. For the common interest privilege to attach, the two parties must have in common an identical interest in securing legal advice related to the same matter, and the communications must be made to advance their shared interest in securing legal advice on that common matter. The "common interest" privilege is limited to communication between counsel and parties with respect to legal advice in a pending or reasonably anticipated litigation in which the parties have a common legal interest. The party asserting the privilege must establish that (1) the communications were made in the course of a joint defense effort, (2) the communication was designed to further the effort, and (3) neither party has waived the privilege. Courts examining this issue have found that the shared interest must be "legal," not solely commercial, financial, or related to a mutual business strategy. Some courts also have noted that the doctrine does not protect a joint business strategy that happens to include a concern about litigation. Some courts have given credit to parties' memorialization of their common interest in a Common Interest Agreement or a Joint Defense Agreement. *See Beneficial Franchise Co., Inc. v. Bank One, N.A.*, 205 F.R.D. 212 (N.D. Ill. 2001); *Tobaccoville USA, Inc. v. McMaster*, 692 S.E.2d 526 (S.C. 2010). However, other courts have stated that a private agreement by the parties to protect communications cannot create a privilege. *Aetna Cas. & Sur. Co. v. Certain Underwriters at Lloyd's London*, 676 N.Y.S.2d 727 (N.Y. Sup. Ct. 1998).

Either way, Precipice Foundation LLC should memorialize its intent to protect communications that legitimately fall under the "common interest" umbrella (i.e., legal issues, rather than solely commercial, financial, or business strategy issues) in a Common Interest Agreement. In the event of a pending or reasonably anticipated litigation, the client should execute a Joint Defense Agreement.

Example 2 (E-mail Forwarding a Research Memorandum)

At times, the supervising attorney might want you to transmit a lengthy law office memorandum using a cover e-mail, which might look like this:

TO: rkbrowning@browningclayllp.com
FROM: clagrande@browningclayllp.com
DATE: September 11, 2017
RE: **Precipice Foundation LLC; Research Memorandum Regarding Enforceability of Forum Selection Clauses**

Rick: Attached please find the legal research memorandum you requested regarding the enforceability of forum selection clauses in the various states in which our client, Precipice Foundation LLC, conducts business. Please let me know whether you have any questions or need additional follow-up research. Thank you very much. Cassidy

III. Administrative E-mails Within the Law Office Environment

In addition to conveying substantive research results to a supervising attorney via e-mail, you likely will need to communicate electronically with law office personnel regarding tangential and administrative issues (e.g., requesting additional assignments, clarifying the scope of an assignment, transmitting timesheets). These types of e-mails should be written in the same tone, style, and manner as the substantive e-mails discussed above.

Example 1 (E-mail Requesting Additional Assignments)

TO: rkbrowning@browningclayllp.com
FROM: clagrande@browningclayllp.com
DATE: September 11, 2017
RE: Workload

Rick: I completed the Precipice Foundation LLC memorandum and am available for additional assignments at your convenience. Please let me know whether you have any research projects with which you need assistance. Thank you very much. Cassidy

Example 2 (E-mail Requesting Clarification on an Assignment)

TO: rkbrowning@browningclayllp.com
FROM: clagrande@browningclayllp.com
DATE: September 11, 2017
RE: Precipice Foundation LLC; Question Regarding Scope of Research

Rick: I have begun researching the issue of the enforceability of forum selection clauses for our client, Precipice Foundation LLC, and had a quick question regarding the scope of the assignment. Did you want me to limit my research to California case law or expand the scope of the research to all jurisdictions in which the client conducts business? Thank you very much. Cassidy

Example 3 (E-mail Requesting a Time to Meet)

TO: rkbrowning@browningclayllp.com
FROM: clagrande@browningclayllp.com
DATE: September 11, 2017
RE: Precipice Foundation LLC; Brief Meeting Regarding Scope of
          Research

Rick: I have begun researching the issue of the enforceability of forum selection clauses for our client, Precipice Foundation LLC, and had a quick question regarding the scope of the assignment. Could I schedule a brief appointment with you this afternoon to obtain clarification on two issues before I get too far along in the research? I am available anytime at your convenience and can come to your office. Thank you very much. Cassidy

Example 4 (E-mail Transmitting Timesheets)

TO: rkbrowning@browningclayllp.com
FROM: clagrande@browningclayllp.com
DATE: September 11, 2017
RE: **August 2016 Timesheets**

Rick: Attached please find my timesheets for August. Please let me know whether you have any questions. Thank you very much. Cassidy

---

When e-mailing in the law office environment, consider these guidelines:

- Always make sure you use the correct e-mail address for the intended recipient. Much of the information you will be conveying via e-mail as an attorney will be protected by the attorney-client privilege and/or attorney work product doctrine. You do not want to inadvertently waive a privilege by e-mailing a confidential legal analysis to the wrong person outside the scope of the privilege. Be very careful as you type e-mail addresses. Check that the "Autofill" in your e-mail program does not insert the incorrect recipient name. Consider drafting your e-mail without any recipients listed, proofread it carefully, and then add (and double-check) the recipient names just before you send the e-mail, to prevent sending the e-mail too early or to an unintended individual or party.
- Always include an e-mail reference line that refers to the client and the precise subject matter of the e-mail. Busy attorneys receive numerous e-mails each day; a helpful reference line enables lawyers to better search for an e-mail based on subject matter within a voluminous Inbox. If the law office represents the same client on many matters, consider referencing the client name, the particular case you are working on (perhaps the name of the opposing party), as well as the substance of the e-mail.
- Use a proper (professional) greeting. Greet the supervising attorney as you would in a meeting; if you are on a first-name basis, use the attorney's first name. If you are not yet on a first-name basis, use a more formal title such as "Mr. Quinn," or "Ms. Volterra."
- Use the first sentence of the e-mail to remind the supervising attorney what he or she asked you to research: "You asked me to research . . ."
- State the results of your research clearly and concisely. Avoid cutting and pasting citations into e-mails; retype them instead. Cutting and pasting citations changes the fonts and makes text difficult to read.
- When signing off, you might offer to perform any necessary follow-up research.

- Use good judgment when drafting e-mails to supervising attorneys. Every e-mail you send reflects your professional persona. Proofread and spellcheck before sending every e-mail, especially if you are writing on an iPad or iPhone, which are notorious for inserting inadvertent spelling and typographical errors. Check your capitalization. Never use lowercase "i" for the pronoun "I" or the abbreviation "u." Be very careful with attempts at humor and with the overall tone.
- E-mails are easily forwarded. In fact, busy attorneys often forward e-mails internally within the law office and even to clients. Never write anything you would not want to see reprinted elsewhere.
- Be aware that many law offices include the following boilerplate language at the end of every e-mail: "Confidentiality Notice: The information contained in this e-mail and any attachments may be legally privileged, confidential and/or otherwise exempt from disclosure and is intended only for the recipient named above. If you are not an intended recipient, you are hereby notified that any dissemination, distribution, or copying of this e-mail is strictly prohibited. If you have received this e-mail in error, please notify the sender and permanently delete the e-mail and any attachments immediately." You should ask your supervising attorney whether your e-mail signature block needs to include this language.

Part 2

Persuasive Writing

Section 7

Context

Introduction to Part 2
Transitioning from Predictive to Persuasive Legal Writing

As lawyers, we wear many different hats in our relationships with our clients. One role we play is one-on-one counselor, offering (hopefully) sage advice to our clients in times of conflict or opportunity. When we communicate in a confidential, privileged, or private manner with our clients, or about our client's circumstances with our colleagues in a law office environment, we perform *predictive* legal analysis—analyzing the strengths *and* weaknesses of our client's position on a legal issue in light of the applicable rule and then anticipating the most likely outcome. Thus, in the first semester of law school, professors and students typically embark upon legal writing instruction by focusing on *predictive* legal writing—analyzing our client scenarios in an objective manner, looking at legal issues from all angles. Then, in the second semester of law school, we usually transition to *persuasive* legal writing, which serves a different purpose and audience than predictive analysis. Now donning the hat of advocate rather than counselor, attorneys use persuasive legal writing to communicate externally with opposing counsel (in a litigation or business transaction), policy makers (legislators or other governmental entities), or decision makers (judges, arbitrators, or juries).

This book offers one method to master the lawyer's technique of persuasive legal writing. Many legal writing professors call upon the wisdom of Aristotle to introduce students to three key elements of rhetorical persuasion: *logos, pathos*, and *ethos*—logic, emotion, and credibility. This book seeks to situate Aristotle's triptych in our Millennial legal environment, providing law students and new lawyers with practical advice on how to incorporate his wisdom into everyday lawyering tasks.

Logic

To convince opposing counsel or a decision maker that a client's position is the correct one, a lawyer must—at a minimum—offer a logical argument. To do so, persuasive legal writers build upon the foundational steps of predictive writing by using structural frameworks like IREAC (Issue, Rule, Explanation, Application, Conclusion) or CREAC (Conclusion, Rule, Explanation, Application, Conclusion), or variations thereof. Persuasive legal writers pinpoint the client's narrow legal issue, research the applicable rule to extract key elements or factors, select helpful (and ideally, favorable) precedent to illustrate this rule, and then apply the rule to the client's facts. Here, instead of weighing the strengths and weaknesses of the client's position and then objectively predicting an outcome (as a lawyer would in an internal law office memorandum), persuasive legal writers focus on the strengths of the client's position and lead the reader down a logical path toward the desired result, stating a concrete conclusion that favors the client. To enhance logic, or *logos,* in a piece of persuasive writing, lawyers use a clear organizational structure, create rule frameworks identifying elements or factors, include well-crafted Rule Explanations of cases (using formulas like Facts + Holding + Rationale and Signal + Cite + Explanatory Parenthetical), and use Rule Applications to link the elements or factors of the rule to the client's facts in a way that demonstrates to the reader that the desired outcome makes sense. To convert a good piece of legal writing into a great one, a logical legal writer avoids making flawed assumptions about the breadth of the reader's knowledge and—like a good roadmap or global positioning system (GPS)—adds signposts, prompts, directions, and smooth transitions so the reader can follow a well-hewed path to the desired result.

Emotion

In predictive legal writing, lawyers often adopt a neutral tone, weighing good and bad facts in light of both favorable and unfavorable law to predict a likely outcome. In persuasive writing, to convince a reader, effective legal writers paint a vivid picture of the client's story, injecting an appropriate level of emotion—or *pathos*—into the narration of the client's circumstances. To tap into *pathos,* lawyers shape a theme, or a "theory" of the case, that will resonate with the reader. Theme-crafting might flow more readily when a lawyer represents a person who suffered a grave injury or a tragic loss at the hands of another, or when handling criminal matter where concepts like freedom and punishment are at stake. However, mindful lawyers representing seemingly impersonal corporate or business clients in financial transactions also employ case themes to foster an emotional connection between the third-party audience and the client's circumstances. For example, lawyers litigating contract disputes might brainstorm meaningful themes about promises kept, economic growth, or the American dream. Attorneys representing clients in intellectual property disputes might innovate case themes about ingenuity, encouragement of ideas, and respect for hard work and originality. The *pathos* aspect of persuasion gives a lawyer permission to flex her creative muscles and construct the equivalent of a 30-second Super Bowl ad for a case—one that can be woven into briefs, oral arguments, and trials and convey a consistent message about why the client's preferred result in the case is the just one.

Credibility

An argument with *logos* and *pathos* aplenty will fall flat if the audience does not trust or believe the messenger. Thus, an effective persuasive writer establishes credibility with the reader through (1) accurately describing the parties' factual circumstances; (2) conducting thorough research about the legal rules; (3) making intelligent choices about which precedent (favorable and unfavorable) to illustrate; (4) respecting and adhering to court rules and procedures; (5) mindfully proofreading and cite-checking; and (6) conveying professional courtesy to opposing counsel and the ultimate decision maker(s). In Chapter 2 invites law students and new lawyers to consider their professional personas. As we learn how to become persuasive legal writers, we will revisit the concept of professionalism as a tool for enhancing the *ethos* of persuasive legal writing.

*   *   *

While this book will touch on all three components of being a persuasive legal writer—*logos*, *pathos*, and *ethos*—persuasive style will bloom in different forms for each writer. During this learning process, take time to consider your personality and style of persuasion. When you want something—either for yourself or for another—how do you communicate most effectively with other human beings? Are you tough? Collaborative? Subtle? Solution oriented? Crafty? Methodical? Passionate?

Drawing upon the theme of mindfulness, this book encourages you to be the most influential version of your *authentic* self as you write persuasively. Not every attorney needs to be a podium-pounding orator to convince opposing counsel, a judge, or a jury to embrace a client's position. You will serve your clients best by tapping into and developing your personal persuasive strengths; yours might be elegant writing, well-reasoned logic, creative theme development, or collaborative problem solving. As you work through the second half of this book to understand the important structural framework of persuasive legal writing, be open to the process of learning about yourself, identifying strengths that you might not yet realize you have, and honing those skills to develop your persuasive legal voice.

CLASSROOM EXERCISE #1

Write a one-page, single-spaced, persuasive argument about anything for which you feel passionately that is *not* related to law school or practice in any way. For example, you may choose to persuade your reader that your favorite football player should be selected for the Pro Bowl, that your takeout Indian restaurant is the best, that your favorite indie film should win an Oscar, that your landlord should not raise your rent, that Adidas shoes are better than Nike or vice versa, etc. Try to employ *logos*, *pathos*, and *ethos* to persuade your reader of your position. One page. Single-spaced. Write.

CLASSROOM EXERCISE #2

List the television or movie characters playing the role of lawyers that you like and dislike the most. Why are they your favorite and least favorite?

Favorite: _____

Least Favorite: _____

What persuasive techniques do these lawyers use to convince their colleagues, opposing counsel, judges, or juries of their positions?

_____

Is your personality similar to or different from these lawyers' personas? How?

_____

CLASSROOM EXERCISE #3

Think about four brands or advertising/marketing campaigns that you find the *most* persuasive. What makes them persuasive? Is it their logic? Emotional appeal? The credibility of the messenger?

Brand/Campaign #1:

Description: _____

Logos? _____

Pathos? _____

Ethos? _____

CLASSROOM EXERCISE #3

Brand/Campaign #2:

Description: _____

Logos? _____

Pathos? _____

Ethos? _____

Brand/Campaign #3:

Description: _____

Logos? _____

Pathos? _____

Ethos? _____

Brand/Campaign #4:

Description: _____

Logos? _____

Pathos? _____

Ethos? _____

Now, think of four brands/campaigns you find to be the *least* persuasive. Why?

Brand/Campaign #1:

Description: _____

Logos? _____

Pathos? _____

Ethos? _____

Brand/Campaign #2:

Description: _____

Logos? _____

Pathos? _____

Ethos? _____

CLASSROOM EXERCISE #3

Brand/Campaign #3:

Description: _____

Logos? _____

Pathos? _____

Ethos? _____

Brand/Campaign #4:

Description: _____

Logos? _____

Pathos? _____

Ethos? _____

Chapter 22

Types of Legal Documents Lawyers Use to Persuade

The *Merriam-Webster* dictionary defines the verb "persuade" as "to cause (someone) to do something by asking, arguing, or giving reasons" or "to cause (someone) to believe something."[1] An attorney uses persuasion when drafting a letter on behalf of a client to a third party to request or demand that the individual or entity do or stop doing something, such as pay overdue rent or cease conducting construction work after dark. Lawyers also utilize persuasive writing to convince opposing counsel to agree to proposed contract terms, produce factual documents or other information being withheld in litigation discovery, negotiate case deadlines or time extensions, or even settle a case. Attorneys employ legal writing to prompt judges and arbitrators to establish a workable case management schedule, reconcile discovery disputes that counsel cannot settle themselves, choose whether certain exhibits or witnesses are admissible at trial or an arbitration hearing, decide objections to evidence, and rule on motions that will narrow the issues to debate at trial or arbitration, or even dispose of a case entirely. As evidenced by the foregoing examples, lawyers use persuasive legal writing in representing clients both in transactional relationships with third parties and in litigation and arbitration.

Refreshing our recollection the phases and progression of a typical client representation—in either a transaction or a litigation—will provide helpful context to grasp the important role each piece of persuasive legal writing plays. While Chapter 1 provided an introduction to the types of legal writing lawyers perform in the various stages of client representation, this chapter focuses on persuasive written work product.

---

[1] http://www.merriam-webster.com/dictionary/persuade (last visited February 5, 2016).

Persuasive Legal Writing in the Transactional Context

In the transactional legal arena, clients often seek legal advice in negotiating, drafting, and executing a contract such as a lease, a prenuptial agreement, a property sale, a loan, or a corporate acquisition. The client conveys information to the attorney about the parameters of the transaction, including key points such as the subject matter, timing, price or value, the location of the transaction, representations that the parties are making to one another, and any conditions. Armed with this material, the lawyer might reach out to counsel representing the other party to obtain additional information, and then one of the attorneys begins the legal writing process of drafting the transactional agreement. Persuasion comes into play in the transactional context when the attorneys begin the dance of convincing one another (and their clients) to accept proposed language and terms. Lawyers might negotiate the parties' promises to one another and summarize them in a **term sheet**. After that, these points must be memorialized in actual contractual language. Every word matters. A single word or item of punctuation can change the tenor of an agreement. Thus, lawyers **"redline" contract drafts** and transmit them back and forth, using persuasion to bargain over the precise language reflected in the agreement. This process can take days or even months, depending on the complexity of the transaction and the personalities of the persuading attorneys. Logic, the appropriate amount of passion, and credibility are key to a successful negotiation in a transactional setting. Transactional attorneys use logic to substantiate their reasons for insisting upon certain contractual terms, passion to emphasize the importance of the particular deal point to the party or the transaction itself, and credibility to bolster the party's position. Integrity is key: lawyers who stubbornly cling to a deal point just for the sake of posturing might win the battle but lose the war.

The work product generated by attorneys throughout this negotiation volley includes e-mails and letters identifying deal points that each side proposes, term sheets summarizing negotiated terms of the transaction, redlined drafts of agreements containing suggested language, additional e-mails and letters debating the proposed language, and the ultimate final version of the **contract**.

Persuasive Legal Writing in the Dispute Resolution Context

In your first semester of law school, you may have learned the basics of how litigation works.[2] Before leaping into the techniques of persuasive writing, let's

---

[2] Chapter 1 describes the typical phases of litigation from start to finish.

refresh our recollection about the typical phases of a lawyer's representation of a client in litigation and how persuasive legal writing fits within that progression.

Prelitigation Persuasive Demand Letters, Settlement Letters, and Settlement Agreements

A client might contact an attorney or a law firm[3] before a dispute rises to the level of actual litigation or before a complaint or another type of "legal pleading" has been filed in a court. Even if no pleadings have yet been filed, a client might call a lawyer and describe the circumstances of a blossoming or ongoing dispute with a third party. Perhaps the client is disgruntled over unpaid rent, a landlord's refusal to perform promised repairs, a shipment of defective products, or an invasion of privacy.

The first type of persuasive legal writing that a lawyer might undertake in the dispute resolution context is a letter or e-mail to a third party to resolve a conflict prior to litigation. These are called **demand letters**. The lawyer drafts the letter on behalf of the client to the third party, and then, using persuasive structure, language, and tone, identifies the legal issue, sets forth the applicable rule governing the issue (perhaps either a contract term, a statute or regulation, or a common law rule derived from precedent), presents the arguments for why the client seeks (and believes he is entitled to) a particular result, and then directly asks the third party to take a particular action, either to do something or stop doing something. A good demand letter provides a deadline for compliance and identifies the next steps that the client will take in the event of inaction by the third party. Demand letters are discussed in Chapter 23.

A variation of the demand letter is a prelitigation **settlement letter**. This document differs from the demand letter in that it seeks to resolve the client's dispute without resort to litigation by proposing a concrete monetary figure or a compromise action. If the receiving party accepts the proposal (or makes a counterproposal that is accepted), the parties can put an end to the disagreement and avoid possibly costly and protracted litigation or arbitration. If the opposing party agrees to the monetary settlement amount or the tendered compromise, the attorneys engage in the transactional process of negotiating a **settlement agreement**—a written contract encompassing the terms of the resolution of the dispute such as timing and amount of payment, releases or waivers of further claims, and penalties for noncompliance. The persuasive aspects of transactional negotiation, discussed previously in this chapter, would govern that process. Settlement letters and agreements are discussed in Chapter 23.

---

[3] At the first client contact, the attorney conducts a conflicts check to make sure there are no ethical conflicts of interest in representing the client. The lawyer also might have the client sign an engagement or retainer agreement, outlining the scope and terms of the attorney-client relationship.

Persuasive Pleadings

If the parties to a legal dispute cannot resolve their conflict through a settlement agreement, one of the parties might proceed to the next step of filing a **pleading** in the appropriate court. If the parties have a contract that requires dispute resolution through arbitration, a form of alternative dispute resolution (ADR), the pleading is called a **demand for arbitration**. In litigation, the initial pleading filed by the party pursuing a lawsuit typically is called the **complaint**.

In civil cases, procedural rules such as the Federal Rules of Civil Procedure, and their counterparts in state courts, require legal complaints to contain certain necessary information to provide the opposing party with adequate notice of the allegations against it. The complaint-drafting process is another opportunity for a lawyer to be persuasive—both to the opposing party and to the ultimate decision maker. Complaints start with a case **caption**, identifying the court exercising proper jurisdiction over the lawsuit, the correct names of the parties, and a designation of who is the plaintiff or the complaining party and who is the defendant. The court eventually will assign a docket or case number to the matter, which is included in the caption on every subsequent pleading. The complaint contains the title of "Complaint."

Below the caption, the filing party uses numbered paragraphs to describe (1) the basis for the court's jurisdiction over the matter; (2) the parties, their states of citizenship, any corporate parties' principal places of business, and the nature of the parties (i.e., who they are, what they do, and how they know each other); (3) the background facts; (4) the various causes of action, usually in numbered "counts" (i.e., Count I: Breach of Contract, Count II: Fraud, etc.); and (5) the damages or remedies sought. The attorney drafting the complaint exercises persuasion, balancing *logos*, *pathos*, and *ethos*, in:

- establishing the court's proper jurisdiction over the matter, citing the appropriate statute or other applicable rule granting the court authority over the type of case being presented (*ethos*)
- describing the background facts accurately yet vividly, to demonstrate to the opposing party why the filing party perceives the conflict, and to engage the interest of the decision maker (*ethos* and *pathos*)
- demonstrating a thorough knowledge of the governing rules of law, itemizing the required elements or range of factors in each cause of action that will determine the outcome (*logos* and *ethos*)
- properly tying the rules of law to the facts, as much as required by the pleading rules of the particular jurisdiction (*logos*, *pathos*, and *ethos*)
- asserting the desired outcome in the form of damages or other remedies sought (*logos*, *pathos*, and *ethos*)

The complaint includes a signature block that the attorney signs. Some jurisdictions also require the client to verify the complaint through a signature.

Aristotle's concept of *ethos*—credibility and integrity of the persuader—is reinforced by court rules such as Federal Rule of Civil Procedure 11 or its state counterpart. Rule 11 indicates that, by signing the signature block of a complaint, the lawyer is promising that:

- the complaint is not being presented for any improper purpose, such as to harass, cause unnecessary delay, or needlessly increase the cost of litigation
- the claims in the complaint are warranted by existing law or by a nonfrivolous argument for extending, modifying, or reversing existing law, or for establishing new law
- the factual contentions in the complaint have evidentiary support or, if specifically identified as such, will likely have evidentiary support after a reasonable opportunity for further investigation or discovery.[4]

If any of the foregoing representations turns out to be untrue, the lawyer as signatory may be subject to sanctions by the court, which could include monetary penalties, or some other action that will "deter repetition of the conduct or comparable conduct" by other attorneys.[5]

Once the complaint is ready, the lawyer files it with the appropriate court and then serves it on the opposing party, perhaps through a process server or other means authorized by the applicable court rules. The responding party then has a certain number of days dictated by the court's rules to file a **motion to dismiss** the complaint[6] or file an **answer**. In federal court, the time period for filing is 21 days from the date of service of the complaint; state court rules may have different deadlines.

In drafting an answer to the complaint, the attorney does not need to use persuasive techniques in responding to the numbered paragraphs of the complaint; typically, attorneys simply state the words "Admitted" or "Denied" in response to each numbered allegation in the complaint. However, if the defendant has a valid **counterclaim** against the plaintiff, the attorney uses the techniques of persuasive pleading-drafting in setting forth the facts, accurate rules of law for each cause of action pled, and the damages or remedies sought. The responding attorney must sign the signature block, also in accordance with Rule 11.

Additionally, the defendant's attorney may bring a third party into the lawsuit by filing a **third-party complaint**, following similar steps performed in drafting the counterclaim against the plaintiff. Third parties then file an answer or a motion to dismiss or even a **cross-claim** against a different party. Co-parties also may file cross-claims against one another.

---

[4] Fed. R. Civ. P. 11.
[5] Fed. R. Civ. P. 11.
[6] Motions to dismiss are described in the section entitled "Pleadings Phase: Persuasive Motions to Dismiss," later in this chapter, and in Chapter 28.

A well-written persuasive pleading might convince the opposing party to settle the dispute without resort to a trial. Further, the document can establish a favorable tone, theme, and storyline on behalf of the client for the judge or arbitrator. Tips for drafting persuasive pleadings are provided in Chapters 24, 25, and 26.

Persuasive Motions and Briefs

At many points in a litigation or arbitration before the ultimate trial or hearing, attorneys have the opportunity to persuade opposing counsel, judges, and arbitrators to decide certain aspects of the dispute (either procedurally or substantively) in their clients' favor. The vehicle for this mode of persuasion is a **motion** and/or **brief**.

Pleadings Phase: Persuasive Motions to Dismiss

Once an initial pleading is filed in a case, the party served with the complaint has the choice whether to file a **motion to dismiss**[7] or to file an answer.[8] A motion to dismiss, and the accompanying brief, are documents that explain to the judge why the party is entitled to dismissal of the action. The motion is usually a short (perhaps one page) document requesting the court to dismiss the case; the brief (also called a *memorandum of points and authorities* or a *memorandum in support of the motion to dismiss*) is a longer document setting forth the issue, the applicable rule, precedent illustrating the rule, the party's arguments, and the precise reasons why the case should be dismissed. In a civil case, a defendant might seek dismissal if (1) the court lacks jurisdiction over the subject matter of the dispute or the parties, (2) the case was filed in the wrong venue, (3) the plaintiff improperly served the defendant with the pleadings or failed to serve the defendant, (4) the complaint fails to state a claim upon which relief can be granted, or (5) the plaintiff failed to join a necessary party to the case.[9]

During this phase of the case, neither party likely has conducted much, if any, discovery, which involves the exchange of documents related to the subject matter of the dispute, interrogatories (written questions answered by a party under oath), depositions (interviews of witnesses conducted under oath and transcribed by a court reporter into a written transcript in Q and A format), physical or mental examinations, or requests for admissions (written statements admitted or denied by a party). Thus, a motion to dismiss typically is limited to a discussion of the content of the pleading documents rather than a litany of external case facts.

---

[7] Different jurisdictions might use other terminology for this procedural action.

[8] In federal court, a defendant could also file a motion to strike the pleadings if it contains "redundant, immaterial, impertinent, or scandalous matter" (Fed. R. Civ. P. 12(f)), or a motion for a more definite statement if the complaint was "so vague or ambiguous that the party cannot reasonably prepare a response" (Fed. R. Civ. P. 12(e)).

[9] Fed. R. Civ. P. 12.

In writing this type of motion and brief, mindful legal writers persuasively identify the issue(s), describe the facts of the case, establish the accurate rule governing the legal issue(s), strategically choose precedent to illustrate the rule(s), and then assert a strong, logical, and appropriately passionate argument as to why the party is entitled to dismissal. Credibility is established through accurate recitation of the facts, legal rules, and case citations and descriptions and through professional presentation (i.e., proofreading, cite-checking, format-ting, and complying with the court's rules for submittal of briefs). The attorney signs the motion and accompanying memorandum, files them with the court, and then serves them upon the opposing party or his counsel if represented.

The responding party has a specific number of days designated in the court rules to draft, file, and serve an **opposition to the motion to dismiss**. The **opposition brief** is the responding attorney's opportunity to be just as persuasive as the initial brief writer (also called the "moving party") in pointing out to the judge (and opposing counsel) all the reasons why the case should *not* be dismissed. The responding attorney likewise describes the key facts, the accurate governing rules, and the reasons why the case should progress forward. The responding attorney signs and files the opposition brief and serves it upon opposing counsel.

Next, the moving party might have a certain number of days prescribed in the court rules to file a **reply brief** in response to the opposition brief. Reply briefs are usually shorter than both the initial and opposition briefs. All three briefs likely will have a page or word count limit enforced by the court.

The court may or may not invite oral argument on the motion to dismiss. If the court does grant or require oral argument, both parties' attorneys have the opportunity to reinforce their positions through persuasive arguments in person, usually limited to 10 or 15 minutes per side. Ultimately, the court rules on the motion—either at the end of the oral argument or later—and issues an **order** stating whether the motion is granted or denied. If the motion is granted, the case ceases as to that portion of the case, or the entire case ends if the court dis-misses all the causes of action in the complaint. If the motion to dismiss is denied, the case moves forward. The defendant then must file an **answer** within a certain number of days, and the parties proceed to the scheduling phase[10] of the case and to discovery. A party who is unsuccessful on a motion may consider filing a **motion for reconsideration.**

---

[10] As explained further in Chapter 27, after the pleadings are filed in a case, many courts require counsel for all the parties to meet and confer (either in person or on the telephone) to map out a timeline of important deadlines in the case to: add new parties; serve requests for production of documents, interrogatories, or requests for admissions; conduct and complete all fact depositions; conclude all fact discovery; exchange expert reports; conduct expert depositions; file pretrial substantive motions; file evidentiary motions; file other pretrial submissions such as jury instructions, if applicable; and select a trial date and duration. The parties typically submit a joint proposed *case scheduling order* (also called a *case management order* or *case structuring order*) to the court. The court will either approve or reject the proposed timeline or modify it to comport with the court's own schedule and docket. Once the case scheduling order is in place, it can be difficult to obtain time extensions from the court, so attorneys should be sure to adhere to the deadlines. Otherwise, they risk waiving the right to file motions or take certain litigation actions identified therein.

Fact Discovery Phase: Persuasive Discovery Motions

Fact discovery is the phase of litigation in which lawyers become investigators, hunting for evidence to prove their client's case and support their client's defenses. Procedural rules govern what types of discovery parties may seek from one another. Typically, litigants serve written requests for discovery upon one another in the form of (1) requests for production of documents or physical things; (2) interrogatories; (3) requests for admissions; (4) notices of depositions; or (5) requests for physical or mental examinations. In *requests for production of documents and things,* lawyers seek tangible items like contracts, letters, photographs, videotapes, logs, diaries, blueprints, e-mails, and receipts or they request site visits to observe conditions of property or accident locales. *Interrogatories* are written questions that an opposing party must answer in writing, under oath, such as, "At what exact time of day did you witness the car accident at the intersection of Hanover and Water Streets?" *Requests for admissions* are statements that an opposing party must either admit or deny, such as "Exhibit 1 is a true and accurate copy of the contract between Gartner Enterprises and Precipice Foundation dated April 3, 2017." *Depositions* are interviews by a lawyer of a witness in which the questions and answers are transcribed by a court reporter into a written transcript in Q and A format. In a deposition, opposing counsel may "defend" the "deponent" and object to the form of the questions being asked, in order to preserve the record. The witness testifies under oath. Unlike other discovery methods, *requests for physical and mental examinations* must be approved by the court through a motion, and they are useful in cases in which a person's physical or mental condition is in question.

Discovery is an essential part of any litigation, yet unfortunately it can breed disputes among lawyers. Litigants often seek to withhold key documents on the basis of attorney-client privilege, the attorney work product doctrine, or their proprietary nature; opposing parties may disagree with the party's basis for withholding pivotal information. To resolve disputes during discovery, lawyers use persuasive writing first by crafting strong demand letters calling for the production of documents being withheld, witnesses who failed to appear for a deposition, or supplemental responses to evasive answers to interrogatories or requests for admissions. If a lawyer is unsuccessful in obtaining the discovery sought through a persuasive demand letter, she would follow the steps outlined in the court rules for resolving discovery disputes and ultimately file a **motion to compel**. This type of motion is accompanied by a short brief; judges do not want to read lengthy tomes describing lawyers' inability to resolve discovery conflicts. Instead, judges or magistrates designated to resolve discovery battles prefer a concise layout of the issue and the alleged basis for the party's entitlement to the discovery sought. Additionally, many courts require a lawyer filing a motion to compel to attach a certification of her prior attempts to meet and confer with opposing counsel to resolve the conflict. The lawyer should be as persuasive and succinct as possible in this type of motion. Opposing counsel then has an opportunity to file an opposition brief, which might warrant an even shorter reply brief filed by the moving party, and the court may (or may not) hear oral argument.

Expert Discovery Phase: Persuasive Motions in Limine

A lawyer's presentation of his party's case to a judge or a jury might benefit from the assistance of one or more experts to explain a concept that is beyond the experience of the average layperson. Evidentiary rules govern the admissibility of expert testimony at trial; a landmark case entitled *Daubert v. Merrell Dow Pharmaceuticals, Inc.*[11] set the eligibility standard for experts to testify in court. Typically, to qualify as an expert, an individual must possess the requisite amount of knowledge, skill, experience, training, or education regarding a particular concept[12]—such as blood spatter evidence, handwriting, fingerprints, deoxyribonucleic acid (DNA) evidence, metallurgy, archaeology, surgical techniques, or accents. During the expert discovery phase of a case, parties identify the experts that they plan to call as witnesses at trial, exchange written expert reports, and then conduct expert depositions. In some courts, such as federal district courts, the written expert reports must include (1) a description of the opinions that the expert will render at trial and the reasons supporting those opinions; (2) the facts or data reviewed and relied upon by the expert; (3) any exhibits that the expert will use to summarize or support her opinions; (4) the expert's qualifications; (5) the expert's publications in the past ten years; (6) a list of all other legal cases during the previous four years in which the expert testified at trial or in a deposition; and (7) the amount of money that the party is paying the expert.[13]

An expert need not have earned a Ph.D. from a highly ranked institution to qualify to testify about a case issue. In fact, experts can qualify to testify in a wide range of capacities, as long as the individual has the appropriate level of knowledge, skill, experience, training, or education. If a case involves a bus accident, a bus driver might qualify as an expert. If an individual was injured operating a high-tech commercial espresso machine, a party might present an experienced coffee barista to educate the trier of fact about the machine. Experts may be permitted to testify about art authenticity, engineering, car mechanics, winemaking, and a wide range of other topics.

However, just like in the fact discovery phase of a litigation, expert discovery can generate conflict between opposing counsel, prompting another vehicle of persuasive writing called the **motion in limine**. *In limine* is Latin for "at the threshold" or "at the beginning." A party often challenges an opponent's experts *before* trial in order to preclude these individuals from testifying, on the grounds

---

[11] 43 F.3d 1311 (9th Cir. 1995). The *Daubert* case involved expert testimony regarding the linkage, or lack thereof, between a pharmaceutical drug and birth defects.
[12] Fed. R. Evid. 702.
[13] Fed. R. Civ. P. 26(a)(2)(B).

that they do not meet the qualification standards. Parties write persuasive motions in limine and accompanying briefs to challenge proffered experts on the following bases:

- the individual does not possess the appropriate degree of knowledge, skill, experience, training, or education required under the rules
- the proposed testimony is not beyond the understanding of the average layperson
- the expert did not review sufficient facts or data before rendering opinions
- in developing her opinions, the expert relied on facts or data not typically evaluated by other experts in the same field or industry
- the expert used unreliable methods or principles to arrive at the opinions
- the expert applied her methods or principles to the client's circumstances in an unreliable manner
- the expert is biased (i.e., only represents a certain type of party, is paid an exorbitant or inappropriate amount by the law firm who engaged the expert, etc.)
- the expert's opinions are irrelevant to the legal matter
- the expert's opinions are less probative than prejudicial
- the expert's testimony will confuse or mislead the jury or judge
- the expert's testimony will delay the trial or waste the court's time
- the expert's testimony is cumulative of other evidence
- the expert's report omitted an opinion that he intends to present at trial
- the party's disclosure of the expert's identity, or the expert report, was late.[14]

If a lawyer believes that any of the foregoing arguments are valid, she writes a persuasive motion in limine, accompanied by a short brief articulating the reasons why the court should exclude the expert from testifying at trial. The lawyer cites the rule and standard governing the admissibility of expert testimony—typically the *Daubert* standard and the corresponding rule of evidence in the particular jurisdiction[15]—and illustrates the rule through examples of case law in which courts have precluded similar proposed experts from testifying at trial. The lawyer then articulates the most persuasive reasons why the expert should be barred from testifying.

In response, the opposing party files an opposition brief, which may warrant a short reply. The court may (or may not) hear oral argument.

---

[14] Fed. R. Civ. P. 702; Fed. R. Evid. 401, 403; *Daubert*, 43 F.3d at 1311.
[15] Fed. R. Civ. P. 702 and its state court counterparts.

Pretrial Phase: Persuasive Motions for Summary Judgment and Motions in Limine

Once the litigants have completed all fact and expert discovery, the case transitions to the pretrial phase, in which the parties prepare for trial. During this phase, many courts require the parties to submit pretrial filings, such as lists of exhibits and witnesses; excerpts from depositions to be read into evidence; jury instructions; and proposed "voir dire" questions to ask jurors during jury selection. The parties exchange these documents in advance of trial by the deadline set in the court's case scheduling order. During this phase, lawyers often file additional persuasive motions in limine that seek to preclude a party from presenting certain documents or witnesses at trial.

An additional important type of persuasive writing that lawyers submit during this pretrial phase is a **motion for summary judgment**. In federal court, a party may obtain *summary judgment* if there are no genuine disputes of material facts and the moving party is entitled to judgment as a matter of law.[16] In other words, the moving party must establish that the key facts bearing on the cause of action are undisputed *and* that all the required elements of the rule governing the cause of action are met (or if trying to defeat a cause of action, that the opposing party cannot prevail on at least one of the required elements). A **motion for summary judgment** is accompanied by a lengthy brief in which the lawyer summarizes—in numbered paragraphs if required by the local court's rules—all the pertinent facts gathered in discovery that are not in dispute, providing citations to the record. The lawyer then relays the legal rule governing the cause of action that is the subject of the brief and applies the rule to the undisputed facts to demonstrate to the court that the party is entitled to judgment, and there is no need for a trial. These briefs are often long, can address more than one cause of action in the case, and typically include numerous attachments of documents to verify the undisputed facts.

In response to a motion for summary judgment, the opposing party files an opposition brief, identifying, in corresponding numbered paragraphs, material facts that the responding party claims *are* in dispute. The lawyer attaches exhibits to her opposition brief to demonstrate the disputed nature of the fact(s) to the court. In this likewise lengthy brief, the responding lawyer applies the applicable rule to the parties' facts, persuasively demonstrating why the moving party is *not* entitled to judgment as a matter of law and why the case should move forward. The initial moving party may have the opportunity to file a reply brief, and the court may (or may not) hear oral argument. Parties often file cross-motions for summary judgment and also sometimes file motions for partial summary judgment on limited aspects of the case. These types of motions, if successful, can dramatically narrow the scope of trial, or eliminate the need for trial altogether, saving the parties and the court time and money.

---

[16] Fed. R. Civ. P. 56.

Trial Phase: Persuasive Trial Motions

The trial is the "big show" of litigation—an opportunity for the lawyers to persuasively present the facts of their case to the judge and possibly a jury, in tandem with the applicable law. Lawyers deliver persuasive opening statements, and then the trial proceeds with the presentation of evidence through exhibits and witness testimony. During trial, lawyers continue to submit persuasive briefs; unresolved evidentiary and substantive issues often arise during a trial, and judges request briefings. Lawyers might conduct a trial all day and then sit down at night and write short briefs for submission to the court for resolution the following day. These could be additional motions in limine concerning objections to exhibits or testimony or substantive motions on legal issues in the case.

Once a party has concluded its case-in-chief, the opposing party might file a **motion for a directed verdict**, a **motion for judgment as a matter of law**, or another style of procedural motion to obtain a judgment in its favor based upon the opposing party's failure to prove its case. The court might require the parties to brief an oral motion fully before the judge will rule on the matter.

Posttrial Phase: Persuasive Posttrial Motions and Appellate Briefs

Once a trial ends, a lawyer's persuasive role does not cease. If the lawyer wins a favorable judgment or verdict for the client, she might have the opportunity to file persuasive **posttrial motions** to obtain prejudgment interest or an award of attorneys' fees and costs, depending on whether a contract or statute allows recovery of such additional expenses. These motions are accompanied by persuasively written briefs that establish the party's entitlement to such supplementary compensation—under a governing rule, often a contract provision or statute—and provide detailed factual information (and possibly exhibits) to support the dollar amounts sought. The opposing party has the right to file an opposition brief, which may warrant a short reply brief.

A party that receives an unfavorable judgment or verdict may file a **motion for a new trial** or a **motion for relief from a judgment**. The nonprevailing party also might have the right to appeal. If so, he must file a notice of appeal by the deadline established in the court rules and could consider filing a **motion for stay of enforcement** of the trial court's judgment pending the appeal.

Appellate advocacy is another avenue of persuasion. As a case transfers from the trial court to the appellate court, the ultimate decision maker shifts from one trial judge or the jury to a panel of appellate judges. An appeal does not involve the presentation of evidence through exhibits and testimony; instead, the appellate lawyer files an often lengthy **appellate brief**, identifying the legal issues on appeal, appending the trial factual record, stating the applicable rules of law, and applying those rules to the evidence presented at trial to demonstrate to the panel of appellate judges why the appealing party (the *appellant*) believes that she is entitled to a different result.

In an appellate brief, the appellant must provide the court with the correct "standard of review." Because the trial court already spent days, weeks, or months adjudicating the dispute, judicial resources would be unnecessarily wasted if the appellate court rehashed the entire case from start to finish. Thus, appellate review of a case invokes the concept of "deference" to the lower court. *Deference* is the appropriate degree of respect that an appellate court must give to a decision rendered by the lower court. Our judicial system is—in part—based on the notion that trial courts are in the best position to judge the facts of a case; the trial judge is physically present in the courtroom with the witnesses and the tangible pieces of evidence and can see and engage with the human beings and documents. Accordingly, appellate courts tend to give a large amount of deference to the lower court on issues of *fact*. However, part of the appellate court's role is to facilitate consistency in the application of rules of law, to establish clear precedent within a jurisdiction. Thus, on issues of *law*, an appellate court might grant less, or no, deference to the lower court and instead review a legal issue with fresh eyes. This standard is called *de novo*, a Latin term meaning "from the new." The following chart summarizes some of the standards of review that appellate courts use:

No Deference: Appellate court considers the issue "afresh" or "anew"	Lots of Deference: Appellate court is reluctant to disturb the lower court's ruling
De novo: Used for questions of law or mixed questions of fact and law	Abuse of discretion (to be overturned, the lower court must have abused its discretion in making a decision): Used for discretionary decisions made by lower court, i.e., evidentiary rulings
	Clearly erroneous (to be overturned, the lower court's decision must be arbitrary and capricious): Used for judicial findings of fact; i.e., the facts found by the lower court are not supported in the record
	Arbitrary and capricious (to be overturned, the lower tribunal's decision must be arbitrary and capricious): Often used in administrative agency decisions; i.e., Equal Employment Opportunity Commission (EEOC), immigration
	No substantial evidence (to be overturned, there must be no substantial evidence to support the jury's decision): Used for jury-made findings of fact
WHY? Appellate courts are responsible for consistency in the LAW	*WHY? Trial courts are in the best position to evaluate the* FACTS

An appellate brief differs from a trial-level brief in that it has the following distinctive component parts: (1) a cover page (containing the case caption and title of the brief); (2) a table of contents; (3) a table of authorities; (4) the question(s) presented; (5) a statement of the case (including the procedural history and a statement of the facts, with citations to the appellate record); (6) argument, which includes the standard of review, point headings, the rules of law, explanation and application of the rules; and (7) a conclusion and "prayer for relief."

The responding party—called the *appellee* or *respondent*—files a responsive brief containing similar substantive sections as the initial brief, which usually warrants a reply brief as well. Often, the appellate court will hear oral argument on the appeal.

ADR: Mediation and Arbitration Papers

As an alternative to litigation, parties might agree—either in a contract or when conflict arises—to resolve disputes through mediation or arbitration. *Mediation* is a somewhat informal process in which the parties mutually select a mediator, often an individual with substantive knowledge of the type of subject matter involved in the dispute, such as a construction claim, a disagreement over a sports contract, or a divorce settlement. The parties may submit mediation papers—either confidential and only submitted to the mediator, or mutually exchanged—which are similar to briefs. These documents describe the facts of the matter from the submitting party's point of view, state the applicable rule(s) of law, and articulate the reasons why the party believes that it will prevail if the matter proceeds to trial. A mediation paper is intended to persuade the mediator and the opposing party that the submitting party has a strong position. If agreed to by the parties and requested by the mediator both sides submit these documents in advance of a scheduled mediation date—either unilaterally solely to the mediator or mutually to one another. On the day of the mediation, the mediator convenes with the parties privately in side meetings called "caucuses"; in each caucus, a good mediator will identify the strengths and weaknesses of each party's case and discern whether compromise is achievable. Throughout a day of mediation, the mediator might alternate between caucusing with the parties separately and then bringing them together to negotiate a compromise. Mediators require parties to bring a representative with full settlement authority to the mediation or have such an individual accessible by phone. If the mediation achieves a settlement of the matter, the parties draft the deal points of a settlement agreement while still in one another's presence and sign the document before departing. Later, the lawyers can draft a formal settlement agreement for signature by the parties.

Arbitration is more formal than a mediation, and comparable to a trial, except without a jury. The parties may choose a single arbitrator or a panel of arbitrators. Like mediators, arbitrators often possess substantive experience in the industries relevant to the dispute. An arbitration may involve similar phases as a standard litigation: pleadings, scheduling, fact and expert discovery, prehearing motions, and a hearing. Discovery is often more restricted than in litigation, and parties have no right to appeal. Throughout the arbitration phases, the parties might submit motions and briefs to educate the arbitrator(s) about the issues in the case and persuade the arbitrator(s) to rule a certain way on procedural and substantive issues.

*   *   *

Overall, whether a lawyer is representing a client in a transactional or a litigation setting, persuasive legal writing is a critical tool used to convince an opposing party, opposing counsel, or a decision maker that the lawyer's client is entitled to the result, remedy, or relief that it seeks.

CHECKLIST OF TYPES OF PERSUASIVE LEGAL WRITING

Transactional Context

- ☑ Negotiation E-mails and Letters
- ☑ Term Sheets
- ☑ Redline Drafts of Agreements

Litigation Context

- ☑ Demand Letter
- ☑ Settlement Letter
- ☑ Settlement Agreement
- ☑ Pleadings (Complaint, Answer, Counterclaim, Third-Party Complaint, Cross-Claim)
- ☑ Motion to Dismiss (plus Opposition Brief and Reply Brief)
- ☑ Discovery Demand Letter
- ☑ Motion to Compel Compliance with Discovery Requests (plus Opposition Brief and Reply Brief)
- ☑ Motion in Limine (plus Opposition Brief and Reply Brief)
- ☑ Motion for Summary Judgment (plus Opposition Brief and Reply Brief)
- ☑ Motion for Directed Verdict (plus Opposition Brief and Reply Brief)
- ☑ Motion for Judgment as a Matter of Law (plus Opposition Brief and Reply Brief)
- ☑ Motion for a New Trial (plus Opposition Brief and Reply Brief)
- ☑ Motion for Relief from a Judgment (plus Opposition Brief and Reply Brief)
- ☑ Motion for Reconsideration (plus Opposition Brief and Reply Brief)
- ☑ Posttrial Motions for Prejudgment Interest or Attorneys' Fees and Costs (plus Opposition Brief and Reply Brief)
- ☑ Motion for Stay of Enforcement of a Judgment (plus Opposition Brief and Reply Brief)
- ☑ Appeals (Initial Briefs, Responsive Briefs, and Reply Briefs)

CLASSROOM EXERCISE

In writing persuasively on behalf of a client, lawyers balance logic, emotion, and credibility to convey an influential message or theme, much as advertisers and politicians do when trying to sway consumers or voters. In our digital era, in which social media reigns supreme, the hashtag has become a medium for transmitting a message in a succinct word or phrase. For each of the following legal scenarios, create a hashtag of one to ten words that best captures the message or theme of the legal predicament.

Example: A band of college-aged computer whizzes hacked into the NYC Transit Authority computer system and wrought havoc throughout the subway lines across the five boroughs of New York. No one was injured, but trains were delayed for days, affecting workers' commutes. The city lost millions of dollars in revenue, and individuals and families suffered income losses. The hackers were arrested and charged with felonies. The prosecutor wanted to argue that these talented computer whizzes should be using their skills for something positive that would contribute to society, instead of jeopardizing the safety and livelihood of their fellow citizens.

Hashtag Theme? #useyourskillsforgoodnotevil

Create your own hashtag legal themes for the following scenarios:

1. The daughter of a single mother turned 16 and, in a rebellious episode, ran away from home. The mother immediately began searching for her throughout the country and discovered—after a year—that the daughter had been swept into a drug and weapons trafficking ring. In order to rescue her daughter, the mother had to infiltrate the ring, committing several crimes in doing so. She succeeded in retrieving her daughter, but she was arrested in the process. You are her defense attorney.
   Hashtag theme? _____

2. A well-known, formerly reputable, bank was caught skimming a penny from each of its customers' accounts each month, which over a period of five years added up to several millions of dollars. You are the prosecutor filing charges against the bank for fraud and embezzlement.
   Hashtag theme? _____

3. A respected construction contractor was hired to build a much-needed power plant in a community. The power plant would run on energy generated from water, not coal, and was intended to be as environmentally friendly as possible, generating a great amount of cost-efficient energy, as well as a large number of jobs, for the local community. The contractor agreed to build the project for a certain price and accepted all the risk of encountering unanticipated site conditions. During construction, the contractor stumbled upon an area of woodland that housed a protected species of bird that neither the contractor

nor the owner knew lived there. Cutting down the woodland would detrimentally affect the bird species, but working around the woodland to construct the project would cost the contractor hundreds of thousands of dollars, unanticipated in its budget. You are the lawyer representing the contractor, arguing that the project owner should renegotiate the contract price to account for these increased costs.

Hashtag theme? _____

Section 8

Writing Persuasive Letters in the Litigation Context

Chapter 23

Writing Persuasive Letters to an Opposing Party or Counsel

In the litigation context, lawyers use persuasive writing skills to craft convincing letters to opposing parties or their counsel at several stages of a case for various purposes:

- before a lawsuit is filed, to induce an individual or an entity to do something, or stop doing something, that affects the client
- to settle a dispute before a lawsuit is filed
- once a lawsuit is filed, to prompt the opposing party or counsel to comply with a discovery request (i.e., turn over documents, produce an uncooperative witness, or allow a site visit) or agree on the admissibility of particular evidence (i.e., exhibits or fact/expert witnesses) at trial
- to settle a dispute before trial.

A persuasive letter to an opposing party or counsel balances *logos* (logic), *pathos* (emotion), and *ethos* (credibility). *Logos* is achieved through clear organization of points and arguments, using a formula like IREAC or CREAC: (1) identifying the issue in dispute and asserting the client's contention, position, or conclusion; (2) asserting the governing rule, whether the rule comes from a contract the parties signed or a statute, regulation, or common law rule; (3) if necessary (depending on the sophistication of the letter recipient), explaining the rule through case examples; (4) applying the rule to the parties' facts; and (5) stating the precise result that the client seeks. An effective letter also provides a timeline or deadline for the requested follow-up action and indicates potential consequences or next steps if the recipient fails to perform the requested act.

Pathos is engendered through choosing engaging language and weaving the client's theme (either subtly or overtly) into the message. Lawyers must consider the tenor of the client's relationship with the opposing party and the nature of the attorneys' interaction when deciding whether to adopt a tone of antagonism, heavy-handedness, reasoned assertiveness, collaboration, or problem solving in a letter.

Ethos is bolstered through accurate recitation of the parties' factual circumstances, thorough research and presentation of the applicable rule(s) and supportive precedent (if included), and a credible stance on the follow-up action requested of the recipient. The letter writer's credibility is furthered by professional presentation, through proofreading, cite-checking, and proper formatting.

Letter Formatting and Structure

A professional legal letter appears on law office letterhead, providing the name and address of the attorney sending the letter. If proof of transmittal is needed, the letter indicates that it was sent via U.S. mail, e-mail, FedEx, or other means. A legal letter always contains the date (important for establishing the timeline/deadline for responsive action) and the correctly spelled name, title (Mr., Ms., Esq., Jr., etc.), and address of the recipient. Next, the letter includes a reference line, denoted by the abbreviation "Re:," indicating the client's name and a concise reference to the subject matter of the letter. If the letter is directed to opposing counsel rather than the party itself, the opposing party's name should be incorporated into the reference line. The letter commences with "Dear _____:" (legal letters use a colon rather than a comma to greet the recipient).

To present a logical and persuasive argument, good legal letters follow this organizational structure:

- An introductory sentence introducing the client and noting the author's representation of that client: "Our office represents _____ ("[*abbreviate client name in parentheses after the full name*]") regarding _____"
- A statement of the legal issue or nature of the dispute
- The governing rule, either from a contract signed by the parties, a statute (or regulation, code, or ordinance), or a common law rule derived and synthesized from case law
- If necessary and appropriate, an explanation of the rule, perhaps through a case or a collection of cases from the relevant jurisdiction

- An application of the rule to the parties' circumstances, focusing on the strengths of the client's position with the goal of convincing the opposing party (or counsel) of the validity of the client's argument
- A conclusion identifying the precise action that the letter requests
- A deadline or timeline for compliance
- If appropriate, the potential or actual consequences of noncompliance by the deadline or within the stated timeline
- A professional sign-off, such as "Sincerely," "Very truly yours," "Regards," or "Respectfully"
- The signing attorney's full name
- If appropriate, a "cc:" to the client and any other relevant individuals (i.e., an insurance company, in-house counsel, etc.)
- The word "Attachment(s)" if any relevant attachments are referenced in the letter and can be attached without logistical difficulty.

Writing a Persuasive Prelitigation Demand Letter

A persuasive demand letter can be an effective vehicle for settling a nascent dispute between a client and another individual or entity. Lawyers send these types of letters before either camp files a lawsuit. Consider this scenario: A client calls your office. She explains that she has been renting a condo in a New York City high-rise apartment building for four years without any problems or disturbance. She paid rent monthly to a management company. Last year, the property owner sold her apartment to an investor who resides in a foreign country. A few days after the sale, her ice maker malfunctioned and needed to be fixed. She called the building superintendent, as usual. The building declined to perform the maintenance work—as it had previously done without question or argument for four years—stating that it now needed authorization from the new owner before undertaking any repairs. The tenant e-mailed the new owner, who requested an estimate of the repair costs before he would approve the expense. The tenant obliged. Ten days passed. Ultimately, the new owner approved the repair but asked the tenant to pay the cost out of her own pocket and deduct the charge from the next month's rent. Unfortunately, the actual repair charge exceeded the estimate by $150. She deducted the total amount of the repair cost from her rent. Six months later, when the tenant moved out of her apartment into a loft in Brooklyn, her landlord deducted the extra $150 from her security deposit refund. The client has asked you to draft a demand letter to the landlord seeking repayment of the $150, which she believes was erroneously withheld.

Your letter might look like this:

Tigre & Hammerhead, LLP
3 West 26th Street, Suite 45
New York, NY 10326

March 26, 2017

Via E-Mail and Certified Mail

> Mode of Delivery

Mr. Victor Cascais
c/o SC Property Management
147 River Drive
Riverside, NY 12365

> Re: Tamryn Callahan; Tenant at 99 Stephan Street, # 72B, New York; Erroneous Withholding of Full Security Deposit Refund

> Reference Line

Dear Mr. Cascais:

> Greeting

Our office represents Tamryn Callahan ("Callahan"), your former tenant at the apartment located at 99 Stephan Street, # 72B, New York, NY. Ms. Callahan has informed us that, after she vacated the apartment at the expiration of her lease, you erroneously withheld $150 from the refund of her security deposit, purportedly representing the difference between the actual cost and the estimate for the repair of the Liebherr ice maker. Ms. Callahan disputes this withholding and hereby requests prompt reimbursement of the $150.

> Client Identification

> Issue

> Demand

Article 15.2 of the Lease between you and Ms. Callahan (a copy of which is attached hereto) states: "At the expiration of the Lease Term, the Tenant shall be entitled to remittance of the security deposit plus accrued interest, less any amounts necessary to repair damage to the floors, walls, appliances, permanent fixtures, and windows. Amounts to repair ordinary use and wear-and-tear shall not be deducted. If the Owner withholds any amounts from the security deposit, it shall provide Tenant with an itemized listing of the dollar amount and nature of such damages and necessary repairs, accompanied by photographs."

> Rule

As you are aware, the Liebherr ice maker malfunctioned through ordinary use and wear-and-tear. At your direction, Ms. Callahan obtained an estimate of the repair from the appliance repairperson of $405. She was without use of the ice maker for ten days while communicating with you, obtaining the estimate, and scheduling the repair. She incurred actual out-of-pocket expenses of $555 to facilitate such repairs, carried the $555 charge on her credit card for a month, and properly deducted such amount from her next month's rent. The excess of $150 was not

> Application of Rule to Client Facts

at all her fault. The repairs to the ice maker were in the ordinary course of her habitation of the property for four-and-a-half years.

Ms. Callahan was an excellent tenant, always paid her rent on time, and kept the apartment in fine shape for the duration of her residence. It is unjust for you to withhold $150 from her security deposit simply because the appliance repair company underestimated the repair costs.

> *Pathos*

At this time, Ms. Callahan requests prompt reimbursement of the $150 via cashier's check or wire transfer to her account at Kensington Trust Bank, by no later than April 7, 2017. If this amount is not received in full by this date, Ms. Callahan will have no choice but to seek reimbursement through the appropriate legal channels, and will also seek recovery of interest, attorneys' fees, and costs in accordance with Article 17.4 of the Lease.

> Specific Action Requested

> Consequences of Failure to Comply

We hope that you will make Ms. Callahan whole so that neither party has to endure the costs, inconvenience, and stress of legal action. Please do not hesitate to contact us if you have any questions regarding the foregoing. We look forward to your prompt cooperation in this matter.

> *Pathos* and *Logos*

Very truly yours,

TIGRE & HAMMERHEAD, LLP

> Respectful Sign-off

Grady H. Anderson

Grady H. Anderson

> Copy to Client

cc: Tamryn Callahan

Attachment

> Reference to Lease as Attachment

Writing a Persuasive Prelitigation Settlement Letter

A persuasive settlement proposal letter is another opportunity for an attorney to resolve a case effectively prior to either party filing a lawsuit. This letter is sent later than an initial demand letter in the timeline of the interaction between the client and the opposing party; perhaps initial demands have already been made, yet the opposing party has failed or refused to comply with the client's requests or demands. A lawyer may transmit a settlement proposal letter at the point at which no viable solution remains other than the opposing party accepting the settlement or the client proceeding with litigation. For this letter to function as intended, its tone must be assertive and authoritative enough to induce the opposing party to accept the proposed settlement terms (or make a counteroffer); otherwise, the client must be ready to proceed with filing the legal complaint in the appropriate court. Sometimes attorneys prepare a draft complaint and attach it to the settlement letter to demonstrate to the opposing party (or counsel) that the client is serious about the alternative to settlement. However, at the same time, depending on the nature of the relationship between the parties and counsel, the letter writer should resist asserting an overly antagonistic tone that might derail any possibility of conflict resolution. The proper posture of a settlement letter is always a judgment call and depends upon the personalities and temperaments of the various individuals involved.

A prelitigation settlement letter is similar in structure to the demand letter described above, except, if the author represents a potential plaintiff in a civil lawsuit, the document incorporates (1) details about the legal causes of action that the client plans to pursue in a lawsuit, (2) the reasons why the client believes she will prevail in such causes of action at trial, (3) the amount of damages or the remedy or remedies the client will seek at trial, and (4) a proposed compromise of the amount of damages or the remedy or remedies that the client will accept instead of proceeding with litigation. Conversely, if the letter writer represents a potential defendant in a civil lawsuit, the letter anticipates the causes of action that the potential plaintiff is likely to pursue and states the reasons why the client believes that the plaintiff will not prevail, any defenses the defendant plans to assert, and a compromise dollar figure or alternative remedy that the defendant offers on the condition that the plaintiff agrees to forego the lawsuit.

A prelitigation settlement letter should also contain a sentence stating that the letter's contents are for the purposes of settlement and compromise only and cannot be used as evidence at trial. Parties may disclose facts or details, admit certain information, or make particular concessions in a settlement letter—purely for the purposes of conflict resolution—that they might not want a judge or a jury to hear in a later trial. Because courts seek to encourage and foster settlement between parties to reduce the number of cases filed and thin crowded court dockets, rule makers have enacted evidentiary rules governing this exact issue. For example, Rule 408(a) of the Federal Rules of Evidence states in part:

> Evidence of the following is not admissible—on behalf of any party—either to prove or disprove the validity or amount of a disputed claim . . . :
>
> (1)   furnishing, promising, or offering—or accepting, promising to accept, or offering to accept—a valuable consideration in compromising or attempting to compromise the claim; and
> (2)   conduct or a statement made during compromise negotiations about the claim . . .

Many states have mirrored this language in their evidentiary rules, some with modifications. For example, Virginia's Rule of Evidence 2:408 states in part:

> Evidence of offers and responses concerning settlement or compromise of any claim which is disputed as to liability or amount is inadmissible regarding such issues. However, an express admission of liability, or an admission concerning an

independent fact pertinent to a question in issue, is admissible even if made during settlement negotiations.

Section 48.105 of Nevada's Evidence Code indicates:

Evidence of: (a) Furnishing or offering or promising to furnish; or (b) Accepting or offering or promising to accept, a valuable consideration in compromising or attempting to compromise a claim which was disputed as to either validity or amount, is not admissible to prove liability for or invalidity of the claim or its amount. Evidence of conduct or statements made in compromise negotiations is likewise not admissible.

While ultimately, the appropriate court will exercise its authority and discretion in applying the applicable rules to decide whether a settlement letter or its contents are admissible as evidence at trial, lawyers are wise to include in such letters an express reference to the applicable evidentiary rules, to bolster a later argument that the correspondence was written for settlement purposes only.

A persuasive prelitigation settlement demand letter might look like this:

ROBINSON AND JUSTICE, LLP
7 Central Park
Baltimore, MD 21218

November 8, 2017

| Mode of Delivery |

E-Mail and U.S. Mail

Miranda Fawcett, CEO
Fawcett Constructors, Inc.
29 Heron Road
Easton, MD 21610

Re: The Meyer Family Residence; 4414 Seaview Way, | Reference Line |
      Oxford, MD; Breach of Contract

Dear Ms. Fawcett: | Greeting |

Our office represents Leif and Stella Meyer (the "Meyers") with regard to the construction of their residence located at 4414 Seaview Way, Oxford, Maryland (the "Project"), and the | Client Identification | construction contract (the "Contract") they signed with Fawcett Constructors, Inc. ("Fawcett") on April 9, 2016. The Project is behind schedule and Fawcett has incorporated materials into the | Issue | Project that do not comply with the applicable building codes.

As you are aware, Article 3.2 of the Contract requires the Project | Rule | to be substantially completed by November 1, 2017. Further, Article 5.1 provides that, if the Project is delayed for reasons that were | Rule | within Fawcett's control, Fawcett shall be liable to the Meyers for liquidated damages in the amount of $2,000 per day of delay. As of the date of this letter, the Project is not substantially complete.

Additionally, Article 17.1 of the Contract provides that all materials used in construction of the Project will fully comply with all applicable building codes. The Meyers have discovered that the wood used by Fawcett in constructing the deck attached to the rear side of the structure fails to comply with Ordinance 4.867 of the Oxford Building Code, which requires fireproofing. An independent wood expert has confirmed this code violation.

> Rule

> Rule

Article 22 of the Contract authorizes the Meyers to terminate the Contract in the event of a material default by Fawcett, which includes a delay to the Project completion date, and/or placement of materials on the site which violate applicable building codes. Article 23 of the Contract entitles the prevailing party in a litigation resolving a dispute arising from or relating to the Contract to recover its reasonable attorneys' fees and court costs.

> Rule

> Rule

The elements of a cause of action for breach of contract under Maryland law include: (1) a contractual obligation; (2) a material breach of that obligation; and (3) damages. *LPS Default Solutions, Inc. v. Friedman & MacFayden, P.A.*, No. WDQ–13–0794, 2013 WL 4541281, at *3 (D. Md. Aug. 23, 2013). Under the express terms of the Contract, Fawcett had a duty to complete the Project in a timely manner by November 1, 2017, and provide code-compliant construction materials. It is undisputed that the Project is not yet complete and the deck materials violate Ordinance 4.867.

> Rule

> Application of Rule to Client Facts

Presently, liquidated damages have accrued for late completion in the amount of $14,000 (7 days of delay through the date of this letter), and will continue to accrue daily at a rate of $2,000 per day until Project completion. Additionally, an independent estimate reveals that the cost to hire a third party to remove and replace the noncompliant deck wood will total $26,000. As you are further aware, the timing of Project completion—which Fawcett represented it could achieve— was directly tied to the Meyers' plan to host their daughter's wedding reception at the new residence on New Year's Eve. The late completion is detrimentally affecting the wedding plans, forcing the Meyers to consider forfeiting deposits on tent rentals and outdoor sound system equipment in the event that they must relocate the wedding to an alternative venue. The Meyers would also incur the costs of notifying all guests of the change in the reception site.

> Pathos

At this time, the Meyers demand the following: (1) a written guarantee from Fawcett that the Project will be completed within the next 14 days, including the deck repair and replacement, which will be paid for by Fawcett; and (2) payment of $42,000 in liquidated damages for 21 days of Project delay. If Fawcett does not

> Specific Action Requested

accept these terms and make such payment, the Meyers will have no choice but to terminate the Contract pursuant to Article 22, hire a replacement contractor to finish the Project and perform the deck repair work, and file a cause of action for breach of contract in a Maryland court. If the Meyers are forced to proceed with litigation, they will seek damages in excess of $100,000, plus attorneys' fees and costs, under Article 23 of the Contract.

> Conse-
> quences of
> Failure to
> Comply

We hope that you will cooperate fully with the Meyers and fulfill the foregoing terms in a timely manner so that both parties can avoid the cost, time consumption, and burden of litigation and that the Project can be completed to the mutual satisfaction of both parties as originally intended. The Meyers hired Fawcett because of its reputation and stated philosophy to work collaboratively to create the home of its customer's dreams. Please stand by your mission statement and fulfill your contractual obligations.

> *Pathos*

This offer remains valid until 5 p.m. EST on November 11, 2017. If acceptance and payment are not received by that time, the Meyers will proceed with terminating the Contract and filing a Complaint in Maryland state court.

Under Maryland Rule of Evidence 5-408, this letter is offered for the sole purpose of compromising or attempting to compromise this claim and shall not be admissible at trial to prove the validity, invalidity, or amount of the claim. Thank you for your cooperation and anticipated timely response.

> Statement
> Regarding
> Admissibility
> of
> Settlement
> Comm-
> unications

Very truly yours,

ROBINSON AND JUSTICE, LLP

> Respectful
> Sign-off

Sam Justice

Sam Justice

> Copy to
> Client

cc: Leif and Stella Meyer

Persuasive Letters During Litigation to Resolve Discovery Disputes

Now imagine that you and your client unfortunately were unable to resolve a legal conflict with an opposing party prior to one side's filing a complaint in court.[1] Either you or opposing counsel filed the complaint, the receiving party filed an answer, the court issued a case management order (also called a scheduling

---

[1] Chapter 24 explains how to write a persuasive complaint.

order), and discovery commenced. *Discovery* is the phase of litigation in which lawyers draft and serve requests for production of documents or physical items, interrogatories, and requests for admissions. Each side serves objections and responses to these discovery requests and then uses the exchanged factual documents or items as exhibits in depositions. This process can take months, and often lawyers disagree on the scope or volume of discovery, arguing over logistical and substantive issues such as the following: (1) whether a party has produced its complete files and records; (2) whether a party's claims of attorney-client privilege or work product protection are valid; (3) whether a party will produce certain out-of-town witnesses for depositions; (4) how long each deposition should take and the scope of questioning; and (5) the timing and scheduling of depositions. Lawyers try to negotiate these issues over the phone or in person, but if they cannot reach a resolution, they must create a paper trail before seeking the court's intervention. Many courts have established rules governing discovery disputes, which require lawyers to meet and confer to resolve discovery disagreements on their own before seeking the court's assistance. The letters exchanged by counsel during this phase of a case serve as proof that the parties have attempted to meet and confer on discovery matters. Thus, when writing persuasive letters to opposing counsel to convince them to agree to the client's stance on a discovery issue, mindful lawyers envision the judge as an eventual additional audience.

Discovery letters follow the same general structural format as demand and settlement letters:

- First, remind opposing counsel which client you represent and which case the letter concerns, further referencing the opposing client's name. Opposing counsel likely has numerous cases pending, so an informative opening sentence referencing the lawyers' respective parties and the particular case is helpful.
- State the discovery issue in dispute and identify exactly what your client wants.
- Identify the governing rule(s)—i.e., the sections of the court's case management order (or scheduling order) stating the discovery parameters, and the jurisdiction's discovery rules.
- If appropriate for the length of the letter, succinctly describe any cases that illustrate the rule(s) and favor your client's position.
- Apply the rule(s) to the discovery that your client seeks or wants to preclude.
- Reiterate the precise result that your client wants.
- Establish a deadline or timeline for compliance or a response.
- Indicate any potential consequences for failure to comply or respond.
- Insert appropriate *pathos* to persuade opposing counsel to resolve the issue prior to seeking the court's intervention.
- Include an appropriate sign-off and signature.
- Add a "cc:" to the client and any other pertinent recipients of the letter.

An example of a letter attempting to persuade an opposing party (and counsel) to comply with a reasonable discovery request, and produce documents that have been wrongfully withheld, might look like this:

Solomon & MacKenzie, LLP
111 Reasonable Way
Naples, FL 34101

July 5, 2017

E-Mail and U.S. Mail

Mode of
Delivery

Christopher Severin, Esq.
Kelly & Casey, LLP
51 Holland Drive
Chicago, IL 60290

Reference
Line

    Re: *Messi Enterprises v. Gartner Insurance Company;* Case
         No. 16-4414; Request for Production of Documents
         Served on June 1, 2016

Dear Mr. Severin:

    As you are aware, we represent Messi Enterprises ("Messi") in the lawsuit against your client, Gartner Insurance Company ("Gartner") pending in the United States District Court for the Northern District of Florida, Case. No. 17-4414. On June 1, 2017, we served Messi's First Request for Production of Documents upon Gartner. According to Fed. R. Civ. P. 34(b)(2)(A), Gartner's written objections and responses were due on July 1, 2017. Your client provided written objections to nearly all the Requests for Production on the erroneous ground that all documents authored by Gartner's in-house counsel are protected by the attorney-client privilege. We disagree with your assertion of the attorney-client privilege and hereby demand production of all responsive documents within Gartner's possession, custody, and control. Fed. R. Civ. P. 37(a)(1) and 37(d)(1)(B), and Paragraph 14 of the court's scheduling order, require litigants to confer in good faith with the party failing to make disclosures or produce discovery in an effort to obtain the withheld documents or information without court action. Please consider this letter to be our good faith attempt to meet and confer to resolve this discovery dispute in advance of seeking the court's intervention, pursuant to Rule 37 and Paragraph 14 of the case scheduling order.

Client
Identification

Rule

Issue

Specific
Action
Requested

    When a party withholds information otherwise discoverable by claiming that the information is privileged, Fed. R. Civ. P. 26(b)(5)(A) requires the party to "describe the nature of the documents, communications, or tangible things not produced or disclosed—and do so in a manner that, without revealing information itself privileged or protected, will enable other parties to assess the claim." Normally, this is accomplished through a privilege log. You have failed to provide any such log identifying the documents that you claim were authored or received by Natalie Pritchett ("Pritchett"), in-house counsel for Gartner, an insurance company. Further, under Florida law, when an insurance company's in-house counsel acts in the ordinary course of the insurer's business in the role of a claims adjuster, her documents are not protected from disclosure by the attorney-client privilege. For example, in *Cutrale Citrus Juices USA v. Zurich American Ins. Group*, No. 5:03-CV-420, 2004 WL 5215191 (M.D. Fla. Sept. 10, 2004), an insurance company withheld documents from a claims file produced during discovery, including investigative materials prepared by the insurer's in-house counsel. The court explained the rule—in the context of insurance companies—that the attorney-client privilege does not apply to documents generated when an attorney performs investigative work in the capacity of an insurance claims adjuster rather than as a lawyer. *Id.* at *3. The court ordered the production of the investigative file. *Id.* Similarly, Pritchett clearly was acting in the role of an insurance claims adjuster rather than an attorney when she reviewed Messi's claim file in the ordinary course of business, to render an initial coverage decision. She analyzed Messi's insurance claim in light of its insurance policy and its exclusions—an action undertaken by claims adjusters every day without the need for legal interpretation or advice.

> Rule

> Application of Rule to Client Facts

> Rule

> Rule Explanation Paragraph

> Application of Rule to Client Facts

Accordingly, we request that you comply with your discovery obligations under Fed. R. Civ. P. 34 and 26 and produce all of Ms. Pritchett's files within fourteen (14) days of the date of this letter. Any delay in production of Gartner's complete file on this matter will only delay and disrupt the commencement of depositions and affect the court's scheduling order and discovery cutoff dates.

> Specific Action Requested

If you do not comply with your discovery obligations by producing such documents in a timely manner, we will have no choice but to file a motion to compel production of the documents, in accordance with the case scheduling order, and will seek sanctions in the form of all costs associated with filing the motion pursuant to Fed. R. Civ. P. 37(d)(1)(A)(ii).

> Consequences of Failure to Comply

Thus far in this litigation, we have appreciated your cooperation in negotiating the dates proposed to the court for discovery deadlines and our mutual agreement on production of electronic documents. We are perplexed by this recent change in tone and hope that you will reconsider your position in light of the foregoing rules, so that discovery can proceed for both parties in as cost-efficient a manner as possible.

> Pathos

We look forward to your anticipated cooperation in resolving this dispute without court intervention.

Very truly yours,

> Respectful Sign-off

Solomon & MacKenzie, LLP

R.G. MacKenzie

Rick MacKenzie

> Copy to Client

cc: Matteo Messi

From the opposing perspective, a persuasive letter explaining to opposing counsel why she is *not* entitled to the discovery sought might look like this:

Kelly & Casey, LLP
51 Holland Drive
Chicago, IL 60290

July 8, 2017

E-Mail and U.S. Mail

> Mode of Delivery

Rick MacKenzie, Esq.
Solomon & MacKenzie, LLP
111 Reasonable Way
Naples, FL 34101

Re: *Messi Enterprises v. Gartner Insurance Company;* Case No. 17-4414; Interrogatories Served on June 1, 2017, and July 7, 2017

> Reference Line

Dear Rick:

> Greeting

As you know, we represent Gartner Insurance Company ("Gartner") in the above-referenced case involving your client, Messi Enterprises ("Messi") pending in the United States District Court for the Northern District of Florida, Case No. 17-4414. We have received Messi's First Set of Interrogatories, served on June 1, 2017, and Second Set of Interrogatories, served on July 7, 2017. Reading all the interrogatories together, including their numerous subparts, Messi has exceeded the permissible number of interrogatories under the Federal Rules of Civil Procedure.

> Client Identification

> Issue

As you should be aware, Fed. R. Civ. P. 33(a)(1) states, "Unless otherwise stipulated or ordered by the court, a party may serve on any other party no more than 25 written interrogatories, including all discrete subparts." By our count, your First Set of Interrogatories totaled 23 (including discrete subparts). Your second set greatly exceeds the number allotted by the rules; the numbered items total an additional 9 questions, and each question contains at least three subparts.

Rule

Application of Rule to Client Facts

As stated in *Oliver v. City of Orlando*, No. 6:06-CV-1671, 2007 WL 3232227 (M.D.Fla. Oct. 31, 2007), if a subpart of an interrogatory question is sufficiently logically related to the information sought in the primary question, the question and subparts are to be counted as a single interrogatory. *Id.* at *3. In *Oliver*, a disputed interrogatory first asked a primary question regarding whether the responding party had paid certain claims. Then, the interrogatory continued; if the answer to the primary question was "yes," the subparts requested names, addresses, claim numbers, and amounts paid. *Id.* The court concluded that the subparts were discrete and should be noted as separately quantifiable interrogatories in the total count. *Id.* Messi's interrogatories follow the same pattern: first, a primary question about whether Gartner has paid certain insurance claims, and second, if so, subpart questions requesting names, addresses, claim numbers, and amounts claimed. Thus, Messi has exceeded its allotted number of interrogatories.

Rule Explanation Paragraph

Application of Rule to Client Facts

In accordance with our discovery obligations, we have already taken the time to prepare written objections and detailed responses to your First Set of Interrogatories. However, given your violation of the discovery rules, it is unfair to impose the burden and legal expense on Gartner to draft objections to your second set. Thus, at this time, we request that you withdraw your second set, redraft them in compliance with the 25-interrogatory limit, and we will respond within the 30-day time period prescribed in Fed. R. Civ. P. 33(b)(2).

Pathos

Specific Action Requested

Please let us know if you agree to such withdrawal by the close of business on Friday, July 14, 2017. If we do not hear from you by then, we will seek the court's intervention via a Motion to Compel Messi to Withdraw Its Second Set of Interrogatories and will seek appropriate costs incurred in filing such Motion.

Consequences of Failure to Comply

We hope that we can continue the spirit of cooperation that has characterized the discovery process in this case to date and resolve this matter expeditiously. Please do not hesitate to contact me if you wish to discuss this over the phone.

	Pathos

Very truly yours,

Kelly & Casey, LLP

	Respectful Sign-off

Christopher Severin

Christopher Severin

cc: Natalie Pritchett, Esq.

	Copy to Client

Persuasive Letters During Litigation to Resolve Evidentiary Disputes

During the discovery or pretrial phases of a case, lawyers on opposing sides also might disagree on whether evidence unearthed through the exchange of documents or during depositions will be admissible at trial. Sometimes lawyers write persuasive letters to negotiate evidentiary issues, to avoid the expense of filing motions in limine or having to inform the court about the evidentiary dispute. An example of a letter seeking to resolve an evidentiary matter related to, for instance, expert testimony might look like this:

Onde & Cavalloni, LLP
45 Surf Way
Honolulu, HI 96813

August 29, 2017

E-Mail and U.S. Mail

	Mode of Delivery

Madigan Rounds, Esq.
Rounds & Farmington, LLP
19 Four Arch Way
Laguna Beach, CA 92651

Re: *Mayle v. Rodham Landscaping Design;* Negligence Claim; Mutual Agreement to Exclude Expert Testimony Regarding Standard of Care

	Reference Line

Dear Madigan:

	Greeting

Thank you for our productive phone call earlier today. As you are aware, my client, Peyton Mayle ("Mayle"), is the plaintiff in

	Pathos

the negligence cause of action against your client, Rodham Landscaping Design ("Rodham"), pending in the United States District Court for the District of Hawaii. We are writing with regard to Rodham's expressed intent to present at trial an expert witness who is unnecessary for the adjudication of this case. The court rules, specifically Fed. R. Civ. P. 26(a)(2) and the Court's Scheduling Order, require the parties to disclose the identity of any testifying expert witnesses by September 16, 2017, and conduct expert depositions by November 11, 2017. If experts are not disclosed in accordance with the rules, such designations are waived.

| Client Identification |
| Issue |
| Rule |

On August 26, 2017, you identified Mark Santino, of Santino Landscaping Consultants, as a potential testifying expert on the subject of the standard of care for landscaping hydration in the Hawaii climate. However, we contend that, because this is an ordinary negligence case and Mayle has not made any allegations of professional negligence or malpractice in his complaint against Rodham, expert testimony on the standard of care is not required.

| Issue |

As the court explained in *Reimer v. Kuki'o Golf & Beach Club, Inc.*, No. 12-00408, 2014 WL 1643260 (D. Haw. April 22, 2014), under Hawaii law, expert testimony is not necessary to establish the applicable standard of care in an ordinary negligence case. Even in a case involving medical evidence, the *Reimer* court held that the jurors were capable of determining the standard of care based on their common knowledge or ordinary experience. *Id.* at *2. The court emphasized that the jurors did not need specialized knowledge, technical training, or background to determine the standard of care in that case. *Id.* Likewise, in the instant matter, Hawaiian jurors will not need specialized knowledge, technical training, or background to understand the principles of landscaping hydration.

| Rule and Rule Explanation Paragraph |
| Application of Rule to Client Facts |

Accordingly, at this time, I hope that we can reach a mutual agreement that neither party will submit expert testimony at trial regarding the standard of care for landscaping hydration in Hawaii. I also request that you withdraw your expert designation of Mr. Santino, and we will forego scheduling any depositions of him.

| Specific Action Requested |

Please indicate your consent to this proposal by the close of business on September 2, 2017. This is the prudent course of action for both parties, to avoid incurring the unnecessary expense of retaining such experts and paying for the production of expert reports, preparation for and participation in expert depositions, and filing and responding to related motions in limine. In the unfortunate event that you do not agree to this reasonable and well-founded proposal based on Hawaii law, we will have no

| *Pathos* |
| Consequences of Failure to Comply |

choice but to file a motion in limine to prevent the submission of Mr. Santino's testimony at trial.

We look forward to your cooperative response.

Very truly yours,

Onde & Cavalloni, LLP

P. Onde

Pietro Onde

Respectful
Sign-off

Copy to
Client

cc: Peyton Mayle

Writing Persuasive Letters to Settle a Dispute After Discovery and Before Trial

Once litigating parties have exhausted at least a majority of their discovery efforts, reviewed key documents, taken pivotal depositions, and vetted one another's experts, lawyers often make another attempt to settle the case before undertaking the expense and attendant risk of a trial. To do so, the plaintiff's lawyer writes a letter articulating the reasons why his client likely will prevail at trial, yet indicating that, if the opposing party will agree to pay a certain amount of money now or perform an alternative remedial action, the plaintiff will forego the trial. Alternatively, a defendant's lawyer might write a letter itemizing the reasons why the plaintiff would be taking a huge risk in proceeding with the trial, further pointing out the weaknesses in the plaintiff's case, and yet offering to settle for a reduced amount if the plaintiff will dismiss the case.

These letters focus on the required elements of the rule(s) of law governing the cause(s) of action in the lawsuit and use the key pieces of evidence obtained in discovery to argue persuasively why the rule elements either will or will not be met. The plaintiff's lawyer presents the client's strengths and highlights the defendant's weaknesses, and vice versa. Strengths and weaknesses might relate to the evidence, the credibility of witnesses, and public relations concerns.

A persuasive letter attempting to settle a case after the conclusion of discovery but before trial might look like this:

Fiducioso & Giustizia, LLP
5 Shore Way
Bay Head, NJ 08742

December 2, 2017

E-Mail and U.S. Mail

Jack Caparbio, Esq.
Caparbio & Associates
56 Main Street
Bay Head, NJ 08742

  Re: *Capri Motor Works, LLC v. Bedrock Insurance Company;* Settlement Proposal

Dear Jack:

  Thank you for sending Bedrock Insurance Company's ("Bedrock") supplemental responses to our client Capri Motor Works' ("Capri") Third Set of Interrogatories. At this time, according to the court's Case Management Order, all fact and expert discovery is now complete and Capri is ready to proceed to trial. However, given the information gathered in document discovery, the damaging admissions of former Bedrock insurance claims personnel in depositions, the adverse findings of Capri's expert witnesses, and the unfortunate notorious reputation that Bedrock has earned in the local community, it clearly would be in Bedrock's best interest to settle this case prior to trial.

  As you are aware, Capri had no choice but to sue Bedrock, its insurer for 21 years, for breach of contract and breach of the implied duty of good faith and fair dealing, based upon Bedrock's unfounded decision to deny coverage of valid insurance claims submitted after Capri endured significant property and financial losses from Hurricane Josselyn. Bedrock had accepted insurance premium payments for 21 years without a single claim filed by Capri, and yet, when Capri needed the support of its insurer most, Bedrock fell short. Under New Jersey law, the elements of a cause of action for breach of contract are: (1) a duty, (2) a breach of that duty, and (3) damages. *Coyle v. Englander's*, 488 A.2d 1083, 1088 (N.J. Super. 1985). Further, every contract under New Jersey law includes an implied covenant of good faith and fair dealing. *Wilson v. Amerada Hess Corporation*, 773 A.2d 1121, 1126 (N.J. 2001). An insurer owes its insured a duty to cover claims properly brought under an insurance agreement and which are not subject to any exclusion. *Flomerfelt v. Cardiello*, 997 A.2d 991, 1004 (N.J. 2010).

<table>
<tr><td>Mode of Delivery</td></tr>
<tr><td>Reference Line</td></tr>
<tr><td>Greeting</td></tr>
<tr><td>Client Identification</td></tr>
<tr><td>Issue</td></tr>
<tr><td>Pathos</td></tr>
<tr><td>Rule</td></tr>
<tr><td>Rule</td></tr>
<tr><td>Rule</td></tr>
</table>

The plain language of the insurance agreement executed 21 years ago between Capri and Bedrock demonstrates that the property and economic losses sustained by Capri during and after the hurricane were exactly the types of losses covered by Capri's insurance policy. Bedrock failed to provide such coverage and ignored its own claims investigation and analysis procedures and policies in rejecting Capri's claim. This constitutes a breach. Further, Capri incurred: (1) out-of-pocket damages in the amount of $1.2 million, (2) additional business losses resulting from Bedrock's refusal to provide coverage, which forced Capri to close its doors for eight months while securing financing, and (3) attorneys' fees and costs in bringing this action—totaling $3.3 million.

> Application of Rule to Client Facts

If this case proceeds to trial, Bedrock will not fare well. The documents obtained in discovery, including e-mails exchanged between Bedrock claims handlers, will reveal Bedrock's strategy of denying coverage for no legitimate reason in hopes that its "lesser sophisticated" insureds will "just go away quietly." We plan to call as witnesses Bedrock's former claims adjusters, who were fired when they challenged the ethics and legality of the foregoing strategy. Further, Capri's expert witness, an insurance professional with over 30 years of industry experience, will testify about the impropriety of Bedrock's procedures in light of industry standards.

> *Pathos*

Based upon the foregoing, and a mountain of additional evidence obtained during discovery, we are fully prepared to proceed with the trial of this action. We further anticipate a large jury verdict and judgment in Capri's favor. However, in the interests of minimizing additional attorneys' fees and court costs, Capri would be willing to settle this case now for a lump sum payment of $2.5 million, payable by wire transfer no later than December 16, 2017. This offer will expire at 5 p.m. EST on that date.

> Specific Action Requested

We look forward to receiving your response. If you have any questions regarding the foregoing, please do not hesitate to contact me.

> Consequences of Failure to Comply

Very truly yours,

> Respectful Sign-off

Fiducioso & Giustizia, LLP

Ronna Giustizia

Ronna Giustizia

cc: Penelope Wyatt, Esq.

> Copy to Client

Pathos and *Ethos* in Letter Writing

When writing letters to opposing parties and counsel, lawyers consider the nature of the client's relationship with the opposing party and the letter writer's relationship with opposing counsel. The tone of the letter will differ depending on whether such relationships will continue in the future after the case is resolved and depending upon the personalities and temperaments of the opposing parties. Consider the differences in tone in the following sentences asking for the same action by the letter recipient:

Example 1 (Aggressive Tone)

Your dilatory behavior throughout discovery is nothing more than a veiled attempt to postpone and delay a resolution of this dispute for as long as possible. We can no longer tolerate your unreasonable and unjustified refusal to produce the entire project file. If you do not transmit the complete set of project records by the close of business on Friday, July 28, 2017, we will proceed with filing a motion to compel and will seek monetary and substantive sanctions to the fullest extent permitted under the court rules.

Example 2 (Good-Faith Attempt to Resolve the Issue)

We understand that this dispute has been stressful, costly, and burdensome to both parties. Nonetheless, both clients are obligated under the applicable discovery rules to produce their complete project files. Your client's inexplicable delay in production of the file is now affecting our ability to prepare for depositions and resolve this case in a cost-efficient and timely manner. Please advise as to why you and your client are unable to meet this straightforward request. We are willing to work with you perhaps on a sequenced or phased production, but we have been more than patient and reasonable in affording you and your client extra time to comply with your discovery obligations and can wait no longer. If we do not receive a good-faith response to this letter by the end of the week, we will have no choice but to pursue judicial intervention, which will only result in additional costs and burden to both parties.

Depending upon the parties' and counsel's relationships, personalities, and temperaments, either one of the foregoing versions—or many variations thereof—might be appropriate under the given circumstances. Regardless of a lawyer's own disposition and default mode of communicating, mindful legal writers consider the bigger picture when drafting litigation letters—pairing the appropriate level of *pathos* with *logos*, and always maintaining a level of *ethos* to preserve one's own integrity and credibility as a client advocate.

Exercise

Recall the legal research memoranda assignments that you wrote in your first semester of law school—in which you focused on objective/predictive legal analysis. Choose your favorite memorandum topic, and write a demand letter on behalf of your client to the opposing party, asking the individual or entity to take a certain action or cease taking a certain action. First, create your own (hypothetical) law office letterhead. Then, use the following structure to draft the content of your letter:

- Date the letter.
- Decide and indicate how you will transmit the letter (U.S. Mail? E-mail? FedEx?).
- Include the opposing party's or counsel's proper name and address.
- Add an informative reference line (your client's name, the opposing party's name, and the name of the case/matter).
- Insert a professional greeting to the letter recipient (i.e., Dear [*Insert Name*] and add a colon).
- Write an introductory sentence identifying your client and noting the nature of your representation of that client: "Our office represents _____ ("[*abbreviate client name*]") regarding _____." Mention the opposing party (with an appropriate abbreviation) if the sentence logic requires.
- Concisely state the legal issue or nature of the dispute that is the subject of the letter.
- Recite the governing rule(s), either from a contract the parties signed, a statute (or regulation, code, or ordinance), or a common law rule derived and synthesized from case law.
- If necessary and appropriate, explain or illustrate the rule(s), perhaps through a case or a few cases in the relevant jurisdiction.
- Apply the rule(s) to the parties' factual circumstances, focusing on the strengths of your client's position and convincing the opposing party (or counsel) of the validity of your argument.
- Balance *logos, pathos,* and *ethos* throughout the letter.
- Conclude by identifying the precise action that you request or demand the letter recipient to take.
- Include a deadline or timeline for compliance.
- If appropriate, identify the potential or actual consequences for noncompliance by the deadline or within the stated timeline.
- Include a professional sign-off, such as "Sincerely," "Very truly yours," "Regards," or "Respectfully."
- Include your full name.

- If appropriate, add a "cc:" to your client and any other relevant individuals (i.e., an insurance company, in-house counsel, etc.).
- Add the word "Attachment(s)" if any relevant attachments are referenced in the letter and would be reasonable and helpful to attach.

Professional letters are single-spaced, with the first line of each paragraph indented one tab space and an extra space between paragraphs. Try to avoid dangling headings or one-line sentences at the bottom of a page. Insert page breaks to make the letter more visually pleasing. If the letter is more than one page, all pages after the first page should include a header at the top left corner with the name of the recipient, the date, and a page number. Proofread, spell-check, and cite-check. When you sign your name to a legal demand letter, you want it to reflect the utmost professionalism. Always keep in mind that a judge might eventually read the letter if it is attached as an exhibit to a motion.

Section 9

Writing Persuasive Pleadings
in the Litigation Context

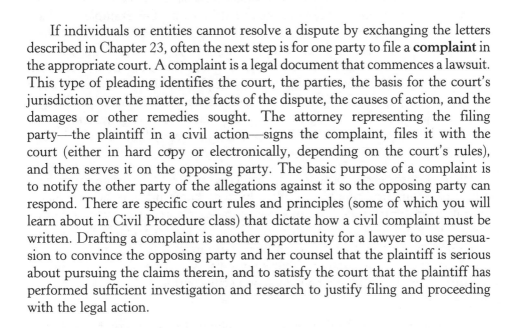

Chapter 24
Drafting a Persuasive Complaint

If individuals or entities cannot resolve a dispute by exchanging the letters described in Chapter 23, often the next step is for one party to file a **complaint** in the appropriate court. A complaint is a legal document that commences a lawsuit. This type of pleading identifies the court, the parties, the basis for the court's jurisdiction over the matter, the facts of the dispute, the causes of action, and the damages or other remedies sought. The attorney representing the filing party—the plaintiff in a civil action—signs the complaint, files it with the court (either in hard copy or electronically, depending on the court's rules), and then serves it on the opposing party. The basic purpose of a complaint is to notify the other party of the allegations against it so the opposing party can respond. There are specific court rules and principles (some of which you will learn about in Civil Procedure class) that dictate how a civil complaint must be written. Drafting a complaint is another opportunity for a lawyer to use persuasion to convince the opposing party and her counsel that the plaintiff is serious about pursuing the claims therein, and to satisfy the court that the plaintiff has performed sufficient investigation and research to justify filing and proceeding with the legal action.

Jurisdiction

In your first semester of law school, you learned about the doctrine of *stare decisis* and precedent—principles upon which our common law legal system is based. In adjudicating new cases, judges rely upon prior court decisions. Whether such past decisions are mandatory or persuasive legal authority depends upon which court in which jurisdiction decided the particular case. Judicial decisions are mandatory authority if they were rendered by a court of higher ranking within the same jurisdiction; i.e., a trial court must follow the decisions of the appellate court in the same jurisdiction. The appellate court must follow the decisions of the Supreme Court, or the highest court in the jurisdiction if the court of last resort is called something other than the Supreme Court (as in the State of New York where the trial court is the Supreme Court and the highest court is the Court of Appeals).

When drafting a complaint, a lawyer must consider the appropriate jurisdiction in which to file the pleading. This decision may, at first glance, seem obvious, but the opposing party (the defendant) can file a motion to dismiss the complaint for lack of jurisdiction if the case is filed in the wrong court. In your Civil Procedure class, you likely will learn about subject matter jurisdiction and personal jurisdiction. *Subject matter jurisdiction* means that the court has authority to adjudicate the substance of the dispute. *Personal jurisdiction* means that the court has authority over the parties because they have sufficient contacts with the particular location, perhaps through residency or conducting business there.

When drafting a complaint and choosing a jurisdiction, lawyers first evaluate whether the case should be filed in state or federal court. For example, a federal district court has jurisdiction if a civil case involves the U.S. Constitution, a federal law, or a treaty in which the United States is a participant. Or, if the case involves citizens of two different states (i.e., the plaintiff is a citizen of Wisconsin and the defendant is a citizen of Nevada) and the plaintiff seeks damages in excess of $75,000, the plaintiff may file the case in federal court based on the principle of "diversity jurisdiction." A state court has jurisdiction over disputes concerning, for example, property located within the state, divorces, child custody, inheritance matters, contract disputes, and personal injury.

Why does the choice of state or federal court matter? First, state and federal courts have different procedural rules. Further, some litigants believe that a federal court forum might be more advantageous for out-of-state corporate parties, to avoid in-state parties having a "home team advantage." Also, the jury selection process may differ between the state and federal courts even in the same geographical location. The judges also vary. These are all issues to research to determine whether a federal or a state court is the appropriate choice for your case.

In addition to the federal-state court distinction, lawyers research which geographical locale is the proper one for the case. If the plaintiff is a citizen of Delaware who purchased a defective item over the Internet from a company in Michigan for $1000, would the litigant rather file in Delaware or in Michigan? Does the parties' purchase agreement designate a choice of forum? Is the choice-of-forum clause mandatory or permissive? Which state has jurisdiction over the parties? Was the contract executed in a certain state? How does the electronic nature of the transaction affect the location where the contract was executed? Did an accident take place in a certain location?

Another consideration when choosing the appropriate court within which to file a complaint is the convenience of the forum to the parties. In many states, the federal court system is divided into different districts. For example, the Commonwealth of Virginia has two districts: the Eastern District of Virginia and the Western District of Virginia. These districts have separate divisions. The Eastern District of Virginia covers the geographical areas of Alexandria, Newport News, Norfolk, and Richmond. The Western District has courthouses in Abingdon, Big Stone Gap, Charlottesville, Danville, Harrisonburg, Lynchburg, and Roanoke. When evaluating the proper venue, courts and litigants consider geographical convenience to the parties and witnesses. Overall, lawyers drafting a complaint conduct thorough research before choosing the proper court in which to file the pleading.

Case Caption

The *caption* of the complaint is the part of the pleading that helps the court clerk organize all the documents filed in a particular case and distinguish one legal matter from another. The caption contains the court name, the proper full names of the parties, a designation of the parties as plaintiff or defendant, and the docket or case number assigned by the clerk once the complaint is filed. When drafting and filing the complaint, attorneys leave the case/docket number blank. When the complaint is filed, the clerk stamps the complaint with the assigned docket number.

Lawyers must identify the proper full names of the parties, whether they are individuals, corporations, or governmental entities. Some companies conduct business under several different names; lawyers must perform adequate research to identify the parties in the case correctly. A defendant could file a motion to dismiss the complaint if it is filed against the wrong individual or entity name.

Some courts also require the caption to identify whether the plaintiff is requesting a jury trial; if the dispute involves a contract, the complaint drafter must check the contract to determine whether the parties waived the right to a jury trial. Without a contractual waiver, lawyers consider whether a judge trial (also called a *bench trial*) or a jury trial would be more beneficial for their clients.

Title

The complaint must bear the title "Complaint" so the court clerk, the judge, and the opposing party know what type of pleading it is.

Introduction

The first sentence of the complaint identifies the party filing it, plus the opposing party, and uses introductory language such as "Plaintiff Riggins

Garment Company ('Riggins'), by counsel, for its Complaint against Cornerstone Insurance Company ('Cornerstone'), hereby states as follows." Just as lawyers assign abbreviations to party names in the first sentence of the persuasive letters discussed in Chapter 23, lawyers establish an appropriate abbreviation for the parties' names in the first sentence of a complaint, to avoid having to repeat lengthy names and titles throughout the pleading.

Numbered Paragraphs

When drafting a complaint, lawyers strive to be persuasive in using *logos*, *pathos*, and *ethos*, but they also must keep in mind the applicable court rules for drafting pleadings. Fed. R. Civ. P. 8(a), which governs complaint drafting in federal court,[1] states:

> A pleading that states a claim for relief must contain:
>
> (1) a short and plain statement of the grounds for the court's jurisdiction, unless the court already has jurisdiction and the claim needs no new jurisdictional support;
> (2) a short and plain statement of the claim showing that the pleader is entitled to relief; and
> (3) a demand for the relief sought, which may include relief in the alternative or different types of relief.

Thus, a federal complaint should include numbered paragraphs that describe the basis for the court's jurisdiction and the chosen venue, a simple description of the parties, the relevant facts giving rise to the dispute, the causes of action, and the damages or other remedies sought. Some lawyers like to include headings to divide each part of the complaint, such as "Jurisdiction and Venue," "Parties," "Facts," "Count I," "Count II," etc., and "Relief Sought," as described below.

Jurisdiction and Venue

The first few numbered paragraphs below the introductory sentence of the complaint should state the basis for the court's jurisdiction and the chosen venue. For example, if the plaintiff is filing the complaint in federal court based on diversity jurisdiction, the lawyer would write numbered paragraphs explaining the following:

---

[1] Lawyers drafting complaints to be filed in state court will check the state court pleading requirements.

1. This court has jurisdiction over this action pursuant to 28 U.S.C. § 1332 because there is complete diversity of citizenship between the parties and the amount in controversy exceeds $75,000.

2. Venue is proper in the United States District Court for the Southern District of New York pursuant to 28 U.S.C. § 1391(b) because the property damage and financial losses that are the subject of this dispute occurred in Lower Manhattan.

Through legal research, lawyers identify the particular statute or other rule that grants the chosen court authority to exercise jurisdiction and to support the venue selection.

Parties

The next few consecutively numbered paragraphs describe the parties, who they are, what they do or their roles in society, their states of citizenship, and perhaps their relationship to one another. For individuals, citizenship is determined by place of domicile—where they reside with an intent to remain.[2] Corporations are citizens of their state of incorporation and the locale of their principal place of business.[3] The citizenship of a partnership or limited liability company is determined by the citizenship of its partners or members.[4]

For example, numbered paragraphs describing the parties might state as follows:

3. Plaintiff Riggins is a company incorporated in the State of New York that imports fabrics and textiles and manufactures garments that it sells to key players in New York's fashion industry. Its principal place of business is located on Front Street in the South Street Seaport area of Lower Manhattan.

4. Defendant Cornerstone is an insurance company that has been operating in Boston, Massachusetts, for over 100 years. It provides various types of insurance to small businesses, including but not limited to professional liability insurance, fire insurance, general comprehensive liability insurance, worker's compensation insurance, and business interruption insurance. It was incorporated in Massachusetts, and its principal place of business is in Boston.

---

[2] *McEntire v. Kmart Corp.*, No. CIV 09-0567 JB/LAM, 2010 WL 553443, at *3 (D.N.M. Feb. 9, 2010).
[3] 28 U.S.C.A. § 1332(c)(1).
[4] *Boise Cascade Corp. v. Wheeler*, 419 F. Supp. 98, 100 (S.D.N.Y. 1976); *Agility Logistics Corp. v. Elegant USA, LLC*, No. 09 Civ. 4719(DLC), 2009 WL 3094898, at *1 (S.D.N.Y. Sept. 25, 2009).

Facts

As stated in Fed. R. Civ. P. 8(a) mentioned above, a lawyer drafting a complaint must provide "a short and plain statement of the claim showing that the pleader is entitled to relief." Not all the facts giving rise to the dispute may be known to the plaintiff at the time the complaint is drafted; the discovery phase of the case will give the parties the opportunity to unearth additional facts. However, Fed. R. Civ. P. 11(b) is an ethical rule that requires the lawyer signing the complaint to certify to the best of the lawyer's "knowledge, information, and belief, formed after an inquiry reasonable under the circumstances," that:

- the pleading is not being presented for any improper purpose, such as to harass, cause unnecessary delay, or needlessly increase the cost of litigation;
- the claims and other legal contentions are warranted by existing law or by a nonfrivolous argument for extending, modifying, or reversing existing law or for establishing new law; and
- the factual contentions have evidentiary support or, if specifically so identified, will likely have evidentiary support after a reasonable opportunity for further investigation or discovery.[5]

Additionally, you likely will learn in Civil Procedure class that courts have certain standards for determining whether a complaint includes enough detail to withstand a motion to dismiss.[6] When drafting a complaint, lawyers must research the applicable standard in the jurisdiction for writing pleadings with sufficient specificity to withstand a motion to dismiss.

The factual section in a complaint should itemize, in numbered paragraphs, the acts and events that gave rise to the dispute. Consider the following excerpt from a dispute between a garment company and its insurer:

5. Plaintiff Riggins has been in the garment industry since 1990, importing textiles from countries like India, Bangladesh, Cambodia, and Mexico, and using them to manufacture garments and clothing lines for designer labels in New York's fashion industry.
6. The company was founded by a married couple named John and Fiona Riggins. John and Fiona are members of the company's board of directors. The board also includes John's sister, Maia Mandell ("Mandell") who is an attorney and serves as in-house counsel to the company.
7. The company leases a warehouse space in a brick building located on Front Street in the historic South Street Seaport area of Manhattan.

---

[5] Fed. R. Civ. P. 11.
[6] "Threadbare recitals of the elements of a cause of action, supported by mere conclusory statements, do not suffice." *Ashcroft v. Iqbal*, 556 U.S. 662, 678 (2009). Only complaints that state a "plausible claim for relief" can survive a Rule 12(b)(6) motion to dismiss. *Id.* at 679.

8. When the company was first founded in 1990, Mr. Riggins purchased comprehensive general liability (CGL) and business interruption insurance policies from Defendant Cornerstone. To purchase the policy, the company was required to complete a detailed application.

9. Upon approval by Cornerstone's insurance risk analyst, Jamie Plunkett, the insurance company issued a full coverage insurance policy (Policy No. 3261970) to Plaintiff Riggins which was designed to cover comprehensive business operations, including losses due to property damage, personal injury, and third-party lawsuits. The policy provided coverage limits of $5 million per occurrence. The policy also provided that Defendant Cornerstone would defend the insured, Plaintiff Riggins, in all third-party lawsuits covered under the policy.

10. Beginning in 1990, Plaintiff Riggins paid an annual premium of $24,000 to Defendant Cornerstone, paid in monthly installments. This premium increased gradually each year. Currently, Plaintiff Riggins pays a monthly premium of $2,900, for an annual premium of $34,800.

11. For 23 years, Plaintiff Riggins paid its insurance premiums on time. In fact, to date, Defendant Cornerstone has cashed checks in the total amount of over $635,000 from Plaintiff Riggins.

12. Until 2013, Plaintiff Riggins had never once filed an insurance claim.

13. Over the 23 years Plaintiff Riggins has been in business, the company has grown its success, expanding to several floors of its warehouse facility on Front Street. Its clients include several premiere fashion designers in New York City, including Howell + Brown and EHD Brand. The company also provides clothing lines for several musical artists for their tours, including Bronwyn D and The Inchi Band.

14. In October 2012, Hurricane Sandy hit the East Coast and had devastating effects in New York City, especially in the South Street Seaport area.

15. Many of the historic buildings in the Seaport area were damaged substantially due to floodwaters, as the storm surge from the East River flooded many buildings up to the second floor. Almost all the buildings on Front Street—including numerous restaurants, coffee shops, apartment buildings, and businesses—were ordered evacuated and closed, pending water rehabilitation work and subsequent environmental and safety inspections.

16. Rehabilitation work commenced immediately once the storm had subsided; however, throughout the remainder of 2012 and much of 2013, many of the buildings on Front Street remained closed.

17. When the storm hit in October 2012, Plaintiff Riggins took steps to protect its warehouse stock; however, the floodwater damaged the entire first floor of the warehouse, destroying inventory, textiles, files, computers, manufacturing equipment, furniture and artwork, etc. Plaintiff Riggins estimates property damage losses in the amount of $1.1 million due to water and mold.

18. Further, Plaintiff Riggins had to shut down its importing and manufacturing operations for a period of four months until March 1, 2013, when it secured temporary alternative workspace in Williamsburg, Brooklyn. Plaintiff Riggins moved as much of the undamaged textiles as it could from the Front

Street location to the Williamsburg location and attempted to resume its importing and manufacturing operations in March 2013 as best it could.

19. During the period of closure, Plaintiff Riggins was unable to perform several contracts for clothing lines for several of its customers. Unfortunately, Plaintiff Riggins was unable to fill an order for designer Howell + Brown in advance of Fashion Week in February 2013. Further, Plaintiff Riggins was unable to fill an order for The Inchi Band, for costumes for backup dancers needed for an April 2013 tour. Both Howell + Brown and The Inchi Band filed lawsuits in New York state court against Plaintiff Riggins, alleging breach of contract damages exceeding a combined total of $500,000. One lawsuit was filed in May 2013 and the other in July 2013. The New York state court granted Plaintiff Riggins time extensions to file Answers in both lawsuits, pending submission of the claims to Defendant Cornerstone.

20. By August 31, 2013, the NYC Department of Buildings had authorized several Front Street businesses to resume occupancy of their facilities after water and mold remediation was complete, and the structures passed environmental and safety inspections.

21. Plaintiff Riggins began to move back into its Front Street facility.

22. In September 2013, Plaintiff Riggins directed its in-house counsel, Mandell, to review the terms of its insurance policies and begin filing claims for insurance coverage of its losses in accordance with the policy terms and notice requirements.

23. Plaintiff Riggins filed its claims for coverage of its property damage losses with its insurer on September 15, 2013.

24. Also on September 15, 2013, Plaintiff Riggins filed claims for coverage of the potential damages from the two lawsuits pending against it, and also submitted a formal request for Defendant Cornerstone to provide and fund a legal defense against both actions, in accordance with the insurance policy terms.

25. For three months, Plaintiff Riggins received no communication from its insurer, despite repeated calls, letters, and follow-up e-mails from in-house counsel Mandell to the company's insurance representative listed on the 2013 premium statements, Todd Nicks ("Nicks").

26. On December 18, 2013, in-house counsel Mandell called the insurance company and was told by an administrative assistant, Jeremy Connor, that Nicks no longer worked for the company, and the policies had been transferred to a new representative, Nadine Valentino.

27. On December 27, 2013, a different insurance representative named Sam Manning sent an e-mail to Mandell indicating that the insurance claims had been further referred to Defendant Cornerstone's claims adjuster and in-house counsel, Madeline Hewes ("Hewes"), for follow-up investigation and evaluation.

28. On January 2, 2014, the insurer sent Plaintiff Riggins a one-page letter denying coverage for all of the alleged property damage losses and refusing to defend the insured against the two lawsuits pending in state court.

29. The letter was signed by Hewes, as Defendant Cornerstone's claims adjuster and in-house counsel.

30. The letter denied coverage and declined to defend the lawsuits on the following alleged grounds:
   a. "The insured failed to make timely insurance premium payments."
   b. "The insured made false misrepresentations in its original policy application."
   c. "The insured failed to comply with the insurance policy's notice requirements and deadlines for filing claims."
   d. "The losses claimed by the insured are not covered losses."
   e. "The insured failed to mitigate its damages and further exacerbated its own losses, nullifying the insurance coverage."
   f. "The losses claimed are excluded under numerous policy exclusions."

31. On January 3, 2014, Plaintiff Riggins sent a letter to the insurer, signed by in-house counsel Mandell, asking it to reconsider its denial of coverage, and requesting the insurer to honor its coverage responsibilities and duty to defend its insured against the two lawsuits.

32. The insurer failed to respond to the letter.

33. On January 6, 2014, Mandell telephoned the insurer and was informed by Brandi Caldwell, assistant to claims adjuster and in-house counsel, Madeline Hewes, that the insurer would not reconsider its position.

34. Plaintiff Riggins' in-house counsel, Mandell, filed Answers to the Complaints filed in the two lawsuits, which are now proceeding to the discovery phase.

Fed. R. Civ. P. 8(d) states that "each allegation must be simple, concise, and direct. No technical form is required." A strong factual section of a complaint uses all three techniques of persuasion: *logos, pathos,* and *ethos.* The recitation must be logical, perhaps relaying the facts in chronological order so the readers—the judge and the opposing party—can understand what the plaintiff contends occurred. It can, and should be, emotionally engaging to a reasonable degree. The lawyer drafting the factual section of a complaint already should be considering a workable theme, or a case theory, for the plaintiff's case and should weave this theme/theory (in a reasonable manner) into the description of the facts. In the example above, the theme might be: a small business owner performed the responsible act of purchasing business insurance and paying thousands of dollars in premiums for 23 years, and when disaster struck, the insurance company abandoned its insured.

Ethos is also important to keep in mind, in light of Fed. R. Civ. P. 11 and its state court counterparts. A lawyer should never stretch the case facts to inspire *pathos* and thereby compromise *ethos.* At the same time, however, the lawyer should not recite the facts so robotically or matter-of-factly that the story ignites no emotion in the reader.

Consider these three contrasting recitations of the same fact:

Too Bland: The insurance company denied the insured's claim.
Too Dramatic: After extorting money from the innocent insured for two decades, absconding with insurance premiums knowing full well that it never had any intention of making good on its promises, the insurance

company abandoned the insured in its time of need, outright rejecting the insured's valid claim, leaving it high and dry, on the brink of financial ruin.

Just Right: The insurance company accepted over $635,000 in insurance premiums over the past 23 years from its insured, who had never previously filed a claim. When disaster struck in the form of Hurricane Sandy, Plaintiff Riggins—for the first time—filed claims seeking coverage of its significant damages and losses, in accordance with the insurance policy terms. Without any legitimate explanation, the insurance company refused coverage and denied the claims.

Mindful persuasive legal writers use their legal research skills to determine the required components of the applicable rule(s) governing the plaintiff's claims against the defendant and employ language to describe the facts of the case in a way that demonstrates the presence of the required elements or the factors of the rule.

Counts/Causes of Action (Elements, Factors)

In the next section of the complaint, the lawyer identifies the various causes of action that the plaintiff plans to pursue against the defendant. The persuasive technique of *ethos* is invoked first through performing thorough legal research. A lawyer must consider all the different possible causes of action that the plaintiff might have against the defendant, evaluating contractual causes of action, torts, statutory causes of action, and other potential claims. If you were researching viable causes of action to include in a pleading for the first time, you might place your law school contracts, torts, and property textbooks on your desk and scan the tables of contents to make a list of all the possible causes of action that a plaintiff may have against a defendant. You could also research sample complaints in electronic legal research databases to identify alternative causes of action that lawyers have pursued in factual circumstances similar to your client's.

After identifying plausible causes of action, the lawyer must perform legal research in the appropriate jurisdiction to identify the applicable rule governing each cause of action and the required elements or components of the rule or factors implicated by the rule. In drafting this part of the complaint, the lawyer inserts headings to distinguish the various "counts"—i.e., Count I (Breach of Contract), Count II (Bad Faith), Count III (Violation of the Consumer Protection Act: N.Y. Gen. Bus. Law § 349). Then the numbered paragraphs beneath each heading describe how the applicable rule is satisfied for each cause of action.

For example, under New York law, the required elements for a cause of action for breach of contract are (1) the existence of a contract, (2) the plaintiff's performance of its obligations under the contract, (3) the defendant's breach of that contract, and (4) resulting damages.[7] In a complaint against an insurance company for breach of contract, an insured might describe the breach of contract count as follows:

Count I: Breach of the Contractual Duty to Provide Coverage and Defend its Insured

35. Plaintiff Riggins incorporates the allegations in the above paragraphs of this Complaint as though fully alleged herein.

36. Valid insurance contracts existed between Plaintiff Riggins and the insurer.

37. Plaintiff Riggins fully performed all of the obligations and conditions required of it under the insurance policies or has been excused from performing such obligations and conditions as a result of the insurer's breach of its duty to provide coverage and defend its insured.

38. By selling the insurance policies, the insurer agreed to, and assumed a contractual duty to, provide coverage for property damage and provide a defense for suits seeking damages for "personal injury and property damage" and financial losses therefrom, as defined in the policies.

39. Plaintiff Riggins suffered significant financial losses and property damage as a result of the floodwaters resulting from Hurricane Sandy and has been sued for additional property damage and financial losses in the two pending lawsuits.

40. These losses are exactly the types of losses covered under the insurance policies, triggering the insurer's duty and obligation to provide coverage and a defense.

41. The insurer has failed to provide coverage for the property damage, and it has refused to provide a defense for the two lawsuits.

42. Nonetheless, the insurer has accepted over $635,000 in insurance premiums from Plaintiff Riggins for the past 23 years. Plaintiff Riggins has received nothing in return for these premiums.

43. As such, the insurer has breached its duties of coverage and defense.

44. Plaintiff Riggins has been damaged by such breach and shall continue to be further damaged by the insurer's wrongful withholding of insurance coverage for these losses.

The lawyer would repeat this general framework for each count of the complaint, using the rule framework for each separate cause of action. Lawyers can include several different counts in a complaint. This is called "pleading in the alternative." Fed. R. Civ. P. 8(d)(2) states that "[a] party may set out 2 or more statements of a claim . . . alternatively." Further, Fed. R. Civ. P. 8(d)(3) indicates that "[a] party may state as many separate claims . . . as it has, regardless of consistency."

---

[7] *Harsco Corp. v. Segui*, 91 F.3d 337, 348 (2d Cir. 1996).

Damages or Other Remedies/Relief Sought

Fed. R. Civ. P. 8(a)(3) also requires a complaint to include "a demand for the relief sought, which may include relief in the alternative or different types of relief." The lawyer drafting the complaint can describe the damages or other remedies or relief sought either beneath each count or in a section at the end of the complaint called the "prayer for relief." If the complaint is being filed in federal court based on diversity jurisdiction, the amount of damages sought must exceed $75,000, excluding interest and court costs. If there is no required jurisdictional threshold for damages, lawyers often will state that the plaintiff seeks damages "in an amount that will be proven at trial" or "in an amount according to proof."

If the plaintiff believes that she is entitled to recover attorneys' fees based on a contract provision or statute, the lawyer should include that contract provision or statutory reference in a request for attorneys' fees. A plaintiff also may be entitled to seek prejudgment interest. Finally, many lawyers add the phrase "and any other relief which the court deems just and proper" at the end of the "prayer for relief."

Different types of nonmonetary remedies or forms of relief also might be wise to consider or pursue. What if a monetary payment will not make the plaintiff whole for damages resulting from a breach or a wrong committed by a defendant? Is the plaintiff entitled to specific performance of a contract? To rescission of an object wrongfully taken away? To an injunction barring the defendant from continuing to do something that is hurting the plaintiff? To cancellation of an unfair contract obtained under duress? Lawyers conduct substantial legal research to consider all the possible remedies and forms of relief that will make their clients whole.

Here is an example of a "prayer for relief":

WHEREFORE, Plaintiff Riggins requests judgment in its favor on Count I in an amount to be determined at trial, plus prejudgment and postjudgment interest, attorneys' fees and costs to the extent allowable by law, and such further relief as this Court deems just and proper.

Signature (Fed. R. Civ. P. 11) and Verification (if Required)

According to Fed. R. Civ. P. 11(a), every complaint "must be signed by at least one attorney of record in the attorney's name—or by a party personally if the party is unrepresented." The signature block contains the signer's mailing address, e-mail address, and telephone number and a designation that the lawyer is "Counsel for Plaintiff." Unless a rule or statute mandates otherwise, a complaint does not need to be verified by the client; verification means that the client signs a statement or an affidavit stating that the facts and allegations in the complaint are true and correct to the best of the client's knowledge and belief. Lawyers should research whether a statute or rule requires the particular complaint (e.g., a complaint seeking a temporary restraining order) to be verified.

Here is an example of a signature block:

Dated: January 7, 2016

Respectfully submitted,
McGee & Rollins, LLP
Bridget Stanton

Bridget Stanton
100 William St., Suite 44
New York, NY 10005
800-555-4718
bstanton@mcgeerollins.com
Counsel for Plaintiff

Exhibits

Sometimes lawyers will attach key exhibits to a complaint, such as a contract that is the subject of the dispute. If the lawyer plans to attach exhibits, such documents must be designated within the body of the complaint as "Exhibit 1," "Exhibit 2," and so on. The exhibits become a permanent part of the record. Instead of attaching only portions or excerpts from a lengthy exhibit, it is better to provide exhibits in their complete form.

Finalizing the Complaint and Filing and Serving It

Once the draft of the complaint is complete, the lawyer spends a significant amount of time editing, revising, and proofreading it. He may circulate the draft to the client for review and input. He cross-checks the complaint against the standard for sufficiency of pleadings in the appropriate jurisdiction and the required elements or the factors of the rule for each cause of action. He makes sure that each numbered paragraph is as clear and concise as possible. He proofreads the entire pleading several times for spelling, citation, and formatting errors. He makes sure that the presentation looks professional, including headings, line spacing, indentation, paragraph length, page numbering, font, and margins.

When it is ready to go, he signs the document, files the required number of copies with the court (some courts require an original and a number of additional copies), pays the appropriate filing fee, and then serves the complaint upon the opposing party. The applicable court rules include instructions for how to properly serve the complaint on the defendant and whether a legal summons is required, notifying the opposing party of how many days it has to file a **motion to dismiss** or an **answer**.

A sample complaint is included in Appendix G.

PERSUASIVE COMPLAINT-WRITING CHECKLIST

Caption

☑ Research and choose the proper jurisdiction and venue. (*Logos* and *Ethos*)

☑ Identify the proper parties. (*Logos* and *Ethos*)

☑ Decide whether the client requests a jury trial. (*Pathos*)

☑ State the title of the pleading and the party filing it.

Introduction

☑ Identify the name of the filing party and the name of the defendant.

Jurisdiction and Venue

☑ Research the proper statutes or other rules to support the assertions of jurisdiction and venue. (*Logos* and *Ethos*)

☑ Cite the proper statutes or other rules supporting jurisdiction and venue. (*Logos* and *Ethos*)

☑ In separate numbered paragraphs, state the facts that support the selected jurisdiction and venue. (*Logos* and *Ethos*)

Parties

☑ In separate numbered paragraphs, identify the names of each party and the pertinent facts, to give the court and opposing party context: state of citizenship (residence for individuals and where they intend to remain; state(s) of incorporation and principal place of business for corporate entities), the parties' respective functions in society, their relationship to each other. (*Logos, Pathos, Ethos*)

Facts

☑ In separate numbered paragraphs, tell the client's story and lay the factual groundwork for the causes of action. (*Logos, Pathos, Ethos*)

☑ Be accurate but engaging. (*Logos, Pathos, Ethos*)

Causes of Action

☑ Research all the potential causes of action that the plaintiff may have against the defendant (a complaint may plead "in the alternative"). (*Logos* and *Ethos*)

☑ Consider causes of action based on contract, tort, property, consumer protection statutes, unfair trade practices statutes, intellectual property rights, etc. (*Logos* and *Ethos*)

☑ Research the required elements or other components of the rule governing each cause of action (i.e., breach of contract includes (1) the existence of a contract; (2) the plaintiff's performance of its obligations under the contract; (3) the defendant's breach of the contract; and (4) damages). (*Logos* and *Ethos*)

☑ In separate numbered "counts" and separate numbered paragraphs beneath each count heading, set forth the allegations that demonstrate that each of the required elements or other components of the rule for each cause of action is satisfied. (*Logos, Pathos, Ethos*)

Damages, Remedies, and Other Relief Sought

☑ Assess the dollar value of the damages that the plaintiff seeks; if the amount is unknown, research whether there is a required dollar amount threshold in the selected jurisdiction (i.e., federal court based on diversity jurisdiction requires the matter in controversy to exceed the sum or value of $75,000). (*Logos* and *Ethos*)

☑ Research all the other remedies potentially available to the plaintiff (i.e., equitable remedies like restitution, rescission, preliminary injunction, temporary restraining order, etc.). (*Logos* and *Ethos*)

☑ Research other relief that potentially is available to the plaintiff (i.e., interest, attorneys' fees if a contract or statute provides for such recovery, costs, etc.). (*Logos* and *Ethos*)

Signature Block

☑ Review Fed. R. Civ. P. 11 (or the state court equivalent) and understand what it means for an attorney to sign a complaint. (*Ethos*)

☑ Include the signer's name, law office name, and contact information.

☑ Add a signature line and designation "Counsel for Plaintiff."

☑ Add the date that the complaint is being filed.

Verification

☑ Research whether the complaint needs to be verified (signed under oath) by the client.

☑ If so, prepare a verification signature block.

Exhibits

- ☑ Research whether the court allows exhibits or attachments to the complaint.
- ☑ Decide whether it would be helpful to the court and the opposing party to attach a document or several documents as exhibits (i.e., a contract). **(Logos)**

Filing and Service

- ☑ Research whether the court requires electronic or hard-copy filing.
- ☑ If hard-copy filing is required, research the number of required copies.
- ☑ Research the filing fee.
- ☑ Research whether any other cover sheets or forms must accompany the complaint.
- ☑ Research the methods allowed by the court for serving the complaint upon the opposing party (or parties).
- ☑ Research the number of days that the opposing party has to file an answer or a motion to dismiss (add the final deadline date to the law office's calendar).

Chapter 25
Drafting a Persuasive Answer

After a plaintiff files a complaint in the court clerk's office and serves it upon the opposing party, the recipient (the defendant) typically reaches out to his lawyer or law firm for advice on how to handle the pleading. When representing an individual or a corporate entity that has received a complaint—perhaps from a process server—lawyers often are asked to explain what the document means and what the required next steps are. Clients can become anxious upon being served with a legal complaint, yet they do not always contact counsel right away. Thus, a lawyer's first task in rendering legal advice to a client who has received such a pleading is to check the court rules for the deadline for filing a **motion to dismiss** or an **answer**. This can be a very short window of time, and there can be significant research involved in preparing a "responsive pleading"; smart lawyers nail down the timeline quickly.

In a motion to dismiss the case, the defendant seeks to persuade the court that the complaint should be dismissed, either in part or entirely, because (1) the plaintiff filed the case in the wrong jurisdiction or venue, (2) the court does not have subject matter jurisdiction over the dispute or personal jurisdiction over the parties, (3) the complaint was not served properly upon the defendant in accordance with the required procedures, or (4) the complaint "fails to state a claim upon which relief may be granted."[1] Each of these grounds for disposal of the case requires substantial legal research so that the attorney filing the motion can satisfy the court's standards for dismissal. Both the structure and substance of a motion to dismiss will be explored in Chapter 27.

---

[1] Fed. R. Civ. P. 12(b).

This chapter focuses on how to craft a persuasive answer to a complaint. If a defendant does not believe that she has a proper ground for filing a motion to dismiss, instead she files an answer to the complaint within the deadline stated in the court rules. A defendant who fails to file a timely answer might be subject to a default judgment; therefore, it is crucial to file an answer on time.

Drafting a persuasive answer is not so much about the *pathos* of language choices and emotional engagement as in the complaint, but instead, the legal writer focuses more on logical and methodical handling of each allegation and ethically responding to the factual and legal claims in the complaint.

Caption, Title, and Introduction

A lawyer drafting an answer uses the same case caption that appears on the complaint, adding the docket or case number assigned by the clerk. The title of the pleading is "Answer." If the plaintiff did not request a jury trial, and there is no contractual or other waiver of or bar to a jury trial, the defendant may request a jury trial in the caption.

The first sentence of the answer identifies the filing party and introduces the responsive pleading. Here is an example:

IN THE UNITED STATES DISTRICT COURT
FOR THE SOUTHERN DISTRICT OF NEW YORK

Riggins Garment Company,   )   Case No. Y16-044-AML
     a New York Corporation,   )   The Honorable Laila Hewson
     Plaintiff,   )
)   ***ANSWER***
v.   )
)
Cornerstone Insurance Company,   )   Jury Trial Requested
     a Massachusetts corporation,   )
     Defendant.   )
_____)

COMES NOW Defendant Cornerstone Insurance Company ("Cornerstone") by counsel, and for its Answer to the Complaint filed by Plaintiff Riggins Garment Company ("Riggins"), states as follows:

Using Numbered Paragraphs to Admit or Deny the Allegations in the Complaint

Fed. R. Civ. P. 8(b)[2] states that "[i]n responding to a pleading, a party must: . . . (B) admit or deny the allegations asserted against it by an opposing party." Further, Fed. R. Civ. P. 8(b)(3) explains that "[a] party that intends in good faith to deny all the allegations of a pleading—including the jurisdictional grounds—may do so by a general denial. A party that does not intend to deny all the allegations must either specifically deny designated allegations or generally deny all except those specifically admitted." Many lawyers drafting an answer typically will sit down with a copy of the complaint and read each numbered paragraph—word-for-word—deciding whether each paragraph can be admitted or must be denied either in part or in whole. Sometimes a numbered paragraph in the complaint will contain certain information that can be admitted and other information that must be denied. It is important to read every word of the plaintiff's allegation and only admit the portion of a sentence or paragraph that can be admitted. The plaintiff's lawyer may have used vague or inaccurate nouns or verbs that change the tenor of a factual statement; each word matters.

For example, consider a scenario in which the precise date upon which an employee ceased working for a company is a key fact in a case. The plaintiff may have included a numbered paragraph in the complaint stating, "The employee left the company on November 8, 2016." However, before admitting or denying this allegation, a diligent attorney drafting the answer should consider questions like: (1) What was the date that the employee submitted her resignation letter? (2) Was her resignation effective immediately upon the date of her letter or did she provide a month's notice, continuing to work until the month's duration expired? (3) Could the word "left" be construed as physically departing the building premises rather than resigning from her position? Fed. R. Civ. P. Rule 8(b)(4) allows a defendant to admit part of an allegation and deny the rest: "A party that intends in good faith to deny only part of an allegation must admit the part that is true and deny the rest." Thus, in the foregoing example, if the factual circumstances warrant, the attorney could admit that the employee terminated her employment but deny that the date she severed ties with the company was November 8, 2016.

Practical Tip: When specifically admitting or denying each numbered paragraph of a complaint, the attorney must check that the numbered paragraphs in the complaint and the answer align accurately so that the defendant will not be deemed to have admitted the wrong allegations. If a statement is not denied, it will be deemed admitted.

---

[2] While the rules referenced in this chapter are federal civil procedure rules, each state court has its counterpart of procedural rules that may mirror or differ from the federal rules. Lawyers drafting answers to complaints review the applicable procedural rules before preparing responsive pleadings.

Lacking Knowledge or Information to Admit or Deny an Allegation

Sometimes a complaint will include statements that a defendant cannot admit or deny without engaging in discovery. Fed. R. Civ. P. (8)(b)(5) allows the defendant to state, in the corresponding numbered paragraph, that he "lacks knowledge or information sufficient to form a belief about the truth of an allegation." The court will treat this statement as a denial.

Here is an example of numbered paragraphs in an answer admitting or denying specific allegations in a complaint:

Example of Numbered Paragraphs in an Answer to a Complaint

Jurisdiction and Venue

1. Admitted.
2. Admitted as to proper venue. The remaining allegations in this paragraph are denied.

Parties

3. Admitted.
4. Admitted.

Facts

5. Admitted.
6. Defendant lacks knowledge or information sufficient to form a belief about the truth of the allegations in this paragraph.
7. Admitted.
8. Admitted.

Defenses and Affirmative Defenses

In addition to admitting or denying each numbered allegation in the complaint, a defendant may assert defenses against the plaintiff's causes of action. Fed. R. Civ. P. 8(a)(1)(A) requires the defendant to "state in short and plain terms its defenses to each claim asserted against it." This task necessitates legal research to determine all the possible defenses that a party may have to the various contract, tort, property, or perhaps statutory causes of action asserted in the complaint. For example, two possible defenses to a breach of contract claim are that the contract itself was void because it was executed under duress or that it was induced by fraud. A potential defense to a defamation lawsuit might be that the alleged inflammatory public statement made by the defendant about the plaintiff was true, not false. A viable defense to a claim of trespassing by the defendant on the plaintiff's property could be that the alleged interloper had consent to enter the land. The lawyer drafting an answer may include the various legal defenses to the specific causes of action within corresponding numbered paragraphs beneath the headings for the individual counts. For example, the lawyer will admit or deny the statement made in the corresponding numbered paragraph in the complaint and then add language stating the defense to the cause of action.

Further, there are certain defenses called *affirmative defenses,* which a defendant must include in an answer or they are waived. These defenses are listed in a separate section of the answer, under the heading "Affirmative Defenses." *Black's Law Dictionary* defines the term *affirmative defense* as "[a] defendant's assertion of facts and arguments that, if true, will defeat the plaintiff's or prosecution's claim, even if all the allegations in the complaint are true."[3] Fed. R. Civ. P. 8(c) lists 18 affirmative defenses: accord and satisfaction, arbitration and award, assumption of risk, contributory negligence, duress, estoppel, failure of consideration, fraud, illegality, injury by fellow servant, laches, license, payment, release, res judicata, statute of frauds, statute of limitations, and waiver.[4] For example, if through legal research, the defendant's attorney realizes that the plaintiff waited too long to file a medical malpractice claim—beyond New Jersey's two-year statute of limitations set forth in N.J. Stat. § 2A-14-2(a)—the attorney would assert an affirmative defense based on the statute of limitations. Or, in an action for breach of contract for failure to pay a debt, if the defendant contends that the plaintiff agreed to, and subsequently did, accept a lower amount in satisfaction of the debt, the defendant's attorney would assert an affirmative defense of accord and satisfaction. Additional affirmative defenses—other than those set forth in Fed. R. Civ. P. 8(c)—include failure to exhaust administrative or contractually prescribed remedies or notice requirements, failure to satisfy conditions precedent, failure by the plaintiff to seek recourse under a mandatory mediation

---

[3] Black's Law Dictionary (2014).
[4] Heidi K. Brown, *Fundamentals of Federal Litigation* § 2:50 (2009) defines each of these affirmative defenses in detail. It can be accessed on Westlaw in the FFLIT database.

or arbitration clause in a contract with the defendant, failure to mitigate damages, sovereign immunity, champerty and maintenance, unclean hands, and the economic loss doctrine.[5]

Here is an example of a section of an answer listing applicable affirmative defenses:

Example: Affirmative Defenses

1. The Plaintiff breached its insurance contract, and therefore is not entitled to coverage and/or a defense, by misrepresenting facts in its insurance policy application.
2. The Plaintiff breached its insurance contract, and therefore is not entitled to coverage and/or a defense, by failing to make timely insurance premium payments.
3. The insured is guilty of "laches" and failed to comply with the insurance policy's notice requirements and deadlines for filing claims.
4. The losses claimed by the insured are not covered losses, based on express policy exclusions.
5. The insured failed to mitigate its damages and further exacerbated its own losses, nullifying the insurance coverage.
6. The doctrine of estoppel bars Plaintiff's claims.
7. The doctrine of waiver bars Plaintiff's claims.

Pleading Alternative Defenses

Just as a plaintiff may allege alternative counts or causes of action in a complaint, a defendant's answer may assert alternative theories of defense. Fed. R. Civ. P. 8(d)(2) states that "[a] party may set out 2 or more statements of a . . . defense alternatively or hypothetically, either in a single . . . defense or in separate ones." Further, Fed. R. Civ. P. 8(d)(3) indicates that "[a] party may state as many separate . . . defenses as it has, regardless of consistency."

Prayer for Relief

Similar to the prayer for relief in the complaint, the last part of the answer asks the court to dismiss the complaint, find in favor of the defendant, possibly award fees and costs if permitted by law, and requests "such other and further relief as the court may deem just and proper."

---

[5] Heidi K. Brown, *Fundamentals of Federal Litigation* § 2:50 (2009).

Counterclaims and Third-Party Claims

When drafting an answer, a lawyer often will realize that her client has viable counterclaims against the plaintiff or claims against third parties who are not yet parties to the plaintiff's lawsuit. Techniques for persuasively drafting these pleadings are described in the next chapter. Depending on the court's procedural rules, a counterclaim may be part of the answer or may be set forth in a separate document; a third-party claim is a separate pleading that is served on that party.

Signature Block and Certificate of Service

The lawyer filing the answer includes a date and signature block at the end of the answer, identifying the signer's name, law office name, contact information, and a designation of "Counsel for Defendant." The lawyer signing the answer is subject to the same ethical considerations under Fed. R. Civ. P. 11(b) (or the state court's counterpart) as the plaintiff's lawyer signing the complaint. That is, the lawyer must certify that:

(1) The answer is not being presented for any improper purpose, such as to harass, cause unnecessary delay, or needlessly increase the cost of litigation.
(2) The defenses and other legal contentions are warranted by existing law or by a nonfrivolous argument for extending, modifying, or reversing existing law, or for establishing new law.
(3) The denials of the factual contentions are warranted on the evidence or, if specifically so identified, are reasonably based on belief or a lack of information.[6]

The defendant's lawyer includes a Certificate of Service, indicating how the answer shall be served upon the plaintiff. Here is an example of a signature block and a Certificate of Service:

---

[6] Fed. R. Civ. P. 11.

Dated: January 10, 2016

Respectfully submitted,
Rodriguez & Jess, LLP
Michael Pineda
Michael Pineda, Esq.
200 Leonard St., Suite 2
New York, NY 10013
800-555-1000
mpineda@rodriguezjessllp.com
Counsel for Defendant

Certificate of Service

I hereby certify that the foregoing Answer to the Complaint of Plaintiff Riggins Garment Company was served via e-filing, with a courtesy copy via e-mail, on January 10, 2016, upon the following:

Bridget Stanton, Esq.
McGee & Rollins, LLP
100 William St., Suite 44
New York, NY 10005
800-555-4718

Bridget Stanton
Bridget Stanton

bstanton@mcgeerollins.com

The lawyer files the answer with the court—either electronically or in hard copy, depending on the court's rules—and then serves the answer on the opposing party, or counsel, in accordance with the court's rules.

A sample answer is included in Appendix H.

PERSUASIVE ANSWER-WRITING CHECKLIST

Caption

☑ Research and decide if the plaintiff chose the proper jurisdiction and venue in filing the complaint. (**Logos** and **Ethos**)

☑ Determine if the plaintiff identified the proper parties and party names. (**Logos** and **Ethos**)

☑ Decide whether the defendant wants to request a jury trial, if the plaintiff did not already. (**Pathos**)

☑ Add the docket or case number assigned by the court clerk when the plaintiff filed the complaint.

☑ State the title of the pleading and the party filing it.

Introduction

☑ Identify the name of the filing party.

Jurisdiction and Venue

☑ Research the proper statute or other rules to determine if the plaintiff's allegations of jurisdiction and venue are correct. (**Logos** and **Ethos**)

☑ Admit or deny the facts regarding the selected jurisdiction and venue. (**Logos** and **Ethos**)

Parties

☑ In numbered paragraphs directly corresponding to the numbered paragraphs in the complaint, admit or deny the facts alleged regarding the parties. (**Logos, Pathos, Ethos**)

☑ Carefully review each word of the party descriptions to determine whether each allegation can be admitted in full or should be denied in part or in whole. (**Ethos**)

Facts

☑ Carefully review each word of the factual statements to determine whether each allegation can be admitted in full or should be denied in part or in whole. (**Ethos**)

☑ In numbered paragraphs directly corresponding to the numbered paragraphs in the complaint, admit or deny the facts alleged. (**Logos, Pathos, Ethos**)

Causes of Action

☑ Research the causes of action alleged by the plaintiff. (**Logos** and **Ethos**)

☑ Research the required elements or other components of the rule governing each cause of action (i.e., breach of contract = (1) the existence of a contract; (2) the plaintiff's performance of its obligations under the contract; (3) the defendant's breach of the contract; and (4) damages). (**Logos** and **Ethos**)

☑ Carefully review each word of the allegations in each cause of action to determine whether each allegation can be admitted in full or should be denied in part or in whole. (**Ethos**)

☑ In numbered paragraphs directly corresponding to the numbered paragraphs in the complaint, admit or deny the allegations regarding each of the required elements or other components of the rule for each cause of action. (***Logos* and *Ethos***)

☑ Note whether the plaintiff failed to assert particular elements or components of the rule for each cause of action. (***Logos* and *Ethos***)

☑ Research and add defenses to each cause of action in the appropriate numbered paragraph. (***Logos, Pathos, Ethos***)

Damages, Remedies, and Other Relief Sought

☑ In numbered paragraphs directly corresponding to the numbered paragraphs in the complaint, admit or deny liability or responsibility for the damages, remedies, or other relief sought. (***Logos* and *Ethos***)

Affirmative Defenses

☑ Research applicable affirmative defenses. (***Logos* and *Ethos***)

☑ Under a separate heading, and in separate numbered paragraphs, assert affirmative defenses to the causes of action pled by the plaintiff. (***Logos, Pathos, Ethos***)

Signature Block

☑ Review Fed. R. Civ. P. 11 (or the state court equivalent) and understand what it means for an attorney to sign an answer. (***Ethos***)

☑ Include the signer's name, law office name, and contact information.

☑ Add a signature line and designation "Counsel for Defendant."

☑ Add the date when the answer will be filed.

Prayer for Relief

☑ State the relief requested from the court. (***Logos, Pathos, Ethos***)

Filing and Service

☑ Research whether the court requires electronic or hard-copy filing.

☑ Research the methods allowed by the court for serving the answer upon the opposing party or parties.

Chapter 26

Drafting a Persuasive Counterclaim, Third-Party Claim, or Cross-Claim

After a plaintiff files a complaint, in addition to preparing the answer and affirmative defenses, the defendant's attorney also might consider whether the client has any viable claims against the plaintiff to assert in a **counterclaim**. Further, as mentioned in Chapter 25, the defendant may realize that he has claims against a third party who is not yet part of the lawsuit. The defendant may consider filing a **third-party claim** against a new individual or entity, joining the new party to the litigation. Further, if the lawsuit already involves more than one defendant, the defendants might file **cross-claims** against one another.

Drafting the substance of these types of pleadings—counterclaims, third-party claims, or cross-claims—is a similar exercise to drafting the initial complaint. The lawyer creating the pleading must (1) establish the court's jurisdiction over the subject matter of the claim (and if a third party is being added, over that party); (2) describe the background facts giving rise to the claim; (3) research and then state the causes of action being pursued; (4) provide sufficient detail regarding the allegations to demonstrate that the elements or factors of the particular rule(s) governing each cause of action are (or will be) established; and (5) indicate the damages or other remedies sought. Depending upon the court's procedural rules, the responding lawyer might attach a counterclaim to the defendant's answer and affirmative defenses—in a separate section of the same pleading. A third-party claim and a cross-claim comprise separate pleadings, each containing the case caption, the title of the document, an introductory sentence identifying the filing party, the five substantive components listed above, and a signature block noting the name and contact information of the filing attorney.

Court deadlines restrict the time allotted for filing these additional pleadings, so it is important for an attorney to check the court rules. Also, many courts have issued rules regarding which types of additional claims are "compulsory" (i.e., must be brought by a certain time or are waived) or "permissive" (i.e., may be brought at a later time or in a separate litigation).

Once the counterclaim, third-party claim, or cross-claim is filed, the receiving party has a certain number of days prescribed in the rules to file an answer or a motion to dismiss. The same principles governing the drafting of an answer to a complaint apply in the context of these pleadings as well.

Section 10

Persuasion in the Scheduling Phase of Litigation

Chapter 27

Persuasively Negotiating a Case Schedule

After all the parties to a litigation have filed pleadings—complaint, answer plus affirmative defenses, and counterclaims, cross-claims, and/or third-party claims—the case proceeds to the scheduling phase, and then discovery commences. Case scheduling is not often discussed or taught in law school, but junior lawyers often play a pivotal role in the early stages of a lawsuit when the litigation timeline is established. Thus, it is important for law students and junior attorneys to understand the scheduling component of a case that is pending in state or federal court. Many jurisdictions require the lawyers for all parties to coordinate with one another early in the case to attempt to map out a timeline, interim deadlines, and a logical progression of how the parties will conduct the case. For example, in federal court, Fed. R. Civ. P. 26(f) requires the lawyers for all parties to "confer" at least 21 days before the court convenes a scheduling conference. The lawyers may assemble in person or on the phone, and they must jointly discuss (1) the nature and basis of their claims and defenses; (2) the potential for settling the case; (3) the mutual exchange of mandatory disclosures of case information, such as names of persons with knowledge about the case, categories of relevant documents, damages summaries, and insurance coverage; (4) preservation of discoverable information; and (5) a proposed plan for the discovery phase of the case.[1] Within 14 days of this conference, the lawyers are required to submit a joint written plan to the court.[2] Now, as any aspiring lawyer can imagine, facilitating consensus among two or more attorneys about all the foregoing issues can pose quite a challenge. Thus, it is important for lawyers to

---

[1] Fed. R. Civ. P. 26(f)(2).
[2] Fed. R. Civ. P. 26(f)(2).

consider the role of persuasion when convincing opposing counsel to agree on a workable litigation schedule for any case, simple or complex, or low or high stakes.

Real-Life Anecdote

When the author of this book was a junior associate at her first law firm—only two years out of law school—a supervising partner asked her to negotiate a proposed "Case Management Order" with opposing counsel in a federal case. When she asked for advice on how to approach the assignment, the lawyer mused, "If opposing counsel wants trial in two years, you want trial in six months. If they want trial in six months, you want it in two years." The young associate returned to her office, perplexed. This seemed like unhelpful advice—fighting just for the sake of fighting, at the beginning of a case? Instead, she sat down and evaluated the lawsuit: the potential number of witnesses, documents, and tangible discovery items and their geographical location; the volume of documents to review for privilege and substance; the complexity of the legal issues; the number of experts needed on both sides; the client's budget; and the number of days/weeks likely needed for trial. Then, in a phone conference with opposing counsel (with a calendar handy), she collaborated with the other party's lawyer to lay out a workable schedule for fact and expert discovery (including travel throughout many states), the timing of pretrial motions, trial preparation, and several weeks of trial (plus reasonable time for trial team members' respective vacations sometime during the case progression!). The judge adopted the parties' proposed plan, and the case ran (relatively) smoothly thereafter.

Further, according to Fed. R. Civ. P. Rule 26(f)(3), in a case scheduling conference, the parties' lawyers also must negotiate the following:

- the timing and nature of the initial disclosures that all parties are required to make about (1) the names of persons with knowledge about the case, (2) the categories of documents that bear on the facts of the case, (3) the categories and amounts of damages claimed, and (4) any potential insurance coverage
- the subjects of, timing of, or any limits on, discovery
- the parameters of electronic discovery (e-mails, computer files, and other electronic records), which requires more technical expertise than gathering, reviewing, and exchanging hard-copy documents
- how the lawyers will handle claims of privilege or attorney work product protection for documents.[1]

Once the lawyers agree on all (or at least most) of the foregoing topics, one lawyer takes the lead in drafting the proposed plan. The lawyers then might

---

[1] Fed. R. Civ. P. Rule 26(f)(3).

exchange redlined edits of the plan until all parties accept the version to be submitted to the court. If the lawyers ultimately cannot agree on a certain term, the plan drafter can include the parties' respective positions on the item, such as "Plaintiff's counsel requests that depositions of all witnesses be limited to one day of seven (7) hours; Defendant's counsel requests that standard depositions be limited to one day of seven (7) hours, but that depositions of corporate designees have a time limit of two days, at fourteen (14) hours total."

Under Fed. R. Civ. P. 16(b), the court reviews the parties' proposed submission and subsequently issues a Scheduling Order, also called a Case Management Order or a Case Structuring Order. The order governs the timing of most of the litigation tasks throughout the case. Once the case timeline is established, it may be difficult to request or obtain time extensions that could affect a judge's already overcrowded docket. Thus, the official Scheduling Order becomes an important document for a lawyer's day-to-day workload and monthly, or even yearly, planning. A single case's deadlines and time limits can affect a lawyer's ability to balance the workloads for other clients, as well as her personal life and stress level. Thus, when negotiating the proposed case plan with opposing counsel, it is important to consider the timing of the following additional matters:

- Decide if any other parties should be joined to the lawsuit, and prepare pleadings to add them
- Decide if the pleadings should be amended, and draft such amendments
- Draft and serve discovery requests, including requests for production of documents and physical objects, interrogatories, and requests for admissions, on opposing counsel
- Object and respond to written discovery requests, including requests for production of documents and physical objects, interrogatories, and requests for admissions, served by opposing counsel
- Review the client's documents (hard copy and electronic) for privilege, and organize and produce nonprivileged documents to opposing counsel
- Review documents (hard copy and privileged) produced by opposing parties, to identify issues and to use as exhibits in depositions
- Decide which individuals with knowledge about the case should be deposed, and prepare and serve deposition notices or subpoenas
- Prepare for and conduct depositions of opposing-party or third-party witnesses
- Defend depositions of the client's witnesses
- Decide whether experts would be helpful to explain aspects of the subject matter of the case to the trier-of-fact
- Engage experts, provide appropriate data and documentation to enable them to render opinions, review and transmit expert reports, and defend expert depositions
- Review the opposing parties' expert reports and take expert depositions
- Prepare and respond to motions to compel a party's compliance with the discovery rules

- Prepare pretrial motions, such as motions for summary judgment and motions in limine
- Decide which witnesses and exhibits to present at trial
- Prepare and exchange pretrial submissions, such as juror *voir dire* questions, jury instructions, witness lists, and exhibit lists
- Prepare trial outlines, opening statements, and witness examination and cross-examination outlines.

The lawyers also must consult their calendars and evaluate appropriate dates for pretrial conferences and the actual trial date. The court's docket might be congested, so there is no guarantee that the court will grant the dates requested, but it helps to have a logical plan and sequencing of these necessary events.

Unfortunately, some lawyers do not take the scheduling conferences seriously enough or put sufficient thought into their advance planning. These conferences and the jointly proposed plan submitted to the court are a tremendous opportunity for a lawyer to demonstrate logical persuasion and establish credibility with opposing counsel and the court. In doing so, the attorney can obtain a workable schedule for the months (or, quite possibly, years) that she will be working on the case. Most lawyers manage more than one case at a time—and have personal lives to consider. A well-thought-out litigation schedule makes all the difference in ensuring that an attorney has ample time to focus on each litigation task, represent her client to the best of her ability, and maintain a healthy work-life balance.

Smart lawyers use the persuasive techniques of *logos* and *ethos* when negotiating case scheduling plans. *Logos* requires lawyers to be logical while realistically considering (1) the subject matter of the case; (2) the volume of potential discovery; (3) the length of time it will take to prepare for the exchange of such discovery and perform its subsequent subject matter review; (4) the geographical scope of the case (i.e., will the lawyers be traveling from state to state to review documents and conduct fact and expert depositions?); (5) the legal issues in the case and whether they will merit extensive substantive briefing; and (6) the length of a trial (i.e., will there be few witnesses testifying about a handful of exhibits, or do the facts require presentation of a parade of witnesses testifying about a mountain of paperwork). The lawyer who considers all of these questions in advance of a scheduling conference with opposing counsel will have the strength of logic on her side when negotiating realistic timelines, deadlines, and cutoff dates.

Accuracy and truthfulness are also essential to establish *ethos*, or credibility, in negotiating a proposed schedule, not only with opposing counsel but likewise with the judge. Lawyers who fight for the sake of fighting (as the supervising partner suggested doing in the "Real-Life Anecdote" above) might win certain battles by blustering and posturing, but they often lose the war. Opposing counsel will not trust a lawyer who exaggerates the scope of discovery needed or purposefully underestimates or overestimates the number of days needed for trial. Likewise, lawyers who lose the trust of a judge may never earn it back.

A lawyer seeking to persuade opposing counsel to agree to her proposed timeline, deadlines, and trial schedule might take the initiative in several critical ways:

- Be the first party to reach out to the opposing party or parties and propose mutually convenient times to conduct the scheduling conference.
- Take the lead on circulating the conference call dial-in number, establishing herself as the conference leader, or invite counsel to his office to conduct an in-person conference.
- Arrive at the conference (either on the phone or in person) first, and establish a role as the leader, providing an agenda for participants of topics to discuss and include in the jointly proposed scheduling order.
- Take accurate notes of the agreements achieved in the scheduling conference, and take the lead on preparing the first draft of the jointly proposed order.
- Establish credibility by accurately capturing the agreements from the scheduling conference, including those issues upon which the parties could not agree, summarizing each side's position on the disputed items in a straightforward manner.
- Reinforce credibility by editing the proposed plan accurately, without trying to "sneak one by" opposing counsel during back-and-forth redlined edits of the document before finalization.
- Further buttress credibility by proofreading and polishing a final professionally presented piece of work product before submitting it to the court.

Judges and opposing counsel will appreciate thoughtful advocacy and will respect a credible lawyer who uses reasonable logic and precision to facilitate agreement on a case schedule. Such a lawyer establishes a professional tone from the outset of a case, so all parties involved can put their best foot forward for their clients.

The following is a sample Case Scheduling Order:

IN THE UNITED STATES DISTRICT COURT
FOR THE SOUTHERN DISTRICT OF NEW YORK

RIGGINS GARMENT COMPANY,) a New York Corporation,)	Case No. Y14-044-AML The Honorable Laila Hewson
) Plaintiff,))	
v.)	**SCHEDULING ORDER**
) CORNERSTONE INSURANCE) COMPANY,)) a Massachusetts corporation) Defendant.) _____)	

The parties submitted a proposed Case Management Plan in accordance with Fed. R. Civ. P. 26(f)(3), and the Court hereby issues this Scheduling Order in accordance with Fed. R. Civ. P. 16(b)(3).

1. The parties consent to conducting proceedings before a United States Magistrate Judge for resolution of discovery disputes and for settlement conferences.
2. The parties have not yet engaged in settlement discussions.
3. The parties have conferred pursuant to Fed. R. Civ. P. 26(f) to discuss a Discovery Plan.
4. At this time, pleadings are closed. The parties may not file amended pleadings or join additional parties except with permission of the Court. Any motion to amend or to join additional parties shall be filed within forty-five (45) days from the date of this Scheduling Order.
5. The parties shall exchange initial disclosures pursuant to Fed. R. Civ. P. 26(a)(1) no later than fourteen (14) days from the date of this Order.
6. The parties shall conclude all fact discovery no later than June 6, 2014.
7. The parties shall agree upon a mutually acceptable procedure for disclosure or discovery of electronically stored information.
8. The parties shall conduct discovery in accordance with the Federal Rules of Civil Procedure and the Local Rules of the Southern District of New York, and in accordance with the following deadlines:
    a. The parties shall serve Initial Requests for Production of Documents by 2/7/14.
    b. The parties shall serve all Interrogatories by 3/7/14.
    c. The parties shall serve all Requests for Admissions by 5/9/14.
    d. All requests for inspection of property must be served by 5/9/14.
    e. Fact depositions shall be completed by 6/6/14.
9. All expert discovery, including disclosure of expert reports, production of underlying documents, and depositions shall be completed by 8/1/2014. The parties shall agree on dates for exchange of expert reports and any necessary rebuttal reports.
10. All motions and applications, including Motions to Compel Discovery and to resolve discovery disputes, shall be governed by the Court's Individual Rules.
11. The parties must meet to discuss settlement within fourteen (14) days following the completion of all discovery. Unless otherwise ordered by the Court, settlement discussions shall not stay or modify any date in this Order.
12. Motions for Summary Judgment and Motions in Limine must be filed within 30 days of the completion of all discovery.
13. The Court shall set a trial date within 90 days of the completion of all discovery.
14. Fourteen (14) days prior to the trial date set by the Court, the parties shall file a Joint Pre-Trial Report prepared in accordance with the Court's Individual Rules and Fed. R. Civ. P. 26(a)(3), along with proposed *voir dire*, jury instructions, and a verdict form.

15. If any party asserts a claim of attorney-client privilege or work product protection for documents or information withheld from discovery, the party shall provide a privilege log pursuant to Fed. R. Civ. P. 26(b)(5) and shall "describe the nature of the documents, communications, or tangible things not produced or disclosed—and do so in a manner that, without revealing information itself privileged or protected, will enable other parties to assess the claim."

This Order may not be modified or the dates herein extended, except by a Court Order. A party requesting the Court to modify or extend the dates herein shall file a motion in accordance with the Court's Individual Rules at least ten (10) business days prior to the deadline sought to be extended. Absent exceptional circumstances, the Court will grant no extensions after deadlines have already passed.

The next Case Management Conference is scheduled for 6/13/14 at 11:00 a.m.

SO ORDERED.

Dated: 1/14/14   The Honorable Laila Hewson
                                            New York, New York

PERSUASIVE CASE SCHEDULING NEGOTIATION CHECKLIST

☑ Research the dates that the court rules stipulate that the parties must (1) confer about the case scheduling plan, and (2) submit the jointly proposed plan.

☑ Research the court rules governing the required content of the jointly proposed plan.

☑ Identify the foregoing deadlines on your calendar, and then contact opposing counsel to schedule the initial conference.

☑ Review the pleadings to identify the complexity of the legal issues in the case.

☑ Evaluate whether the pleadings suggest that additional parties should be joined or whether the pleadings should be amended to add allegations, causes of action, or defenses.

☑ Determine whether your client has a budget limitation for the case (this can affect scope of discovery, experts, research and drafting of briefs, and length of trial).

☑ Make a list of all the potential witnesses on all sides of the case and their geographical locations (if known).

☑ Estimate the volume of documents (hard copy and electronic) in your client's files that you will need to first review for attorney-client privilege, then produce, and finally review for substance to prepare for depositions.

☑ Try to anticipate the volume of documents (hard copy and electronic) that the opposing party or parties likely will produce, which you will need to review for substance in preparation for depositions.

☑ Consider the potential number of depositions that will be taken by all parties and their geographical locations (which will affect travel time).

☑ Consider all types of discovery requests that you likely will draft to serve on opposing counsel, and those that opposing parties likely will serve on your litigation team, necessitating the drafting of objections and written responses.

☑ Evaluate whether the subject matter of the case requires the engagement of experts.

☑ Anticipate the time required for engaging experts, having the experts evaluate the facts, preparing, exchanging, and reviewing expert reports, and taking and defending expert depositions (in various geographical locations).

☑ Decide whether the case merits a site visit of any kind.

☑ Anticipate whether the case potentially could be resolved, even in part, through pretrial motions (such as motions for summary judgment or motions in limine to address evidentiary issues).

☑ Evaluate how much time you might need to prepare required pretrial submissions; i.e., juror *voir dire* questions, jury instructions (these can be lengthy if the case involves numerous legal issues), witness lists, exhibit lists, etc.

☑ Consider how much time your litigation team might need for trial preparation; i.e., drafting opening statements, crafting witness examination and cross-examination outlines, preparing exhibits (including demonstrative trial exhibits), and meeting with witnesses.

☑ Try to calculate how many days, weeks, or months the trial realistically should take; i.e., how many witnesses will testify for each party, how many exhibits will be offered into evidence, and how many legal issues the trier-of-fact needs to decide.

☑ Research whether opposing counsel has a reputation for cooperating during discovery and pretrial or whether you anticipate needing time to draft and file motions to compel compliance with discovery or respond to motions filed by opposing counsel to resolve discovery disputes.

☑ Look at your personal and professional calendar for the next year or two, and consider your workload for other cases and any personal/family obligations, such as scheduled vacations.

Section 11

Writing Persuasive Motions and Briefs in the Litigation Context

Chapter 28

Types of Persuasive Motions Written by Lawyers

After the scheduling phase of a litigation, the judge issues the scheduling order and the parties proceed with fact and expert discovery and then move on to pretrial activities and eventually trial. From the pleadings phase through the end of trial, lawyers use persuasion in writing motions and briefs on a variety of procedural and substantive issues. A *motion* is an important piece of legal writing in which a lawyer procedurally "moves," or asks, the court to take a certain action in the case (i.e., dismiss the complaint, resolve a discovery dispute, exclude or permit evidence at trial, or render judgment on part or all of the causes of action alleged in the pleadings). *Briefs* are the vehicle in which a lawyer (1) identifies the precise legal issue or issues before the court; (2) if applicable, explains the standard governing the action requested of the court; (3) describes the relevant facts in an engaging manner; (4) outlines the governing rules derived from a contract, statutes, regulations, or case law; (5) illustrates the rules through explanations of prior precedent; (6) applies the governing rules to the client facts; and (7) argues persuasively why the court should rule in the client's favor. The brief specifically indicates the result or relief that the client seeks, so the court can make a definitive ruling and move the case forward. A motion and the accompanying brief include the case caption, a title of the document, the foregoing components of the argument, a date, and a signature block.

Overall Components of a Brief

- Case Caption
- Title of Brief
- Introduction (Issue)

- Standard for Prevailing on Motion (Rule)
- Relevant Facts
- Elements or Factors of the Substantive Rule(s) Governing the Legal Issue
- Explanation of the Rule(s)
- Application of the Rule(s) to the Case Facts (using persuasive arguments/techniques)
- Specific Request for Relief
- Date
- Signature Block

Because different motions occur in different procedural phases of a case, a lawyer needs to understand the distinction among the various types of motions and the different functions that they serve at various points along the litigation timeline.

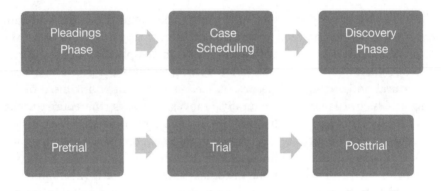

Motions to Dismiss

When a plaintiff files a complaint against a defendant, before filing an answer, the defendant's lawyer should analyze the pleading to determine whether it is more appropriate to file a motion to dismiss the complaint in part (i.e., as to only certain causes of action) or in its entirety. In federal court, Fed. R. Civ. P. 12 provides several grounds on which a lawyer can file a motion to dismiss during the pleadings phase of the case:

- The court lacks jurisdiction over the subject matter of the case (e.g., the case should be brought in state court instead of federal court because the matter involves a state law rather than a question of federal law and the parties lack diversity of citizenship).

- The court lacks personal jurisdiction over a party (i.e., the party does not have sufficient contacts with the forum state such that being forced to litigate there would be fair).
- The particular court is the wrong venue within the chosen jurisdiction (i.e., a different court within the same state or geographical area would be more convenient and equitable to the parties).
- The plaintiff failed to serve the defendant properly (i.e., served the wrong entity or delivered the complaint to the wrong address).
- Certain required documentation for service with the complaint (e.g., a summons) was missing or contained inaccurate information.
- The complaint failed to state a claim upon which relief can be granted.
- The plaintiff failed to join a party required for the lawsuit to proceed.

In a Rule 12(b)(6) motion for failure to state a claim upon which relief may be granted, for example, a lawyer might argue that one or more required elements of the rule governing a count or cause of action are not properly alleged or are missing altogether from the complaint. When evaluating motions and briefs, courts strive for consistency in their rulings on each type of motion; to facilitate this goal of consistency, courts apply legal "standards." To succeed in persuading a court to dismiss a case for failure to state a claim, the lawyer must demonstrate that the circumstances satisfy the court's standard for dismissal, or stated another way, that the complaint fails to satisfy the standard for sufficiency of the pleading. The legal standard applicable to a Rule 12(b)(6) motion to dismiss in federal court can appear rather confusing to new practitioners. The two key cases that provide the standard for a Rule 12(b)(6) motion are *Ashcroft v. Iqbal*[1] and *Bell Atl. Corp. v. Twombly*.[2] Based upon these two federal cases, in order for a complaint filed in federal court to survive a Rule 12(b)(6) motion to dismiss, the pleading must state a "plausible claim for relief" against the opposing party.[3] A claim is plausible "when the plaintiff pleads factual content that allows the court to draw the reasonable inference that the defendant is liable for the misconduct alleged."[4] A plaintiff must show "more than a sheer possibility that a defendant acted unlawfully"[5] and cannot rely on mere "labels and conclusions" to support a claim.[6]

If a lawyer representing the defendant believes that the plaintiff's complaint (1) fails to assert facts demonstrating that the required elements of the rule governing a particular cause of action are, or can be, met, (2) lacks facts that would allow the court to infer that the defendant is liable, or (3) contains mere legal labels and conclusions, the lawyer might draft a motion to dismiss the complaint in its entirety or as to certain causes of action included therein. To do so, the attorney would start by researching cases in the applicable jurisdiction in which litigants have won similar motions.

---

[1] 556 U.S. 662 (2009).
[2] 550 U.S. 544 (2007).
[3] *Iqbal*, 556 U.S. at 679.
[4] *Id.* at 678.
[5] *Id.*
[6] *Twombly*, 550 U.S. at 555.

Then, in the motion and the accompanying brief,[7] the attorney would:

1. Identify the causes of action in the complaint that the party is asking the court to dismiss.
2. Cite the standard relied upon by the court in granting motions to dismiss in other cases.
3. Describe the pertinent facts of the case that are relevant to the motion, using *pathos* in a manner that will resonate with the judge.
4. State the substantive legal rules governing the causes of action subject to dismissal, including any required elements or applicable factors.
5. Illustrate the rules through case law that is favorable to the client.
6. Possibly distinguish any unfavorable case law that serves as mandatory precedent in the jurisdiction.
7. Provide logical arguments as to why the court should dismiss the particular causes of action, applying rules and precedent to the client facts.
8. State the precise relief the moving party seeks (i.e., dismissal).

In a brief supporting a motion to dismiss, a persuasive legal writer uses *logos* by following an organized IREAC/CREAC formula, presenting issues, rules, rule explanations (case illustrations, described in Chapter 29), arguments, and conclusions in a logical structure. The writer employs *pathos* to reveal the emotional nuances of the case, weaving the theme of the client's case through the brief in an appropriate manner. The author of a persuasive brief in support of a motion to dismiss also exhibits *ethos*—credibility—by accurately citing the standard for the motion, the applicable rules, and the governing precedent. *Ethos* is furthered by respecting and following all applicable court rules governing the format, length, and style of the motion, adhering to citation rules, and proofreading to avoid any typographical, grammatical, or other unsightly demerits in professionalism.

The defendant's attorney files the motion to dismiss and accompanying brief with the court within the deadline set forth in the court rules and then serves it upon opposing counsel, either electronically or in hard copy, depending upon the court's required procedures. The receiving party then has a certain number of days to file an opposition brief—which likewise uses *logos, pathos,* and *ethos* to argue persuasively why the complaint, or causes of action therein, should *not* be dismissed. Chapter 30 offers one strategy for drafting opposition briefs. Once an opposition brief is filed and served upon the party who initially filed the motion, the moving party may have the option to file a reply brief, which is often much shorter, and responds solely to key points in the opposition brief meriting a response. Tips for crafting persuasive reply briefs are provided in Chapter 30 as well.

The court will take time to review the motion and all three briefs and may hear oral argument from the attorneys on the issues. Ultimately, the judge will issue a decision (often in a written opinion) whether to grant the motion. If the

---

[7] The format of these two separate documents (the motion and the brief) will be explained in Chapter 29.

motion is granted as to an entire complaint, the case is dismissed and ends. If the motion is denied, whether in whole or in part, the case proceeds. The defendant then must comply with the deadline prescribed in the court rules for filing an answer and any affirmative defenses. Once the answer and any counterclaims, cross-claims, or third-party claims are filed, the parties and the court establish the case schedule, and discovery commences.

Discovery Motions

As discussed in previous chapters, *discovery* is the phase of a case in which parties exchange requests for the production of documents and physical items, interrogatories, and requests for admissions and conduct depositions of fact and expert witnesses. During the discovery phase, lawyers often disagree over the scope of discovery sought by the opposing parties, or they become frustrated at a litigant's unwillingness to produce documents, respond fully to interrogatories or requests for admissions, or cooperate during depositions. A **motion to compel** compliance with the court's scheduling order, discovery rules, and the parties' discovery requests becomes an important persuasive tool during the discovery phase of a case.

A word of caution: some discovery disputes stem from stubborn counsel's inability to resolve personality conflicts rather than bona fide disagreements over their legal interpretations of the discovery rules. A request by a party for the court to step in and referee a fight between uncooperative lawyers distracts from the adjudication of a case's substance. Thus, many courts require attorneys to attempt—through initial procedural steps—to resolve discovery conflicts on their own before seeking judicial intervention and include such requirements in their court rules or in the case scheduling order or case management order. Typically, courts require attorneys to "meet and confer" to resolve discovery disputes, and only if their good-faith attempts are unsuccessful may one party file a motion to compel, certifying the parties' compliance with the meet-and-confer rule.

A brief in support of a motion to compel is a piece of legal writing, often shorter than a "dispositive"[8] motion (such as a motion to dismiss), which:

1. Identifies the nature of the discovery dispute (e.g., which set of documents or which witness the opposing party will not produce, the particular interrogatories that a party failed to sufficiently answer, or the fact that a party exceeded the interrogatory number limit)
2. States the rules governing the particular discovery issue (e.g., what types of documents the attorney-client privilege or the work product doctrine protects

---

[8] A dispositive motion "disposes" of a portion or all of the case.

from disclosure to the opposing party, or the limit on the number of interrogatories permitted per party)

3. Summarizes favorable case law illustrating the particular rules (and distinguishing any adverse mandatory authority)

4. Applies the rules and precedent to the client's case

5. Incorporates arguments based on *logos* and *pathos* to persuade the judge to rule in the client's favor

6. States the precise result the client seeks (e.g., an order directing the opposing party to produce the stated categories of documents by a particular date, an order mandating the opposing party to supplement its prior dilatory responses to interrogatories, or an order directing the party to revise its set of interrogatories to comply with the numerical limit)

The motion to compel also contains the case caption, a signature block, and a certification that the filing party has complied with the meet-and-confer requirement. A motion to compel typically also includes exhibits: the discovery requests, objections, and responses (or excerpts therefrom if the originals are overly voluminous), plus the pertinent e-mails or letters demonstrating the parties' attempts to resolve the dispute without judicial intervention. As noted in Chapter 23, when writing letters to opposing counsel, lawyers must always consider the possibility that their correspondence might end up attached to a motion read by the judge. Professionalism and proper tone matter.

To keep these types of filings short, courts may impose page limits (or word-count limits) on briefs accompanying motions to compel. Once the motion to compel and brief are filed and served, the receiving party has a certain number of days to file an opposition brief, asserting arguments to persuade the judge to rule against the movant and not grant the result sought. The court might permit the moving party to file a reply brief, which is even shorter than the original briefs. The judge may or may not hear oral argument on discovery motions. Once the court rules on the discovery motions, the parties usually have a certain number of days to comply with an order directing a certain action. A party who fails to comply with the order might be subject to sanctions (such as fines, penalties, or waiver of claims or the right to use evidence at trial), defined by the court rules.

A contrasting motion that attorneys often file during the discovery phase of a case is a **motion for a protective order**. A party may believe that an opposing party's discovery requests are beyond the scope of the rules, are overly burdensome or intrusive, or seek privileged or proprietary information. If so, the attorney can draft a motion asking the court to grant an order "protecting" the party from being compelled to produce the requested information, documents, or witnesses, or restricting the way the opposing party may use the information, documents, or witnesses if produced. A protective order might require the parties to physically label the identified documentation or information as proprietary or confidential and require the recipient to certify that it will use the content solely for the purposes of the case, without disseminating it to any third party, news outlet, or competitor. A brief in support of a motion for a protective order reflects a general structure similar to the brief in support of a motion to compel, but it argues for the *prohibition* of the discovery sought by the opposing party, or restrictions on its scope, instead of *compliance* with the discovery rules. In a brief in support of a motion for a protective order, a persuasive lawyer will focus on the governing rules and provide examples of similar cases in which the court granted motions for protective orders under similar circumstances. A recipient of a motion for a protective order likely will file an opposition brief, and the moving party may be permitted to file a reply. The judge may or may not hear oral argument. If a case generates several discovery-related disputes among counsel, the judge might schedule a single hearing to address all discovery issues at the same time, so the case can proceed unimpeded thereafter.

Evidentiary Motions

Once the parties have engaged in discovery and evaluated documents, interrogatory responses, admissions, deposition testimony, and expert reports, attorneys might identify certain topics or pieces of evidence that they believe should be excluded from trial. Evidence (including documents, responses to discovery, or witness testimony) can properly be excluded from trial for many reasons, including:

- The evidence is more prejudicial to a party than "probative of" (i.e., tending to prove) the legal issues.[9]
- The evidence is being offered only to inflame the jury.
- The evidence is hearsay (defined as an out of court statement offered for the truth of the matter asserted), which lacks sufficient reliability.[10]
- The evidence is irrelevant to the legal issues in the case.[11]
- The evidence (i.e., handwriting, documents, checks, e-mails, artwork, etc.) cannot be properly authenticated.[12]

The type of motion (and accompanying brief) that lawyers write to persuade a judge to exclude certain evidence at trial is known as a **motion in limine.** *Limine* means "at the start." Evidentiary issues ideally are resolved before the trial commences to minimize confusion, delay, and prejudice to the parties.

One particular aspect of litigation that invites motions in limine is the use of experts. During the expert phase of discovery, as mentioned in Chapter 22, parties:

1. Identify whether the legal issues in the case require the assistance of qualified individuals to explain scientific, technical, or other specialized aspects of the case to the trier of fact.

---

[9] Fed. R. Evid. 403.
[10] Fed. R. Evid. 801.
[11] Fed. R. Evid. 402.
[12] Fed. R. Evid. 901.

2. If so, engage experts in the necessary fields.

3. Identify to all opposing parties those experts who will testify at trial.

4. Exchange expert reports, analyzing the facts and rendering opinions.

5. Take and defend expert depositions.

Once a lawyer has evaluated the topic or topics for which the opposing party has designated an expert to provide opinions, reviewed the expert's written report, and questioned the expert at a deposition, the lawyer might believe that the expert should be precluded from testifying at trial for one or more of the reasons identified in Chapter 22. The procedural avenue for excluding the expert is the motion in limine.

In a brief in support of a motion in limine, the legal writer identifies the specific piece or category of evidence, or the name of the fact or expert witness, that he requests the court to exclude from trial. Then, using *logos*, the lawyer tries to persuade the court to exclude the evidence by (1) stating the applicable evidentiary rule (e.g., the legal definition of relevance, the standard for the admissibility of expert testimony, the legal definition of hearsay, or the standard for analyzing whether a piece of evidence is more prejudicial than probative); (2) illustrating the rule by summarizing prior cases in the appropriate jurisdiction that have excluded similar evidence from trial, describing the facts, holding, and court's rationale of each of those cases; (3) applying the rule and precedent to the piece of evidence; and (4) stating the precise result that the lawyer seeks—the exclusion of the evidence, or perhaps in the alternative, a limitation on the use of such evidence. Briefs in support of motions in limine tend to be shorter than briefs in support of "dispositive" motions, especially if the lawyer is filing multiple motions in limine on different items of evidence. The motions include the case caption, a title such as "Plaintiff's Motion in Limine to Exclude Tax Returns" or "Defendant's Motion in Limine to Preclude the Testimony of Plaintiff's Automotive Expert," a date, and a signature block. If practical, the lawyer might attach the specific piece of evidence to the motion as an exhibit.

The opposing party has the opportunity to file an opposition brief within a certain number of days prescribed in the court rules, and the initial moving party may be permitted to file a reply brief. Ideally, the court will render a decision on all the evidentiary motions before the trial commences. The case scheduling order usually contains a cutoff date for filing motions in limine, so the parties can properly prepare their exhibits and witnesses for trial without confusion over whether such documents and witness testimony are likely to be admissible.

Motions for Summary Judgment

Another type of motion that lawyers file after completing at least a substantial portion of the discovery phase of a case, but before trial, is a **motion for summary judgment**. *Summary judgment* means that a court can grant a judgment in favor of one party on part or all of a case in advance of trial, if the key facts are undisputed and a party demonstrates that she is entitled to prevail as a matter of law. In federal courts, as mentioned in Chapter 22, Fed. R. Civ. P. 56(a) describes the standard for summary judgment as follows:

> The court shall grant summary judgment if the movant shows that there is no genuine dispute as to any material fact and the movant is entitled to judgment as a matter of law.

This rule and its state court counterparts require two angles of focus for the brief-writer: (1) the material facts and (2) the required elements of the cause(s) of action for which summary judgment is sought. Thus, drafting a brief in support of a motion for summary judgment is usually much more time-consuming than writing some of the other briefs described in this chapter. The lawyer must review all the key documents obtained in discovery (e.g., contracts, e-mails, letters, correspondence, photographs, etc.), responses to interrogatories, written admissions, and deposition testimony in order to identify documentary or testimonial support in the case record for every material fact. This exercise is critical to identify the material facts that are *not* in dispute and the documentary or testimonial evidence that supports that contention. Then, the lawyer must review all the required elements or other components of the rules governing the causes of action for which summary judgment is sought and link the undisputed facts to the required rule elements to prove that judgment in the client's favor is warranted because either (1) all the required elements are met, or (2) if the lawyer is defending against the cause of action, at least one element fails.

To craft a persuasive summary judgment brief, the lawyer:

1. Identifies for the court the specific legal causes of action in the complaint (or counterclaim) upon which summary judgment is sought
2. Researches and then describes and cites the standard for summary judgment in the appropriate jurisdiction (i.e., Fed. R. Civ. P. 56 in federal courts)
3. Includes a separate section in the brief—in numbered paragraphs if required by the court rules—listing all the material facts pertinent to the particular cause of action with citations to the documentary and/or testimonial evidence demonstrating that such facts are not in dispute
4. Relays the rules governing the particular cause of action, listing the required elements or the factors considered by the court
5. Illustrates the rules by summarizing previous case law granting summary judgment, showing similar factual circumstances, the court's holding, and the court's rationale in those cases (also distinguishing any adverse mandatory precedent)
6. Applies the rules and precedent to the undisputed facts of the client's case, persuading the judge that summary judgment is proper by demonstrating that all the required elements of the cause of action are met or, if defending a cause of action, that one or more elements cannot be met
7. Stating the exact result that the moving party seeks: judgment in its favor on all or part of the complaint (or counterclaim).

If a lawyer seeks summary judgment for more than one count or cause of action in the complaint (or counterclaim), a mindful legal writer uses *logos* to craft separate informative headings and IREAC/CREAC structures in the brief for each count or cause of action. The motion for summary judgment and accompanying brief contain the case caption, the title of the document, and a signature block.

Preparing a summary judgment for filing does not end when the motion and brief are completed, edited, cite checked, and proofread. The lawyer must organize and attach—as exhibits—the documentation from the record that demonstrates the undisputed nature of the material facts. This can be a time-consuming process; it involves (1) making copies of documents, interrogatory responses, written admissions, deposition excerpts, and affidavits; (2) organizing them in the correct order to correspond with the relevant material facts; (3) designating each exhibit with a number or letter; and (4) attaching the exhibits to the brief. Many courts require electronic filing, which means that the lawyer may be required to scan and prepare Portable Document Format (PDF) copies of the foregoing exhibits and upload them to the court's electronic filing system.

The court rules will designate the number of days within which the opposing party must file an opposition brief. The lawyer opposing a motion for summary judgment must demonstrate either (1) there *is* a genuine dispute over at least one material fact or (2) the moving party is *not* entitled to judgment as a matter of law (i.e., at least one of the required elements of a cause of action *cannot* be met, or if the moving party is arguing that a cause of action alleged by the responding party fails, all the required elements of a cause of action *can* be met). The lawyer drafting the opposition brief must review all the evidence obtained in discovery in order to extract documents, testimony, or discovery responses demonstrating that a material fact *is* in dispute, cite to such excerpts, and provide such evidence as exhibits. Often lawyers will respond to the moving party's list of material facts by providing counterfacts in corresponding numbered paragraphs to show that at least some of the alleged undisputed facts actually are in dispute.

Chapter 30 focuses on how to craft a legal argument in an opposition brief; there is an art to persuasively responding to a moving party's arguments and shifting the court's view in the responding party's favor. Mindful lawyers thoughtfully consider how to chronologically organize legal issues that are outlined first in an opposing lawyer's initial brief and then respond to each argument in the opposition brief using *logos* and *pathos*.

Once the opposing lawyer files the opposition brief, the moving party usually has an opportunity to file a reply brief. After the judge rules on the motion for summary judgment, the parties have a clearer idea of which issues have been resolved prior to trial in one party's favor and which remaining matters will proceed to trial.

Practice Tip: There are few moments more satisfying in the legal world than winning an entire case based on a summary judgment brief. Thus, smart lawyers take these oeuvres of legal writing very seriously.

Trial Motions

At some point in every litigator's life, the big day arrives: the first day of trial. Before this day, the lawyers have exchanged exhibit lists, witness lists, proposed jury *voir dire* questions, and jury instructions. In a jury trial, the judge and lawyers start by engaging in jury selection. Once a jury is seated, the lawyers deliver opening statements. The plaintiff calls the first witness, and the case proceeds. During trial, outside the presence of the jury, lawyers continue to make and file motions on issues that arise during the case. Trial motions involve procedural matters (such as a motion to exclude witnesses from the courtroom until they are called to testify), follow-up evidentiary motions that were not resolved previously, and substantive motions (such as a motion for a directed verdict at the end of a party's case-in-chief, also called a *judgment as a matter of law* in federal court). Procedural and evidentiary motions made during trial tend to be short documents; often, the lawyers draft these briefs at night after a long day of trial and an evening of preparation for the next day's proceedings. Substantive trial motions, such as for a directed verdict or for judgment as a matter of law, might be lengthier, pulling facts and law from past briefs such as a motion for summary judgment that the judge might have denied as premature earlier in the case. Regardless of the nature of the trial motion, good legal writers use *logos, pathos,* and *ethos,* constructing arguments based on an IREAC/CREAC framework:

1. Identifying the legal issue(s)
2. Describing the governing rule(s)
3. Illustrating the rule(s) through case law in which the court in the appropriate jurisdiction ruled in favor of the client's position
4. Distinguishing any adverse mandatory precedent
5. Applying the rule(s) and precedent to the client's circumstances
6. Asking for the specific relief sought (e.g., an order excluding witnesses from the courtroom, excluding evidence, or granting judgment in favor of the moving party)

Each brief contains the case caption, the title of the document, and a signature block.

During a fast-paced trial, a party opposing a motion often has a short window to file a written response. Reply briefs may not even be necessary or permitted, depending on the timing of the court's decision.

Posttrial Motions

Once a trial concludes, a judge in a bench trial renders a decision, or a jury in a jury trial delivers a verdict. Often the lawyers—win or lose—are ready for a long vacation. But they cannot rest quite yet. After trial, lawyers file additional motions. If a lawyer's client receives a negative outcome (an adverse judgment or verdict), she might consider filing one of the following:

- a renewed motion for judgment as a matter of law
- a motion for a new trial
- a motion to amend the court's findings (in a bench trial)
- a motion to amend or alter a judgment
- a motion for relief from a judgment
- a motion for a stay of enforcement of a judgment.[13]

Even after a successful verdict or judgment, the prevailing party is not finished yet either; the victorious lawyer may consider filing one of the following:

- a motion to amend the court's findings (in a bench trial)
- a motion to alter or amend a judgment (perhaps to add interest to the damages award)
- a motion for costs and attorneys' fees

Each of these types of motions has different legal standards that the lawyer must research in the appropriate jurisdiction, describe in the accompanying brief, and then demonstrate through persuasive argument how the standard is met. Good legal writers use a well-structured IREAC/CREAC framework to:

1. State the issue.
2. Outline the standard required for the particular motion (the applicable rule).
3. Illustrate the standard/rule through case law showing circumstances in which the same courts have granted the same types of motions in the past (also distinguishing any adverse mandatory precedent).
4. Apply the standard/rule to the client's scenario.
5. Ask the court for the precise result or relief sought.

The motion and brief contain the case caption, the title of the document, and a signature block. The court rules will prescribe the number of days within which the opposing party must file an opposition brief and whether a reply brief may be filed (and if so, the deadline).

---

[13] Of course, the nonprevailing party can also file a notice of appeal (usually a one- or two-page form).

Appellate Briefs

A nonprevailing party in a trial may have the opportunity to appeal the verdict or judgment. Court rules govern parties' rights to appeal an adverse decision. Typically, courts require an appealing party (called an *appellant*) to file a notice of appeal within a certain number of days after the adverse judgment. Once the appellate court assumes jurisdiction over the appeal, the court issues a briefing schedule. An appellate court reviews a case solely upon briefs submitted by the lawyers and possibly oral argument; it does not hear testimony from witnesses or conduct a new trial. Thus, appellate briefs are a critically important vehicle of persuasion in an appeal. Appellate courts have very specific rules mandating the required components of an appellate brief that differ from a trial brief; often, appellate briefs are longer than trial briefs. For example, in a federal appellate court, a brief must include:

- a corporate disclosure statement that identifies—for nongovernmental parties—any parent corporation and any publicly held corporation that owns 10 percent or more of the appealing party's stock or that states that there is no such corporation (so that the appellate justices can determine whether they have a conflict of interest)[14]
- a table of contents, with page references to where the headings and subject matter can be found within the body of the argument section of the brief
- a table of authorities—including cases (alphabetically arranged), statutes, and other authorities—with references to the pages of the brief where such sources of law are cited
- a statement of the basis for the court's jurisdiction, including:
  - the basis for the trial court's subject-matter jurisdiction (i.e., federal question, diversity jurisdiction), with citations to the applicable statutory provisions and stating relevant facts establishing jurisdiction
  - the basis for the court of appeals' jurisdiction, with citations to the applicable statutory provisions and stating relevant facts establishing jurisdiction
  - the filing dates verifying that the appeal was filed on time
  - an assertion that the appeal is from a final order or judgment that disposes of all parties' claims (so that the appellate court can determine that the appeal is ripe)
- a statement of the legal issues presented for review
- a concise statement of the case
  - describing the facts relevant to the issues submitted for review
  - summarizing the relevant procedural history, and

---

[14] Fed. R. App. P. 26.1.

  o identifying the rulings presented for review, with appropriate
    references to the record
 ● a summary of the argument, containing a succinct, clear, and accurate
   statement of the arguments made in the body of the brief
 ● the argument, which must contain:
   o the appealing party's arguments and the reasons for them, with
     citations to the authorities and facts in the trial record on which the
     appellant relies
   o for each issue, a concise statement of the applicable standard of review
 ● a short conclusion stating the specific relief sought
 ● a certificate stating that the brief complies with the page or word count
   limitation in the court's rules.[15]

The standard of review in an appeal is an important consideration, but it can be confusing at first for law students and new lawyers. Recall from Chapter 22 that because the trial court already invested days, weeks, or months adjudicating the dispute (while the lawyers presented exhibits and witness testimony), it would not serve the interests of judicial economy for the appellate court to rehear the entire case from start to finish. Thus, appellate review considers the concept of deference to the lower court. Deference is the degree of respect that an appellate court must give to a decision of the lower court. Chapter 22 provides a chart summarizing a few of the standards of review that an appellate court might consider, including de novo review, the arbitrary and capricious standard, the clearly erroneous standard, the no substantial evidence standard, and the abuse of discretion standard.

Good legal writers research the standard of review applicable to each legal issue in the appeal, recite the rule explaining each pertinent standard in the appellate brief (with correct citations to the source of the rule), and illustrate the governing standard of review through case law that favors the client's position.

---

[15] Fed. R. App. P. 28.

Chapter 29

Drafting a Persuasive Trial-Level Brief

Logos, Pathos, and *Ethos* in a Persuasive Brief

In your first semester of law school, your Legal Writing course probably focused on predictive or objective legal writing, analyzing a legal issue from all sides, balancing strengths and weaknesses, and anticipating how a court likely would determine the outcome. In contrast, in brief writing, lawyers engage in persuasive writing; other than oral argument in open court or in a judge's chambers, briefs are the sole mode of communication between a lawyer and a judge. Briefs present an opportunity for lawyers to educate the court about the facts and legal issues in a client's case, capture the judge's attention, hopefully cause the client's circumstances to resonate with the reader on some emotional level, and then motivate the court to render a decision on a legal issue in a way that benefits the client. Briefs also afford lawyers a chance to convince opposing counsel of the strengths of the client's case, and, in that regard, can facilitate settlement or narrow issues for trial.

While legal research memoranda address both the strong and weak aspects of a client's case and are circulated internally within a law office environment or within the confines of the attorney-client relationship, briefs focus solely on the strengths of a client's position and are transmitted externally to opposing counsel and the decision maker in the case. When researching and drafting a brief, good lawyers keep in mind how the audience, tone, purpose, and format of this form of legal writing differ from a memorandum. The goal of the brief writer is to invoke *logos, pathos,* and *ethos* to convince a busy judge that the right result is the one that the client seeks. Just as supervising attorneys expect to see legal memoranda written in a certain format (Header, Question Presented, Brief Answer, Statement of Facts, Discussion—which includes Rules, Rule Explanations, and Rule Applications—and a Conclusion), opposing counsel and judges expect briefs to follow a particular structure. Smart lawyers use this tried-and-true framework to convey legal concepts efficiently and clearly to a legal audience. This is part of the *logos* component of brief writing. Good lawyers exhibit *logos* through carefully and thoroughly researching the applicable rules and then explaining those governing rules through a well-crafted Issue, Rule, Explanation, Application, Conclusion (IREAC) or Conclusion, Rule, Explanation, Application, Conclusion (CREAC)[1] structure. Thoughtful legal writers impart the rules to the reader through workable lists of elements or factors. Then, they make smart decisions about which cases to use to illustrate the rules through Rule Explanations (using a framework of Facts, Holding, and Rationale). Finally, they apply the rules to the client facts, and lead the reader down a logical path toward the desired result.

Some novice brief writers initially bristle at the thought of being required—yet again—to adhere to a seemingly rigid structure in brief writing; however, the concept of *pathos* grants each brief writer a certain amount of leeway to inject personality and passion into the legal writing piece. Good lawyers utilize *pathos* to captivate and engage the reader by carefully choosing the right language to describe the client facts in a visual manner, experimenting with tone, and employing grammatical techniques—such as using active voice instead of passive voice—to highlight a key point. Additionally, taking time to ponder a stimulating theme for each brief can provide a creative outlet for attorneys feeling stifled by structure; a thought-provoking theme can convert even the most mundane brief topic (e.g., a motion to resolve a deposition scheduling dispute or to settle disagreements over the transmittal of electronic documents) into a vehicle for forging a bond between the decision maker and the client. Win the small battles, win the war.

Finally, *ethos* is a critical ingredient in brief writing—perhaps the most essential, in fact. A well-written brief serves as a lawyer's calling card in the courtroom. When an attorney signs a brief, under Fed. R. Civ. P. 11 (or the state court equivalent), he places his integrity on the line. Brief writers must make smart ethical choices when writing about good and bad client facts and favorable and adverse precedent. A drafter should be both persuasive and ethical, highlighting the strengths of a party's case while being truthful and thorough, so that the judge has access to the entire story and can make an informed decision about the legal issues. A brief writer's integrity is conveyed also through professional presentation: perfect proofreading, impeccable legal citation, visually pleasing formatting, and compliance with the court's rules regarding substance and form.

---

[1] Some legal writers (and legal writing professors) switch acronyms from IREAC to CREAC in brief writing, reflecting a conscious and intentional conversion from the more neutral initial I (representing the issue in memo writing) into a more persuasive C to denote the parties' contention or conclusion requested on the issue in a brief. Whichever acronym is used, the important point is that good brief writers always use a logical structure to convey their persuasive arguments.

Briefs cannot be produced in a single all-nighter. These forms of legal writing take time and deep thinking, balancing and processing *logos, pathos,* and *ethos* to craft an elegant, effective message to the decision maker.

Components of a Single-Issue Trial-Level Brief

Courthouses process hundreds, perhaps even thousands, of cases across our nation every day. Judges and their clerks are busy people, and lawyers must be efficient in communicating with them; otherwise, we risk losing the attention of our audience. Lawyers over decades have developed a standard structure for legal briefs that enables the writer to transmit the most pertinent information about the facts and law governing a case in a concise manner. Through this fundamental organizational framework, the readers—opposing counsel and the judge—can grasp the facts and rules quickly and understand the requested responsive procedural and substantive action. Of course, like any form of writing, briefs differ from author to author in language choice and style, but the basic structural skeleton should remain the same whether the brief is a 5-page discovery motion or a 40-page motion for summary judgment.

A trial brief[2] typically includes these components:

Case Caption
- Court name
- Parties' names (and designation as Plaintiff, Defendant, etc.)
- Docket number (assigned by the court clerk when the complaint is filed)

Title
- Party filing the brief
- Type of brief (e.g., Plaintiff's Motion to Compel Defendant to Produce Documents)

Introduction
- First sentence (party filing the brief, type of brief, rule governing the type of brief (if applicable))
- Theme sentence
- Identification of the legal issue(s)
- Governing rule(s)
- Brief statement of the reasons why the moving party should prevail
- Concise statement of result/relief sought

---

[2] Later in this chapter, we will discuss the format and substance of the 1- or 2-page procedural motion that accompanies a brief. The first part of this chapter focuses on the substance and format of a brief in support of a motion.

Statement of Facts
- Description of the pertinent client facts relevant to the motion
- Procedural background of the case (if relevant to the motion)
- Citations to the factual or procedural record (if applicable)

Argument (IREAC/CREAC → may have more than one, depending on the number of legal issues in the brief)
- Persuasive headings introducing each key argument point (if applicable)
- Statement of the issue (if more than one, one at a time)
- Governing rule(s) (if more than one, one at a time, and broken into workable elements or factors, if possible)
- Rule Explanations (thoughtful selection of case law to illustrate the rule)
- Signal cites + explanatory parentheticals (to fit additional case law into the brief concisely)
- Rule Application (applying rule elements/factors to client facts, presenting a logical argument leading to the result sought)
- Mini-Conclusion

Conclusion
- Specific result/relief sought

Date and Signature Block
Exhibits (if necessary)

If the focus of the brief is limited to a single legal issue, the brief writer might structure the argument around a lone IREAC/CREAC. However, if a single-issue brief involves a rule with more than one element or a set of factors, the drafter might organize the argument section around one IREAC/CREAC *per element or factor*. If the brief tackles more than one legal issue, a good legal writer crafts persuasive headings to introduce each distinct legal issue and addresses each issue through individual IREAC/CREAC analyses beneath each appropriate heading. Outlining and organizing the argument section of a brief around the legal rules is a critical step in the brief-writing process.

But where does the legal writer begin? Before focusing on the legal issue and researching the applicable substantive rules, the first step that every mindful lawyer takes when preparing to write a brief is to **check the governing court rules** for instructions, restrictions, and requirements for filing a brief in that court.

Avoiding the Dreaded "Benchslap"

To manage the thousands of pages of case pleadings, motions, and briefs filed in courthouses daily, judges (and their clerks) enforce rules and requirements addressing the substance contained in, and the procedure controlling, documents submitted by lawyers. In your first semester of law school, you may have felt that a page- or word-count limit on a memorandum assignment seemed arbitrary, even unfair. After all, you had so much to say about the legal issue; why should your analysis be restrained by such a seemingly random constraint? Well, page- and word-count limits on legal research memoranda in the first semester of law school are designed to prepare you for the reality that most judges impose standards, instructions, and requirements for the motions and briefs submitted to their courts, including restrictions on length. These rules accomplish two goals. First, they educate lawyers about the substance and content that a judge expects to find in a brief, enabling the court to process complex and voluminous intellectual material efficiently and "forge enlightened decisions."[3] Second, rules requiring all attorneys to prepare and submit motions and briefs in a consistent structural and procedural format promote "fairness and orderliness" in the judicial process.[4]

Mindful lawyers readily embrace rules governing the substance and procedure of filing briefs.

Substantive Brief-Writing Rules

For a novice brief writer unsure how to start the brief-drafting process, court rules identifying the required substantive components of a motion and accompanying brief are most helpful. For example, federal civil courts require lawyers to follow Federal Rules of Civil Procedure addressing the general content of certain motions, like Rule 56, which governs the substance of a motion for summary judgment. Specifically, Rule 56 requires the brief writer to (1) identify each claim or defense on which summary judgment is sought; (2) demonstrate that there is no genuine dispute as to any material fact (by citing to depositions, documents, affidavits, admissions, interrogatory answers, or other materials); and (3) show the client is entitled to judgment as a matter of law. Some local courts promulgate even more specific rules about how such content should be presented, so the judge can understand the case and so opposing counsel can respond in an efficient manner. If lawyers on both sides of the case comply with the rules, ideally the court will have all the information it needs to rule fairly on the legal issue. For instance, in its local version of Rule 56(b), the federal district court in Maine requires a lawyer filing a summary judgment motion and accompanying brief to describe the undisputed facts in the following specific form:

- The lawyer must include a separate, short, and concise statement of material facts, each set forth in a separately numbered paragraph or paragraphs, as to which the moving party contends there is no genuine issue of material fact to be resolved at trial.

---

[3] As the United States Court of Appeals for the First Circuit explained so succinctly in *Reyes-Garcia v. Rodriguez & Del Valle, Inc.*, 82 F.3d 11, 14 (1st Cir. 1996), "rules establish a framework that helps courts to assemble the raw material that is essential for forging enlightened decisions." The court also noted that deficiencies in legal writing "frustrate any reasonable attempt to understand [a party's] legal theories." *Id.*

[4] *Id.* Courts' procedural rules "ensure fairness by providing litigants with a level playing field. They ensure orderliness by providing courts with a means for the efficient administration of crowded dockets." *Id.*

- Each fact asserted in the statement shall be simply and directly stated in narrative, without footnotes or tables, and shall be supported by a record citation.

These types of specific substantive rules are valuable resources to help new legal writers ensure they include in the brief all of the key information bearing on the legal issues. For other types of motions and briefs, courts leave the scope of the content of the document to the discretion of the writer. Nonetheless, smart lawyers always check to see if any substantive rules govern the filing, so the court does not reject the motion or brief or issue a "benchslap"—the term that legal bloggers and some legal writing professors use to describe a written judicial opinion in which a judge admonishes an attorney for submitting a substandard brief.[5]

If you log onto an electronic legal research database like Westlaw, Lexis, or Bloomberg Law and search in published and unpublished court decisions for derivations of phrases like "poorly written brief" or "failure to follow court rules," you will find an alarming multitude of case opinions in which judges openly chastise lawyers for submitting shoddy briefs or flouting nonnegotiable substantive and procedural rules. Embarrassing consequences can ensue if a lawyer forgets or fails to check the court's rules before filing a motion and accompanying brief. Appendix A provides a comprehensive survey of judges' "benchslaps"—providing a taste of the extent of judges' frustration with lawyers who disregard brief-writing rules!

Formatting and Procedural Rules

To efficiently manage the mountain of paperwork judges must read each week and keep the playing field even so that all parties share equal opportunity for communicating with judges about the pivotal legal issues in their cases, many courts issue strict formatting and procedural rules for motions and briefs. For instance, Rule 7 of the Local Rules for the United States District Court for the District of Maine imposes the following formatting requirements for motions and briefs:

- All memoranda[6] in support of motions must be typed, in a font of no less than size 12 point, and shall be double-spaced on 8-1/2 × 11-inch paper or printed.

---

[5] According to the Urban Dictionary, the term "benchslap" was popularized by David Lat of Above the Law (http://www.abovethelaw.com) when he was blogging for Underneath Their Robes. *See* Article III Groupie, Underneath Their Robes, *Bench-Slapped! Reinhardt v. O'Scannlain*, http://underneaththeirrobes.blogs.com/main/2004/06/greetings_welco.html (June 24, 2004, 1:07 p.m.); *see also* Josh Blackman, Josh Blackman's Blog, *The 8 Best Benchslaps of 2012*, http://joshblackman.com/blog/2012/12/18/the-8-best-benchslaps-of-2012/ (Dec. 18, 2012).

[6] Some courts refer to the briefs submitted in support of motions as "Memoranda of Points and Authorities."

- Footnotes shall be in a font of no less than size 10 point, and may be single spaced.
- All pages shall be numbered at the bottom.
- No memorandum of law in support of or in opposition to a nondispositive[7] motion shall exceed 10 pages.
- No memorandum of law in support of or in opposition to a motion to dismiss, a motion for judgment on the pleadings, a motion for summary judgment, or a motion for injunctive relief shall exceed 20 pages.
- No reply memorandum shall exceed 7 pages.

Similarly, regarding technical formatting and presentation, Rule 10 of Maine's federal court rules requires that:

- All pleadings, motions, and other papers filed with the Clerk or otherwise submitted to the Court, except exhibits, shall bear the proper case number and shall contain on the first page a caption . . . and immediately thereunder a designation of what the document is and the name of the party on whose behalf it is submitted.
- All such documents shall be typed in a font of no less than size 12 point, and shall be double-spaced or printed on 8-1/2 × 11-inch paper.
- Footnotes shall be in a font of no less than size 10 point, and may be single spaced.
- All pages shall be numbered at the bottom.

Why would a court care about the font size selected by an attorney in preparing a document? Well, this formatting rule is a matter of readability and fairness. Judges devote significant time to reading tomes of briefs in the gamut of cases comprising their docket. From a practical standpoint, briefs must be physically readable; certain fonts enhance the visual presentation of these intellectually challenging papers so that judges can process and absorb the words efficiently. Further, imposing limitations or requirements on font size, line spacing, margins, footnotes, page numbering, and total page or word count ensures that all parties filing briefs on the same topic have an even playing field in presenting the facts and law to the decision maker. It would be unfair to allot one party 40 pages to advance legal arguments but limit the other party to 25 pages. Likewise, in the context of a 10-page limit, it would be inequitable to allow one party to submit a brief containing 3000 words presented in a tiny font but restrict the other party to 2300 words using a larger readable font.

---

[7] A nondispositive motion is one that will not "dispose" of a legal issue in the case. These types of motions address discovery or evidentiary disputes. In contrast, a dispositive motion may include, for example, a motion to dismiss or a motion for summary judgment, which have potential to "dispose" of or resolve certain legal issues in the case.

Professionalism Counts

Unfortunately, some lawyers erroneously believe that their writing is unique or deserves special treatment. They creatively circumvent the rules, or simply ignore them. As noted above, Appendix A provides a survey of judicial opinions in which judges have critiqued lawyers of all experience levels for their disregard of substantive and procedural legal writing rules. On a positive note, this appendix also summarizes cases in which judges have praised lawyers for their adherence to the rules and explained why such respect for writing submission mandates helps facilitate the administration of justice. Appendix A summarizes the following eight different circumstances in which legal writers run the risk of a benchslap from a judge by ignoring or flouting legal writing guidelines or rules:

- Lack of clarity (in structural logic or phrasing)
- Missing required substantive components
- Poor handling of the case facts, including inaccurate or missing citation to the factual record
- Faulty treatment of the applicable law, including imprecise citation to legal sources or failing to cite mandatory precedent
- Defiance of procedural and formatting rules, such as page/word limits, line spacing, margins, and font size
- Rampant typographical, grammatical, or general proofreading errors
- A disrespectful tone toward the court, opposing counsel, or other parties
- Late filings

Where to Find Courts' Legal Writing Rules

Sources of Brief-Writing Rules

- Systemwide rules
- Local rules
- Judge's rules
- Case scheduling order

Before you begin any brief-writing project, use your legal research skills to track down all applicable court rules governing your work product. If your case is pending in federal court, check the Federal Rules of Civil Procedure or the Federal Rules of Criminal Procedure. If you are handling a case in state court, check the state system's general civil or criminal rules. Then check your court's local rules, if any. Next, research whether your judge has issued her own set of rules. Your case's scheduling order or case management order also might impose requirements on written work product filed with the court. Look for rules that dictate what substantive content must be presented in the brief, any required sections of the brief (e.g., statement of facts, standard of review, etc.), formatting requirements (font, line spacing, margins, footnotes, page numbers, page- or word-count limits), and procedural submission requirements (electronic versus paper submissions, how many copies, format of attachments, etc.). Also, determine the deadline for filing the brief, and build time into your calendar for completing various interim drafts, editing, cite-checking, proofreading, and finalizing the document for filing.

Once you have all this information, consider creating a document template in your word processing system that contains the correct case caption and title of the brief and adheres to the court's formatting requirements. Then you are ready to start researching and drafting.

The Brief-Writing Process

Like the memorandum drafting process typically taught in the first semester of a law school Legal Writing curriculum (starting with identifying the legal issue and the pertinent rule), lawyers do not commence the brief-writing process by sitting down at a laptop, typing the first word of the caption, and continuing on through the last word of the signature block. To build a logical persuasive argument, lawyers write briefs from the inside out—first identifying the narrow legal issue, researching the rule, breaking the rule down into workable parts (elements, or factors, if possible), and choosing the best cases to explain the rule to the reader. Good legal writers use some variation of IREAC or CREAC to build a framework around the issue and the rule, illustrating the rule through strategically selected cases described in Rule Explanation (RE) paragraphs (and signal cites plus explanatory parentheticals). Then the legal writer applies the rule methodically to the client facts, leading the reader down a path toward the only logical outcome: the conclusion. The IREAC/CREAC framework can evolve in myriad different ways; this book offers three initial options, depending on the complexity of your legal issue and governing rule(s)s:

1. A single-issue brief governed by one simple rule (one IREAC/CREAC)
2. A single-issue brief governed by one rule with *multiple* elements or factors (one IREAC/CREAC for each element/factor, introduced by persuasive descriptive headings presenting each part of the rule)
3. A multi-issue brief governed by a *different* rule for *each* issue (separate IREAC/CREAC analyses for each issue, divided by persuasive and descriptive headings introducing each issue)

After writing the argument section of the brief, applying the rule components to the client facts in Rule Application (RA) paragraphs and asserting the result or remedy sought in the conclusion, the brief writer then goes back to the chronological beginning of the document and writes the formal introduction to the entire brief and the Statement of Facts. It is difficult to write a strong introduction without first having written the arc of the persuasive argument. Thereafter, a good legal writer edits the brief several times from start to finish, working through a twelve-step editing and proofreading process to enhance the professionalism of the document. This drafting process takes time, but if performed mindfully, thoughtfully reflecting on ways to integrate *logos*, *pathos*, and *ethos* throughout the document, ultimately the brief will represent the lawyer's finest effort to convince the decision maker that the result sought for the client is the right one.

Identifying and Narrowing the Issue in a Brief

Judges review piles of pleadings, motions, and briefs for many different cases addressing multitudinous areas of the law, including, for example, contractual disagreements, torts, property disputes, and intellectual property issues. Smart lawyers use legal writing as a vehicle to streamline the judge's job in the particular case, first by narrowing the focal point of the pertinent legal issue. Whether the client's case is simple or complex overall, each of the many briefs potentially filed in a case comprises only one small piece of the whole case puzzle. Think of each brief as a small battle in a greater war or, to use a more positive analogy, one brick in the construction of a larger wall or one dot in a Monet tableau. For the judge to grasp the legal question quickly, understand your proposed resolution, and make an informed and efficient decision, each brief must laser-focus on the precise legal issue it addresses rather than rambling or "throwing in everything but the kitchen sink." Smart lawyers use briefs to help the judge bushwhack through the jungle of distraction and pinpoint the primary issue of attention.

When you receive a brief-writing assignment, take time to discern the precise legal question. Perhaps your client has been sued for the tort of negligence. You recall that negligence has four elements: (1) duty; (2) breach; (3) causation; and (4) damages. Your client contends that there was no duty toward the complaining party in the first place. Your summary judgment brief might center around the narrow issue of the existence of a duty—one small piece of a larger legal pie.

Or perhaps your client, a valet parking attendant, has been accused of vehicle theft. A California statute, Cal. Veh. Code § 10851 (West 2011), states:

> Any person who drives or takes a vehicle not his or her own, without the consent of the owner thereof, and with intent either to permanently or temporarily deprive the owner thereof of his or her title to or possession of the vehicle, whether with or without intent to steal the vehicle . . . is guilty of a public offense. . . .

To determine the precise legal issue, first you break down the elements of the crime of vehicle theft into:

1. driving or taking,
2. a vehicle,

3. that is not one's own,

4. without consent of the owner,

5. with the intent to permanently or temporarily deprive the owner of title to or possession of the vehicle.

From your fact-gathering efforts, you learn that your client *drove* a *customer's car* off a parking lot and took it for a 30-minute joyride. Elements (1), (2), and (3) are satisfied; he *drove* a *car* that was *not* his own. However, did the owner give *consent* by handing his keys to the valet? Also, if the client intended to, and ultimately did, return the car to its owner, is element (5) satisfied, or does it fail? By breaking the rule down into its component parts and applying the facts, you have narrowed the legal issues in question down to *consent* and *intent to deprive the owner of title or possession*.

Let's consider another example. In a discovery dispute, a party stubbornly withholds documents on a shaky claim of attorney-client privilege. You want to file a motion to compel production of the documents. The legal issue in your brief might be whether the attorney-client privilege protects the unique category of documents sought. Or, in an evidentiary dispute, if you wish to file a motion in limine to preclude the opposing party's expert from testifying at trial on the grounds that she is not qualified, your legal issue in the brief may be whether the expert is sufficiently qualified by knowledge, skill, experience, training, or education.

Invest time in isolating the precise and narrow legal issue or issues that your brief will address. Perhaps the issue involves a legal definition (by statute or synthesized from case law) or a single element or factor of a rule governing one cause of action in the client's multifaceted case. Get laser-focused. The legal issue is not whether your client should *win* the overall case or—procedurally—whether he is entitled to an *order* granting the motion. The legal issue revolves around a single aspect of the *rule of law*.

Let's examine a hypothetical case scenario that we will use as a guide throughout this chapter for preparing a single-issue brief involving a simple straightforward rule. Later, we will ramp up the complexity of the brief-writing process by attacking a *single-issue* brief with a *multi-part* rule, and a *multi-issue* brief. For now, though, let's start with the basics.

Imagine that you represent a garment manufacturing company with a home office in a warehouse building in downtown New York City in the South Street Seaport area near the East River. An unexpected hurricane causes massive flooding to the seaport and the warehouse, causing the client to suffer substantial business losses, including property damage and an inability to fulfill customer orders. Fortunately, the company has insurance; it has been paying premiums to the same insurance company for 20 years and has never previously filed a claim. However, when the client telephones its insurer to file a claim, the insurance company denies coverage and refuses to reimburse the company for its losses. The owners of the garment company are understandably upset, after paying premiums for all those years. They feel that they have no choice but to sue the insurer for breach of contract.

The company hires you as counsel. Using the techniques discussed in Chapter 24, you prepare and file the complaint, alleging a cause of action for breach of contract. The insurance company files an answer. The parties meet and confer to plan a case timeline, and the court issues a case scheduling order. Discovery commences. During discovery, you learn that the insurance company possesses many e-mails and memoranda exchanged between the insurer's in-house counsel and its claims adjusters about the hurricane-related claims filed by many of the company's insureds, your client's particular insurance claims, and the insurer's decision to deny coverage of your client's losses. You want to review those claim-related documents, believing that they will shed light on the propriety of the insurance company's decision to deny insurance coverage to your client. You serve a Request for Production of Documents, specifically requesting the foregoing records. The insurance company subsequently refuses to produce the documents, arguing that the e-mails and memoranda are protected by the attorney-client privilege; they were sent to or from in-house counsel. You perform preliminary legal research and learn that there is an exception to the attorney-client privilege rule governing in-house counsel working for insurance companies: documents and communications generated by or exchanged with an insurance company's in-house counsel are *not* privileged if the in-house attorney was serving in the role of a claims analyst *in the ordinary course of the insurance company's business* instead of in a legal advisory role. You plan to file a motion to compel production of the documents. In the brief, your legal issue is *not:* Should the client prevail in its overall claim for breach of contract against the insurer? It is *not:* What duties does an insurer owe its insured? It also is *not:* What does the attorney-client privilege govern? Your legal issue is much narrower: Does the attorney-client privilege protect communications and documents generated by or exchanged with an insurance company's in-house counsel? Laser-focus.

When identifying the legal issue for a brief, consider using the following pyramid:

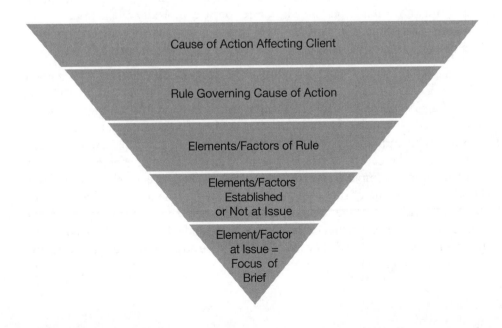

Cause of Action Affecting Client

Rule Governing Cause of Action

Elements/Factors of Rule

Elements/Factors Established or Not at Issue

Element/Factor at Issue = Focus of Brief

Identifying and Describing the Rule Governing the Issue in a Brief

As you may be able to discern from the upside-down pyramid, the legal issue and the governing rule go hand in hand. In fact, the rule often drives the legal issue that is the subject of a brief.

Let's look at examples of rules in three different brief-writing scenarios: (1) a discovery motion; (2) an evidentiary motion; and (3) a dispositive motion, such as a summary judgment motion that will dispose of a key aspect of a case. Recall from the first semester of law school that sources of rules include the U.S. Constitution or state constitutions, statutes, regulations, and common law derived from cases.

Identifying a Rule in a Brief Supporting a Discovery Motion

Using the example of the insurance dispute discussed above, let's imagine that you represent the garment manufacturer whose insurance company denied coverage of property damage and business losses stemming from a hurricane that flooded the client's warehouse. You filed the complaint alleging a cause of action for breach of contract. The insurer filed an answer denying responsibility and asserting defenses. The court issued the case scheduling order, and discovery commenced. In accordance with the discovery rules, you served a request for production of documents upon the insurer, asking for the client's claims evaluation file. You asked for all documents related to the insurance company's decision to deny coverage—a logical query. The insurer refused to produce a subset of those documents, asserting protection by the attorney-client privilege based on the fact that the communications were prepared by and/or for the insurance company's in-house counsel. However, as mentioned above, your research revealed that such privilege is inapplicable when an insurer's in-house attorney serves in a claims evaluation role in the ordinary course of business of the company—rather than in performing her function as a legal advisor.

A good legal writer presents the rule structure for the judge in a logical, easy-to-understand manner. Because a rule might have several parts, it is important to relay them methodically. In this example, the writer first would define the attorney-client privilege in the applicable jurisdiction:

> "The attorney-client privilege protects from disclosure those communications made in confidence between an attorney and a client for the purpose of facilitating the attorney's rendering of legal services to the client." *See Byrnes v. Empire Blue Cross Blue Shield*, No. 98CV8520(BSJ)(MHD), 1999 WL 1006312, at *1 (S.D.N.Y. Nov. 4, 1999).

Second, the writer would state the rule that specifically applies to attorneys working as in-house counsel for insurance companies:

> However, in the insurance context, the attorney-client privilege does not apply when an attorney acts as a claims adjuster, claims process supervisor, or claims investigation monitor, rather than a legal advisor. *See Amerisure Ins. Co. v. Laserage Tech. Corp.*, No. 96-CV-6313, 1998 WL 310750, at *1 (W.D.N.Y. Feb. 12, 1998).

Then, to illustrate the rule, the writer would select cases differentiating the in-house lawyer's two distinct roles: (1) legal advisor and (2) claims adjuster, claims process supervisor, or claims investigation monitor.

The brief writer tapers each legal rule from general, narrower, to precise.

Identifying a Rule in a Brief Supporting an Evidentiary Motion

Now, let's consider a different brief-writing scenario. Imagine that an opposing party seeks to introduce—as evidence in a jury trial—a newspaper article that describes your client in an unfavorable light. You object to the introduction of this so-called evidence at trial because you believe it constitutes nothing more than a piece of exaggerated tabloid journalism, riddled with rumor and unproven innuendo. In performing your legal research, you discovered a valid objection to the introduction of a newspaper article as evidence at trial on the grounds that it constitutes inadmissible hearsay. Now, laypersons use the term "hearsay" in everyday speech, but lawyers use a legal definition. To relay the governing rule in a brief in support of a motion in limine submitted to the judge, the brief writer first would recite the legal definition of hearsay in the particular jurisdiction:

> The Federal Rules of Evidence govern the admissibility of evidence in federal court. Fed. R. Evid. 801(c) defines hearsay as "a statement, other than one made by the declarant while testifying at the trial or hearing, offered in evidence to prove the truth of the matter asserted." In other words, hearsay is "a declarant's out-of-court statement offered for the truth of the matter asserted." *United States v. Torres*, 794 F.3d 1053, 1059 (9th Cir. 2015).

Then, to tailor this rule to newspaper articles, the writer would cite the narrower rule:

> Newspaper articles are considered hearsay under Rule 801(c) when offered at trial as evidence of the truth of the matter asserted therein. *Green v. Baca*, 226 F.R.D. 624, 637 (C.D. Cal. 2005).

The writer would illustrate these rules by describing cases in which courts barred the introduction of newspaper articles as evidence at trial because they (1) constituted out-of-court statements, (2) were made by a declarant, and (3) were offered as evidence of the truth of the matters asserted in the newspaper text.

Identifying a Rule in a Brief Supporting a Dispositive Motion

The foregoing rules regarding discovery and the admissibility of evidence were relatively straightforward: the writer first recites the definition of a legal term like "privilege" or "hearsay," and then applies the definition more narrowly to a particular context. Often, however, a statute provides a rule, but the statutory language needs further interpretation in order to extract a workable rule to apply to the client's facts. In that circumstance, lawyers look to case law applying the statutory rule in various factual scenarios in order to synthesize a more helpful subrule. In the brief, the legal writer first would state the overall statutory rule and then describe the more detailed subrule in a list of elements or factors gleaned from applicable case law. This multi-step analytical process is an exercise lawyers routinely undertake in outlining and drafting complex briefs such as motions to dismiss or motions for summary judgment.

Let's consider an example. Suppose that your client is a doctor who has been sued for medical malpractice in Minnesota. You believe that your client has a defense to the claim based upon the applicable statute of limitations. In other words, the allegedly injured patient waited too long to file the complaint, and, under the applicable statute of limitations, the claim is now time-barred. You want to file a motion for summary judgment asserting that the malpractice action is precluded based on the applicable statute of limitations.

To recite the rule, the brief writer first would refer to the statute designating the time period within which an injured party must file a medical malpractice action in Minnesota:

> An action by a patient against a health care provider alleging malpractice must be commenced within four years from the date the cause of action accrued. Minn. Stat. Ann. § 541.076 (1999).

Next, the writer would state the rule defining when a malpractice cause of action "accrues" in Minnesota:

> The cause of action accrues when the physician's treatment for the particular condition ceases. *Noland v. Freeman*, 344 N.W.2d 419, 420 (Minn. 1984).

Then, to fully flesh out the rule, the writer must list the factors that courts consider when determining *the date when treatment ceases:*

> Minnesota courts consider three factors in determining the date when treatment ceases: (1) whether there is a relationship between the physician and the patient with regard to the illness; (2) whether the physician still is attending and examining the patient; and (3) whether there is anything more the physician may do for the patient with regard to the illness. *Grondahl v. Bulluck*, 318 N.W.2d 240, 243 (Minn. 1982).

Good legal writers do not just relay the basic rule and leave readers to fend for themselves in interpreting legal **terms of art** embedded within the rule. Thoughtful legal writers recite the main governing rule and then drill down each definition or component part to provide an even narrower subrule, making the framework of the law as clear as possible. This is the *R* part of an IREAC or CREAC scaffold. Later, in the *E* section, the brief writer illustrates the rules in Rule Explanations (abbreviated REs), summarizing the Facts, Holding, and Rationale of carefully chosen examples of cases (and possibly signal cites plus explanatory parentheticals). Then the brief writer applies the rule to the client facts (in the Rule Application (abbreviated as RAs), to persuade the judge to issue an order granting the result sought.

In summary, when researching, describing, and narrowing the rule controlling the legal issue in your brief, the inverted pyramid structure is useful:

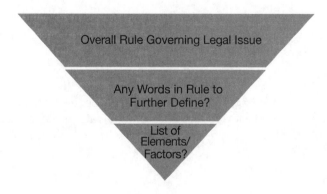

Overall Rule Governing Legal Issue

Any Words in Rule to Further Define?

List of Elements/ Factors?

Explaining the Rule in a Brief (Rule Explanation or RE)

During the brief-drafting process, mindful lawyers invest significant time in researching and finding case law to illustrate the applicable rule. A brief writer's goal is to use vivid case examples to convince the judge (and opposing counsel) that the client's position is sound and the result sought is supported by precedent. While researching, lawyers hunt for cases in the governing jurisdiction in which courts have applied the same rule and dictated outcomes favorable to the client. More often than not, brief writers stumble upon unfavorable case law as well, but thoughtful lawyers ponder ways to distinguish such cases based on differences between the client's facts and the parties' circumstances in the precedent cases or policy reasons why the former precedent should not govern the client's matter. Legal research may reveal a mere handful of cases that are "on point" or dozens of cases. The brief writer's job includes paring down a large collection of cases unearthed during the legal research process to a manageable number of cases to write about in the brief. Lawyers look for (1) "landmark" cases, which perhaps established the rule in the first place or applied it to a novel set of facts for the first time; (2) recent cases confirming that the rule is up-to-date; (3) a spectrum of cases to illustrate the rule under a variety of circumstances; and (4) patterns within the cases to demonstrate to the eventual brief reader that the rule should yield the result sought by the brief writer. Ethical rules obligate lawyers to inform the court of adverse mandatory precedent, i.e., cases in the governing jurisdiction in which a higher court resolved the legal issue in a manner that, on the case's face, disfavors the client. Thus, it is important during the legal research process to ensure that you have read a wide range of cases applying the rule.

If the rule is broad (e.g., the definition of negligence under Nevada state law), you likely will find dozens and dozens of cases on point. Then the decision-making process boils down to choosing the most useful cases to illustrate through Rule Explanation (RE) paragraphs in the brief (perhaps tucking a few extra into the brief through signal cites plus explanatory parentheticals). If the brief topic is narrower (e.g., the accrual date of the statute of limitations in an architectural malpractice action), your research might yield a handful of cases, simplifying the case selection process. Either way, performing a thorough job in the legal research component of the brief-writing process will enhance the *ethos* element of persuasion: bolstering the credibility and integrity of the brief writer.

Effective legal writers use the composition techniques of REs (using a formula containing the Facts, Holding, and Rationale of the case) and signal citations plus explanatory parentheticals to weave additional case law seamlessly into a brief. Through the REs and signal cites, lawyers ethically advise the court about the rule governing the legal issue and demonstrate how courts in the particular jurisdiction have favored parties with similar facts to the client's. Legal writers use cases to persuade the judge that the result sought is the correct one.

Consider the following options when selecting cases to include in RE paragraphs in your brief (the E component of IREAC or CREAC):

- Choose the landmark case (i.e., the first major case to address the rule), plus three to five more recent favorable cases to illustrate the rule.
- Contrast two or more favorable cases with one unfavorable case (distinguishing the unfavorable one).[8]
- Describe the spectrum of cases (with varying results based on different factual circumstances) explaining the rule, and demonstrate to the court where the client's case fits into the spectrum.
- Choose three or more favorable cases to illustrate the rule, and then use the citation technique of Signal Cite + Explanatory Parenthetical to contrast favorable and unfavorable cases (distinguishing the unfavorable ones).

The option or options that you choose, as well as the total number of cases that you decide to include and illustrate in a brief, will depend upon (1) the complexity of the legal issue; (2) the wealth or dearth of case law on point; and (3) the page- or word-count limit of the brief. Mindful brief writers do not list and describe every case ever written on the legal issue; they make strategic choices about which, and how many, cases to write about, to clearly explain the rule to the decision maker in as thorough, accurate, ethical, yet concise a manner as possible.

Drafting Logical RE Paragraphs

Legal writers illustrate legal rules to judges (and opposing counsel) through case law. However, due to page- or word-count restrictions, lawyers must be selective about how many cases to rely on and describe in a brief and how much information to incorporate about each case. As you may remember from writing legal research memoranda in the first semester of law school, lawyers use a writing formula often called a Rule Explanation or an "RE" (alternatively called Case Explanations or Case Illustrations[9]). Whether you are writing objectively (in a predictive legal research memorandum) or persuasively (in a brief), RE paragraphs follow the same structure. The legal writer's goal in an RE is to convey the facts of the precedent case, the court's holding on the same legal issue affecting the client, and the rationale behind the court's reasoning in a concise yet informative manner, enabling the brief reader to quickly grasp what happened in the

---

[8] The jurisdiction's ethical rules may require you to include adverse case law if it is mandatory authority. Good legal writers thoughtfully consider how to distinguish unfavorable case law from the client's circumstances, explaining to the court how the seemingly adverse outcome does not defeat the result sought by the client.
[9] Your legal writing professor may use different terminology to refer to this brief component, but the same principles described herein apply whenever a brief writer describes a precedent case in a brief.

precedent case and draw links or note differences between the precedent case and the client's circumstances. Strong REs follow this structure:

- A smooth transition to the RE—perhaps a narrower recitation of the rule than the more detailed rule contained in the *R* part of the IREAC/CREAC, or if such subrule is unnecessary, a succinct transition word or phrase, like "For example, in *Brown v. Miller* . . . ."
- A description of the legally significant facts of the precedent case (in a few sentences).
- The court's holding: The court held ____.
- The court's reasoning: The court emphasized ____. The court reasoned ____________________. The court explained ____________________.

Let's look at an annotated example:

Annotation	Example text
Rule/Transition	Under New York law, a landowner cannot be held liable for a person's injuries on leased property unless the landowner retains control over the premises.
Full Case Cite	*Carvano v. Morgan*, 703 N.Y.S.2d 534 (N.Y. App. Div. 2000).
Facts	In *Carvano*, an employee slipped and fell on an accumulation of ice in his company's parking lot. The company rented the property from the landowner pursuant to a lease. The employee brought an action against the out-of-possession landowner, alleging that the owner was negligent in allowing the condition to occur and failing to cure it. *Id.* at 535.
Holding	However, the court held that the landowner was not liable. *Id.*
Rationale	The court relied upon an express statement in the lease stating that the landowner was not contractually obligated to remove the snow and ice; instead, the company/lessee bore responsibility for snow and ice removal. *Id.* The court emphasized that, even though the landowner retained a contractual right to reenter the premises to repair or inspect it if the tenant failed to do so, the landowner did not retain control over the parking lot. *Id.*

Notice the following in the example above:

- The first sentence introducing this RE is a general statement of the law regarding landowner liability. It is not so specific that it applies only to the parties in the precedent case; rather, it could apply to both the precedent parties and the key players in the client's scenario.
- The first time that the case is cited, the legal writer uses the full cite of the case (if this is the first time within the brief that the case is cited). Thereafter, the writer uses the shortened case name within the subsequent sentence, and "*Id.*" cites thereafter to refer to specific page numbers where the facts, holding, and rationale are found within the judicial opinion (called *pinpoint cites, pin cites,* or *jump cites*).

- The legal writer does not use the actual names of the parties in the factual description of the precedent case. A thoughtful and mindful legal writer only wants the judge to have to remember the names of the parties in the *client's* case. It is too confusing (and unnecessary) for a judge to be tasked with distinguishing client party names from the precedent case parties; thus, smart legal writers use easily understandable labels or roles for the parties in the precedent cases that readily can be transferred to the key players in the client scenario. Consider labels/roles like landowner, tenant, employee, athlete, celebrity, truck driver, pedestrian, teacher, parking attendant, etc.
- Lawyers write the facts, holding, and rationale of REs in the past tense.
- The facts summarize only the *legally significant* facts that bear on the court's holding, not *every* fact.
- The court's holding should be very simple. Start with the words "The court held _____," and then state the court's decision on the exact same legal issue affecting the client. Avoid describing any procedural outcome (e.g., granted summary judgment, denied the motion to dismiss) unless absolutely relevant to your client's case.
- To describe the court's rationale, lawyers use introductory phrases like "The court emphasized . . . ," "The court evaluated . . . ," "The court reasoned . . . ," or "The court relied upon . . ." to describe the pertinent reasons for the court's holding.
- To enhance *ethos*, lawyers use pinpoint page cites (using "*Id.* at _____") to note the exact pages within the case where the judge and opposing counsel can locate the cited information.

Let's look at another example with an alternate introduction/transition:

Rule/Transition	For example, in *Del Giacco v. Noteworthy Co.*, 572 N.Y.S.2d 784 (Sup. Ct. App. Div. 1991), an employee slipped and fell on snow and ice
Full Cite	while exiting his automobile in the parking lot of his place of employment. He sued the out-of-possession landowner who had leased the property to his employer. *Id.* at 785. The landowner moved for
Facts	summary judgment, contending that, through the lease to the employer, it had transferred possession and control of the land to its lessee and had not retained or assumed any responsibility over the premises. *Id.* The
Holding	court held that the landowner was not liable. *Id.* at 786. The court reasoned that the employee failed to show that the out-of-possession landowner exercised any control over the land. *Id.* Further, the court
Rationale	emphasized that the landowner was not contractually obligated to repair the premises, did not assume responsibility by a course of conduct to maintain any portion of the property, and did not create the dangerous condition. *Id.*

In the example above, note the following:

- Here, the transition to the RE is simply "For example, in *Del Giacco* . . . ." The rule already would have been stated in the prior paragraph (in the *R* component of the IREAC or CREAC). If the legal writer believes that there is no need to repeat the rule or include a subrule when introducing the RE, the writer instead inserts a simple transition to signal a shift to the case illustration: "For example, in *Del Giacco* . . . ."

- If this is the first time that the case is cited in the brief, the writer includes the full cite of the case. Thereafter, the writer uses "*Id.*" to denote pinpoint cites after each pertinent fact, holding, and rationale sentence, indicating to the brief reader where such information can be found within the body of the judicial opinion.
- The writer includes only the *legally significant* facts of the precedent case, using labels or roles to identify the parties (instead of the names of the parties in the precedent case): "employee," "landowner," "employer."
- The holding starts with "The court held . . ." and answers the legal question of landowner liability.
- The rationale provides the key reasons why the court ruled the way it did.
- The writer uses the past tense to describe the facts, holding, and rationale of the precedent case.

When writing an RE for a key precedent case in your brief, use the following guidelines to determine the critical information to include in the RE paragraphs:

Introduction/Rule Statement (or Transition): In the IR or CR parts of your IREAC or CREAC, you already introduced the legal issue and the governing rule (tapering from general principles to narrower definitions, elements, or factors of the rule). To introduce an RE, decide whether you should craft a new rule statement that differs from the rule sentences you already wrote or whether you can simply use a transition phrase like, "For example, in *Davidov v. Harper,* . . . ." Can you draft a sentence that provides new information about the rule or perhaps a subrule? The transition that introduces the RE should be distinct from any other sentences already describing the rule and must be phrased using language that applies both to the parties in the precedent case and to the client. Let's look at an example:

Main Rule (already described in the R part of IREAC or CREAC):

To assess whether an out-of-possession landowner retained control over a property and can be held liable for injuries to a visitor to the premises, courts focus on (1) language in a contract between the landowner and a lessee, and (2) course of conduct. Courts will consider contractual language discussing the landowner's right of reentry to make repairs but will not hold such landowner liable, even in light of a right of reentry, unless the parties' course of conduct indicates that the landowner exercised that right in a manner that demonstrated ongoing control of the land.

More Narrow Rule Statement/Transition to RE:

In analyzing course of conduct, courts specifically evaluate how often the landowner visited the property and whether the landowner actually performed repairs to the property. For example, in *Gronski v. County of Monroe*, 18 N.Y.3d 374 (N.Y. 2011) . . . .

Alternate Transition to RE:

If you believe that you already did a solid job of describing the rule in the R section of the IREAC or CREAC, you do not need to craft a new rule statement to introduce the RE. Instead, use a simple transition, such as "For example, in *Capri v. Positano*, . . ." or "For instance, in *Roma v. Firenze*, ..." The important consideration is to include at least some form of transition between the rule and the RE, so the reader does not feel any choppiness or an abrupt shift in content.

Facts: What are the key, legally significant facts that yielded the court's decision in the precedent case? Start with identifying who the key players were, giving them labels or roles:

Who was involved? _____

What labels/roles can you assign the key players (to avoid using their names) (e.g., police officer, pilot, mechanic, teacher, taxi driver, boxer, politician, manufacturer)? _____

What happened between the parties?_____

Who sued whom?_____

Why did the one party sue the other? _____

What was the legal issue between the parties?_____

Holding: What was the court's decision on the same exact legal issue affecting your client? The court held _____.

Rationale: Why did the court make the decision it did?

The court relied upon _____.

The court evaluated _____.

The court emphasized _____.

The court explained _____.

The court reasoned _____.

Citation: Is this RE the first time that you are mentioning the case in your brief? If so, use the full cite of the case right after the rule statement/introductory sentence or within the transition sentence:

[Case name (*italicized* or underlined)], [Volume] [Reporter] [Initial page of case] ([Court] [Year]).

Or have you cited the case earlier in the brief? If so, the first time you cite the case in the RE, use the short cite:

[Name of first party in the case (*italicized* or underlined)], [Volume] [Reporter] at [Pinpoint page cite].

Thereafter, starting in the fact section, use "*Id.* at _____." or "*Id.*" to cite to specific pages where the facts, holding, and rationale principles can be found in the judicial opinion. Use "*Id.* at _____." each time you switch to a new page, or simply "*Id.*" if the information is found on the same page as the previous cite.

For unpublished cases, always check the court rules to determine whether citation of unpublished cases in a brief is permitted, and if so, whether the court requires you to attach a copy of each unpublished case as an exhibit to the brief. The formula for citation of unpublished cases is:

Full cite: [Case name (*italicized* or <u>underlined</u>)], [Docket number], [Database ID and document number], at * [Pinpoint page number] ([Court and Full date]).

Example: *Byrnes v. Empire Blue Cross Blue Shield*, No. 98CV8520(BSJ)(MHD), 1999 WL 1006312, at *1 (S.D.N.Y. Nov. 4, 1999). (Note the asterisk before the page number, signifying that this is an electronic page, not a real page in a book.)

Short cite: *Byrnes*, 1999 WL 1006312, at *1.

Id. cite: *Id.* at *3.

Transitions Between REs

A final note on RE paragraphs: You likely will include more than one RE in a brief. Mindful legal writers insert transitions between REs. As you end one RE and begin another, take time to craft a new informative rule statement/introduction for the second RE, either by extracting a new aspect of the rule from that particular case or highlighting a specific element or factor of the rule that is illustrated in the new case. Alternatively, if the next RE merely builds upon the prior one, use a transition word or phrase like "Further, in *Nogueras* . . ." or "Similarly, in *Rana* . . . ." If the subsequent RE contrasts with the prior RE, you could use a transition like "In contrast, in *Levy* . . . ." Transitions help transform a decent brief into an excellent one.

Signal Cites Plus Explanatory Parentheticals

Brief writers also use a creative citation technique to tuck additional case support into a brief in a concise manner without writing full RE paragraphs: the Signal Cite + Explanatory Parenthetical. The formula looks like this:

[Appropriate signal introducing the cite] [Case citation: parties' names, volume, reporter, initial page number, court, year] [Well-structured parenthetical capturing the facts, holding, and rationale of the case in four lines of text or less].

Here is an example:

Signal and citation	*See, e.g., Lo v. Burke, 455 S.E.2d 9, 13 (Va. 1995)* (holding that a statute of limitations for medical malpractice began to run on the date of onset of a disease in the patient's pancreas rather than the date of a
Explanatory Parenthetical	misread CT scan).

The following critical points distinguish excellent signal cites (plus explanatory parentheticals) from mediocre ones:

- The choice of an appropriate signal to introduce the citation (the range of signal choices is explained below)
- Proper and accurate citation form
- A concise but well-structured parenthetical with the following characteristics:
  - It starts with a gerund (a verb ending in "-ing").
  - The parenthetical captures the facts, holding, and rationale of the case in four lines of text or less.
  - Regarding punctuation, it includes no internal periods; commas are permitted, and semicolons can link two separate concepts if absolutely necessary.
- The writer attaches each signal cite to the *end* of a prior RE (signal citations should never interrupt an ongoing RE of a different case).

Choosing the Proper Signal

The *Bluebook* explains the different types of signals in R1.[1] New legal writers should consider choosing from the following signal options:

Signal	Usage
No signal	The following case contains the direct quote just stated in the brief or stands for the exact rule or principle just recited in the brief.
See	The following case or cases stand for, or illustrate, the rule or principle just stated.
See also	The following case or cases show additional support for the rule or principle that the previously cited case just illustrated or supported.

---

[1] The Bluebook: A Uniform System of Citation.

But see	The following case or cases contrast with the statement just made or the cases just cited.
See, e.g.,	The following case or cases provide an example or examples of the rule or proposition just stated.
Compare [case] *with* [case]	These two cases show opposite holdings by courts applying the same rule or illustrate the rule through two contrasting sets of facts.

To cite a case to support a statement just made in a brief, either use no signal and then cite the case, or use *See* to introduce the case. To contrast a new case with a statement just made in a brief, use *But see*. To add additional support, use *See also*, or *See, e.g.,*. The *"Compare . . . with . . ."* formula is a little trickier and advanced, but it is a neat way to contrast two cases in a brief concisely.

Signals are either italicized or underlined; choose the same typeface style that you use for your case name citations. Do not flip-flop back and forth between italics and underlining within the body of the brief. Also notice how "*See, e.g.,*" is the only signal that contains commas.

Citing the Case

After the signal, use standard citation form to cite the case. If this is the first time that you are citing the case in the brief, use the full citation. If you already have cited the case in the brief, use the short citation form. If you are quoting directly from the case, include a pinpoint page citation that provides the exact location of the quote within the body of the judicial opinion (in the full cite, add a comma after the initial page and then include the pinpoint page cite; in the short cite, omit the initial page of the case and insert "at [the pinpoint page number]"). If citing the case for a general proposition, you do not need a pinpoint page citation, but if you are citing the case for a specific fact, rule, holding, or rationale, it helps the brief reader to know exactly where those principles can be found within the body of the judicial opinion.

Crafting a Helpful Parenthetical

Crafting a concise but helpful parenthetical takes patience and care. Remember that the purpose of a signal cite plus explanatory parenthetical is to tuck additional case law into a brief without expending precious words writing an entire RE to illustrate the judicial opinion. Thus, parentheticals that exceed four lines of text defeat that goal and become unwieldy for the reader. However, it can be challenging to distill an entire case into four lines. Here are some tips:

1. Identify the court's holding on the exact legal issue that is the subject of your brief.

2. Extract the key legally significant facts in the precedent case that pertain to the legal issue and that drove the court's decision.

3. Determine one to three critical reasons why the court held the way it did.

Now, try to fit those key pieces of information into the following formula, starting with a gerund (e.g., holding that, finding that, determining that, etc.):

Formula: (holding that [*insert the court's holding here*] when [*insert the legally significant facts here*] because [*insert the court's rationale here*]).

Example: *See, e.g., Green v. City of New York*, 906 N.Y.S.2d 587 (N.Y. App. Div. 2010) (holding that an out-of-possession landowner was not liable when a mall customer sustained injuries while riding an elevator in a building leased to the mall because the landowner retained no daily control over the premises and was not contractually obligated to repair unsafe conditions).

In the example, notice the following points:

- The parenthetical starts with a gerund (you could also use "finding that" or "deciding that").
- The parenthetical states the holding (the landowner was not liable).
- The parenthetical tells the basic factual story (a mall customer was injured in an elevator).
- The parenthetical provides the legal rationale for the holding (the court relied upon factors such as the landowner's lack of daily control over the premises and lack of contractual obligation to perform repairs).
- The parenthetical occupies no more than four lines of text.

Consider these two additional examples, addressing the same legal issue of landowner liability:

Example: *See also Vijayan v. Bally's Total Fitness*, 733 N.Y.S.2d 703 (N.Y. App. Div. 2001) (holding that a landowner was not liable when a patron slipped and fell on icy outdoor steps leading up to a gym because the property owner expressly relinquished control over the premises to the gym owner in a lease).

Example: *See, e.g., Alnashmi v. Certified Analytical Group, Inc.*, 929 N.Y.S.2d 620 (N.Y. App. Div. 2011) (holding that a building owner who leased the premises to a tenant-employer was not liable when an employee slipped and fell on water that had accumulated in a hallway because the lease placed responsibility for maintenance and repair squarely on the tenant-employer).

Expanding a Signal Cite to a String Cite

Sometimes a brief writer might wish to tuck a series of extra cases into a brief through a signal cite, to show the court that even more precedent supports a rule, a proposition, or a trend in the judicial decision making on the pertinent legal issue. Savvy brief writers use another advanced signal technique called a *string cite*. In this writing device, lawyers "string" together more than one case, using the signal-cite-plus-explanatory-parenthetical formula but linking a group of cases through semicolons.

> Example: *See, e.g., Alnashmi v. Certified Analytical Group, Inc.*, 929 N.Y.S.2d 620 (N.Y. App. Div. 2011) (holding that a building owner who leased premises to a tenant-employer was not liable when an employee slipped and fell on water that had accumulated in a hallway because the lease placed responsibility for maintenance and repair squarely on the tenant-employer); *Green v. City of New York*, 906 N.Y.S.2d 587 (N.Y. App. Div. 2010) (holding that a property owner was not liable when a mall customer sustained injuries while riding an elevator in a building leased to the mall because the landowner retained no daily control over the premises and was not contractually obligated to repair unsafe conditions); *Vijayan v. Bally's Total Fitness*, 733 N.Y.S.2d 703 (N.Y. App. Div. 2001) (holding that a landowner was not liable when a patron slipped and fell on icy outdoor steps leading up to a gym because the property owner expressly relinquished control over the premises to the gym owner in a lease).

Note how, in the example, only one signal introduces the string cite. The writer replaces the periods at the end of the first two cites with semicolons and ends the entire string cite with a period. Obviously, string cites create rather long, citation-heavy paragraphs that can become tedious for a reader, so good legal writers use this technique sparingly in a brief (perhaps once or twice in a brief under ten pages).

The *Bluebook* prescribes rules governing the order of cases in a string cite:

- Federal cases precede state cases.
- Federal cases are cited in the following order: U.S. Supreme Court cases, courts of appeals cases, district court cases.
- Cases decided by the same court are cited in reverse chronological order.
- Cases from several states are cited alphabetically by state and then by court rank within each state.[2]

Choosing Cases for REs and Signal or String Cites

If your legal research yielded only a handful of cases addressing your brief topic, you might be able to include all the pertinent cases within the body of your

---

[2] The Bluebook: A Uniform System of Citation at R1.

argument. However, if your legal research yielded a voluminous number of cases—some favorable and others adverse—you must thoughtfully consider how many, and which, cases to include in REs or signal or string cites. Page- and word-count limits affect how many cases brief writers can include in an argument; additionally, a legal reader does not need a survey of every case on point. Achieving the right balance of case law takes care and practice.

Consider constructing a case selection chart or matrix to help you make strategic decisions on which cases to include:

Case Name	Favorable Outcome for Client?	Less Favorable or Adverse Outcome for Client?	Landmark Case or *Mandatory* Precedent That *Must* Be Cited (check ethical rules)?	Case Provides Helpful, Easy-to-Understand, Logical Legal Analysis of the Issue (i.e., good for full RE?)	Case Provides Only Cursory Legal Analysis of the Issue (i.e., better for a signal or string cite?)

Once you complete the chart, group together the favorable cases, and consider (1) whether they are landmark cases or mandatory precedent that must be included in the brief; (2) whether they are informative cases that provide a helpful detailed analysis of the legal issue, and therefore would be beneficial in a full RE; or (3) whether they merely touch on the legal issue and provide a favorable result but without much analysis, and therefore would be better suited for a signal or string cite. Then conduct the same analysis for the unfavorable cases and decide whether, under the ethical rules, they must be included in the brief (because they are mandatory authority). If they are mandatory precedent and ethical rules require their citation, think strategically about how to distinguish the cases from the favorable cases and your client's case. A case may be distinguishable on its facts, new societal circumstances that did not exist when the case was decided, or recent developments in the rule.

Organizing the E Part of IREAC or CREAC

There are many ways to organize the REs and signal or string cites in the Rule Explanation section of an argument. There is not just one "correct" way of organizing the law in your brief. Consider some of the following options:

Option 1
(using 4 cases—showing consistent holdings)

Legal Issue (Position on the Issue → Contention/Conclusion)

Rule

RE 1 illustrating the rule

RE 2 (with a similar holding as RE 1) illustrating the rule

RE 3 (with a similar holding as REs 1 and 2) illustrating the rule
Signal Cite + Explanatory Parenthetical (case with a similar holding as REs 1, 2, and 3)

Option 2
(using 4 cases—showing contrasting holdings)

Legal Issue (Position on the Issue → Contention/Conclusion)

Rule

RE 1 illustrating the rule

RE 2 (with a similar holding as RE 1) illustrating the rule
Signal Cite + Explanatory Parenthetical (case with a similar holding as REs 1 and 2)

RE 3 (with a holding contrasting REs 1 and 2) illustrating the rule as applied to a distinguishable set of facts

Option 3
(using 7 cases—showing contrasting holdings)

Legal Issue (Position on the Issue → Contention/Conclusion)

Rule

RE 1 illustrating the rule

RE 2 (with a similar holding as RE 1) illustrating the rule
String Cite + Explanatory Parentheticals (two cases with holdings similar to REs 1 and 2)

RE 3 (with a holding contrasting REs 1 and 2 and the String Cite) illustrating the rule as applied to a distinguishable set of facts

RE 4 (with a similar holding as RE 3) illustrating the rule as applied to a distinguishable set of facts
Signal Cite + Explanatory Parenthetical (case with a similar holding as REs 3 and 4)

Applying the Rule in a Brief (Rule Application or RA)

So far in the brief-writing process, you have learned how to identify the legal issue, state the applicable rule, extract the components of the rule that the court will need to apply to decide the outcome, and illustrate the rule through strategically selected cases described in RE paragraphs (linked by transitions) and signal or string citations plus explanatory parentheticals. The next section of the brief (the A in IREAC or CREAC, also called the Rule Application or RA) applies the rule components to the client's facts in a persuasive manner to convince the court that the outcome sought by the brief writer is the correct one. In this section of the brief, thoughtful legal writers intertwine *logos, pathos,* and *ethos.* The Rule Application section leads the reader down a logical path toward the requested result while capturing the reader's attention with engaging and resonating facts and arguments. Writers engender credibility by balancing passionate advocacy with a respectful tone toward the court, opposing counsel, the parties, and the legal system in general. The RA can include rule-based reasoning, analogical reasoning, policy-based reasoning, or all three.

Rule-Based Reasoning

To logically apply the rule components to the client's facts, good legal writers structure the RA around the organizational framework of the rule itself, mirroring the chronology of the rule components illustrated in the REs. Let's use the example of a legal rule governing the circumstances in which an "out-of-possession" landowner may be held liable for injuries to third parties that occur on property leased to or managed by a person or company other than the landowner. Suppose, in the R section of the brief, the brief writer included the following rule:

> Under New York law, an out-of-possession property owner is *not* liable for injuries to a third-party resulting from a dangerous condition existing on a premises unless the landowner: (1) *created* the dangerous condition; (2) assumed responsibility to *maintain* any portion of the premises; (3) was contractually obligated to *repair* the unsafe condition; or (4) retained *control* of the property.

A lawyer must address the rule's four components—creation, maintenance, repair, and control—to convince the judge to rule in her client's favor. On one hand, if the lawyer represents the *out-of-possession landowner* and seeks a ruling that the client is *not* liable for an injury that occurred on property that he leased to a company, the brief writer must apply all four parts of the legal rule and demonstrate that *none* of the four prongs is satisfied by the client's particular facts. On the other hand, if the brief writer represents the *injured party* and requests a ruling that the landowner is indeed liable, the lawyer likewise must analyze all four rule components in the brief. The injured party's attorney ideally would argue that all four prongs (creation, maintenance, repair, and control) are satisfied under the case facts; however, the rule requires satisfaction of only *one* prong for liability to attach (note the word "or" in the rule). Thus, if the client's facts are weak on one or more of the rule components, the lawyer might decide strategically to concede one or more points to enhance credibility. These types of decisions invoke the *ethos* prong of persuasive writing; the brief writer must consider whether her integrity or credibility will be tarnished by making shaky arguments.

In rule-based reasoning, the brief writer applies each part of the rule (in the same chronological order that the rule components appear in the R and RE sections of IREAC or CREAC, so the reader has a logical framework to follow) to the facts of the client's case and makes the strongest argument possible for why the court should rule in the client's favor. To ensure that all the legally significant facts are woven into the RA section of the argument, you might consider creating a comparison chart:

Rule Component (Element? Factor? Definition?)	Strong Client Facts That Support the Client's Position	Weak Client Facts That Possibly Undermine the Client's Position

In persuasive writing, lawyers emphasize and spotlight the strongest facts supporting the client's position on each rule component. Just like when addressing unfavorable case law, lawyers must exercise professional judgment when deciding how to handle weak client facts. Unlike adverse mandatory precedent, lawyers have no ethical obligation to inform the court of every adverse or unfavorable fact. However, lawyers may not misrepresent facts. Thus, if omission of a weak fact would effectively constitute a misrepresentation to the court, the writer should disclose it. Additionally, a writer might gain a strategic advantage by revealing a negative fact before the opponent does, taking control, and explaining to the court why (1) the fact is not actually unfavorable when viewed through the correct lens or (2) the fact is not dispositive or determinative (in other words, it is not relevant to the court's decision on the legal issue, or other facts should be weighed more heavily). Some lawyers prefer to take charge of a weak fact by proactively revealing it to the court, instead of defensively responding to the other side's illumination of it in an opposition brief. These decisions require strategic thinking and professional judgment.

In the RA, good brief writers thoughtfully consider how to present the facts and arguments chronologically within each component of the rule. If both strong and weak facts must be addressed, the lawyer can decide whether weaker facts should be sandwiched between stronger facts or whether another organizational structure would be more effective. Overall, good brief writers start and end the RA with a flourish of strength.

Analogical Reasoning

In addition to applying each component of the governing rule methodically to the client facts to demonstrate why the result the brief writer seeks is the logical and correct one, lawyers persuade further by comparing and contrasting the client's circumstances to the case law illustrated in the REs and signal or string cites. This technique is called *analogical reasoning:* using case law analogies to convince the judge to rule in the client's favor. In everyday communications, we draw analogies between pairs of objects or concepts to show similarities and differences: "Your argument is as shaky as a bowl of lime Jello." "The investment banker is as crooked as Lombard Street in San Francisco." "The courthouse was as busy as Grand Central Station the day before Thanksgiving." Lawyers undertake the same exercise with case law. For example, if the *Simmons* precedent case involved facts similar to the client's facts, and the *Simmons* court ruled in favor of the litigant who played a similar role to that of the client in his dispute, the lawyer would state:

> Similar to the landowner in *Simmons,* which the court found not liable for the trespasser's injury because the property owner did not retain control over the premises, here Browning relinquished control over the management, maintenance, and repair of the beach house to his tenant, Christopher.

Or

> Just like the contractor in *Meyer,* which the court held had waived its claim to delay damages by failing to submit the proper paperwork within the 21-day deadline specified in the contract, here Chambliss Contractors waited too long to submit its time extension request, violating the contractual notice requirements.

The lawyer's goal in using analogical reasoning is to show the court how similar the client's circumstances are to the cases with favorable outcomes and to distinguish the client's situation from the cases with unfavorable outcomes. When distinguishing unfavorable cases in the RA, lawyers focus on differences in factual circumstances between the precedent case and the client's case or societal changes or evolutions in the rule that render the precedent case outdated in some way. Innovative brief writers use case law to demonstrate a spectrum of results and show the court where the client's case fits along the continuum. Further, good briefs weave rule-based reasoning and analogical reasoning together. Examples of this technique can be found in the sample briefs in Appendices L and M.

Policy-Based Reasoning

In addition to rule-based reasoning and analogical reasoning, brief writers often engage in policy-based reasoning. To craft a policy argument, a brief writer momentarily steps away from the drafting process and invests time thinking about why the result sought is the fair one, not only for the client but for society or the legal system as a whole. Public policy considerations include concepts of fairness, equality, clarity in the law, efficiency, economy, conservation of resources, ethics, morality, and other societal notions. A good first step in constructing a policy argument is to think about the intention and objective that the lawmakers had when creating the rule: Was it to promote fairness? Equity? Order? An economic benefit? Safety? Health? Consider adding a paragraph in the Rule Application section of the brief that integrates a discussion of the public policy behind the rule and how the outcome sought by your client furthers that public policy purpose.

For example, if you are writing a motion in limine to exclude a hearsay document from being admitted into evidence, research the policy underlying the exclusionary hearsay rule (i.e., to prevent the admission of unreliable out-of-court statements). Then, in the brief, you could focus on the *unreliable* nature of the particular evidence that the opposing party seeks to introduce at trial, weaving in a policy-based argument about how such feeble evidence undermines the integrity of the fact-finding process.

Alternatively, if you are drafting a motion to dismiss or a motion for summary judgment to enforce a statute of limitations, first research the public policy underlying statutes that restrict the time period for an aggrieved party to file a lawsuit (i.e., preventing individuals "from having to defend unanticipated lawsuits brought after a long delay" and fostering fairness and judicial economy by precluding "lawsuits where evidence may have become lost or stale due to the passage of time").[10] Or, if you are crafting a motion to dismiss a complaint based on the plaintiff's failure to comply with a contractual agreement to arbitrate disputes rather than litigate, research the public policy of encouraging individuals' freedom of contract and respecting bargained-for choices of dispute resolution mechanisms.

Some brief writers incorporate public policy arguments into a brief in a separate section from rule-based arguments and analogical reasoning (perhaps under a distinct heading). Others intertwine such arguments with the rule-based and analogical reasoning within the RA. Either way, the brief writer's goal is to persuade the court that the result sought not only makes logical sense under the applicable rule and is supported by the case law but also furthers public policy.

Structuring an RA

Mindful brief writers signal the shift from the RE part of the argument section of a brief to the RA through a transition sentence, foreshadowing and concluding the ultimate outcome on the legal issue as a whole or the distinct

---

[10] *Miller v. Fortis Benefits Ins. Co.*, 363 F. Supp. 2d 700, 705 (D.N.J. 2005).

component of the legal issue being addressed in that section of the brief. Readers need a signpost to mentally segue from the rules to facts/persuasive arguments. A transition sentence introducing an RA might look like this:

- Applying the foregoing rule regarding attorney-client privilege to the documents being erroneously withheld by Cornerstone Insurance Company, the privilege does not shield from discovery the documents generated by in-house counsel acting in the role of a claims adjuster.
- Applying the factors of the *Daubert* standard applicable to expert witnesses, Dr. Meadows unequivocally fails to meet the test of admissibility of an expert at trial.
- Applying the definition of hearsay under the Federal Rules of Evidence, the newspaper article must be excluded from trial as an unreliable out-of-court statement offered for the truth of the matter asserted.

Each of the foregoing examples states a concrete conclusion about the legal issue being addressed in that IREAC or CREAC analysis. After the conclusory transition, the brief writer analyzes each element, factor, or definitional component of the rule in distinct paragraphs. Effective RAs use separate paragraphs to address each component of a rule. Each paragraph should have (1) an introduction, identifying which part of the rule is being analyzed next; (2) a middle (using rule-based and analogical reasoning, applying the rule to the client facts and comparing and contrasting the facts to the case law); and (3) a mini-conclusion, stating the resolution of the individual component part of the rule. Next, the writer inserts a paragraph break and then repeats the pattern and structure with the next prong of the rule and continues until all rule components are analyzed.

A good RA leads the reader down a logical path toward the desired result, framing the analysis around the rule and showing whether and how the elements, factors, or definitional components are satisfied (or not satisfied) and how that calculation drives the ultimate result sought. Consider these logic trails:

- The rule governing a breach of contract has four required elements: (1) existence of a contract; (2) the plaintiff's performance of the contract or excuse for nonperformance; (3) the defendant's breach of the contract; and (4) resulting damage to the plaintiff. If even one of these elements is missing, the cause of action for breach of contract fails.
  - Because the plaintiff must prove that *all four* required elements are met, the plaintiff's RA on the issue of breach of contract would cover four separate analyses, arguing one-by-one why each distinct element is met. The overall conclusion would be that, since all four required components are established, the plaintiff prevails.
  - In contrast, to defeat the plaintiff's cause of action for breach of contract, the defendant only needs to prove that *one element* fails. Ideally, a defendant might want to point out how all of the components fail, but if that is not realistic, it is fine to concede—for purposes of

ethos—clearly established elements, while strongly contending why at least once critical element falls short.

The last sentence of each RA paragraph (or RA section addressing each distinct rule component, if more than one paragraph is necessary to address that particular prong of the rule) should affirmatively state the party's mini-conclusion on the rule component discussed therein.

Using Language to Persuade in an RA

In addition to using *logos* to apply the rule components to the client facts in a logical manner and compare and contrast the case law to the client's circumstances in the RA, mindful legal writers employ the techniques of *pathos* and *ethos* by carefully selecting language to engage and captivate the reader while at the same time fostering the credibility of the writer. Brief writers thoughtfully consider phrasing choices that will invoke an emotional connection between the reader and the client's circumstances, while conveying *ethos:* credibility and integrity. The RA is the section of a brief that offers the writer the most leeway and creative license in the drafting process. Some writers push this freedom a bit too far and use overly dramatic language to describe the client's facts and arguments—an easy way to undermine the lawyer's credibility. Indeed, new legal writers should experiment with their "lawyer voice," considering language, grammar, and punctuation choices that can enhance the persuasive nature of a brief. However, brief writers should always balance passion for the client's cause with mindful respect for the truth, the parties in the case, the reader, opposing counsel, the court, and the judicial process. The following sections demonstrate how different language choices affect the *pathos* and *ethos* of a brief.

Language Choices in a Brief Supporting a Discovery Motion

Consider the following three ways of phrasing an argument that opposing counsel has wrongfully withheld documents in discovery:

Option 1: True to form, counsel continues its shameless ruse of hiding behind the attorney-client privilege to prevent ABC Corporation's e-mails from ever seeing the light of day. Counsel has distorted and warped the definition of privilege in a flawed attempt to suppress pivotal documents that undoubtedly will expose ABC Corporation's outright fraud against its shareholders.

Critique: Too dramatic? Accuses opposing counsel of wrongdoing? Potentially undermines the writer's credibility?

Option 2: Counsel has refused to provide e-mails to which the shareholders are entitled pursuant to the discovery rules.

Critique: Too boring and bland? Accurate, but . . . will anyone care?

Option 3: Counsel erroneously asserts the attorney-client privilege to prevent the shareholders' discovery of highly relevant e-mails that will shed light on ABC Corporation's deception. A closer look at the authors and recipients of the wrong-fully withheld documents reveals that the privilege simply does not apply: no attorney authored or received the documents in question. Accordingly, ABC Corporation has no viable claim of privilege and must produce these documents.

Critique: Better than the last two. Focuses on the law. Demonstrates the error in opposing counsel's privilege assertion without accusing the lawyer of an ethical violation.

Language Choices in a Brief Supporting an Evidentiary Motion

Consider the following three ways of phrasing an argument that an expert should be precluded from testifying at trial because he is not qualified:

Option 1: It would be an outright travesty of justice to allow Dr. Chauncey Meadows—who openly flaunts the title of "Dr." but who obtained his medical license from a mail-order catalog—to opine about the so-called victim's pur-ported injuries. Meadows has never penned a single article in any reputable med-ical journal about knee injuries, has not once qualified as an expert in any court in this country, and never even examined the "victim" in person, relying solely upon out-of-date X-rays.

Critique: Too dramatic? Disrespectful? Inappropriately sarcastic?

Option 2: The doctor is unqualified to render a medical opinion. He fails to meet any of the criteria in Fed. R. Evid. 702.

Critique: Too boring and bland? No interesting detail? Will anyone care?

Option 3: Because juries afford high deference to opinions rendered by experts, the court exercises an essential gatekeeping function, allowing only those experts who meet the qualifications of Fed. R. Evid. 702 and the *Daubert* standard to render opinions at trial. Unfortunately, Dr. Meadows lacks the requisite educa-tional and professional attributes to qualify as a medical expert under *Daubert*. His medical degree and license cannot be verified; he did not graduate from a medical school accredited by the American Medical Association, nor is he licensed in any state within the United States or any foreign country with reciprocal accreditation. Further, he is not recognized by peers as an expert on knee injuries, having written no scholarly articles, spoken at no conferences, and testified as an expert in no court proceedings. Finally, Dr. Meadows performed a mere cursory review of the employee-plaintiff's injuries solely by viewing outdated X-rays, notwithstanding his opportunity to examine the allegedly injured party last week.

Critique: Better than the last two. Focuses on the law. Applies the facts to the legal standard in a more respectful tone.

Language Choices in a Brief Supporting a Dispositive Motion (i.e., Motion to Dismiss or Motion for Summary Judgment)

Consider the following three ways of phrasing an argument that a former gym employee stole trade secrets from his company as soon as he learned of his impending termination:

Option 1: The jilted gym employee was nothing more than a bandit, stealing customer contact lists and membership reports from his generous employer the very nanosecond he knew that he was being fired for rampant lateness. He pilfered proprietary data from the front desk computer by e-mailing confidential files to his Gmail account and smuggled confidential client mailing lists off the premises in his backpack.

Critique: Overly dramatic? Inappropriate use of criminal terminology?

Option 2: The gym employee took trade secrets from the company by e-mailing computer data to himself and leaving the fitness center with confidential files.

Critique: Too boring and bland? Will anyone care?

Option 3: In retaliation for his impending termination by his fitness center employer for lateness, the gym employee, hurt and embarrassed, made a pointed error in judgment. He misappropriated vital trade secrets and valuable intellectual property by intentionally transmitting data from the front desk computer to his personal e-mail account and secretly removing proprietary files from the gym premises.

Critique: Better than the prior two—states the facts in a manner that mainly focuses on the act rather than the actor.

Bringing a Brief to Life Through Language Choices

Language choices in brief writing are a matter of individual style, and it takes years of experimentation and practice to develop one's personal writing voice.

Each writing assignment in law school presents an opportunity to explore persuasive language choices. For example, you might thoughtfully consider the many ways to describe each player, act, or object in a client scenario:

- **Injured party:** Depending on which side of the case you represent, what word best captures the essence of the injured party for purposes of your client's position? Victim? (Nameless) Plaintiff? Pedestrian? Trespasser? Burglar? Elena?
- **Teenager:** Juvenile delinquent? Emancipated youth? Orphan? Defendant? Adolescent? Victim? Prodigy? Lindsay?
- **Drunk driver:** Father? Husband? Former lawyer? Criminal? Widower? Mike?
- **Embezzlement:** Theft? Heist? Misunderstanding? Misappropriation? Pilfer? Misplacement of funds? Borrowing? Loan?
- **Assault:** Beating? Battering? Bump? Knock? Tap? Pounding? Jostle?
- **Stiletto shoe:** Weapon? High-heel? Fashion accessory? Bludgeon?

Also consider alternative ways of asking the court for the result that you seek (some language choices are more respectful than others):

- The court must . . . . The Court should . . . . (Note: We need to be careful about telling the court what it must or should do.)
- ABC Corporation respectfully requests the court to . . . .
- Based upon the foregoing law, ABC Corporation is entitled to . . . .
- Justice requires . . . .
- Based upon the foregoing, ABC Corporation must produce the requested documents . . . .
- Based upon the foregoing, ABC Corporation should be required to produce the documents by . . . .

Smart lawyers ponder the most appropriate way to request the court to grant the result or remedy sought while demonstrating respect for the decision maker and the process.

CLASSROOM EXERCISE	Using persuasive and engaging phrasing (vivid nouns, action verbs, etc.), rewrite these case facts from *opposing* points of view in under 60 words: first, from the alleged victim's perspective, and second, from the alleged wrongdoer's perspective:
	1. A flight from Boston to Florida was delayed five hours due to weather issues. A passenger was becoming increasingly upset that, due to the flight delay, he was likely to miss his cousin's bachelor party. He began yelling at a gate attendant. The passenger was wearing a t-shirt with a profanity on it.

When the flight finally boarded, the passenger jostled a seat-mate while taking his seat. He apologized to the seat-mate. After the flight attendants had closed the plane's doors upon completion of the boarding process, the passenger got up from his seat and attempted to use the restroom; a flight attendant told him to sit down as the flight was moments away from take-off. The passenger muttered a derogatory statement about the flight attendant in response. He then attempted to retrieve a piece of luggage from the overhead compartment, but the same flight attendant told him to leave the bag where it was and sit down. He refused. Eventually, the flight attendant sought the assistance of the pilot, who ultimately directed the passenger to gather his belongings and deplane. Embarrassed and humiliated, and distraught over missing his flight entirely, he later sued the airline for the tort of intentional infliction of emotional distress.

Passenger's Point of View:

_____

_____

Airline's Point of View:

_____

_____

2. A newly married couple bought a townhouse in an urban neighborhood and decided to launch a community farmer's market on the weekends. The neighborhood was subject to an ordinance that prohibited residents from owning or housing farm animals without a license. The farmer's market quickly gained popularity and was well-received by the community; local proprietors began offering fresh produce and home-made desserts, ciders, and other seasonal treats. To entertain the neighborhood children, the married couple hired a local farmer to bring a few sheep, goats, rabbits, and a pig to the farmer's market each weekend, to provide a small petting zoo. Local newspapers wrote articles about how the farmer's market was providing a much-needed sense of community to the neighborhood. One weekend, a neighborhood child was playing with one of the goats in the petting zoo, and the goat kicked the child, bruising his arm. The child's parent sued the couple. The local authorities fined the couple for violating the farm animal ordinance.

Child's Parent's Point of View:

_____

_____

Couple's Point of View:

_____

CLASSROOM EXERCISE

3. A college student decided to participate in an "Occupy Wall Street"-style protest of "the ills of corporate America" in a business district within the university town. To maintain the peace during the protest, the town dispatched police officers to the location where the protest was taking place. The police officers were part of an equestrian unit, riding horses. The college student joined a group of protesters who were throwing pennies in the direction of a particular corporation's front door. The college student happened to be throwing a handful of pennies at the door when a police officer riding a horse trotted by him. The pennies hit the horse, who became startled, reared its legs and knocked the college student to the ground. The police officer arrested the college student for assaulting an officer. The college student claimed wrongful arrest and assault and battery.

Police Officer's Point of View:

_____

_____

College Student's Point of View:

_____

_____

Drafting the Conclusion in a Brief

After the Rule Application section of the brief, the final step in building the IREAC or CREAC structure is to craft the overall conclusion. Here, the brief writer asks the court for the specific relief sought—substantively and procedurally. Each RA paragraph (or section covering each distinct prong of a multi-part rule) already will have provided a mini-conclusion, asking the court to find that the pertinent component of the rule is either satisfied or not satisfied, depending on the client's position. Then, in the ultimate conclusion of the brief, the writer asks for specific relief on the overall legal question, a request for the appropriate procedural action to enforce the substantive finding, and a request for costs, if appropriate to the motion. Brief writers must be as specific as possible when requesting the court to take action. Consider this example:

V. Conclusion

Based upon the foregoing facts and law, Daphneto respectfully requests the court to find that Barberini's expert, Dr. Sanders, is not qualified to testify as an expert at trial. Accordingly, Daphneto requests the court to issue an Order precluding Dr. Sanders from testifying at the trial of this matter.

Dated: April 9, 2017

Respectfully submitted,

BRISTOW & SUMMERS, LLP

Rhianna Bristow

Rhianna Bristow, Esq.
745 Coppola Street
Athens, Georgia 30601
(965) 555-0364
rbristow@bristowsummers.com
Counsel for Plaintiff Daphneto, Inc.

The example pinpoints the substantive ruling requested of the court (that the expert is not qualified) and the procedural action (an order precluding the expert's testimony).

Take a look at this second example:

V. Conclusion

Based upon the foregoing facts and law, Riggins respectfully requests the court to find that the attorney-client privilege does not protect Cornerstone's documents prepared by or for in-house counsel Madeline Hewes, as the documents were generated in the context of her role as an insurance adjuster, rather than in the function of rendering legal advice. Accordingly, Riggins requests the court to issue an Order[11] compelling Cornerstone to produce the documents erroneously withheld on its privilege log and to award Riggins its attorneys' fees and costs in filing this motion, pursuant to Fed. R. Civ. P. 37(a)(5)(A).

---

[11] Some courts require the lawyer submitting the brief to prepare a proposed order that the judge can sign. A sample proposed order is provided later in this chapter.

Dated: May 24, 2017

Respectfully submitted,

McGEE & ROLLINS, LLP

Bridget Stanton

Bridget Stanton, Esq.
100 William Street Suite 44
New York, NY 10005
800-555-4718
bstanton@mcgeerollins.com
Counsel for Plaintiff

The second example likewise includes a conclusion on the substantive legal issue (that the attorney-client privilege does not protect the documents being withheld by the insurer) and a conclusion on what procedural action the party requests the court to take (an order compelling production). Further, the lawyer added a request for an award of its costs in preparing and filing the motion, pursuant to an applicable court rule.

Date and Signature Block

The date of the brief and a signature block appear below the text of the conclusion. The signature block contains the phrase "Respectfully submitted," plus the law office name, a signature line, and the signer's name, state bar number (if required), address, phone number, e-mail address, and a designation of "Counsel for Plaintiff" or "Counsel for Defendant."

The first time that a new legal writer signs a brief and files it with the court can be a momentous occasion. Many new lawyers start their careers ghostwriting briefs for supervising attorneys to sign; it is a big transitional step to serve as the actual signer of a brief for the first time, and one with ethical connotations. Remember that under Fed. R. Civ. P. 11 (and its state counterparts), every time an attorney signs a brief, he is certifying that to the best of his knowledge, information, and belief, formed after a reasonable inquiry:

- The brief is not being presented for any improper purpose, such as to harass, cause unnecessary delay, or needlessly increase the cost of litigation.
- The claims, defenses, and other legal contentions in the brief are warranted by existing law or by a nonfrivolous argument for extending, modifying, or reversing existing law or for establishing new law.
- The factual contentions have evidentiary support or, if specifically so identified, will likely have evidentiary support after a reasonable opportunity for further investigation or discovery.

● The denials of factual contentions are warranted on the evidence or, if specifically so identified, are reasonably based on belief or a lack of information.[12]

Drafting the Introduction to a Brief

In the brief-drafting process, this chronological progression might seem counterintuitive, but legal writers often write the introduction to a brief *last*—after finishing the first draft of the IREAC or CREAC argument framework. An effective introduction to a brief includes the following components:

● A first sentence, identifying WHO, WHAT, and WHY: which party is filing the brief, what type of brief is being submitted, and, if applicable, the procedural rule authorizing the submission (i.e., a court rule, the case scheduling order, or another judge-issued directive in the case)
● A second sentence, stating the THEME
● A third sentence, stating the ISSUE (some lawyers reverse the order of the Issue and Theme sentences)
● The rule framework
● Three to five reasons why the party submitting the brief should prevail
● The specific result sought.

First Sentence of the Introduction

Because courts receive so many briefs filed in numerous cases every day, the first sentence of the introduction to a new brief needs to convey critical information: who is filing the brief, what type of brief is being filed, and, if applicable, the procedural rule authorizing the filing of the brief.

Consider the following examples:

COME NOW Plaintiffs Molly Booker ("Booker") and Bryan Salmon ("Salmon"), by counsel, and hereby submit this Pretrial Brief pursuant to the Court's Order dated February 28, 2017.

COMES NOW Defendant Perez Preparatory School Board ("Perez"), by counsel, and hereby submits this Motion in Limine to exclude expert testimony, pursuant to Local Rule 45.2.

---

[12] Fed. R. Civ. P. 11.

Plaintiff Riggins Garment Company ("Riggins"), by counsel, hereby submits this Motion for Summary Judgment in accordance with Fed. R. Civ. P. 56.

Defendant Coxland Corporation ("Coxland"), by counsel, hereby submits this Motion to Dismiss Defendant Maynard Farms' ("Maynard") Complaint for breach of contract, under Fed. R. Civ. P. 12(b)(6).

In the foregoing examples, note the following:

- Some lawyers still use traditional introductory language like "COME NOW" (for plural parties filing a brief) or "COMES NOW" (for a singular party) to introduce the party or parties filing the brief. Others view this language as too antiquated. Unless the preferences of the applicable court dictate otherwise, either style is fine.
- The initial sentence of the brief is the first time, other than in the caption and the title of the brief (described later in this chapter), that the reader learns the names of the party or parties involved in the particular brief including the filing party. It is important to use the full name of the party submitting the brief and then establish—in parentheses and quotation marks—an appropriate abbreviation to use throughout the rest of the document. Be careful about using acronyms; choose a respectful abbreviation for the client's name (and the opposing party's name if mentioned in the first sentence of the brief).
- The examples above denote the type of brief being filed: Pretrial Brief, Motion in Limine, Motion for Summary Judgment, Motion to Dismiss.
- The first sentence of the introduction should, if applicable, provide the procedural rule authorizing the filing of the brief: either a court order instructing the parties to file the particular type of brief or a court rule allowing or requiring the type of brief.

Theme Sentence

The subsequent two sentences of the brief's introduction relay the party's "theme" and the legal issue addressed in the document. Legal writers share different preferences on whether the theme or the issue should appear first. The chronological order does not really matter so long as both items are woven into the early part of the introduction. The theme sentence captures the reader's attention and, in a concise but engaging manner, conveys the general subject matter and nature of the case—distinguishing the client's legal matter from the other cases pending on the court's docket. The issue sentence states the precise legal issue (or issues, if more than one) that will be addressed in the brief and decided by the judge.

A theme sentence is comparable to a 30-second television commercial for a new show or a movie trailer. Consider these examples of theme sentences from real trial and appellate briefs and decide if they intrigue you:

- "This case is about a subterfuge. . . . This case is about conspiracy to deprive civil rights."[13]
- "This case is about pornography being pushed on children and unconsenting adults. This case is not about 'censorship.'"[14]
- "This case is about this Court's role as a guarantor of justice for a person with no prior felony record whose offense likely resulted from a substance abuse problem."[15]
- "This case is about a tenant intent on playing games, involving intentional violations of park rules and disingenuous attempts to avoid legal consequences, all to the detriment of the landlord and the other tenants."[16]
- "This case concerns hard money, not soft money."[17]
- "This case is about the narrow issue of whether [a bar patron] was habitually addicted to any or all alcoholic beverages, whether the Defendant served him alcohol with knowledge of [the] habitual addiction, and whether [the patron] became intoxicated as a result of Defendant's alcohol service prior to the subject accident."[18]
- "This case is about credibility. This case is about motives and bias."[19]

If your case involves, for example, a construction contract dispute, your theme sentence might state, "This case concerns a contract between a project owner and a contractor to build a water treatment plant for a local community in need, and the owner's breach of its promise to pay for the work." Or, "This case involves an architect who failed to exercise diligence and care in designing a sophisticated, high-end hotel complex, risking the safety of the facility's employees and guests."

If your case involves an insurance dispute, your theme sentence might read, "This case concerns a hard-working small business owner who paid insurance premiums for years, only to be abandoned by its insurance company in its time of need." If your case concerns property damage, your theme sentence might state, "This case is about a rotting tree which, left untended by a

---

[13] *Diedrich v. Newport News,* 2004 WL 2812092 (U.S. 2004) (Appellate Petition).
[14] *Alliance for Community Media, et al. v. Federal Communications Commission,* 1996 WL 56348 (U.S. 1996) (Appellate Brief).
[15] *The People of the State of New York v. Rickenbacker,* 2003 WL 25557214 (N.Y. App. Div. 2003) (Appellate Brief).
[16] *Emerald Coast, Inc. v. Davis,* 2009 WL 6835874 (Or. App. 2009) (Appellate Brief).
[17] *Federal Election Commission v. Colorado Republican Federal Campaign Committee,* 2000 WL 33976599 (U.S. 2000) (Appellate Petition).
[18] *Wilde v. Okeechobee Aerie 4137,* 2014 WL 4254402 (Fla. Cir. Ct. 2014) (Trial Motion).
[19] *Donicht v. Sandoval,* 2008 WL 8191426 (Nev. Dist. Ct. 2008) (Trial Motion).

neighboring property owner, fell on a homeowner's car. Luckily, she was not in it." Regardless of whether your case involves an emotionally layered legal dispute between individuals, invoking a natural level of intrigue, or a seemingly interpersonal dispute between commercial or corporate parties, good legal writers craft a theme sentence that—in just a few words—captures the attention of the reader and sets the tone for the rest of the brief. The goal of the theme sentence is to convey the subject matter area of the law (Contract? Tort? Real property? Constitutional law? Insurance? Intellectual property?) and plant a seed in the reader's mind to begin to answer the question: Why should I care about this case?

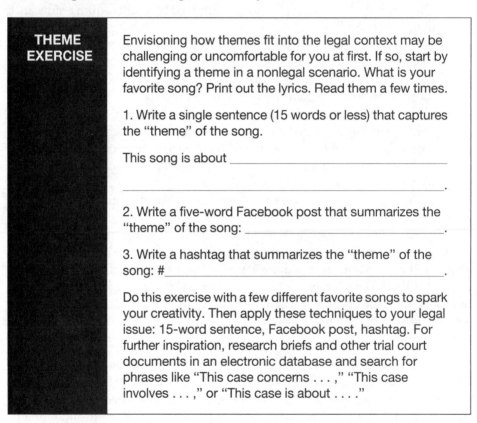

THEME EXERCISE

Envisioning how themes fit into the legal context may be challenging or uncomfortable for you at first. If so, start by identifying a theme in a nonlegal scenario. What is your favorite song? Print out the lyrics. Read them a few times.

1. Write a single sentence (15 words or less) that captures the "theme" of the song.

This song is about _____

_____.

2. Write a five-word Facebook post that summarizes the "theme" of the song: _____.

3. Write a hashtag that summarizes the "theme" of the song: #_____.

Do this exercise with a few different favorite songs to spark your creativity. Then apply these techniques to your legal issue: 15-word sentence, Facebook post, hashtag. For further inspiration, research briefs and other trial court documents in an electronic database and search for phrases like "This case concerns . . . ," "This case involves . . . ," or "This case is about . . . ."

An impactful theme sentence (1) reveals the subject matter area of the law governing the client's case, (2) foreshadows the client's key factual circumstances, and (3) also if possible, introduces an overarching societal goal or concern. Even the most seemingly mundane legal conflicts involve at least some important consideration of fairness. Does the client's case involve justice? Equality? Freedom? Respect? A broken promise? An injury? Discrimination? Oppression? Racism? Improper invasion of privacy? Fraud? Homeland security? Democracy? Protection of the environment? A greater good? Experiment with crafting theme sentences that capture the attention of the reader.

Issue Sentence

Either before or after the theme sentence, the brief writer states the precise legal issue (or issues, if more than one) that the brief will address, for the purpose of informing the court of the brief's narrow focus. Remember that a single litigation might involve numerous brief filings. Each distinct legal issue in a brief is like one tree in a forest or a single dot in a Monet painting. Here are some examples of issue sentences:

- In the Complaint, Plaintiff asserted seven causes of action against Defendant Daughtry Hospital, each of which turns solely on whether the ambulance staff and the paramedics breached the standard of care in handling a patient who was injured when she fell off a gurney. The undisputed facts demonstrate that neither the ambulance staff nor the paramedics in any way breached the standard of care.
- The winemaker's liability for breach of the celebrity's right of privacy turns on whether the image printed on a wine bottle label constitutes a "portrait or picture" of the celebrity, which would violate N.Y. Civ. Rights Law §§50 and 51.
- The issue before the court is whether the crime-fraud exception to the attorney-client privilege—which negates privilege protection of communications to an attorney by a client who intends to commit a crime—mandates the production of documents being erroneously withheld by NTP Inc.
- This case turns on whether a patient alleging medical malpractice must establish the standard of care of an attending doctor by presenting expert testimony or whether the alleged treatment procedures are within the common knowledge of nonmedically trained personnel, eliminating the need for expert witnesses.

In describing the legal issue for the court, brief writers identify the key players in the client's scenario and boil down the focal point of the brief into the precise legal question that the judge will decide. If the brief involves a discovery dispute, the writer identifies the legal question determinative of whether the documents, information, or witness should be disclosed or made available to the other side. If the brief addresses an evidentiary dispute, the writer pinpoints the legal question governing whether the document or person may be presented at trial or must be excluded. If the brief seeks to dismiss a cause of action, or obtain summary judgment on a cause of action, the writer highlights the legal question that drives whether the moving party should prevail.

Simple briefs might concentrate on a single legal issue; more complex briefs might tackle multiple issues. If a brief addresses several legal issues, the introduction should present them all. For example:

Defendant Cornerstone Insurance Company erroneously has withheld documents on its privilege log on two misplaced grounds: (1) the attorney-client privilege and (2) the attorney work product doctrine.

Or

The issue before the court is whether an "out-of-possession" landowner can be held liable for injuries to a third party that occur on a property managed by a tenant or a lessee. In evaluating whether an out-of-possession property owner can be liable under these circumstances, courts analyze whether the landowner (1) created a defective condition; (2) assumed a contractual duty to maintain the premises; (3) owed a contractual duty to repair defects; or (4) retained or relinquished control over the land.

Rule Framework

Next in the introduction, the brief writer introduces the general rule governing the legal issue, in a concise manner, since the rule will be described and illustrated more fully through the R and E parts of the IREAC or CREAC formula in the argument section of the brief. Consider these examples:

- An airline's right to remove a passenger from a flight depends on whether the passenger is "inimical to safety." 49 U.S.C. § 44902(b).
- Insurance companies are not entitled to shield documents from discovery under a claim of attorney-client privilege if the correspondence and written communications were prepared by in-house counsel serving in a claims adjuster role in the ordinary course of the insurer's business, rather than in the role of providing legal advice.
- "Hearsay" is defined as an out-of-court statement made by a declarant offered for the truth of the matter asserted. Fed. R. Evid. 801(c).
- Under Federal Rule of Evidence 702, a party seeking to offer the testimony of an expert witness at trial must demonstrate that the individual is qualified by knowledge, skill, experience, training, or education.

In the introduction, the brief writer may not need to cite statutes or cases unless quoting from the source or there is a particular reason to highlight the name of the statute or case for the judge from the beginning of the brief. Otherwise, good brief writers succinctly state the governing rule that will drive the judge's decision—ideally in one or two sentences.

Concise List of Reasons the Filing Party Should Prevail

After the rule framework, the brief writer states the three (to five) primary reasons why the filing party is entitled to the result sought. This can be accomplished in a few sentences or in a numbered list. Consider these examples:

Examples of Reasons in Sentence Form

- Riggins is entitled to discovery of the documents erroneously withheld on Cornerstone's privilege log. Cornerstone's in-house counsel, Madeline Hewes ("Hewes"),[20] was acting in the role of an insurance claims adjuster, in the ordinary course of the insurance company's business, when she authored and received the documents. She was not serving in the role of rendering legal advice. Insurance companies cannot be permitted to hide behind the cloak of privilege to insulate documents generated in the ordinary course of making insurance coverage decisions.
- Unfortunately, Dr. Meadows lacks the requisite educational and professional qualifications of a medical expert, and therefore, he should be precluded from testifying at trial. His medical degree and license cannot be verified. Further, he is not recognized by any peers as an expert on knee injuries, having written no scholarly articles, spoken at no conferences, and testified as an expert in no court proceedings. Finally, Dr. Meadows gave a mere cursory review of the employee-plaintiff's injuries through viewing outdated X-rays rather than conducting a live examination.

Examples of Reasons in Numbered List Form

- Under New York law, Precipice Foundation is an "out-of-possession" landowner of Longacres Farms and cannot be liable for injuries to a third party that occurred on the premises leased to a tenant because (1) the landowner did not create the allegedly dangerous condition in the barn that was newly constructed by the tenant; (2) the farm lease expressly stated that the tenant assumed responsibility to maintain the premises; (3) Precipice Foundation had no contractual obligation under the lease to repair unsafe conditions on the farm; and (4) by virtue of the lease, the landowner relinquished all control of the premises to the tenant.
- The wine bottle label containing an artistically blurred image of a former New York Knicks basketball player cannot be deemed a "portrait or picture" of the athlete, thereby violating his right of privacy under N.Y. Civil Rights Law §§ 50 and 51, because (1) the pixilated nature of the

---

[20] If the introduction is the first time a key player in the client's story is introduced to the reader, the brief writer establishes an abbreviation (if an individual, usually the person's last name) to use throughout the document. If the key player is a company, a brief writer may use a shortened version of the company name or a respectful acronym (e.g., ABC Corporation ("ABC")).

image, distorting his face and jersey number, prevented any recognizable likeness; (2) the image in the context of a wine label instead of in a basketball arena failed to capture the essence of the athlete; and (3) there was no accompanying text sufficient to trigger a link to the athlete's persona in the public's mind.

Statement of the Exact Result Sought

In the last sentence of the introduction to the brief, the brief writer states exactly what action the party is asking the court to take, substantively and procedurally. The writer informs the court precisely how the moving party would like the court to decide the pivotal legal issue and then asserts the procedural action necessary to enforce that determination. For example:

- Based upon the foregoing, Riggins respectfully requests the court to find that the documents withheld by Cornerstone on its privilege log are not protected by the attorney-client privilege. Riggins requests the court to grant this Motion to Compel and order Cornerstone to produce the documents within ten days of the date of the court's ruling.
- Based upon the foregoing, Precipice Foundation respectfully requests the court to find that because it is an "out-of-possession" landowner under New York law, it cannot be held liable for Plaintiff's injuries. Accordingly, Precipice Foundation requests the court to grant this motion and issue an order of dismissal of the Complaint in its entirety.
- Based upon the foregoing, Daughtry Hospital respectfully requests the court to find that Dr. Meadows does not meet the standard for the admissibility of expert testimony in this court, as he does not have the requisite knowledge, skill, experience, training, or education. Accordingly, Daughtry Hospital requests the court to grant this motion in limine and issue an order precluding Dr. Meadows from testifying at trial.

Brief Introduction Checklist

- First sentence (identifies the party filing the brief, introduces the appropriate name abbreviation, states the type of brief, and specifies the procedural rule authorizing the filing)
- Theme sentence
- Sentence stating the precise legal issue (or issues) the brief addresses
- General rule framework
- Three to five primary reasons why the filing party should prevail and why the result sought is justified (either in sentences or a numbered list)
- Statement of the precise result sought, substantively and procedurally

Writing a Persuasive Statement of Facts in a Brief

The factual section of a brief is a prime opportunity for a legal writer to balance *logos*, *pathos*, and *ethos* in conveying the client's story to the judge (and opposing counsel). Although it might be tempting to draft the statement of facts early in the brief-writing process, often it helps to write this brief component *after* you have written the IREAC or CREAC argument section, so you are keenly aware of the facts that are legally significant to the analysis. Keeping in mind the page- or word-count limit of the brief, the fact section should strive to accomplish the following:

- Start by capturing the essence of the parties' dispute in a phrase or a sentence or two (e.g., breach of a promise, argument over property ownership, disagreement over the origin of an idea, deprivation of one party's rights or freedom, infringement on one party's privacy, discrimination against one party, etc.).
- Chronologically relay the sequence of key events that led to the dispute.
- Summarize the facts essential to the determination of the legal issue (this part of the statement of facts will vary among the briefs filed in the same case—one brief might focus on the parties' disagreement over the scope of discovery, while another might dwell on an item of evidence sought to be introduced at trial, while still another might address whether one required element of the rule governing a cause of action in the complaint is satisfied by the facts).
- Enliven even the most mundane facts through vivid description, humanizing the key players, captivating the reader's attention, and invoking a degree of empathy for the parties' circumstances.
- Reinforce the integrity of the brief writer by portraying the facts accurately, including the facts that support the client's position, but also incorporating weaker facts if relevant to the legal analysis and ethically necessary to tell the full story.
- If required by the court rules or helpful to the reader without being distracting, cite the source of each fact from the documentary record in the case.
- If pertinent to the purpose of the brief, summarize the procedural history of the case (i.e., the pleadings filed, causes of action and defenses alleged, discovery performed to date, motions filed, and orders issued).

A logical progression of the legally significant facts lays the foundation in the reader's mind for why the filing party is entitled to the result sought, enhancing *logos*. A brief writer's choice of language and storytelling techniques, bringing the client scenario to life, spark *pathos*; the writer's goal is to spur the reader to care about the legal matter at hand and the parties involved. Triggering an emotional reaction in the reader might be an easier feat if the litigants are grappling with pain and suffering, a personal injury, a devastating emotional loss, a divorce, or a death, but thoughtful brief writers can inject passion even into corporate disputes or seemingly less emotive conflicts, over, for example, taxes, software, construction, or insurance.

Finally, *ethos* resonates from truthful storytelling (from the advocacy perspective of the client), relaying the parties' narrative ethically—balancing zealous representation of the client's interests with the lawyer's duty to be honest and forthright.

Lawyers balance *logos*, *pathos*, and *ethos* through language choices. Consider these contrasting examples of sentences describing the same fact:

Example 1 (mundane fact; no detail): The pilot removed the passenger from the plane.

Example 2 (vivid detail from the airline's point of view): In an effort to expedite takeoff and mitigate further delays to the cooperating passengers, FlyGreen's pilot made the difficult decision to remove the disruptive passenger from the flight. The passenger exhibited signs of inebriation, disregarded flight attendants' safety instructions, refused to stow his luggage, murmured derogatory slurs at a seatmate, and attempted to enter the first class cabin several times.

Example 3 (vivid detail from the passenger's point of view): Without any investigation or basis whatsoever, the airline deprived Joseph Anderson of his right to fly, manhandling him and ejecting him from the plane, forcing him to purchase a costly new ticket, miss his best friend's wedding, and suffer humiliation and stress.

Now consider this range of descriptions of the same event:

Example 1 (mundane fact; no detail): The project to construct the new high school fell behind schedule. The project owner terminated the construction contract and hired a new contractor to finish building the school.

Example 2 (from the project owner's point of view): As the new school year rapidly approached, the project owner had no choice but to terminate its contract with the builder who was behind schedule. The project owner scrambled to find a replacement contractor to finish the project in time for commencement of the school year. The local community had relied upon the project owner's promise that the new school would be available to accommodate the growing number of elementary age children in the surrounding neighborhoods. The project owner made every effort to help the contractor mitigate its project delays, but in the end, the contractor's mismanagement of its workers, failure to promptly remedy construction deficiencies, and rampant safety violations forced the owner to take the drastic measure of termination.

Example 3 (from the construction contractor's point of view): Without any justification whatsoever, the project owner breached the construction contract by terminating the contractor with only a month remaining until project completion. The contractor's work was impacted by extraordinary weather delays, the owner's slow payments, unforeseen subsurface obstructions, and late material deliveries, all of which were beyond the contractor's control. The owner failed to give the contractor sufficient opportunity to mitigate project delays. With the right amount of cooperation and support from the owner, the contractor could have completed the job on time. Instead, the owner has withheld hundreds of thousands of dollars in payment, pushing the contractor to the brink of bankruptcy.

Practice Tips

- When drafting the statement of facts, brief writers must include all the key facts relied upon in the RA section of the IREAC or CREAC argument. It can be confusing to a reader to encounter a new fact for the first time in an RA that was not relayed initially in the statement of facts earlier in the brief. To ensure that you do not inadvertently omit a fact from the statement of facts that you relied upon in an RA, go through each RA and physically highlight each client fact. Then cross-check those facts against the statement of facts, highlighting the sentences in the statement of facts that contain the RA facts. This exercise will help you determine whether any RA facts are missing from the statement of facts.
- In drafting the statement of facts, check to make sure that you have not made any faulty assumptions about your reader's breadth of knowledge of the case, parties, key players, tangible items, events, or abbreviations. Do not assume that the judge or opposing counsel will go back and reread the complaint and answer before reviewing the brief; write every brief with the mindset that it is your job to remind the audience who the parties are, the nature of their relationship, the background of the dispute, the names of the key players and their roles, any physical items at issue, major events, and any abbreviations or acronyms referenced in the brief.

Putting the Parts of the Brief Together

Up to now, you have learned how to craft the introduction, the statement of facts, the IREAC or CREAC argument, the conclusion, and the signature block of the brief. Now let's put together all the components and make it look like a brief. Then we will commence the foolproof 12-step editing and proofreading process.

Caption and Title

Every brief contains the case caption so the court clerk and the judge recognize which case is associated with the filing. Lawyers often create a case caption template early in the timeline of each litigation and then use the form repeatedly when drafting each subsequent pleading, motion, and brief. The caption includes the court, the parties' names and designations as plaintiff or defendant (or other appropriate terminology, such as cross-claimant or third-party defendant), and the docket number assigned to the case. Here is an example:

UNITED STATES DISTRICT COURT
FOR THE SOUTHERN DISTRICT OF NEW YORK

Riggins Garment Company,)	
)	Case No. Y14-044-AML
Plaintiff,)	The Honorable Laila Hewson
)	
v.)	
)	
Cornerstone Insurance)	
Company,)	
)	
Defendant.)	
_____)	

Next, the brief writer includes the document title. The title of each brief is important; it distinguishes among the many pleadings, motions, and briefs filed in a single case. The title also indicates to the court whether the brief is filed by the plaintiff or defendant (or another party), helping to differentiate initial briefs from opposition and reply briefs. Titles can be placed beneath the docket number within the caption or under the caption, with the first letter of each word capitalized and the entire title underlined or bolded. Remember that in most cases, a party filing an initial brief (as contrasted with an opposition or reply brief discussed in Chapter 30) submits both a Motion and an accompanying brief.[21] The initial filing party is "moving" the court to take a certain procedural action, which is facilitated through the Motion rather than the accompanying brief (which provides the substantive legal justification for the procedural action requested). Tips on how to draft the Motion itself (a short document) are included at the end of this chapter. Thus, the accompanying brief in support of the Motion is called a *Memorandum of Points and Authorities* or a *Memorandum of Law*. Consider these titles for briefs accompanying Motions:

- Defendant Cornerstone Insurance Company's Memorandum of Points and Authorities in Support of its Motion to Dismiss the Complaint

---

[21] Sometimes, a trial court will request parties to submit trial briefs analyzing and presenting the law on various legal issues pending in the case—which would not require an accompanying Motion. In that circumstance, the court simply wants briefing on the law but is not asking either party to "move" for a particular procedural action. The parties would not need to draft a Motion to accompany the brief but would file just the brief itself. The title of such a brief would be "Plaintiff's Trial Brief," or "Defendant's Trial Brief."

- Plaintiff Riggins Garment Company's Memorandum of Law in Support of its Motion to Compel the Production of Documents Withheld on Defendant Cornerstone Insurance Company's Privilege Log
- Defendant Daughtry Hospital's Memorandum of Points and Authorities in Support of its Motion in Limine to Exclude Dr. Chauncey Meadows from Testifying as an Expert Witness
- Plaintiff Precipice Foundation's Memorandum of Law in Support of its Motion for Summary Judgment

Smoothing Transitions

Another technique to convert a good brief into a great one is to smooth the transitions between brief components, IREAC or CREAC sections, and paragraphs within each section—using headings, transition phrasing, thesis sentences, and mini-conclusions. Headings (described further in the next section) signal to the reader that a change in subject matter is approaching. Brief writers use headings—numbered, indented, and bolded or underlined—to distinguish a brief's major components: the introduction, statement of facts, argument section, and conclusion. In lengthier briefs, or even in short briefs analyzing distinct legal issues governed by separate rules or discrete components of a rule, headings are useful to announce to the reader a shift in substantive focus.

Other less obvious spots where transitions enhance readability include:

- Between separate REs, introducing a new RE with either a novel rule statement or subrule, or a simple transition phrase or word like "Additionally, in *Hartwell v. Gartner*," "Similarly, in *Oberlin v. Aquino*," or "In contrast, in *Forster v. Nardi*."
- Between the last RE and the beginning of the RA, using a thesis sentence[22] to signal to the reader that the recitation of the law is complete, and the brief now will shift to applying the components of the rule to the client's facts, such as "Based upon the foregoing rule, Precipice Foundation unequivocally is an 'out of-possession' landowner that cannot be held liable for injuries occurring on the property," or "Applying the foregoing rule to the dispute between Riggins Garment Company and Cornerstone Insurance Company, the insurer undeniably breached its duty to cover its insured's losses." These thesis sentences state the brief writer's position on the overall legal issue.
- Between paragraphs of the RA section of the argument, ending each distinct paragraph with a mini-conclusion on the particular rule

---

[22] In legal writing, a thesis sentence is a "persuasive topic sentence." Kirsten K. Davis, *Persuasion Through Organization*, 42-SEP Ariz. Att'y 50 (2005) ("A thesis sentence not only gives the topic of the paragraph it introduces, it also furthers the writer's argument on a particular point.").

component being applied to the client facts, and starting a new paragraph with a thesis sentence (a conclusory statement as to the client's position on the next component of the rule), such as, "Accordingly, the element of the 'out-of-possession' landowner rule regarding creation of the defective condition fails. [Insert paragraph break] Regarding the element of a duty to maintain or repair the premises, the lease expressly dictates that the lessee farm retain all responsibility for maintenance and repair."

Drafting Persuasive Substantive Headings

A single-issue brief may require headings only for the introduction, statement of facts, argument, and conclusion, with Roman numerals numbering each heading. Lawyers often capitalize the initial letter of each word in the heading and then bold or underline the text. However, if the argument section of the brief is lengthy or has distinct subparts (multiple legal issues or discrete parts of a legal rule requiring separate analysis), brief writers craft persuasive headings as signposts or interim billboards for the reader. Persuasive headings signal to the reader what topic is coming next, but in a way that foreshadows the client's position on that subject matter. For example, using the out-of-possession landowner example discussed above, a brief writer might use the following persuasive headings to convey the party's position on the four subparts of the legal rule, i.e., whether the property owner (1) created a defective property condition, (2) had a contractual obligation to maintain the premises, (3) owed a duty to repair defects, or (4) exercised or relinquished control over the land:

I. **Precipice Foundation Played No Role in Designing, Purchasing, Creating, or Constructing the Barn**

II. **Under the Lease, the Farm as Tenant Retained Sole Responsibility for Maintaining the Safety of the Premises**

III. **Under the Lease, the Farm as Tenant Assumed Complete Responsibility for Repairs to the Property**

IV. **Precipice Foundation Relinquished All Control of the Premises to the Farm**

New legal writers sometimes mistakenly assume that one-, two-, or three-word headings are sufficient to convey information to the reader, like:

I. **The Condition's Creation**

II. **Duty to Maintain**

III. **Duty to Repair**

IV. **Control**

However, such abbreviated headings presume (misguidedly) that the reader already is familiar with the applicable law and rule terminology. As legal writers discussing and debating our research results and legal arguments with our colleagues in the classroom or law office, we might use shorthand to refer to legal terms of art or rule components; however, when we communicate those same concepts to a reader who may be unfamiliar with the statutes and case law, we must be precise and thorough with word choice and phrasing.

Good brief writers use informative headings to break up long passages of text, separate distinct legal issues or analyses of rule components in an IREAC or CREAC argument section, and persuade the reader by foretelling the client's position on the legal topic referenced. Brief writers try to limit headings to two or three lines of single-spaced text to avoid eyestrain for the reader; long, single-spaced headings can clutter the page, especially when they are capitalized and bolded or underlined. Avoid capitalizing entire headings; stick to initial capitalization of each key word. Note of caution: brief writers never use headings like "Rule Explanation" or "Rule Application." These phrases are for legal writing instruction and learning only.

If you are not sure whether headings are necessary in your brief, review your brief's introduction and the three to five reasons you asserted as to why your client should prevail and why the result sought is justified. Evaluate whether you can convert these reasons into strong persuasive headings in the argument section of the brief.

Weaving the Case Theme Throughout the Brief

Another task that mindful brief writers undertake when putting all the components of the brief together is to weave the case theme throughout the brief. Various spots where theme cues could go include the introduction, the statement of facts, the headings, the RE and RA, and the conclusion. For example, if your case theme centers on a broken promise, you can invoke that theme for the first time in the theme sentence of the introduction. The broken promise concept can be woven through the statement of facts, describing the covenant made in the contract, how one party broke its pledge, and the effect on the client. You can further reinforce the premise of the broken promise in the RE and RA sections of the argument, emphasizing how case law reinforces the public policy of enforcing contracts as written and then applying the elements of the breach of contract rule and its underlying policy to the client's facts. Finally, in the conclusion, you can reprise the theme before asking the court to find in your client's favor and take the requisite procedural action to remedy the broken promise.

Alternatively, perhaps your case involves infringement of your client's intellectual property rights; your theme reflects the notion of protecting the originality of ideas. You can introduce this theme in the brief's introduction, describe the creativity and innovation of your client's idea in the statement of facts, explore the policy underlying protection of intellectual property rights when relaying and explaining the rule in the REs, reiterate the originality of your client's intellectual work in the RA, and then echo the theme in the conclusion before asking the court to take action.

Twelve-Step Editing and Proofreading Process

After completing the first draft of a brief, thoughtful legal writers undertake a serious editing and proofreading process, generating numerous additional iterations of the document before even thinking about filing the final version. If you invest time in the following 12-step editing progression, your brief will be logical, clear, engaging, concise, and professional. Many legal writers benefit from performing each of these editing phases by printing the brief out in hard copy, instead of viewing it on a computer screen. Printing the brief in hard copy allows the editor to see the document as a whole; writers often catch substantive and formatting gaps, mistakes, or glitches that previously went unnoticed by stepping away from technology and viewing the physical pages of a brief. Experiment with this tactic, printing a fresh hard-copy version of the document with each editing review.

The 12 phases of a thorough editing and proofreading process are as follows:

Step 1: Check the applicable court rules again to make sure that you have included all substantive components required by the court.

Step 2: Read the brief as a whole to make sure that the IREAC or CREAC logic makes sense to an unfamiliar reader. Have you made any erroneous assumptions about the breadth of the readers' knowledge of the case, the parties, the facts, the legal issues, or the rules? Check your logic flow against the framework of the rule. If the rule has several required elements, have you explained clearly how each element is satisfied by the client facts (or not satisfied, if your client's position is that the opposing party's cause of action based on the rule fails)? If the rule consists of a set of factors to be weighed and balanced, have you demonstrated that most (if not all) of the factors are fulfilled by the client's facts (or are not fulfilled, if your client's position is that the opposing party's cause of action based on the rule fails)? Once you are comfortable that the logic of your overall argument makes sense, set the brief aside. Take a break from it and return to the document later, with fresh eyes, to continue to the next step.

Step 3: Review each stand-alone section of the brief for its distinct function. Read the introduction separately. Does it make sense? Then read the statement of facts separately. Do the same with each subsequent section of the argument. Finally, read the conclusion on its own. You will more likely catch a logic error or an awkward paragraph when reviewing each building block of the brief for its own purpose rather than reading a 5-page, 8-page, 10-page, or even 25-page brief from start to finish. Once you have completed the stand-alone section review, set the brief aside again. Take a break from it, and return to the document later, with fresh eyes, for the next step.

Step 4: Read the entire brief again to perform a theme and persuasion review. Have you introduced the case theme in the introduction of the brief and then reprised that theme enough in various subsequent components of the brief? Will the brief pass the "Why do we care?" test? Are there areas of the brief that read too perfunctorily, or matter-of-factly, and could use some added flavor, zest, or enthusiasm? Of course, this is a balancing act; you do not want to be too dramatic when expressing the case theme. But reviewing the brief solely for the purpose of determining whether it will resonate with a reader could reveal opportunities for enhancing its persuasion. Once you have completed the theme/persuasion review, set the brief aside again. Take a break from it, and return to the document later, with fresh eyes, for the next step.

Step 5: Review each paragraph of the brief as an individual unit. Does each paragraph have a beginning, a center, and a conclusion? Do any paragraphs occupy almost an entire page? If so, they probably are too long and combine more than one topic. Can you break long paragraphs into two, starting each paragraph with a topic or thesis sentence introducing a distinct issue, analyzing the single issue, and then ending the paragraph with a conclusory statement about that issue? Are any paragraphs too short, perhaps only a sentence or two? Do they truly merit standing alone, perhaps for dramatic effect, or do they fit within the subject matter of another short paragraph, inviting a linking of the two? Each paragraph throughout the brief should boost the persuasive nature of the document, moving the reader paragraph by paragraph down a logical path toward the result sought by the filing party. Once you have completed the paragraph review, set the brief aside again. Take a break from it, and return to the document later, with fresh eyes, for the next step.

Step 6: Review each sentence of the brief, one at a time. Try to stop your eyes (and brain) from skimming too quickly to the next sentence. Read aloud if you need to, and stop at the end of each sentence. Concentrate on the phrasing of each sentence individually. Does the message make sense? Does the sentence have a strong subject and an active verb (rather than a vague subject and a passive verb?)[23] Are any sentences too long? Should they be split into two distinct thoughts? Are any sentences too short (or do they constitute sentence fragments, missing a subject or verb)? Have you used interesting nouns and verbs to relay the client's story and persuade the judge? Is your punctuation accurate?[24] Once you have completed the sentence review, set the brief aside again. Take a break from it, and return to the document later, with fresh eyes, for the next step.

Step 7: Read the brief through again, purely for tone. Are there any spots in the brief that sound sarcastic, disrespectful, or cynical? If so, revise the language in those areas to reflect your best professional self. Once you have completed the

---

[23] If you are not sure of the difference between active verb voice and passive verb voice, consider these two choices: "The issue was decided by the court." *or* "The court granted the party's motion." The latter is active—you can almost hear the judge hammering the gavel and declaring, "Motion granted!" Note the difference between "The draft of the brief was eaten by the dog." and "The dog ate the draft." Look how much shorter and more concise the latter active version is (five words instead of ten).

[24] Some new legal writers struggle with punctuation rules. Many judges and lawyers (and legal writing professors) are precise and picky when it comes to proper grammar and punctuation. Check English grammar rules for usage of apostrophes (to show possession), commas, semicolons, and quotation marks. If you have two nouns next to each other in a sentence, one of them probably possesses the other; you need an apostrophe. Also check English grammar rules for (1) how to handle apostrophes at the end of plural nouns and singular nouns that end with "s"; (2) whether punctuation at the end of a quote goes inside or outside the quotation mark (periods and commas go inside); and (3) when to use semicolons rather than commas (semicolons join two standalone sentences with related concepts and also can be used between items in a numbered list).

tone review, set the brief aside again. Take a break from it, and return to the document later, with fresh eyes, for the next step.

Step 8: If you want to be sure to catch every pesky typographical error and punctuation glitch in a brief, you must read the document on a word-by-word basis, and ideally *backward to forward* instead of starting on the first page. When reading a document seven or more times (in the steps listed above) for substantive editing and proofreading purposes, legal writers inevitably miss typographical errors. These blemishes get filed along with the final version of the document, only to appear glaringly obvious when, a month later, in preparing for oral argument, the lawyer picks up the filed brief and immediately sees a luminescent typo flashing like a neon light on the first page. "How in the world did I miss that?" we groan. It is difficult for an editing brain that is processing substance to multitask and peruse a piece of writing for tiny typographical mistakes. Our eyes and brains naturally leap forward from sentence to sentence. To catch these smaller (in visual size) mistakes, we must jolt the brain out of its substantive review mode. When reading a brief backward, the brain cannot focus on substantive logic; instead, it will notice, for the first time, typographical errors that spellcheck will not highlight: "statue" versus "statute," "contact" versus "contract," "trail" versus "trial" (and many more embarrassing misprints). Print out the document, grab a pen, flip to the last page of the brief, start with the last word at the bottom of the page, and move right to left. You will catch words that have no logical place in the brief (are you really writing about a statue? A contact? A trail?). You will also notice punctuation glitches, such as missing quotation mark pairs or odd spacing before a semicolon. Once you have completed the word review, set the brief aside again. Take a break from it, and return to the document later, with fresh eyes, for the next step.

Step 9: Next, take a printed version of the brief and check only the citations. Have you used accurate full citation form (full name of the case, volume number, reporter, and page number, court name, and date), as needed? Are the pinpoint cites correct? Once you have cited the case in full once, did you use proper short cites thereafter? If you flipped back and forth between cases, are your subsequent "*Id.*" citations pointing to the correct cases? Did you stick with one typeface style, either underlining or italicizing your case names—not flipping back and forth between styles? Do your citation signals (in signal cites and string cites) use that same typeface style? Check to make sure that your word processing system did not automatically capitalize the *A* in "at" after each "*Id.*" Once you have completed the citation review, set the brief aside again. Take a break from it, and return to the document later, with fresh eyes, for the next step.

Step 10: This editing/proofreading phase is the easiest on a hardworking legal writer's brain: checking for formatting errors. Print the document out (a hardcopy version is essential for this step because you will not be able to notice formatting glitches on a computer screen), and flip through each page, scrutinizing:

- Consistency in tab spacing/indenting at the beginning of each paragraph
- Line spacing

- Dangling headings or paragraph starts at the bottom of a page (insert a page break, if possible so the heading or lone line of text moves to the top of the next page—which is more visually pleasing to the reader)
- Consistency in heading formatting (including numbering, capitalization, bold or underlining, indentation, spacing, and grammatical structure)
- Page numbering
- Margins

Once you have completed the formatting review, set the brief aside again. Take a break from it, and return to the document later, with fresh eyes, for the next step.

Step 11: Read the brief through again, solely checking for consistency in terminology when referencing items like (1) party names (use the same abbreviation for each party that you established in the introduction), (2) the court (are you capitalizing "Court" or not throughout the document?), and (3) the motion (are you capitalizing "Motion" or not throughout the document?). Once you have completed the terminology consistency review, set the brief aside again. Take a break from it, and return to the document later, with fresh eyes, for the next step.

Step 12: The final phase of the brief editing and proofreading process is to check the document against the court's submission rules, verifying compliance with any page- or word-count limits (including any written certifications), and directives about margins, line spacing, font, footnotes, accompanying documents or exhibits, and the procedure for filing the brief with the court. Once you are comfortable that the brief complies with the rules, you are almost ready to submit.

Attachments and Exhibits

Depending upon the type of brief, its content, and the applicable court rules, a brief writer may be entitled (or required) to attach key factual documents or transcript excerpts to the brief as exhibits. One exception is a motion to dismiss a complaint, which typically is decided based solely on the parties' pleadings—the complaint and answer. However, for other briefs, it might be helpful (or mandated by the court rules) to include copies of contracts, letters, e-mails, photographs, transcript excerpts, and other materials. If the brief writer relies on factual record documents to relay the client's story in the statement of facts within the brief, she cites to the case record by identifying these documents as Exhibit 1, Exhibit 2, etc., or Attachment A, Attachment B, etc. For clarity, brief writers label the attachments accordingly within the body of the statement of facts and then physically label such documents when they are appended to the end of the brief.

Practice Tips

- If citing from and attaching a lengthy document as an exhibit, you should balance concerns about appending overly bulky attachments against the risk of being criticized for only including excerpts instead of the complete document (lawyers have been known to accuse opposing counsel of picking and choosing only favorable parts of a lengthy document if it is not attached in its entirety, and courts sometimes note that parties have not provided complete copies of important documents for review).
- If citing from and attaching transcripts (from depositions or trials), you should cite to the exact page and line numbers (e.g., David Evans Deposition Transcript, March 26, 2017, 45:1-7).
- If court rules require electronic filing of the brief and its attachments, the rules may require exhibits to be submitted separately in Portable Document Format (PDF) form; it is important to label electronically filed exhibits clearly so that the clerk knows which brief they correspond to and important documents do not disappear.

Preparing a Certificate of Service

Briefs must be served upon opposing counsel. Court rules require attorneys to attach a Certificate of Service to the brief, verifying how and when the document was transmitted to opposing parties. A Certificate of Service for a brief that is electronically filed with the court and served upon opposing counsel looks like this:

CERTIFICATE OF SERVICE

I hereby certify that on the 4th day of April, 2017, I caused an electronic copy of Plaintiff Riggins Garment Company's Motion to Compel to be properly submitted to the court's electronic filing system. Pursuant to Local Rule 44.1, this filing and the Notice of Docket Activity subsequently generated by the electronic case filing system shall satisfy Plaintiff's duty to serve Defendant Cornerstone Insurance Company's registered attorney, although a courtesy copy was served via e-mail upon:

Michael Pineda, Esq.
Rodriguez & Jess, LLP
200 Leonard Street, Suite 2
New York, NY 10013
646-555-1000

mpineda@rodriguezjessllp.com

David H. Evans

David H. Evans

Drafting a Proposed Order

Local court rules may require parties to submit a proposed Order along with a brief, so the judge may rule on the Motion and simply sign one of the parties' proposed Orders. A proposed Order might look like this:

IN THE UNITED STATES DISTRICT COURT
FOR THE SOUTHERN DISTRICT OF NEW YORK

Riggins Garment Company,	)	
	)	
Plaintiff,	)	
	)	
v.	)	Case No. Y14-044-AML
	)	The Honorable Laila Hewson
Cornerstone Insurance Company,	)	
	)	
Defendant.	)	
————————————————	)	

ORDER

Upon consideration of Plaintiff's Motion to Compel, the parties' briefs in support and opposition, and reply memoranda, and the entire record herein, and it appearing that the relief sought should be granted, it is hereby:

ORDERED that:

- Defendant shall produce the eleven documents withheld on its privilege log within ten (10) days of the date hereof.
- Defendant shall pay Plaintiff its reasonable costs and attorneys' fees incurred in preparing, submitting, and arguing this motion.
- Plaintiff shall produce documentation to support its claim of costs and fees within ten (10) days of the date hereof.

SO ORDERED.

Entered this date of: _____   _____
                                                                  United States District Judge

---

Requesting Oral Argument

Local court rules often indicate whether the court will allow the parties to present oral argument on the issues involved in the briefs. If so, brief writers either

(1) indicate a request for oral argument in the caption of the Motion (stating "Oral Argument Requested"), or (2) if the court rules prescribe, submit a separate filing containing the request, and possibly a statement of why oral argument would be helpful to resolve the issues in the brief. For example, regarding oral argument, Rule 1.6-2(d) of New Jersey's state court rules explains in part:

> Except as otherwise provided . . . , no motion shall be listed for oral argument unless a party requests oral argument in the moving papers or in timely-filed answering or reply papers, or unless the court directs. . . . If the motion involves pretrial discovery or is directly addressed to the calendar, the request shall be considered only if accompanied by a statement of reasons and shall be deemed denied unless the court otherwise advises counsel prior to the return day. As to all other motions, the request shall be granted as of right.

Similarly, Rule 3.A of the Rules of Montana's Sixteenth Judicial Circuit states:

> When counsel desire oral argument on a motion, other than a motion for summary judgment, they shall so state within their motion, response, or reply, including therein the reasons in support of oral argument. Counsel shall include a proposed Order Granting Oral Argument. . . . If the Court determines on its own motion that oral argument would be beneficial to a determination of the motion, it shall so order and will notify the parties of the time and date of hearing.

Oral argument is a unique opportunity for lawyers on both sides of the case to communicate directly—in person—with the judge deciding the issues in the brief and elaborate on the written arguments. Tips for how to prepare for and conduct an oral argument are addressed in Chapter 32.

Single-IREAC/CREAC Versus Multi-IREAC/CREAC Briefs

If a brief involves a single legal issue and a straightforward governing rule (i.e., without multiple elements or factors), a brief writer likely can structure the argument section around one IREAC or CREAC framework. As described earlier in this chapter, the introduction to the brief would outline the theme of the party's case, the issue, the governing rule, the three to five reasons why the filing party should prevail and why the result sought is justified, and the precise decision and action requested of the court. Then, after the statement of facts, the argument section—using an IREAC or CREAC structure—would state the legal issue again (asserting the filing party's position on the issue), describe the rule, use cases to explain the rule in RE paragraphs, apply the rule in RA paragraphs, and build toward a logical conclusion that the result requested is proper.

There are at least two circumstances in which a brief writer might choose to write a brief organized around more than one IREAC or CREAC framework: (1) if a single-issue brief involves a rule with multiple required elements, or a range of factors, each meriting separate analysis and an exploration of case law on the distinct element or factor or (2) if the brief involves more than one legal issue, each governed by discrete rules and perhaps based on completely unrelated subject matter.

Using an example discussed earlier in this chapter, if a lawyer is writing a motion for summary judgment on an injured plaintiff's cause of action for negligence brought against an "out-of-possession" landowner based on injuries that occurred on the landowner's property, the rule regarding out-of-possession landowner liability requires analysis of four subissues:

1. Whether the landowner created the dangerous condition
2. Whether the landowner had a duty to maintain the property
3. Whether the landowner was contractually responsible for repairs to the premises
4. Whether the landowner retained or relinquished control over the land

To assist the reader, the brief writer could structure the argument section of the brief around four separate IREAC or CREAC analyses, each labeled with persuasive informative headings tied to each subrule. Beneath the heading on the first subrule addressing whether the landowner created the dangerous condition, the brief writer would fully analyze the issue of creation, illustrating the subrule through REs of cases that focus on the creation of land conditions (rather than maintenance, repair, or control that are addressed in the subsequent three subrules). The RA would focus on the facts supporting the party's allegation that the landowner did not create the dangerous condition. The IREAC or CREAC would end with a mini-conclusion asserting that the creation prong of the rule fails.

In the next three sections, each introduced by a persuasive heading, the brief writer would address one by one the maintenance, repair, and control prongs of the rule, illustrating each rule component through REs of cases discussing each topic in the context of "out-of-possession" landowners. Of course, some of the cases might address overlapping topics and can be used more than once in the brief. Within each separate IREAC or CREAC, the RA would focus on the client facts related to the specific rule prong being addressed: either maintenance, repair, or control. The brief writer would end each section with a mini-conclusion on that particular rule prong.

Separating the four subrule analyses into distinct IREAC or CREAC frameworks helps the reader follow the logic path of one subrule at a time, closing the loop on that subissue before moving on to the next topic. Strong headings are essential to inform the reader about the part of the rule being addressed in each section of the argument. The chronology of the headings in the argument should mirror the sequence of subissues outlined in the brief's introduction. Finally, the conclusion of the brief should reiterate the client's position on all four subissues and assert the overall result requested.

An example of how a brief writer might organize the foregoing brief looks like this:

- **Caption and Title**
- **Introduction**
  - First sentence (filing party, type of brief, procedural rule authorizing the filing of the brief)
  - Theme sentence: Fairness in liability resulting from property ownership
  - Overall issue/contention: The out-of-possession landowner is not liable for injuries to individuals occurring on premises leased to, or managed by, a third party.
  - Governing rule: For a landowner to be liable, the landowner must have (1) created the allegedly dangerous condition, (2) assumed a duty to maintain the premises, (3) retained a duty to repair defects, or (4) maintained control over the property.
  - Subissues before the court:
    - Subissue 1: Did the landowner create the allegedly dangerous condition?
    - Subissue 2: Did the landowner have a duty to maintain the property?
    - Subissue 3: Did the landowner have a duty to repair defects on the premises?
    - Subissue 4: Did the landowner retain or relinquish control over the property?
  - Reasons why the filing party should prevail:
    - The landowner did not create the dangerous condition.
    - The landowner had no duty to maintain the property.
    - The landowner had no duty to repair the property.
    - The landowner relinquished control over the property.
  - Ask the court to find the landowner not liable; grant summary judgment.
- **Statement of Facts**
- **Argument**
  - Issue/contention: An out-of-possession landowner is not liable for injuries occurring on premises leased to, or managed by, a third party.

- Governing rule: For a landowner to be liable, the landowner must have (1) created the allegedly dangerous condition, (2) assumed a duty to maintain the premises, (3) retained a duty to repair defects, *or* (4) maintained control over the property.
- Theme
- **Persuasive Heading:** The landowner did *not* create the allegedly dangerous condition.
  - Issue: Creation
  - Rule: A landowner who created the condition can be liable.
  - RE: Provide case examples of landowners held *not* liable because they did not create the condition.
  - RA: Describe facts showing that the client landowner did not create the condition.
  - Mini-conclusion: The creation prong of the rule is *not* satisfied.
- **Persuasive Heading:** The landowner had *no* duty to maintain the property.
  - Issue: Maintenance
  - Rule: Courts evaluate the landowner's contract and course of dealing.
  - RE: Provide case examples of landowners held *not* liable because they had no duty to maintain the property and exercised no such course of dealing.
  - RA: Describe facts showing that the client landowner did not have a contractual duty to maintain the property and did not do so in its course of dealing with the premises.
  - Mini-conclusion: The maintenance prong of the rule is *not* satisfied.
- **Persuasive Heading:** The landowner had *no* duty to repair defects on the premises.
  - Issue: Repair
  - Rule: Courts evaluate the landowner's contract and course of dealing.
  - RE: Provide case examples of landowners held *not* liable because they had no duty to repair the property and exercised no such course of dealing.
  - RA: Describe facts showing that the client landowner did not have a contractual duty to repair the property and did not do so in its course of dealing with the premises.
  - Mini-conclusion: The repair prong of the rule is not satisfied.
- **Persuasive Heading:** The landowner relinquished control over the property.
  - Issue: Control
  - Rule: Courts evaluate the landowner's contract and course of dealing.

- RE: Provide case examples of landowners held *not* liable because they relinquished control of the property.
- RA: Describe facts showing that the client landowner relinquished control of the property.
  - Mini-conclusion: The control prong of the rule is not satisfied.
- **Conclusion:** Landowner is not liable.
- Signature Block
- Attachments/Exhibits
- Certificate of Service
- Proposed Order

The foregoing is an example of a *single-issue* brief (analyzing whether the landowner is liable) involving a rule with *multiple* components (creation? maintenance? repair? control?), each of which merits separate analysis and recitation of case law on the distinct subissue and subrule. Now, let's look at an example of a brief involving *multiple legal issues* governed by discrete rules.

Imagine that an opposing party has refused to produce documents in discovery, asserting two distinct bases: (1) the application of the attorney-client privilege and (2) protection under the attorney work product doctrine. The party's decision to withhold the documents from discovery on these grounds invokes two distinct rules. The attorney-client privilege allows a party to withhold confidential communications between the client and his lawyer given for the purpose of obtaining and rendering legal advice.[25] In contrast, the attorney work product doctrine permits a party to withhold documents from discovery that were prepared in anticipation of litigation or for trial, by or for another party or its representative (including the other party's attorney, consultant, surety, indemnitor, insurer, or agent).[26] The work product doctrine shields from disclosure the "mental impressions, conclusions, opinions, or legal theories of a party's attorney or other representative concerning the litigation."[27] A brief in support of a motion to compel the production of the withheld documents must address the two separate issues and rules.

A brief writer might organize the brief like this:

---

[25] *See, e.g., McArthur v. Robinson*, 98 F.R.D. 672, 674 (E.D. Ark 1983) ("In order for the attorney-client privilege to apply, the material must involve (1) a communication, (2) which concerns the seeking of legal advice, (3) between attorney and client acting as such, (4) relating to legal matters, and (5) is being protected at client's insistence).

[26] Fed. R. Civ. P. 26(b)(3)(A).

[27] Fed. R. Civ. P. 26(b)(3)(B).

- **Caption and Title**
- **Introduction**
  - First sentence (filing party, type of brief, procedural rule authorizing the filing of the brief)
  - Theme sentence: Fairness and even playing field in litigation
  - Overall issue/contention: The filing party is entitled to the withheld documents, as the privilege and work product doctrine do not apply.
  - Governing rule: The opposing party can properly withhold the documents only if they are protected by the attorney-client privilege *or* the work product doctrine.
  - Rule regarding attorney-client privilege (confidentiality, communications between attorney and client, for purposes of rendering or obtaining legal advice)
  - Rule regarding work product doctrine (documents prepared by or for the party or its representative, in anticipation of litigation)
  - Concise statement of reasons why attorney-client privilege does not apply
  - Concise statement of reasons why work product doctrine does not apply
  - Statement of exact relief sought: Production of the withheld documents, plus the fees and costs of filing the motion
- **Statement of Facts**
- **Argument**
  - Overall introduction of the two issues (attorney-client privilege and work product doctrine)
  - Reiteration of theme (fairness and even playing field in litigation)
  - **Persuasive Heading:** The attorney-client privilege does not apply.
    - Issue: Applicability of the privilege
    - Rule: Confidential communications, between attorney and client for purposes of rendering/obtaining legal advice
    - RE: Provide case examples of erroneous claims of privilege rejected by the court; documents ordered produced.
    - RA: Describe facts showing that the documents were not confidential, not exchanged solely between the attorney and client, *or* not for purposes of rendering/obtaining legal advice.
    - Mini-conclusion on attorney-client privilege
  - **Persuasive Heading:** The work product doctrine does not apply.
    - Issue: Applicability of the doctrine
    - Rule: Prepared by or for party or counsel, in anticipation of litigation
    - RE: Provide case examples of erroneous claims of work product protection rejected by the court; documents ordered produced.
    - RA: Describe facts showing that the documents were not prepared by or for the party at the direction of counsel and that litigation was not reasonably anticipated.
    - Mini-conclusion on work product doctrine

- **Conclusion:** The withheld documents must be produced.
- Signature Block
- Attachments/Exhibits
- Certificate of Service
- Proposed Order

If you are writing a brief that involves a rule with multiple parts, consider whether each part might warrant its own IREAC or CREAC analysis. Likewise, if you are writing a brief addressing more than one distinct legal issue, you most likely will need to structure the brief around more than one IREAC or CREAC because different rules will govern the individual legal topics. With each brief that you write, experiment with different structures, always keeping in mind the importance of guiding the reader down a logical path toward the desired result, enhancing *logos*.

Drafting a Motion to Be Supported by a Brief

This chapter has focused primarily on the process of drafting a trial-level brief, along with a Certificate of Service and a proposed Order. Unless the brief constitutes a stand-alone trial brief that the court requests both parties to file to explain certain legal issues in the case, most trial-level briefs are written in support of a Motion—a short 1- or 2-page document that identifies the procedural action requested of the court—e.g., a Motion to Dismiss, a Motion to Compel, a Motion in Limine, or a Motion for Summary Judgment. The brief then accompanies the Motion and is entitled, for example, "Memorandum of Points and Authorities in Support of Plaintiff's Motion to Dismiss the Complaint," or "Memorandum of Law in Support of Defendant's Motion to Compel the Production of Documents."

The actual Motion is usually a much shorter document than the brief and looks like this:

IN THE UNITED STATES DISTRICT COURT
FOR THE SOUTHERN DISTRICT OF NEW YORK

Riggins Garment Company,	)	
Plaintiff,	)	Case No. Y14-044-AML
	)	The Honorable Laila Hewson
v.	)	
	)	
Cornerstone Insurance Company,	)	ORAL ARGUMENT
	)	REQUESTED
Defendant.	)	
	)	

PLAINTIFF RIGGINS GARMENT COMPANY'S
MOTION TO COMPEL
PRODUCTION OF DOCUMENTS WITHHELD IN DISCOVERY

COMES NOW Plaintiff Riggins Garment Company ("Riggins") and hereby submits this Motion to Compel documents erroneously withheld from discovery by Defendant Cornerstone Insurance Company ("Cornerstone"), pursuant to Fed. R. Civ. P. 37(a)(3)(B)(iv) and Local Rule 37.1. A Memorandum of Points and Authorities in support of this Motion is attached hereto, along with a proposed Order.

Dated: May 7, 2017

Respectfully submitted,

MCGEE & ROLLINS, LLP

Bridget Stanton

Bridget Stanton, Esq.
100 William St., Suite 44
New York, NY 10005
800-555-4718
bstanton@mcgeerollins.com
Counsel for Plaintiff

BRIEF-WRITING CHECKLIST

Getting Started

☑ Check the court rules for:
  o Filing deadline
  o Page- or word-count limit

o Margins
o Font size
o Rules on footnotes
o Required substantive components (if any)
o Required attachments (if any)
o Submission requirements and procedure

☑ Check with supervising attorney regarding:
o Internal deadlines
o Any limits on number of hours billed to the writing assignment
o Any restrictions on research methods (electronic?)
o Ideal or preferred length of brief

Identifying the Issue and Case Theme

☑ What legal issues should the brief address?
o Is there one legal issue?
o Are there multiple legal issues?

☑ What theme captures the essence of the party's lawsuit, your client's position, and the crux of the brief?

Researching the Rule

☑ What rule governs the legal issue or issues in the brief?

☑ Is there a governing statute (or regulation)?
o Can you break the statute down into elements or factors?
o Does the statute include legal definitions of terms?
o Do you need case law to help synthesize a list of elements or factors or to define a legal term?

☑ Are there cases applying the rule?
o Are there cases that favor your client's position?
o Are there cases that disfavor your client's position?
o Which cases are mandatory authority?
o Which cases would be most effective in a full RE?
o Which cases would be useful in a signal or string cite plus explanatory parenthetical?

Organizing an IREAC or CREAC Framework

☑ Can the argument section of the brief be organized around a single IREAC or CREAC structure, or would more than one IREAC or CREAC be helpful to the reader (to address a multipart rule or multiple legal issues)?

☑ For each IREAC or CREAC:
o Pinpoint the precise legal issue.

- Outline the rule framework:
  - State the overall rule.
  - List any required elements or range of factors that courts analyze.
  - Define any legal terms that need further explanation.
- Decide which cases to use in full RE paragraphs and which to use in string or signal cites.
  - Consider the cases in terms of:
    - Landmark cases establishing the rule or applying it for the first time to a particular set of facts
    - Recent cases confirming the current state of the rule
    - Mandatory versus persuasive precedent
    - Favorable versus less favorable outcomes
    - Comparable versus contrasting facts (as analogized to the client facts)
    - Cases with helpful thorough analysis versus cases that only tangentially touch on the legal issue
- Organize the client facts that support each rule component.
- Organize the cases to compare and contrast to the client facts.
- Identify any policy arguments.

Writing the IR or CR Part of the IREAC or CREAC

- ☑ Beneath the Argument heading (or a more engaging substantive heading to introduce the argument), do the following:
  - Identify the legal issue for the court.
  - State the overall governing rule.
  - Outline the rule framework:
    - List any required elements or range of factors that courts analyze.
    - Define any legal terms that need elaboration.
  - Weave the case theme into the beginning of the argument section.

Writing the REs and Signal or String Cites (Plus Explanatory Parentheticals)

- ☑ Transition to the first RE through a rule statement (explaining an aspect of the rule that builds upon the prior recitation of the overall governing rule, or a subrule) or a transitional phrase (like "For example, in *Jameson v. Three Trees, Inc.*").
- ☑ Cite the case (in full if this is the first time you are citing the case in the brief; short-cite the case if it has been cited previously).
- ☑ Describe the legally significant facts of the case (in the past tense).
- ☑ State the court's holding on the same legal issue affecting your client ("The court held . . .").

☑ Describe the court's reasoning in a few sentences ("The court explained . . . ," "The court evaluated . . . ," "The court relied upon . . . ," or "The court emphasized . . .").

☑ Use *Id.* to insert pinpoint cites to support the facts, holding, and rationale sentences of the RE with page references to their location within the judicial opinion.

☑ Avoid using the names of the parties in the precedent cases; instead, use descriptive labels that will vividly paint the scene and that readily can be applied to the client's scenario: e.g., athlete, celebrity, company, employer, vehicle owner, passenger, pilot, etc.

☑ When transitioning to the next RE, insert a new rule statement *or* use a transitional phrase like "Similarly, in *Ortega v. Edmonds* . . . ," or "In contrast, in *Bartholemew v. Colmans* . . . ."

☑ Attach signal cites to the end of a prior RE; never interrupt an RE with a signal cite of a new case.

☑ Choose appropriate signals and properly cite the case (use a full cite if it is the first time citing the case in the brief; short-cite if the case has been cited previously).

☑ Craft helpful parentheticals starting with an *-ing* word ("holding that . . .") and capture the facts, holding, and rationale of the case in fewer than four lines of text.

☑ Use *ethos*, informing the court of mandatory precedent and properly citing to sources of law.

Writing the RA Section of an Argument in a Brief

☑ Transition between the RE section of the argument to the RA by inserting a paragraph break and a thesis sentence foreshadowing the conclusion on the legal issue that is the focus of the IREAC or CREAC.

☑ Write separate paragraphs analyzing each distinct component of the rule (element, factor, or definition):
  ○ Draft each paragraph with an introduction, a middle, and a mini-conclusion on the particular component of the rule.
  ○ Use rule-based reasoning.
  ○ Use analogical reasoning (comparing and contrasting the client facts to/with the case law).
  ○ Use policy-based reasoning (if applicable).

☑ Make sure the logic of the RA section builds toward the ultimate conclusion favoring the client:
  ○ Show that all rule elements are met (if your client seeks a result governed by a rule with a checklist of required elements).

- ○ Show that at least one rule element fails (if your client seeks a result in which the opposing party cannot satisfy all prongs of a governing rule with a checklist of required elements).
- ○ Show that the majority of factors favors a finding that the rule is satisfied (if your client seeks a result governed by a rule with a balancing test of factors).
- ○ Show that the majority of factors favors a finding that the rule is not satisfied (if your client seeks a result in which the opposing party cannot satisfy a governing rule with a balancing test of factors).
- ☑ Inject *pathos* into the factual descriptions and RA portion of the argument, forging an emotional connection between the reader and the client's position.
- ☑ Reinforce *ethos*, by balancing zealous representation of the client with respectful tone and language, integrity, and professionalism.
- ☑ Reiterate the theme of the case where appropriate.
- ☑ Include a mini-conclusion on the legal issue that is the subject of the IREAC or CREAC.

Repeat the foregoing steps if the brief involves more than one IREAC or CREAC.
- ☑ Consider drafting persuasive informative headings to distinguish among multiple IREAC or CREAC sections.

Writing the Brief's Conclusion

- ☑ At the tail end of the brief (after the IREAC or CREAC or the last of multiple IREACs or CREACs), reiterate the following:
  - ○ The substantive decision or decisions that you want the court to make on the legal issue or issues
  - ○ The procedural action that should follow (typically an order granting the motion and enforcing the action sought: e.g., compelling production of documents, excluding a witness or piece of evidence from trial, dismissing the case, entering summary judgment or partial summary judgment, etc.)
  - ○ If appropriate under a statute, an applicable rule, or a contract provision, a statement of whether you are requesting an award of attorneys' fees and costs associated with the motion
  - ○ A statement of whether any additional relief is proper
- ☑ Reiterate the theme of the case.

Creating the Signature Block

- ☑ Date the brief.
- ☑ Add the phrase, "Respectfully submitted."

☑ Add a line for a signature.

☑ State the signing attorney's name, law office name, law office address, phone number, and e-mail address.

☑ Add a designation ("Counsel for Plaintiff" or "Counsel for Defendant").

Crafting the Caption and Title

☑ Use the same case caption that appeared on the complaint and answer:
  o Court name
  o Party names
  o Designation as plaintiff and defendant (plus any additional parties joined to the case)
  o Docket number assigned by the clerk

☑ Insert the proper title of the brief and which party is filing it (e.g., "Plaintiff's Memorandum of Points and Authorities in Support of its Motion to Compel Production of Documents," "Defendant's Memorandum of Law in Support of its Motion for Summary Judgment," etc.).

☑ If appropriate under the court rules, state "Oral argument requested" beneath the docket number in the caption.

Drafting the Introduction

☑ First sentence: State the name of the party filing the brief, the type of brief, and, if applicable, the procedural rule authorizing the filing of the brief (court rule, judge's case management order, etc.).

☑ Establish appropriate abbreviations for the parties' names that will be used throughout the brief.

☑ Include a theme sentence (this can be the second or third sentence) to set the brief in the context of the overall case and engage the reader with the client's point of view.

☑ State the legal issue or issues that are the focus of the brief (this can be the second or third sentence—swapped with the theme sentence—the order of these two sentences is the judgment call of the brief writer).

☑ Describe the overall governing rule or rules.

☑ State the three to five most persuasive reasons why the filing party should prevail and obtain the result sought.

☑ Identify the exact result sought on the substantive legal issues.

☑ State the procedural action requested of the court.

Writing the Statement of Facts

- ☑ Tell the client's story.
- ☑ Identify the key players, any relevant tangible physical items, and events—chronologically (to enhance *logos*).
- ☑ Engage the reader's attention by using *pathos*—describing the facts as vividly as possible (use strong nouns and active verbs).
- ☑ Establish *ethos* by including all legally significant facts, handling any weak facts appropriately and ethically (including them if they are relevant to the court's analysis but placing them in context with stronger facts).
- ☑ Cross-check the statement of facts against the client facts described in the RAs and make sure that all client facts relied upon in the RAs are included in the statement of facts.
- ☑ Cite to the record sources of the facts (if appropriate or required by the rules, labeling the sources with exhibit numbers if they will be attached to the brief).

Inserting Smooth Transitions

- ☑ Insert standard headings within the body of the brief: introduction, statement of facts, argument, conclusion (with Roman numerals, and the text bolded or underlined, with only initial letters of each word capitalized).
- ☑ If appropriate for the length and complexity of the brief, consider crafting persuasive and informative subheadings for the argument section of the brief to use as signposts or billboards to signal to the reader shifts between multiple issues or analyses of sequential rule components.
- ☑ Insert transitions between separate REs.
- ☑ Insert a transition between the RE section of an IREAC or CREAC arc and the RA, using a thesis sentence to assert the ultimate conclusion on the issue or component of the rule being discussed.
- ☑ Insert transitions between RA paragraphs, using mini-conclusions at the end of one paragraph and strong thesis sentences at the beginning of the next paragraph.

Checking for Theme Reiteration

- ☑ Introduce the theme in the brief's introduction.
- ☑ Weave the theme into the statement of facts, using *pathos* and descriptive vivid language to describe the client's story.
- ☑ Reiterate the theme in the RE and RA sections of the argument.
- ☑ Reprise the theme in the conclusion.

Preparing Attachments

- ☑ If allowed or required under the court rules, prepare any attachments of record sources relied upon in the statement of facts, labeling them Exhibit 1, Exhibit 2, etc. or Attachment A, Attachment B, etc.
- ☑ Prepare a Certificate of Service to show how the brief is served on opposing counsel.
- ☑ Draft a proposed Order if allowed or required under the rules.

Twelve-Step Editing and Proofreading Process

- ☑ Check the applicable court rules to ensure that all required substantive components are included in the brief.
- ☑ Review the brief as a whole for IREAC or CREAC logic.
- ☑ Review each stand-alone section of the brief separately.
- ☑ Read the entire brief for theme and persuasion.
- ☑ Review each paragraph of the brief separately.
- ☑ Review each sentence of the brief separately.
- ☑ Review the brief for professionalism in tone.
- ☑ Proofread on a word-by-word basis, ideally backward to forward.
- ☑ Check all citations.
- ☑ Check for formatting errors.
- ☑ Check for consistency in terminology in references to party names, the court, the motion, etc.
- ☑ Perform a final check of the document against the court's submission rules:
  - o Page- and word-count limits
  - o Margins
  - o Line spacing
  - o Font
  - o Handling of footnotes
  - o Accompanying documents or exhibits
  - o Procedure for filing the brief with the court

Drafting the Motion

- ☑ Using the same caption as the brief, create the cover Motion that identifies the party filing the Motion and the title of the Motion.
- ☑ State whether oral argument is requested.
- ☑ Indicate that an accompanying Memorandum of Points and Authorities, or Memorandum of Law, in Support of the Motion is attached.

Filing and Serving

☑ Follow the court's rules in filing the motion and brief with the clerk, including required number of copies, electronic versus hard-copy filing, etc.

☑ Serve the motion and brief on opposing counsel, completing a Certificate of Service.

Chapter 30

Drafting Persuasive Opposition and Reply Briefs

After one party files an initial brief and serves it on the opposing party, the receiving party has the opportunity to file an opposition brief. Then, in response to the opposition brief, the initial party may have the chance to file a shorter reply brief before the court schedules oral argument or issues a written decision. In law school, we tend not to focus much attention on how to craft persuasive opposition or reply briefs. This chapter provides guidance on the process of reviewing an opponent's brief, outlining a response, and persuasively arguing to the court why the opposing party's contentions fail but the responding party's position should prevail.

Following Court Rules

Many courts issue rules specifying the content and formatting of, and any restrictions on, opposition and reply briefs. If you receive an initial brief from opposing counsel, the first step in the responsive brief-writing process is to check the court rules to determine the deadline for filing an opposition, any substantive content requirements, formatting directives, and page- or word-count limits. Likewise, if you represent the moving party and you submitted the initial brief, upon receipt of the opposition brief, you would check the court rules governing the parameters of the reply brief. Courts typically allot opposition briefs the same number of pages or words as the initial brief. However, reply briefs are much shorter—sometimes half the number of pages or words of the initial and opposition briefs. It is essential to know these constraints before beginning the responsive brief-writing process.

For example, California Rule of Court 3.1113(d) states:

> Except in a summary judgment or summary adjudication motion, no opening or responding memorandum may exceed 15 pages. In a summary judgment or summary adjudication motion, no opening or responding memorandum may exceed 20 pages. No reply or closing memorandum may exceed 10 pages. The page limit does not include exhibits, declarations, attachments, the table of contents, the table of authorities, or the proof of service.

Similarly, Rule 7.1(b)(2) of the Local Rules of the United States District Court for the District of Utah limits opposition and reply briefs as follows:

> Memoranda in opposition to motions made pursuant to Fed. R. Civ. P. 12(b),[1] 12(c),[2] 56,[3] and 65[4] must not exceed twenty-five (25) pages, exclusive of any of the following items: face sheet, table of contents, concise introduction, response to the statement of elements and undisputed material facts, any statement of additional elements and/or undisputed material facts, table of exhibits, and exhibits.
>
> Reply memoranda must be limited to ten (10) pages, exclusive of face sheet, table of contents, any additional facts, and exhibits and must be limited to rebuttal of matters raised in the memorandum opposing the motion.
>
> Response memoranda related to all motions that are not listed above must not exceed ten (10) pages, exclusive of any of the following items: face sheet, table of contents, concise introduction, statements of issues and facts, table of exhibits, and exhibits.

Identifying Issues in an Initial Brief Warranting Response in an Opposition or Reply

When a lawyer receives a brief from an opposing party—either through electronic filing, or through e-mail or regular mail—after checking the court rules, the next step in the responsive brief-writing process is to read the brief and highlight the following:

- The legal issue or issues
- Any themes asserted by opposing counsel
- Inaccurate statements of the governing rule or rules (this step might require research as indicated in the next section of this chapter)
- Inaccurate factual statements
- Accurate factual statements that are unfavorable to the responding lawyer's client

---

[1] Motions to Dismiss.
[2] Motions for Judgment on the Pleadings.
[3] Motions for Summary Judgment.
[4] Motions for Injunction or Restraining Order.

- Factual admissions that favor the responding lawyer's client
- Missing facts
- Illogical or weak arguments
- Persuasive arguments that are unfavorable to the responding lawyer's client

Lawyers often jot notes in the margins of a hard copy of the opponent's brief, highlight or circle key sentences, and mark exclamation points near statements that cause concern or merit a response.

Checking the Law

The next step in the responsive brief-writing process is to check the accuracy of the governing law and rules cited and relied upon by the opposing party for each legal issue. After identifying the legal issue or issues in the initial brief, the responding lawyer lists the statutes, regulations, and case law cited by opposing counsel and then conducts fresh research on the legal issue or issues to determine the pertinent rules and cross-check them against the legal authority cited by the opponent. Did opposing counsel cite the correct statute or regulation? Was it the most up-to-date version? Did she cite the correct rule in its entirety or only a favorable excerpt? Did opposing counsel relay to the court the correct required elements of the rule, range of factors, or accurate legal definitions of terminology within the rule? What jurisdiction's law governs the case? Did the opposing party omit any key mandatory precedent from the applicable jurisdiction? Did opposing counsel rely on cases from the wrong jurisdiction?

Next, the responding lawyer KeyCites, Shepardizes, or BCites all the cases cited in the initial brief to check and make sure that they are still good law. Have any of the cases been overturned on appeal? Reversed? Vacated? Modified? Distinguished? The responding lawyer then reads the cases cited by opposing counsel. Do the cases truly stand for the propositions cited in the opponent's brief? Has opposing counsel described the facts, holding, and rationale of each case accurately? Did opposing counsel rely on cases that *favor* the responding lawyer's client? Can any unfavorable cases be distinguished factually or temporally (perhaps society views have shifted or evolved since the case was decided)?

Checking the Facts

After identifying the legal issue or issues in the opponent's brief, conducting fresh research to identify the governing rules (including statutes, regulations, and cases), and then vetting the law relied upon by opposing counsel, the next step in the responsive brief-writing process is to check the facts of the opponent's brief. Has opposing counsel misstated or exaggerated any client facts? Did the brief writer omit legally significant facts necessary to tell the parties' complete story? Has opposing counsel cited accurate facts that disfavor the responding lawyer's client and need to be addressed? Did the brief writer admit or concede facts that are helpful to the responding lawyer's client? Can any of the facts be restated in a light more favorable to the responding lawyer's client, without undermining their accuracy?

Single-Issue Versus Multiple-Issue Opposition/Reply Briefs

Once the responding brief writer has reviewed the text of the opponent's brief, identified the legal issue or issues, vetted the law, and checked the facts, the next step is to organize this information into the most persuasive responsive framework. The higher the quality of writing in the opponent's brief, the easier it is to organize a responsive brief. And the converse is true as well: the more poorly organized the opponent's brief is, the more work a responding lawyer must undertake to re-arrange the opponent's points into a logical progression and then frame responsive arguments.

Just as Chapter 29 emphasized the importance of structuring an initial brief around the legal issue or issues and governing rules, responsive brief writers must make thoughtful assessments and decisions about whether the opposition or reply brief merits a single IREAC or CREAC or more than one. Lawyers writing single-issue briefs involving straightforward legal rules without numerous component parts likely can construct the argument section of the brief using just one IREAC or CREAC arc. However, single-issue briefs based on multipart rules and multiple-issue briefs probably require more than one IREAC or CREAC framework to present the key information logically and clearly to the reader. While the initial brief writer took the lead on choosing an organizational framework to present her arguments, the responsive brief writer is not bound by that structure; in fact, one of the most pivotal decisions the responsive brief writer can make is whether to write the opposition or reply brief using the same chronology of issues, rules, rule components, and arguments as the opponent's brief or to re-organize the responsive brief in a different logical progression. As long as the end result is the reader's understanding of the issues, governing rules, and both parties' arguments, either approach is fine.

The R and E Sections of IREAC or CREAC in an Opposition Brief

An opposition brief includes the same general sections as the initial brief: caption, title, introduction, statement of facts, argument, conclusion, and signature block. As noted above, the argument section may contain one or more IREAC or CREAC sections, depending on the complexity of the subject matter of the brief and the governing rules. Responsive brief writers use persuasive and informative headings throughout the argument section to help the reader navigate through multiple IREAC or CREAC frameworks.

For each legal issue raised in the initial brief, the responding brief writer should inform the court of the governing rule and use case law to illustrate how the rule impacts the responding party. If opposing counsel stated the rule *correctly* in the initial brief, the responding lawyer will repeat the same rule. However, even the recitation of the rule presents an opportunity for the responsive brief writer to persuade. If the moving party (who filed the initial brief) bears the burden of proving that, for example, all five required elements of a rule are satisfied, the responsive brief writer should emphasize—in explaining the rule—that if *just one* element fails, the court must find in favor of the responding party. Likewise, if the rule involves a list of factors that must be weighed, the responsive brief writer should reiterate that if the majority of factors weigh in favor of the responsive party, the court must find in favor of the responding party instead of the moving party. Mindful responsive brief writers use *logos* when describing the rule and its elements or factors, planting a seed in the judge's mind about why the responsive brief, and the result sought therein, makes more *logical* sense than the initial brief. Of course, if opposing counsel misstated the rule, omitted a key element or factor, or misdescribed a legal definition, the responsive brief writer points out the discrepancy and corrects it in the R portion of the IREAC or CREAC.

In the RE section of the IREAC or CREAC in a responsive brief, lawyers make strategic decisions about which cases to describe in full RE paragraphs and which to weave into the brief using signal or string cites plus explanatory parentheticals. The responsive brief writer must (1) explain the governing rule through cases that favor the client; (2) inform the court of the mandatory precedent pertinent to the legal issue; and (3) distinguish any adverse case law cited by opposing counsel. Good responsive brief writers are assertive and affirmative rather than defensive. They approach the RE section of the argument just as if they were writing the initial brief, choosing the cases that explain the rule in a way that favors the client's position. They thoughtfully select landmark cases, more recent cases that thoroughly and vividly explain the rule and reveal results favorable to the client, and/or perhaps a spectrum of cases showing a range of outcomes, ultimately illustrating how the client's scenario fits into the favorable end of the continuum.

An added task in writing an opposition brief that is not required during the initial brief-writing process is to distinguish any adverse case law cited by opposing counsel. Brief writers who do not undertake this important step run the risk of the judge relying wholly on the adverse case law if the initial brief is adequately persuasive. Responsive brief writers read opposing counsel's adverse case law carefully and look for discrepancies and distinctions in the facts and surrounding circumstances. Two cases rarely involve identical facts. Thoughtful lawyers can use legally significant distinctions to explain to the court why the adverse case law is irrelevant or unpersuasive in the client's context. Further, perhaps the adverse precedent is outdated, addressing societal circumstances that have evolved since the court's decision. Additionally, a responsive brief writer should emphasize if the case was decided in a lower court or a different state and therefore is not mandatory precedent. Responsive brief writers also use research tools such as KeyCite, Shepard's, and BCite to see if other courts have distinguished the adverse precedent and then make similar arguments.

Brief writers can distinguish the adverse precedent cited by opposing counsel by writing an RE about the case and then explaining why it is inapplicable to the client's circumstances. Alternatively, if the initial brief contains a series of adverse cases that must be addressed, the responsive brief writer can craft a string cite with helpful explanatory parentheticals demonstrating why all such cases are inapplicable to the client's situation. Consider these two examples:

Example of How to Use an RE to Distinguish Adverse Precedent

> Introductory sentence indicating the distinction

> Transition and Case Citation

> Facts

> Holding

> Rationale

The cases relied upon by Plaintiff Willows are distinguishable based on the level of control exercised by the "out-of-possession" landowner over the premises. For example, in *Gronski v. County of Monroe*, 18 N.Y.3d 374 (N.Y. 2011), relied upon by Willows, the County owned a waste recycling center, operated by a waste management company. A management company employee injured on the premises sued the County. *Id.* at 377. An Operations and Maintenance Agreement governed the relationship between the County and the management company, stating that the management company "shall have complete charge of and responsibility for the Facility and Facility Site." *Id.* The agreement assigned all responsibility for repair, maintenance, and safety at the Facility to the management company. The County retained "the right of access to the Facility in order to determine compliance by the [management company] with the terms and conditions of this Agreement, and . . . the right . . . to take visitors and group tours through . . . the Facility." *Id.* The County moved for summary judgment, arguing that, like an "out-of-possession" landlord, it had relinquished control over the maintenance and operations of the Facility to the management company pursuant to the Agreement, and was not contractually obligated to repair unsafe conditions on the premises. *Id.* at 378. The *Gronski* court held that an issue of fact existed as to whether the County retained sufficient control over the Facility such that it owed the injured party a duty to prevent the condition that resulted in injury. *Id.* at 382. The court focused on the following facts: (1) the County maintained a visible and vocal presence at the Facility; (2) the

County availed itself of its contractual access to the Facility through regular public tours and routine unannounced inspections; and (3) a County representative took specific supervisory actions, for example, when he observed workers not wearing hard hats. *Id.* at 381. These facts are readily distinguishable from Precipice Foundation's circumstances; Precipice Foundation's course of conduct indicates it had no presence whatsoever at the farm. Other than collecting rent from Daughtry Farms once a month, Precipice Foundation had no contact with the farm, did not visit the premises, and had no interaction with the workers or patrons.

Distinction between the precedent case and the client's facts

Notice how the formula for the RE is the same as in an initial brief (transition, citation, facts, holding, rationale). The responsive brief writer distinguishes the facts of the precedent case from the client's facts in the last few sentences of the paragraph. Responsive brief writers use words like "distinguishable" and "inapposite" or phrases like "Plaintiff Willows' reliance on the *Gronski* case is misplaced" to indicate that adverse precedent cited in an initial brief should not be followed. Here is another example using a string cite plus explanatory parenthetical:

Example of How to Use a String Cite to Distinguish Adverse Precedent

Introductory sentence indicating the distinction

Signal and Citation

Explanatory parenthetical

Citation

Explanatory parenthetical

All of the cases relied upon by Cornerstone for the proposition that communications prepared by an insurance company's in-house counsel are discoverable are distinguishable, as they involve circumstances in which the lawyers were rendering legal advice, not performing a claims adjuster role. *See, e.g., Anacapri Clothiers, Inc. v. Liberty Protection Insurance*, 326 F.3d 2016 (S.D.N.Y. 2018) (denying motion to compel production of e-mails authored by insurer's in-house counsel when rendering legal advice in drafting policy language rather than in a claims evaluation function); *Pompeii Tours v. Rainbow Insurance Trust*, 49 F.3d 1994 (S.D.N.Y. 2018) (denying motion to compel production of in-house attorney's meeting minutes compiled in the role of rendering legal advice regarding changing coverage language in new policy forms, rather than in the role of adjusting claims).

The A Section of IREAC or CREAC in an Opposition Brief

In the RA section of the IREAC or CREAC in the argument section of an opposition brief, the responsive brief writer explains persuasively and methodically why the facts of the client's case do or do not satisfy the components of the applicable rule. The organization of the RA paragraphs in a responsive brief should follow the same logical progression described in Chapter 29 in applying the rule to the client facts in an initial brief. However, wherever possible, the responsive brief writer should react to, correct, dispute, clarify, or challenge the initial brief writer's factual contentions and arguments. The RA in a responsive brief is the ideal opportunity to remedy any inaccuracies in opposing counsel's factual recitations, highlight missing legally significant facts, address unfavorable facts and describe such details in a light more favorable to the client, and emphasize the flaws in opposing counsel's logic. The RA is also a prime occasion in the responsive brief to assert any policy reasons why opposing counsel's arguments are flawed and why the result requested in the responding brief makes more sense.

At the end of each IREAC or CREAC, the responding brief writer asserts a mini-conclusion on the issue or rule component addressed in that section of the argument.

Drafting Persuasive Conclusions and Requests for Relief in an Opposition Brief

Brief writers conclude the opposition brief by stating the specific result sought—usually the opposite result (both substantively and procedurally) from the one requested by opposing counsel in the initial brief. Responsive brief writers indicate the requested ruling of the court on the substantive legal issues and then request the procedural action necessary to enforce that ruling. For example, if the initial brief requested the court to grant a motion to compel production of documents withheld in discovery, the responsive brief asks the court to find that the documents are *not discoverable* because, for example, they are protected by the attorney-client privilege. Then, the responding party asks the court to issue an order *denying* the motion to compel. Alternatively, if the initial brief requested the court to grant a motion in limine to exclude an expert from testifying at trial, the opposition brief asks the court to find that the expert is indeed qualified under the rules and applicable standard for the admissibility of expert testimony and requests the court to issue an order denying the motion in limine.

After the conclusion, the responsive brief writer includes the date of the brief and the signature block described in Chapter 29, with a designation of whether the signing lawyer is "Counsel for Plaintiff" or "Counsel for Defendant." The ethical considerations of Fed. R. Civ. P. 11 (or its state counterparts) govern opposition and reply briefs as well.

Caption, Title, and Introduction in an Opposition Brief

The caption of a responsive brief is the same as the caption of the initial brief, including the court name, parties' names, designations as plaintiff and defendant, and docket number. If the moving party did not request oral argument, but the court rules allow the responding party to make such a request, the responsive brief writer should follow the rules for requesting the oral argument either in the caption of the opposition brief or in a separate filing.

The title of the responsive brief states the name of the filing party and denotes that the responsive brief is submitted in opposition to the initial brief. For example, the title might read, "Defendant Cornerstone Insurance Company's Brief in Opposition to Plaintiff Riggins Garment Company's Motion to Compel Production of Documents." Or "Defendant Andrea Willows' Brief in Opposition to Plaintiff Precipice Foundation's Motion for Summary Judgment."

The introduction in an opposition brief should include the same components as the introduction in an initial brief described in Chapter 29, incorporating *logos* and *pathos* to persuade the reader that the result sought in the responsive brief is the proper resolution of the legal issue, while the result sought in the moving party's brief is incorrect. The introduction should contain the following components:

- A first sentence, identifying WHO, WHAT, and WHY: which party is filing the brief, what type of brief is being submitted, and the procedural rule governing the submission (i.e., a court rule, the case scheduling order, or another directive in the case)
- A second sentence, stating the THEME
- A third sentence, stating the ISSUE (some lawyers reverse the order of the issue and theme sentences)
- The framework of the rule governing the legal issue (or issues)
- Three to five reasons why the party submitting the responsive brief should prevail
- The specific result sought

In the initial sentence, the responsive brief writer establishes the name of the party filing the brief, the title of the responsive brief (so that the court can link the opposition brief to the correct initial brief), and any procedural rule governing the filing of the responsive brief. In this first sentence, the responsive brief writer also designates any abbreviations of the parties to be used throughout the brief. If the responsive brief writer disagrees with the way that opposing counsel abbreviated the party names in the prior brief, he can use his own appropriate abbreviations.

When crafting the introduction of a responsive brief, the brief writer should discern whether opposing counsel's brief invoked any particular theme about the parties' case. If the opposing counsel's brief lacked a theme, the responsive brief writer should incorporate a theme about the case to capture the attention of the judge. If opposing counsel did weave a theme into the brief, the responsive brief writer should consider a contrasting theme, in order to shift the reader's attention from the *pathos* of the opposing party's position. Consider these themes reflecting two sides of the same legal dispute:

- Plaintiff insured suggests a theme of deep-pocketed insurance companies abandoning their insureds in time of need by denying coverage of valid claims; Defendant insurer responds with a theme of protecting the general public from insurance rate increases due to expensive fraudulent claims by carefully vetting requests for coverage.
- Plaintiff student asserts the theme of violation of his First Amendment right to freedom of speech when a high school censored his online postings; Defendant high school responds with the theme of protecting other students from cyberbullying.
- Plaintiff airline passenger asserts the theme of discrimination and violation of her right to travel; Defendant airline responds with the theme of fostering airline safety and protecting other passengers from disruptive and potentially dangerous travelers.
- Plaintiff movie theater asserts the theme of improper censorship of artists' freedom of expression; Defendant parents' group responds with the theme of protecting children from graphic images of violence and sexual acts.

The introduction to the responsive brief is an ideal location to introduce either the first theme asserted in the case if opposing counsel did not weave one into the initial brief, or a contrasting theme. If the opposing party's initial brief did not clearly describe the legal issue or issues and governing rules to the court, the responsive brief writer should do so. Then, in the next part of the introduction, the responsive brief writer relays the three to five reasons why the judge should rule in the responding party's favor. *Logos* is important here, to demonstrate why the opposing party's logic fails and the client's position is the only sound solution. If the moving party argued that all the required elements of a rule were met, the responding party must demonstrate why at least one (and hopefully more than one) element fails. If the moving party contended that the case facts satisfy the majority of a set of factors balanced by the court, the responding party must sway the pendulum of persuasion back in favor of the client and show how those factors are actually *not* met. The responding brief writer outlines this logic in its three to five reasons in the introduction to the brief and later explains this reasoning in more detail in the argument section.

The introduction to the responsive brief concludes with a specific request of the substantive ruling and procedural action sought from the court, such as:

Based upon the foregoing, Defendant Cornerstone respectfully requests the Court to find that the documents that it has withheld from discovery and properly identified on its privilege log are protected by the attorney-client privilege and the attorney work product doctrine and should not be produced. Further, Cornerstone requests the Court to issue an Order denying Plaintiff Riggins' Motion to Compel and to award Cornerstone its costs in defending the Motion.

Or

Based upon the foregoing, Plaintiff Willows respectfully requests the Court to find that Defendant Precipice Foundation has failed to establish immunity from liability as an "out-of-possession" landowner as a matter of law, because there is a material fact in dispute as to whether the landowner relinquished control over the farm to its tenant. Accordingly, Plaintiff Willows requests the Court to issue an Order denying Defendant's Motion for Summary Judgment.

Statements of Facts in an Opposition Brief

After the introduction, the statement of facts in an opposition brief is a second opportunity to interlace a theme that will help persuade the court that the responding party's position is the sound one. In the statement of facts, the responsive brief writer must (1) fix any inaccuracies in opposing counsel's statement of facts, (2) assert any essential favorable facts that were omitted in the initial brief, and (3) address any unfavorable facts raised in the initial brief, casting them in the most favorable light possible for the client (balancing *pathos* and *ethos*). The responsive brief writer can reorganize the facts in a chronological order that differs from that of the initial brief. As long as the facts make logical sense to the reader, the writer can use persuasive techniques to highlight the strengths of the client's case, set weaknesses in context, and fill in gaps left by the opposing party.

Responding to the factual allegations in a *motion for summary judgment*, in particular, presents a greater workload than other opposition briefs for the responsive brief writer. Recall that Fed. R. Civ. P. 56 (and state counterparts) requires the moving party to demonstrate, in part, that there is no genuine dispute as to any material fact pertinent to the legal issue. The lawyer seeking summary judgment in federal court must support its assertion that a fact cannot be "genuinely disputed" by "citing to particular parts of materials in the record, including depositions, documents, electronically stored information, affidavits or declarations, stipulations (including those made for purposes of the motion only), admissions, interrogatory answers, or other materials."[5] Some courts' local rules require the moving party to list the undisputed material facts in distinct numbered paragraphs, with citations to the documentary support. Thus, when drafting an opposition to a motion for summary judgment, the responsive brief writer must, in turn, show that there *are* material facts in dispute. To do so, the responsive brief writer must explain the nature of the parties' disagreement on a particular material fact and provide documentary support to show the parties' differing contentions. For example, imagine that one of the critical issues in a lawsuit is the date upon which a contract was formed. In the motion for summary judgment, the moving party asserted that the contract was formed on the date it was signed by one party and e-mailed to the opposing party whose administrative assistant acknowledged the transmission via e-mail; the moving party attaches to

---

[5] Fed. R. Civ. P. 56.

the brief an affidavit of the signing party authenticating the e-mail exchange. In response, the opposing party asserts that the date of contract formation is a material fact *in dispute*, providing counterdocumentation through (1) the contract itself, showing a different date that the receiving party's president physically executed the agreement, and (2) an affidavit from the president attesting to the later contract execution date. Responding to a statement of material facts in a motion for summary judgment takes time and logistical coordination; the responsive brief writer must carve out time to contest each material fact that is in dispute and then collect the documentary record to support the challenge.

Drafting Persuasive Headings in an Opposition Brief

As explained in Chapter 29, a single-issue brief may only require headings for the introduction, statement of facts, argument, and conclusion, with Roman numerals numbering each heading (capitalizing the first letter of each key word and bolding or underlining the text of each heading). However, if the argument section of the brief is lengthy or has distinct subparts (multiple legal issues or discrete parts of a compound legal rule each requiring separate analysis), brief writers craft persuasive headings as interim signposts or billboards for the reader. In a responsive brief, headings should broadcast the party's position on each legal issue or rule component and urge the reader down a logical path to the desired result. Consider these persuasive headings in a responsive brief:

I. **The Attorney-Client Privilege Protects the Documents Drafted by Cornerstone's In-House Counsel in Her Role as Legal Advisor**

II. **The Attorney Work Product Doctrine Shields the Documents Generated by Cornerstone's In-House Counsel in Anticipation of Litigation**

III. **Plaintiff Riggins Failed to Establish That Cornerstone's In-House Counsel Was Acting in the Role of a Claims Adjuster Rather Than a Legal Adviser When She Drafted the Documents**

Headings in responsive briefs can foster *logos*, *pathos*, and *ethos*—motivating the reader in the direction toward the only logical substantive result, reprising and reinforcing the case theme, and challenging the opposing party's contentions (using a respectful and professional tone).

Language Choices in a Responsive Brief

Depending on the tone, language, and level of confrontation in an opposing party's brief, a responding brief writer might be tempted to launch a counter-attack in a responsive brief, using heated or accusatory language or adopting entrenched positions and arguments. However, no matter how argumentative, aggressive, or provocative an opponent's brief may be, a responsive brief writer usually benefits from "taking the high road," using *logos*, *pathos*, and *ethos* in drafting an opposition or reply, instead of lobbing linguistic grenades back at opposing counsel. Every legal writer eventually encounters an opposing attorney who insists on making ad hominem (personal) attacks on the lawyer or the client, maligns the lawyer's or the client's character, wrongfully accuses the lawyer or client of wrongdoing, or takes the *pathos* element of legal writing too far, exaggerating the drama of the parties' dispute. When these unfortunate legal writing flare-ups do occur, responsive brief writers are wise to resist the initial emotional reaction and instead take a deep breath, grab a highlighter and pen, and outline strong, law-based, well-reasoned responses to the opponent's allegations. Good brief writers exhibit strength not through hollow rhetoric but instead through exhaustive legal research, impactful themes, thoughtful choices of case law to illustrate rules through REs and signal or string cites, well-structured IREACs or CREACs, powerful logic, and language choices reflecting the writer's integrity and respect for the reader and the legal system.

That being said, there are artful ways of pointing out improprieties in an opposing party's brief. Consider these phrasing options:

- Plaintiff's strident and accusatory tone distracts from the important legal issue before the court.
- Rather than focusing on the legal issues at hand, Defendant persists in its campaign to malign the character of Plaintiff.
- Instead of addressing the legal issues in question, Defendant attempts to cast Plaintiff in a nefarious light. However, the crux of the parties' dispute centers on whether there was a legal duty that was breached.
- Plaintiff attempts to obfuscate the narrow legal issue pending before the court through a litany of irrelevant and inflammatory facts. Defendant will set the record straight to assist the court in making a reasoned decision based on the factual record—not smoke and mirrors.

Special Tips for Reply Briefs

As noted above, while court rules typically allot opposition briefs an equal number of pages or words as the initial brief, reply briefs are shorter—sometimes only half (or less than half) the length of the initial and opposition briefs. While reply briefs are a marvelous opportunity for a brief writer to voice the last word on the legal issue before the court, lawyers must take care to use reply briefs for their intended purpose: rebutting statements, allegations, and arguments propounded in the opposition brief and succinctly restating the result sought in the initial brief. Reply brief writers should not rehash all the arguments made in the initial brief but instead should use the steps outlined in this chapter to (1) identify any new legal issues raised in the opposition brief that warrant a response; (2) address any facts, rules, cases, arguments, or themes discussed in the opposition brief that merit a response, explanation, or distinction; and (3) reiterate any key points or arguments from the initial brief that may have been clouded by the contentions in the opposition brief. The reply brief ends with a clear restatement of the substantive ruling and procedural action requested of the court.

Editing and Proofreading an Opposition or Reply Brief

After completing a draft of the opposition or reply brief, the responsive brief writer should undertake the 12-step editing and proofreading process outlined in Chapter 29. One way to have a judge view an opposition or reply brief more favorably than the opposing party's brief is through impeccable presentation. If an opponent's brief is missing required component parts or incorporates faulty IREAC or CREAC logic, misshapen paragraphs, run-on sentences, inaccurate citations, rampant typographical errors, and formatting glitches, a responsive brief writer does his client an enormous service by presenting a responsive brief without any of those flaws. When the presentation is perfect, the substance can shine.

CHECKLIST FOR DRAFTING OPPOSITION BRIEFS

Getting Started

☑ Receive the initial brief from the opposing party.
☑ Check the court rules for:
  ○ Filing deadline
  ○ Page- or word-count limit
  ○ Margins
  ○ Font size
  ○ Rules on footnotes
  ○ Required substantive components (if any)
  ○ Required attachments (if any)
  ○ Submission requirements and procedure
☑ Check with supervising attorney regarding:
  ○ Internal deadlines
  ○ Any limits on number of hours billed to the writing assignment
  ○ Any restrictions on research methods (electronic?)
  ○ Ideal or preferred length of the brief

Reviewing the Initial Brief

- ☑ What legal issue or issues does the initial brief address?
- ☑ What arguments does the opposing party make?
- ☑ Are the factual allegations correct? Are any facts misstated?
- ☑ Are key favorable facts missing?
- ☑ Does the opposing party admit or concede any key facts?
- ☑ Are any weak client facts included that must be rebutted or explained?
- ☑ What rules are cited as governing the legal issue or issues?
  - o Research: Does the opposing party accurately cite the rules?
  - o Can each rule be broken down into elements or factors?
  - o Do the rules include legal definitions of terms?
- ☑ What cases does the opposing party cite?
  - o Research:
    - o Did the opposing party omit any mandatory precedent that is favorable to the client?
    - o Did the opposing party rely on case law from the wrong jurisdiction?
    - o Do any of the adverse cases relied upon by the opposing party constitute merely persuasive authority rather than mandatory authority?
    - o Does the opposing party accurately cite the cases?
    - o Are the cases cited by the opposing party still "good law"?
    - o Does the opposing party accurately describe the facts, holding, and rationales of the cases?
    - o Can any adverse cases be distinguished from the client's case?
    - o Research new cases and decide which would be most effective in full REs in the responsive brief.
    - o Which cases would be useful in a signal or string cite plus explanatory parenthetical?
- ☑ Does the opposing party assert a theme?
  - o Brainstorm: contrasting theme
- ☑ Does the opposing party make any policy arguments?
  - o Brainstorm: contrasting policy arguments
- ☑ What result or relief does the opposing party seek?
- ☑ To achieve the result, does the opposing party need to satisfy a checklist of elements or demonstrate that a majority of factors in a rule are met?
  - o Do any of the required elements fail? Can the responding party show that a majority of the factors favor the client rather than the opposing party?

Identifying the Issue and Case Theme

☑ What legal issue or issues should the responding brief address?
  o Is there one legal issue?
  o Are there multiple legal issues?
☑ What theme captures the essence of the party's lawsuit, the client's position, and the crux of the brief?

Organizing and Writing the IREAC or CREAC

☑ Can the argument section of the brief be organized around a single IREAC or CREAC structure, or would more than one IREAC or CREAC be helpful to the reader (to address a multipart rule or multiple legal issues)?
  o If more than one IREAC or CREAC is necessary, craft persuasive and informative headings as interim signposts or billboards for the reader.
☑ Should the issues and arguments in the responsive brief track the chronology of issues and arguments in the opposing party's brief, or would a different sequence make more sense to the reader or be more persuasive for the client?
☑ For each IREAC or CREAC:
  o Pinpoint the precise legal issue.
  o Reprise the theme, where appropriate.
  o Outline the rule framework.
    o State the overall rule.
    o List any required elements or range of factors courts analyze.
    o Define any legal terms that need further explanation.
    o Point out if the opposing party misstated the rule or omitted a key component.
  o Decide which cases to use in full RE paragraphs and which to use in string or signal cites.
    o Consider the cases in terms of:
      o Landmark cases establishing the rule or applying it for the first time
      o Recent cases confirming the current state of the rule
      o Mandatory versus persuasive precedent
      o Favorable versus less favorable outcomes
      o Comparable versus contrasting facts (as analogized to the client facts)
      o Cases with helpful thorough analysis versus cases that only tangentially touch on the legal issue
    o After using the case law to make the strongest argument on the client's behalf, distinguish any adverse case law cited and relied upon in the opposing party's brief.
  o Organize the client's facts that support a favorable application of each rule component.

o Organize the cases to compare and contrast to the client facts.

o Identify any policy arguments.

Enhancing the REs and Signal or String Cites (Plus Explanatory Parentheticals)

☑ Transition to the first RE through a rule statement (explaining an aspect of the rule that builds upon the prior recitation of the overall governing rule, or a subrule) or a transitional phrase (like "For example, in *Leeuwen v. Three Trees, Inc.* . . .").

☑ Cite the case (in full if this is the first time you are citing the case in the brief; short-cite the case if it has been cited previously).

☑ Describe the legally significant facts of the case (in the past tense).

☑ State the court's holding on the same legal issue affecting your client ("The court held . . .").

☑ Describe the court's reasoning in a few sentences ("The court explained . . .," "The court evaluated . . .,""The court relied upon . . .," "The court emphasized . . .").

☑ Use *Id.* to insert pinpoint cites to support the facts, holding, and rationale sentences of the RE with page references to their location within the judicial opinion.

☑ Avoid using the names of the parties in the precedent cases; instead, use descriptive labels that will vividly paint the scene and that readily can be applied to the client's scenario: e.g., athlete, celebrity, company, employer, vehicle owner, passenger, pilot, etc.

☑ When transitioning to the next RE, insert a new rule statement *or* use a transitional phrase like "Similarly, in *Ortega v. Edmonds* . . ." or "In contrast, in *Bartholemew v. Colmans* . . ."

☑ Attach signal cites to the end of a prior RE; never interrupt an RE with a signal cite of a new case.

☑ Choose appropriate signals and properly cite the case (use a full cite if it is the first time citing the case in the brief; short-cite if the case has been cited previously).

☑ Craft helpful parentheticals starting with an *-ing* word ("holding that . . ."), and capture the facts, holding, and rationale of the case in fewer than four lines of text.

☑ Use *ethos*, informing the court of mandatory precedent and properly citing to sources of law.

Enhancing the RA Section of an Argument in a Brief

☑ Transition from the RE section of the argument to the RA by inserting a paragraph break and a thesis sentence foreshadowing the conclusion on the legal issue that is the focus of the IREAC or CREAC.

☑ Write separate paragraphs analyzing each distinct component of the rule (element, factor, or definition):
  o Draft each paragraph with an introduction, a middle, and a mini-conclusion on the particular component of the rule.
  o Use rule-based reasoning.
  o Use analogical reasoning (comparing and contrasting the client facts to/with the case law).
  o Use policy-based reasoning (if applicable).

☑ Make sure that the logic of the RA section builds toward the ultimate conclusion favoring the client:
  o Show that all rule elements are met (if your client seeks a result governed by a rule with a checklist of required elements).
  o Show that at least one rule element fails (if your client seeks a result in which the opposing party cannot satisfy all prongs of a governing rule with a checklist of required elements).
  o Show that the majority of factors favor a finding that the rule is satisfied (if your client seeks a result governed by a rule with a balancing test of factors).
  o Show that the majority of factors favor a finding that the rule is *not* satisfied (if your client seeks a result in which the opposing party cannot satisfy a governing rule with a balancing test of factors).

☑ Inject *pathos* into the factual descriptions and RA portion of the argument, forging an emotional connection between the reader and the client's position.

☑ Reinforce *ethos* by balancing zealous representation of the client with a respectful tone and language, integrity, and professionalism.

☑ Reiterate the theme of the case where appropriate.

☑ Include a mini-conclusion on the legal issue that is the subject of the IREAC or CREAC.

Repeat the foregoing steps if the brief involves more than one IREAC or CREAC.

☑ Consider drafting persuasive informative headings to distinguish among multiple IREAC or CREAC sections.

Writing the Brief's Conclusion

☑ At the tail end of the brief (after the IREAC or CREAC, or the last of multiple IREACs or CREACs), reiterate the following:
  o The substantive decision or decisions that you want the court to make on the legal issue or issues
  o Why the opposing party's argument/contention fails (being succinct)
  o The procedural action that should follow (typically an Order denying the opposing party's motion, enforcing the action sought: e.g., compelling production of documents, excluding a witness or piece of

evidence from trial, dismissing the case, entering summary judgment or partial summary judgment, etc.)
- o If appropriate under a statute, an applicable rule, or a contract provision, a statement of whether you are requesting an award of attorneys' fees and costs associated with opposing the motion
- o A statement of whether any additional relief is proper
- ☑ Reiterate the theme of the case.

Creating the Signature Block

- ☑ Date the brief.
- ☑ Add the phrase, "Respectfully submitted."
- ☑ Add a line for a signature.
- ☑ State the signing attorney's name, law office name, law office address, phone number, and e-mail address.
- ☑ Add a designation ("Counsel for Plaintiff" or "Counsel for Defendant").

Crafting the Caption and Title

- ☑ Use the same case caption that appeared on the complaint and answer:
  - o Court name
  - o Party names
  - o Designation as plaintiff and defendant (plus any additional parties joined to the case)
  - o Docket number assigned by the clerk
- ☑ Insert the proper title of the brief and which party is filing it (e.g., "Plaintiff's Brief in Opposition to Defendant's Motion to Compel Production of Documents," "Defendant's Brief in Opposition to Plaintiff's Motion for Summary Judgment," etc.).
- ☑ If appropriate under the court rules, state "Oral argument requested" beneath the docket number in the caption.

Drafting the Introduction

- ☑ First sentence: State the name of the party filing the brief, the type of brief, and, if applicable, the procedural rule authorizing the filing of the brief (court rule, judge's case management order, etc.).
- ☑ Establish appropriate abbreviations for the parties' names that will be used throughout the brief.
- ☑ Include a theme sentence (this can be the second or third sentence) to set the brief in the context of the overall case and align the reader with the client's point of view.

☑ State the legal issue or issues that are the focus of the brief (this can be the second or third sentence—swapped with the theme sentence—this is the judgment call of the brief writer).

☑ Describe the overall governing rule or rules.

☑ State the three to five most persuasive reasons why the opposing party's arguments fail and why the responding party's position is the sound one.

☑ Identify the exact result sought on the substantive legal issue or issues.

☑ State the procedural action requested of the court.

Writing the Statement of Facts

☑ Tell the client's story.

☑ Identify the key players, any relevant tangible physical items, and events—chronologically (to enhance *logos*).

☑ Engage the reader's attention by using *pathos*—describing the facts as vividly as possible (use strong nouns and active verbs).

☑ Establish *ethos* by including all legally significant facts.

☑ Handle any weak facts emphasized in the opposing party's brief by explaining them appropriately and ethically (placing them in context with stronger facts).

☑ Identify any favorable key facts omitted in the opposing party's brief.

☑ Correct any misstatements of facts in the opposing party's brief.

☑ Cross-check the statement of facts against the client facts described in the RAs and make sure that all client facts relied upon in the RAs are included in the statement of facts.

☑ Cite to the record sources of the facts (if appropriate or required by the rules, labeling the sources with exhibit numbers if they will be attached to the brief).

Inserting Smooth Transitions

☑ Insert standard headings within the body of the brief: introduction, statement of facts, argument, conclusion (with Roman numerals, and the text bolded or underlined, with only initial letters of each word capitalized).

☑ If appropriate for the length and complexity of the brief, consider crafting persuasive and informative subheadings for the argument section of the brief, to use as signposts or billboards to signal to the reader shifts between multiple issues or analyses of sequential rule components.

☑ Insert transitions between separate REs.

☑ Insert a transition between the RE section of an IREAC or CREAC arc and the RA, using a thesis sentence to assert the ultimate conclusion on the issue or component of the rule being discussed.

☑ Insert transitions between RA paragraphs, using mini-conclusions at the end of one paragraph and strong thesis sentences at the beginning of the next paragraph.

Checking for Theme Reiteration

☑ Introduce the theme in the brief's introduction.

☑ Weave the theme into the statement of facts, using *pathos* and descriptive vivid language to describe the client's story.

☑ Reiterate the theme in the RE and RA sections of the argument.

☑ Reprise the theme in the conclusion.

Preparing Attachments

☑ If allowed or required under the court rules, prepare any attachments of record sources relied upon in the statement of facts, labeling them Exhibit 1, Exhibit 2, etc. or Attachment A, Attachment B, etc.

☑ Prepare a Certificate of Service to show how the brief is served on opposing counsel.

☑ Draft a proposed order if allowed or required under the rules.

Twelve-Step Editing and Proofreading Process

☑ Check the applicable court rules to ensure that all required substantive components are included in the brief.

☑ Review the brief as a whole for IREAC or CREAC logic.

☑ Review each stand-alone section of the brief separately.

☑ Read the entire brief for theme and persuasion.

☑ Review each paragraph of the brief.

☑ Review each sentence of the brief.

☑ Review the brief for professionalism in tone.

☑ Proofread on a word-by-word basis, ideally backward to forward.

☑ Check the citations.

☑ Check for formatting errors.

☑ Check for consistency in terminology in references to party names, the court, the motion, etc.

☑ Perform a final check of the document against the court's submission rules:
   o Page- or word-count limits
   o Margins
   o Line spacing
   o Font
   o Handling of footnotes

o Accompanying documents or exhibits
o Procedure for filing the brief with the court

Filing and Serving

☑ Follow the court's rules in filing the brief with the clerk, including required number of copies, electronic versus hard-copy filing, etc.

☑ Serve the brief on opposing counsel, completing a Certificate of Service.

Chapter 31
Drafting an Appellate Brief

After the court enters a final judgment in a case—after either a jury verdict or a bench trial—the parties may have the right to appeal. An appeal may be granted as a matter of right, or a party may need to seek permission from the court to appeal the judgment. Either way, a notice of appeal must be filed within the deadline established in the court rules.

On occasion, a party may be able to appeal a court's decision in the middle of, rather than at the end of, a case. This is called an *interlocutory appeal*. In federal court, according to 28 U.S.C. § 1292(b):

> When a district judge, in making in a civil action an order not otherwise appealable under this section, shall be of the opinion that such order involves a *controlling question of law* as to which there is *substantial ground for difference of opinion* and that an immediate appeal from the order may *materially advance the ultimate termination of the litigation*, he shall so state in writing in such order. The Court of Appeals which would have jurisdiction of an appeal of such action may thereupon, in its discretion, permit an appeal to be taken from such order, if application is made to it within ten days after the entry of the order. [Emphasis added]

Thus, to obtain an interlocutory appeal from a decision of the trial court, three criteria must be established: (1) the court's order must involve a controlling question of law; (2) there must be a substantial ground for difference of opinion on the controlling question of law; and (3) an immediate appeal might materially advance the ultimate termination of the litigation.

Whether the appeal is interlocutory or occurs after final judgment, a party must comply with the court-imposed deadlines for filing the notice of appeal. Once the appellate court accepts jurisdiction, the appellate rules establish the timeline for filing initial briefs, responsive briefs, and reply briefs and the date of oral argument, if requested and allowed. An appeal does not involve a retrial of the case; lawyers do not present witnesses or exhibits in the courtroom. An appeal is reviewed by a panel of judges, who read the parties' briefs and possibly hear oral argument. Thus, persuasive legal writing is of the utmost importance in the appellate process.

The tasks involved in writing appellate briefs are very similar to those regarding trial-level briefs discussed in Chapters 29 and 30, with three exceptions: (1) appellate court rules require legal writers to include a few extra substantive sections in appellate briefs that are not required in trial-level briefs; (2) the appellate brief writer must understand, research, and apply the appropriate "standard of review"; and (3) the appellate brief writer must prepare and attach the trial court record, including trial transcripts, exhibits, motions, trial-level briefs, and court orders.

Substantive Sections of an Appellate Brief That Differ from a Trial-Level Brief

Once a party files a notice of appeal and the appellate court accepts jurisdiction, the first step in the appealing party's brief-writing process is to check the court rules for (1) the deadline to file the initial brief, and (2) a list of the required substantive components of the initial brief. Many courts of appeal require substantive components that differ from a trial brief, and if a filing party omits any of the required parts, the appellate brief could be rejected. Let's consider a few examples.

At the state level, New York's Appellate Division, First Department, requires brief writers to include the following sections in an appellate brief:

- An index or table of contents stating the headings of the points asserted in the brief, indicating the pages of the brief where the headings are found
- A table of cases (alphabetically arranged), statutes, and other authorities, indicating the pages of the brief where the sources of law are cited
- A concise statement, not exceeding two pages, of the legal questions involved in the appeal, without names, dates, amounts, or particulars; each question must be numbered, set forth separately, and followed immediately by the answer (if any) to the question by the lower court from which the appeal is taken
- A concise statement of the nature of the case and of the facts necessary to determine the legal questions involved, with supporting references to pages in the record or the appendix
- The appellant's argument, divided into points by appropriate headings distinctively printed

Similarly, Rule 16 of the Massachusetts Rules of Appellate Procedure requires the appealing party to include the following substantive sections in an appellate brief:

- A table of contents, with page references
- A table of cases (alphabetically arranged), statutes, and other authorities cited, with references to the pages of the brief where the sources of law are cited
- A statement of the issues presented for appellate review
- A statement of the case, indicating briefly the nature of the case, the course of proceedings, and its disposition in the lower court
- A statement of the facts relevant to the legal issues presented for review, with appropriate references to the trial record
- The argument, containing the appellant's contentions on the legal issues presented, and the reasons therefor, with citations to the authorities, statutes, and parts of the record relied on, with the following parameters:
  - In a brief with more than 24 pages of argument, the brief-writer also must include a short summary of argument:
    - Using suitable paragraphs
    - Containing page references to later material in the brief dealing with the same subject matter
    - Condensing the argument actually made in the body of the brief and not merely repeating the headings in the argument
- Finally, a short conclusion stating the precise relief sought

In federal appellate courts, Rule 28 of the Federal Rules of Appellate Procedure requires brief writers to include the following substantive components:

- A corporate disclosure statement, if applicable (to ensure that none of the presiding justices has any conflicts of interest with any corporate parties)
- A table of contents, with page references
- A table of authorities—cases (alphabetically arranged), statutes, and other authorities—with references to the pages of the brief where the sources of law are cited
- A jurisdictional statement, including:
  - The basis for the district court's subject matter jurisdiction, with citations to applicable statutory provisions and stating relevant facts establishing jurisdiction
  - The basis for the court of appeals' jurisdiction, with citations to applicable statutory provisions and stating relevant facts establishing jurisdiction
  - The filing dates establishing the timeliness of the appeal or petition for review
  - An assertion that the appeal is from a final order or judgment that disposes of all parties' claims or information establishing the court of appeals' jurisdiction on some other basis

- A statement of the legal issues presented for review
- A concise statement of the case, which:
  - o Sets out the facts relevant to the issues submitted for review
  - o Describes the relevant procedural history
  - o Identifies the rulings presented for review
  - o Includes appropriate references to the record
- A summary of the argument, containing a succinct, clear, and accurate statement of the arguments made in the body of the brief and not merely repeating the argument headings
- The argument, containing:
  - o The appellant's contentions and the reasons for them, with citations to the authorities and parts of the record on which the appellant relies
  - o For each issue, a concise statement of the applicable standard of review (which may appear in the discussion of the issue or under a separate heading placed before the discussion of the issue)
- A short conclusion stating the precise relief sought
- A certificate of compliance affirming that the brief complies with the type-volume limitation (i.e., page- or word-count limits)

As the foregoing rules indicate, appellate briefs can differ from trial briefs in the requirement that they include a table of contents, a table of authorities, jurisdictional statements, a separate section describing the legal issues or questions involved in the appeal, a statement of the case (similar to the statement of the facts in a trial brief, but with citations to the record plus a summary of the procedural history of the case), summary of the argument, and a description of the applicable standards of review.

Table of Contents

Unless a trial-level brief is lengthy—like a brief in support of a motion to dismiss or a motion for summary judgment—it likely would not require a table of contents. Appellate briefs inevitably are long documents and thus, as indicated from the rules cited above, require a table of contents. Appellate brief writers craft the table of contents *after* writing the entire brief and conducting the 12-step editing and proofreading process discussed in Chapter 29; the wording of the headings within the table of contents needs to reflect the actual final wording of the headings in the brief. The phrasing of headings and the brief's page numbering can change repeatedly throughout the various steps of the editing process, so it is wise to wait until the tail end of the proofreading process to construct the final table of contents. All major and minor brief headings, numbered or lettered accordingly, should be included in the table of contents. The page numbers of the table of contents and table of authorities themselves should appear in lowercase Roman numerals (i, ii, iii, etc.).

Table of Authorities

In an appellate brief, the table of authorities lists the statutes, regulations, cases, and any other legal authorities divided into the foregoing categories (with headings) and then organized alphabetically within each category. The citations for statutes, regulations, and cases should be in full citation form (not short-cites). The table of authorities cross-references the page numbers in the appellate brief where each particular source of legal authority is found. For example, if a case is full-cited for the first time on page 3, then short-cited on pages 4, 9, and 15, the table of authorities should include page references to 3, 4, 9, and 15 for that case.

Jurisdictional Statement (If Required)

As indicated by Rule 28 of the Federal Rules of Appellate Procedure above, some appellate courts require brief writers to include a jurisdictional statement. Rule 28 specifically describes the content of this required statement in federal appellate courts. First, the brief writer must describe the basis for the district (trial) court's subject matter jurisdiction. For example, if the trial court exercised diversity jurisdiction over the lawsuit, the appellate brief writer would cite to the federal diversity jurisdiction statute, 28 U.S.C. § 1332, explaining that the amount in controversy in the case exceeds $75,000, exclusive of interest and costs, and the lawsuit is between citizens of different states (identifying the citizenships of the various parties). Next, the brief writer would indicate the basis for the court of appeals' jurisdiction; for example, if the trial took place in the United States District Court for the Southern District of New York, the United States Court of Appeals for the Second Circuit has jurisdiction over the appeal. Further, the brief writer would establish the timeliness of the appeal, stating the date that the Notice of Appeal was filed and indicating that the filing occurred within the requisite number of days after the entry of the final order or judgment. If the appeal is based on an order or judgment that was not final (i.e., an interlocutory appeal), the brief writer needs to assert the basis of the appellate court's jurisdiction over the interlocutory appeal (e.g., 28 U.S.C. § 1292 (the federal statute authorizing interlocutory appeals under appropriate circumstances)).

Statement of the Issues or Questions Involved in an Appeal

One of the most critical components of an appellate brief—and an item that is not required in a trial-level brief—is a separate statement of the legal issues or questions presented in the appeal. As the First Department of New York's Appellate Division's rules demonstrate, courts may require the issues or questions to be presented in a particular format; as discussed above, the First Department requires the questions to be numbered, followed by the trial court's answer (if any) to each question, with a page limit of two pages. Other courts are less precise in their preferred formatting. The function of the statement of the issues is to identify each distinct legal issue that the party requests the appellate court to decide, framing the issue in the light most favorable to the client. The art of crafting an issue statement or "question presented" involves clearly defining the legal issue while foreshadowing the result sought by the appealing party. Lawyers use various grammatical formats when constructing issue statements or questions presented; the two most popular are (1) question format and (2) a statement starting with the word "whether." Consider these two alternate examples:

- Is a property owner considered an "out-of-possession" landowner, immune from liability for injuries to third-party visitors, when the landowner did not create a defective condition on its land, bore no contractual responsibility to maintain or repair the premises, and relinquished control of the land to a tenant or management company?
- Whether a property owner is considered an "out-of-possession" landowner, immune from liability for injuries to third-party visitors, when the landowner did not create a defective condition on its land, bore no contractual responsibility to maintain or repair the premises, and relinquished control of the land to a tenant or management company.

Notice how both options (1) state the legal issue (whether the property owner should be deemed an "out-of-possession" landowner), (2) incorporate the applicable rule (which has four elements: creation, maintenance, repair, and control), and (3) subtly imply the outcome sought (that since none of the four elements are satisfied, the appellant landowner should prevail; the appellate court should overturn the lower court's decision that the landowner was not "out-of-possession" and should reverse the judgment of liability for injuries to a person visiting the property). Consider these two additional alternate examples of issue statements and questions presented:

- Was an airline's decision to remove a passenger from a flight arbitrary and capricious and, therefore, discriminatory when the passenger ignored safety instructions, refused to stow his carry-on luggage, entered the first class cabin without permission, and physically disrupted other travelers?
- Whether an airline's decision to remove a passenger from a flight was arbitrary and capricious and, therefore, discriminatory when the passenger ignored safety instructions, refused to stow his carry-on luggage, entered the first class cabin without permission, and physically disrupted other travelers.

Again, both of the foregoing examples (1) state the legal issue (whether the airline's decision was arbitrary and capricious and, therefore, discriminatory),

(2) incorporate the relevant factors of the applicable rule (ignoring safety instructions, refusing to follow airline rules, and disrupting other passengers), and (3) subtly imply the outcome sought (the factors weigh in favor of a finding that the airline properly removed the passenger from the flight and did not act in an arbitrary and capricious, or discriminatory, manner).

Statement of the Case

The statement of the case in an appellate brief is similar to the statement of facts in a trial-level brief but with a few additions and enhancements. A strong statement of the case persuasively relays the legally significant facts pertinent to the issues on appeal. The appellate brief writer uses *logos*, *pathos*, and *ethos* to chronologically convey the client's story in a logical manner, engage the appellate justices through vivid description and language choices to bring the story to life (invoking emotional resonance), and describe the facts accurately and thoroughly while still advocating the client's interests. The same general principles discussed in Chapter 29 regarding drafting a statement of facts in a trial-level brief apply to the fact-drafting process in an appellate brief. However, the appellate brief writer also must summarize the relevant procedural history of the case and its progression to the appeal stage. The lawyer should explain the claims and defenses asserted in the trial court pleadings, the result of the trial court's proceedings, the rulings of the trial court presented for review, and the timely filing of the notice of appeal. Finally, appellate brief writers are required to cite—throughout the statement of the case—to the record (i.e., the pleadings, the trial transcripts, the motions, the trial-level briefs, the lower court's orders, the exhibits, etc.). As explained below, part of the appellate brief writer's job is to assemble the complete trial court record for the appellate court, gathering pleadings, transcripts, motions, trial-level briefs, exhibits, and orders and then organizing them, paginating them, and appending them to the appellate brief. Throughout the statement of the case, appellate brief writers cite to the pages of the record or appendix using notations like "R-65" or "A-78." Further guidance on preparing the record is included later in this chapter.

Summary of the Argument (If Required)

Some appellate courts also require a summary of the argument. For example, as noted above, Rule 16 of the Massachusetts Rules of Appellate Procedure states that in a brief with more than 24 pages of argument, the brief writer must include a short summary of argument "suitably paragraphed with page references to later material in the brief dealing with the same subject matter." The summary "should be a condensation of the argument actually made in the body of the brief, and not a mere repetition of the headings under which the argument is arranged." Likewise, Rule 28 of the Federal Rules of Appellate Procedure requires "a summary of the argument, which must contain a succinct, clear, and accurate statement of the arguments made in the body of the brief, and which must not merely repeat the argument headings."

The summary of the argument in an appellate brief can mirror the structure of the introduction in a trial-level brief described in Chapter 29:

- Identify which party is filing the appeal.
- Invoke a theme and describe the factual nature or subject matter of the case.
- Clearly identify the legal issue or issues decided in the lower court on which the party seeks appellate review.
- Summarize the rule framework for each issue.
- State the reasons why the party submitting the brief should prevail on each issue.
- Request a specific result (e.g., reversal of the lower court's decision on each issue).

The summary of the argument should be concise yet persuasive, following a pattern for each legal issue: issue, rule, convincing reasons why the party should prevail, and finally the specific result sought. The formula can be repeated in separate paragraphs for each issue pending on appeal. Depending on the length of the argument section of the brief, appellate brief writers should aspire to limit the summary to a page or two at most.

Standards of Review

The goal of an appellate brief is to convince the appellate justices to correct an error (or multiple errors) made in the lower court proceedings—either a factual conclusion, a decision on an issue of law, an application of the law to the party's facts, or a resulting procedural ruling. As noted in Chapters 22 and 28, because the trial court already spent days, weeks, or months adjudging the parties' conflict, it would be a waste of time and judicial resources for the appellate court to re-hear the entire case from beginning to end. Thus, appellate review of a case honors the concept of "deference" to the lower court. *Deference* is the appropriate degree of respect that an appellate court must give to a decision of the lower court. As noted in Chapters 22 and 28, our judicial system is, in part, based on the concept that trial courts are in the best position to judge the *facts* of a case; the trial judge is present in the courtroom hearing witness testimony and observing the tangible pieces of evidence, engaging with the human beings and physical documents. Thus, appellate courts afford great deference to the lower court on issues of *fact*. However, one of the roles of appellate courts is to promote consistency in the application of rules of law for the purpose of establishing clear precedent within a jurisdiction. Accordingly, on issues of *law*, an appellate court might give less deference to the lower court and instead review a legal issue anew, taking a fresh look. An appellate brief writer must research and then provide the appellate court with the correct "standard of review" for the issues being appealed. Different standards of review might apply to distinct aspects of the appeal.

In the argument section of an appellate brief, the writer must relay to the court the appropriate standard of review for each legal issue on appeal and then perform the IREAC or CREAC analysis of that issue, showing how the application of the standard of review warrants the result requested. Ascertaining the correct standard of review for each distinct legal issue on appeal is an extra aspect of legal research that appellate brief writers must perform, in addition to the legal research on the applicable substantive rules and case law. The following few sections of this chapter describe some of the common standards of review addressed in appellate briefs.

The *De Novo* Standard of Review

If the appellate court is reviewing an aspect of a case with fresh eyes, this standard is called *de novo*, a Latin term meaning "from the new." Again, because part of the appellate court's role is to foster consistency and predictability in the application of rules within a jurisdiction, the court of appeals evaluates questions of law or mixed questions of law and fact anew, with a fresh perspective, and is not required to defer to the lower court's legal findings. The appellate justices consider the issue or issues of law raised in the parties' briefs, evaluate the applicable rules, and then answer the legal questions posed. If the appellate court must analyze a fact or set of facts to render a decision on the legal question, it refers to the case record, which is provided by the brief writer in a voluminous appendix (remember, in an appeal, lawyers cannot present witness testimony or exhibits other than those transcripts or documents contained in the appendix). Ultimately, if the appellate court determines that the lower court made an error in ruling on the question of law or mixed question of law and fact, the appellate court will overturn and reverse the lower court's decision.

Recall from your studies in the first semester of law school that the appellate court is higher in the judicial hierarchy than the trial courts in the same jurisdiction. Thus, a decision by the appellate court on an issue of law becomes mandatory authority that the trial courts must follow.

The Arbitrary and Capricious Standard of Review

Courts apply the "arbitrary and capricious" standard of review in appeals of decisions rendered by administrative agencies, such as the Federal Labor Relations Authority, U.S. Citizenship and Immigration Services, and Securities and Exchange Commission. According to the U.S. Supreme Court, "[t]he scope of review under the 'arbitrary and capricious' standard is narrow, and a court is not to substitute its judgment for that of the agency."[1] The Supreme Court explained the standard as follows:

> [W]e must "consider whether the decision was based on a consideration of the relevant factors and whether there has been a clear error of judgment." . . . Normally, an agency rule would be arbitrary and capricious if the agency has relied on factors which Congress has not intended it to consider, entirely failed to consider an important aspect of the problem, offered an explanation for its decision that runs counter to the evidence before the agency, or is so implausible that it could not be ascribed to a difference in view or the product of agency expertise. The reviewing court should not attempt itself to make up for such deficiencies: "We may not supply a reasoned basis for the agency's action that the agency itself has not given." . . . We will, however, "uphold a decision of less than ideal clarity if the agency's path may reasonably be discerned."[2]

In other words, the "arbitrary and capricious" standard binds an appellate court to uphold an agency decision unless the appellant can demonstrate a clear mistake in judgment. This is a difficult standard.

The Clearly Erroneous Standard of Review

Courts apply the "clearly erroneous" standard of review in appeals relating to a trial court's findings of *fact*—distinguished from decisions on questions of *law*, which are subject to the *de novo* standard described above. Under Fed. R. Civ. P. 52(a)(6), "[f]indings of fact, whether based on oral or other evidence, must not be set aside unless clearly erroneous, and the reviewing court must give due regard to the trial court's opportunity to judge the witnesses' credibility." Again, according to the Supreme Court, "[a] finding is 'clearly erroneous' when although there is evidence to support it, the reviewing [body] on the entire evidence is left with the definite and firm conviction that a mistake has been committed."[3] The clearly erroneous standard is "significantly deferential" to the lower court's findings of fact.[4]

The No Substantial Evidence Standard of Review

Appellate courts review a jury's findings of fact under the "no substantial evidence" standard. A court of appeals will not overturn a jury's verdict "unless

---

[1] *Motor Vehicle Manufacturers Association of the United States, Inc. v. State Farm Mutual Automobile Insurance Company*, 463 U.S. 29, 43 (1983).
[2] *Id.* (internal citation omitted).
[3] *Concrete Pipe and Products of California, Inc. v. Construction Laborers Pension Trust for Southern California*, 508 U.S. 602, 622 (1993).
[4] *Id.* at 623.

it is based upon a jury's findings of fact that are unsupported by substantial evidence."[5] In applying the substantial evidence standard to a jury's decision and assessing whether the factual determination was reasonable, the appellate court reviews the evidence presented at trial.[6]

Additionally, a party seeking to overturn certain administrative agency decisions may argue that the determination is not supported by substantial evidence. Commentators explain that the "arbitrary and capricious" standard described above applies to appellate review of *informal* agency actions, while the "no substantial evidence" standard governs review of *"formal* record-producing agency actions."[7] Courts have defined substantial evidence in this context as "such relevant evidence as a reasonable mind might accept as adequate to support a conclusion."[8]

The Abuse of Discretion Standard of Review

An appellate court reviews a trial court's decisions on matters such as the scope of discovery and the admissibility of evidence under an "abuse of discretion" standard. A trial court abuses its discretion "when it relies upon clearly erroneous findings of fact or when it improperly applies the law or uses an erroneous legal standard."[9]

The Argument Section of an Appellate Brief

The techniques for drafting the argument section of an appellate brief are very similar to those employed in drafting a trial-level brief, except that the brief writer must first assert the applicable standard of review for each issue and then weave the application of the standard into the IREAC or CREAC discussion. Appellate brief writers should follow the steps suggested in Chapter 29 for organizing the argument (with the addition of the standard of review):

- Identify the legal issues to be decided by the appellate court.
- Research the applicable standard of review for each issue.
- Research the rules governing each issue.

---

[5] *Baxter Healthcare Corporation and Utah Medical Products, Inc. v. Spectramed, Inc.*, 49 F.3d 1575, 1584 (Fed. Cir. 1995).
[6] *Quaker City Gear Works, Inc. v. Skil Corporation*, 747 F.2d 1446, 1455 (Fed. Cir. 1984).
[7] Matthew J. McGrath, *Convergence of the Substantial Evidence and Arbitrary and Capricious Standards of Review During Informal Rulemaking*, 54 Geo. Wash. L. Rev. 541 (May 1986) (emphasis added).
[8] *American Tower LP v. City of Huntsville*, 295 F.3d 1203, 1207 (11th Cir. 2002).
[9] *Crable v. Brown*, 124 F.3d 197, at *1 (6th Cir. 1997) (Unpublished).

- Decide if each legal issue warrants a single IREAC or CREAC or if a rule including multiple required elements or a range of factors merits more than one IREAC or CREAC.
- Choose case law to illustrate the rule in full Rule Explanations and select other cases to incorporate in signal or string cites plus explanatory parentheticals.
  o Make decisions about how to handle adverse precedent.
- Identify potential policy arguments.
- Choose the facts from the record to support the application of the rule components to the client facts.
- Determine the precise result sought for each issue.

After undertaking the foregoing steps to organize the brief, the appellate brief writer can employ the persuasive writing techniques described in Chapter 29 to craft the entire argument section, including informative headings and subheadings to distinguish among the different arguments and guide the appellate justices down a logical path toward the result sought. Within each mini-conclusion to a section of the argument devoted to a distinct issue, the brief writer should be sure to remind the court of the standard of review and why the result sought on that issue is appropriate.

The Appellate Record

The appellate court will neither re-hear witness testimony nor observe the live presentation of exhibits as the trial court did. Thus, appellate brief writers must undertake the time-consuming task of preparing the appellate record such that the justices have all the evidence and testimony collated and located in one convenient spot for their reference while reviewing the briefs. The party filing the initial appellate brief is responsible for gathering all the trial transcripts (certified by the court reporter), all parties' trial exhibits, and the pleadings, motions, trial-level briefs, and court orders, and assimilate them into well-organized chronological volumes. The record or appendix volumes are filed with the court and served on the opposing party along with the initial brief. The appellate record is paginated with consecutive numbered pages, like a book. Instead of citing to the individual trial or lower court documents, appellate brief writers cite to the particular page of the record or appendix, using notations like R-23 or A-65 to denote specific pages. An appellate record can be voluminous and take a substantial amount of time to prepare to ensure that it is complete and organized. Many lawyers enlist appellate service companies to assist with (1) collecting and collating transcripts, exhibits, pleadings, motions, trial-level briefs, and orders, (2) paginating the record, (3) printing and binding the requisite number of copies for filing with the court of appeals, and (4) serving the briefs and record volumes on opposing counsel.

Drafting Opposition and Reply Briefs in the Appellate Context

The appellate court sets the deadlines for the party responding to the appeal (often called the *appellee* or the *respondent*) to file an opposition brief, and for the appellant to file a reply brief. Rule 28 of the Federal Rules of Appellate Procedure indicates that, in federal court, the opposition brief must include the same substantive components as the initial brief, except that the responding party need not include the jurisdictional statement, the statement of the issues, the statement of the case, or the statement of the standard of review, unless the appellee is dissatisfied with the appellant's versions of those items.

The federal appellate rules require reply briefs to contain a table of contents and table of authorities, but there are no other substantive requirements. Lawyers representing appellants in state courts of appeals should check the court rules for instructions and requirements on submitting reply briefs. Reply briefs are much shorter than the initial and opposition briefs. Brief writers submitting opposition and reply briefs at the appellate level can follow the same substantive advice provided in Chapter 30 for outlining, researching, and drafting opposition and reply briefs.

* * *

A sample appellate brief is included as Appendix L.

Section 12

Persuasion Through Oral Argument

Chapter 32

Preparing for and Delivering an Oral Argument

Purpose of Oral Argument

Lawyers are not permitted to communicate with the judge presiding over a case in an *ex parte* manner—which means independently of the other party or parties in a case. The only scenario in which a lawyer may communicate orally with a judge about a case is when all parties are present or represented by counsel. A hearing on a motion or an appeal is an example of such a verbal exchange. Judges may decide a motion or an appeal strictly on the briefs submitted by the lawyers. Or judges or the parties may request oral argument. A party's request for oral argument is not always granted. A lawyer seeking oral argument on a motion or appeal should follow the court rules for requesting oral argument, which may require submission of a written statement of the reasons why argument beyond the briefs would be helpful to the court's resolution of the legal issue or issues pending.

An effective oral argument does not simply rehash the contentions in the briefs; rather, it narrows the focus of the lawyer's interaction with the judge to the key points supporting the party's position, the theme of the case, and any public policy reasons that reinforce the desired result. Judges use oral argument to test the strengths and weaknesses of the parties' positions so the written decisions issued by the court can withstand review by a higher court. In preparing for oral argument, lawyers pare down their legal and factual contentions into persuasive sound bites. Further, they anticipate questions from the trial judge or appellate panel of judges about the weaknesses of their clients' positions, crafting responses that will resolve any concerns that the judge or appellate panel may have about ruling in the party's favor.

Logistics of an Oral Argument in the Law School Setting

Most law school Legal Writing course curricula focused on persuasive writing culminate with an oral argument assignment. Students prepare a brief on a legal issue, or perhaps more than one issue, and then are paired against a student representing the opposing side of the issue or issues to argue for 10 or 15 minutes before a panel of judges. The arguments may take place in a classroom, a mock courtroom, or a school conference room. The judges often include the students' Legal Writing professor, other professors or law school administrators, members of the school's moot court or trial teams, and alumni.

At the scheduled argument time, the students enter the room and take their respective seats. When the judges are ready to proceed, the chief judge calls the first advocate to the podium. The student who is arguing first approaches the podium, and when the chief judge indicates that it is time to begin, the student commences the argument. The chief judge might "call the case" by stating the names of the parties. A bailiff (perhaps another law student) keeps track of the allotted time by holding up flashcards that count down the advocate's time remaining, with 2-minute or 1-minute warning signs near the end, and then a STOP sign when the advocate's time has expired. During the argument, judges interrupt the presentation with questions about the case law, the case theme, legally significant facts, the weaknesses of the party's position, and the strengths of the opponent's position. The student answers the judges' questions and, after each response, returns to the argument as smoothly as possible. The initial advocate may reserve 1 or 2 minutes of rebuttal time to respond to the opponent's arguments.

Once the initial argument is complete, the second student stands up and approaches the podium. The first student sits down and takes notes on the opponent's argument, culling out two or three points meriting a response in rebuttal. The second student progresses in the same manner as the first advocate, delivering the argument and responding to the judges' questions. The bailiff uses the flashcards to count down the time remaining. Once the second student's time has expired, the first student resumes the argument with the short period of time reserved for rebuttal, responding to two or three key points raised in the opponent's argument. The judges might ask questions during the rebuttal as well.

Once the rebuttal is complete, the argument is finished. The judges may give immediate feedback, or the Legal Writing professor may wait until later to comment.

Logistics of an Oral Argument in a Courtroom Setting

An oral argument in a trial or appellate court setting often is more formal than a law school setting. The lawyers arrive at the courthouse with enough time to navigate through any required security procedures (most courthouses have metal detectors, and some require visitors to check their cell phones) and find the correct courtroom where the arguments will convene. The trial judge or appellate panel might hear numerous arguments on a lengthy docket of cases on the same day. Other lawyers and clients likely will comprise the audience, and each pair of advocates may have to wait their turn to argue while many other cases run their course.

Eventually, the trial judge or chief justice of an appellate panel will call the particular case. The court will indicate how many minutes each side is allotted or requested for the argument, or may allow the advocates to propose a time duration within the boundaries of the rules. The lawyers proceed one at a time in delivering arguments at the podium or from counsel's table, and the judge or judges typically interrupt with questions. The trial judge or chief justice will stop each lawyer when the time allowed has expired, although each lawyer is expected to keep track of time as well. A judge may decide the legal issues contemporaneously, or the court may take the matter under advisement and deliver a written decision at a later date.

Substantive Preparation for Oral Argument

To prepare for oral argument, lawyers use their carefully crafted brief and the opponent's brief (and any reply brief) to outline the points to reinforce, anticipate the judges' questions, and review the applicable statutes and case law. Lawyers might draft three items when preparing for oral argument: (1) the argument outline, (2) a case law "prompt sheet," and (3) a judge's question "prompt sheet." All three documents should be printed in a larger-than-usual font, for ease in reading from a podium or counsel's table.

Drafting the Argument Outline

In drafting the argument outline, lawyers typically begin with a "road map" introduction with the following components:

- "May it please the court,[1] my name is _____ and I represent _____."
- "This case concerns _____." (*introduce the subject matter of the legal dispute and the party's case theme*)
- "The issues before the court here today are: _____."

---

[1] This introductory language may seem old-fashioned, but lawyers still use this phrasing in many courtrooms to introduce an oral argument.

- "[*Name of Party*] requests the court to find _____ because: [*insert the key three to five reasons why the party should prevail*]."

A lawyer might use the headings from her brief to extract the three to five key reasons why her client should prevail. A 10- or 15-minute argument is too short a period of time to reiterate all the points made in a lengthy brief. Thus, lawyers need to be choosy about the areas of focus for the argument. Attorneys highlight the three to five main rationales to support the result requested and then craft sound bites to support each contention. They might pinpoint a key precedent case or a policy reason why the argument makes sense and leads logically to the result sought. The IREAC or CREAC structure works just as well for oral argument as it does in organizing a brief; an oral advocate should identify the legal issue for the court, concisely state the applicable rule (and any required elements, range of factors, or definitions), briefly explain the rule (perhaps through an illustrative precedent case or two), apply the rule to the client's facts, and then assertively state the conclusion sought.

Attorneys plan arguments around the entire allotted 10- or 15-minute time slot, but they also should anticipate that the judges' questions may consume some of these minutes; therefore, parts of the argument may need to be condensed or omitted. When a lawyer notes that she is running out of time (perhaps with approximately 30 seconds remaining), she should transition quickly to her overall conclusion, reminding the court of the specific result sought and, if she has time, her case theme that supports the requested action.

Case Law Prompt Sheet

As indicated in Chapters 29, 30, and 31, in preparing initial, opposition, and reply briefs, lawyers often rely on and cite numerous precedent cases. Remembering all the facts, holdings, and rationales from a substantial number of judicial opinions can be challenging. Because judges may ask oral advocates specific questions about the cases, some lawyers prepare case law prompt sheets: listing the cases in alphabetical order (for easy accessibility) and summarizing the jurisdiction and year of the decision, a concise, bullet-point factual recitation, the court's holding on the key legal issue, and a succinct set of reasons underlying the court's decision. The keys to a useful case law prompt sheet are brevity and ease of reading. A lawyer delivering an argument at a podium does not have time or physical space to flip through reams of paper to locate the answer to a judge's question. Codifying the cases in alphabetical order allows a lawyer in the thick of an argument to glance down at the prompt sheet, readily locate the case, and relay the information sought by the judge in a smooth seamless manner.

A useful case law prompt sheet also identifies whether each case is favorable or adverse to the party; if the case is adverse, the lawyer can add a bullet point distinguishing the case from the client's matter on its facts or time in history.

Some lawyers color-code case law prompt sheets to differentiate favorable from adverse cases.

Judges' Questions Prompt Sheet

Well-prepared oral advocates anticipate the potential questions judges may ask about the weaknesses of the client's position, unfavorable case law or facts, or policy reasons supporting the opponent's position. Because oral argument scenarios can be intense or nerve-wracking, and it may be hard to remember coherent responses to all the possible questions that judges could ask, some lawyers prepare prompt sheets containing short labels for each anticipated question (like "*Nicholas* Case" or "Judicial Economy Argument" or "Slippery Slope Risk") and then bullet points of well-crafted logical responses. For example, when a judge interrupts the argument with a question about the Judicial Economy Argument, the lawyer can artfully scan the prompt sheet, locate the abbreviated label tied to that anticipated topic, quickly recall the key points to emphasize in answering the question, and then deliver the response.

Logistical Preparation for an Oral Argument

Even for the most prepared advocate, the oral argument experience can be intimidating, and this is definitely so for law students or lawyers who prefer quietly writing over engaging in a Socratic-style verbal exchange. In addition to the substantive preparatory tools suggested in the prior sections of this chapter, lawyers can take other steps to prepare logistically and mentally for the experience, with the goal of reducing stress and anxiety and allowing substance to shine. First, lawyers should find out in advance, if possible,[2] exactly where the argument will take place. In the law school context, the student should try to determine if the argument will convene in a classroom, in a mock courtroom, or in a school conference room. In the litigation context, the lawyer should identify the courtroom in which the argument will occur and take a field trip there to understand the logistics involved, such as parking, security procedures, and courtroom layout.

To quell the anxiety of a nervous advocate, it helps to know certain logistics and parameters in advance: Does the room have a podium? Are there counsel tables? Does the podium or table have a microphone? How big is the room? Is the lighting bright or dim? Is the room noisy? How far away from the judge or appellate panel do the advocates sit or stand? Where do the lawyers sit while awaiting their turn to speak? Who is the trial judge or who are the judges on

---

[2] Sometimes the oral argument location may not be determined until the last minute.

the appellate panel? In the law school context, are the judges students? Professors? Alumni? Will they be wearing robes? What are the judges' personalities? Who is the opposing lawyer, and what is his personality? Will anyone else be present (e.g., a bailiff)?

In the logistical preparation, lawyers evaluate the podium or the table from which they will deliver the argument, checking whether there is enough room on the reading platform for the three preparation documents: the argument outline, the case law prompt sheet, and the judges' question prompt sheet? Well-prepared advocates consider the best logistical manner to arrange these useful outlines on the lectern so they can be accessed without shuffling or other distraction. Some lawyers like to attach all three documents to the various sides of a manila folder for ease in maneuvering during the argument.

What Else to Bring to an Oral Argument

Other than the three preparation documents discussed earlier in this chapter, a lawyer should not bring substantive materials to the podium or counsel's table: no books, case law printouts (unless the cases are unpublished and the judge might ask for a copy), or factual documents (unless absolutely relevant to the argument). Typically, oral advocates have no time to consult written materials during the argument other than their outlines and prompt sheets; good advocates avoid shuffling papers while delivering the presentation and answering the judges' questions. The only other physical item that a lawyer should bring to the podium or counsel's table is a writing implement—one that does not click. When judges interrupt with questions, lawyers can subtly use a highlighter, a nonclicking pen, or a pencil to mark the place in the argument outline where they paused, to help them seamlessly return to the argument flow after answering the judge's question. A writing implement and a blank legal pad are also important when listening to the opponent's argument and mapping out two to three points meriting a response on rebuttal.

Rebuttal

If the initial advocate reserved time for rebuttal, he should takes notes while opposing counsel is speaking. Some nervous orators are so relieved when they finish the initial argument that they sit back down and accidentally tune out their opponents; other advocates return to their seats and revisit the ups and downs of their own argument instead of listening to their opponents and the questions from the bench. However, mindful advocates consciously strive to focus on their opponent's arguments and jot down two or three points meriting a response in rebuttal. The briefs that the parties exchanged in advance already will have signaled the strengths of the opponent's argument, so lawyers can prepare potential counterarguments to present in rebuttal, adjusting them in real time based on the opponent's live argument and the judge's questions.

To deliver the rebuttal, the advocate returns to the podium or stands at the counsel's table, waits for the signal from the bench to proceed, and then states: "Your Honor, there are two/three points I will address on rebuttal. First, ..." The rebuttal will be short—only a few minutes usually—so the lawyer should be mindful of the allotted time, make her points succinctly, answer any judge's questions assertively, and then conclude by reminding the court of the result sought.

Handling Challenging Aspects of an Oral Argument

If you are anxious about the oral argument experience, you are not alone. Many law students and even seasoned lawyers struggle with anxiety around the oral argument experience. Feelings of angst about oral advocacy are absolutely no indication of one's future success as a lawyer. Many lawyers initially hesitant about oral advocacy enjoy remarkable achievements in that arena once they tap into their authentic lawyer voices.[3]

The first step in preparing mentally for an oral argument is to remember that the actual speaking part of this experience will consume less than 10 or 15 minutes of your life. Those minutes will fly by. Judges will interrupt the argument flow to ask questions, and time will tick off the clock. Nervous advocates may benefit from considering the argument less of a performance and more of a dialogue with another human being: "Your Honor, yes, that is true because . . . ." "Your Honor, no, I respectfully disagree because . . . ." No conversation in real life transpires exactly according to script; that is alright. Rely on the *logos* of your argument outline, the *pathos* of the theme of the client's case, and the *ethos* of the effort exerted in writing the briefs, contemplating the cases, considering the parties' strengths and weaknesses, and preparing for the argument. Your sole mission is to do the best job you can in the 10 or 15 minutes allotted. Anticipate and embrace the imperfections. Be authentic and real. It will work.

Mind Going Blank

Many professors, mentors, and public speaking pundits urge, "Don't rely on your notes! The best speakers memorize!" That may be true for some, but when law students and novice attorneys are tackling their first oral argument experiences, notes are essential. When nerves intervene, there is nothing wrong with

---

[3] The author of this book has written two articles devoted specifically to this topic: *Empowering Law Students to Overcome Extreme Public Speaking Anxiety: Why "Just Be It" Works and "Just Do It" Doesn't*, 53 Duquesne Law Review 182 (Winter 2015); *The "Silent but Gifted" Law Student: Transforming Anxious Public Speakers into Well-Rounded Advocates*, 18 Leg. Writing 291 (2012).

relying on the argument outline and prompt sheets to keep yourself talking. That is exactly why you wrote these items down. If you wrote them down, they are already phrased perfectly.

If anxiety begins to rattle you as you take your place at the podium and your mind goes blank, take a deep breath, glance down and read the first line of your road map introduction, "May it please the court, my name is . . . ." Even if you are continuing to read, look up periodically, make eye contact with the judges, and continue. Slow down, breathe, and keep going. You can deliver a masterful oral argument even by referring to your notes if you breathe, remain calm, keep talking, make eye contact, and inject the appropriate level of passion into the delivery.

Periodic Stumbles

Many oral advocates trip on words. It happens. Sometimes they forget their next thought. It does not matter. The goal is to keep going. Remember that, as noted above, a real conversation or dialogue is not a perfectly delivered script. Be authentic. If you trip over your words or misstate a phrase, pause, take a breath, and start the sentence again.

Difficult Questions from the Judges

Judges are going to interrupt every advocate at some point. Some might do it nicely, and others will do it in a manner that might feel challenging. That's fine. Instead of worrying about the tone of the judges' questions, embrace their substance; you planned for this. You created your judges' questions prompt sheet. Use it.

Occasionally, and inevitably, a judge might ask you a question that you do not understand or to which you do not know the answer. There are several options in such a circumstance. If you do not understand the question, it could simply be because it is inartfully phrased; you could respond, "I'm sorry, Your Honor, I'm not sure I understand the question. Could you please repeat it?" A nice judge likely will rephrase it using different language that hopefully you will understand or will break a compound question into parts. If the judge for some reason does not rephrase the question, or if you do not know the answer, use your case "themes." Try to link some aspect of the question—a legal term, phrase, rule, case, or policy—to your client's theme and say, "Your Honor, I believe you are focusing on X. That is a key point because . . . [*insert discussion of the theme of your case*]." If the judge is not satisfied by your answer, she will ask another question. Do your best and keep going. After you answer a question to the best of your ability, do not wait for approval to move onward to a new point in your argument. Return to where you left off in your argument outline, and keep pushing forward. Keep an eye on the timekeeper (if any) or the clock, and try to hit all your key points before time runs out.

Pausing to Think

There is nothing wrong with pausing to collect your thoughts before transitioning to a new point or thinking before you respond to a judge's question. Taking a couple of seconds to craft a coherent response is perfectly fine; in fact, that will give your brain the space to process the advance preparatory work you included in your case law or judges' questions prompt sheet and retrieve the key information that can fuel your riposte.

Ending the Argument

Once the arguments have concluded, in the law school context, the judges may give immediate feedback, although the Legal Writing professor may reserve detailed evaluative comments until he has had time to reflect on his notes. In the courtroom context, the judge may rule immediately on the legal issue, or she might indicate that she will issue a written decision at a later date. Either way, at the conclusion of the argument, say thank you. Thank the judge or appellate panel and shake your opposing counsel's hand. You did it.

Other Oral Argument Tips

- Adopt a balanced physical stance at the podium or counsel's table. Avoid crossing your legs and arms, leaning sideways, or shifting your weight too often. A balanced stance will help you breathe calmly, think clearly, and avoid distracting the judges.
- Avoid pen-clicking or twirling.
- Try to control saying "um" and "uh" during your speech. (Many advocates who struggle with these speech habits videotape practice arguments to notice how often and when these words appear. Others envision their sentences being printed on a transcript as they say them aloud, to catch the onset of repetitive words or phrases and begin to edit this language out of their speech.)
- Refer to the judge as "Your Honor": "Yes, Your Honor." "No, Your Honor."
- Refer to your opponent as "Counsel for Plaintiff" or "Counsel for Defendant" or "Counsel for Appellant" or "Counsel for Respondent," as appropriate.

- Never interrupt a judge. Even if the judge interrupts you, stop speaking immediately. Let the judge ask the question, and then when the judge stops talking, you may speak.
- Never ask for permission to continue with the argument after answering a judge's question. Do not ask, "Did I answer your question?" or "May I continue?" Simply transition back into your argument. If the judge has a follow-up question, he will ask it.
- If a judge asks a question, do the best you can to answer it, right then. Do not say, "Your Honor, I'll get to that later." If you do not understand the question, say "Your Honor, I'm not sure I understand the question. Will you please repeat it?" If the judge asks the same question or you do not know the answer to the question, try to tie your answer to the theme of the case.
- When your allotted time expires, stop your argument. Stop. You may respectfully ask, "You Honor, I see that my time is up. May I briefly conclude?" If the judge says yes, leap immediately to your conclusion, concisely reiterate the result you seek, and if time, your case theme. Then stop, say thank you, and sit down. If the judge says no, say thank you and sit down.
- Always be respectful to the judge or appellate panel, and opposing counsel, and the bailiff. Do not be sarcastic, crack jokes, roll your eyes, or become antagonistic. Engage in a calm, intellectual dialogue.
- Be prepared. Prepare enough materials for the entire allotted time period—in the event that the judge or appellate panel does not ask many questions—but be flexible and ready to adjust your argument to hit your key points even if the judge or appellate panel occupies your time with a barrage of questions.
- Dress professionally.
- Be on time. (Actually, be early.)
- Say thank you, to everyone.

Section 13

Drafting Persuasive Mediation/Arbitration Papers

Chapter 33
What Is Mediation?

Sometimes parties seek to settle or resolve a disagreement or a legal dispute before, or instead of, resorting to litigation, through alternative dispute resolution (ADR) measures, including such options as mediation or arbitration. Some courts mandate mediation before a trial. In a mediation, the parties engage the services of a neutral party, called a *mediator*. Often the parties select a mediator who has significant experience in the particular industry related to the parties' conflict. The mediator does not necessarily have to be an attorney. There are various mediation services and organizations throughout the country, some tailored to specific types of disputes, such as family law issues, sports, construction, and other subject matter areas. If parties decide to mediate a dispute, they typically agree to share the costs of the mediator equally. Mediation costs may include the mediator's daily expenses, travel, and fees to reserve a meeting locale for the day, or several days, that the mediation takes place.

Once the parties select a mediator, the mediation coordinator usually sends a letter summarizing the parameters of the mediation, including the scheduled dates and times, the fees and costs, whether the mediator requests any written documentation from the parties in advance (such as corporate disclosure statements and the names of the parties with settlement authority who will attend the mediation), and whether any "mediation statement" (like a brief) must be submitted confidentially by each party to the mediator or whether the parties will exchange mediation statements.

If the parties desire, or the mediator requires, the mediation statements can remain confidential, and the parties will submit them only to the mediator, not to each other. Alternatively, the parties may agree to, or the mediator may require, the mutual exchange of mediation statements. Mediation statements, like briefs, persuade the mediator and the opposing party of the strengths of the submitting party's case and the likelihood of success at trial or arbitration, but also advise the mediator and the opposing party whether settlement is realistic or feasible.

When drafting a persuasive mediation statement, lawyers consider the audience and how the document will be used in the potential settlement of the dispute. To do so, it is important to understand how an actual mediation works.

On the scheduled mediation date, the two (or more) parties arrive at the mediation locale, often accompanied by their lawyers and at least one person with settlement authority. If parties participate in a full day of mediation but the representatives for one side lack settlement authority, the mediation can be a waste of time and money for everyone. A mediator often starts the day's session by having each party or their counsel present a short summary of their position, perhaps in a Microsoft PowerPoint slideshow. Then the mediator convenes "caucuses," meeting with each party individually in separate rooms, to suss out strengths, weaknesses, and areas of potential compromise. The mediator may bring the parties back together periodically throughout the day or may continue to volley back and forth between the parties, attempting to induce and facilitate compromises on various claims, demands for reimbursement of damages, or other requests for relief. With this logistical backdrop in mind, the mediation statement submitted to the mediator (and possibly the opposing party) before the mediation date should describe the following:

1. The factual background of the parties' relationship
2. The events giving rise to the dispute
3. The procedural status of the parties' dispute so far
4. Any settlement discussions to date
5. The parties' claims against one another, and defenses against one another's claims
6. Terms of any contract governing the parties' relationship
7. The rules of law governing the parties' claims and defenses
8. The submitting party's position on each claim and defense
9. A limited amount of case law supporting the submitting party's position (typically, mediators and opposing parties do not expect to see as much case law in a mediation statement as a judge would expect in a brief)
10. The damages or other remedies sought, with supporting documentation to substantiate damage amounts
11. Any counterarguments to the opposing party's anticipated assertions or positions
12. Any potential barriers to settlement (e.g., the opposing party's misunderstanding of the contract or the law, disagreement over financial terms, emotional considerations, personality conflicts, posturing, etc.)
13. Suggestions for possible resolution of the barriers to settlement

The last two components differentiate mediation statements from briefs filed in court; drafters can address nonlegal issues that stand in the way of conflict resolution and propose methods of eliminating these obstacles.

The mediation statement can be structured like a brief, but drafters of these documents have more leeway in organizational style than brief writers do. The mediator may suggest drafting guidelines, but there is no one standard way for drafting a mediation paper. As with any persuasive legal writing project, a good mediation paper clearly introduces the mediator to the parties, explains their relationship to one another, provides sufficient background facts, states the legal issues, identifies the correct governing rules, and then applies the rules to the facts, persuading the mediator (and the opposing party) of the strengths of the submitting party's case. The writer also reinforces the case theme throughout the document—overall balancing *logos*, *pathos*, and *ethos*.

In a confidential mediation statement submitted solely to the mediator, a party may reveal information, contentions, or arguments it would not necessarily disclose to the other party, perhaps even indicating potential areas or ranges of compromise to assist the mediator in finding neutral ground, in hopes of achieving a settlement. In contrast, if the parties are mutually exchanging mediation statements, each party likely only will focus on the strengths of its position, much like a typical brief. If the drafter anticipates that the decision maker for the opposing party is likely to read the mediation paper (and such decision maker is not a lawyer), the drafter should write the paper for both a legal and nonlegal audience—another difference between a brief filed with the court and a mediation statement (briefs are written primarily for a legal audience). Either way, a well-written mediation statement, combining *logos*, *pathos*, and *ethos*, will help the mediator understand the logic of the party's position, engage with the theme of the party's case, and trust in the integrity of the drafter of the document. To set a productive agenda for the mediation day, the drafter adopts a respectful tone, balancing the spirit of conflict resolution and compromise while still advancing the submitting party's interests. A sample mediation statement can be found in Appendix M.

Notably, Federal Rule of Evidence 408 protects from disclosure at trial settlement offers and certain statements made during settlement negotiations if the parties do not achieve a compromise. The rule reads:

> Evidence of the following is not admissible—on behalf of any party—either to prove or disprove the validity or amount of a disputed claim or to impeach by a prior inconsistent statement or a contradiction:
>
> **(1)** furnishing, promising, or offering—or accepting, promising to accept, or offering to accept—a valuable consideration in compromising or attempting to compromise the claim; and
> **(2)** conduct or a statement made during compromise negotiations about the claim—except when offered in a criminal case and when the negotiations related to a claim by a public office in the exercise of its regulatory, investigative, or enforcement authority.

Many state courts have similar evidentiary rules. Thus, settlement offers and statements made during mediation may be protected from disclosure later at trial if the mediation fails or a settlement falls through. Parties often include the following sentence in their mediation statements to preserve this protection: "This mediation statement is offered for the sole purpose of compromising or attempting to compromise this claim and shall not be admissible at trial to prove the validity, invalidity, or amount of the claim."

If the mediation results in a settlement, the parties write out the terms of the settlement while still in one another's presence—even in handwritten form if necessary—so there is no confusion, disagreement, misunderstanding, or later attempt to backpedal from the agreed-upon terms. Subsequently, the attorneys draft a formal settlement agreement, incorporating (1) the settlement terms, (2) timing requirements for payment, transfer of property, or other remedial action, (3) the consequences if one party breaches the settlement agreement, and (4) confidentiality considerations. The written document may also include any timing requirements for withdrawing or dismissing any pending lawsuit between the parties. A sample settlement agreement can be found in Appendix N.

Chapter 34
What Is Arbitration?

Another method of dispute resolution that presents an alternative to litigation is arbitration. In an arbitration, parties forego a judge or jury trial, instead agreeing to have their dispute resolved by a single arbitrator or a panel of three arbitrators. Arbitrators often are retired judges, attorneys, or individuals with substantial experience in the particular industry that is the subject of the parties' dispute. The parties mutually select a single arbitrator, or if they prefer a panel of three arbitrators, each party chooses one arbitrator and then the two arbitrators pick the third one. Parties often agree in advance on which side shall pay the initial filing fee and how the arbitrators' daily fees shall be paid, and then individual parties typically bear their own costs of arbitration, including attorneys' fees, expert and consultant expenses, and other costs. While many parties believe that arbitration is less costly than litigation, the arbitration process still involves (1) filing of a demand for arbitration, and responsive answers and counterclaims; (2) discovery, including exchange of documents and participation in taking and defending depositions; (3) submission of prehearing statements, like briefs; (4) hearings in which parties present witnesses and exhibits; and (5) possibly posthearing statements—all of which can be expensive. While there are fewer structural guidelines and less rigid requirements for how arbitration documents should be drafted (as compared to federal and state court rules on submission of pleadings, motions, and briefs), lawyers still must balance *logos*, *pathos*, and *ethos* to persuade the arbitrator or arbitrators, opposing counsel, and the other party or parties of the strengths of the client's case. Parties in an arbitration should follow the same guidelines provided in the earlier chapters of this book for drafting persuasive letters, pleadings, motions, and briefs.

After arbitration hearings conclude and the parties submit any posthearing statements, the arbitrator or arbitrators issue an award, which is usually final and binding on the parties, without any right to appeal.

Section 14

Persuasive Writing in the Transactional Context

Chapter 35
Persuasion in Transactional Lawyering

Outside the litigation arena, lawyers in the transactional context use persuasive writing techniques when communicating with opposing parties and counsel about proposed and agreed-upon contract terms, summarizing negotiated deal terms and unresolved issues, and drafting final contract language. The progression of a negotiated transaction might go as follows:

1. Parties express interest in engaging in a transaction with one another.
2. The principals of the parties agree on the general parameters of the deal, such as subject matter, timing, price, assumption of contractual risks, insurance, indemnity, dispute resolution procedures, etc.
3. Parties or their attorneys draft and exchange a deal term sheet.
4. The attorneys begin crafting the language of the formal written contract that will memorialize, administer, and enforce the terms of the deal.
5. One attorney creates the initial draft of the contract and sends it to opposing counsel for review.
6. Opposing counsel accepts non-objectionable language in the draft and redlines language the party will not accept, deleting disagreeable terms and inserting proposed alternative language.
7. The parties (or their attorneys) might conduct rounds of conference calls to negotiate terms and language remaining in dispute, or they may continue to exchange and circulate evolving redlined drafts.
8. The parties (or their attorneys) might pare down terms or language remaining in dispute by creating a side-by-side matrix summarizing both sides' positions.
9. The parties (or their attorneys) eventually resolve all contested language and arrive at a final version of the contract agreed upon by all parties.
10. The parties execute the contract with their signatures.

Transactional attorneys must balance *logos*, *pathos*, and *ethos* when drafting term sheets, preliminary contract language, evolving versions of the formal written agreement, side-by-side position matrices, and final executable contracts. Transactional lawyers use *logos* to establish the logic of their clients' positions on terms and contractual language, *pathos* to invoke themes such as fairness, equality, compromise, mutual agreement, and collaboration in transactional negotiation, and *ethos* to reinforce the integrity, honesty, dignity, and reliability of the negotiators. When summarizing agreed-upon terms, using *ethos*, attorneys must accurately portray the parties' agreements and concessions, or they risk jeopardizing the parties' negotiations or even the entire deal through a lack of trust by the opposing party. Also when categorizing areas of disagreement in a negotiation in, for example, a side-by-side matrix of the parties' divergent positions, lawyers must correctly capture the two sides' propositions.

The following is an example of a deal term sheet on a relatively simple construction transaction.

Term Sheet

The parties, OBX Beach Homes, Inc. ("Owner") and GKB Construction, LLC ("Contractor"), hereby agree on the following terms of their contract for construction of a hotel called Hotel Meyer to be located in Duck, North Carolina ("Construction Contract"):

- **Project Description:** 24-room boutique hotel with pool, spa, and restaurant
- **Scope of Services:** All construction and services required by the final plans and specifications (hereinafter "Design Documents"), including all labor, materials, equipment, and services to fulfill the Contractor's obligations, and all work necessary to provide a finished, functioning, and occupiable facility (hereinafter "Work")
- **Contract Price:** $11,326,170
- **Contract Time:** 14 months from the issuance of a Notice to Proceed by the Owner
- **Liquidated Damages for Delayed Completion:** $4000 per day of delay
- **Early Completion Bonus:** $2000 per day
- **Contract Form:** Guaranteed Maximum Price (GMP) including actual costs of the construction Work and a Contractor Fee of 5% of the costs of the Work
- **Insurance:** Contractor-Provided (included as a cost of the Work)
- **Form of Disputes Resolution:** Mandatory mediation prior to litigation
- **Choice of Law:** North Carolina
- **Choice of Forum:** Federal Courts of North Carolina
- **Interest on Late Payment:** Prevailing Bank Rate

- **Lender:** KDH County Bank
- **Warranty:** Three Years

This Term Sheet is intended to be binding on the parties. The parties agree to negotiate in good faith and execute the full Construction Contract within thirty (30) days of the execution of this Term Sheet. The rights and obligations of the parties under this Term Sheet shall terminate upon the execution of the full Construction Contract.

Date: _____

By:

_____   _____
OWNER (Signature)   CONTRACTOR (Signature)

_____   _____
(Printed name and title)   (Printed name and title)

Contract Drafts

Lawyers often "redline" contract drafts using a word processing feature called "Track Changes," which shows, in contrasting colors, deletions and additions to text. Tracking editorial changes is the most transparent way for all parties to observe the "real time" evolution of a negotiated agreement. Lawyers might also insert margin comments to explain the *logos* or *pathos* behind a particular edit, to streamline negotiations and give context to a drafting change. The following is an example of redlined contract terms:

- The Contractor will commence the Work promptly following ~~on~~ the date established in a notice to proceed from Owner (the "Notice to Proceed"). Owner shall issue ~~a~~ the Notice to Proceed ~~within__days of the Effective Date~~ on or before April 9, 2018.
- This Contract will be interpreted and construed in accordance with the laws of the ~~state in which the Project is located~~ State of North Carolina. The parties expressly agree that litigation can only be brought in a court of competent jurisdiction located in the ~~jurisdiction in which the Project is located~~ State of North Carolina. The courts of the ~~jurisdiction in which the Project is located~~ State of North Carolina shall be the sole and exclusive forum for resolution of all claims, disputes, causes of action, or other legal matters between the parties, arising from or relating to this Agreement and the Project.

Negotiation Matrix

Sometimes the process of drafting and negotiating contract language can drag on for weeks or even months, with a continuous volley of dueling drafts back and forth between counsel, such that an evolving redlined document can contain so many colors of changed text, it resembles a Picasso painting. To cull down lingering drafting issues into a manageable format for lawyers and parties to discuss in a negotiation conference call or in a face-to-face meeting, one attorney might draft a side-by-side matrix, identifying the contract provisions remaining in dispute and accurately summarizing the parties' respective positions on each issue. The following is an example of a side-by-side position matrix for use in resolving disagreements during a contract negotiation:

Issue	Owner Position	Contractor Position
Article 3.6.2.2 (Insurance)	Contractor pays premiums	Owner pays premiums
Article 4.1 (Amount of Initial Installment of Preconstruction Fee)	25%	50%
Article 7.4 (Notice to Proceed)	Proposes the following language: "The Owner will issue a Notice to Proceed within 14 days of the Contract's execution date."	Proposes the following language: "The Owner shall issue Notice to Proceed by September 11, 2018. If the Owner fails to issue the Notice to Proceed by that date, the Contract Time shall be extended by Change Order."
Article 32 (Disputes Resolution)	• 21-day notice requirement for all claims or disputes (notice must be provided to the other party within 21 days of the event giving rise to the dispute, or the claim is waived) • Parties must give 30 days' notice of intent to file a lawsuit (so parties can attempt to resolve the dispute first)—no mediation required • Choice of Forum: Litigation in federal courts of North Carolina • Prevailing party in any litigation is entitled to recover its reasonable attorneys' fees and costs	• Modify notice requirement to 60 days after the event giving rise to the claim (Contractor reasonably needs more time) • Mediation must be a condition precedent to arbitration • Arbitration rather than litigation • No prevailing party clause

Negotiation Letter

As indicated above, parties and their lawyers often clash on the substance of particular contract terms or the appropriate manner in which to phrase them to enforce the parties' mutual intent. If disagreements persist, lawyers write letters or e-mails, setting forth the reasons why the attorney believes the other side's position is flawed and memorializing the evolution of negotiated terms. Consider this example of such a letter:

December 5, 2018

Daphne Rhodes, Esq.
Manning & Paul, LLP
648 Benning Way
Duck, North Carolina 27949

Re: OBX Beach Homes, Inc.; GKB Construction, LLC; Final Contract
     Terms

Dear Daphne:

As you are aware, our clients, OBX Beach Homes, Inc. ("Owner") and GKB Construction, LLC ("Contractor"), have been negotiating the substantive terms and language of the contract for construction of the Hotel Meyer project ("Contract) for three months now. We have made significant progress in overcoming business-related and legal hurdles and in moving the contract documents toward finalization and execution. However, your latest round of edits poses an unfortunate setback. After our two-hour conference call last week, we believed that the parties were in full agreement on the precise language of the warranty, indemnity, and disputes resolution provisions. We made every effort to capture the express wording that our respective clients verbalized on the conference call, and we inserted the precise phrasing into our last redlined agreement. However, your most recent edits backtrack from that agreed-upon phrasing and change the tenor of those important risk-shifting provisions to an extent to which my client cannot agree. To avoid unnecessary delays in finalizing the contract documents and the additional risk of jeopardizing the funding for the construction project due to a delayed loan closing, we request that you accept the edits to these three provisions made in our November 30, 2018, version of the agreement. We then will prepare a clean copy of the contract for the parties' final review and execution.

We look forward to your continued cooperation in finalizing this important agreement for our clients so that the loan may close and construction may commence on time. Please do not hesitate to contact me if you have any questions or concerns regarding the foregoing.

Very truly yours,

Krista McGinn

Krista McGinn

cc: GKB Construction, LLC

***

Overall, the keys to a successful contract negotiation, drafting process, and finalization are as follows:

1. Listening to clients to understand their strong preferences, potential deal breakers, and concerns
2. Listening to the opposing parties to ascertain their potential areas of compromise and points of contention
3. Taking the lead on drafting contract language that advances the clients' interests but also accurately reflects wording and phrasing mutually agreed upon by the parties
4. Being transparent in language additions and deletions during the editing process (using change-tracking word processing tools)
5. Carefully reading each new version of the contract circulated by opposing counsel, noting every wording change
6. Explaining clearly and logically—either in margin comments, an issues matrix, or a follow-up letter or e-mail—why a client disagrees with the opposing party's proposed term or phrasing, and offering alternate text to move the negotiations forward
7. Using *logos*, *pathos*, and *ethos* to advance the contract to finalization
8. Creating a clean proofread final version of the contract for the parties to sign

Appendices

Appendix A: Converting Benchslaps to Backslaps

Instilling Professional Accountability in New Legal Writers by Teaching and Reinforcing Context

Heidi K. Brown[*]

A search in published and unpublished court decisions for derivations of phrases like "poorly written brief" or "failure to follow court rules" yields an alarming multitude of case opinions in which judges admonish lawyers of all levels of experience for shoddy briefs or for flouting non-negotiable substantive and procedural rules. Legal bloggers have affectionately dubbed these public reprimands "benchslaps."[1] Lawfirm hiring partners often remark that many new lawyers do not yet know how to write well. However, it is not only novice attorneys who are being "benchslapped" by courts; experienced litigators are often the regrettable recipients of judges' rebukes.

Still, despite access to professors' comprehensive instruction, one-on-one writing conferences, and detailed grading rubrics, some law students submit written work product that lacks key substantive components and violates clear procedural and formatting requirements. Benchslap opinions demonstrate that, for many lawyers, a laissez-faire approach toward legal writing can unfortunately continue beyond law-school graduation. As the case law reveals, attorneys who have been practicing law for decades represent some of the more egregious offenders. This problem goes beyond fundamental writing ability; it signifies at least some level of disregard for court-imposed instructions and guidelines—an interesting phenomenon in a profession swathed in rules.

---

[*] Heidi K. Brown was formerly an Associate Professor of Law at New York Law School where she taught Evidence, Legal Practice, and Deposition Skills. She is the incoming Director of the Legal Writing Program, and an Associate Professor of Law, at Brooklyn Law School. Professor Brown graduated from the University of Virginia School of Law and subsequently practiced commercial litigation and arbitration of complex construction disputes for over fifteen years in Washington, D.C., and New York. She is the author of six editions of *Fundamentals of Federal Litigation*, a litigation manual for new lawyers based upon the Federal Rules of Civil Procedure and selected Federal Rules of Evidence, published by Thomson-West. This article was funded by a summer research grant generously provided by New York Law School. It was originally published in 11 J. Legal Comm. & Rhetoric 109 (2014). Only Section 1 of the article has been excerpted here.
[1] According to the Urban Dictionary, the term "benchslap" was popularized by David Lat of *Above the Law* (http://www.abovethelaw.com) when he was blogging for Underneath Their Robes. *See* Article III Groupie, Underneath Their Robes, *Bench-Slapped! Reinhardt v. O'Scannlain*, http://underneaththeirrobes .blogs.com/main/2004/06/greetings_welco.html (June 24, 2004, 1:07 p.m.); *see also* Josh Blackman, Josh Blackman's Blog, *The 8 Best Benchslaps of 2012*, http://joshblackman.com/blog/2012/12/18/the-8-best-benchslaps-of-2012/ (Dec. 18, 2012).

489

Of course, a notable percentage of law students graduates with a portfolio of "law-firm quality" memoranda and briefs, and has the writing aptitude necessary to represent a client well. However, this article focuses on strategies for reaching the cadre of law students and new lawyers who unfortunately are not embracing the challenge of legal writing in a way that will produce quality work product for legal employers and clients.

This article considers the threshold possibility that law students and new lawyers fall short in their written communications and periodically ignore substantive, procedural, and formatting mandates (from professors, supervising attorneys, or courts) because they do not understand the *context* of why these conventions matter. Ideally, if new lawyers and law students comprehend more fully *why* their legal communications need to be written a certain way, they will be more motivated to fulfill, if not exceed, their intended audience's expectations. Novice writers need to learn that an author's adherence to a particular structural logic increases the likelihood of the reader's understanding of complex legal analysis. Likewise, while procedural and formatting rules might seem overly pesky, they facilitate the information's transportation to the reader's hands in a medium he or she expects. If new legal writers grasp the bigger picture of how a standalone writing assignment fits into a client's case—and the legal system—as a whole, they might take greater ownership in how their written word can serve as an advocacy tool, rather than treating a writing project as just another activity to cross off a "to do" list.

Section I of this article provides a contextual background that professors and practitioners can share with rookie legal writers, using judicial opinions to demonstrate the eight most-common ways that attorney work product falls short of judges' expectations and, more importantly, how those deficiencies detrimentally affect the legal process and client advocacy. On a positive note, this section also provides examples of judges' appreciation for good legal writing that facilitates the court's understanding and evaluation of a case.

Section II briefly considers several philosophical reasons why individuals ignore or flout rules in general, even intelligent, accomplished individuals like ambitious law students and seasoned legal practitioners. This section is designed to provide law professors and supervising attorneys with context as to why new practitioners might behave a certain way, so that we can inspire change.

Section III suggests practical ways for professors and practitioners to communicate and reinforce to law students and new attorneys why substantive–structural and procedural–formatting rules of legal writing are important. With the goal of inspiring and cultivating better-written work product across the profession, this article concludes with proposals for broad-scale legal communities (such as civil-procedure rule-makers and state bar associations) and small-scale legal communities (like law offices) to motivate new lawyers to invest more care into the written word. These considerations include whether (a) civil-procedural rules should include more-express language concerning the quality of legal writing in court submissions and clarify the ramifications of not following substantive mandates and procedural rules; (b) the oaths that new attorneys take in the fifty state bars across the country should incorporate a commitment to quality legal writing and rule compliance as an overt covenant of professionalism; and (c) state bar Continuing Legal Education (CLE) requirements should be modified to integrate an annual legal writing component, just as many states impose an annual ethics or professionalism requirement.

I. Benchslap Fodder: Work Product that Flouts Courts' Substantive, Procedural, and Formatting Rules

Litigators often transmit client e-mails riddled with writing errors and submit briefs to the court that opposing counsel, the judge, or his or her clerks, first need to decipher before taking responsive action. Some law students challenge their legal writing professors' critiques about clarity, structure, or rampant proofreading errors, a few even asserting, "No one minded when I turned in papers like this in college, and professors gave me A's." This approach toward one of the most effective and powerful modes of advocacy can be disturbing to those who take pride in their written word.[2] However, simply telling these writers that good legal writing is important is obviously not effective enough to motivate change. Until they experience negative professional repercussions, and still even then, they might not realize or understand exactly how terrible writing and rule-flouting negatively affect the legal system and their clients. This article suggests that, through learning a richer context earlier—and seeing examples from real cases about the broader effect of sub-par written work on various aspects of, and players in, the legal system—new legal writers hopefully will envision their important role in the legal process on a broader scale.

Judges in state and federal courts provide a wealth of insights as to how and why poor legal writing affects the efficiency and efficacy of the legal system. The next section of this article extracts excerpts from cases to explain the disadvantageous impacts of (a) unclear structural logic and hazy phrasing in written work product submitted to courts; (b) missing substantive components in pleadings and briefs; (c) poor handling of the case facts, including slack citation to the factual record; (d) faulty treatment of the applicable law, including imprecise citation to legal sources; (e) express defiance of procedural and formatting rules, including page or word limits, line spacing, margins, and font size; (f) rampant typographical, grammatical, or general proofreading errors; (g) a disrespectful tone directed toward the court, opposing counsel, or other parties; and (h) late filings.

---

[2] Lawyers who fail to take pride in their written work product can truly rile a court. For example, in *Negrón-Santiago v. San Cristobal Hospital*, 764 F. Supp. 2d 366, 373 (D.P.R. 2011), the court criticized an attorney for filing "bad, even bordering on terrible" pleadings. The lawyer had "cut and pasted" parts of the complaint from prior cases pending before the same judge, failing to remove the names of unrelated co-defendants. *Id.* The court called this behavior "the opening salvo in a barrage of incompetence." *Id.*

Two themes permeate this survey of judicial opinions: First, good substantive legal writing enables courts to process complex intellectual material efficiently, so judges can "forge enlightened decisions."[3] Second, written work product submitted in compliance with court procedural rules ensures "fairness and orderliness" in the judicial process.[4] Conversely, poor legal writing hampers judges' ability to understand parties' claims and render fair decisions; written work product that defies procedural rules detrimentally affects courts' functional ability to process substance, adding to court-staff workload, and prejudicing opposing counsel who follow the rules. As explained further in section III, we can invite discussion and raise awareness with new legal writers about these issues by sharing some or all of the judicial opinions explained here.

A. Lack of Clarity in Written Work Product Can Force Judges to Read Pleadings and Briefs Multiple Times, Inviting Unfavorable Rulings

Although a courtroom judge might grant counsel a bit of creative leeway if a closing argument takes a meandering road to get to a point, a judge forced to hunt for substance in a written brief like an elusive "truffle"[5] will not likely be as generous. Unclear legal writing forces judges to read pleadings and briefs multiple times and can result in adverse rulings if the court—as the decision maker—cannot understand the attorney's claims.

For example, in *Ochoa v. Cook County Sheriff*, a plaintiff's attorney submitted a particularly "poorly written and virtually unintelligible" brief in response to a defendant's motion to dismiss.[6] Even after reading the plaintiff's complaint and opposition brief multiple times, the court still was unclear about what causes of action plaintiff's counsel was attempting to set forth.[7] Ultimately, the court granted the defendant's motion to dismiss.

Interestingly, on the same day as the *Ochoa* case, in *Sambrano v. Mabus*,[8] Judge Easterbrook of the United States Court of Appeals for the Seventh Circuit

---

[3] As the United States Court of Appeals for the First Circuit explained so succinctly in *Reyes-Garcia v. Rodriguez & Del Valle, Inc.*, 82 F.3d 11, 14 (1st Cir. 1996), "rules establish a framework that helps courts to assemble the raw material that is essential for forging enlightened decisions." The court also noted that deficiencies in legal writing "frustrate any reasonable attempt to understand [a party's] legal theories." *Id.* Further, "[s]ince appellate judges are not haruspices, they are unable to decide cases by reading goats' entrails. They instead must rely on lawyers and litigants to submit briefs that present suitably developed argumentation." *Id.* at 12.

[4] *Id.* at 14. Courts' procedural rules "ensure fairness by providing litigants with a level playing field. They ensure orderliness by providing courts with a means for the efficient administration of crowded dockets." *Id.*

[5] *U.S. v. Dunkel*, 927 F.2d 955, 956 (7th Cir. 1991) ("Judges are not like pigs, hunting for truffles buried in briefs.").

[6] No. 11 C 5544, 2011 WL 5404150, at *2 (N.D. Ill. Nov. 8, 2011).

[7] *Id.*

[8] 663 F.3d 879 (7th Cir. 2011).

referred to a lawyer's brief as "almost unintelligible,"[9] and parts of it as "wretched."[10] Among other unclear passages, the attorney's statement of appellate jurisdiction was "incoherent."[11] The court ordered the attorney to show cause why he should not be subject to monetary sanctions and why he should not be "censured, suspended, or disbarred."[12] The court emphasized, "Judges are better able than clients to separate competent from bungling attorneys, and we have a duty to ensure the maintenance of professional standards by members of our bar."[13]

Further, in *Donnelly v. Chicago Park District*, a defendant submitted both a brief in support of a motion for summary judgment and a reply brief; the court described both as "inadequate and disappointing."[14] The court stated that the brief in support of the motion for summary judgment "provided, at best, only the most minimal assistance to the court. Indeed, in a number of instances, it was of no help at all."[15] The quality of the briefs rendered it "impossible to make an informed judgment" about one of the counts in the complaint for which the party sought summary judgment.[16] The court emphasized the effects of deficient "quality of briefing at all levels of the judicial system" as follows:

> Under inclusive and inadequate presentations shift the responsibility to the court to do the lawyer's work. That's a risky business, for it requires the judge to be clairvoyant or intuitively to know the contours of the unmade argument. And, it rests on the hope that the judge will explicate the arguments that the briefs have left undeveloped, rather than resorting to the rule that superficial, skeletal, and unsupported arguments will be deemed waived or forfeited.[17]

As the foregoing cases demonstrate, poorly organized and convoluted legal writing can inhibit the court from finding a justification to rule in a client's favor. Judges have no obligation to do idle lawyers' work[18] and may view cases a completely different way if left to ascertain the facts and law on their own.

---

[9] *Id.* at 880.

[10] *Id.* at 881.

[11] *Id.*

[12] *Id.* at 882.

[13] *Id.*

[14] 417 F. Supp. 2d 992, 994 (N.D. Ill. 2006).

[15] *Id.*

[16] *Id.* The court noted that it could simply deny the motion on this count but that "enough questions appear to be implicated that it would not be institutionally responsible to take that course, which would necessitate a trial where perhaps there should be none." *Id.* The court thus gave the defendant the option to file an additional brief on that count, directed to the specific questions discussed in the opinion. *Id.*

[17] *Id.* at 993–94 (citing *United States v. Cusimano*, 148 F.3d 824, 828 n. 2 (7th Cir. 1998)).

[18] *See also Latsko v. Shinseki*, No. 09–2617, 2011 WL 3557234 at *4 (Vet. App. Aug. 15, 2011) (noting the court's refusal to address arguments that were "baseless, undeveloped, and at times mystifying"); *Reyes-Garcia*, 82 F.3d at 15 ("[E]ven if we were inclined to do [the party's] homework—and that is not our place—[the party's] substantial noncompliance with the rules would hamstring any attempt to review the issues intelligently.").

B. Omitting Key Substantive Components from Briefs Stifles the Court's Understanding of a Party's Claims

Many law-school professors, whether in the legal writing classroom or in doctrinal law classes, introduce law students to the basics of written legal analysis through structural formulae.[19] Seasoned attorneys might not recall these structural blueprints from law school, but subconsciously use them because such frameworks present a legal analysis in a logical way. Law students and new lawyers need to embrace this structure fully so the logic of their thought process leads the reader down a substantive path toward a well-reasoned conclusion. A writer who skips steps in logic inevitably loses the reader along the way. Legal writing formulae are simple, but they work. Yet, for some reason, many lawyers stray from using any type of logic formula in their writing, leaving the reader guessing and potentially frustrated and annoyed.

Poor legal writing, however, goes beyond an attorney's decision to reject a rigid formulaic structure. A legal reader will be confounded equally at a pleading or brief that is missing anticipated substantive components. In fact, many courts promulgate official rules that list key substantive elements that must appear in particular types of work product filed with the court. These rules are based on judges' vast experience in knowing exactly what they—and opposing parties— need to see in a party's pleadings and briefs in order to understand the facts and legal issues in the case and recognize what responsive action to take.

For example, the Federal Rules of Civil Procedure require a Complaint to include three items: (1) "a short and plain statement of the grounds for the court's jurisdiction . . . ," (2) "a short and plain statement of the claim showing that the pleader is entitled to relief," and (3) "a demand for the relief sought. . . ."[20] Likewise, a party filing an Answer to a Complaint in federal court must (1) "state in short and plain terms its defenses to each claim asserted against it" and (2) "admit or deny the allegations asserted against it."[21] Regarding motions for summary judgment, many local court rules require the parties to include a separate section itemizing undisputed material facts; for example, the United States District Court for the District of New Jersey requires the moving party to list such facts "in separately numbered paragraphs citing to the affidavits and other documents submitted in support of the motion."[22] Further, in appellate briefs, for example,

---

[19] *See e.g.* Linda H. Edwards, *Legal Writing: Process, Analysis, and Organization* chs. 7, 10, 19, 20 (5th ed. 2010) (discussing IREAC and various legal writing formulae). These might include various iterations of IRAC (Issue, Rule, Application–Analysis, Conclusion), IREAC (Issue, Rule, Explanation, Application–Analysis, Conclusion) or CREAC (Conclusion, Rule, Explanation, Application–Analysis, Conclusion). Even professors who do not have an affinity for IRAC likely still expect students to use some logical analytical structure in their writing, even if it does not echo the traditional acronym.

[20] Fed. R. Civ. P. 8(a).

[21] Fed. R. Civ. P. 8(b).

[22] U.S. Dist. Ct. D.N.J. Civ. R. 56.1 Furthermore, "[t]he opponent of summary judgment shall furnish, with its opposition papers, a responsive statement of material facts, addressing each paragraph of the movant's statement, indicating agreement or disagreement and, if not agreed, stating each material fact in dispute and

the Alabama Rules of Appellate Procedure require appellants to include eleven items: (1) a statement requesting oral argument (if desired), (2) a table of contents, (3) a statement of jurisdiction, (4) a table of authorities, (5) a statement of the case, (6) a statement of the issues, (7) a statement of the facts, (8) a statement of the standard of review, (9) a summary of the argument, (10) the argument, and (11) a conclusion.[23] If an attorney fails to submit any of these required substantive items, neither the court nor opposing counsel has all the raw materials necessary to take responsive action.

Courts know what they need from an attorney in order to get up to speed quickly on the facts and the law of a client's case and to convey these requirements to the litigants in local and system-wide rules. Some attorneys still ignore these directives. Unfortunately, an attorney's failure to follow express court instructions can leave a negative impression on the judge making key legal decisions in the case.

A federal case entitled *Scott v. Arrow Chevrolet, Inc.*[24] offers a particularly embarrassing example of a court's admonition for poor legal writing and a failure to follow court rules. The court declared that "counsel have established themselves as prime candidates for the Worst Federal Pleading of the Year Award."[25] In drafting an answer to a complaint, the lawyer failed to follow the Federal Rules of Civil Procedure and neglected to properly admit or deny the numbered allegations in the Complaint, instead making allegedly nonsensical statements about the substance in the pleading.[26] In response, the court struck the entire answer and required counsel to "to send a copy of this opinion to [the] client together with a letter advising that no charge will be made for any time and expense incurred in correcting counsel's own errors. . . ."[27] The court demonstrated that an Answer that fails to follow the substantive requirements in the rules and properly admit or deny each allegation in the Complaint is virtually worthless to the court and the opposing party.

Likewise, in *Skybridge Spectrum Foundation v. F.C.C.*,[28] in ruling on a party's motion for summary judgment, the court rejected the responding party's Cross-Statement of Material Facts Not in Dispute, because it "flatly contravene[d]" the court's scheduling order by failing "to respond to each of the . . . factual assertions 'with a correspondingly numbered paragraph, indicating whether that paragraph is admitted or denied.'"[29] Without responses to assertions of undisputed material facts tied to corresponding numbered paragraphs, it was impossible for the court or opposing counsel to tell whether the party accepted or

---

citing to the affidavits and other documents submitted in connection with the motion; any material fact not disputed shall be deemed undisputed for purposes of the summary judgment motion." *Id.*
[23] Ala. R. App. P. 28.
[24] No. 01 C 7489, 2001 WL 1263498 (N.D. Ill. Oct. 22, 2001).
[25] *Id.* at *1.
[26] *Id.*
[27] *Id.* at *2.
[28] 842 F. Supp. 2d 65 (D.D.C. 2012).
[29] *Id.* at 70 n.1.

rejected the undisputed nature of a particular fact. The attorney's failure to follow the substantive rules precluded the court from narrowing the issues in dispute, which, of course, was the fundamental function of the motion for summary judgment.[30]

Similarly, in *Moore v. State of Indiana*,[31] a lawyer submitted an appellate brief without an accurate Statement of the Case, an express requirement under the Indiana Rules of Appellate Procedure.[32] The court emphasized that the purpose of the substantive requirement of the Statement of the Case in the appellate rules was to assist the court by encapsulating the procedural posture of the case.[33] The court admonished that adherence to the standards set forth in the appellate rules is not optional.[34] Without the Statement of the Case, the court could not refer readily to the procedural posture of the case, which it needed to fully understand the nature of the appeal. The court ordered a rebriefing, concluding that the attorney's originally filed brief was a "disservice to his client and this court."[35]

Recently, in *United States v. Johnson*,[36] Judge Easterbrook of the United States Court of Appeals for the Seventh Circuit again pointed out how attorneys' failure to include substantive materials in compliance with court rules "hampered our ability to evaluate the arguments for both sides."[37] Even though the court rules required the appellant to attach the trial court's decision to the appellate brief, the party failed to do so.[38] When one lawyer falsely certified that all such materials had been filed with his brief, the court issued a public "rebuke" and assessed a $2,000 sanction.[39]

As these cases demonstrate, an attorney's failure to include required substantive components in attorney work product precludes the court and opposing parties from fully grasping the nature of the case, impeding their ability to move the case forward.[40]

---

[30] *Id.*

[31] 426 N.E.2d 86 (Ind. Ct. App. 1981).

[32] *Id.* at 89. Further, the attorney's substantive arguments were "predominantly bald assertions," and failed to include citations to the record. *Id.* at 90.

[33] *Id.* at 89.

[34] *Id.* at 90.

[35] *Id.*

[36] No. 13-1350, 2014 WL 466084 (7th Cir. Feb. 6, 2014).

[37] *Id.* at *3.

[38] *Id.*

[39] *Id.* at *4.

[40] Pro se litigants are also held to these standards. In *Means v. Housing Authority of the City of Pittsburgh*, 747 A.2d 1286 (Pa. Cmmw. 2000), the court explained that "the Pennsylvania Rules of Appellate Procedure exist to ensure that litigants present appeals of sufficient clarity to allow appellate courts to evaluate those appeals with the benefit only of the record below." *Id.* at 1289. In this case, a brief submitted by a pro se litigant (not a licensed attorney) ignored the rules applicable to his appellate brief by failing to provide a statement of scope and standard of review, a statement of the case, and a summary of the argument. *Id.* at 1287. These failures impaired the court's "ability to discern his issues and arguments, and preclude[d] any meaningful appellate review of this case." *Id.* at 1289.

C. Poor Handling of the Case Facts Adds to the Court's Workload and Could Thwart a Judge's Willingness or Ability to Address a Particular Factual Claim

Law students and practicing attorneys sometimes groan at the burden of providing accurate pinpoint citations to pages (and line numbers) in a voluminous case transcript to identify factual support for a claim. However, courts routinely explain that an attorney's failure to handle case facts properly and provide precise citations to the factual record forces court staff members to perform excess work to find the references in bulky transcripts, or worse, to *guess*—which could result in the court's having no choice but to decline to address unsupported claims or arguments.[41]

For example, in *Jones v. Jones*,[42] the court criticized a lawyer for failing to comply with the rules and provide the exact reference to the pages of the record supporting his alleged facts.[43] The court declared, "The rules are more than suggestive, and it is the duty of the members of the Bar to comply therewith."[44] Similarly, in *Commonwealth v. Stoppie*,[45] when an attorney failed to provide record citations in a brief, the court described the monumental task involved in having to fill in the blanks to confirm facts:

> The argument in this brief is 134 pages long and contains innumerable references to evidence and other matters in the record. Yet, there is not one place in the argument where counsel refers us to the page in the record where we may find the subject matter that he is discussing. The trial in this case covered ten days. . . . The Notes of Testimony from the trial alone cover 680 pages and the testimony in other proceedings . . . cover just over 200 pages.[46]

The court noted that "it is a cause of continuing frustration to appellate judges and their staffs to find incomplete and inaccurate citations."[47] The court emphasized that a lawyer's failure to cite to the factual record forces the court to "perform, to a certain extent, the duties of appellate counsel and search the record in an attempt to discover what counsel is talking about."[48]

The court in *State v. Dillard*[49] reiterated the point that the lawyer's failure to properly cite to the record adds to the court's workload: "An appellate Court is

---

[41] Further, misstating the factual record undermines attorneys' credibility and can warrant disciplinary action. *In re Disciplinary Action of Raymond P. Boucher*, 850 F.2d 597 (9th Cir. 1988) (censuring attorney whose brief went beyond the bounds of proper advocacy in characterizing the factual record).

[42] 202 S.W.2d 746 (Ky. 1947).

[43] *Id.* at 748.

[44] *Id.* at 749.

[45] 486 A.2d 994 (Pa. Super. 1984).

[46] *Id.* at 996.

[47] *Id.*

[48] *Id.*

[49] No. 2005AP2696, 2007 WL 115872 (Wis. App. Jan. 17, 2007).

improperly burdened where briefs fail to consistently and accurately cite to the record."[50]

When confronted with poor record citation, a court may feel compelled to speculate,[51] or the court may simply limit its review. In *Murken v. Solv-Ex Corp.*,[52] the court explained that the lawyers' failure to include specific cites to the sizable record restricted the scope of the court's review.[53] The particular record covered "approximately eight years and 4,712 pages of litigation."[54] The court declined to review the party's "arguments to the extent that it would have to comb the record to do so."[55]

Likewise, in *Benford v. Minneapolis*,[56] the court criticized the quality of the record citations in an attorney's brief, noting it was "rife with incomplete sentences and blank citations to the record" and that some citations referred "to irrelevant deposition testimony or documents, or to only a single page from a larger passage of relevant testimony."[57] Explaining how the attorney's failure to use proper citation added to the court's workload, the court stated, "Although the Court has attempted to locate relevant portions of the record on its own, the task of sifting through several thousand pages of documents to support Plaintiffs' claims is not the Court's function. The Court will not advocate for Plaintiffs by mustering the evidence and making arguments when their counsel has neglected to do so."[58]

Poor citation, quite simply, prevents judges from accessing key information that can facilitate a ruling in a party's favor. As stated in *Kentucky–Indiana Municipal Power Assn v. Public Service Co. of Indiana*,[59] the rules are for the "benefit of the court" so that it can retrieve key information from the record, and "facilitate review and utilization of the transcript in determining the appeal."[60] Further, the rules are designed to afford a level playing field to opposing parties; "opposing counsel may be disadvantaged in rebutting or explaining assertions" that are unsupported with accurate cites to the record.[61]

---

[50] *Id.* at *2 (citing *Weiland v. Paulin*, 259 Wis. 2d 139). *See also Hurlbert v. Gordon*, 824 P.2d 1238, 1245 (Wash. App. Div. I 1992) (Typographical errors in record cites create more work for the court: there were "numerous references to clerk's papers which were either non-existent, or difficult if not impossible to find, because of typographical errors in the references."); *Moore*, 426 N.E. 2d at 88 (Counsel's failure to place marginal notations on each page of the record pursuant to the rules "makes our examination of the transcript of evidence especially burdensome.").

[51] *See Latsko* 2011 WL 3557234 at *3 (Failure to provide a record citation left "the Court with the task of engaging in blind guessing.").

[52] 124 P.3d 1192 (N.M. Ct. App. 2005).

[53] *Id.* at 1194.

[54] *Id.* at 1196.

[55] *Id.*

[56] No. 10–04539 ADM/LIB, 2012 WL 6200365 (D. Minn. Dec. 12, 2012).

[57] *Id.* at *2.

[58] *Id. See also Northwestern Natl. Ins. Co. v. Baltes*, 15 F.3d 660, 662–63 (7th Cir. 1994) ("District judges are not archaeologists. They need not excavate masses of papers in search of revealing tidbits—not only because the rules of procedure place the burden on the litigants, but also because their time is scarce. Other parties, who live by the rules, have a priority claim on the judge's attention. Lawyers and litigants who decide that they will play by rules of their own invention will find that the game cannot be won.").

[59] 393 N.E.2d 776 (Ind. App. 3d Dist. 1979).

[60] *Id.* at 784.

[61] *Id.*

Because of the impact on courts' and opposing counsel's ability to do their jobs, some judges might impose sanctions upon attorneys who ignore record citation rules. For instance in *Hurlbert v. Gordon*,[62] the court rebuked an attorney for "laissez-faire" legal briefing replete with factual statements lacking citation to the record.[63] The court had to cull through 6000 pages of clerk's papers, exhibits and transcripts.[64] The court imposed $750.00 in sanctions, explaining that the briefing errors "wasted the time of opposing counsel and hampered the work of the court."[65]

Though it is tedious to comb through tomes of transcripts to find exact cites for factual documents, new attorneys need to understand the importance of doing so—to enable judges and their clerks to review the factual support for arguments made, and afford opposing counsel a fair opportunity to respond. It is neither the judge's nor the clerks' job to conduct such a search, and lawyers should not assume that they will fill in the blanks.

D. Deficient Citation to Legal Authority Hampers the Court's Ability to Evaluate the Merits of a Case and Undermines an Attorney's Credibility

Law students often find legal citation rules to be onerous, and some perceive professors as overly nitpicking in penalizing Bluebooking errors. Some frustrated students remark, "As long as the reader can find the case, isn't that sufficient?" From a practical standpoint, it would seem logical that a lawyer's improper citation of statutes and cases would add to a judicial clerk's workload in preparing a bench memo for a judge, requiring him or her to first take the time to track down accurate cites and pinpoint page numbers instead of immediately proceeding to review the applicable law and verify that the cases actually stand for the propositions set forth in the brief.[66] Citation errors certainly add an extra step during a legal writing professor's grading process; when a student quotes from, or references a proposition in, a case, and yet provides the wrong citation, the professor cannot check the student's substantive accuracy without first having to do the initial work to fix the citation.

An example of a court's frustration with a brief plagued by sloppy citation is *Hurlbert v. Gordon*.[67] In *Hurlbert*, an attorney's brief contained case citations with typographical errors as well as references to cases that "did not support the

---

[62] 824 P.2d 1238 (Wash. App. Div. 1 1992).
[63] *Id.* at 1245–46.
[64] *Id.* at 1245.
[65] *Id.* at 1246.
[66] Worse, an attorney's intentional citation of a case that does not support the contentions asserted in a brief, or a lawyer's failure to cite adverse authority on point, immediately undermines the offending attorney's credibility.
[67] 824 P.2d at 1238.

positions for which they were cited."[68] The court explained that the purpose of the citation rules is "to enable the court and opposing counsel efficiently and expeditiously . . . to review the relevant legal authority."[69] Similar to an attorney's failure to cite to the factual record, the court stated that "the violations of the rules will not go unnoticed and unsanctioned."[70]

Similarly, in *Bradshaw v. Unity Marine Corp., Inc.,*[71] the court colorfully chastised two lawyers for poor legal writing and deficient legal citation:

> [T]his case involves two extremely likable lawyers, who have together delivered some of the most amateurish pleadings ever to cross the hallowed causeway into Galveston, an effort which leads the Court to surmise but one plausible explanation. Both attorneys have obviously entered into a secret pact ¾ complete with hats, handshakes and cryptic words ¾ to draft their pleadings entirely in crayon on the back sides of gravy-stained paper place mats, in the hope that the Court would be so charmed by their child-like efforts that their utter dearth of legal authorities in their briefing would go unnoticed. Whatever actually occurred, the Court is now faced with the daunting task of deciphering their submissions.[72]

The judge frowned upon both lawyers' scarcity of citation to mandatory precedent,[73] their inaccurate citations, and the shortage of pinpoint cite page numbers—which forced the court to search through a forty-page legal decision to locate legal support for the lawyer's arguments.[74]

Further, in *Hnot v. Willis Group Holdings,*[75] the court reprimanded a lawyer's overt failure to cite many relevant cases that ran contrary to the party's position in a motion *in limine* seeking to exclude an expert's testimony at trial.[76] The court ultimately denied the lawyer's motion, cautioning that "[a]lthough lawyers are expected to make the strongest argument possible for their clients, they undermine their own credibility when they ignore authority unhelpful to their position."[77] The judge referred to the attorney's brief as "disappointing" and his behavior as verging on "disingenuous."[78]

New legal writers need to understand that learning Bluebook rules is not just an annoying rite of passage and a fussy category on a professor's grading rubric.

---

[68] *Id.* at 1245.

[69] *Id.*

[70] *Id.* at 1246.

[71] 147 F. Supp. 2d 668 (S.D. Tex. 2001).

[72] *Id.* at 670.

[73] *Id.* at 670–71; *see also Yun Shou Xie v. Board of Immigration Appeals,* 186 Fed. Appx. 88, 91 (2d Cir. 2006) ("[T]he brief filed by petitioner's counsel is seriously deficient. . . . The argument section is only two pages long and fails to cite a single case from this Court or any other court or a single statute or regulation.").

[74] *Bradshaw,* 147 F. Supp. 2d at 670–71.

[75] No. 01 CIV 6558, 2007 WL 1599154 (S.D.N.Y. June 1, 2007).

[76] *Id.* at *4; *see also Donnelly,* 417 F. Supp. 2d at 994 (expressing dissatisfaction with a lawyer's brief because it failed to assist the court, instead taking the "ostrich-like tactic" of omitting relevant, potentially dispositive legal authority).

[77] *Hnot,* 2007 WL 1599154 at *4.

[78] *Id.*

A well-cited brief enhances the court's ability to review and apply the law efficiently and further boosts the credibility of an advocate.

E. Disregarding Procedural and Formatting Rules May Be Perceived as an Attempt to Garner an Unfair Advantage

Law students sometimes consider procedural rules imposed by their professors, such as page limits or word-count limits, to be unfairly arbitrary. Some undertake creative formatting maneuvers to circumvent such rules, via miniscule font and eye-straining line spacing. Others simply submit papers that exceed the word-count or page limit, accepting a grading penalty instead of making the effort to shave the excess through dogged editing. Many practitioners also flout court rules regarding font, line spacing, and footnotes, assuming that substance will trump these bothersome limitations. However, courts have specific logical and logistical reasons for imposing these requirements, not the least of which is to level the playing field for litigants.[79]

Noting a disturbing trend of lawyers' ignoring appellate-brief-writing rules, the court in *Commonwealth v. Stoppie* reprimanded an attorney who completely ignored the court-imposed word-count restrictions and page limits.[80] The lawyer submitted (1) a thirteen-page Statement of Questions, defying an express fifteen-line limit; (2) an eight-page Summary of Argument, disobeying a two-page limit; and (3) a brief exceeding the maximum page limit by ninety pages.[81] The court explained that the purpose of these limits is fairness; lawyers who ignore the rules have an unfair advantage over counsel "who conscientiously attempt to comply, as judicial resources are needlessly devoted to cases involving noncompliance."[82] The court warned that "where gross deviations from the appellate rules, which substantially impair our ability to exercise the power of review, are present, we will not hesitate to suppress the party's brief and quash the appeal."[83]

The goal of an even playing field was also emphasized in *Hawkins v. Miller*.[84] In *Hawkins*, a party appeared *pro se*, but had vast legal experience in over thirty lawsuits filed in Kentucky federal and state courts.[85] The *pro se* litigant's briefs disregarded the Kentucky Rule of Civil Procedure requiring briefs to be double-spaced; he instead crammed thirty-five lines of text onto each page, violating the twenty-three-line per page limit.[86] The court explained the repercussions: "Such

---

[79] *See, e.g. Stann v. Levine*, 180 N.C. App. 1, *6–*7 (2006) ("*[A]d hoc* application of the rules, with inconsistent and arbitrary enforcement, could lead to allegations of favoritism for one counsel over another.").
[80] *Stoppie*, 486 A.2d at 996.
[81] *Id.*
[82] *Id.* at 997.
[83] *Id.* (citing *Commonwealth v. Taylor*, 451 A.2d 1360 (Pa. Super. 1982).
[84] 301 S.W.3d 507 (Ky. 2009).
[85] *Id.* at 508 n.1.
[86] *Id.* at 508.

a disregard of the rule puts him at an advantage over the Appellees, who complied with the rule."[87] The court struck his briefs.[88]

Like law professors, courts are not blind to lawyers' not-so-surreptitious attempts to outwit the rules. In *Murken v. Solv-Ex Corp.*, the court critiqued a brief that contained too many footnotes, an obvious attempt by the drafter to circumvent the page limits.[89] The court stated, "While this court appreciates having briefs under the page limit, it does not enjoy receiving briefs with one hundred eleven footnotes. Nor does it enjoy receiving footnotes that are single spaced and in very small print."[90] The court described the lengthy footnotes as "aggravating."[91]

As the foregoing cases indicate, courts may perceive attorneys who disregard court-imposed procedural and formatting rules as trying to garner an unfair advantage. Law students and new lawyers might be more inclined to follow procedural and formatting rules if they understand the negative message their defiance sends to their audience.

F. Proofreading Errors Can Cause Courts to Question Attorneys' Competence in Client Representation

Some law students scurrying to meet deadlines shrug off the importance of proofreading a memo or brief and seem ruffled when they lose precious grading points for spelling and grammatical errors. Similarly, new attorneys sometimes think a senior partner is being "uptight" for ranting about typographical errors appearing in an e-mail to a client or opposing counsel. Again, these novice legal writers just might not grasp the potential repercussions of submitting attorney work product abounding with embarrassing punctuation, spelling, and grammar mistakes. Several courts have emphasized that unprofessionally presented work product causes the bench to question the competency of the attorney's representation of his or her client.

For example, in *In re Jacoby Airplane Crash Litigation*,[92] the court criticized a lawyer's work product, noting that it was "consistently replete with grammatical and typographical errors."[93] The court pointed out numerous misspellings, musing, "[t]he reader of this is left to wonder" about an incomplete sentence in the

---

[87] *Id.*

[88] *Id. See also Barry v. Lindner*, 81 P.3d 537, 544 (Nev. 2003) (Noting it would "not permit flagrant violations of the Nevada Rules of Appellate Procedure," the court fined an attorney $500 for, among other brief-writing violations, failing to doublespace the text and hand-writing page numbers.).

[89] 124 P.3d 1192, 1196 (N.M. App. 2005).

[90] *Id.*

[91] *Id.* at 1197. *See also Lundy v. Farmers Group, Inc.*, 750 N.E.2d 314, 318 (Ind. App. 2d Dist. 2001) (Quoting court rules discouraging footnotes and stating they should be used "sparingly," the court recognized a party's overuse of footnotes as an obvious attempt to avoid exceeding the page limit and struck all the footnotes.).

[92] No. 99-6073, 2007 WL 5037683 (D.N.J. Aug. 27, 2007).

[93] *Id.* at *41 n.28.

Argument.[94] Further, in *Kuzmin v. Thermaflo, Inc.*,[95] the court stated that "counsel's brief is poorly written, replete with improper spelling and bad formatting. By submitting a poorly written brief, the attorney fails the court as well as the clients."[96]

An attorney's written work product is a reflection of the individual's professionalism and competence; every word matters. Spelling, grammatical, and typographical errors cause the reader to question the care with which the attorney prepared the document. A reader's concerns about presentation can trigger doubts about substance as well.

G. Briefs That Vent Their Authors' Frustration and Attack the Court, Opposing Counsel, or Adverse Parties, Undermine the Public Trust in the Legal System

Unfortunately, it is not a new trend for lawyers to show disrespect to the bench, opposing counsel, or opposing parties in written submissions.[97] Even in cases decided over a hundred years ago, attorneys were reprimanded for projecting a brazen tone toward the court and counsel.[98] Of course, litigation can be vexing, and there are often times when a court's decision might seem unfair, biased, or flat-out wrong, but attorneys cannot use written advocacy to display their exasperation and rail against the court or their opponents for perceived injustices; instead, they must make well-reasoned persuasive arguments. Law students and new practitioners need to understand that attorneys who use the written word to disrespect the court and their fellow members of the bar undermine the public trust in the legal system.[99]

---

[94] *Id. See also State v. Dillard*, 2007 WL 115872 at *2 (Wis. App. 2007) (pointing out that a lawyer's brief contained typographical and collating errors); *Yun Shou Xie* 186 Fed. Appx. at 91 ("[C]ounsel's brief is replete with typographical errors."); *Moore*, 426 N.E.2d at 87 n. 1 ("The brief contains many grammatical, semantic and typographical errors; we suggest appellant carefully proof his next brief."); *Simmons v. John F. Kennedy Medical Centers*, 727 F. Supp. 440, 444 (N.D. Ill. 1989) (admonishing "counsel for both parties to proofread their briefs for typographical and spelling errors before filing").

[95] No. 2:07CV00554, 2009 WL 1421173 at *2 n. 6 (E.D. Tex. May 20, 2009).

[96] *Id.*

[97] For example, in *Miles v. Miles*, 994 P.2d 1139 (Mont. 2000), a lawyer submitted briefs in which he made accusations against opposing counsel and attacked the judge for alleged *ex parte* communication with opposing counsel. The court concluded that the briefs were "some of the worst we have read in terms of being uncivil and demeaning toward the District Court, the personal representative, and opposing counsel." *Id.* at 1147. The court emphasized that "an attorney who engages in this sort of behavior is not properly representing his client. He brings public discredit to the legal profession. He wastes the time and resources of the courts, of opposing counsel and of the parties." *Id.* at 1148.

[98] *See e.g. Rahles v. J. Thompson & Sons Mfg. Co.*, 119 N.W. 289, 289 (Wis. 1909) (criticizing an attorney's language in a brief for a rehearing as "mere scolding" and in violation of Wisconsin Supreme Court Rules); *Rose v. Campbell*, 77 S.W. 707 (Ky. 1903) ("We decline to consider the questions attempted to be presented by the petition for rehearing, because of its offensive and disrespectful tone and language."); *Anderson v. Cook*, 65 P. 113, 113 (Mont. 1901) (striking a disrespectful brief from the record).

[99] In *Attorney General v. Superior Court of the Commonwealth of the Northern Mariana Islands*, No. 99–001, 1999 WL 33992417 *3 (N. Mar. Is. June 28, 1999), a lawyer used language offensive toward parties in a brief. Counsel also criticized the trial court judge, accusing him of "refus[ing] to follow the law." *Id.* The court noted that the rules of professional conduct help to ensure that false statements by a lawyer will not "unfairly undermine public trust and confidence in the administration of justice" through criticism of the judiciary. *Id.* at *4.

1. Attacking the Integrity of the Court

In *Rahles v. J. Thompson & Sons Manufacturing. Co.*, a lawyer challenged a court ruling and submitted a brief that suggested that the court had "utterly disregard[ed] the jury's findings," "usurp[ed]" the role of the jury, and "substi-tute[d]" its own factual findings.[100] The court deemed the language disrespectful to the court and took the time to explain—in eloquent fashion—the distinction between "argument" and "mere scolding":

> "Argument" is a connected discourse based upon reason; a course of reasoning tending and intended to establish a position and to induce belief. "Scolding" is mere clamor, railing, personal reproof. Argument dignifies the orator and instructs and convinces the auditor. Scolding relieves somewhat the hysteria of the scolder, but only amuses or irritates the hearer. Argument is the professional weapon of the lawyer; scolding that of the communis rixatrix. Argument is enjoyed and welcomed in a brief for rehearing; scolding has no proper place therein.[101]

The lawyer should have presented persuasive arguments demonstrating the flaws in the ruling; the attacks on the integrity of the court distracted from the pertinent legal issues.[102]

Further, in *Dabney v. Ledbetter*,[103] a lawyer filed a brief challenging an opin-ion issued by the Supreme Court of Oklahoma, suggesting that the court had concocted a set of facts beyond the record.[104] In reviewing the brief, the court concluded that the "language employed is too harsh, critical, and carries with it an attitude of disrespect."[105] The court described attorneys who engage in such behavior as "a destructive factor in our institutions of government."[106] Noting the societal effects of an attorney's attacks on the court via written advocacy, the court explained,

> Public confidence and respect for courts of justice are indispensable requisites of a democratic form of government. Where attorneys do not evince a proper respect and confidence, the public cannot be expected to do so. Thus the threat to organized government becomes grave and of no little concern.[107]

---

[100] 119 N.W. at 289.

[101] *Id.* at 290; *see also Anderson*, 65 P. at 113 (striking a brief and denying the underlying motion when the lawyer employed language and tone which was disrespectful to the court, using terminology such as "absurd," and challenging the court's "legal or moral right" to make a certain ruling).

[102] *Id.*; *see also Strowbridge v. City of Chiloquin*, 277 P. 722, 723 (Or. 1929) ("Abuse is not argument; calumniation is not convincing; defamation is not determinative of an issue; perversion of speech is not persuasive.").

[103] 18 P.2d 1085 (Okla. 1933).

[104] *Id.* at 1086.

[105] *Id.* at 1087.

[106] *Id.*

[107] *Id. See also White v. Priest*, 73 S.W.3d 572, 580 (Ark. 2002) (per curiam), in which an attorney's "continued strident, disrespectful language used in his pleadings, motions, and arguments, and his repeated refusal to recognize and adhere to precedent" resulted in the court's striking his 70-page brief, and referring him to the Professional Conduct Committee. Also, in *People v. Maynard*, 238 P.3d 672 (Colo. 2009), an attorney was suspended from the practice of law for a year for misconduct. A concurring judge noted the

More recently, in *Ligon v. McCullough*,[108] an attorney filed a motion to abate a $550 fine imposed by the Professional Conduct Committee.[109] The motion contained "unnecessary, strident, and disrespectful language" toward the Executive Director of the Committee.[110] The court struck the motion in its entirety, cautioning "attorneys from filing motions containing irrelevant, disrespectful, and caustic remarks that only serve to vent a party's emotions such as anger or hostility."[111] The court referred the lawyer to the Committee for disciplinary action.[112]

Finally, in *Cruz v. Commissioner of Social Security*,[113] the court noted several unprofessional comments in an attorney's brief in which he accused an administrative law judge of misconduct.[114] The court explained, "Heated rhetoric like this does nothing to advance a client's cause. It serves only to distract attention from the merits and to call counsel's judgment into question."[115] The court indicated it could "no longer tolerate the pollution of appellate practice that these repeated *ad hominem* attacks represent."[116] The court referred the attorney to the Court's Standing Committee on Attorney Discipline.[117]

From a teaching and learning standpoint, professors and practitioners should alert new legal writers to anticipate times in their legal careers when courts may seem partial to an opposing party or appear to have made flawed decisions. However, novice practitioners should be counseled to refrain from using a brief to launch caustic attacks on the integrity of the court and instead be encouraged to craft persuasive arguments that respectfully challenge a court decision through logical reasoning and clear phrasing.

---

lawyer's "repeatedly intemperate, unprofessional and vitriolic language in briefs and other court filings, directed at the trial judge, opponents and opposing counsel." *Id.* at 693 (Holme, J., concurring). The lawyer referred to the judge by last name and used terms like "revolting level of cronyism," "lie," and "outrageous abuse of power."*Id.* at 694. Citing *In the matter of Lester T. Vincenti*, 458 A.2d 1268, 1275 (N.J. 1983), the concurring judge emphasized, "Bullying and insults are no part of a lawyer's arsenal." *Id.* at 696.

[108] 247 S.W.3d 868 (Ark. 2007).

[109] *Id.* at 869.

[110] *Id.*

[111] *Id.*

[112] *Id. See also Prudential Ballard Realty Co. v. Weatherly*, 792 So.2d 1045, 1060 (Ala. 2000) (per curiam) ("[Counsel's] remarks . . . are indicative of a growing trend among some attorneys who feel that an application for rehearing provides them with a bully pulpit for venting their frustrations after receiving an adverse decision. Whether some attorneys believe it to be necessary to spew this venom for the benefit of their unhappy clients or to take the spotlight off their own inadequacies as legal practitioners, such childish behavior is uncivil and beneath the members of a professional bar association and it is a dangerous method of appellate advocacy.").

[113] 244 Fed. Appx. 475 (3d Cir. 2007).

[114] *Id.* at 482–83.

[115] *Id.* at 483.

[116] *Id.* at 484.

[117] *Id. See also U.S. v. Venable*, 666 F.3d 893, 904 n. 4 (4th Cir. 2012) ("[A]dvocates . . . do themselves a disservice when their briefs contain disrespectful or uncivil language directed against the district court, the reviewing court, opposing counsel, parties, or witnesses," including disdainful language, sarcasm, and use of words like "absurd" and "charlatan."); *Davidson & Schaaff, Inc. v. Liberty National Fire Ins. Co.*, 69 F.3d 868, 871–72 (8th Cir. 1996) ("[S]everal unwarranted, unprofessional aspersions" in a party's briefs directed at the district court's treatment of the case "were totally uncalled for and far beyond the pale of responsible advocacy."); *Exigence, LLC v. Baylark*, 367 S.W.3d 550, 557–58 (Ark. 2010) (cautioning counsel about rules that prohibit the use of disrespectful language, including counsel describing the circuit court's decision as "a flagrant case of retaliatory abuse of discretion").

2. Personal Attacks on Opposing Counsel or an Adverse Party

Similarly, all new attorneys need to realize the reality that, at some point in their careers, they will encounter an opposing party or its counsel that causes endless frustration and possibly even infuriation. Discovery disputes, negotiations, and arguments outside the courtroom can become heated and intense, and lawyers might feel tempted to bring to the court's attention certain nefarious behavior of an opposing party or counsel. As hard as it might be to "take the high road," restraint and respect are the best course of action. Courts never appreciate having to referee counsel who cannot get along. Using a disrespectful tone toward an opponent in a written submission might feel cathartic at the time, but the court most likely will view a lawyer's written words differently.[118]

For example, in *U.S. Neurosurgical, Inc. v. Chicago*,[119] a lawyer submitted a brief that—in the court's view—made unnecessary and unfounded attacks on opposing counsel.[120] In striking portions of the brief, the court explained, "Not only are such attacks unnecessary and distracting from the issues in the case, they do not assist the court in resolving the matter and give the impression, whether accurate or not, that the position taken by [the party] is unsupported by the law or facts because it has resorted to such distractions."[121] Further, as noted in the Seventh Circuit's Preamble to the Standards for Professional Conduct, "[c]onduct that may be characterized as uncivil, abrasive, abusive, hostile, or obstructive impedes the fundamental goal of resolving disputes rationally, peacefully, and efficiently. Such conduct tends to delay and often to deny justice."[122]

In *Thomas v. Tenneco Packaging Co.*,[123] the court affirmed the district court's sanctioning of an attorney who submitted documents to the court that contained "abusive and offensive remarks" directed at opposing counsel.[124] The court emphasized, "[h]aranguing and offensive tactics by lawyers interfere with the orderly administration of justice and have no proper place in our legal system."[125]

---

[118] *See e.g. Anderson v. Federal Cartridge Corp.*, 156 F.2d 681, 686 (8th Cir. 1946) (briefs containing language that is disrespectful to the court or opposing counsel—such as claims of malicious conspiracy—may be stricken); *Davidge v. Simmons*, 266 F. 1018, 1020 (D.C. Cir. 1920) (court took issue with disrespectful language in a brief directed at an opposing party and struck the brief); *Anderson v. Coolin*, 27 Idaho 334 (1915) (striking a brief "devoted largely to personalities, vituperation, and abuse directed against one of the attorneys," because it was "of no assistance to this court in reaching a correct determination of the legal questions involved"); *Grathwohl v. Garrity*, 871 N.E.2d 297, 299 n. 1 (Ind. App. 2007) (noting the disrespectful tone toward opposing counsel in briefs and calling counsel's writing "convoluted" and "nearly incoherent," including language that is "inappropriate and does not assist this court in resolving the issues on appeal"); *Hoosier Outdoor Advertising Corp. v. RBL Management, Inc.*, 844 N.E.2d 157, 162 (Ind. App. 2006) (The court deemed an attorney's brief using terms like "scheme," "cockamamie theory," "obtuse if not foolhardy," and "shell game" to describe his opposing counsel's arguments to be disrespectful, stating, "[V]itriol is inappropriate and not appreciated by this court, nor does it constitute effective appellate advocacy.").

[119] No. 02 C 4894, 2006 WL 752970 (N.D. Ill. Mar. 21, 2006).

[120] *Id.* at *1–3.

[121] *Id.* at *1.

[122] *Id. See also Dranow v. U.S.*, 307 F.2d 545 (8th Cir. 1962) ("[A]ll calumnious, defamatory, disrespectful, derogatory, impertinent and scandalous matter contained in appellant's briefs directed toward or denunciatory of the Trial Judge or Counsel for the Government is hereby ordered stricken.").

[123] 293 F.3d 1306 (11th Cir. 2002).

[124] *Id.* at 1308.

[125] *Id.* at 1323.

Similarly, in *Lockheed Martin Energy Systems, Inc. v. Slavin*,[126] a lawyer's personal attacks on opposing counsel were so appalling to an Administrative Law Judge that she referred to the lawyer's style of practicing law as "a prime example of the continuing problem of lack of civility in litigation," and outright barred the attorney from appearing before her.[127] The court censured the attorney, directed the clerk to send a copy of the opinion to each bar of which the attorney was a member, ordered a written apology, and imposed a suspended monetary sanction of $10,000 "for the great amount of judicial resources wasted in this case" in the event of the attorney's non-compliance with the court's directives.[128]

Certain opposing counsel or adverse parties simply will behave despicably. Spending countless hours and the client's money responding to such behavior—either in discovery or during trial—can be exasperating. However, law students and new lawyers need to know that briefs to the court are not the appropriate forum for "tattling" on opposing counsel via a disrespectful or attacking tone. Instead, lawyers must try to remove personal feelings from the equation and maintain a level of professionalism at all times, focusing instead upon the merits of the case via well-written, persuasive, advocacy pieces.

H. Flouting Filing Deadlines or Expecting Special Treatment Is Disrespectful to the Court and Opposing Counsel

Some law students present myriad excuses for submitting assignments late, often assuming that their circumstances are unique and that a waiver of the professor's penalty is warranted. In parallel fashion, some lawyers disregard filing deadlines and submit pleadings and briefs late, often expecting a judge or opposing counsel to act leniently and grant time extensions. It is essential for law students and new attorneys to realize that court deadlines are not suggestions; they are rules and serve important purposes such as judicial efficiency and fairness to litigants.[129]

In *Williams v. Chicago Bd. of Education*,[130] the court explained several factors that judges should consider when deciding whether to dismiss a case for failure to

---

[126] 190 F.R.D. 449 (E.D. Tenn. 1999).
[127] *Id.* at 460.
[128] *Id.* at 461–63.
[129] *See e.g. Brill v. New York*, 814 N.E.2d 431, 433 (N.Y. 2004) (explaining that the purpose of a summary-judgment deadline was to minimize impacts to judicial economy and prejudice to opposing counsel: "Eleventh-hour summary judgment motions, sometimes used as a dilatory tactic, left inadequate time for reply or proper court consideration, and prejudiced litigants who had already devoted substantial resources to readying themselves for trial.").
[130] 155 F.3d 853 (7th Cir. 1998).

prosecute, including (1) the frequency and magnitude of an attorney's failure to comply with court deadlines; (2) the impact of these failures on the court's time and schedules, and (3) the prejudice to other litigants.[131] The *Williams* court dismissed the plaintiff's case after her counsel "repeatedly disregarded the court's orders and deadlines and wasted the court's time and resources despite numerous warnings that further dilatory behavior would result in dismissal."[132] Likewise, in *Andrea v. Arnone, Hedin, Casker, Kennedy and Drake, P.C.*,[133] the court affirmed the dismissal of a case because of a lawyer's inability to meet deadlines.[134] The judge emphasized, "Litigation cannot be conducted efficiently if deadlines are not taken seriously, and we make clear again, as we have several times before, that disregard of deadlines should not and will not be tolerated."[135]

Prejudice to other parties was the paramount consideration in *Pacific Information Resources, Inc. v. Musselman*.[136] In *Pacific Information*, the plaintiff's counsel repeatedly submitted late filings, prompting the court to assert, "some form of sanction is necessary to discourage plaintiff and its counsel from continuing to engage in the sort of conduct which is tantamount to requiring the defendants to aim at a moving target."[137] Similarly, in *Donald v. Cook County Sheriff's Department*, the court urged, "The requirement that parties who simply ignore deadlines make a showing of excusable neglect should be taken seriously by the district courts, precisely because of the prejudice to the other party, exemplified here, which may result from untimely filings."[138]

Law students and new lawyers need to understand that untimeliness of written work product affects other individuals and entities; late filings affect both professors' and courts' efficiency in processing substantive review, and distract such readers from focusing on timely submissions from students or lawyers who complied with the deadlines. Although certain circumstances might warrant a court's understanding and leniency, new practitioners need to evolve from any previous "excuse" mindset and instead show respect for the court and opposing counsel by submitting documents on time.

---

[131] *Id.* at 857.

[132] *Id.* at 857–58.

[133] 840 N.E.2d 565 (N.Y. 2005).

[134] *Id.* at 566.

[135] *Id.* at 569. *See also Levine v. Shackelford, Melton & McKinley, L.L.P.*, 248 S.W.3d 166 (Tex. 2008) (per curiam) (refusing to set aside a default judgment entered because of the attorney's pattern of ignoring deadlines).

[136] No. C06-2306, 2008 WL 2338505 (N.D. Cal. June 4, 2008).

[137] *Id.* at *2.

[138] 95 F.3d 548, 558 (7th Cir. 1996) (emphasizing the "dilatory tactics" of the defendant in responding late to a complaint and finding that the district court's *sua sponte* enlargement of the time period for the defendant to respond to the complaint "seriously prejudiced" the plaintiff's prosecution of his case); *see also Kovacic v. Tyco Valves & Controls*, 433 Fed. Appx. 376, 381–82 (6th Cir. 2011) (dismissing a case in which plaintiff's "counsel's conduct was extremely dilatory" and "defendant was prejudiced by opposing counsel's delay"); *McLaurin v. East Jordan Iron Works, Inc.*, 666 F. Supp. 2d 590, 593 (E.D.N.C. 2009) (acknowledging the defendants' frustration with plaintiffs' counsel's failure to comply with case-management deadlines, and warning that future late filings will result in the imposition of sanctions); *Kalispel Tribe of Indians v. Moe*, No. CV–03–423–EFS, 2008 WL 2273286 (E.D. Wash. June 2, 2008) (affirming imposition of sanctions against counsel when a late-filed summary-judgment response forced plaintiff's counsel to incur unnecessary expenses drafting an additional reply brief).

I. Backslaps: When the Pleadings or Briefs Are Well Written and Facilitate the Service of Justice, Judges Say So

In stark contrast to judges' expressed frustration with poor legal writing, they articulate their appreciation for well-written submissions that streamline the judicial process. For example, in *In re Law Offices of James Sokolove, LLC*,[139] the Supreme Court of Rhode Island stated, "We wish to express our sincere appreciation for the articulate arguments and well-written briefs submitted by counsel for both sides in this case, as well as for the insightful *amicus curiae* briefs submitted in this case."[140]

In demonstrating gratitude for well-written briefs, courts emphasize their effectiveness in assisting the court.[141] For instance, in *Cisneros v. Corpus Christi Independent School District*,[142] the court highlighted the helpfulness of the efforts exerted by counsel in preparing quality written work in a complex case involving the politically charged issue of school desegregation. Near the start of the opinion, the court stated,

> Because it is an important case I want again to express my appreciation for the efforts of the attorneys who have appeared here, not only for their cooperation in

---

[139] 986 A.2d 997 (R.I. 2010).

[140] *Id.* at 1006 n. 14. *See also East Greenwich School Committee v. East Greenwich Educ. Ass'n*, 982 A.2d 1049, 1049 n. 1 (R.I. 2009) ("We hasten to express our sincere appreciation for the articulate arguments and well-written briefs submitted by counsel for both sides in this case, as well as the amicus curiae brief submitted."). Other state and federal courts also have complimented the quality of attorneys' legal writing. *See, e.g. Gauer v. Genesco, Inc.*, No. C-73-1375, 1975 WL 429, at *1 (N.D. Cal. Aug. 1, 1975) ("[T]he court wishes to express its appreciation to counsel for each of the parties for their very well-written briefs and the incisive arguments contained therein"); *Brunswick Corp. v. U.S.*, No. 07 C 3792, 2008 WL 5387086, at *12 (N.D. Ill. Dec. 22, 2008) ("The court also thanks all counsel for their exceptionally thorough and well-written briefs."); *Kennedy Ship &Repair, L.P. v. Loc Tran*, 256 F. Supp. 2d 678, 687 (S.D. Tex. 2003) ("The Court appreciates the informative and well-written briefs that it has received from Parties' counsel in this case."); *Carpenter v. Mattes Electric*, No. 96A–07–005 WTQ, 1997 WL 528044, at *1 n. 1 (Del. Super. Apr. 9, 1997) (The court appreciated "the well-written and well-argued briefs of both parties."); *Templeton Coal Co., v. Shalala*, 855 F. Supp. 990, 994 (S.D. Ind. 1993) ("[T]he parties have done a remarkably good job of compiling documents and well written briefs for the court's consideration."); *Watts v. Winn Parish School Bd.*, 66 So. 2d 350, 355 (La. App. 2d Cir. 1953) ("The lengthy well written briefs of both counsel have been read with interest, and we express our appreciation for them."); *Scuderi v. Monumental Life Ins. Co.*, 344 F. Supp. 2d 584, 586 n. 1 (E.D. Mich. 2004) ("The Court commends and thanks counsel for the thoroughness and clarity of their well[-]written briefs."); *Quirk v. Premium Homes, Inc.*, 999 S.W.2d 306, 310 n. 5 (Mo. App. E. Dist. 1999) ("We would be remiss if we failed to make public our appreciation for the well written briefs, superior arguments and, above all, exemplary courtesy and professionalism exhibited by counsel for both parties."); *Tait v. North America Equitable Life Assurance Co.*, 194 N.E.2d 456, 457 (Ohio Com. Pl. 1963) ("The Court at the outset wishes to thank and to express its sincere appreciation to both counsel for their excellent, well-written and very comprehensive briefs."); *Anderson v. State*, 905 S.W.2d 367, 368 (Tex. App.–Fort Worth 1995) ("The well written briefs and cogent arguments of both State and Appellant are appreciated by the court.").

[141] *See e.g. Dewey v. Allstate Ins. Co.*, 588 F. Supp. 479, 483 (D. Kan. 1982) (acknowledging that a trial brief "was well written and helpful to the Court"); *Livingood v. Townsend*, 422 F. Supp. 24, 28 (D. Minn. 1976) ("The court appreciates the excellent assistance afforded by all counsel in the form of well written briefs and candid oral presentations."); *Verizon Directories Corp. v. Yellow Book USA, Inc.*, No. 04–CV–0251, 2004 WL 1598917, *1 (E.D.N.Y. July 19, 2004) ("The court thanks the parties for their full, well-written and helpful briefs and other materials"); *Trenda v. Astrue*, 2009 WL 5184344, *2 (D.N.D. 2009) (acknowledging that "briefs were well written, addressed numerous issues, and provided substantial assistance to the court"); *Indiana-American Water Co., Inc. v. Indiana Off. of Util. Consumer Counselor*, 844 N.E.2d 106, 109 n. 1 (Ind. App. 2006) ("We thank the parties for their well-organized and well-written briefs, which greatly facilitated our review of the Commission's 127–page order and the twenty-two-volume record.").

[142] 324 F. Supp. 599 (S.D. Tex. 1970).

providing the court with all the relevant and pertinent evidence, voluminous data and statistics, but also for wellwritten briefs, and also for the expeditious manner in which the evidence was presented.[143]

The court explained that it had the arduous task of reviewing voluminous statistical data, exhibits and testimony, and that it found the plaintiffs' submissions to be "accurate and very illuminating."[144] The court likewise complimented the statistical calculations offered by the defendants, stating, "[T]he court is deeply appreciative of the cooperation, and of the long, tiresome work that the school administration had to undertake to furnish this data."[145] The court relied heavily on the voluminous evidence clearly presented by both parties in rendering its decision on this pivotal subject matter.

Law students and new attorneys might be more motivated to generate quality briefs if they are exposed to similar examples of how attorney work product made the court's job easier in rendering decisions, and see the real impact their own typewritten words can have on creating law in this country.

---

[143] *Id.* at 600.
[144] *Id.* at 601.
[145] *Id.* at 602.

Appendix B: Sample Single-Issue Legal Office Memorandum

MEMORANDUM

TO: Olivia Ramos, Esq.
FROM: Sloan McDonald, Associate
DATE: July 1, 2017
RE: Dylan Fontaine; File No. 3-26; Definition of "Deadly Weapon"
        Under Ohio Law

QUESTION PRESENTED

Under Ohio law, will our client Dylan Fontaine ("Fontaine") likely be found guilty of the crime of felonious assault with a deadly weapon when (1) she removed a Jimmy Choo high-heel stiletto shoe from her foot and threw it at a local bartender, Jamie Dunham ("Dunham"); (2) she yelled curse words at Dunham while throwing the shoe; and (3) the pointed heel of the stiletto shoe hit Dunham in the forehead, causing a deep gash requiring emergency medical attention?

BRIEF ANSWER

Yes, Fontaine likely will be found guilty of felonious assault with a deadly weapon. Under Ohio Rev. Code § 2903.11(A) (2011), the felonious assault statute states that "[n]o person shall knowingly . . . [c]ause or attempt to cause physical harm to another . . . by means of a deadly weapon or dangerous ordnance." Ohio Rev. Code § 2923.11(A) defines a "deadly weapon" as "any instrument, device, or thing capable of inflicting death, and designed or specially adapted for use as a weapon, or possessed, carried, or used as a weapon." It is undisputed that Fontaine knowingly caused physical harm to Dunham by throwing her Jimmy Choo high-heel stiletto shoe directly toward him. Therefore, the sole question is whether the shoe qualifies as a "deadly weapon" under the Ohio statute.

When evaluating whether an otherwise innocuous item qualifies as a deadly weapon under the felonious assault statute, Ohio courts consider (1) the size and weight of the item, (2) the shape and design of the item, (3) the ability of the item to be grasped in the hands of the user in such a way that it may be used on or directed against the body of another, and (4) the ability of the item to be used in a manner and with sufficient force to kill the other person. Applying these factors to

Fontaine's high-heeled shoe, a court likely will construe the stiletto to be a deadly weapon based on its size, weight, shape, design, and ability to be thrown in such a way and with such force as to kill a person. Thus, Fontaine likely will be found guilty of the crime of felonious assault with a deadly weapon.

STATEMENT OF FACTS

Fontaine is a twenty-seven-year-old resident of Cleveland, Ohio, where she works for an advertising and marketing agency. She is a frequent patron of an upscale wine bar called Enoteca located in Shaker Heights, Ohio. On New Year's Eve, Fontaine attended a party at the wine bar. Prior to midnight, she ordered a bottle of Spanish wine from the bartender, Dunham. At midnight, she still had not received the bottle of wine she ordered and began to get agitated; she felt the bartender was ignoring her requests. She requested the bottle again. Finally, Dunham responded to Fontaine, "Dylan, I can't serve you any more. I'm cutting you off." Fontaine reacted angrily. A few moments later, witnesses saw her remove from her foot a size 7 champagne-colored suede Jimmy Choo high-heel stiletto shoe. The shoe was a platform "peep-toe" stiletto constructed of suede, leather, and steel. The heel measured 3.9 inches in height and was plated in a gold-colored metal; the point of the heel was affixed to a small rubber sole. The platform part of the shoe was less than half an inch wide.

Witnesses observed Fontaine throw the shoe with force at Dunham while yelling curse words. The pointed heel of the stiletto shoe hit Dunham directly in the forehead. He immediately fell backwards and into the bar, and then collapsed onto the floor. The point of the stiletto heel caused a deep gash in his forehead. Bystanders called paramedics to the scene. Police arrived as well, and they arrested Fontaine for felonious assault. Dunham's forehead required emergency medical attention, including stitches and treatment for a concussion. He was transported to the hospital where he spent one night; he was released the next afternoon.

DISCUSSION

Our client seeks legal advice regarding whether she likely will be found guilty of the crime of felonious assault with a deadly weapon, as defined under Ohio law. Ohio Rev. Code § 2903.11(A)—the felonious assault statute—states that "[n]o person shall knowingly . . . [c]ause or attempt to cause physical harm to another . . . by means of a deadly weapon or dangerous ordnance." Ohio Rev. Code § 2923.11(A) defines a "deadly weapon" as "any instrument, device, or thing capable of inflicting death, and designed or specially adapted for use as a weapon, or possessed, carried, or used as a weapon." It is undisputed that Fontaine knowingly caused physical harm to Dunham by throwing her Jimmy Choo high-heel stiletto shoe directly at him. The sole question is whether the shoe qualifies as a "deadly weapon" under Ohio law.

When evaluating whether an otherwise innocuous item qualifies as a deadly weapon under the felonious assault statute, Ohio courts consider (1) the size and weight of the item, (2) the shape and design of the item, (3) the ability of the item to be grasped in the hands of the user in such a way that it may be used on or directed against the body of another, and (4) the ability of the item to be used in a manner and with sufficient force to kill the other person. Applying these factors to Fontaine's shoe, a court likely will construe the stiletto to be a deadly weapon. Thus, Fontaine likely will be found guilty of the crime of felonious assault with a deadly weapon.

Courts have applied the foregoing factors to numerous household items that normally would not be considered weapons in their everyday uses. For example, in *State v. Redmon*, No. CA-7938, 1990 WL 94745 (Ohio Ct. App. June 25, 1990), a home intruder, who had smoked cocaine earlier in the evening, broke into a house, picked up a wicker rocking chair, approached the homeowner who was sitting on her couch, and told her that he was going to kill her. *Id.* at *1. The intruder swung the rocker at the woman's face. While she was able to duck and run into the kitchen, the intruder continued swinging the chair as he made his way to the kitchen. He swung the rocker at the homeowner again, missed, and finally threw the object away. *Id.* After an ongoing struggle and a 911 call, eventually the police arrived and arrested the intruder for the crime of felonious assault. *Id.*

The intruder argued that the wicker rocking chair was not a deadly weapon. *Id.* However, the court held that the chair was indeed a deadly weapon as defined by Ohio law. *Id.* at *2. The court explained that "[a]n instrument, no matter how innocuous when not in use, is a deadly weapon if it is of sufficient size and weight to inflict death upon a person, when the instrument is wielded against the body of the victim or threatened to be so wielded." *Id.* The court considered the following factors: (1) the size and weight of the chair, (2) the shape and design of the chair, (3) the ability of the chair to be grasped in the hands of the intruder and swung at the victim, and (4) the ability of the chair to be used in a manner and with sufficient force to kill the victim. *Id.* Applying these factors, the court emphasized that the intruder swung the wicker rocking chair at the victim's head while telling her that he was going to kill her. She ducked and the chair missed her face by one-and-a-half feet. These factors supported the court's finding that the chair constituted a deadly weapon. *Id.*

Similarly, in *State v. Ware*, No. 57546, 1990 WL 151499 (Ohio Ct. App. Oct. 11, 1990), an ex-boyfriend entered his ex-girlfriend's home and, as she was putting a broom behind a door, he struck her on the head with an iron and said, "I am going to kill you." *Id.* at *1. The man continued to strike the woman with the iron while she screamed for help. She struggled toward her bed and grabbed a pillow to protect herself from the blows of the iron. The man continued to swing the iron, hitting her and the wall, until the iron fell apart. Eventually, she got away. *Id.* The ex-boyfriend was charged with felonious assault with a deadly weapon. He argued that the iron did not qualify as a "deadly weapon." *Id.*

The court held that the iron was a deadly weapon. *Id.* at *6. Applying the above-mentioned factors to determine whether the iron was capable of inflicting death, the court emphasized that the ex-boyfriend used the iron in such a manner by striking the victim several times and caused her to sustain multiple abrasions and lacerations, requiring several stitches. The court found this sufficient to qualify the iron as capable of inflicting death. *Id.*

Further, in *State v. Maydillard*, No. CA99-06-060, 1999 WL 988822 (Ohio Ct. App. Nov. 1, 1999), an inmate at a correctional institution in Ohio entered the cell of another inmate carrying a plastic shaving razor from which he had removed the plastic guards to expose the blades. The first inmate brandished the razor at the second inmate in an attempt to collect a debt owed. *Id.* at *1. A struggle ensued. Guards arrived at the cell, pulled the inmates apart, and handcuffed them. During a pat-down search, a guard found the razor. The inmate was charged with possession of a deadly weapon while under detention. *Id.*

In applying the statutory definition of a "deadly weapon" to the razor, the *Maydillard* court held that the razor possessed by the inmate was a "deadly weapon" by the manner of its use or adaptation. *Id.* at *4. The court explained that cases that have found a razor not to be a deadly weapon involve circumstances where the razor was used or possessed in a manner consistent with its legitimate purpose, such as a barber's razor or a pocket knife used for cutting packing tape and rope. *Id.* at *3. However, this inmate had adapted the razor, by removing the plastic guards, to function as a deadly weapon. *Id.* at *4. Further, he brandished it as a weapon. Finally, the court emphasized that the inmate presented no testimony that he was using the razor in a manner consistent with its legitimate purpose. *Id.*; *see also State v. Salinas*, No. F-84-8, 1985 WL 7568 (Ohio Ct. App. July 26, 1985) (holding that a jury reasonably could find that a baseball bat constituted a deadly weapon when the perpetrator swung the bat at a victim, causing injury to his jaw, ribs, and arms); *State v. Deboe*, 406 N.E.2d 536 (Ohio Ct. App. 1977) (holding that a club-like instrument three inches in diameter wrapped in spongy material, which the perpetrator swung rapidly at the victim, hitting him 15 or 20 times on the head, arms, back, shoulders, and kidneys, causing black and blue welts and bruises, constituted a deadly weapon).

In contrast, in *State v. Kaeff*, No. 20519, 2004 WL 2245095 (Ohio Ct. App. Sept. 24, 2004), a husband was indicted for one count of domestic violence and one count of felonious assault with a deadly weapon, after using only his hands to attempt to strangle the victim, his wife. *Id.* at *1. The husband filed a motion to dismiss the count of felonious assault on the ground that a person's hands cannot, as a matter of law, be considered a deadly weapon. The trial court granted the motion and dismissed the count. The prosecution appealed the court's ruling. *Id.*

The prosecution argued that hands (1) fit within the definition of an "instrument," (2) are capable of inflicting death, and (3) can be used as a weapon. However, the court held that hands do not meet the definition of a deadly weapon. *Id.* at *4. The *Kaeff* court reasoned that the factors defining a deadly weapon suggest the use of an object apart from one's own body. Thus, one's hands are not within the scope of the statutory definition. *Id.*

In evaluating whether Fontaine's Jimmy Choo stiletto qualifies as a deadly weapon, a court will consider (1) the size and weight of the shoe, (2) the shape and design of the shoe, (3) the ability of the shoe to be grasped in the hands of the user in such a way that it may be used on or directed against the body of another, and (4) the ability of the shoe to be used in a manner and with sufficient force to kill the other person. Applying the foregoing factors, the court likely will find the stiletto constitutes a deadly weapon. Regarding the size and weight of the shoe, the facts indicate that Fontaine's "instrument" was a size 7 champagne-colored Jimmy Choo high-heel stiletto shoe. The shoe was constructed of suede and leather, and was a platform peep-toe stiletto. The heel height measured 3.9 inches and was constructed of steel with a gold-colored point attached to a small rubber sole. The platform part of the shoe was less than half an inch. The shoe was neither lightweight nor small. Further, the pointy shape of the nearly four-inch metal heel, and the weight of the platform peep toe structure, rendered the shoe capable of causing harm when thrown with force. Fontaine was able to grasp the heavy unwieldy shoe in her hand and hurl it toward the body of Dunham, specifically his head. The weight and shape of the shoe, when thrown in the manner Fontaine propelled it, likely had sufficient force to kill another person.

Unlike the perpetrator in *Maydillard* who modified an everyday razor by removing plastic safety guards, Fontaine did not modify or adapt the shoe from its original purpose. Further, unlike the assailants in *Redmon*, *Ware*, and *Deboe*, who swung their respective weapons—a rocking chair, an iron, and a sponge-covered bat—numerous times against the body of their victims, Fontaine heaved the shoe only one time at Dunham.

Nonetheless, given the shoe's size, weight, shape, design, and ability to be grasped by Fontaine in such a way to be hurled at Dunham with sufficient force to gravely injure him and possibly kill him, a court likely will find that the shoe meets the definition of a "deadly weapon."

CONCLUSION

Because Fontaine knowingly caused physical harm to Dunham by means of a deadly weapon, she is likely to be found guilty of felonious assault under Ohio Rev. Code § 2903.11(A).

Appendix C: Sample Multi-Issue Legal Office Memorandum

MEMORANDUM[1]

TO: Francesca Volterra, Esq.
FROM: Rodney Belknap
DATE: November 19, 2017
RE: Wynter Slade; File No. 2-10; Whether a Passenger's Removal from a FlyGreen Flight Was Arbitrary and Capricious

Question Presented

Under 49 U.S.C.A. § 44902(b) (2014), was the airline FlyGreen's decision to remove our client Wynter Slade ("Slade") from a recent flight arbitrary and capricious when Slade (1) is a practicing Wiccan, (2) was transporting harmless powders in a Ziploc bag and jokingly dangled them in front of two passengers, (3) made a sarcastic statement regarding putting a "hex" on two passengers, (4) was on a flight that was rushing to take off to avoid an incoming storm, and (5) interacted with a surly flight attendant who had a short employment history with the airline and a possible bias against passengers?

Brief Answer

Yes, a court likely would find that FlyGreen's decision to remove our client from the aircraft was arbitrary and capricious. Under 49 U.S.C.A. § 44902(b), an air carrier may (1) refuse to transport, (2) a passenger or property, (3) whom the carrier decides is, or might be, inimical to safety. To determine whether a passenger was inimical to safety, or if the airline's decision was arbitrary and capricious, courts consider (1) the facts known to the airline at the time of its decision, (2) any time constraints affecting the flight's takeoff, (3) the general national security climate at the time of the flight, and (4) the reasonableness of the pilot's reliance on a flight attendant's representations.

At the time FlyGreen made this particular decision to deplane Slade, the flight attendant told the pilot that Slade had threatened two passengers, but the pilot did not know the specific language of such alleged threats. Additionally, although the pilot may have examined the contents of a satchel Slade carried, and

---

[1] This sample memorandum was adapted from a final memorandum submitted by Courtney Weinstein, a New York Law School student.

517

observed powders therein, he could not possibly have found any dangerous items. Her satchel merely contained herbs and spices. The pilot was in a rush to take off due to an incoming storm; however, the flight ended up departing on time. The destination of the flight was Florida, which is not a typical target for terrorism. On the date of the incident, more than 30 years since the 9/11 attacks, and FlyGreen had never had any previous security issues. The flight attendant whom the pilot relied on was new to the airline and had not actually witnessed the altercation between Slade and her fellow passengers. The flight attendant also had overtly expressed disdain for the passengers. Based on the foregoing, a court likely would find that the airline's decision to remove Slade was arbitrary and capricious.

Statement of Facts

On September 26, 2014, Slade, a newly practicing Wiccan, was traveling onboard a FlyGreen flight from JFK to Florida to attend her cousin's wedding the following day. The flight was departing at 4:45 p.m. Slade arrived at the airport at 3:30 p.m. She was carrying a satchel and a duffel bag, and checked no bags.

While navigating through security, Slade emptied her satchel and placed jars of colored powders, a candle, and Wicca books into a plastic bin. Slade noticed two women staring at her and whispering.

After clearing security, Slade went to Starbucks where she mentioned to the barista that the Starbucks logo resembled a Wiccan goddess. Slade noticed the same women staring again. Slade proceeded to her gate and heard an announcement that the flight might be delayed due to an incoming storm.

At the gate, a female flight attendant arrived and introduced herself to a male flight attendant and the pilots. Slade overheard the female attendant tell the male attendant that it was her first week working with FlyGreen as she recently left another airline. She said she was "tired of whacko passengers and arrogant pilots" and that she was "in no mood to deal with nutjobs today." The two male pilots were within earshot of this conversation, but they did not participate. While waiting for the flight, Slade read her Wicca book and took out her harmless powders, which were herbs and spices commonly used in rituals in the Wiccan religion. She began arranging the powders on the next seat while studying her book. The two women began whispering and staring again. Slade placed the powders into a Ziploc bag and jokingly dangled it in their direction.

Eventually, the flight attendants began the boarding process. During boarding, the flight attendants began rushing people to their seats to expedite departure to avoid an incoming storm. Slade arrived at her seat, which coincidentally was next to the two women. She struggled to stow her luggage quickly. Her jacket fell from the overhead bin and her satchel knocked one of the women. The woman said, "Watch it, you weirdo!" and "Keep your crazy witchcraft junk away from me." Slade muttered back, "Why don't you just shut up and mind your own business . . . unless you want to find out the hard way how a hex works." The women pressed the attendant call button. One of the women said to the female attendant, "I can't sit next to this person. She has a bag full of hocus-pocus, and she just threatened me." The flight attendant said, "Another day, another nut-job," and grabbed Slade's satchel. She took it to the cockpit and within minutes the attendant returned with the pilot. Without discussion, the pilot directed Slade to deplane. Passengers began clapping.

Security personnel interrogated Slade for twenty minutes. Ultimately, she was released, with an admonition to place her powders in her checked luggage the next time she flies. The flight took off on time without Slade. There were no remaining direct flights to Florida that day with available seats. Slade did not arrive in Florida until the next day. She missed her cousin's wedding.

Discussion

I. Introduction

Our client Slade seeks legal advice regarding whether FlyGreen acted properly in removing her from a flight. Under 49 U.S.C.A. § 44902(b), an air carrier may (1) refuse to transport, (2) a passenger or property, (3) whom the carrier decides is, or might be, inimical to safety. To determine whether a passenger was inimical to safety, or whether the airline's decision was arbitrary and capricious, courts consider (1) the facts known to the airline at the time of its decision, (2) any time constraints impacting the flight's takeoff, (3) the general security climate at the time of the flight, and (4) the reasonableness of the pilot's reliance on the flight attendant's representations. Applying the foregoing factors, a court likely would find that FlyGreen's decision was arbitrary and capricious.

II. Courts Consider the Facts Known to the Airline at the Time of the Decision to Deplane a Passenger

When evaluating facts known to the airline at the time of a decision to deplane a passenger, in deciding whether an airline's decision to remove a passenger was arbitrary and capricious, courts consider passenger behavior that is obnoxious, offensive, dangerous, or intimidating. For example, in *Zervigon v. Piedmont Aviation, Inc.*, 558 F. Supp. 1305 (S.D.N.Y. 1983), a band was traveling to Florida. *Id.* In the airport, the band exhibited loud and boisterous behavior. *Id.* at 1306. A passenger overheard a band member remark in Spanish about landing in the "capital city"; passengers interpreted this reference as Havana, Cuba, which was not the flight's destination. *Id.* at 1307. Once onboard, a band member twisted a flight attendant's arm. *Id.* She reported this assault to the captain. *Id.* A passenger who had overheard the discussion about Cuba while in the airport informed the flight attendant, who relayed this information to the pilot. *Id.* The pilot entered the cabin and asked the passenger for a description of what he heard; the pilot decided to remove the band from the flight. *Id.* The court held that the airline's decision to remove the band was not arbitrary and capricious based on the facts known to the captain at the time the decision was made. *Id.* The court relied on the pilot's assessment that the continued presence of the band may have subjected others to grave danger, based on the band's disruptive behavior, odd remarks about the plane's destination, and physical engagement with the flight attendant. *Id.*

Similarly, in *Ruta v. Delta Airlines, Inc.*, 322 F. Supp. 2d 391 (S.D.N.Y. 2004), a passenger's flight to Florida was delayed due to weather. *Id.* at 394. The passenger cut in front of other passengers at the boarding gate, interrupted the gate agent, and used foul language. *Id.* Travelers observed the passenger drinking alcohol prior to boarding. *Id.* Once on board, the passenger shouted "free booze," appeared intoxicated, and smelled like alcohol. *Id.* The passenger also kicked a flight attendant while the attendant was in the aisle. *Id.* The flight attendant informed the pilot of this behavior; he removed the passenger from the flight. *Id.* The court held that the airline's decision to remove the passenger was not arbitrary and capricious due to the pilot's knowledge of the passenger's disruptive and intoxicated behavior, and her physical interaction with a crew member. *Id.* at 395.

Applying this factor to Slade's circumstances, a court likely would find that FlyGreen was not justified in removing Slade from the flight. In contrast to the passenger in *Ruta*, Slade was sober and minding her own business in the terminal. While organizing her harmless powders, she was not exhibiting any obnoxious or insulting behavior, unlike the passengers in *Zervigon* and *Ruta*. In contrast, the two other female passengers were acting rudely by whispering. This provoked Slade to dangle the harmless powders in their direction, a fact that— importantly—was not known to any of the flight crew. Once onboard, Slade's jacket and satchel accidentally bumped one of the women. The woman said, "Watch it, you weirdo! Keep your crazy witchcraft junk away from me." This comment was offensive and intimidating to Slade, naturally causing her to mumble sarcastically about putting a hex on them. The fellow passengers provoked Slade's behavior on both occasions. Further, the foregoing specific reference to a "hex" was not relayed to the flight attendant; the women just stated that Slade had threatened them. Unlike the travelers in *Zervigon* and *Ruta*, Slade did not have any physical contact with any of the flight crew. Thus, this factor weighs in favor of a finding that FlyGreen's decision to remove Slade was arbitrary and capricious.

III. Courts Consider Any Time Constraints Affecting the Flight's Takeoff

When evaluating whether an airline's decision to remove a passenger was arbitrary or capricious, courts also consider whether the airline was under any time constraints affecting takeoff and, therefore, had limited time to evaluate the circumstances. *See, e.g., Christel v. AMR Corp.*, 222 F. Supp. 2d 335 (E.D.N.Y. 2002) (holding that the decision to refuse a passenger transportation was not arbitrary and capricious because, while the plane was about to take off the passenger became angry when asked to move a carry-on bag, acted in a hostile manner toward the flight attendant, ignored the crew's instructions, and became disorderly).

In FlyGreen's case, the flight takeoff time was indeed affected by weather; the pilot and crew were reacting to a pending storm that was causing them to expedite boarding. However, the flight ultimately ended up taking off on time—even considering Slade's removal. Overall, because FlyGreen was not holding up air traffic control, the pilot could have taken a few more minutes to investigate Slade's perspective on her interaction with the female passengers, had her explain the powders, and allowed her to provide any other information necessary to reassure the pilot that she posed no threat. Accordingly, this factor weighs in favor of a finding that the airline's decision was arbitrary and capricious.

IV. Courts Consider the General National Security Climate at the Time of the Flight

When evaluating the general national security climate at the time of the flight in determining whether an airline's decision to remove a passenger was arbitrary and capricious, courts consider prior hijackings as well as the intended destination of the flight. For example, in *Al-Qudhai'een v. American West Airlines, Inc.*, 267 F. Supp. 2d 841 (S.D. Ohio 2003), a passenger was traveling to Washington, D.C. *Id.* Later the passenger was informed there would be an unscheduled layover in Ohio, which irritated him. *Id.* Once on board, the passenger disregarded instructions regarding changing seats, he touched the cockpit door while using the first-class bathroom, and he anxiously asked the flight attendants questions about the length of the layover and whether the passengers would be switching aircrafts. *Id.* at 844. The flight attendants relayed this disconcerting information to the pilot, who ultimately decided to remove the passenger. *Id.* The court held that the decision to remove the passenger was not arbitrary and capricious because the event occurred only two years after 9/11, the flight destination was Washington, D.C.—a terrorism target—and the passenger made strange flight inquiries. *Id.*; *see also Dasrath v. Cont'l Airlines, Inc.*, 467 F. Supp. 2d 431 (D.N.J. 2006) (holding that an airline's decision to remove passengers was not arbitrary and capricious because the incident took place within five years of 9/11, the passenger was anxiously moving his bag around his seat area, and his wife had recently become employed by the airline).

Further, in *Shqeirat v. U.S. Airways Group, Inc.*, 645 F. Supp. 2d 765, 771 (D. Minn. 2009), six American passengers of Middle Eastern origin were traveling to Minneapolis. Three of the passengers had been traveling on one-way tickets. *Id.* at 772. At the boarding area, the passengers prayed loudly from the Koran and cursed U.S. involvement with Saddam Hussein. *Id.* Once onboard the flight, a few of the passengers switched seats in a disruptive manner. *Id.* The flight attendant informed the pilot of this behavior, and ultimately he engaged the police to remove the passengers from the flight. *Id.* at 774. The court held that the decision to remove the passengers was not arbitrary and capricious because the passengers purchased one-way tickets, checked no luggage, made anti-American remarks, and switched seats in an obtrusive manner while on the plane. *Id.* at 785.

In Slade's case, the United States had experienced no airline security issues in more than 30 years. Further, FlyGreen had never had any prior security-related events. Slade purchased a round-trip ticket to Florida, which is not a typical terrorist target. Although Slade did not check any bags, both of her carry-on bags cleared security. Additionally, although Slade made a sarcastic remark about putting a hex on the two female passengers, she made no comments or inquiries regarding the aircraft, flight, or destination and did not make any negative comments regarding the United States. An analysis of this factor weighs in favor of a finding that FlyGreen's decision to remove Slade from the flight was arbitrary and capricious.

V.   Pilots Are Entitled to Reasonably Rely on the Representations of the Flight Crew But Must Perform At Least a Cursory Inquiry

When evaluating the reasonableness of the pilot's reliance on the representations of a crewmember in determining whether an airline's decision to remove a passenger was arbitrary and capricious, courts consider whether it was proper for the pilot to make the decision without even the most cursory inquiry. For example, in *Cordero v. Cia Mexicana De Aviacion, S.A.*, 681 F.2d 669 (9th Cir. 1982), a passenger was traveling on a nonstop flight from Los Angeles to Mexico City. *Id.* at 670. After flight delays, passengers boarded the plane. The pilot made an announcement that the flight would be stopping in Mazatlan. *Id.* Frustrated, another traveler yelled insults directed at the pilot. *Id.* The pilot came out and warned that traveler to stop. *Id.* Inside the Mazatlan terminal, the original passenger circulated a petition complaining about the unscheduled stop. *Id.* As the passenger attempted to reboard the plane, airline personnel informed him that he would not be allowed to board because he had insulted the captain and crew (when in fact they had confused him with the other traveler who had been yelling insults). *Id.* The court held that the decision to remove the passenger was arbitrary and capricious because the pilot did not make even a cursory inquiry to determine the identity of the passenger who disrupted the flight. *Id.* at 672. *But see Cerqueira v. Am. Airlines, Inc.*, 520 F.3d 1, 15 (1st Cir. 2008) (holding that an experienced pilot's decision to remove a passenger was not arbitrary and capricious because the passenger spent an extended period of time in the bathroom, showed odd interest in the flight attendant's duties, and repeatedly requested to sit next to the emergency exit; a responsible decision maker could make this decision without additional inquiry).

In Slade's case, the pilot based his decision to deplane her strictly on a cursory scan of the contents of her satchel and full reliance on the word of the flight attendant about threats against the female passengers. However, the pilot had never met the flight attendant before that flight, as she was new to the airline. Further, the flight attendant had made rude and derogatory remarks about passengers and pilots in the gate area, calling into question her credibility and integrity. Because no responsible decision maker would rely on the new flight attendant without making at least a cursory further inquiry, this factor weighs in favor of a finding that FlyGreen's decision to remove Slade was arbitrary and capricious.

VI.   Conclusion

Applying the foregoing factors, it is likely that a court will find that FlyGreen's decision to remove Slade was arbitrary and capricious.

Appendix D: Legal Office Memorandum-Drafting Checklist

Step 1 (Gather the Client Facts)

- ☑ Review factual documents provided.
- ☑ Make a bullet-point list of facts (a chronology).
- ☑ Identify key characters, events, tangible items, and dates.
- ☑ Take note of any logic gaps in the client's narrative, for later follow-up.
- ☑ Interview the client (if possible) and take notes, adding to the chronology and filling gaps.
- ☑ Begin creating a client case file.

Step 2 (Identify the Client's Legal Issue)

- ☑ Determine what jurisdiction governs the client's case, situation, or opportunity.
- ☑ Identify the legal *question(s)* raised by the client.
- ☑ Write down: What exactly does my client want to know?
- ☑ Have I been provided any statutes, regulations, or case law as a starting point?
- ☑ Do these statutes, regulations, and/or case law help narrow the precise legal *issue?*

Step 3 (Conduct Additional Research)

- ☑ Is there a statute on point?
- ☑ Is there a regulation on point?
- ☑ Are there cases on point? Do the cases interpret a statute or regulation?
- ☑ Do I need to review secondary sources to get a bigger picture of the legal issue?
- ☑ From case cites, use Headnotes and Key Numbers, and check digests to find additional cases.
- ☑ Make sure the cases are still good law (use KeyCite, *Shepard's*, or BCite).

Step 4 (Brief Cases and Synthesize Rule)

- ☑ Brief each case:
  - ○ Parties (Roles in society? Relationship to one another?)
  - ○ Full citation

o Jurisdiction (important for determining whether the case is mandatory or persuasive authority)
o Date of decision
o Legal issue(s)
o Facts (procedural, substantive)
o Rule
o Parties' arguments
o Holding (there might be only one holding, or there may be two or more holdings on two or more different issues)
o Rationale underlying each holding
o Judgment

☑ If research yields numerous cases on the same issue, create a comparison chart:
o What are the holdings of each case?
o Are there similar facts? Different facts? Circle similar facts/themes/elements/factors.
o How do different facts/themes/elements/factors impact the court's decision in each case? Are there patterns?

☑ After reviewing a sufficient amount of case law, begin synthesizing the rule.

☑ Does the rule of law have required *elements*?

☑ Does the rule of law have a list of *factors* the court weighs?

Step 5 (Begin Outlining/Drafting the Discussion)

☑ Identify the elements/factors from the rule of law.

☑ For each element/factor at issue, jot down the names of the cases that best explain that element/factor.

☑ Select appropriate cases to illustrate each part of the rule in Rule Explanations plus signal cites + explanatory parentheticals.

☑ Outline a logical chronology of the case law to be discussed in the memo. (e.g., considering favorable/unfavorable holdings, clear/confusing judicial opinions, deep analysis/mere mention of the rule, etc.).

☑ Draft a Rule Explanation for at least one case for each element/factor:
o Rule statement (state a rule or subrule that will be applied from the case(s))
o Facts (explain the legally significant facts of the case; "In *Halstead*, . . .")
o Holding ("The *Halstead* court held . . .")
o Rationale ("The court reasoned . . .")
o Draft transitions between Rule Explanations

☑ Draft signal cites + explanatory parentheticals to add additional case law within the rule/Rule Explanation sections.

☑ Create a chart to compare the rule elements/factors to the client facts in the Rule Application section.

☑ Draft a Rule Application(s) section applying the rule to the client's facts:
  ○ Start with a transition/introductory sentence foreshadowing the ultimate conclusion on the part of the legal rule being addressed.
  ○ Apply the element(s)/factor(s) from the rule one by one.
  ○ Consider comparing/contrasting cases ("Similar to the victim in *Del Toro*, . . ." "In contrast to the victim in *Del Toro*, . . ." or "Like the claimant in *Halstead*, . . ." "Unlike the claimant in *Halstead*, . . .).
  ○ Draw a mini-conclusion on each element/factor

☑ If necessary for a multi-part rule, repeat the RA structure for each part of the rule.

☑ Draft an overall conclusion for the entire memorandum ("Based on the foregoing rule, the court likely will find . . .").

Step 6 (Draft the Umbrella Paragraph)

☑ Write an umbrella paragraph to the discussion section laying out
  ○ the client's legal issue,
  ○ the rule(s) (itemizing the elements/factors; identifying any aspects of the rule that are not at issue),
  ○ brief application of the rule to the client scenario, and
  ○ the overall conclusion(s).

Step 7 (Draft the Question Presented)

☑ "Under/Does/When" formula—introduce the governing law, the client's legal question, and the legally significant facts:

  Example: "Under _____ law, does our client _____, when: (1) _____, (2) _____ and (3) _____?"

Step 8 (Draft the Brief Answer)

☑ Answer the question presented, providing the reasons for the answer:
  ○ Give a one- or two-word answer, with a supportive concrete conclusory statement
  ○ State the rule (identifying elements/factors, and explaining the excludsion of the parts of the rule not at issue)
  ○ Briefly apply the rule to the client facts
  ○ State the conclusion on the legal question presented

Step 9 (Draft the Statement of Facts)

☑ Summarize the background and legally significant facts:
  ○ Will it make the most sense to the reader to recite the facts in chronological order?
  ○ Would it make better sense to link facts by issue/element/factor/theme?

☑ Summarize the relevant procedural facts if the case has proceeded to a formal legal action, via filing a complaint or petition. (Who sued whom? What are the allegations or causes of action in the complaint? Are there defenses raised by a party in an answer? Have the parties engaged in discovery? Was there a trial? What action did the trial court take? Did someone win on a motion to dismiss or summary judgment? Was there a jury trial or a bench trial? Who appealed? What did the appellate court do?)

Step 10 (Put It All Together)

☑ Make sure all the required sections of the memorandum are present.
☑ Add helpful numbered or lettered section headings and subheadings, if necessary (in a longer memo).
☑ Add smooth transitions between paragraphs and sections.
  o Add transitions between REs.
  o Add transitions between RA paragraphs (topic/thesis sentences and mini-conclusions).

Step 11 (Add Overall Conclusion)

☑ Restate the answer to the client's question.

Step 12 (Edit! Edit! Edit!)

☑ Review numerous times for different purposes:
  o Substance/logic review (read the document as a whole to make sure the legal conclusion makes sense overall)
  o Paragraph and section structure, logic, and clarity
  o Sentence-level clarity review
  o Word-by-word proofreading
  o Visual formatting review
    o Check heading numbering, indentation, and spacing.
    o Check that underlining/boldface/italics are used consistently.
    o Check that no headings or one-line sentences dangle alone at the bottom of a page. (If they do, insert a page break.)
    o Check margins, font, line spacing, page numbering.
  o Professional and respectful tone
  o Reader engagement (is it interesting to read?)
  o Citation review
  o Submission rules (e.g., adhere to word count or page limits)

Appendix E: "Bring It, Socrates!"

Conquering Anxiety About the Socratic Method and Public Speaking in Law School

During the fall semester of the first year of law school, most students experience at least some low-grade anxiety about being called on in class and queried by a law professor about a complex legal case or rule. However, if individually you are struggling with a more *extreme* sense of anxiety about your professors' use of the Socratic method or other modes of public speaking in the law school arena (including the oral argument in the Spring semester of the 1L year), you are not alone. Some students mistakenly assume that their fear of public speaking is more severe than that of other students and that a hesitance to jump into the classroom fray somehow means they are not cut out to be lawyers. These assumptions are not true at all. Extreme public speaking anxiety in the law school context is an obstacle students definitely can overcome—with the right help and encouragement.[1] Some students unknowingly bring buried stressors from childhood, adolescence, high school, college, and postcollege experiences to law school. Others simply might be introverts who naturally prefer thinking and writing over responding instantaneously to a question they are not quite ready to answer. Others may have been confident and extroverted in college classes, but law school somehow triggers insecurities from the distant past that these students have not yet adequately worked through to resolution.[2]

If you fit in any of the foregoing categories, this appendix first encourages you to consider addressing the origins of your individual public speaking anxiety (everyone has a different life story), and then offers five tangible steps you can take to prepare for a Socratic classroom dialogue. Chapter 32 specifically addresses how to prepare for an oral argument.

---

[1] The author of this book personally suffered from extreme public speaking anxiety—in law school, in a 15-year litigation career, and as a novice law professor. After transitioning to academia, she began to intensely study the psychology underlying this fear and finally was able to conquer it herself, after two decades of struggle. The helpful resources she found, as well as citations to two articles she has written on this topic, are included at the end of this appendix.

[2] As many of the references in the bibliography at the end of this appendix suggest, considering the roots of public speaking anxiety is an important step for students who truly desire to conquer this difficulty; the anxiety might be coming from a deeper place, and students who wish to make lifelong changes must be willing to self-reflect, dig up the root, and send it to the compost heap. However, for some this may require the assistance of someone more skilled in professional counseling. There is nothing wrong with asking for help to figure out what might be holding you back from "finding your lawyer voice."

I. Consider Exploring the Roots of Your Public Speaking Anxiety

Some students experiencing an inordinate amount of angst toward the Socratic method or other law school public speaking experiences try to cope by opting out, taking a "pass," seeking accommodations, or accepting a grade reduction for nonparticipation. However, as the author of this book can personally attest, avoidance certainly may feel better temporarily, but a much more effective long-term solution is to (1) probe and then address the roots of the anxiety in a safe environment, (2) establish a conscious plan for approaching public speaking experiences in law school, (3) work through each public speaking opportunity with thoughtful and mindful self-support and mentorship, (4) anticipate experiencing the rise and fall of the anxiety symptoms in each public speaking encounter and managing them through mental and physical routines, and (5) realize that you can indeed speak successfully about the law. Your delivery does not need to be perfect; just be present and do your best.

If you are interested in investigating and addressing the roots of your public speaking anxiety, consider reading the following sources:

Heidi K. Brown, *Empowering Law Students to Overcome Extreme Public Speaking Anxiety: Why "Just Be It" Works and "Just Do It" Doesn't*, 53 Duq. L. Rev. — (2015).

Heidi K. Brown, *The "Silent but Gifted" Law Student: Transforming Anxious Public Speakers into Well-Rounded Advocates*, 18 Legal Writing 291 (2012).

Susan Cain, *Quiet: The Power of Introverts in a World That Can't Stop Talking* (2012).

Steve Flowers, *The Mindful Path Through Shyness* (2009).

Erika B. Hilliard, *Living Fully with Shyness and Social Anxiety* (2005).

Barbara G. Markway, Cheryl N. Carmin, C. Alec Pollard & Teresa Flynn, *Dying of Embarrassment: Help for Social Anxiety and Phobia* (1992).

Barbara G. Markway & Gregory P. Markway, *Painfully Shy: How to Overcome Social Anxiety and Reclaim Your Life* (2001).

Ivy Naistadt, *Speak Without Fear* (2004).

Once you have begun examining possible causes of your particular anxiety, try the techniques set forth below for consciously preparing for a law school public speaking experience, such as a Socratic dialogue in the classroom. As you commence this journey toward conquering extreme public speaking anxiety— which *will* be a successful one—just take a deep breath and give yourself time to find, and develop, your "lawyer voice." The author of this book strongly contends that the legal industry needs to make greater space for the quiet thinkers: you.[3]

II. Prepare for Class with the Dialogue in Mind

A. What Types of Questions Can I Expect?

Many students prepare for the Socratic method simply by plowing through the assigned reading. However, students experiencing public speaking anxiety need to do more than review and highlight the substantive material; they need to deconstruct the question-and-answer process in advance and develop a plan for handling a back-and-forth interaction with a professor (especially an intimidating one) in a calm and mindful manner—being aware of what is happening mentally and physically, during the anticipation phase and the actual event, remaining present throughout the ups and downs of the communication exchange, and focusing on doing their best even when the repartee does not go perfectly. The first step in getting ready for a Socratic dialogue is to think about what types of specific questions the professor might ask and then tailor the class preparation accordingly. In the first few weeks of law school, rather than writing down other students' answers to Socratic questions about the law and rules, take notes instead on the types of questions the professors ask. Can you detect a pattern or rhythm of phrases and inquiries that help you understand what information each professor wants to know?

To begin a Socratic dialogue, about a judicial decision, a professor might ask you some easy questions such as the parties' names and relationship (and perhaps their roles in society), the jurisdiction, the date, and the basic facts of the case. You welcome these questions because they are easy to answer if you have read the homework; they are not trick questions. You can get into a rhythm or volley of a dialogue and calm yourself down by answering these questions, giving you time to catch your breath and slow a rapid heart rate.

Then the professor will delve deeper. The IRAC formula should help you prepare for the tougher questions in advance. Focus on the *issues* in the case before the court, the *rule* applied by the court, the *application* of that rule to the facts of the case, and then the court's holding, or *conclusion*. As you do your homework, use IRAC to help you brainstorm questions the professor will ask. Take notes in "IRAC form" on your assigned reading.

On a more complex level, your professor might ask you to explain each party's theory of the case. What arguments did each side make? Can you

---

[3] See Heidi K. Brown, *Empowering Law Students to Overcome Extreme Public Speaking Anxiety: Why "Just Be It" Works and "Just Do It" Doesn't*, 53 Duq. L. Rev. 182 (Winter 2015).

glean a theme from the case? Is the case about fairness? Equality? Property rights? Unkept promises? Sometimes trying to devise a theme helps simplify a legally complicated case. If you had to describe the case in a Twitter tweet, on a car bumper sticker, in a Facebook post, in a magazine ad, on a t-shirt, or in a 30-second commercial spot on television, what would the message be?

Make sure you are clear as to what the court held on the legal issue; focus on the answer to the substantive legal question rather than the procedural result. Professors also like to dig into the court's rationale, or reasoning, for its holding; in other words, "Why did the court rule the way it did?" Can you think of any public policy reasons for the decision? Public policy is just a fancy term for considerations of fairness, equality, clarity and consistency in the law, efficiency, conservation of resources, ethics, morality, and similar concerns.

The most rigorous Socratic questions might involve applying the same rule you just discussed to a *new* hypothetical set of facts. This type of interchange requires students to "think on their feet" a bit more—which can be difficult for reticent public speakers. In your preparation, try to brainstorm alternate sets of facts and see whether you can apply the same rule to new scenarios.

Also get into the habit of looking up words in the casebook that you do not know. Keep a running list of the definitions; your professor might ask you to define them.

B. Structure Your Case Briefs and Class Preparation Notes So They Are Easy to Access and Use in Class

Make sure your case briefs or class preparation notes are easy to read and organized with headings such as "Issue," "Rule," "Holding," and "Theme" so you can quickly locate answers to the professor's questions. You do not want to have to flip through pages of case material to find the answers you carefully framed at home. Consider printing out your case briefs and class preparation notes, so you do not have to search for the answers on your computer.

C. Have a Plan in Case You Get Stumped by a Question

Students experiencing extreme public speaking anxiety tend to dread that precise moment when they realize they do not know how to answer the professor's question, their mind goes blank, silence ensues, and they feel a sea of eyes staring at them as every additional millisecond passes. But consider this reality: The law is complex, and throughout our legal careers there will be numerous times when we do not know the answer to a question off the top of our head, and we need to think about it. This does not make us bad lawyers or unintelligent; it makes us thinkers, and smart ones at that. Professors also experience this situation; often students ask interesting questions that the professor has never previously considered, and therefore needs time to ponder to come up with the appropriate answer. Do not fear; instead, anticipate that there will be a moment in which you do not know how to answer a professor's question and have a plan to deal with it. In the event you get stumped by a professor's question, return to your theme of the case. If you do not know the legal answer to a question, you might offer what you believe is the theme of the case and see whether that helps you get to the answer she seeks. Again, case themes might include preserving equity, following through on a promise, protecting property, or antidiscrimination. You might respond honestly, "Well, I'm not exactly sure of the answer to the question posed, but the theme of this case seems to be X, and therefore . . . ." No one can judge you for being your authentic truthful self.

D. Practice Answering Questions Aloud at Home

Try practicing answering questions aloud at home too. Just hearing your own voice saying those legal words out loud will show you that you do indeed know what you are talking about and already "sound like a lawyer."

III. Be Realistic

Many times, anxiety blossoms when we take an everyday event and blow it up in our minds into something greater than it actually is. If you were in medical school, it is likely that no one would ask you to perform quadruple bypass surgery in your first week; instead you would probably start anatomy class with something less high-stakes. Likewise, in law school, it might feel like you are being expected to argue before the Supreme Court on day one, but you are not. Consider your first year of Socratic dialogue like dissecting a frog in a science class: supremely tragic for the poor frog, yes indeed (!), but a low-stakes learning experience—and one of many. Try to be realistic about the classroom "on-call experience." It is just a dialogue between you and a professor—just another human being—who is there to help you learn in a different way. Just like any other conversation you participate in every hour of every day, if you do not understand the question, it is okay to say so (respectfully, of course). If you were conversing with your professor in the elevator and did not understand the way he phrased a question, you might simply say, "I'm not sure I understand the question. Do you mind asking it again?"

Another way in which we overintensify a classroom Q&A session in our minds into the pressure equivalent to delivering a Superbowl halftime show is that we imagine the eyes of all our peers on us, scrutinizing our every syllable. It is important to realize that not everyone in the class is hanging on our every word. Unfortunately, some students are probably surreptitiously (or not) multitasking.

Others are probably relieved that they were not called on, and their brains are distracted momentarily by feelings of liberation. Still others are rooting for you to successfully handle the questions so the professor does not move on to another candidate. So while we may anticipate judgment from our peers, in reality, not everyone is following what we are saying, and those who are listening are likely hoping that our Socratic experience is an easy and pleasant one.

So, try to be more realistic about the stakes involved. If you do not know the answer, it is not the end of your legal career; actually, it is the beginning. Ask the professor, respectfully, to perhaps repeat or rephrase the question. Or mention your theme of the case, as discussed above. Just do your best. You are dissecting a theoretical frog, not performing quadruple bypass surgery.

IV. Consider Your "Happy Place"

Another technique for handling the Socratic dialogue in a law school class is to remind yourself how 100 percent competent you are at verbal communication in other venues or at other activities in your life. Perhaps you feel most confident in your kickboxing class at the gym, or regaling your friends with funny tales while sharing a pizza, or hanging out with your family. Try to bring some of that confidence into your classroom persona. You probably would not be intimidated if someone asked you a confusing or difficult question at the gym, or around a table at your favorite restaurant, or at a family get-together. You would simply ponder your response, engage in a conversation, and ask for clarity if you did not understand a question or needed more information.

You are a capable, confident, smart human being. Just remind yourself of a place outside school in which you thrive and try to bring a little piece of that environment into the classroom with you.

V. Use Your Physical Body to Help Your Brain

An aspect of public speaking that affects us deeply (because we think we cannot control it) is the physical manifestation of anxiety. Our heart pounds; we become short of breath; we may turn red, start sweating, break out in hives, or shake. We do not really understand what is happening to us, much less how to stop it, and we are worried that everyone can see us unraveling.

A very effective technique for assuming some control over our public speaking anxiety is to study, and become aware of, what is happening to our physical bodies when we are nervous. Ivy Naistadt, author of *Speak Without Fear* (2004), provides a wonderful description in Chapter 7 of her book of how anxiety manifests in our physical selves; she then reveals simple adjustments we can make in our physical posture and positioning during a public speaking opportunity that have dramatically helpful effects on our breathing and blood flow. Physical manifestations of anxiety differ from person to person. However, it is phenomenal how much control we can assert over our mental angst when we try subtle physical alterations, like adopting a balanced physical stance (whether standing or seated) and consciously slowing our breathing. Think about how athletes like boxers, martial artists football players, tennis players, golfers, and ballroom dancers adopt a steady stance before starting a movement.

Read Chapter 7 of Naistadt's book and follow her suggested techniques. For example, when you are called on in class, make sure you are sitting squarely in your chair without crossed legs, with your feet on the floor. Uncross your arms. The more you open up your physical self, the more your breath and blood can move, giving you oxygen you need to think clearly. Take three or four slow breaths in and out before saying your first words; you can raise your hand to acknowledge your presence to the professor while you are doing so, but that nonverbal interaction will last mere seconds and no one will notice you breathing (with mindful intention). When you begin speaking, amplify your voice to the person farthest away from you in the room. Make eye contact with the professor. Pretend this is just a normal conversation between two people.

If you turn red or feel blotchiness or heat rising up your neck, tell yourself, "So what if I'm red. Who cares?" Take a full breath before every single response to a professor's question and project your voice. Again, this will open up, instead of restrict, your air and blood flow, and give your brain the tools to do its job. If you continue to feel the physical effects of your anxiety, be mindful of them, be present with them, and do not try to control them; acknowledge that, "okay, I am short of breath, but in a minute or two my breath will come back." Note that, "my face feels hot, but in a few minutes it will feel normal again." Let the physical manifestations run their course; they always will revert back to "normal." For your growth in tackling this challenge, it is important to understand that each public speaking opportunity at the beginning inevitably will bring a rise and fall of these natural biological reactions, but you will survive each experience, and eventually (as you conquer the mental side of public speaking anxiety) the physical symptoms will subside faster.

VI. Allow Only Positive Internal Messages to Enter Your Mindset

In the seconds that tick away between the moment the professor calls your name and when you start speaking, messages might flood your brain: "I can't do this! I hate this! I'm going to fail! Get me out of here! Everyone is looking at me! I'll never make it as a lawyer! Everyone in here is smarter than I am!"

Instead of allowing those negative missives to cloud your thinking, as you plan ahead for a Socratic dialogue or an upcoming public speaking event, make a list of realistic, positive messages—in your own words. Write them on an index card and place it in front of you, or at least have it tucked away in your notebook. You are going to tell yourself mantras similar to the following:

- This is not quadruple bypass surgery; I am merely dissecting a tiny theoretical frog.
- Not everyone in this room is paying attention to what I am about to say, and most everyone else is rooting for me.
- I engage in normal stress-free intelligent conversations with people every hour of every day. This is just another conversation.
- If I don't understand the question, it's okay to say so.
- If I don't know the answer to the question, there are other things that I *do* know and can talk about, like my own theme of the case.
- This classroom conversation is only ten minutes of my three-year law school education.
- I am smart.
- I am successful.
- I am doing my best.
- Someday I am going to be a tremendous lawyer because I will have empathy for people who experience anxiety like me.

If any harmful mantras creep in, just turn them away. Try that for ten seconds. And keep doing it for another ten seconds when the next question comes. And so on.

Note from the Author

People who do not suffer from public speaking anxiety might casually advise tell you that the best way to overcome public speaking anxiety is to don your pair of Nikes and yell, "Just do it!", as you psychologically bungee-jump your way to an anxiety-free existence. As a litigator and law professor who struggled with extreme public speaking anxiety throughout a 20-year legal career, I respectfully disagree. Mantras like "Just do it!" and "Fake it till you make it!" do not not work for this particular obstacle (trust me, I've tried); instead, you have to "Just be it" while you mindfully work through the kinks of public speaking anxiety and "find your lawyer voice." It is very important to acknowledge that this fear is genuine and has deep roots that might not be easy to yank out on the first try. That is okay. The fact that you may have public speaking anxiety has exactly zero correlation with how successful you will be as an attorney. You need to give yourself permission to explore where this anxiety comes from (possibly seeking guidance from a law school mentor or a qualified professional counselor), and then cut yourself some slack to practice some of the foregoing strategies for conquering each public speaking opportunity one at a time.

If you have any questions or need advice on how to get started, please feel free to contact me at heidi@theintrovertedlawyer.com. I have been in your shoes and know how scary it can feel. But I promise, you can do it.

VII. BIBLIOGRAPHY

Resources for Assisting Law Students in Overcoming Extreme Public Speaking Anxiety

Heidi K. Brown, *Empowering Law Students to Overcome Extreme Public Speaking Anxiety: Why "Just Be It" Works and "Just Do It" Doesn't*, 53 Duq. L. Rev. 182 (2015).

Heidi K. Brown, *The "Silent but Gifted" Law Student: Transforming Anxious Public Speakers into Well-Rounded Advocates*, 18 Legal Writing 291 (2012).

Susan Cain, *Quiet: The Power of Introverts in a World That Can't Stop Talking* (Crown Publishing Group 2012).

Susan Cain, *The Rise of the New Groupthink*, N.Y. Times, Jan. 13, 2012.

Sophia Dembling, *The Introvert's Way: Living a Quiet Life in a Noisy World* (Penguin Group 2012).

Carol S. Dweck, *Mindset: The New Psychology of Success* (Ballantine Books 2008).

Janet E. Esposito, *In the Spotlight: Overcome Your Fear of Public Speaking and Performing* (Strong Books 2000).

M. F. Fensholt, *The Francis Effect: The Real Reason You Hate Public Speaking and How to Get over It* (Oakmont Press 2006).

Steve Flowers, *The Mindful Path Through Shyness* (New Harbinger Publications 2009).

Laurie Helgoe, *Introvert Power: Why Your Inner Life Is Your Hidden Strength* (Sourcebooks, Inc. 2008).

Erika B. Hilliard, *Living Fully with Shyness and Social Anxiety* (Da Capo Press 2005).

Jennifer Kahnweiler, Ph.D., *Quiet Influence: The Introvert's Guide to Making a Difference* (Berrett-Koehler Publishers 2013).

Jennifer Kahnweiler, Ph.D., *The Introverted Leader: Building on Your Quiet Strength* (Berrett-Koehler Publishers 2013).

Jane Korn, *Teaching Talking: Oral Communication Skills in a Law Course*, 54 J. Legal Educ. 588 (2004).

Arnie Kozak, Ph.D., *The Everything Guide to the Introvert Edge* (Adams Media 2013).

Marti Olsen Laney, Psy.D., *The Introvert Advantage: How to Thrive in an Extrovert World* (Workman Publishing 2002).

Barbara G. Markway, Cheryl N. Carmin, C. Alec Pollard & Teresa Flynn, *Dying of Embarrassment: Help for Social Anxiety and Phobia* (1992).

Barbara G. Markway & Gregory P. Markway, *Painfully Shy: How to Overcome Social Anxiety and Reclaim Your Life* (2001).

Ivy Naistadt, *Speak Without Fear* (Harper Perennial 2004).

Sarah E. Ricks, *Some Strategies to Teach Reluctant Talkers to Talk About Law*, 54 J. Legal Educ. 570 (2004).

Natalie H. Rogers, *The New Talk Power* (Capitol Books 2000).

Appendix F: Six Tips for Converting a Law School Writing Assignment into a Job Search Writing Sample

(1) **Choose work product that best reflects your legal writing and analytical abilities.** In your 1L legal writing class, over the course of a year, you typically will produce two objective legal memoranda and two persuasive briefs. Your legal writing proficiency likely will improve as each semester progresses, and your analysis presumably will become more sophisticated. When selecting written work product for a writing sample, choose a memo or brief that best represents your ability as a legal writer. You also might think about the substance of the written work and decide which piece of writing you would feel most comfortable discussing in a potential interview.

(2) **Consider a document of appropriate length for your intended reader.** Attorneys responsible for hiring law students for summer jobs are busy and have limited free time. Do not submit an overly long writing sample. Some employers impose page limits on writing samples. Even if there is no page limit, ideally you should provide a five- to eight-page (double-spaced) sample of your writing that demonstrates your aptitude for fully analyzing a legal question. If the memo or brief that you believe best reflects your writing ability exceeds eight pages because it addresses more than one legal question, consider editing the document to limit the discussion to a single substantive issue. This does not mean you can simply delete a second issue and submit the document. Make sure you read the entire document and edit the introduction, facts, headings, umbrella paragraph(s), and conclusion to reflect the adjusted focus to one isolated issue.

(3) **Read your professor's grading comments and revise the document accordingly.** In grading your work product, your legal writing professors spend a significant amount of time providing comments and a constructive critique to help you improve your writing. You should review these comments (and your scores on any grading rubric provided) in detail, to grasp how you can enrich the document. Then set aside time to do some serious editing, including (1) studying the comments to determine what aspects of the paper need revision, (2) incorporating your professor's suggestions *throughout* the document (not just in the particular sentences or paragraphs where he or she made margin comments), and (3) making your writing sample the best it can be.

(4) Consider whether party names or factual details should be modified or made more formal for a potential employer. Sometimes law professors design legal writing assignments to involve clients with humorous names or wild fact patterns to keep class discussion fun and interesting. Prior to submitting a law school assignment to a legal employer, review your work product to determine whether any humorous names or zany fact details should be adjusted in tone or formality for a practicing attorney as your audience. If you change names or details, proofread carefully to ensure you have done so consistently throughout the document.

(5) Proofread, proofread, proofread. A busy legal employer might make an adverse summer employment decision based on a quick scan of a candidate's writing sample, rather than a deep read of the substance. Maximize your chances of getting hired by presenting a perfectly proofread document. One cursory proofread is insufficient. As recommended in Chapter 18, consider reading the document several different times for distinct purposes to catch any and all grammatical, typographical, citation, and logic errors:

(a) Check the sample memorandum against drafting checklists provided by your professor and the checklist in Appendix D. For sample briefs, check to make sure all the expected substantive components are included.

(b) Read the document *overall*, for IREAC/CREAC logic and clarity. Read the document out loud for this purpose. Ask yourself whether the analysis will make sense to a reader unfamiliar with the subject matter or whether you have made assumptions about your reader's background knowledge that necessitate revision.

(c) Read the document at the *section and/or paragraph level*, focusing on the substantive logic of each standalone section and/or paragraph: Does each section and/or paragraph have a natural arc from topic/thesis sentence, to analysis, to conclusion?

(d) Read the document at the *sentence* level to tighten phrasing by deleting unnecessary repetition of language, eliminating extraneous introductory text (such as "there is a possible argument that . . .") and converting passive to active voice. Ask yourself whether each sentence will make sense to a reader unfamiliar with the subject matter. Do you need to convert "legalese" to plain English? Have you used proper grammar and punctuation in every sentence?

(e) Consider reading the document backwards (yes, backwards!) on a *word-by-word* level to catch typographical and punctuation errors that writers inadvertently miss when reading a document numerous times for substance (e.g., trial v. trail, statute v. statue, contract v. contact).

(f) Review the document for professional and respectful *tone* and *formality*.

(g) Review the document for its *interest level*: Is it engaging to read? Does the client's story resonate?

(h) Visually scan the document at the *page* level to catch formatting errors (e.g., dangling headings; inconsistent font, spacing, indentations, or margins; missing page numbers) and to ensure paragraphs are of appropriate length.

(i)   Focus solely on checking the legal *citation* throughout the document.

(j)   Make sure the document conforms to any specific *rules or guidelines* provided by the potential legal employer for submission of writing samples—length, format (Microsoft Word v. PDF), electronic v. hard copy.

(k)   Finally, have someone else read the document—ideally a lawyer or business professional who is unfamiliar with the assignment—and have him or her identify if and where the document falls short in clarity and professional presentation. (When submitting documents to your professor for a grade, you should always follow your school's policies against plagiarism and obtaining editing/proofreading assistance outside the classroom. However, when submitting a writing sample for a job interview, there typically is no prohibition against having a trusted third party review the document before submission to a potential employer. When in doubt, check with your Career Services Department.)

(6)   Give your reader context. When you transmit the document to a potential legal employer, consider whether the reader might appreciate a two- or three-sentence summary of the context of the writing sample, such as the following:

> This writing sample is a legal office memorandum I wrote for my Legal Practice course at New York Law School this past semester. I represented an airline passenger who was involuntarily removed from a flight on the airline FlyGreen for an alleged discriminatory reason. My eight-page memorandum summarizes federal law regarding the circumstances under which an airline may remove a passenger from a flight for safety reasons without incurring liability.

The foregoing process will take considerable effort, so set aside an appropriate block of time to focus on creating a strong writing sample to amplify your employment opportunities. You might consider dedicating a full day for the substantive editing process, then shelve the document for a day or two, and return to it with fresh eyes for each phase of editing and proofreading. Best of luck!

Appendix G: Sample Complaint

IN THE UNITED STATES DISTRICT COURT
FOR THE SOUTHERN DISTRICT OF NEW YORK

Riggins Garment Company, a New York Corporation, Plaintiff, v. Cornerstone Insurance Company, a Massachusetts corporation, Defendant.	) Case No. Y14-044-AML))) **COMPLAINT**))) REQUEST FOR JURY TRIAL)))

COMES NOW Plaintiff Riggins Garment Company ("Riggins") by counsel, and for its Complaint against Defendant Cornerstone Insurance Company ("Cornerstone") states as follows:

Jurisdiction and Venue

1. This court has jurisdiction over this action pursuant to 28 U.S.C. § 1332 because there is complete diversity of citizenship between the parties and there is more than $75,000 in controversy in this action.

2. Venue is proper in the United States District Court for the Southern District of New York pursuant to 28 U.S.C. § 1391(b) in that the property damage and financial losses which are the subject of the insurance policies at issue in this case occurred in this District. Further, two underlying lawsuits filed against Plaintiff Riggins by third-parties, for which Plaintiff Riggins sought legal defense and insurance coverage from its insurer Defendant Cornerstone, which the insurer wrongfully denied, were filed in state court in this geographical District. Further, Defendant Cornerstone owed its insured, Riggins, insurance coverage and a defense in this District based on an insurance policy sold to Plaintiff Riggins in the State of New York for business operations conducted here.

-1-

Parties

3. Plaintiff Riggins is a company incorporated in the State of New York that imports fabrics and textiles, and manufactures garments which it sells to key players in New York's fashion industry. Its principal place of business is located on Front Street in the South Street Seaport area of Lower Manhattan.

4. Defendant Cornerstone is an insurance company that has been operating in Boston, Massachusetts for over 100 years. It provides various types of insurance to small businesses, including but not limited to professional liability insurance, fire insurance, general comprehensive liability insurance, worker's compensation insurance, and business interruption insurance.

Facts

5. Plaintiff Riggins has been in the garment industry since 1990, importing textiles from countries like India, Bangladesh, Cambodia, and Mexico, and using them to manufacture garments and clothing lines for designer labels in New York's fashion industry.

6. The company was founded by a married couple named John and Fiona Riggins. John and Fiona are members of the company's Board of Directors. The Board also includes John's sister, Maia Mandell ("Mandell"), who is an attorney and serves as in-house counsel to the company.

7. The company leases a warehouse space in a brick building located on Front Street in the historic South Street Seaport area of Manhattan.

8. When the company was first founded in 1990, Mr. Riggins purchased a comprehensive general liability (CGL) and business interruption insurance policy from Defendant Cornerstone. To purchase the policy, the company had to complete a detailed application.

9. Upon approval by Cornerstone's insurance risk analyst, Jamie Plunkett, the insurance company issued a full coverage insurance policy (Policy No. 3261970) to Plaintiff Riggins which was designed to cover comprehensive business operations, including losses due to property damage, personal injury, and third-party lawsuits. The policy provided coverage limits of $5 million per occurrence. The policy also provided that Defendant Cornerstone would defend the insured, Plaintiff Riggins, in all third-party lawsuits covered under the policy.

10. Beginning in 1990, Plaintiff Riggins paid an annual premium of $24,000 to Defendant Cornerstone, paid in monthly installments. This premium increased gradually each year. Currently, Plaintiff Riggins pays a monthly premium of $2,900, for an annual premium of $34,800.

11. For 23 years, Plaintiff Riggins paid its insurance premiums on time. In fact, to date, Defendant Cornerstone has cashed checks in the total amount of over $635,000 from Plaintiff Riggins.

12. Up until 2013, Plaintiff Riggins had never once filed an insurance claim.

13. Over the 23 years that Plaintiff Riggins has been in business, the company has grown its success, expanding to several floors of its warehouse facility on Front Street. Its clients include several premiere fashion designers in New York City, including Howell + Brown and EHD Brand. The company also provides clothing lines for several musical artists for their tours, including Bronwyn D and The Inchi Band.

14. In October 2012, Hurricane Sandy hit the East Coast and had devastating effects in New York City, especially in the South Street Seaport area.

15. Many of the historic buildings in the Seaport area were damaged substantially due to floodwaters, as the storm surge from the East River flooded many buildings up to the second floor. Almost all the buildings on Front Street—including numerous restaurants, coffee shops, apartment buildings, and businesses, were ordered evacuated and closed, pending water rehabilitation work and subsequent environmental and safety inspections.

16. Rehabilitation work commenced immediately once the storm had subsided; however, throughout the remainder of 2012 and much of 2013, many of the buildings on Front Street remained closed.

17. When the storm hit in October 2012, Plaintiff Riggins took steps to protect its warehouse stock; however, the floodwater damaged the entire first floor of the warehouse, destroying inventory, textiles, files, computers, manufacturing equipment, furniture and artwork, etc. Plaintiff Riggins estimates property damage losses in the amount of $1.1 million due to water and mold.

18. Further, Plaintiff Riggins had to shut down importing and manufacturing operations for a period of four months until March 1, 2013 when it secured temporary alternative workspace in Williamsburg, Brooklyn. Plaintiff Riggins moved as many of the undamaged textiles as it could from the Front Street location to the Williamsburg Brooklyn location, and attempted to resume importing and manufacturing operations in March 2013 as best it could.

19. During the period of closure, Plaintiff Riggins was unable to perform several contracts for clothing lines for several of its customers. Unfortunately, Plaintiff Riggins was unable to fill an order for designer Howell + Brown in advance of Fashion Week in February 2013. Further, Plaintiff Riggins was unable to fill an order for The Inchi

Band, for costumes for backup dancers needed for an April 2013 tour. Both Howell + Brown and The Inchi Band filed lawsuits in New York state court against Plaintiff Riggins, alleging breach of contract damages exceeding a combined total of $500,000. One lawsuit was filed in May 2013, and the other in July 2013. The New York state court granted Plaintiff Riggins time extensions to file Answers in both lawsuits, pending submission of the claims to Defendant Cornerstone.

20. By August 31, 2013, the NYC Department of Buildings had authorized several Front Street businesses to resume occupancy of their facilities after water and mold remediation was complete, and the structures passed environmental and safety inspections.

21. Plaintiff Riggins began to move back into its Front Street facility.

22. In September 2013, Plaintiff Riggins directed its in-house counsel, Mandell, to review the terms of its insurance policies and begin filing claims for insurance coverage of its losses in accordance with the policy terms and notice requirements.

23. Plaintiff Riggins filed its claims for coverage of its property damage losses with its insurer on September 15, 2013.

24. Also on September 15, 2013, Plaintiff Riggins filed claims for coverage of the potential damages from the two lawsuits pending against it, and also submitted a formal request for Defendant Cornerstone to provide and fund a legal defense against both actions, in accordance with the insurance policy terms.

25. For three months, Plaintiff Riggins received no communication from its insurer, despite repeated calls, letters, and follow-up emails from in-house counsel, Mandell, to the company's insurance representative listed on the 2013 premium statements, Todd Nicks ("Nicks").

26. On December 18, 2013, in-house counsel, Mandell, called the insurance company and was told by an administrative assistant, Jeremy Connor, that Nicks no longer worked for the company, and the policies had been transferred to a new representative, Nadine Valentino.

27. On December 27, 2013, a different insurance representative named Sam Manning sent an e-mail to Mandell indicating that the insurance claims had been further referred to Defendant Cornerstone's claims adjuster and in-house counsel, Madeline Hewes ("Hewes") for follow-up investigation and evaluation.

28. On January 2, 2014, the insurer sent Plaintiff Riggins a one-page letter denying coverage for all of the alleged property damage losses and refusing to defend the insured against the two lawsuits pending in state court.

29. The letter was signed by Hewes, as Defendant Cornerstone's claims adjuster and in-house counsel.

-4-

30. The letter denied coverage and declined to defend the lawsuits on the following alleged grounds:
    a. "The insured failed to make timely insurance premium payments."
    b. "The insured made false misrepresentations in its original policy application."
    c. "The insured failed to comply with the insurance policy's notice requirements and deadlines for filing claims."
    d. "The losses claimed by the insured are not covered losses."
    e. "The insured failed to mitigate its damages and further exacerbated its own losses, nullifying the insurance coverage."
    f. "The losses claimed are excluded under numerous policy exclusions."
31. On January 3, 2014, Plaintiff Riggins sent a letter to the insurer, signed by in-house counsel Mandell, asking it to reconsider its denial of coverage, and requesting the insurer to honor its coverage responsibilities and duty to defend its insured against the two lawsuits.
32. The insurer failed to respond to the letter.
33. On January 6, 2014, Mandell telephoned the insurer and was informed by Brandi Caldwell, assistant to claims adjuster and in-house counsel, Hewes, that the insurer would not reconsider its position.
34. Plaintiff Riggins' in-house counsel, Mandell, filed Answers to the Complaints filed in the two lawsuits, which are now proceeding to the discovery phase.

Count I: Breach of the Contractual Duty to Provide Coverage and Defend its Insured

35. Plaintiff Riggins incorporates the allegations in the above paragraphs of this Complaint as though fully alleged herein.
36. Valid insurance contracts existed between Plaintiff Riggins and the insurer.
37. Plaintiff Riggins fully performed all of the obligations and conditions to be performed by it under the insurance policies, or has been excused from performing such obligations and conditions as a result of the insurer's breach of its duty to provide coverage and defend its insured.
38. By selling the insurance policies, the insurer agreed to, and assumed a contractual duty to, provide coverage for property damage and provide a defense for suits seeking damages for "personal injury and property damage" and financial losses therefrom as defined in the policies.
39. Plaintiff Riggins suffered significant financial losses and property damage as a result of the floodwaters flowing from Hurricane Sandy, and has been sued for additional property damage and financial losses in the two pending lawsuits.

40. These losses are exactly the type of losses covered under the insurance policies, triggering the insurer's duty and obligation to provide coverage and a defense.
41. The insurer has failed to provide coverage for the property damage, and has refused to provide a defense for the two lawsuits.
42. Nonetheless, the insurer has accepted over $635,000 in insurance premiums from Plaintiff Riggins for the last 23 years. Plaintiff Riggins has received nothing in return for these premiums.
43. As such, the insurer has breached its duties of coverage and defense.
44. Plaintiff Riggins has been damaged by such breach and shall continue to be further damaged by the insurer's wrongful withholding of insurance coverage for these losses.

WHEREFORE, Plaintiff Riggins requests judgment in its favor on Count I in an amount to be determined at trial, plus pre-judgment and post-judgment interest, attorneys' fees and costs to the extent allowable by law, and such further relief as this Court deems just and proper.

Count II: Bad Faith Denial of Coverage and Refusal to Defend

45. Plaintiff Riggins incorporates the allegations in the above paragraphs of this Complaint as though fully alleged herein.
46. In issuing its contracts of insurance, the insurer agreed to pay covered claims in a timely manner, and to adhere to the inherent contractual obligation to interact with its insured, including the Plaintiff, in good faith and in a fair manner—the implied covenant of "good faith and fair dealing."
47. By accepting insurance premiums for over two decades from its insured and yet denying coverage and refusing to defend its insured in actions clearly covered under the insurance policies, the insurer has breached its covenant of good faith and fair dealing.
48. Further, upon information and belief, the insurer did not conduct an adequate and thorough investigation of the claims in question, and instead simply denied coverage and refused to defend its insured for no justifiable reason.
49. None of the reasons listed in the coverage denial letter have any validity or basis in fact, and the insurer is simply issuing its denial based upon boilerplate reasons for coverage rejection which have nothing to do with the Plaintiff in this case.
50. Upon information and belief, the insurer merely instituted an internal company policy of simply denying coverage and refusing to defend without properly evaluating its insured's claims, in hopes that the insured would simply accept this erroneous coverage decision.

51. Upon information and belief, the insurer also failed to notify its insured that its insurance representative no longer worked for the company, and failed to take seriously Plaintiff Riggins' request for coverage and a defense by assigning a dedicated insurance representative to the insured's file.

52. These business practices constitute bad faith by the insurer against the insured.

WHEREFORE, Plaintiff Riggins requests judgment in its favor on Count II in an amount to be determined at trial, plus pre-judgment and post-judgment interest, attorneys' fees and costs to the extent allowable by law, and such further relief as this Court deems just and proper, including punitive damages.

Dated: January 7, 2016   Respectfully submitted,

                                          McGee & Rollins, LLP

                                          Bridget Stanton

                                          Bridget Stanton, Esq.
                                          100 William St., Suite 44
                                          New York, NY 10005
                                          800-555-4718
                                          bstanton@mcgeerollins.com
                                          Counsel for Plaintiff

Appendix H: Sample Answer

IN THE UNITED STATES DISTRICT COURT
FOR THE SOUTHERN DISTRICT OF NEW YORK

Riggins Garment Company, a New York Corporation, Plaintiff, v. Cornerstone Insurance Company, a Massachusetts corporation, Defendant.	) Case No. Y14-044-AML) The Honorable Laila Hewson)) **ANSWER**))))))

COMES NOW Defendant Cornerstone Insurance Company ("Cornerstone") by counsel, and for its Answer to the Complaint filed by Plaintiff Riggins Garment Company ("Riggins"), states as follows:

Jurisdiction and Venue

1. Admitted.
2. Admitted as to proper venue. The remaining allegations in this paragraph are denied.

Parties

3. Admitted.
4. Admitted.

Facts

5. Admitted.
6. Defendant lacks knowledge and information sufficient to answer the allegations in this paragraph.

-1-

551

7. Admitted.
8. Admitted.
9. Admitted that Defendant Cornerstone issued insurance policies to Plaintiff Riggins. The terms of the policies speak for themselves.
10. Admitted.
11. Denied.
12. Admitted.
13. Defendant lacks knowledge and information sufficient to answer the allegations in this paragraph.
14. Admitted.
15. Admitted.
16. Admitted.
17. Defendant lacks knowledge and information sufficient to answer the allegations in this paragraph.
18. Defendant lacks knowledge and information sufficient to answer the allegations in this paragraph.
19. Defendant lacks knowledge and information sufficient to answer the allegations in this paragraph.
20. Admitted.
21. Defendant lacks knowledge and information sufficient to answer the allegations in this paragraph.
22. Defendant lacks knowledge and information sufficient to answer the allegations in this paragraph.
23. Admitted.
24. Admitted that Plaintiff Riggins filed coverage claims and a request for a defense. Denied as to the remainder of the allegations in this paragraph.
25. Denied.
26. Admitted.
27. Admitted.
28. Admitted that such a letter was sent. The content of the letter speaks for itself.
29. Admitted.
30. Admitted.
31. Admitted that such a letter was sent. Denied as to all other allegations in this paragraph.
32. Denied.
33. Admitted.
34. Defendant lacks knowledge and information sufficient to answer the allegations in this paragraph.

Count I: Breach of the Contractual Duty to Provide Coverage and Defend its Insured

35. See responses to paragraphs above.
36. Denied.
37. Denied.
38. The policies speak for themselves.
39. Defendant lacks knowledge and information sufficient to answer the allegations in this paragraph.
40. Denied.
41. Denied as phrased. Admitted that the insurer has declined coverage and a defense.
42. The first sentence is admitted. The second sentence is denied.
43. Denied.
44. Denied.

Count II: Bad Faith Denial of Coverage and Refusal to Defend

45. See responses to paragraphs above.
46. Denied as phrased. The policies speak for themselves.
47. Denied.
48. Denied.
49. Denied.
50. Denied.
51. Denied.
52. Denied.

Affirmative Defenses

1. The Plaintiff breached its insurance contract, and therefore, is not entitled to coverage and/or a defense, by misrepresenting facts in its policy application.
2. The Plaintiff breached its insurance contract, and therefore, is not entitled to coverage and/or a defense, by failing to make timely insurance premium payments.
3. The insured is guilty of "laches," and failed to comply with the insurance policy's notice requirements and deadlines for filing claims.
4. The losses claimed by the insured are not covered losses, based on express policy exclusions.
5. The insured failed to mitigate its damages and further exacerbated its own losses, nullifying the insurance coverage.
6. The doctrine of estoppel bars Plaintiff's claims.
7. The doctrine of waiver bars Plaintiff's claims.

Prayer for Relief

WHEREFORE, Cornerstone requests:

1. That Riggins' Complaint be dismissed with prejudice;
2. That Riggins take nothing by its action;
3. An award of costs; and
4. Such other and further relief as the Court may deem just and proper.

Dated: January 10, 2016.

Respectfully submitted,
Rodriguez & Jess, LLP

Michael Pineda
Michael Pineda, Esq.
200 Leonard Street, Suite 2
New York, NY 10013
646-555-1000
mpineda@rodriguezjessllp.com

Counsel for Defendant

Certificate of Service

I hereby certify that the foregoing Answer to the Complaint of Plaintiff Riggins Garment Company was served via e-filing, with a courtesy copy via e-mail, on January 10, 2016, upon the following:

Bridget Stanton, Esq.
McGee & Rollins, LLP
100 William St., Suite 44
New York, NY 10005
800-555-4718
bstanton@mcgeerollins.com
Counsel for Plaintiff

Rafaela Barba
Rafaela Barba
Paralegal to Michael Pineda, Esq.

Appendix I: Sample Motion to Compel and Accompanying Memorandum of Points and Authorities

---

IN THE UNITED STATES DISTRICT COURT
FOR THE SOUTHERN DISTRICT OF NEW YORK[1]

Riggins Garment Company,
  a New York Corporation,
  Plaintiff,
	)
	)
	)	

	)	Case No. Y14-044-AML
	)	The Honorable Laila Hewson
v.	))	

Cornerstone Insurance Company,
  a Massachusetts Corporation,
  Defendant.
	)
	)
	)
	)	

PLAINTIFF RIGGINS GARMENT COMPANY'S
MOTION TO COMPEL PRODUCTION
OF DOCUMENTS WITHHELD IN DISCOVERY

COMES NOW Plaintiff Riggins Garment Company ("Riggins") and hereby submits this Motion to Compel documents erroneously withheld from discovery by Defendant Cornerstone Insurance Company ("Cornerstone"), pursuant to Fed. R. Civ. P. 37(a)(3)(B)(iv) and Local Rule 37.1. Cornerstone has hindered Riggins' ability to investigate the insurance company's denial of its insurance claims by erroneously withholding relevant documents based on unfounded claims of attorney-client privilege and the work product doctrine. A Memorandum of Points and Authorities in support of this Motion, and a proposed Order, is attached hereto. Riggins respectfully requests the Court to compel Cornerstone to produce Documents #1, 2, 3, 4, 5, 6, 7, 9,

---

[1] This motion, which has been edited for purposes of this book, was originally written by former New York Law School student and 2015 graduate, Bulent ("Billy") Can.

-1-

and 10 identified on Cornerstone's privilege log and erroneously withheld as attorney-client privileged and work product, within ten (10) days of the Court's Order, and to award fees and costs incurred by Riggins in preparing this Motion.

Dated: May 29, 2016   Respectfully submitted,

MᴄGᴇᴇ & Rᴏʟʟɪɴs, LLP

Bridget Stanton

Bridget Stanton, Esq.
100 William St., Suite 44
New York, NY 10005
800-555-4718
bstanton@mcgeerollins.com
Counsel for Plaintiff

IN THE UNITED STATES DISTRICT COURT FOR THE SOUTHERN DISTRICT OF NEW YORK

Riggins Garment Company, a New York Corporation, Plaintiff, v. Cornerstone Insurance Company, a Massachusetts Corporation, Defendant.	))) Case No. Y14-044-AML) The Honorable Laila Hewson)))))))

PLAINTIFF RIGGINS GARMENT COMPANY'S MEMORANDUM OF POINTS AND AUTHORITIES IN SUPPORT OF ITS MOTION TO COMPEL PRODUCTION OF DOCUMENTS WITHHELD IN DISCOVERY

COMES NOW Plaintiff Riggins Garment Company ("Riggins") and hereby submits this Memorandum of Points and Authorities in Support of its Motion to Compel documents erroneously withheld from discovery by Defendant Cornerstone Insurance Company ("Cornerstone"), pursuant to Fed. R. Civ. P. 37(a)(3)(B)(iv) and Local Rule 37.1. This case involves a small business which has been taken advantage of by a large insurance firm amidst the aftermath of Hurricane Sandy—one of the largest natural disasters to ever strike the New York metropolitan area. Cornerstone has hindered Riggins' ability to prove its claims for breach of the insurance contract in this case by erroneously withholding documents based on unfounded claims of attorney-client privilege and the work product doctrine.

The attorney-client privilege protects communications between an attorney and client made in confidence for the purpose of rendering legal services—while the attorney is acting in the role of legal counsel. Work product protection covers documents created by or for a client or his representative (including his attorney) in anticipation of litigation, but does not apply to correspondence generated in the ordinary course of a company's business.

Riggins is entitled to the production of Documents #1-7 and #9-10 listed on Cornerstone's privilege log because such records were prepared: (1) by or for an attorney while acting in a business-related capacity other than legal counsel, (2) in the ordinary course of the business of the insurer, and (3) prior to the anticipation of litigation. Riggins respectfully requests the Court to order Cornerstone to produce the documents it wrongly withheld.

I. Factual Background

Riggins, a family-owned business engaged in importing fabrics and textiles and manufacturing garments, filed a Complaint for breach of contract in this Court on January 7, 2016 against Cornerstone for: (1) failure to provide coverage of hurricane-related property damage and business losses; (2) refusal to defend Riggins against third-party lawsuits stemming from Hurricane Sandy; and (3) bad faith denial of coverage and refusal to defend. The issue arises in the wake of Hurricane Sandy's aftermath of property damage to Riggins' warehouse space located in the South Street Seaport area of Manhattan (including estimated monetary losses in the amount of $1.1 million) and lawsuits against Riggins for unfulfilled contract orders (exceeding a combined total of $500,000). Cornerstone formally denied Riggins' insurance claim on January 2, 2014.

Cornerstone filed an Answer to Riggins' Complaint in this action. Following a Preliminary Conference, the Court issued a Scheduling Order on January 17, 2016. On February 7, 2016, Riggins served its First Request for Production of Documents, and on February 8, 2016, counsel for Cornerstone served Objections and Responses accompanied by a Privilege Log (Exhibit 1). On April 2, 2016, Riggins served a Demand Letter (Exhibit 2) to Cornerstone seeking production of Documents #1-7 and #9-10 erroneously withheld as attorney-client privileged communications and attorney work product. In a letter dated April 8, 2016 (Exhibit 3), Cornerstone refused to produce the requested documents.

Pursuant to Rule 3 of Judge Hewson's Individual Court Rules, Plaintiff Riggins hereby certifies that it has made a good faith effort to resolve this discovery dispute with opposing counsel, to no avail.

II. Argument

Riggins respectfully requests the court to compel Cornerstone to produce Documents #1-7 and #9-10 erroneously withheld as attorney-client privileged communications and attorney work product for the reasons set forth herein.

A. Documents #1-7 and #9-10 Were Created Outside the Scope of Providing Legal Advice and While the Attorneys were Acting in a Business Capacity Other than Legal Advisors, and Thus are not Privileged

Riggins requests the Court to compel Defendant Cornerstone to produce Documents #1-7 and #9-10 erroneously listed on its privilege log as attorney-client privileged correspondence. Courts have interpreted communications between an attorney and client as privileged when such exchanges are made in confidence for the purpose of rendering legal services, and when the attorney is acting in the role of legal counsel and not in a separate role. *S.E.C. v. Credit Bancorp, Ltd.*, No. 99 CIV 11395IRWS, 2002 WL 59418, *2 (S.D.N.Y. January 16, 2002). Furthermore, in the insurance context, the privilege applies only when the attorney involved is acting as legal counsel, and not as a claims investigator. *Id.* at *3.

For example, in *Amerisure Ins. Co. v. Laserage Tech. Corp.*, No. 96-CV-6313, 1998 WL 310750, *1 (W.D.N.Y. February 12, 1998), an insurer withheld from discovery a memo written by its Vice President of Corporate Claims and transmitted to a corporate consultant, on the grounds that the memo was protected by the attorney-client privilege. *Id.* The vice president was an attorney admitted to practice law in New York. *Id.* at *2. The vice president's memo discussed case law, and the consultant, who was not an attorney, testified that he too would discuss case law with the vice president and make recommendations regarding coverage. *Id.* The *Amerisure* court held that, even though the memo discussed case law, no attorney-client privilege attached to the document. *Id.* The court reasoned that, although it was clear from the record that the vice president was an attorney, he was acting as a corporate employee and as a claims supervisor in a claims coverage evaluation role when he produced the memo. *Id. See also Ten Talents Inv. 1, LLC v. Ohio Sec. Ins. Co.*, No. C12-5849RBL, 2013 WL 1618780, *1 (W.D. Wash. April 15, 2013) (holding that the attorney-client privilege is inapplicable to communications generated while an insurance company's in-house counsel acts in the role of a claims adjuster or supervisor); *S.E.C.*, 2002 WL 59418 at *3 (holding that the attorney-client privilege does not protect claims evaluation documents prepared by outside counsel as part of the regular business of the insurance company); *Chicago Meat Processors, Inc. v. Mid-Century Ins. Co.*, No. 95 C 4277, 1996 WL 172148, *3 (N.D. Ill. April 10, 1996) (highlighting the public policy that insurance companies are in the business of reviewing, processing, and adjusting claims and thus

-3-

should not be permitted to insulate factual findings of investigations by the involvement of an attorney to perform such work).

Applying the foregoing rule to the matter at issue, Cornerstone has improperly withheld Documents #1-7 and #9-10 under the guise of the attorney-client privilege. Similar to the documents in *Amerisure*, Documents #1-3, #6, and #9 were produced while Cornerstone's General Counsel, Madeline Hewes ("Hewes"), was acting as Chief Claims Adjuster in the regular course of business of the insurer; these communications contain material pertaining to her investigation into Riggins' claims. Additionally, Documents #4 and #5 are communications concerning risk assessment and policy coverage of hurricane-related claims not specific to Riggins. This information does not amount to correspondence created by an attorney in the course of providing legal advice, but rather constitutes information gathered in the regular course of business by a claims adjuster. Thus, it does not fall within the realm of the attorney-client privilege.

Furthermore, Document #7, minutes of a meeting attended by Hewes and outside counsel, Roberta Lee ("Lee"), reflects information derived while the attorneys were monitoring the progress of insurance cases; this document was not created in the course of either Hewes or Lee providing legal advice. Lastly, Document #10 (a draft of Cornerstone's coverage denial letter) is not privileged; Cornerstone is in the business of reviewing, processing, and adjusting insurance claims and cannot shield factual findings used to derive a final claims decision by the participation of counsel.

Accordingly, Riggins requests the Court to compel Cornerstone to produce the foregoing documents erroneously withheld as attorney-client privileged, as the communications were created outside the course of providing legal advice and while the attorneys were acting in a capacity other than legal advisors.

B. Documents #4-7 and #9-10 Were Generated in the Ordinary Course of the Insurer's Business Prior to the Anticipated Date of Litigation of January 2, 2014, and Thus are Not Protected Under the Work Product Doctrine

Riggins further requests the Court to compel Defendant Cornerstone to produce Documents #4-7 and #9-10 erroneously listed on its privilege log as protected work product. Courts have afforded work product protection to documents that: (1) "show legal research and opinions, mental impressions, theories, or conclusions of the attorney" or of other representatives of a party; (2) comprise an attorney's "written notes or memoranda of factual statements or investigations"; or (3) constitute formal or written "statements of fact, or other tangible facts, gathered by an attorney in preparation for or in anticipation of litigation." *Panattoni Cons., Inc. v. Travelers Prop. Cas. Co. of Am.*, No. C11-1195RSM, 2012 WL 6567141, *2 (W.D. Wash. December 14, 2012). In the insurance context, courts have narrowed the protection to exclude materials: (1) prepared *prior* to the date that coverage is denied; and (2) prepared during the ordinary course of an insurer's business, such as evaluations or factual inquiries into insurance claims. *Cutrale Citrus Juices USA, Inc. v. Zurich Am. Ins. Grp.*, No. 5:03-CV-420-Oc-10GRJ, 2004 WL 5215191, *2 (M.D. Fla. September 10, 2004).

For example, in *Cutrale*, a fruit juice company was forced to reimburse a major client for losses after a production shutdown and product recall due to the malfunctioning of a piece of equipment used to sterilize tanks that are used for processing fruit juice. *Id.* The fruit juice company made repeated requests to its insurers for coverage, but its requests were denied. *Id.* In discovery in the insured's lawsuit for breach of contract, the insurers withheld virtually all of its claims file documents, including the investigative materials created *prior* to the date of the denial of the fruit juice company's claim–asserting work product protection. *Id.* The fruit juice company filed a motion to compel production of the claims file.

The *Cutrale* court held that, in the insurance context, the proper date after which it is fairly certain there is an anticipation of litigation is the date that coverage is denied by the insurer, and documents generated after that date would be protected as work product; thus documents dated *before* such date would not be protected and must be disclosed. *Id.* The court reasoned that it is the very nature of an insurer's business to investigate and evaluate the merits of claims. *Id.* Documents constituting factual inquiry into or evaluation of such claims, undertaken in order to arrive at a claim decision, are produced in the ordinary course of an insurer's business rather than in anticipation of litigation, and, therefore, are not offered work product protection. *See also Cont'l Cas. Co. v. Marsh*, No. 01CV0160, 2004 WL 42364, *8 (N.D. Ill. January 6, 2004) (emphasizing that materials that are part of an evaluation or investigation into an insured's claims *prior* to a final coverage decision are prepared in the ordinary and routine course of the insurer's business, and thus are not protected as attorney work product); *Mission Nat'l Ins. Co. v. Lilly*, 112 F.R.D. 163 (D. Minn. 1986) (holding that, to the extent outside counsel acted as a claims adjuster, communications will be treated as generated in the ordinary business of the insurer and outside the scope of protected work product; it would not be fair to create a blanket of obstruction to discovery of claims investigations).

Applying the foregoing rule to the matter at issue, Cornerstone has erroneously withheld Documents #4-7 and #9-10 as protected work product. Similar to the documents in *Cutrale*, Documents #4-7 and #9-10 were created *prior* to the claim denial date of January 2, 2014, the date after which it is fairly certain the insurer could have anticipated litigation. Furthermore, Documents #4 and #5 include information regarding Cornerstone's general assessment of claims and were created by or for Lee in the ordinary course of Cornerstone's business. Documents #6 and #7 include standard information regarding coverage of Riggins' claim and not materials or tangible facts collected by an attorney in preparation for or in anticipation of litigation. Lastly, Document #10 contains information regarding the denial of coverage of Riggins' claim, produced in the ordinary course of the insurer's business.

Accordingly, Riggins respectfully requests the Court to compel Cornerstone to produce the foregoing documents erroneously withheld as attorney work product, as the documents were generated in the ordinary course of the insurance company's business *prior* to the anticipated date of litigation.

III. CONCLUSION

Based upon the foregoing, Riggins respectfully requests the Court to compel Cornerstone to produce Documents #1, 2, 3, 4, 5, 6, 7, 9, and 10 erroneously withheld as attorney-client privileged communications and attorney work product. Riggins further requests the Court to order Cornerstone to pay Riggins' fees and costs in preparing this Motion.

Dated: May 29, 2016   Respectfully submitted,

                             McGee & Rollins, LLP

                             Bridget Stanton

                             Bridget Stanton, Esq.
                             100 William St., Suite 44
                             New York, NY 10005
                             800-555-4718
                             bstanton@mcgeerollins.com

                             Counsel for Plaintiff

Certificate of Service

I hereby certify that on this 29th day of May, 2016, I caused a true and correct copy of Plaintiff's Motion to Compel and accompanying Memorandum of Points and Authorities to be sent via U.S. Mail postage prepaid and Electronic Mail to the following individual:

Michael Pineda, Esq.
Rodriguez & Jess, LLP
200 Leonard Street, Suite 2
New York, NY 10013
646-555-1000
Mpineda@rodriguezjessllp.com
Counsel for Defendant

Bridget Stanton
Bridget Stanton, Esq.

IN THE UNITED STATES DISTRICT COURT
FOR THE SOUTHERN DISTRICT OF NEW YORK

Riggins Garment Company, a New York Corporation, Plaintiff,	))) Case No. Y14-044-AML) The Honorable Laila Hewson)
Cornerstone Insurance Company, a Massachusetts Corporation, Defendant.	)))))

Order

This Matter came before the Court on Plaintiff's Motion to Compel and accompanying Memorandum of Points and Authorities, and it appearing to the Court, upon review of the appropriate authorities in this matter, that the Motion should be granted, it is hereby ORDERED that Defendant Cornerstone Insurance Company ("Cornerstone") shall produce Documents #1, 2, 3, 4, 5, 6, 7, 9, and 10 as identified on its privilege log to Plaintiff Riggins Garment Company ("Riggins") within ten (10) days of the date hereof. Cornerstone also shall reimburse Riggins for its reasonable costs and fees incurred in preparing the Motion and Memorandum, and in appearing at the hearing. Riggins shall submit an affidavit of costs and fees, with appropriate supporting documentation, within ten (10) days of the date hereof.

SO ORDERED:

Date: _____   _____
                                 United States District Judge

Appendix J: Sample Opposition to Motion to Compel

IN THE UNITED STATES DISTRICT COURT FOR THE SOUTHERN DISTRICT OF NEW YORK

Riggins Garment Company,
  a New York Corporation,
  Plaintiff,
 	
v.
 	
Cornerstone Insurance Company,
  a Massachusetts Corporation,
  Defendant.
	) Case No. Y14-044-AML
	) The Honorable Laila Hewson
	)
	)
	)
	)
	)
	) ORAL ARGUMENT REQUESTED
	)
	)
	)
	)

DEFENDANT CORNERSTONE INSURANCE COMPANY'S OPPOSITION TO PLAINTIFF RIGGINS GARMENT COMPANY'S MOTION TO COMPEL PRODUCTION OF DOCUMENTS

COMES NOW Defendant Cornerstone Insurance Company ("Cornerstone") and hereby submits this Opposition to Plaintiff Riggins Garment Company's ("Riggins") Motion to Compel Production of Documents, pursuant to Judge Hewson's Rule 3. Unfortunately, Plaintiff's Motion demonstrates its misunderstanding of how the insurance industry works, as well as a lack of recognition of the sanctity of the attorney-client relationship and the critical importance of the attorney work product doctrine in our adversarial litigation process.

The insurance industry in the United States provides much-needed financial solace and peace of mind for businesses to function even in the face of threats of unforeseen disasters, such as theft, fires, floods, and acts of terrorism. However, insurance coverage is not simply a "blank check" for insureds to cash in and recoup hundreds of thousands of dollars any time

-1-

unfortunate events occur. There are procedures and rules in place, to prevent fraudulent and false claims, in order to minimize insurance premium costs for the average hard-working American citizen.

In the instant case, Plaintiff misunderstands the process that insurers nationwide undertake to evaluate claims prior to rendering coverage decisions. Since 9/11, like many other insurance companies, Cornerstone has implemented a process under which its attorneys—including General Counsel, Madeline Hewes ("Hewes"), and its primary outside counsel, Roberta Lee ("Lee") of Sebastian & Forrest, LLP—are intimately involved in high-level legal analyses that bear on claims decisions. The attorney-client privilege is expressly designed to cover these precise types of communication between a client (the insurance company) and its legal counsel (whether in-house or outside counsel) that involve sophisticated legal interpretation of policy terms and exclusions in each coverage determination.

Further, since 9/11, lawsuits against insurance companies have abounded by insureds seeking to "win the lottery" by suing their insurers for frivolous and spurious bad faith claims. As such, Cornerstone has implemented an industry-approved corporate policy and standard procedure to anticipate and prepare for litigation from the moment a coverage event occurs—in this case, the devastating natural disaster of Hurricane Sandy. As such, all documents generated by or for Cornerstone's in-house and outside counsel related to this catastrophic event—and especially those containing the mental impressions and strategies of the legal minds who authored or directed the generation of such documents—are protected by the work product doctrine.

Accordingly, Cornerstone respectfully requests the court to deny Plaintiff's Motion to Compel, and award Cornerstone its costs and fees in responding to the Motion.

I. Statement of Facts

Hurricane Sandy devastated New York and New Jersey in October 2012. From the very onset of the storm, Cornerstone was inundated with requests and demands by insureds for support from the insurance company. Within days of the subsidence of the floodwaters, insurance claims began pouring in, many containing threats of litigation by plaintiffs' lawyers if Cornerstone did not "promptly" provide reimbursement for losses. Obviously, Cornerstone is not a "bottomless pit" of funds. Claims must be evaluated for validity prior to payment, especially in light of the gravity of the damage caused by Hurricane Sandy.

The documents withheld by Cornerstone on its privilege log (Exhibit 1 to Plaintiff's Motion) reflect high-level legal analysis of insurance contract language, policy limits, and exclusions, by individuals who graduated from law school, passed the Massachusetts bar exam, and now spend every day of their professional lives performing complex legal research and written analysis. The documents memorializing these activities are exactly the types of communication intended to be protected by the time-honored doctrines of the attorney-client privilege and work product protection.

II. Argument

Under the bounds of the attorney-client privilege, and given the indispensable importance of the attorney work product doctrine in the context of litigation, Cornerstone has properly withheld Documents 1-11 on its privilege log.

A. All Documents on Cornerstone's Privilege Log That Were Generated by or for In-House Counsel and Outside Counsel Are Privileged

Cornerstone properly has asserted attorney-client privilege protection for all the documents on its privilege log. The attorney-client privilege is the foremost recognized testimonial privilege in both British and American legal history, dating back four centuries, and is regarded as a hallmark of the attorney-client relationship. See Swidler & Berlin v. United States, 524 U.S. 399, 403 (1998); United States v. Bilzerian, 926 F.2d 1285, 1292 (2d Cir. 1991). Indeed, only when communications between an attorney and his client are guaranteed confidentiality can an attorney provide enlightened legal advice. See Upjohn Co. v. United States, 449 U.S. 383, 389 (1981) (The privilege's "purpose is to encourage full and frank communication between attorneys and their clients and thereby promote broader public interests in the observance of law and administration of justice."); In re Rivastigmine Patent Litig., 237 F.R.D. 69, 73 (S.D.N.Y. 2006) ("The attorney-client privilege functions 'to encourage full and frank communications between attorneys and their clients.'"). The party asserting the privilege "must demonstrate that there was: (1) a communication between client and counsel, which (2) was intended to be and was in fact kept confidential, and (3) made for the purpose of obtaining or providing legal advice." United States v. Constr. Prods. Research, Inc., 73 F.3d 464, 473 (2d Cir. 1996).

Cornerstone acknowledges that, in the insurance context, to the extent that an attorney acts solely as a claims adjuster, claims process supervisor, or claims investigation monitor, and not as a legal advisor, the attorney-client privilege may not apply. However, Hewes and Lee were not acting as claims adjusters; they clearly were rendering legal advice to the insurer about the complexities involved in interpreting the policy coverage and legal exclusions set forth in Cornerstone's Comprehensive General Liability (CGL) insurance policy—which is 67 pages long and full of complicated legal concepts. See, e.g., Linder v. Insurance Claims Consultants, Inc., 560 S.E.2d 612 (S.C. 2002) (An insurance adjuster engages in the "practice of law" if he or she advises an insurance company or customers "of their rights, duties, or privileges under an insurance policy regarding matters requiring legal skill or knowledge, i.e., interpret[s] the policy").

In Document 1, dated November 1, 2012, Hewes gave instructional advice to Todd Nicks ("Nicks"), a Cornerstone risk analyst, regarding how to interpret legal language in the standard CGL policy regarding weather exclusions, and provided legal advice regarding what to look for in site visits to properties in the South Street Seaport area. Document 2, dated November 28, 2012, reflects Nicks' minutes of a meeting with Hewes to report the results of his investigation so she could make a legal determination regarding the application of policy exclusions. Document 3, dated December 5, 2012, is a follow-up memo from Nicks to Hewes summarizing results of the investigation and site visit to South Street Seaport. All three of these documents reflect the legal analysis of Hewes in her role as General Counsel addressing a monumental weather event which was giving rise to voluminous legal claims. Moreover, Document 6, dated September 20, 2013, contains an e-mail with a policy analysis memo attached—sent from Nicks to Hewes—further following up on the legal advice Hewes gave Nicks.

Subsequently, Hewes sought legal advice from outside counsel, at the firm of Sebastian & Forrest, LLP. Document 4, dated January 15, 2013, consists of e-mail communications between Hewes and Lee, an associate at the outside counsel law firm, Sebastian & Forrest, LLP—correspondence which clearly encompasses the seeking and rendering of substantive legal advice. Document 5, dated May 15, 2013, includes an e-mail with a legal research memo attached from Lee to Hewes. Lee rendered legal advice to Cornerstone in the form of legal research, analysis, and a written summary thereof. Document 7, dated September 21, 2013, consists of minutes from a meeting among Hewes, Nicks, and Lee, in which Lee continued to render legal advice in her role as outside counsel. Document 8, dated October 23, 2013, comprises e-mail communications and another legal research memo exchanged between Lee and Hewes. All of these exchanges which occurred **between not one—but two—lawyers** are exactly the types of documentation the attorney-client privilege is designed to protect.

Document 9, dated December 28, 2013, is a memo from Hewes to Nadine Valentino ("Valentino"), a Cornerstone claims adjuster, leading up to Cornerstone's denial of coverage of Riggins' claims; this document contains direct legal advice from Hewes to Valentino regarding the legal nature of the reasons for declining coverage, and thus unequivocally is privileged. Document 10 is the draft coverage denial letter containing handwritten notes by both attorneys—again reflecting the legal analysis of **two attorneys**. Finally, Document 11 is plainly privileged, as it constitutes the transmission of the draft Answer to the Complaint from in-house counsel to outside litigation counsel, Michael Pineda, Esq.

As this court itself stated so eloquently in 1986, privileged communications are to be "zealously protected." Standard Chartered Bank PLC v. Ayala Intern. Holdings (U.S.) Inc., 111 F.R.D. 76 (S.D.N.Y. 1986). Accordingly, Cornerstone respectfully requests the court to honor the privileged relationship between and among Hewes, Lee, and Cornerstone, respect the confidential nature of Documents 1-11 on the privilege log, and deny Riggins' Motion.

B. Documents 4-11 on Cornerstone's Privilege Log Are Protected by the Work Product Doctrine Because They Were Prepared in Anticipation of Litigation

Documents 4-11 constitute attorney work product since they were created *after* Cornerstone anticipated that lawsuits would be brought by a veritable army of insureds, including Riggins. According to Fed. R. Civ. P. 26(b)(3)(A), "a party may not discover documents and tangible things that are prepared in anticipation of litigation or for trial by or for another party or its representative (including the other party's attorney, consultant, surety, indemnitor, insurer, or agent)." This well-recognized judicially-created safeguard against discovery, known as the "work product doctrine," was first articulated by the Supreme Court in the case of Hickman v. Taylor, 329 U.S. 495 (1947). There the Court said, in pertinent part:

> In performing his various duties, . . . it is essential that a lawyer work with a certain degree of privacy, free from unnecessary intrusion by opposing parties and their counsel. Proper presentation of a client's case

demands that he assemble information, sift what he considers to be the relevant from the irrelevant facts, prepare his legal theories and plan his strategy without undue and needless interference. . . . This work is reflected, of course, in interviews, statements, memoranda, correspondence, briefs, mental impressions, personal beliefs, and countless other tangible and intangible ways aptly though roughly termed by the Circuit Court of Appeals in this case as the "work product of the lawyer." Were such materials open to opposing counsel on mere demand, much of what is now put down in writing would remain unwritten. . . . Inefficiency, unfairness and sharp practices would inevitably develop in the giving of legal advice and in the preparation of cases for trial.

Id. at 511.

When determining whether and when a party first anticipated litigation, "the tenor of the party's relationship will serve as evidence that a suit was expected to be filed." Penn. Gen. Ins. Co. v. CaremarkPCS, 3:05–CV–0844, 2005 WL 2041969, at *6 (N.D. Tex. Aug. 24, 2005). Courts routinely have held that factual investigations are protected by the work product doctrine. See, e.g., In re Grand Jury Subpoena, 357 F.3d 900, 905 (9th Cir. 2004) (stating that investigation of environmental clean-up by an environmental consultant hired by a lawyer was protected work product); Bickler v. Senior Lifestyle Corp., 266 F.R.D. 379 (D. Ariz. 2010) (finding that an investigation conducted by a human resources department employee at the direction of the company's in-house counsel was performed in anticipation of litigation; virtually from the moment of the incident giving rise to the investigation, the prospect of litigation loomed).

As articulately stated in In re Commercial Financial Services, Inc., 247 B.R. 828, 846 (Bkrtcy. N.D. Okla. 2000), "the work product doctrine preserves attorneys' interests in their own intellectual creations and processes, and promotes the use of the adversary system to settle disputes that are otherwise irreconcilable." Further, because attorneys and their work product are "indispensable parts of our administration of justice," courts must honor the protection of the thought processes and intellectual strategies of counsel seeking to resolve disputes. Cornerstone's lawyers—Hewes and Lee—anticipated litigation from the moment that Hurricane Sandy's storm surge caused the East River to overflow and gush into the South Street Seaport area. Documents 4-11 on Cornerstone's privilege log reflect the mental impressions, conclusions, opinions, and legal theories of the insurer's attorneys—information which is clearly protected under Fed. R. Civ. P. 26(b)(2)(B)'s definition of undiscoverable attorney work product.

Accordingly, Cornerstone respectfully requests the court to deny Riggins' Motion to Compel production of these documents.

III. Conclusion

Based upon the foregoing, Defendant Cornerstone respectfully requests the Court to deny Plaintiff Riggins' Motion to Compel, and award the fees and costs incurred by Cornerstone in preparing this opposition brief.

Dated: June 15, 2016

Respectfully submitted,

Rodriguez & Jess, LLP

Michael Pineda

Michael Pineda, Esq.
200 Leonard Street, Suite 2
New York, NY 10013
646-555-1000
mpineda@rodriguezjessllp.com
Counsel for Defendant

Certificate of Service

I hereby certify that the foregoing Opposition to Plaintiff Riggins Garment Company's Motion to Compel was served hand-delivery on June 15, 2016.

Hansen McMannis

Hansen McMannis
Paralegal to Michael Pineda, Esq.

Appendix K: Sample Motion to Dismiss and Accompanying Memorandum of Points and Authorities

---

UNITED STATES DISTRICT COURT
SOUTHERN DISTRICT OF NEW YORK

RANDALL DUBLIN,	)
	)
Plaintiff,	)
	)
v.	) DOCKET 2017/56436
	)
YORK PROPERTY	)
DEVELOPMENT, LLC,	) Oral Argument Requested
	)
Defendant.	)
_____	)

Defendant York Property Development, LLC's Motion to Dismiss the Complaint for Failure to State a Claim

Defendant York Property Development, LLC ("York"), by counsel, hereby submits this Motion to Dismiss the Complaint for failure to state a claim, pursuant to Fed. R. Civ. P. 12(b)(6). Under New York law, York cannot be held liable for Plaintiff Randall Dublin's ("Dublin") injuries which occurred on property owned by York, because York is an "out-of-possession" landowner. York did not create the alleged condition which gave rise to Dublin's injuries, relinquished responsibility for maintenance and repair of the property to a management company, Brooklyn Sports Complex Management, Inc. ("BSCM"), and exercised no control over the premises either by virtue of the Management Agreement with BSCM or the parties' course of dealing. Accordingly, York requests the court to dismiss the Complaint against it.

-1-

A Memorandum of Points and Authorities and a proposed Order is attached hereto.

Date: December 20, 2017   Respectfully submitted,

Paolo Edmunds

Paolo Edmunds, Esq.
EDMUNDS & LUCY, LLP
436 Spring Street
New York, NY
800-913-8559
p.edmunds@edmundslucy.com
Counsel for York Property
Development, LLC

UNITED STATES DISTRICT COURT
SOUTHERN DISTRICT OF NEW YORK

RANDALL DUBLIN,	)
	)
Plaintiff,	)
	)
v.	) DOCKET 2017/56436
	)
YORK PROPERTY	) Oral Argument Requested
DEVELOPMENT, LLC,	)
	)
Defendant.	)
_____	)

Defendant York Property Development, LLC's Memorandum of Points and Authorities in Support of Its Motion to Dismiss the Complaint for Failure to State a Claim

Defendant York Property Development, LLC ("York"), by counsel, hereby submits this Memorandum of Points and Authorities in support of its Motion to Dismiss the Complaint for failure to state a claim, pursuant to Fed. R. Civ. P. 12(b)(6). Plaintiff Randall Dublin ("Dublin") has asserted a negligence action against York as the owner of a sports stadium complex located in Brooklyn, New York called the Brooklyn Gridiron (the "Facility"). However, under New York law, York cannot be held liable for Dublin's injuries which occurred on the Facility property because York is an "out-of-possession" landowner. York did not *create* the alleged condition which gave rise to Dublin's injuries, relinquished responsibility for *maintenance* and *repair* of the Facility to the Facility's management company, Brooklyn Sports Complex Management, Inc. ("BSCM"), and exercised no *control* over the premises either by virtue of the Management Agreement with BSCM or the parties' course of dealing. The public policy underlying New York's limitation on out-of-possession landowner liability is that "the person in possession and control of property is best able to identify and prevent any harm to others." *Butler v. Rafferty*, 100 N.Y.2d 265, 270 (N.Y. 2003). As York fully surrendered control over the Facility to BSCM, it cannot be liable for Dublin's injuries. Accordingly, York requests the court to dismiss the Complaint against it.

-1-

I. Statement of Facts

Dublin was born in Manhattan and is presently 33 years old. (Complaint ¶ 5). On April 4, 2015, he accepted a job as a maintenance employee with BSCM, the company which manages the Facility in Brooklyn. (Complaint ¶ 6).

Two completely different corporate entities own and manage the Facility. York is a limited liability company—formed in the State of Delaware with its principal place of business in New Jersey[1]—that owns the real estate in Brooklyn where the Facility is located, and the land and structures thereon. (Complaint ¶ 9). York purchased the land, and hired a construction company to build the Facility. (Complaint, Exhibit A, Management Agreement, p.1). As a real estate investment company, York does not operate or manage the sports stadium complex or operations; the separate management company, BSCM, runs the operation completely. (*Id.*). York and BSCM are two separate legal entities. (*Id.*). BSCM is incorporated in the State of Delaware. (*Id.*). York is not the parent company of BSCM, and BSCM is not the parent company of York. (*Id.*). As the Facility's management company, BSCM operates the building, hires the employees, and runs the Facility. (*Id.* at p. 5). The Facility's business operations—including all profits and losses—are owned by BSCM. (*Id.*).

BSCM has the exclusive right to manage the Facility, and controls the property. (*Id.* at p. 7). It employs the stadium's Executive Director, and the administrative, maintenance, security, and housekeeping staff that keeps the stadium property safe and orderly. (*Id.*). BSCM manages the physical plant, the building, the grounds, and the operations of the sports complex at the Facility. (*Id.*). BSCM is responsible for maintenance of the property, the land, and the buildings (including snow and ice removal) and repairs. (*Id.*).

York (as Owner) and BSCM (as Manager) entered into a Management Agreement (Complaint, Exhibit A), which includes the following key terms:

Article 14.1: "Owner hereby appoints Manager and Manager hereby accepts such appointment, subject to the provisions of this Agreement, as the exclusive manager for the day-to-day operation, administration, and management of the Facility. Manager has responsibility and *complete and full control* and discretion in the

---

[1] Dublin filed this action in New York state court. York removed the action to federal court based on diversity jurisdiction.

operation, direction, management and supervision of the Facility." (emphasis added) (*Id.* at p. 9).

Article 14.2: "Facility operations are under the *exclusive direction and control* of Manager." (*Id.*).

Article 14.3: "Manager is responsible for the supply, operation, *maintenance and service* of the Facility, and for planning, executing and supervising all *repairs and maintenance* at the Facility." (emphasis added) (*Id.*).

Article 14.4: "Manager shall comply with *all laws, codes, rules, regulations, and ordinances* governing the *repairs, maintenance,* or operation of the facility." (emphasis added) (*Id.*).

Article 14.5: "Owner shall have access to the Facility at any and all reasonable times for the purpose of inspection or showing the Facility to prospective buyers, investors, lessees, or lenders." (*Id.*).

As the express language of the Management Agreement demonstrates, York hired BSCM to bear all responsibility to maintain and run the property. (*Id.* at p. 9). This is a common circumstance for these types of investment landowners.

In the summer of 2015, BSCM directed the assembly of a portable storage locker on the outskirts of the Facility's property, near the West parking lot. (Complaint ¶ 14). The stadium's Executive Director, Jake Grotto ("Grotto"), an employee of BSCM, ordered the portable storage locker from a company called Storage Locker Depot, LLC ("Depot") on behalf of BSCM. (Complaint, Exhibit B, Purchase Order).

BSCM purchased the storage locker in August 2015 and paid for it via credit card. (Complaint, Exhibit C, Sales Receipt). Depot designed and built the storage locker and a ramp for loading items into the front entrance of the locker. (*Id.*). The front ramp led up to double doors; the storage locker also had two side entrance doors and four windows. (Complaint, Exhibit D, Photo).

Grotto had no communications with York about the storage locker or ramp. There is no evidence that anyone at BSCM communicated with York about the storage locker or ramp, or that York even knew the ramp existed any time between its assembly in August 2015 and November 12, 2015 (the date of Dublin's accident).

On November 12, 2015, Dublin was late to work; several inches of snow had fallen overnight. (Complaint, ¶ 17). Upon arrival at the Facility, he walked to the maintenance room inside the Facility to obtain rock salt to distribute on the Facility's snow-covered sidewalks. (Complaint, ¶ 18). Not finding the rock salt, he then walked to the storage locker located on the outskirts of the Facility near the West parking lot. (Complaint, ¶ 19). There was snow on the ground. (Complaint, ¶ 20). Dublin was wearing Timberland work boots. (Complaint, ¶ 21). Dublin walked up the ramp which was covered in snow, opened the entrance doors, and entered the storage locker. (Complaint, ¶ 22). Inside the storage locker, he located a bag of rock salt. (Complaint, ¶ 23). Turning to leave, he exited the doorway, took one step onto the ramp, slipped, and fell. (Complaint, ¶ 24). He hit his right knee on the doorjamb of the locker. (Complaint, ¶ 25).

After he fell, he returned to the stadium and visited the first aid office. (Complaint, ¶ 26). He was limping, so the first aid attendant called an ambulance which transported Dublin to a nearby hospital, where he was x-rayed and prescribed pain medication. (Complaint, ¶ 27). He had no broken bones and was not bleeding. (Complaint, ¶ 28). He was discharged the same day. (Complaint, ¶ 29). Dublin was advised to take ten days off and return to work on light duty. (Complaint, ¶ 30). Dublin did not return to work again. (Complaint, ¶ 31). Dublin filed a claim against BSCM's workers' compensation insurance for alleged injuries to his knee, and received benefits through 2016. (Complaint, ¶ 37). BSCM's workers' compensation insurance paid for Dublin's medical care. (Complaint, ¶ 39).

Because of his workers' compensation claim, Dublin could not sue his employer, BSCM. Instead, Dublin filed a Complaint against York as property owner, alleging that there existed a dangerous condition on the Facility property, and the condition caused Dublin's injury.

II. Standard for Dismissal of a Complaint Under Fed. R. Civ. P. 12(b)(6)

According to the United States Supreme Court in *Ashcroft v. Iqbal*, 556 U.S. 662, 678 (2008), "[t]o survive a motion to dismiss, a complaint must contain sufficient factual matter, accepted as true, to 'state a claim to relief that is plausible on its face.'" Further, "[a] claim has facial plausibility when the plaintiff pleads factual content that allows the court to draw the reasonable inference that the defendant is liable for the misconduct alleged." *Id.* "[T]he complaint must contain enough factual matter taken as true to raise the right to relief above the speculative level." *In re Saba Enterprises*, 421 B.R. 626, 639 (S.D.N.Y. Bankr. 2009), *citing Bell Atl. Corp. v. Twombly*, 550 U.S. 544, 555 (2007). Dublin's Complaint should be dismissed as it does not state a plausible claim against York for negligence. Instead, applying the doctrine of "out-of-possession" landowner liability, there is no reasonable inference that York is liable for the misconduct alleged.

III. Satisfying All the Criteria of an Out-of-Possession Landowner Under New York Law, York Cannot Be Liable to Dublin

Dublin's Complaint fails to state a plausible claim against York because, as an out-of-possession landowner, York cannot be liable for Dublin's injuries. Under New York law, an out-of-possession property owner *cannot* be liable for injuries that occur on a premises unless the landowner: (1) *created* the dangerous condition; (2) assumed responsibility to *maintain* any portion of the premises; (3) is contractually obligated to *repair* the unsafe condition; or (4) retained *control* of the premises. *Buckowski v. Smith*, 185 A.D.2d 556 (N.Y. App. Div. 1992). A review of the allegations in the Complaint confirms that all four criteria fail in this case.

A. York Did Not Create the Storage Locker or Ramp

York did not create the storage locker or ramp. (Complaint, Exhibit B, Purchase Order). BSCM purchased the storage locker in August 2015 from Depot and paid for it via credit card. (Complaint, Exhibit C, Sales Receipt). Depot designed and built the storage locker and ramp. (*Id.*). Further, there is no evidence that anyone at BSCM communicated with York about the storage locker or ramp, or that York even knew the ramp existed any time between its assembly in August 2015 and November 12, 2015 (the date of Dublin's accident).

B. BSCM Bore Responsibility for Maintenance and Repair of the Premises

Under Article 14 of the Management Agreement, BSCM assumed responsibility for: (1) the daily operation, direction, management and supervision of the Facility; (2) the supply, operation, maintenance, repairs and service of the Facility, and (3) compliance with any applicable laws, codes, rules, regulations, and ordinances for the repairs, maintenance, and

-5-

operation of the Facility. (Complaint, Exhibit A, Management Agreement, p.9). The Facility was under "the exclusive supervision direction and control" of BSCM. (*Id.*). The foregoing terms expressly confirm that BSCM—not York—bore responsibility to maintain and repair the Facility.

C. York's Limited Right of Re-Entry and its Course of Conduct Demonstrate It Relinquished Control of the Facility to BSCM

To assess whether an out-of-possession landowner retained or relinquished control over property, courts focus on: (1) contractual language; and (2) course of conduct. Courts evaluate contractual language discussing a right of re-entry *to make repairs* by the landowner (*broader* than York's right of re-entry to inspect or show the property to buyers, investors, lessees, or lenders in Article 14.5 of the Management Agreement), but will absolve a landowner from liability even in light of such a right of re-entry, unless the parties' course of conduct demonstrates the offsite landowner's ongoing control of the property.

Many New York courts have addressed the issue of control in out-of-possession landowner cases. For example, in *Gronski v. County of Monroe*, 18 N.Y.3d 374 (N.Y. 2011), the County owned a waste recycling center, operated by a waste management company. A management company employee sued for injuries he incurred on the property. *Id.* at 377. An Operations and Maintenance Agreement governed the relationship between the County and the management company, stating that the management company "shall have complete charge of and responsibility for the Facility and Facility Site." *Id.* The agreement assigned all responsibility for repair, maintenance, and safety at the facility to the management company. The County retained "the right of access to the Facility in order to determine compliance by the Contractor with the terms and conditions of this Agreement, and . . . the right . . . to take visitors and group tours through . . . the Facility." *Id.* The County moved for summary judgment, arguing that, like an out-of-possession landlord, it had relinquished control over the maintenance and operations of the Facility to the management company pursuant to the agreement, and was not contractually obligated to repair unsafe conditions on the premises. *Id.* at 378. The court recited the rule that "a landowner who has transferred possession and control is generally not liable for injuries caused by dangerous conditions on the property." *Id.* at 379. Courts "look not only to the terms of the agreement but to the parties' course of conduct—including, but not limited to, the landowner's ability to access the premises—to determine whether the landowner in fact surrendered control over the property such that the landowner's duty is extinguished as a matter of law." *Id.* at 380-381.

The *Gronski* court held that an issue of fact existed as to whether the County retained sufficient control over the Facility such that it owed the injured party a duty to prevent the condition that resulted in injury. *Id.* at 382. The court focused on the following facts indicating ongoing physical contact with the premises: (1) the County maintained a visible and vocal presence at the Facility; (2) the County availed itself of its contractual access to the Facility through regular public tours and routine unannounced inspections; and (3) a County representative took specific supervisory actions, for example, when he observed workers not wearing hard hats. *Id.* at 381. In contrast, the express language of the Management Agreement between York and BSCM demonstrates relinquishment of control over the premises from York to BSCM. Further, Dublin has not alleged, and cannot allege, any facts to demonstrate a course of conduct tying York to the day-to-day operations of the Facility.

Further, in *Michaelov v. 632 Kings Highway Realty Corp,* No. 3969/10, 2012 WL 3322678 (N.Y. Sup. Ct. July 13, 2012), an accident occurred outside a grocery store leased by the building's owner to the store owner. As workers maneuvered an air conditioning unit in a window above the store, a piece of glass fell on a store visitor. Pursuant to the lease, the store owner—not the building owner—was responsible for the repair and maintenance of the premises. *Id.* at *4. The lease specifically stated, "Tenant shall, throughout the term of the lease, take good care of the demised premises . . . and at its sole cost and expense, make all non-structural repairs thereto . . . " *Id.* at *6. The lease also afforded the building owner the right to enter the premises "to examine the same *and to make such repairs, replacements, and improvements as Owner may deem necessary* . . . following Tenant's failure to make repairs." *Id.* (emphasis added). The court reiterated the rule that "an out-of-possession landlord is not liable for injuries sustained at the leased premises unless it has retained control over the premises or is contractually obligated to repair unsafe conditions." *Id.* at *13. The court held that, based on the lease, the owner was <u>not</u> contractually obligated to make non-structural repairs or to maintain the area of the premises where the visitor's accident occurred. *Id.* The court further found no evidence that the owner controlled the premises through course of conduct. There was no proof that he: (1) actually controlled or undertook any repairs, even though the owner visited the premises occasionally to check on the tenant's renovations; (2) visited the premises on a regular basis for the purpose of controlling maintenance or repairs; (3) gave the tenant tools for repairs; or (4) instructed the tenant regarding repairs at the premises. *Id.* Importantly, the lease in *Michaelov* granted the building owner the right of re-entry *to repair* and yet the owner was still held <u>not</u> responsible based on its course of conduct. Notably, York's narrow right of re-entry stated in the Management Agreement with BSCM was limited to inspection and showing the property to potential buyers, investors, lessees, and lenders; it did not encompass a right to repair.

Moreover, in *Vijayan v. Bally's Total Fitness*, 289 A.D.2d 224 (N.Y. App. Div. 2001), a patron slipped and fell on icy steps of a gym, and sued the out-of-possession landowner. The court held that the property owner was not liable because it did not retain control over the premises that was leased to the gym. *Id.* at 225. The court explained that regular visits of the owner's managing agent to the premises to collect rent, lease additional space, and address tenants' concerns did not establish control. *Id.* Further, a reservation of rights to re-enter the premises was insufficient to impose liability. *Id.* Rather, the gym bore the sole contractual responsibility for clearing snow and ice from the premises. *Id.*[2]

In contrast, in *Derienzo v. East New York Club House*, 22 Misc. 3d 1124(A), 2009 WL 415556 (N.Y. Sup. Ct. 2009) (unreported), a landowner retained a contractual responsibility to keep its premises in repair, as well as the right to re-enter and make needed repairs. Indeed, the landlord *had* made repairs to the premises. With respect to the alleged defect which caused the plaintiff's injury, the owner had visited the site, observed the defect, and indicated it would be repaired. *Id.* at *2. Under these circumstances, the court denied the landowner's motion for summary judgment based on "out-of-possession" landowner liability.

Unlike the plaintiffs in *Gronski* and *Derienzo* who contended that the landowners visited their properties regularly, established visibility, and interacted with property personnel regarding repairs or deficiencies, Dublin has not alleged in the Complaint, and cannot prove, that York maintained any presence at the Facility—having relinquished control of the physical premises to BSCM under the Management Agreement. York had no contractual duty to re-enter the premises to perform repairs, and Dublin alleged no course of dealing in the Complaint, and cannot assert any such conduct, contradicting its contractual relinquishment of control to BSCM.

---

[2] *See also Alnashmi v. Certified Analytical Group, Inc.*, 89 A.D.3d 10 (N.Y. App. Div. 2011); *Green v. City of New York*, 76 A.D.3d 508 (N.Y. App. Div. 2010); *Boyd v. Paladino*, 295 A.D.2d 298 (N.Y. App. Div. 2002); *Carvano v. Morgan*, 270 A.D.2d 222 (N.Y. App. Div. 2000); *Del Giacco v. Noteworthy Co.*, 175 A.D.2d 516 (N.Y. App. Div. 1991) (all finding the out-of-possession landowner not liable based on lack of control).

D. York Had No Actual Notice of Any Defects

In an unreported case, *Graybill v. City of New York*, No. 123754/01, 2003 WL 21649704 (N.Y. Sup. Ct. June 23, 2003), the court elaborated on the rule of control in the context of an out-of-possession landowner, stating, "[a]bsent contractually created responsibility, liability requires proof that the out-of-possession landowner retained sufficient control over the premises, had actual or constructive notice of a dangerous or defective condition, and had reasonable opportunity to repair or correct it." *Id.* at *1. All three criteria are required to impose liability: control, notice, and opportunity. According to *Bautista v. 85th Columbus Corp.*, 42 Misc.3d 651 (N.Y. Sup. Ct. 2013), "[a]n out-of-possession landlord may be found liable for failure to repair a *known dangerous condition* on leased premises if the landlord both assumes a duty to make repairs and reserves the right to enter in order to inspect or to make such repairs." (emphasis added). As stated above, York had a right of re-entry, but not to make repairs. York's right of re-entry was limited to inspection and showing the Facility to prospective buyers, investors, lessees, or lenders. Further, Dublin has not alleged any facts in the Complaint supporting a plausible conclusion that York had actual notice of the portable storage locker, or its ramp, let alone that there were any issues with their assembly. New York courts will not impose liability upon a party for circumstances which it did not create, and of which it had no notice.

This rule was illustrated in *Butler v. Rafferty*, 291 A.D.2d 754 (N.Y. App. Div. 2002), *aff'd in* 100 N.Y.2d 265 (N.Y. 2003), in which a child fell from a bunk bed in a tenant's home, and the parents sued a co-owner of the property. The tenant had built a house on the property, and constructed the bunk bed. The co-owner "did not assist in the construction of the bunk bed and knew nothing more about it than that it existed." *Id.* at 755. The court viewed the co-owner as an out-of-possession landlord, reiterating the rule that "an out-of-possession landlord is not liable for injuries resulting from the condition of the demised premises." *Id.* at 756. The court further stated that "application of that rule is particularly apt in this case, given that [the co-owner] took no part in the construction of the portion of the property occupied . . . or of the bunk bed . . . and thus did not have notice of any alleged defect." *Id.* The co-owner even knew the bunk bed existed—in contrast to the lack of any factual assertion in Dublin's Complaint that York knew about the storage locker and ramp—and the court still found the co-owner not liable.

Since Dublin's Complaint does not plead factual content that allows the court to draw the reasonable inference that York had actual notice of the ramp, dismissal of the Complaint is warranted. *See Iqbal*, 556 U.S. at 678.

E. York Had No Constructive Notice of Any Defects

New York also recognizes a tangential constructive notice rule related to the right of re-entry to make repairs. In *Michaelov*, 36 Misc.3d 1228(A), 2012 WL 3322678, the court explained:

> the mere "[r]eservation of a right of entry *for inspection and repair* may constitute sufficient retention of control to impose liability for injuries caused by a dangerous condition . . . *only where liability is based on a significant structural or design defect that violates a specific statutory provision.*" . . . A structural defect is one where the defect violates a statute rather than a regulation . . . . General maintenance of a premises and a failure stemming therefrom, is not akin to a structural defect. . . . In the absence of a statutory duty, a landlord's mere reservation of a right to enter leased premises *to make repairs* is insufficient to give rise to liability for a subsequently arising dangerous condition.

Id. at *13 (internal citations omitted) (emphasis added).[3] "[A]bsent a contractual obligation to repair/maintain the premises, or the right to reenter it to make repairs at the tenant's expense," an out-of-possession landowner may not be charged with constructive notice of a structural defect. *Lucero v. DRK, LLC*, 111 A.D.3d 578, 663 (N.Y. App. Div. 2013).

York could only be charged with constructive notice if: (1) it reserved a right of entry in order to inspect the premises *and make necessary repairs*, and (2) there was a *significant* structural or design defect that (3) violated a specific statutory provision.[4] York's right of access was only to inspect and show the Facility to prospective buyers, investors, lessees, and lenders—not to repair. Further, the Complaint fails to allege any facts to support a reasonable inference that the ramp had a *significant* structural or design defect that violates a specific statutory violation. Since Dublin's

---

[3] *See also David v. HSS Property Corp.*, 1 A.D.3d 153 (N.Y. App. Div. 2003) (an out-of-possession owner can be held liable under a theory of constructive notice only where it has reserved the right to enter the premises to perform *inspection, maintenance and repairs* at the tenant's expense and injury was caused by a *significant* structural or design defect that is contrary to a specific statutory safety provision; owner retained the right to enter and make repairs to a leased office but a floor defect was not a violation of a safety regulation triggering constructive notice); *Hepburn v. Getty Petroleum Corp.*, 258 A.D.2d 504 (N.Y. App. Div. 1999).

[4] *See, e.g., Bautista v. 85th Columbus Corp.*, 42 Misc.3d 651 (N.Y. Sup. Ct. 2013) (sidewalk basement stairway without handrails and without proper tread width and lighting did not constitute a significant structural or defect to warrant liability); *Czerkas v. Jonre Realty Co., Inc.*, 200 A.D.2d 821 (N.Y. App. Div. 1994) (failure to place or maintain a step between a platform and the floor did not appear to be a structural defect in the building for which the owner was responsible); *Quinones v. 27 Third City King Restaurant, Inc.*, 198 A.D.2d 23 (N.Y. App. Div. 1993) (ruts, pitting and holes in the plastic covering of an interior step installed by the tenant did not constitute a *significant* structural defect).

Complaint does not plead factual content that allows the court to draw the reasonable inference that York had constructive notice of the ramp, dismissal of the Complaint is warranted. *See Iqbal*, 556 U.S. at 678.

IV. Conclusion

The New York rule limiting out-of-possession landowner liability is designed to protect property owners from accountability for injuries that occur on premises over which such owners relinquished control to a third-party. York did not *create* the storage locker or its ramp, delegated responsibility in the Management Agreement to BSCM for *maintenance* and *repair* of the Facility, and relinquished *control* of the Facility's operations to BSCM. Further, York had no actual or constructive notice of any defects in the storage locker or ramp. Based upon the foregoing, York respectfully requests the Court to dismiss the Complaint.

Date: December 20, 2017

Respectfully submitted,

Paolo Edmunds

Paolo Edmunds, Esq.
EDMUNDS & LUCY, LLP
436 Spring Street
New York, NY
800-913-8559
p.edmunds@edmundslucy.com
Counsel for York Property
Development, LLC

Appendix L: Sample Appellate Brief

SECOND JUDICIAL DEPARTMENT APPELLATE DIVISION
SUPREME COURT OF THE STATE OF NEW YORK

RANDALL DUBLIN,

   Plaintiff-Respondent,

v.

YORK PROPERTY
DEVELOPMENT, LLC,

   Defendant-Appellant.

DOCKET 2017/56436

ON APPEAL FROM THE SUPREME COURT OF THE
STATE OF NEW YORK
COUNTY OF KINGS

Paolo Edmunds, Esq.
EDMUNDS & LUCY, LLP
436 Spring Street
New York, NY
p.edmunds@edmundslucy.com
800-913-8599

Counsel for York Property Development, LLC

-1-

TABLE OF CONTENTS

TABLE OF AUTHORITIES

QUESTION PRESENTED

Did the trial court err in finding that Defendant-Appellant is not an "out-of-possession" landowner and, therefore, is liable to Plaintiff-Respondent for alleged injuries he sustained in a slip and fall on a snowy ramp that he was responsible for maintaining as an employee of a management company of a sports stadium?

NATURE OF THE CASE

The Plaintiff-Respondent

Plaintiff-Respondent Randall Dublin ("Dublin") was born in Manhattan. (A-22:19-20).[1] He is presently 33 years old. (A-22:18, 25; A-63:1). On April 4, 2015, Dublin accepted a job as a maintenance employee with a management company of a sports stadium complex located in Brooklyn,

---

[1] All cites to the Appendix are referred to herein as "A-__"

New York called the Brooklyn Gridiron (the "Facility"). (A-72:19). The management company is called Brooklyn Sports Complex Management, Inc. ("BSCM").

The Two Different Entities That Own and Manage the Stadium

Two completely different corporate entities own and manage the stadium. York Property Development, LLC ("York") is a limited liability company—formed in the State of Delaware—that owns the real estate in Brooklyn where the Facility is located, and the land and buildings thereon. (A-55:24-25; A-56:1-11; A-91:2-4). York purchased the land (A-57:16-17; A-99:6-8), and hired a construction company to build the stadium. (A-75:12-14). As a real estate investment company, York does not operate or manage the sports stadium complex or operations; a separate management company, BSCM, runs the operation completely (A-35:12-17). York and BSCM are two separate legal entities. (A-71:10-13). BSCM is incorporated in the State of Delaware. (A-71:5-9). York is not the parent company of BSCM, and BSCM is not the parent company of York. (A-70:21-25; A-71:1). As the Facility's management company, BSCM operates the stadium, hires the employees, and runs the Facility. (A-95:24-25; A-105:19-22). The Facility's business operations—including all profits and losses—are owned by BSCM. (A-90:4-8).

Management Company's Role

BSCM has the exclusive right to manage the stadium (A-73:7-8, 25; A-74:1-2), and controls the property. (A-74:6-7). It employs the stadium's Executive Director, and the administrative, maintenance, security, and housekeeping staff that keeps the stadium and property safe and orderly. (A-100:9-15). BSCM manages the physical structure, the building, the grounds, and the operations of the sports complex at the Facility. (A-73:7-11, 19-24). BSCM is responsible for maintenance (A-206:21-23) of the property, the land, and the buildings (including snow and ice removal) (A-206:1-15) and repairs. (A-282:8-20; A-283:3-14; A-117:3-10).

Management Agreement

York (as Owner) and BSCM (as Manager) entered into a Management Agreement (A-488-367; A-38:19-22), which includes the following key terms:

-4-

Article 14.1: "Owner hereby appoints Manager and Manager hereby accepts such appointment, subject to the provisions of this Agreement, as the exclusive manager for the day-to-day operation, administration, and management of the Facility. Manager has responsibility and *complete and full control* and discretion in the operation, direction, management and supervision of the Facility." (emphasis added) (A-408)

Article 14.2: "Facility operations are under the *exclusive direction and control* of Manager." (emphasis added) (A-410)

Article 14.3: "Manager is responsible for the supply, operation, *maintenance* and service of the Facility, and for planning, executing and supervising all *repairs and maintenance* at the Facility." (emphasis added) (A-411)

Article 14.4: "Manager shall comply with *all laws, codes, rules, regulations, and ordinances governing* the *repairs, maintenance,* or operation of the Facility." (emphasis added) (A-440)

Article 14.5: "Owner shall have access to the Facility at any and all reasonable times for the purpose of inspection or showing the Facility to prospective buyers, investors, lessees, or lenders." (A-442)

According to BSCM employee testimony, including that of Louise Cartwright ("Cartwright"), York had a limited right to inspect the property if it wished to bring a potential buyer, investor, tenant, or bank to look at the property. (A-61:16-17; A-69:12-21). This limited inspection right did <u>not</u> include a right to make repairs. (A-69:22-24). York hired BSCM to bear all responsibility to maintain and run the property. (A-100:16-19). This is a common circumstance for these types of investment landowners. (A-100:20-22).

The Storage Locker

In the summer of 2015, BSCM directed the assembly of a portable storage locker on the outskirts of the Facility's property, near the West parking lot. (A-98:21-24). The stadium's Executive Director, Jake Grotto ("Grotto"), an employee of BSCM (A-279:7-9), ordered the portable storage locker from a company called Storage Locker Depot, LLC ("Depot") on behalf of BSCM because it was cheaper than the off-site storage facility the Facility had been using in Queens, New York. (A-391:24-25; A-392:1-8). Grotto also decided he needed a ramp to the storage locker, and asked BSCM for approval. (A-293:3-4; A-417:11-12, 21). BSCM ordered the storage locker installation. (A-90:10-12).

BSCM purchased the storage locker in August 2015 (A-78:21-23; A-987) and paid for it via credit card. (A-395:3-21; A-397:20-25; A-398:1-7,

13-14; A-399:1-14; A-424:17-19; A-688). Depot designed and built the storage locker and a ramp for loading items into the front entrance of the locker. (A-292:15-16; A-593:10-15; A-112:21-23). BSCM was not involved in the storage locker design. (A-296:17-19). The storage locker was prefabricated and arrived in separate pieces; Depot assembled the storage locker on the property (A-393:18-21; A-400:2-3) in late August 2015. (A-289:25; A-290:1-2). The storage locker had a front ramp leading up to double doors; the storage locker also had two side entrance doors, and four windows. (A-290:7-9, 14).

BSCM did not assist Depot with the storage locker and ramp installation. (A-410:6-13). Depot advised BSCM that it could place the storage locker on the stadium property without a permit because it was a portable structure. (A-112:13-16). Grotto was not aware of any codes or regulations that applied to the storage locker or ramp. (A-113:8-10).

Grotto had no communications with York about the storage locker or ramp. (A-110:19-22; A-23:8-10). There is no evidence that anyone at BSCM communicated with York about the storage locker or ramp. Grotto did not consult York to get permission for the ramp (A-393:7-9) or the storage locker. (A-229:7-10; A-140:16-23; A-152:11-13). York never requested (A-320:23-25), approved (A-81:1-2), created, built, or designed the ramp (A-81:7-10), or even knew the ramp existed any time between its assembly in August 2015 and November 12, 2015 (the date of Dublin's accident) (A-149:7-10; A-141:12-14; A-323:25; A-174:1-3, 8-13; A-237:1-5). The relationship between York and BSCM required limited communication; Cartwright testified that if BSCM decided it needed a storage locker, it was not required to communicate that to York. (A-654:11-16). BSCM was 100% in charge of the stadium (A-216:1-7), and did not need York's permission or guidance regarding the stadium or property. (A-336:8-12).

BSCM's Responsibility for the Storage Locker and Ramp

BSCM bore responsibility for the storage locker's maintenance (A-777:19-20) and the ramp's condition. (A-954:14-17). Prior to November 12, 2015 (Dublin's accident), BSCM never received complaints about the ramp (A-215:11-13), and Grotto never had concerns about its condition. (A-827:12-14, 19). Grotto never notified York regarding any concerns about the ramp. (A-805:22-24).

BSCM bore responsibility for ensuring that all property operations conformed to applicable laws. (A-12:7-10). If a city code inspector had visited the property and advised regarding an issue with a ramp (which none ever did), under the Management Agreement, BSCM bore responsibility for repairs. (A-29:3-7). York had no representatives stationed on the property (A-900:16-18), and none visited the property while Grotto was Executive Director. (A-977:13-20). During Grotto's tenure, there was never a need for York to send a representative to the property (A-378:3-5) or perform any periodic inspection of the property because BSCM made all decisions regarding the property. (A-378:14-20). BSCM maintained the property with its own employees. (A-378:21-25; A-479:1-3). No York employee ever performed property maintenance or repairs. (A-279:10-12). York did not direct BSCM's Executive Director regarding how to manage the property. (A-280:18-22; A-628:12-13).

The Incident

On November 12, 2015, Dublin was late to work; several inches of snow had fallen overnight. (A-11:2-8; A-231:17-24). Upon arrival at the stadium, he walked to the maintenance room inside the Facility to obtain rock salt to distribute on the Facility's snow-covered sidewalks. (A-151:25, A-152:1). Not finding the rock salt, he then walked to the storage locker (A-152:18-22) located on the outskirts of the Facility near the West parking lot. (A-781:21-23). There was snow on the ground. (A-93:20-23). Wearing Timberland work boots (A-94:8), Dublin walked to the storage locker; the ramp was covered in snow. (A-94:16-19; A-534:9-11). Even though there were other entrances to the storage locker besides the one at the top of the ramp (A-114:20-21), Dublin walked up the ramp, opened the entrance doors, and entered the storage locker. (A-205:7-10). Inside the storage locker, he located a bag of rock salt. (A-205:13-21). Turning to leave, he exited the doorway, took one step onto the ramp, slipped, and fell. (A-205:24-25). He hit his right knee on the doorjamb of the locker. (A-316:4; A-311:2-3).

After he fell, he returned to the stadium and visited the first aid office. (A-401:22-23). He was limping so the first aid attendant called an ambulance which transported Dublin to a nearby hospital, where he was x-rayed and prescribed pain medication. (A-502:16-20). He had no broken bones and was not bleeding. (A-519:12-16). He was discharged the same day. (A-602:21-23). Dublin was advised to take ten days off and return to work on light duty. (A-703:12-13). He did not return to work again. (A-708:3-8). Dublin filed a claim against BSCM's workers' compensation insurance for alleged injuries to his knee, and received benefits through 2016.

-7-

(A-820:24-25; A-821:2-4, 12-16, 21-24). BSCM's workers' compensation insurance paid for Dublin's medical care. (A-822:1-6).

Dublin's Lawsuit

Because of his workers' compensation claim, Dublin could not sue his employer, BSCM. (A-913:19-22). Instead, Dublin filed a Complaint against York as property owner, alleging that there existed a dangerous condition on the Facility property, and the condition caused Dublin's injury. (A-43-49).

Expert Testimony about the Storage Locker and Ramp

At trial, an engineering expert named Bernard Rowan ("Rowan") testified that he inspected the site in December of 2016—over a year after Dublin's incident. (A-257:17-23). He testified that the storage locker's ramp slope exceeded the allowable grade under the building code, and that New York State building codes and property maintenance codes required handrails for ramps—which the locker's ramp lacked. (A-250:12-18). Rowan testified concerning the New York State Uniform Fire Prevention and Building Code, and Property Maintenance Code, but never concluded that the ramp constituted a *significant* structural defect. (A-1048).

Trial Proceedings Regarding the "Out-of-Possession Landowner" Issue

During trial, York moved for a directed verdict based on the "out-of-possession landowner" doctrine under New York law, asserting that Dublin had failed to prove: (1) that York created the condition; (2) that York retained responsibility for maintenance or repair of the stadium premises; (3) that York controlled the property; or (4) that York had actual or constructive knowledge of the locker or the ramp. (A-948:14-25; A-949:1-7). The trial court denied the motion, finding that York had control over the premises (A-973:2-9; A-973:16-23), and—in contrast to the Management Agreement's express language addressing BSCM's responsibility for repair and maintenance—"the management company had no right to alter the Facility without Owner approval." (A-974:12-14).

Verdict

The jury rendered a verdict in favor of Dublin, finding the ramp was not in a reasonably safe condition, and awarding damages for past and future pain and suffering, past and future lost wages, and past and future medical expenses. (A-862:20-25). The verdict totaled $2,100,000. After the verdict, the trial court indicated it would not yet rule on the out-of-possession landowner issue, but later would issue a written decision. (A-712:10-13).

Post-Trial Motion

York filed a Post-Trial Brief in Support of its Motion for Directed Verdict (A-1331-1339), reiterating that Dublin failed to establish that York: (1) retained sufficient control over the property to impose liability for any negligent condition; (2) created, knew, or had any reason to know of the condition of the ramp; or (3) retained any responsibility for maintenance or repairs of the stadium building. York asserted that, as an out-of-possession landowner, it could not be liable for Dublin's injuries. The trial court denied York's Motion, on the basis that York as Owner "retained the right to access the premises at any time to inspect or show it to prospective buyers, investors, lessees, or lenders." (A-97-98). The trial court emphasized that Dublin's expert stated that the ramp had design defects. (A-98). The trial court concluded that York was not an out-of-possession landowner. (A-101). The court entered judgment on September 29, 2017. (A-1-6). On October 29, 2017, York timely filed its Notice of Appeal. (A-7).

ARGUMENT

I. Introduction

The trial court misapplied New York law limiting the liability of an "out-of-possession" landowner, disregarding clear standards established in case law. It is well-recognized under New York law that an out-of-possession property owner cannot be liable for injuries that occur on a premises unless the landowner: (1) created the dangerous condition; (2) assumed responsibility to maintain any portion of the premises; (3) is contractually obligated to repair the unsafe condition; or (4) retained control of the premises. York did not *create* the storage locker or its ramp, delegated responsibility in the Management Agreement to BSCM for *maintenance* and *repair* of the Facility, and relinquished *control* of the Facility's operations to BSCM. Further, York had no actual or constructive notice of any defects in the storage locker or ramp, and notice cannot be imputed to York because there is no evidence that the ramp had *significant* structural defects as required under New York law. For these reasons, York seeks reversal and *vacatur* of the judgment against it on liability and damages.

II. Standard of Review

Under CPLR 5501(c) (McKinney 1997), "[t]he appellate division shall review questions of law and questions of fact on an appeal from a judgment or order . . . " The Court has expansive authority to review questions of law and fact, and to render new findings of fact.

III. Satisfying All the Criteria of an Out-of-Possession Landowner Under New York Law, York Cannot Be Liable to Dublin

Dublin was employed by BSCM, not York. Because he exhausted his remedies against BSCM through his workers' compensation claim, he sued York. It is well-recognized under New York law that an out-of-possession property owner *cannot* be liable for injuries that occur on a premises unless the landowner: (1) *created* the dangerous condition; (2) assumed responsibility to *maintain* any portion of the premises; (3) is contractually obligated to *repair* the unsafe condition; or (4) retained *control* of the premises. *Buckowski v. Smith*, 185 A.D.2d 556 (N.Y. App. Div. 1992). In deciding that York was not an out-of-possession landowner, the trial court ignored the express language of the Management Agreement and the parties' course of dealing, and misapplied New York law. New York repeatedly has refused to impose liability upon out-of-possession landowners who have much greater contractual obligations and connections to their properties than York did. Analyzing the issues of *creation, maintenance, repair,* and *control,* the verdict and judgment as to liability and damages must be reversed and vacated.

A. York Had No Involvement in Creating the Storage Locker or Ramp

Grotto testified that York did not create the storage locker or ramp. Grotto, a BSCM employee, ordered the storage locker from Depot for BSCM. (A-391:24-25; A-392:1-8). Grotto had no communications with York about the storage locker or ramp. (A-1100:19-22; A-23:8-10). There is no evidence that anyone from BSCM communicated with York about the storage locker or ramp. Grotto did not consult York to get permission for the ramp (A-393:7-9) or the storage locker. (A-229:7-10; A-140:16-23; A-152:11-13). York never requested (A-320:23-25), approved (A-81:1-2), created, built, or designed the ramp (A-81:7-10), or even knew the ramp existed any time between its assembly and Dublin's accident. (A-149:7-10; A-141:12-14; A-323:25; A-174:1-3, 8-13; A-237:1-5).

B. BSCM Was Responsible for Maintenance and Repair of the Premises

In rejecting York's out-of-possession landowner argument, the trial court erroneously concluded that "the management company had no right to alter the Facility without Owner approval." (A-97:12-14). This is a patent contradiction of the plain language of the Management Agreement. Under Article 14 of the Management Agreement, BSCM assumed responsibility for: (1) the daily operation, direction, management, and supervision of the stadium; (2) the supply, operation, maintenance, repairs, and service of the stadium, and (3) compliance with any applicable laws, codes, rules, regulations, and ordinances governing the repairs, maintenance, or operation of the Facility. The foregoing terms expressly confirm that BSCM—not York—bore responsibility to maintain and repair the Facility and comply with all legal requirements.

C. York's Limited Right of Re-Entry and its Course of Conduct Demonstrate It Relinquished Control of the Facility to BSCM

To assess whether an out-of-possession landowner retained or relinquished control over property, courts focus on: (1) contractual language; and (2) course of conduct. Courts evaluate contractual language discussing a right of re-entry *to make repairs* by the landowner (*broader* than York's right of re-entry to show the property to buyers, investors, lessees, or lenders), but will absolve a landowner from liability even in light of a right of re-entry, unless the parties' course of conduct demonstrates the offsite landowner's ongoing control of the property. Article 14.5 of York's Management Agreement with BSCM stated, "Owner or its agents shall have access to the Facility at any and all reasonable times for the purpose of inspection or showing the Facility to prospective buyers, investors, lessees, or lenders." (A-442). The evidence in Dublin's case shows that: (1) York's narrow contractual right of re-entry in Article 14.5 was limited to inspection and showing the property to prospective buyers, investors, lessees, or lenders (A-477:13-20; A-578:3-5; A-642)—wholly distinguishable from New York cases involving landowners possessing a right of re-entry *to conduct repairs*, and (2) no representative from York inspected or visited the property during BSCM's management. (A-993). No requisite control existed to impose liability on York.

Many New York courts have addressed the issue of control in out-of-possession landowner cases. For example, in *Gronski v. County of Monroe*, 18 N.Y.3d 374 (N.Y. 2011), the County owned a waste recycling center, operated by a waste management company. A management company

-11-

employee who was injured on the premises sued for damages. *Id.* at 377. An Operations and Maintenance Agreement governed the relationship between the County and the management company, stating that the management company "shall have complete charge of and responsibility for the Facility and Facility Site." *Id.* The agreement assigned all responsibility for repair, maintenance, and safety at the Facility to the management company. The County retained "the right of access to the Facility in order to determine compliance by the Contractor with the terms and conditions of this Agreement, and . . . the right . . . to take visitors and group tours through . . . the Facility." *Id.* The County moved for summary judgment, arguing that, like an out-of-possession landlord, it had relinquished control over the maintenance and operations of the Facility to the management company pursuant to the Management Agreement, and was not contractually obligated to repair unsafe conditions on the premises. *Id.* at 378. The court recited the rule that "a landowner who has transferred possession and control is generally not liable for injuries caused by dangerous conditions on the property." *Id.* at 379. Courts "look not only to the terms of the agreement but to the parties' course of conduct—including, but not limited to, the landowner's ability to access the premises—to determine whether the landowner in fact surrendered control over the property such that the landowner's duty is extinguished as a matter of law." *Id.* at 380-381.

The *Gronski* court held that an issue of fact existed as to whether the County retained sufficient control over the Facility such that it owed the injured plaintiff a duty to prevent the condition that resulted in injury. *Id.* at 382. The court focused on the following facts indicating ongoing physical contact with the premises: (1) the County maintained a visible and vocal presence at the Facility; (2) the County availed itself of its contractual access to the Facility through regular public tours and routine unannounced inspections; and (3) a County representative took specific supervisory actions, for example, when he observed workers not wearing hard hats. *Id.* at 381. These facts are readily distinguishable from York, whose course of conduct indicates it had no presence at the Facility.

Further, in *Michaelov v. 632 Kings Highway Realty Corp*, No. 3969/10, 2012 WL 3322678 (N.Y. Sup. Ct. July 13, 2012), an accident occurred outside a grocery store leased by the building's owner to the store owner. As workers maneuvered an air conditioning unit in a window above the store, a piece of glass fell on a store visitor. Pursuant to the lease, the store owner—not the building owner—was responsible for the repair and maintenance of the premises. *Id.* at *4. The lease specifically stated, "Tenant shall, throughout the term of the lease, take good care of the demised premises . . . and at its sole cost and expense, make all non-structural repairs thereto . . . " *Id.* at *6. The lease also afforded the building owner the right to enter the premises "to examine the same *and to make such repairs, replacements, and improvements as Owner may deem necessary* . . . following Tenant's failure to make repairs." *Id.* (emphasis added). The court reiterated the rule that "an out-of-possession landlord is not liable for injuries sustained at the leased premises unless it has retained control over the premises or is contractually obligated to repair unsafe conditions." *Id.* at *13. The court held that, based on the lease, the owner was <u>not</u> contractually obligated to make non-structural repairs or to maintain the area of the premises where the visitor's accident occurred. *Id.* The court further found no evidence that the owner controlled the premises through course of conduct. There was no proof that he: (1) actually controlled or undertook any repairs, even though the owner visited the premises occasionally to check on the tenant's renovations; (2) visited the premises on a regular basis for the purpose of controlling maintenance or repairs; (3) gave the tenant tools for repairs; or (4) instructed the tenant regarding repairs at the premises. *Id.* Importantly, the lease in *Michaelov* granted the building owner the right of re-entry *to repair* and yet the owner was still held <u>not</u> responsible based on its course of conduct. Notably, York's narrow right of re-entry stated in the Management Agreement with BSCM was limited to inspection and showing the property to potential buyers, investors, lessees, or lenders; it did not encompass a right to repair.

Moreover, in *Vijayan v. Bally's Total Fitness*, 289 A.D.2d 224 (N.Y. App. Div. 2001), a patron slipped and fell on icy steps of a gym, and sued the out-of-possession landowner. The court held that the property owner was not liable because it did not retain control over the premises that was leased to the gym. *Id.* at 225. The court explained that regular visits of the owner's managing agent to the premises to collect rent, lease additional space, and address tenants' concerns did not establish control. *Id.* Further, a reservation of rights to re-enter the premises was insufficient to impose liability. *Id.* Rather, the gym bore the sole contractual responsibility for clearing snow and ice from the premises. *Id.*[2]

In contrast, in *Derienzo v. East New York Club House*, 22 Misc.3d 1124(A), 2009 WL 415556 (N.Y. Sup. Ct. 2009) (unreported), a landowner retained a contractual responsibility to keep its premises in repair, as well as the right to re-enter and make needed repairs. Indeed, the landlord *had* made repairs to the premises. With respect to the alleged defect which caused the plaintiff's injury, the owner had visited the site, observed the

---

[2] *See also Alnashmi v. Certified Analytical Group, Inc.*, 89 A.D.3d 10 (N.Y. App. Div. 2011); *Green v. City of New York*, 76 A.D.3d 508 (N.Y. App. Div. 2010); *Boyd v. Paladino*, 295 A.D.2d 298 (N.Y. App. Div. 2002); *Carvano v. Morgan*, 270 A.D.2d 222 (N.Y. App. Div. 2000); *Del Giacco v. Noteworthy Co.*, 175 A.D.2d 516 (N.Y. App. Div. 1991) (all finding the out-of-possession landowner not liable based on lack of control).

-13-

defect, and indicated it would be repaired. *Id.* at *2. Under these circumstances, the court denied the landowner's motion for summary judgment based on "out-of-possession" landowner liability.

Unlike the landowners in *Gronski* and *Derienzo* who visited their properties regularly, established visibility, and interacted with property personnel regarding repairs or deficiencies, York maintained no presence at the stadium—having relinquished control to BSCM under the Management Agreement. York stationed no representatives on the property. (A-900:16-18). None visited the property. (A-977:13-20). York performed no repairs or maintenance on the property. (A-279:10-12). BSCM made all property decisions (A-378:14-20) and maintained the property with its own employees. (A-378:21-25; A-479:1-3). York had no contractual duty to re-enter the premises to conduct repairs, and its course of dealing reflected its relinquishment of control to BSCM.

D. York Had No Actual Notice of Any Defects

In an unreported case, *Graybill v. City of New York*, No. 123754/01, 2003 WL 21649704 (N.Y. Sup. Ct. June 23, 2003), the court elaborated on the rule of control in the context of an out-of-possession landowner, stating, "[a]bsent contractually created responsibility, liability requires proof that the out-of-possession landowner retained sufficient control over the premises, had actual or constructive notice of a dangerous or defective condition, and had reasonable opportunity to repair or correct it." *Id.* at *1. All three criteria are required to impose liability: control, notice, and opportunity. According to *Bautista v. 85th Columbus Corp.*, 42 Misc.3d 651 (N.Y. Sup. Ct. 2013), "[a]n out-of-possession landlord may be found liable for failure to repair a *known dangerous condition* on leased premises if the landlord both assumes a duty to make repairs and reserves the right to enter in order to inspect or to make such repairs." (emphasis added). As stated above, York had a right of re-entry, but not to make repairs. The right of re-entry was limited to inspection and showing the stadium premises to prospective buyers, investors, lessees, or lenders. Further, the trial record confirms that York had no actual notice of the portable storage locker, or its ramp, let alone that there were any issues with their assembly. New York courts will not impose liability upon a party for circumstances which it did not create, and of which it had no notice.

This rule was illustrated in *Butler v. Rafferty*, 291 A.D.2d 754 (N.Y. App. Div. 2002), *aff'd in* 100 N.Y.2d 265 (N.Y. 2003), in which a child fell from a bunk bed in a tenant's home, and the parents sued a co-owner of the property. The tenant had built a house on the property, and constructed the bunk bed. The co-owner "did not assist in the construction of the bunk bed and knew nothing more about it than that it existed." *Id.* at 755. The court viewed the co-owner as an out-of-possession landlord, reiterating the rule that "an out-of-possession landlord is not liable for injuries resulting from the condition of the demised premises." *Id.* at 756. The court further stated that "application of that rule is particularly apt in this case, given that [the co-owner] took no part in the construction of the portion of the property occupied . . . or of the bunk bed . . . and thus did not have notice of any alleged defect." *Id.* The co-owner even knew the bunk bed existed—in contrast to York's lack of knowledge of the storage locker and ramp—and the court still found the co-owner not liable.

Grotto never had communications with York about the storage locker or ramp. (A-110:19-22; A-23:8-10). He did not consult York to get permission for the ramp (A-393:7-9) or the storage locker. (A-229:7-10; A-140:16-23; A-152:11-13). York never requested (A-320:23-25), approved (A-91:1-2), created, built, or designed the ramp (A-81:7-10), or even knew the ramp existed any time between its assembly and Dublin's accident. (A-149:7-10; A-141:12-14; A-323:25; A-174:1-3, 8-13; A-237:1). York clearly had no actual notice of the existence of, or defects in, the storage locker or ramp.

E. York Had No Constructive Notice of Any Defects

New York recognizes a tangential constructive notice rule related to the right of re-entry to make repairs. In *Michaelov*, 36 Misc.3d 1228(A), 2012 WL 3322678, the court explained:

> the mere "[r]eservation of a right of entry *for inspection and repair* may constitute sufficient retention of control to impose liability for injuries caused by a dangerous condition . . . *only where liability is based on a significant structural or design defect that violates a specific statutory provision.*" . . . A structural defect is one where the defect violates a statute rather than a regulation . . . . General maintenance of a premises and a failure stemming therefrom, is not akin to a structural defect. . . . In the absence of a statutory duty, a landlord's mere reservation of a right to enter leased premises *to make repairs* is insufficient to give rise to liability for a subsequently arising dangerous condition.

Id. at *13 (internal citations omitted) (emphasis added).[3] "[A]bsent a contractual obligation to repair/maintain the premises, or the right to

---

[3] *See also David v. HSS Property Corp.*, 1 A.D.3d 153 (N.Y. App. Div. 2003) (an out-of-possession owner can be held liable under a theory of constructive notice only where it has reserved the right to enter the premises to perform *inspection, maintenance and repairs* at the tenant's expense and injury was caused by a *significant* structural or design defect that is contrary to a specific statutory safety provision; owner retained the right to enter and make repairs to a leased office but a floor defect was not a violation of a safety regulation triggering constructive notice); *Hepburn v. Getty Petroleum Corp.*, 258 A.D.2d 504 (N.Y. App. Div. 1999).

reenter it to make repairs at the tenant's expense," an out-of-possession landowner may not be charged with constructive notice of a structural defect. *Lucero v. DRK, LLC*, 111 A.D.3d 578, 663 (N.Y. App. Div. 2013).

York could only be charged with constructive notice if: (1) it reserved a right of entry in order to inspect the premises *and make necessary repairs*; and (2) there was a *significant* structural or design defect that violated a specific statutory provision.[4] Both criteria are required to constitute constructive notice, which would then only satisfy one of the three *Graybill* criteria of control, notice, and opportunity. 2003 WL 21649704. First, York's right of access was only to inspect and show the stadium property to prospective buyers, investors, lessees, and lenders—not to repair. Second, there was no evidence at trial, and the trial court did not find, that the ramp had a *significant* structural or design defect of which York possibly could have been aware.

New York law requires a specific statutory violation and a *significant* structural or design defect. The "specific" violation of a building code must impose more than a general duty of repair; general safety provisions cannot support a claim of liability against an out-of-possession landowner. *Bautista*, 42 Misc.3d at 658. Dublin's expert, Rowan, referred to general safety provisions such as Section 650 of the New York State Fire Prevention and Building Code and Section 302 of the Property Maintenance Code (A-1048)—which cannot support a claim of liability. While Rowan alleged violations of Section 765.2 (incline) and 765.4 (handrails) of the Building Code, he never testified that such constituted a *significant* structural defect. *See e.g., Kittay v. Moskowitz*, 95 A.D.3d 451 (N.Y. App. Div. 2012) (Noncompliance with regulations that govern, e.g., tread width and depth does not constitute a *significant* structural or design defect). Under New York law, because York had no right of re-entry to conduct repairs, and there was no analysis at trial, or finding, of whether the ramp had a *significant* structural defect, York cannot be deemed to have constructive notice. All three of the *Graybill* elements fail: control, notice, and opportunity. 2003 WL 21649704.

---

[4] *See, e.g., Bautista*, 42 Misc.3d at 651 (sidewalk basement stairway without handrails and without proper tread width and lighting did not constitute a significant structural or defect to warrant liability); *Czerkas v. Jonre Realty Co., Inc.*, 200 A.D.2d 821 (N.Y. App. Div. 1994) (failure to place or maintain a step between a platform and the floor did not appear to be a structural defect in the building for which the owner was responsible); *Quinones v. 27 Third City King Restaurant, Inc.*, 198 A.D.2d 23 (N.Y. App. Div. 1993) (ruts, pitting and holes in the plastic covering of an interior step installed by the tenant did not constitute a *significant* structural defect).

IV. Conclusion

The New York rule limiting out-of-possession landowner liability is designed to protect property owners from accountability for injuries that occur on premises over which such owners relinquished control to a third-party. York did not create the storage locker or its ramp, delegated responsibility in the Management Agreement to BSCM for maintenance and repair of the Facility, and relinquished control of the Facility's operations to BSCM. Further, York had no actual or constructive notice of any defects in the storage locker or ramp, and notice cannot be imputed to York because no evidence was presented, and the trial court did not find, that the ramp had *significant* structural defects as required under New York law. Based upon the foregoing, York respectfully requests the Court to reverse and vacate the judgment as to liability and damages.

Date: December 20, 2017   Respectfully submitted,

Paolo Edmunds

Paolo Edmunds, Esq.
EDMUNDS & LUCY, LLP
436 Spring Street
New York, NY
p.edmunds@edmundslucy.com
800-913-8599
Counsel for York Property
Development, LLC

Appendix M: Sample Mediation Brief

IN THE UNITED STATES DISTRICT COURT FOR THE
SOUTHERN DISTRICT OF NEW YORK

Riggins Garment Company,)	Case No. Y14-044-AML
a New York Corporation,)	
Plaintiff,)	The Honorable Laila Hewson
)	
v.)	
)	
Cornerstone Insurance Company,)	
a Massachusetts corporation,)	
Defendant.)	

PLAINTIFF'S MEDIATION BRIEF

Plaintiff Riggins Garment Company ("Riggins"), by counsel, hereby submits this Mediation Brief pursuant to Mediator Stella Brunetti's Dispute Resolution Services Memorandum dated August 18, 2017.

I. Factual Background

This case involves an insurance dispute between Riggins and its insurance company, Cornerstone Insurance Company ("Cornerstone"). Riggins is a company incorporated in the State of New York that imports fabrics and textiles, and manufactures garments which it sells to key players in New York's fashion industry. Its principal place of business is located on Front Street in the South Street Seaport area of Lower Manhattan. Cornerstone is an insurance company that has been operating in Boston, Massachusetts for over 100 years. It provides various types of insurance to small businesses, including but not limited to professional liability insurance, fire insurance, general comprehensive liability insurance, worker's compensation insurance, and business interruption insurance.

Riggins has been in the garment industry since 1990, importing textiles from countries like India, Bangladesh, Cambodia, and Mexico, and using

-1-

them to manufacture garments and clothing lines for designer labels in New York's fashion industry. The company was founded by a married couple named John and Fiona Riggins. John and Fiona are members of the company's Board of Directors. The Board also includes John's sister, Maia Mandell ("Mandell"), who is an attorney and serves as in-house counsel to the company. The company leases a warehouse space in a brick building located on Front Street in the historic South Street Seaport area of Manhattan.

When the company was first founded in 1990, Mr. Riggins purchased a comprehensive general liability (CGL) and business interruption insurance policy from Cornerstone. To purchase the policy, the company had to complete a detailed application. Upon approval by Cornerstone's insurance risk analyst, Jamie Plunkett ("Plunkett"), the insurance company issued a full coverage insurance policy (Policy No. 3261970) to Riggins which was designed to cover comprehensive business operations, including losses due to property damage, personal injury, and third-party lawsuits. The policy provided coverage limits of $5 million per occurrence. The policy also provided that Cornerstone would defend the insured, Riggins, in all third-party lawsuits covered under the policy.

Beginning in 1990, Riggins paid an annual premium of $24,000 to Cornerstone, paid in monthly installments. This premium increased gradually each year. Currently, Riggins pays a monthly premium of $2,900, for an annual premium of $34,800. For 23 years, Riggins paid its insurance premiums on time. In fact, to date, Cornerstone has cashed checks in the total amount of over $635,000 from Riggins. Up until 2013, Riggins had never once filed an insurance claim.

Over the 23 years that Riggins has been in business, the company has grown its success, expanding to several floors of its warehouse facility on Front Street. Its clients include several premiere fashion designers in New York City, including Howell + Brown and EHD Brand. The company also provides clothing lines for several musical artists for their tours, including Bronwyn D and The Inchi Band.

In October 2012, Hurricane Sandy hit the East Coast and had devastating effects in New York City, especially in the South Street Seaport area. Many of the historic buildings in the Seaport area were damaged substantially due to floodwaters, as the storm surge from the East River flooded many buildings up to the second floor. Almost all the buildings on Front Street—including numerous restaurants, coffee shops, apartment buildings, and businesses, were ordered evacuated and closed, pending water rehabilitation work and subsequent environmental and safety inspections. Rehabilitation work commenced immediately once the storm had subsided;

however, throughout the remainder of 2012 and much of 2013, many of the buildings on Front Street remained closed.

When the storm hit in October 2012, Riggins took steps to protect its warehouse stock; however, the floodwater damaged the entire first floor of the warehouse, destroying inventory, textiles, files, computers, manufacturing equipment, furniture and artwork, etc. Riggins estimates property damage losses in the amount of $1.1 million due to water and mold. Further, Riggins had to shut down importing and manufacturing operations for a period of four months until March 1, 2013 when it secured temporary alternative workspace in Williamsburg, Brooklyn. Riggins moved as many of the undamaged textiles as it could from the Front Street location to the Williamsburg, Brooklyn location, and attempted to resume importing and manufacturing operations in March 2013 as best it could.

During the period of closure, Riggins was unable to perform several contracts for clothing lines for several of its customers. Unfortunately, Riggins was unable to fill an order for designer Howell + Brown in advance of Fashion Week in February 2013. Further, Riggins was unable to fill an order for The Inchi Band, for costumes for backup dancers needed for an April 2013 tour. Both Howell + Brown and The Inchi Band filed lawsuits in New York state court against Riggins, alleging breach of contract damages exceeding a combined total of $500,000. One lawsuit was filed in May 2013, and the other in July 2013. The New York state court granted Riggins time extensions to file Answers in both lawsuits, pending submission of the claims to Cornerstone.

By August 31, 2013, the NYC Department of Buildings had authorized several Front Street businesses to resume occupancy of their facilities after water and mold remediation was complete, and the structures passed environmental and safety inspections. Riggins began to move back into its Front Street facility.

In September 2013, Riggins directed its in-house counsel, Mandell, to review the terms of its insurance policies and begin filing claims for insurance coverage of its losses in accordance with the policy terms and notice requirements. Riggins filed its claims for coverage of its property damage losses with its insurer on September 15, 2013. Also on September 15, 2013, Riggins filed claims for coverage of the potential damages from the two lawsuits pending against it, and also submitted a formal request for Cornerstone to provide and fund a legal defense against both actions, in accordance with the insurance policy terms.

For three months, Riggins received no communication from its insurer, despite repeated calls, letters, and follow-up emails from in-house counsel,

Mandell, to the company's insurance representative listed on the 2013 premium statements, Todd Nicks ("Nicks"). On December 18, 2013, in-house counsel, Mandell, called the insurance company and was told by an administrative assistant, Jeremy Connor, that Nicks no longer worked for the company, and the policies had been transferred to a new representative, Nadine Valentino.

On December 27, 2013, a different insurance representative named Sam Manning sent an e-mail to Mandell indicating that the insurance claims had been further referred to Defendant Cornerstone's claims adjuster and in-house counsel, Madeline Hewes ("Hewes"), for follow-up investigation and evaluation. On January 2, 2014, the insurer sent Riggins a one-page letter denying coverage for all of the alleged property damage losses and refusing to defend the insured against the two lawsuits pending in state court. The letter was signed by Hewes, as Cornerstone's claims adjuster and in-house counsel. The letter denied coverage and declined to defend the lawsuits on the following alleged grounds:

a. "The insured failed to make timely insurance premium payments."
b. "The insured made false misrepresentations in its original policy application."
c. "The insured failed to comply with the insurance policy's notice requirements and deadlines for filing claims."
d. "The losses claimed by the insured are not covered losses."
e. "The insured failed to mitigate its damages and further exacerbated its own losses, nullifying the insurance coverage."
f. "The losses claimed are excluded under numerous policy exclusions."

On January 3, 2014, Riggins sent a letter to the insurer, signed by in-house counsel Mandell, asking it to reconsider its denial of coverage, and requesting the insurer to honor its coverage responsibilities and duty to defend its insured against the two lawsuits. The insurer failed to respond to the letter. On January 6, 2014, Mandell telephoned the insurer and was informed by Brandi Caldwell, assistant to claims adjuster and in-house counsel, Hewes, that the insurer would not reconsider its position. Riggins' in-house counsel, Mandell, filed Answers to the Complaints filed in the two third-party lawsuits, which are now proceeding to the discovery phase.

II. Procedural Background

Riggins filed a Complaint against Cornerstone in the United States District Court for the Southern District of New York on January 7, 2016 for: (1) failure to provide coverage of hurricane-related property damage and business losses; (2) refusal to defend Riggins against third-party lawsuits stemming from Hurricane Sandy; and (3) bad faith denial of coverage and refusal to defend. On January 10, 2016, Cornerstone filed an Answer to Riggins' Complaint in this action.

Following a Preliminary Scheduling Conference, the Court issued a Scheduling Order on January 17, 2016. On February 7, 2016, Riggins served its First Request for Production of Documents, and on February 8, 2016, counsel for Cornerstone served Objections and Responses accompanied by a Privilege Log. The parties have resolved certain of several ongoing discovery disputes, exchanged documents, and conducted a preliminary round of depositions of key party personnel. Both parties have identified experts who will testify at trial.

III. Causes of Action and Defenses

Riggins has asserted two separate causes of action against Cornerstone: (1) breach of contract; and (2) bad faith refusal to provide coverage and defend its insured. In the breach of contract action, Riggins contends that, by selling the insurance policies, the insurer agreed to, and assumed a contractual duty to, provide coverage for property damage and provide a defense for suits seeking damages for losses as defined in the policies. Further, Riggins indicated that it has suffered significant financial losses and property damage as a result of the floodwaters resulting from Hurricane Sandy, and has been sued for additional losses in the two pending lawsuits.

Under New York law, "an insurance contract is interpreted to give effect to the intent of the parties as expressed in the clear language of the contract." *Bamundo, Zwal & Schermerhorn, LLP v. Sentinel Insurance Company, Ltd.*, No. 13–CV–6672, 2015 WL 1408873, at *3 (S.D.N.Y. March 26, 2015). When analyzing insurance coverage, an insurance company may deny coverage based on a policy exclusion only if it "establish[es] that the exclusion is stated in clear and unmistakable language, is subject to no other reasonable interpretation, and applies in the particular case." *Kingsbay v. Yaakov*, 130 A.D.3d 769, 770 (N.Y. App. Div. 2015). Further, an insurance company's duty to defend its insured against a third-party lawsuit is determined by evaluating the allegations in the complaint in the context of the terms of the policy. *Law Offices of Zachary R. Greenhill P.C. v. Liberty Insurance Underwriters, Inc.*, 128 A.D.3d 556, 559 (N.Y. App. Div. 2015). The foregoing losses alleged by Riggins are exactly the type of losses covered under Cornerstone's insurance policies, triggering its duty and obligation to provide coverage and a defense. The insurer has failed to provide coverage for the property damage, and has refused to provide a defense for the two lawsuits. Nonetheless, the insurer has accepted over $635,000 in insurance premiums from Riggins for the last 23 years. Riggins has received nothing in return for these premiums. As such, the insurer has breached its duties of coverage and defense. Riggins has been damaged by such breach and shall continue to be further damaged by the insurer's wrongful withholding of insurance coverage for these losses.

In the second cause of action, Riggins asserts that, in issuing its contracts of insurance, the insurer agreed to pay covered claims in a timely manner, and to adhere to the inherent contractual obligation to interact with Riggins in good faith and in a fair manner—the implied covenant of "good faith and fair dealing." Under New York law, "[t]he duty of good faith and fair dealing implied in every contract is an integral part of an insurance contract." *Federated Department Stores, Inc. v. Twin City Fire Ins. Co.*, 28 A.D.3d 32, 37 (N.Y. App. Div. 2006).

By accepting insurance premiums for over two decades from its insured and yet denying coverage and refusing to defend its insured in actions clearly covered under the insurance policies, the insurer has breached its covenant of good faith and fair dealing. Further, Riggins contends that the insurer did not conduct an adequate and thorough investigation of the claims in question, and instead simply denied coverage and refused to defend its insured for no justifiable reason. Moreover, none of the reasons listed in the coverage denial letter have any validity or basis in fact, and the insurer simply issued its denial based upon boilerplate reasons for coverage rejection which have nothing to do with Riggins in this case. Riggins believes that the insurer merely instituted an internal company policy of denying coverage and refusing to defend without properly evaluating its insured's claims, in hopes that the insured would simply accept this erroneous coverage decision. Cornerstone also failed to notify its insured that its insurance representative no longer worked for the company, and failed to take seriously Riggins' request for coverage and a defense by assigning a dedicated insurance representative to the insured's file. Riggins intends to prove at trial that these business practices constitute a breach of the duty of good faith and fair dealing by the insurer against the insured.

In its Answer, Cornerstone has asserted affirmative defenses based upon the same grounds set forth in its coverage denial letter. Riggins challenges each of these defenses.

IV. Damages Sought

In its Complaint, Riggins seeks recovery of: (1) its property damage losses of approximately $1.1 million; (2) any damages assessed against Riggins in the two third-party lawsuits, currently estimated at over $500,000;

(3) its attorneys' fees and costs in pursuing this action and in defending against the two third-party lawsuits; and (4) pre-judgment and post-judgment interest.

V. Status of Settlement Negotiations and Perceived Barriers to Settlement

Riggins and Cornerstone met in July 2017 in an attempt to resolve their differences instead of proceeding to trial. The settlement meeting was unfruitful, primarily because Cornerstone failed to bring a representative to the meeting who had requisite settlement authority.

Further, throughout the early stages of this litigation, Cornerstone has been wholly unwilling to cooperate in discovery, forcing Riggins to file several Motions to Compel and incur legal fees and costs in doing so. Frustrated with Cornerstone's dilatory discovery tactics and misrepresentations during the prior settlement meetings, Riggins withdrew a previous settlement offer. Since then, settlement discussions have stalled.

Earlier this month, Cornerstone engaged new outside counsel. The new lawyer, a relative of Cornerstone's Chief Financial Officer, has further impeded settlement discussions, engaging in a letter-writing campaign in the past few weeks riddled with ad hominem attacks on Riggins' principals and attorneys that have distracted from the merits of this dispute. Riggins requests that the mediator consider meeting with the principals of the parties outside of the presence of their attorneys in at least one caucus session during the mediation day, in the hopes of diffusing the disruptive influence of Cornerstone's new counsel and moving this matter forward to resolution.

Pursuant to Federal Rule of Evidence 408, the statements made herein are for the purpose of settlement discussions only, and shall not be admissible as evidence at the trial of this matter.

Dated: September 11, 2017

Respectfully submitted,

MᴄGᴇᴇ & Rᴏʟʟɪɴꜱ, LLP

Bridget Stanton

Bridget Stanton, Esq.
100 William St., Suite 44
New York, NY 10005
800-555-4718
bstanton@mcgeerollins.com
Counsel for Plaintiff

Appendix N: Sample Settlement Agreement

Settlement Agreement

This Settlement Agreement is entered into by and between OBX Beach Homes, Inc. ("Owner") and GKB Construction, LLC ("Contractor") (hereinafter collectively the "Parties"), who entered into a contract (the "Contract") to construct a hotel called Hotel Meyer in Duck, North Carolina (the "Project").

RECITALS

WHEREAS, on November 8, 2015, the Parties entered into the Contract to construct a 24-room boutique hotel plus a pool, spa, and restaurant in the resort area of Duck, North Carolina.

WHEREAS, the Contractor agreed to furnish all construction equipment, materials, and services required by the Project Design Documents, including all labor, materials, equipment, and services to fulfill the Contractor's obligations under the Contract, and all work necessary to provide a complete and functioning facility fit for the purpose intended by the Contract.

WHEREAS, the Contract Price was $11,326,170.

WHEREAS, the Contractor agreed to achieve Substantial Completion of the Project within 14 months from the issuance of a Notice to Proceed by the Owner, which was issued on December 1, 2015.

WHEREAS, the contractually-required Substantial Completion date was February 1, 2017.

WHEREAS, the Contract allowed the Owner to assess liquidated damages for delays to Substantial Completion at a rate of $4,000 per day of delay.

WHEREAS, a dispute arose between the Parties because the Contractor was behind the Project Schedule and, in many instances, failed to perform its Project work in accordance with the Project Design Documents.

WHEREAS, the Contractor failed to achieve Substantial Completion by the contractually-prescribed date.

WHEREAS, the Owner was forced to step in and engage the services of a replacement contractor to complete the Project.

WHEREAS, on November 28, 2017, the Owner filed a lawsuit in the United States District Court for the Eastern District of North Carolina, Case No. 44142017, alleging that the Contractor breached the Contract, asserting damages, including liquidated damages, in the amount of $948,000.

WHEREAS, the Parties have engaged in extended discovery in the federal action, continue to incur substantial legal expenses, and now wish to limit any further expense incurred by both Parties in litigating this matter.

WHEREAS, by virtue of this Settlement Agreement, the Parties hereby wish to resolve any and all disputes between them arising from or relating to the Contract and the Project, including the case pending in the district court, Case No. 44142017.

NOW THEREFORE, in consideration for entering into this Settlement Agreement, the premises set forth above and the promises set forth below, and for good and other valuable consideration, the receipt and sufficiency of which is hereby acknowledged, the Parties hereby agree as follows:

1. In full and complete satisfaction of all claims, lawsuits, disputes, actions, causes of action, demands, liabilities, and/or debts between the Parties, Contractor agrees to pay to Owner the amount of $300,000.00 by wire transfer within fourteen (14) business days of the execution of this Settlement Agreement.
2. Owner agrees to file a Notice of Dismissal of the federal action with the Eastern District Court within five (5) business days of receipt of payment from Contractor.
3. The Parties agree to cooperate with one another and to take any additional steps, or execute any documents, reasonably necessary to obtain a dismissal of the federal court action.
4. The Parties represent that they are not aware of any other existing or pending claims, disputes, actions, causes of action, demands, litigations, arbitrations, liabilities, debts, or lawsuits arising from or relating to the Contract or the Project, including claims against one another or third-party claims.
5. Mutual Release: The Parties hereby mutually agree to release, waive, and forever discharge one another from liability for any and all existing, pending or future claims, disputes, actions, causes of action, demands, litigations, arbitrations, liabilities, debts, or lawsuits, whether known or unknown, arising from or relating to the Contract or the Project.
6. The Parties agree to keep in place all warranties and insurance coverages required under the Contract for a period of four (4) years after the date of this Settlement Agreement.
7. This Settlement Agreement constitutes the entire agreement between the Parties and supersedes any and all prior agreements or understandings, written or oral, between them that pertain to the Contract, the Project, or the federal court action.
8. The law of the State of North Carolina governs the terms and interpretation of this Settlement Agreement.
9. Exclusive Choice of Forum: The Parties expressly agree that any litigation arising from or relating to breach of this Settlement Agreement can only be brought in a court of competent jurisdiction located in the State of North

Carolina. The courts of the State of North Carolina shall be the sole and exclusive forum for resolution of all claims, disputes, causes of action or other legal matters between the Parties, arising from or relating to this Settlement Agreement.

10. Attorneys' Fees and Costs: In the event that a claim for breach of this Settlement Agreement is resolved by judgment or jury verdict in a court of competent jurisdiction, the prevailing party shall be entitled to recover, from the non-prevailing party, its reasonable attorneys' fees and costs of litigation.

11. The Parties warrant that the signatories to this Settlement Agreement have all requisite authority to enter into this Agreement and bind the respective companies to its terms.

IN WITNESS WHEREOF, the Parties hereto have executed this Settlement Agreement.

OBX BEACH HOMES, INC.

Signed: _____

Name: _____

Title: _____

Date: _____

GKB CONSTRUCTION, LLC

Signed: _____

Name: _____

Title: _____

Date: _____

Appendix O: Sample Oral Argument Outline

Roadmap

- Good Afternoon your Honors. May it please the court, my name is Paolo Edmunds, and I represent the Defendant-Appellant in this action, York Property Development, LLC.
- This case is about an employee of a management company of a sports stadium complex located in Brooklyn suing an "out-of-possession" landowner for injuries the employee sustained when he fell on a snowy ramp that he personally was responsible for maintaining as part of his scope of work.
- York owns the real estate where the stadium is located but has no day-to-day involvement with, or control over, the stadium operations.
- The employee sued the out-of-possession landowner (instead of his employer) because worker's compensation laws prevented him from seeking additional compensation from his employer.
- However, the public policy underlying New York's limitation on out-of-possession landowner liability is that "the person in possession and control of property is best able to identify and prevent any harm to others."
  - *Butler v. Rafferty*, 100 N.Y.2d 265, 270 (N.Y. 2003).
- Applying the **four-pronged** rule governing "out-of-possession" landowner liability, York respectfully requests the Court to find that, because York:
  - did not **create** the ramp in question,
  - bore no responsibility for **maintenance** or **repairs** of the sports stadium complex, and
  - relinquished all **control** of the property to a third-party management company—who was the plaintiff's employer—

York cannot be liable for the plaintiff's injuries.

Rule

- It is well-established under New York law that an out-of-possession property owner *cannot* be liable for injuries that occur on a premises unless the landowner:
  - **created** the dangerous condition;
  - assumed responsibility to **maintain** any portion of the premises;
  - is contractually obligated to **repair** the unsafe condition; or
  - retained **control** of the premises.
- *Buckowski v. Smith*, 185 A.D.2d 556 (N.Y. App. Div. 1992).

APPLYING THE **FIRST** PRONG OF THE RULE → **CREATION** OF THE RAMP,

- York did not **create** the ramp that led up to the entrance of a portable storage locker on the stadium property.
- Jake Grotto, an employee of the management company, Brooklyn Sports Complex Management (BSCM), ordered the storage locker and ramp from a company called Storage Locker Depot, LLC.
- Grotto had no communications with York about the storage locker or ramp.
- There is no evidence that anyone else from BSCM communicated with York about the storage locker or ramp.
- Grotto did not consult York to get permission for the ramp or the storage locker.
- York never requested, approved, created, built, or designed the ramp, or even knew the ramp existed any time between its assembly and the plaintiff's accident.

APPLYING THE **SECOND** AND **THIRD** PRONGS OF THE RULE → RESPONSIBILITY FOR **MAINTENANCE** AND **REPAIR** OF THE PREMISES,

- The express language of the Management Agreement between York and the management company (BSCM) demonstrates that BSCM rather than York bore all responsibility for **maintenance** and **repair** of the stadium premises.
- Under Article 14 of the Management Agreement, BSCM assumed responsibility for:
  o the daily operation, direction, management and supervision of the stadium;
  o the supply, operation, maintenance, repairs and service of the stadium, and
  o compliance with any applicable laws, codes, rules, regulations, and ordinances governing repairs, maintenance, or operation of the stadium.
- [If necessary: read exact language from Article 14 of the Management Agreement referring to maintenance and repair]

APPLYING THE **FOURTH** PRONG OF THE RULE → **CONTROL** OVER THE PREMISES,

- To assess whether an out-of-possession landowner retained or relinquished **control** over property, courts focus on:
  o **contractual language**; and
  o **course of conduct**.

- Article 14.5 of York's Management Agreement with BSCM stated, "Owner or its agents shall have access to the Facility at any and all reasonable times for the purpose of inspection or showing the Facility to prospective buyers, investors, lessees, or lenders."
- Courts evaluate **contractual language** discussing a right of re-entry to make repairs by the landowner (broader than York's right of re-entry to show the property to buyers, investors, lessees, or lenders), but will absolve a landowner from liability even in light of a right of re-entry, unless the parties' course of conduct demonstrates the offsite landowner's **ongoing control** of the property.
- The evidence shows that York's narrow contractual right of re-entry in Article 14.5 was limited to inspection and showing the property to prospective buyers, investors, lessees, or lenders—wholly distinguishable from New York cases involving landowners possessing a right of re-entry to conduct repairs.
  - Case Law: *Derienzo v. East New York Club House*, 22 Misc.3d 1124(A), 2009 WL 415556 (N.Y. Sup. Ct. 2009):
    - Landowner retained a contractual responsibility to keep its premises in repair, as well as the right to re-enter and make needed repairs.
    - Landlord had made repairs to the premises (visited the site, observed the defect, and indicated it would be repaired).
    - Distinguishable from York (no right of re-entry to make repairs; no course of dealing visiting or making repairs).
- Further, no representative from York inspected or visited the property during BSCM's management.
- Case Law on Course of Dealing:
  - *Gronski v. County of Monroe*, 18 N.Y.3d 374 (N.Y. 2011):
    - Court denied summary judgment on "out-of-possession" landowner issue because an issue of fact existed over level of control exercised by County over waste management facility—operated by a management company.
    - Course of conduct (distinguishable from York):
      - County maintained a visible and vocal presence at the facility.
      - County availed itself of its contractual access to the facility through regular public tours and routine unannounced inspections.
      - County representative took specific supervisory actions, for example, when he observed workers not wearing hard hats.
  - *Michaelov v. 632 Kings Highway Realty Corp*, No. 3969/10, 2012 WL 3322678 (N.Y. Sup. Ct. July 13, 20120):
    - Right of re-entry to make repairs (distinguishable from York).
    - Holding: Out-of-possession landlord NOT liable.
    - NOT contractually obligated to make non-structural repairs.
    - NO course of conduct indicating control; no proof that landowner:

- actually controlled or undertook any repairs, even though the owner visited the premises occasionally to check on the tenant's renovations.
- visited the premises on a regular basis for the purpose of controlling maintenance or repairs.
- gave the tenant tools for repairs.
- instructed the tenant regarding repairs at the premises.
  - *Vijayan v. Bally's Total Fitness*, 289 A.D.2d 224 (N.Y. App. Div. 2001) (even regular visits of the owner's managing agent to the premises to collect rent, lease space, and address tenants' concerns did not establish control).
  - *Alnashmi v. Certified Analytical Group, Inc.*, 89 A.D.3d 10 (N.Y. App. Div. 2011); *Green v. City of New York*, 76 A.D.3d 508 (N.Y. App. Div. 2010); *Boyd v. Paladino*, 295 A.D.2d 298 (N.Y. App. Div. 2002); *Carvano v. Morgan*, 270 A.D.2d 222 (N.Y. App. Div. 2000); *Del Giacco v. Noteworthy Co.*, 175 A.D.2d 516 (N.Y. App. Div. 1991) (all finding out-of-possession landowner not liable based on lack of control).
- Summary of **Control** Issue:
  - Unlike the landowners in *Gronski* and *Derienzo* who visited their properties regularly, established visibility, and interacted with property personnel regarding repairs or deficiencies, York maintained no presence at the stadium—having relinquished control to BSCM under the Management Agreement.
  - York stationed no representatives on the property.
  - None visited the property.
  - York performed no repairs or maintenance on the property.
  - BSCM made all property decisions and maintained the property with its own employees.
  - York had no contractual duty to re-enter the premises to conduct repairs, and its course of dealing reflected its relinquishment of control to BSCM.

APPLYING TWO TANGENTIAL NEW YORK RULES REGARDING ACTUAL AND CONSTRUCTIVE NOTICE,

- Under *Graybill v. City of New York*, No. 123754/01, 2003 WL 21649704 (N.Y. Sup. Ct. 2003): Absent contractually created responsibility, liability requires proof that the out-of-possession landowner:
  - retained sufficient **control** over the premises,
  - had **actual or constructive notice** of a dangerous or defective condition, and
  - had reasonable **opportunity** to repair or correct it.
- All three criteria are required: **control**, **notice**, and **opportunity.**
- **Actual notice:**

o York had no actual notice of the portable storage locker, or its ramp, let alone that there were any issues with their assembly.

o New York courts will not impose liability upon a party for circumstances which it did not create, and of which it had no notice.

o Case Law: *Butler v. Rafferty*, 291 A.D.2d 754 (N.Y. App. Div. 2002), *aff'd in* 100 N.Y.2d 265 (N.Y. 2003):

> o Facts: A child fell from a bunk bed in a tenant's home, and the parents sued a co-owner of the property. The tenant had built a house on the property, and constructed the bunk bed. The co-owner "did not assist in the construction of the bunk bed and knew nothing more about it than that it existed."
>
> o Holding: The court viewed the co-owner as an out-of-possession landlord, reiterating the rule that "an out-of-possession landlord is not liable for injuries resulting from the condition of the demised premises."
>
> o The court further stated that "application of that rule is particularly apt in this case, given that [the co-owner] took no part in the construction of the portion of the property occupied . . . or of the bunk bed . . . and thus did not have notice of any alleged defect."
>
> o Comparison to York: The *Butler* co-owner even knew the bunk bed existed—in contrast to York's lack of knowledge of the storage locker and ramp—and the court still found the co-owner not liable.

● **Constructive Notice**:

o New York recognizes a tangential constructive notice rule related to the right of re-entry to make repairs.

o *Michaelov*, 36 Misc.3d 1228(A), 2012 WL 3322678:

> o The mere "[r]eservation of a **right of entry for inspection and repair** may constitute sufficient retention of control to impose liability for injuries caused by a dangerous condition . . . only where liability is based on a **significant** structural or design defect that violates a specific **statutory** provision."

o York could only be charged with constructive notice if:

> o it reserved a right of entry in order to inspect the premises **and make necessary repairs**; AND
>
> o there was a **significant** structural or design defect
>
> o that violated a specific **statutory** provision.

o First, York's right of access was only to inspect and show the stadium property to prospective buyers, investors, lessees, and lenders—**not to repair**.

o Second, there was no evidence at trial, and the trial court did not find, that the ramp had a **significant** structural or design defect of which York possibly could have been aware.

o Because York had neither **control** nor **notice**, and therefore no **opportunity** to remedy any defect on the property, it cannot be held liable as an out-of-possession landowner.

Conclusion

Your Honors, for the foregoing reasons, York respectfully requests the Court to find that, because York:

- did not **create** the ramp in question,
- bore no responsibility for **maintenance** or **repairs** of the sports stadium complex, and
- relinquished all **control** of the property to a third-party management company—who was the plaintiff's employer—

York cannot be liable for the plaintiff's injuries.

THANK YOU.

Index